Paul's Language of Grace in its Graeco-Roman Context

James R. Harrison

Paul's Language of Grace
in its Graeco-Roman Context

WIPF & STOCK · Eugene, Oregon

Wipf and Stock Publishers
199 W 8th Ave, Suite 3
Eugene, OR 97401

Paul's Language of Grace in its Graeco-Roman Context
By Harrison, James R.
Copyright©2003 Mohr Siebeck
ISBN 13: 978-1-5326-1346-3
Publication date 1/03/2017
Previously published by Mohr Siebeck, 2003

Preface

This book is a revision of my PhD thesis that was completed at the School of Ancient History, Macquarie University, Sydney in 1996. It was recommended for publication in the WUNT series by the series editor, Professor Martin Hengel, in 1999. I am grateful to Professor Hengel for the honour of being published in such a highly regarded series. I am also thankful to Professor Jörg Frey, the current editor, whose continued interest has encouraged me to complete the project.

The subsequent delay in publication was due to the demands of preparing undergraduate and postgraduate lectures at Wesley Institute and Robert Menzies College School of Christian Studies. However, I feel that the book has benefited from my classroom discussions with students, so I do not regret the lapsed time.

There are two substantial differences between the original thesis and this book. First, on the suggestion of Professor Hengel, I omit discussion of grace in the Dead Sea Scrolls. This is replaced by an exploration of grace in Pseudo-Philo's two synagogal sermons, *De Sampsone* and *De Jona*, which better approximate the Diaspora context of Paul's house churches. Second, at the suggestion of Professor Albrecht Dihle, I examine the 'servant leader' motif of Antisthenes as a backdrop to 2 Corinthian 8:9. These changes, I believe, enable Paul's understanding of grace to be better situated within its Graeco-Roman and Diaspora context.

Many people have contributed to my thinking about the theme of the book. I am grateful to Dr Mark Harding, Dean of the Australian College of Theology, and Professor Judith Lieu, King's College, London, for their help with the Jewish literature. Mr Graham Joyner was invaluable to my early work on the Greek inscriptions, as was Mr Greg Fox with the fragments of Antisthenes.

Dr Christopher Forbes has been a close friend and mentor. His astute advice helped me to steer away from errors and into profitable areas of research. He has always been available and willing to discuss my work and talk about wider scholarly issues.

Emeritus Professor Edwin Judge exercises a profound influence on my research. He is lavish of his time and skills, and this book reflects some of his many interests as a Roman and New Testament social historian. As a mentor, he shows a personal interest that has made this task much easier to complete. Although he retired from the Chair of Ancient History at Macquarie University in 1993, he supervised my thesis until completion and continues generously to offer advice on various issues. This represents an act of grace on his part that goes far beyond the requirements of his official duties.

Three other people deserve special mention. Mrs Beth McPherson and Ms Gill McPherson are proofreaders par excellence and their dedication to their task saved me from many errors. Elisabeth, my wife, never doubted that I would complete this book. In recent months, she spared time from her own academic career to help format it. Like Phoebe, she has been προστάτις and διάκονος and I dedicate this thesis to her with my love and thanks.

Finally, production of a book often reflects a personal journey. Professor Hengel suggested that I emphasise more forcefully than I had in the original thesis the reality of divine love behind divine grace. In this regard, the truth of Galatians 2:20b continues to overpower me each day as I struggle with ingrained character traits that resist the transformation of the new creation.

Jim Harrison
Sydney
June 2003

Contents

Preface	V
Table of Contents	VII
Abbreviations	XI
Introduction to the 2017 Reprint Edition	XVII

Chapter 1: Paul and the Reign of Grace 1
    1.1. Modern Scholarship on Benefaction: The Clue to the First-Century Context of *Charis*? 3
    1.2. Modern Scholarship on *Charis*: A Timeless Construct? 8
    1.3. Patronage and the Social-Scientific Approach: The Way Ahead for New Testament Social Research? 13
        1.3.1. Valuable insights from the social sciences for our understanding of first-century grace 17
        1.3.2. Deficiencies in the social-scientific approach for a historically nuanced understanding of first-century grace 22
    1.4. Purpose and Plan of Study 24

Chapter 2: The Role of *Charis* in the Inscriptions 26
    2.1. The Inscriptions and New Testament Benefaction Terminology 26
    2.2. The Inscriptions, *Charis*, and New Testament Benefaction Studies 33
    2.3. The Nature and Structure of Honorific Decrees 37
    2.4. *Charis* in the 'Manifesto' Clause: Return of 'Favour' or 'Thanks'? 40
    2.5. A Survey of *Charis* in the Inscriptions 44
    2.6. *Charis* and the Ethos of Reciprocity 50
    2.7. *Charis* and the Gods 53
    2.8. A Profile of Benefactors and their Communities 57
        2.8.1. Zosimos of Priene (84 BC) 58
        2.8.2. Antiochus I of Kommagene (Mid first century BC) 59
        2.8.3. Phainios of Gytheion (AD 41/42) 60
        2.8.4. Caligula (AD 37) and Nero (AD 67) 61
        2.8.5. Conclusion: *Charis* in the first century AD 62
    2.9. Conclusion 63

Chapter 3: The Role of *Charis* in the Papyri 64
    3.1. *Charis* and the Ancient Epistolary Theorists 64
        3.1.1. *Charis*, the papyri, and benefaction studies 64
        3.1.2. Papyrological methodology and benefaction studies 66
        3.1.3. The social world of benefaction in the epistolary theorists 68
    3.2. A Survey of *Charis* and Its Cognates 72
        3.2.1. The bestowal of a favour or a gift 72
        3.2.2. The return of gratitude 75

Contents

- 3.2.3. The letter of recommendation and the disposal of favour ... 77
- 3.2.4. *Charis* and its cognates in the Jewish papyri ... 79
- 3.2.5. Conclusion ... 80
- 3.3. *Charis* and the Ethos of Reciprocity in the Papyri ... 80
- 3.4. *Charis* and the Gods in the Papyri ... 85
- 3.5. *Charis* and the Caesar Cult in the Papyri ... 87
- 3.6. *Charis* in the Magical Papyri ... 90
  - 3.6.1. *Charis* and beneficence in the magical papyri ... 92
  - 3.6.2. Thanksgiving in the magical papyri ... 94
  - 3.6.3. Conclusion ... 95
- 3.7. Conclusion ... 95

Chapter 4: The Role of *Charis* in First-Century Judaism ... 97

- 4.1. Grace and First-Century Judaism Post E.P. Sanders ... 97
  - 4.1.1. E.P. Sanders and the 'New Perspective' on Paul: Situating grace in its Jewish context ... 97
  - 4.1.2. The 'new perspective': an adequate portrayal of Judaism and Paul? ... 101
- 4.2. The Use of *Charis* in the LXX ... 106
- 4.3. The Use of *Charis* in the Apocrypha and Pseudepigrapha ... 110
- 4.4. *Charis*, Philo, and Beneficence ... 114
  - 4.4.1. Modern scholars, Philo, and *charis*: A survey ... 115
  - 4.4.2. Grace and the beneficence of God in Philo ... 120
  - 4.4.3. Philo and the ethos of reciprocity ... 128
  - 4.4.4. Philo's critique of *charis* in its benefaction context ... 130
  - 4.4.5. Conclusion ... 133
- 4.5. *Charis*, Josephus, and Beneficence ... 133
  - 4.5.1. Grace and divine beneficence in Josephus ... 135
  - 4.5.2. Grace and human beneficence in Josephus ... 138
  - 4.5.3. Josephus and the ethos of reciprocity ... 140
  - 4.5.4. Josephus' critique of *charis* in its benefaction context ... 144
  - 4.5.5. Conclusion ... 145
- 4.6. Grace in the Jewish Synagogal and Funerary Inscriptions ... 146
  - 4.6.1. Grace in the Jewish synagogal inscriptions ... 146
  - 4.6.2. Grace in the Jewish funerary inscriptions ... 149
- 4.7. Grace in the Jewish Synagogal Sermon ... 151
- 4.8. Grace in the Rabbinic Literature ... 157
  - 4.8.1. Methodological issues ... 157
  - 4.8.2. The rabbinic exegesis of Old Testament grace texts ... 160
- 4.9. Conclusion ... 165

Chapter 5: The Role of *Charis* in the Philosophers ... 167

- 5.1. *Charis*, the Philosophers, and Benefaction Studies ... 167
  - 5.1.1. Paul's exposure to the philosophers' discussions of *charis* ... 167
  - 5.1.2. The contribution of the philosophers to benefaction studies ... 170
- 5.2. A Survey of *Charis* and its Cognates in the Philosophers ... 174
  - 5.2.1. The bestowal of a favour or a gift ... 174
  - 5.2.2. The return of gratitude ... 175
  - 5.2.3. *Charis* outside its benefaction context ... 178
- 5.3. *Charis* and the Ethos of Reciprocity in the Philosophers ... 179

5.4. *Charis* and the Gods of the Philosophers 183
    5.4.1. *Charis* and the gods: a general survey 184
    5.4.2. Grace and the cults 188
    5.4.3. Grace and recompense 190
5.5. The Philosophical Critique of *Charis* 192
    5.5.1. The moral critique of benefaction ideology 192
    5.5.2. Critical responses to the ethos of reciprocity 194
    5.5.3. The critique of the cult 195
    5.5.4. Epicureans, cynics, and the debate on divine beneficence in antiquity 196
5.6. Beneficence in the Roman Moralists: A Study of the Role of *Gratia* 199
    5.6.1. A survey of *gratia* and its cognates in the Roman moralists 199
    5.6.2. *Gratia* and the ethos reciprocity in the Roman moralists 202
    5.6.3. *Gratia* and the gods in the Roman moralists 206
    5.6.4. The philosophical critique of *gratia* in the Roman moralists 208
5.7. Conclusion 209

Chapter 6: Paul and Divine Beneficence 211

6.1. Paul, *Charis*, and the Salvation of God 212
    6.1.1. Graeco-Roman benefaction and the honour-and-shame dynamic of
           Paul's letter to the Romans 214
    6.1.2. Graeco-Roman benefaction and the age of grace: Paul and the
           Roman Christians 220
        6.1.2.1. Paul's solution to the honour-and-shame dynamic in Romans
               does not diminish the demands of divine righteousness 220
        6.1.2.2. Paul's solution to the honour-and-shame dynamic in Romans
               involves a novel understanding of righteousness 223
        6.1.2.3. The gift of divine righteousness is extended to unworthy
               beneficiaries through a dishonoured benefactor 224
        6.1.2.4. The reign of grace in Romans 5:12-22 must be situated as
               much within the Roman eschatology of Augustus as within
               the Jewish apocalyptic literature 226
        6.1.2.5. Paul's metaphor of Christians as obligated beneficiaries in
               Romans 6:12-23 is drawn from the *familia Caesaris* 234
    6.1.3. Graeco-Roman benefaction and the age of grace: Paul and the eastern
           Mediterranean Christians 242
        6.1.3.1. Paul's doctrine of grace in Ephesians is directed against local
               manifestations of counterfeit spirituality at Ephesus 242
        6.1.3.2. Paul and the honorific inscriptions stress the obligation of
               beneficiaries to respond worthily of their benefactor 247
6.2. Paul, *Charis*, and the Impoverished Benefactor Motif 250
6.3. Paul and Antisthenes on the *Charis* of the Enslaved Leader 256
6.4. Paul, *Charis*, and the Body of Christ 269
    6.4.1. *Charis* and gratitude 269
    6.4.2. *Charis* and apostleship 273
    6.4.3. *Charis* and spiritual gifts 279
6.5. Paul, *Charis* and the Gods of the Gentiles 283
6.6. Conclusion 287

Chapter 7: Paul and Human Beneficence 289
7.1. Introduction 289
7.2. Paul, *Charis*, and the Jerusalem Collection 294
   7.2.1. Paul's description of the Jerusalem collection 294
      7.2.1.1. The Jerusalem collection as χάρις 294
      7.2.1.2. The honorific inscriptions and Paul's descriptions of the collection 300
   7.2.2. Theological and social dimensions of the Jerusalem collection 303
      7.2.2.1. The eschatological interpretation 304
      7.2.2.2. The ecumenical interpretation 307
      7.2.2.3. The obligation interpretation 309
7.3. The Jerusalem Collection in its Graeco-Roman Context 314
   7.3.1. Paul and the inscriptional motifs of rivalry and imitation 314
      7.3.1.1. The ἵνα and ὅπως clause in the resolution proper of the honorific inscriptions 315
      7.3.1.2. Paul's redefinition of the inscriptional motifs of rivalry and imitation 318
   7.3.2. Paul and the ethos of reciprocity 321
      7.3.2.1. Paul's critique of the Graeco-Roman reciprocity system 322
      7.3.2.2. Paul's endorsement of the Graeco-Roman reciprocity system 324
7.4. Paul and Corinthian Disputes over Beneficence 332
   7.4.1. Paul's use of benefaction terminology and motifs in 2 Cor 10-13 333
   7.4.2. Paul as the endangered and cowardly benefactor 335
   7.4.3. Paul and the reciprocation of parental favour 340
7.5. Conclusion 343

Chapter 8: Conclusion 345
8.1. The Ethos of Reciprocity 348
8.2 The Χάριτες of the Gods 349
8.3. The Augustan Age of Grace 351

Bibliography 353
Index of Modern Authors 384
Index of Passages 392
   Old Testament 392
   Apocrypha 396
   Pseudepigrapha 398
   Rabbinic Literature 400
   New Testament 402
Index of Ancient Non-Literary Sources 417
Index of Ancient Literary Sources 426
Index of Subjects 439

Abbreviations

AClass	*Acta Classica*
AJP	*American Journal of Philology*
ANRW	*Aufsteig und Niedergang der römischen Welt* ed. H. Temporini
ATR	*Anglican Theological Review*
AusBR	*Australian Biblical Review*
BAR	*Biblical Archaeologist Reader*
BGU	*Berliner greichische Urkunden (Ägyptische Urkunden aus den königlichen Museen zu Berlin)*
Bib	*Biblica*
BJRL	*Bulletin of the John Rylands Library, Manchester*
BMI	*Ancient Greek Inscriptions in the British Museum*
BSac	*Bibliotheca Sacra*
BTB	*Biblical Theology Bulletin*
C&M	*Classica et Mediaevalia*
CBQ	*Catholic Biblical Quarterly*
CIG	*Corpus Inscriptionum Graecarum*
CIJ	*Corpus Inscriptionum Iudaicarum*, ed. J.B. Frey
CIL	*Corpus Inscriptionum Latinarum*
Comm Viat	*Communio Viatorum*
CPh	*Classical Philology*
CPJ	*Corpus Inscriptionum Judaicarum*, ed. V. Tcherikover
CQ	*Classical Quarterly*
CR	*Classical Review*
CurTM	*Currents in Theology and Mission*
DHA	*Dialogues d'histoire ancienne*
Ephesos BMI	*Ancient Greek Inscriptions in the British Museum (Ephesos)*
ETR	*Études théologiques et religieuses*
EvQ	*Evangelical Quarterly*
F.Gr.H.	*Fragmente der griechischen Historiker*, 1932- ed. F. Jacoby
FD	*Fouilles de Delphes. 3. Épigraphie, et al.*, ed. G. Colin

IG	*Inscriptiones Graecae, et al.*, ed. W. Dittenberger
GRBS	*Greek, Roman and Byzantine Studies*
HR	*History of Religions*
HTR	*Harvard Theological Review*
HUCA	*Hebrew Union College Annual*
I. AnkyraBosch	*Quellen zur Geschichte der Stadt Ankara im Altertum*, ed. E. Bosch
I. Assos	*Die Inschriften von Assos*, ed. R. Merkelbach
I. Délos	*Inscriptions de Délos, et al.*, ed. F. Durrbach
I. Ephesos	*Die Inschriften von Ephesos, et al.*, ed. H. Wankel
IGRR	*Inscriptiones Graecae ad res Romanas pertinentes, et al.*, ed. R. Cagnat
I. Iasos	*Die Inschriften von Iasos*, ed. W. Blümel
I. Kalchedon	*Die Inschriften von Kalchedon, et al*, ed. R. Merkelbach
I. Keramos	*Die Inschriften von Keramos*, ed. E. Varinlioglu
I. Kyme	*Die Inschriften von Kyme*, ed. H. Engelmann
I. Kyzikos	*Die Inschriften von Kyzikos und Umgebung*, ed. E. Schwertheim
I. Magnesia	*Die Inschriften von Magnesia am Maeander*, ed. O Kern
I. Mylasa	*Die Inschriften von Mylasa. I.Inschriften der Stadt*, ed. W. Blümel
I. Perge	*Die Inschriften von Perge*, ed. S. Sahin
I. Priene	*Die Inschriften von Priene*, ed. F. Hillier von Gaertringen
I. Prusa Olymp.	*Die Inschriften von Prusa ad Olympum*, ed. T. Corsten
I. Stratonikeia	*Die Inschriften von Stratonikeia*, ed. S. Sahin
I. Tralleis	*Die Inschriften von Tralles und Nysa. I.Die Inschriften von Tralleis*, ed. F.B. Poljakov
Int	*Interpretation*
JAAR	*Journal of the American Academy of Religion*
JAC	*Jahrbuch für Antike und Christentum*
JBL	*Journal of Biblical Literature*
JJS	*Journal of Jewish Studies*
JQR	*Jewish Quarterly Review*
JR	*Journal of Religion*
JRH	*Journal of Religious History*
JRS	*Journal of Roman Studies*

JSNT	*Journal for the Study of the New Testament*
JTS	*Journal of Theological Studies*
Michel	*Recueil d'inscriptions grecques*, ed. by C. Michel
Neot	*Neotestamentica*
New Docs	*New Documents Illustrating Early Christianity*, eds. G.H.R. Horsley (vols 1-5); S.R. Llewelyn (vols 6-9)
NovT	*Novum Testamentum*
NTS	*New Testament Studies*
OGIS	*Orientis Graeci Inscriptiones Selectae*, ed. W. Dittenberger
P & P	*Past and Present*
Pap. Agon.	*Zehn agonistische Papyri*, ed. P. Frisch
P. Ath. Univ. Inv.	*The Carbonised Papyrus of the Institute of Classical Philology at the University of Athens*, ed. N. Livadaras
P. Bon.	*Papyri Bononienses*, ed. O. Montevecci
P. Brem.	*Die Bremer Papyri*, ed. U. Wilcken
P. Erasm.	*Papyri in the Collection of the Erasmus University (Rotterdam)*, eds P.J. Sijpesteijn and P.A. Verdult
P. Fam. Tebt.	*A Family Archive from Tebtunis*, ed. B.A. van Groningen
P. Fuad I Univ.	*Fuad I University Papyri*, ed. by D.S. Crawford
P. Gr.	*Papyrus grecs de la Bibliothèque Nationale et Universitaire de Strasbourg*, ed. J. Schwartz
P. Herc.	*Catalogo dei Papiri Ercolanesi*, ed. M. Gigante
P. Lond.	*Greek Papyri in the British Museum*, eds. F.G. Kenyon & H.I. Bell
P. Louvre	*Notices et extraits des papyrus grecs du Musée du Louvre et de la Bibliothèque Impériale*, ed. J.A. Letronne
P. Mert.	*A Descriptive Catalogue of the Greek Papyri in the Collection of Wilfred Merton, F.S.A., et al.*, H.I. Bell
P. Mich.	*Papyri in the University of Michigan Collection, et al.*, ed. C.C. Edgar
P. Oxy.	*Oxyrhynchus Papyri, et al.*, eds B.P. Grenfell and A.S. Hunt
P. Oxy. Hels.	*Fifty Oxyrhynchus Papyri, et al.* ed. by H. Zilliacus
P. Princ.	*Papyri in the Princeton University Collections, et al.*, ed. A.C. Johnson
P. Ross Georg.	*Papyri Russischer und Georgische Sammlungen*, ed. G. Zereteli

P. Sarap.	*Les archives de Sarapion et de ses fils:une exploitation agricole aux environs d'Hermoupolis Magna*, ed. J. Schwartz
P. Soter.	*Das Archive des Soterichos*, ed. S. Omar
P. Strass.	*Griechische Papyrus der Kaiserlichen Universitäts- und Landesbibliothek zu Strassburg*, ed. F. Preisigke
P. Tebt.	*The Tebtunis Papyri, et al.*, ed. B.P. Grenfell
P. Turner	*Papyri Greek and Egyptian, edited by various hands in honour of Eric Gardner Turner on the occasion of his 70th birthday*
P. Warren	*The Warren Papyri, et al*, ed. M. David
P. Wash. Univ.	*Washington University Papyri, I: Non Literary Texts (nos 1-61)*, ed. V.B. Schuman
P. Würzb.	*Mitteilungen aus der Würzburger Papyrussammlung*, ed. U. Wilcken
P. Wisc.	*The Wisconsin Papyri*, ed. P.J. Sijpesteijn
P. Yale	*Yale Papyri in the Beinecke Rare Book and Manuscript Library I. Et al.*, ed., J.F. Oates
PGM	*Papyri Graecae Magicae. Die griechischen Zauber papyri*, ed. K. Preisendanz
PSI	*Papiri greci e latini, et al*, G. Vitelli
PWSup	*Pauly-Wissowa Supplement*
RAC	*Reallexikon für Antike und Christentum*
ResQ	*Restoration Quarterly*
Rev Exp	*Review and Expositor*
RhM	*Rheinisches Museum*
RHPR	*Revue d'histoire et de philosophie religieuses*
RIDA	*Revue internationale des droits de l'antiquité*
RivB	*Rivista Biblica*
SE	*Studia Evangelica, ed. by F. Cross*
SEG	*Supplementum Epigraphicum Graecum*
SIG³	*Sylloge Inscriptionum Graecarum*, ed. W. Dittenberger
SJT	*Scottish Journal of Theology*
TAM	*Tituli Asiae Minoris, et al.*, ed. E. Kalinka
TAPhA	*Transactions of the American Philological Association*
TDNT	*Theological Dictionary of the New Testament*
TDOT	*Theological Dictionary of the Old Testament*
TynBul	*Tyndale Bulletin*

TZ	*Theologische Zeitschrift*
UPZ	*Urkunden der Ptolemäerzeit*, ed. U. Wilcken
USQR	*Union Seminary Quarterly Review*
VSpir	*Vie spirituelle*
VT	*Vetus Testamentum*
WTJ	*Westminster Theological Journal*
ZAW	*Zeitschrift für die alttestamentliche Wissenschaft*
ZNW	*Zeitschrift für die neutestamentliche Wissenschaft*
ZPE	*Zeitschrift für Papyrologie und Epigraphik*
ZST	*Zeitschrift für systematische Theologie*

Paul's Language of Grace
Introduction to the 2017 Reprint Edition

The Historical Method and the Study of Grace

In the last thirty-five years there has been a resurgence of monographs on the role of grace in the Paul's thought. These have ranged from a study on Paul's language of "overflowing" grace,[1] two comparisons of grace in the thought of Philo and Paul,[2] two general studies on grace and thanksgiving in Paul's letters,[3] an exploration of Paul's language of grace against its Graeco-Roman background,[4] a study of the transformative nature of grace,[5]

---

1. M. Theobald, *Die überströmende Gnade: Studien zu einem paulinischen Motivfeld* (Würzburg: Echter Verlag, 1982). This essay adapts and expands upon my introductory comments in J. R. Harrison, "Paul, Theologian of Electing Grace," in *Paul the Theologian: Pauline Studies Volume III*, ed. S. E. Porter, (Leiden: Brill, 2006), 77–108, at 77–90. The essay's original emphasis on Romans as an important litmus test for Paul's theology of grace is retained in what follows. For the limitations caused by my heavy emphasis on Romans in discussing Paul's understanding of divine χάρις in *Paul's Language of Grace*, see Z. A. Crook, *Reconceptualising Conversion: Patronage, Loyalty, and Conversion in the Religions of the Ancient Mediterranean* (Berlin: Walter de Gruyter, 2004), 146.

2. D. Zeller, *Charis bei Philon und Paulus* (Stuttgart: Verlag Katholisches Bibelwerk GmbH, 1990); O. McFarland, *God and Grace in Philo and Paul* (Leiden/Boston: Brill, 2015), the latter having been a doctoral student of John Barclay.

3. B. Eastman, *The Significance of Grace in the Letters of Paul* (New York: Peter Lang, 1999); D. W. Pao, *Thanksgiving: An Investigation of a Pauline Theme* (Downers Grove: IVP, 2002). See the general work of P. J. Leithart, *Gratitude: An Intellectual History* (Waco: Baylor University Press, 2014).

4. J. R. Harrison, *Paul's Language of Grace in Its Graeco-Roman Context* (Tübingen: Mohr Siebeck, 2003).

5. K. B. Wells, *Grace and Agency in Paul and Second Temple Judaism: Interpreting the Transformation of the Heart* (Leiden/Boston: Brill, 2015), the latter also having been a doctoral student of John Barclay. Additionally, conceptually, see the collection of essays

to, finally, the magnum opus of J. M. G. Barclay, which situates grace in its sociological, theological and Second Temple Judaism context.[6] Two other studies have discussed the patronal backdrop to Paul's understanding of grace, even though each work's theme is more wide-ranging.[7] Also the controversy engendered by the "New Perspective" debate over the covenantal basis of Mosaic law in Second Temple Judaism and its relation to Pauline justification by faith has acutely raised the issue of the place of grace in Paul's thought.[8]

What unites most of these studies (with the exception of Eastman and Theobald) is their use of historical evidence to inform a theological discussion of grace. Harrison provides the most extensive discussion of χάρις and its cognates against the backdrop of the Graeco-Roman reciprocity system, surveying evidence from the inscriptions, papyri, Jewish literature, and the popular philosophers.[9] Barclay conducts a comprehensive investigation of the variegated evidence of Second Temple Judaism by means of a series of penetrating case studies (Wisdom of Solomon, Philo and Pseudo-Philo, 1QHa, 4 Ezra), insightfully unfolding the diverse dynamics of grace in

---

of J. M. G. Barclay and S. J. Gathercole, eds., *Divine and Human Agency in Paul and His Cultural Environment* (London: T&T Clark, 2008).

6. J. M. G. Barclay, *Paul and the Gift* (Grand Rapids: Eerdmans, 2015).

7. D. A. DeSilva, *Honor, Patronage, Kinship and Purity: Unlocking New Testament Culture* (Downers Grove: IVP, 2000), 95-119; Z. A. Crook, *Reconceptualising Conversion: Patronage, Loyalty, and Conversion in the Religions of the Ancient Mediterranean* (Berlin: Walter de Gruyter, 2004), 132-48.

8. For coverage, see Harrison, *Paul's Language of Grace*, 97-106. Additionally, D. A. Carson, ed., *Justification and Variegated Nomism: Volume 2—The Paradoxes of Paul* (Grand Rapids: Baker Academic, 2004), Subject Index s.v. "grace"; S. Westerholm, *Perspectives Old and New on Paul: The "Lutheran" Paul and His Critics* (Grand Rapids: Eerdmans, 2004), 341-51; D. A. Campbell, *The Deliverance of God: An Apocalyptic Rereading of Justification in Paul* (Grand Rapids: Eerdmans, 2009), 96-124; Barclay, *Paul and the Gift*, 151-65; and N. T. Wright, *Paul and His Recent Interpreters: Some Contemporary Debates* (Minneapolis: Fortress, 2015), 64-105.

9. For reviews of *Paul's Language of Grace in Its Graeco-Roman Context*, see P. Tomson, *De stem von het Boek* 15.1 (2004): 14; G. Griffith, *JSNT* 27.7 (2005): 494-96; J. Kloppenborg, *BIAC* 32 (2005): 10-11; K. Ehrensperger, "Review Article: Reading Paul in the Light of Differing Frameworks of Thinking," *JBV* 26.3 (2005): 317-23, at 320; R. S. Ascough, *RSR* 32.1 (2006): 42; L. J. Peerbolte, *TvT* 44.3 (2006): 305-06; U. Schnelle, *TL* 131.11 (2006): 1154-56; D. Zeller, *TZ* 63 (2007): 141-43; E. Eguiarte, *Mayeutica* 33 (2007): 245-46; C. Stenschke, *R&T* 15 (2008): 178-80. The book was the 2005 Winner of the biannual *Biblical Archaeology Society Publication Award* for *Best Book Relating to the New Testament* published in 2003 and 2004.

Paul's first-century context.¹⁰ The quality and depth of Barclay's discussion of the Jewish background is unlikely to be challenged or supplanted for a long time, though Wells provides an excellent coverage of the Second Temple traditions in relation to Deuteronomy 30 and Romans 2:17–29, and the work is equally characterised by fine theological insight and careful exegesis.¹¹ Other studies explore aspects of divine grace in its eastern Mediterranean benefaction context, discussing either Seneca (Griffith, Pao; cf. Blanton, n. 15 *infra*) or Philo (Zeller, McFarland), or employing a selection of literary and documentary evidence (Crook, DeSilva). Last, in two massive volumes N. T. Wright explores the Jewish, Greek and Roman context of the apostle Paul's thought with immense care and exhaustive analysis.¹² As an important player in the "Paul and Empire" debate, Wright brings Paul's epistles into insightful dialogue with the Roman context.¹³ Wright argues that there are conceptual similarities between "Israel's millennium long narrative" of the Abrahamic promises of covenantal grace, now fulfilled in Christ, and the grand imperial narrative moving from Rome's founders (Aeneas/Romulus and Remus) to Augustus.¹⁴

By contrast, systematic and biblical theologies continue to touch on the role of grace in Paul's thought, but they make virtually no reference to the first-century context. This is hardly surprising, given the vastly different methodologies employed by the theological disciplines and exegetically based studies. But the continuing debate about the nature and task of New Testament theology poses a fundamental methodological question for us. How should historical exegesis of Pauline χάρις—as interpreted within the conventions of the LXX and Second Temple Judaism, the eastern Mediterranean reciprocity system, and the reign of Augustan and Neronian grace¹⁵—inform the study of grace in systematic and biblical theologies?¹⁶

10. Barclay, *Paul and the Gift*, 194–328.

11. Wells' book (*Grace and Agency in Paul*) won the Manfred Lautenschlaeger Award for Theological Promise in 2016.

12. N. T. Wright. *Paul and the Faithfulness of God: Parts I and II* (London: SPCK, 2013), 75–347.

13. N. T. Wright. *Paul and the Faithfulness of God: Parts III and IV* (London: SPCK, 2013), 1271–1319.

14. Wright, *Paul and the Faithfulness of God: Parts III and IV*, 1301–14.

15. On Augustan and Neronian grace, see Harrison, *Paul's Language of* Grace, 61–62, 88–89, 226–42, 351–52. For recent studies on Paul and reciprocity, see T. R. Blanton, "The Benefactor's Account Book: The Rhetoric of Gift Reciprocation According to Seneca and Paul," *NTS* 59.3 (2013): 396–414; Leithart, *Gratitude: An Intellectual History*.

16. On the nature and task of New Testament theology, see D. O. Via, *What is New*

Certainly there remains considerable good will regarding the possibility of an integration of disciplines in this regard. In recent years, several biblical scholars have reaffirmed the contribution that the application of historical methodology to the biblical documents makes for our understanding of New Testament and Pauline theology, as well as for our pastoral engagement with contemporary society.[17] In P. F. Esler's New Testament theology, for example, the author has proposed that a meticulous historical examination of Romans—within his proposed hermeneutical framework of interpersonal communication and communion—might throw light on how we can address ethnic violence and genocide within our own era.[18]

But the study of grace in systematic and biblical theologies had remained for a very long while caught in a "time warp" of Reformation dogmatics and has only recently been substantially challenged by the "New Perspective," Campbell's "participationist" approach, and Wright's "covenantal" theology. For too long there has been a disinclination on the part of theological exegetes to enter sympathetically and imaginatively into the struggles of mid-first-century Roman believers when they heard Paul's papyrus letter being read out aloud for the first time in their house churches. What difference, for example, did Paul's doctrine of divine election by grace in Romans 9–11 make to Jewish Christians struggling with the rising anti–Semitism at Rome among the Roman intelligentsia in the late 40's and 50's?[19] Alternatively, what difference did it make to Gentile Christians

---

Testament Theology? (Minneapolis: Fortress Press, 2000); H. Räisänen, *Beyond New Testament Theology* (London: SCM Press, 2000); P. F. Esler, *New Testament Theology: Communion and Community* (London: SPCK, 2005), 11–37; M. Bird, "New Testament Theology Reloaded: Integrating Biblical Theology and Christian Origins," *TynBul* 60.2 (2009): 265–91.

17. J. D. G. Dunn, *The Theology of Paul the Apostle* (Grand Rapids: Eerdmans, 1998); N. T. Wright, *The New Testament and the People of God* (Minneapolis: Fortress Press, 2000); G. Strecker, *Theology of the New Testament* (Louisville: Westminster John Knox, 2000); M. Bird, "New Testament Theology Reloaded."

18. Esler, *New Testament Theology*, 273–82. See Esler's previous commentary on Romans and the extensive attention he gives to ethnicity: idem, *Conflict and Identity in Romans: The Social Setting of Paul's Letter* (Minneapolis: Fortress Press, 2003), 40–76.

19. R. Penna, "The Jews in Rome at the Time of the Apostle Paul," in idem, *Paul the Apostle. Volume 1: Jew and Greek Alike* (Collegeville: Liturgical Press, 1996), 19–47; W. Wiefel, "The Jewish Community in Rome and the Origins of Roman Christianity," in K. P. Donfried, ed., *The Romans Debate: Revised and Expanded Edition* (Peabody: Hendrickson, 1991), 85–101. S. Grindheim's book on divine election (*The Crux of Election: Paul's Critique of the Jewish Confidence in the Election of Israel* [Tübingen: Mohr Siebeck, 2005], 7–76) expertly investigates the Jewish background of Romans 9–11.

living in the capital where the propaganda of Augustus depicted the ruler as the elect Saviour of Providence and the iconic benefactor of the world? We turn now to the understanding of grace in systematic theology.

The Understanding of Grace in Systematic Theology

In exploring the understanding of grace in systematic theology, we acknowledge that the task of theological dogmatics differs markedly from the brief of biblical exegesis. Systematic theologians range across the Old Testament and New Testament. They discuss the theological themes unifying both testaments within their canonical development, utilize the tools and methods of current biblical research, and draw upon the doctrinal traditions of historical theology for further illumination. Additionally, systematic theologians seek to bring their theological investigation into dialogue with contemporary concerns, relating their findings to traditional and emerging academic disciplines and to the pressing social, philosophical and cultural questions of their day.

It is unlikely that a detailed analysis of Paul's theology of grace would emerge from the wide-ranging quest of systematic theology, notwithstanding the wealth of exegetical observation found in Calvin or Barth, for instance. But the "timeless" approach of systematic theology to Paul's language of grace has imposed enduring paradigms upon the study of Paul that have, until only recently, obscured the apostle's versatility as a social and ecclesiastical thinker. A brief survey of systematic interpretations of Paul's theology of grace is therefore important for our purposes.

In late antiquity, Augustine of Hippo articulated his seminal understanding of divine grace in commentaries and treatises that were written in response to the doctrinal threat posed by the Manichees and Pelagius.[20] Whereas Manichaeism repudiated the existence of free will, Pelagius "exaggerated its role in justification."[21] By contrast, Augustine understood the event of justification, as enunciated by Paul, to be inaugurated by *operative grace* (a unilateral act of God), whereas the process of justification was accomplished by *cooperative* grace (a divine renewal that engaged the human

---

20. See P. Brown, *Augustine of Hippo: A Biography* (London: Faber & Faber, 1967); R. L. Fox, *Augustine: Conversions and Confessions* (Milton Keynes: Allen Lane, 2015).

21. A. E. McGrath, *Iustitia Dei: A History of the Christian Doctrine of Justification*, 2nd ed. (Cambridge: Cambridge University Press, 1998), 26.

will).²² Theologians of the early and later medieval period—including Thomas Aquinas, Duns Scotus, and Gabriel Biel—pursued and expanded upon Augustine's conviction that human beings still had a positive role to play in justification, arguing that this occurred through the infusion of grace or by means of the sacraments or via a pact between God and humankind.²³

To some extent, Augustine's polemical approach bore similarities to the tactics of the historical Paul who, centuries earlier, had worked on several ideological fronts in framing his theology. The apostle responds pointedly to cultural and theological perversions of his gospel of grace, Graeco-Roman and Jewish, emanating from inside and outside his house churches. He also critiques, sometimes with intentional precision, other times more obliquely, the competing social and religious ideologies of the eastern Mediterranean basin by means of his careful theological construction of counter symbolic universes. Paul's presentation of the reign of grace in Romans 5:12–21, to return to our engagement with Romans, is as much written against the backdrop of the unparalleled grace of the Julio-Claudian benefactors as the variegated Jewish understandings of covenantal grace and sin, the theological crisis precipitated by Israel's stumbling (Rom 9–11), and the arrogance of Gentile Christians towards their Jewish brothers (11:17–21).²⁴

This is not to suggest that Paul's language of grace was merely an apologetic strategy. The apostle's gospel of justification by electing grace originated from his own Damascus experience of the risen Jesus and from his call to be the apostle to the Gentiles (e.g. Gal 1:14–16 [Jer 1:4–5; Isa 42:1, 6–7; 44:1–2, 24; 49:1, 6; Pss 22:9–19; 71:6]; 2 Cor 4:6; cf. Rom 8:29–30; Eph 1:4–6).²⁵ Undoubtedly, it was also informed by the tradition of Je-

---

22. For Augustine's critique of Pelagius, see *On the Proceedings of Pelagius*.

23. See the magisterial discussion of A. E. McGrath, *Iustitia Dei*, 37–179.

24. For criticism of my position, see C. Breytenbach, "CHARIS and ELEOS in Paul's Letter to the Romans," in *The Letter to the Romans*, ed. U. Schnelle (Leuven: Leuven University Press/Uitgenerij Peeters, 2009), 247–77, at 251–58. As noted above, I had suggested that Paul's language of "overflow" in Romans 5:12–21 probably came conceptually and terminologically from the Julio-Claudian reign of unparalleled and unrivalled grace. Cilliers Breytenbach, however, has convincingly argued that it comes *conceptually* from the LXX Psalms where God's overflowing forgiveness of sinners is effusively enunciated. To illustrate the point by way of a metaphor, the husk of Paul's terminology may still be Graeco-Roman in this instance, as I have argued, but, as Breytenbach has decisively shown, its theological and conceptual kernel was Jewish.

25. See S. Kim, *Paul and the New Perspective: Second Thoughts on the Origin of Paul's Gospel* (Grand Rapids: Eerdmans, 2002), 101–27 etc. for a discussion of the convergence

sus' openness towards the "godless and lost" in his ministry,[26] and by the apostle's own Spirit-renewed understanding (2 Cor 3:8, 17–18), in light of his Damascus experience, of the Old Testament covenantal and prophetic heritage.[27]

In the Reformation, Martin Luther and John Calvin attacked the merit theology of medieval Catholicism, ensuring the triumph of Paul's theology of grace in Protestant thought through their relentless emphasis on justification by faith alone.[28] Two significant developments for Pauline scholarship emerged from this striking theological breakthrough. First, the Reformers dismissed medieval Catholicism as a "works-based" piety with strong parallels, it was alleged, to the meritorious Torah-based religion of Judaism.[29] The caricature of first-century Judaism as a "graceless" religion remained deeply entrenched in New Testament scholarship until G. F. Moore, R. T. Herford, and E. P. Sanders challenged the stereotype over the course of the twentieth century.[30] Second, eternal election—which Calvin saw mirrored in Christ (*Inst.* 3.24.5; cf. Eph 1:4, 9; 2 Tim 1:9)—was singled

of Paul's Damascus experience with the elect Servant of Isaiah.

26. Note the comment of E. Stauffer (*New Testament Theology* [London: SCM Press, 1955], 144–45): "The message of God's grace and of the forgiveness of sins derives from Jesus himself and was the common ground of the primitive Church. But its most powerful representative was the apostle Paul, and its most forceful expression is found in his doctrine of atonement." G. Bornkamm (*Paul* [London: Hodder and Stoughton, 1971], 237–39) also points to the continuity between Jesus and Paul on the issue of justification, but asserts that Paul knew less about the Jesus of history than we do. However, Paul's tantalising reference to the "meekness and gentleness" of Christ (2 Cor 10:1) perhaps indicates that he knows considerably more about the historical Jesus' ministry to "sinners" (e.g. Matt 5:5; 11:28–30) than he initially lets on.

27. Note the revealing comment of A. Richardson (*An Introduction to the Theology of the New Testament* [London: SCM Press, 1958], 272): "Against this religion of pride and merit, the teaching of Jesus and his disciples, notably St Paul, represents a vigorous 'protestant' reformation, a reformation based upon a return to the *sola gratia* of Israel's prophets and to their parallel doctrine of election for service."

28. While the great Reformer, Philip Melanchthon, did not surrender the *sola gratia* of justification, his later theology reflected elements of synergistic thinking. For discussion, see G. C. Berkouwer, *Divine Election* (Grand Rapids: Eerdmans, 1960), 32–33.

29. For a comparison between works-based Judaism and the papists, see P. Melanchton, *Commentary on Romans* (St. Louis: Concordia Publishing House, 1992), 60.

30. G. F. Moore, *Judaism in the First Centuries of the Christian Era: The Age of the Tannaim*, 3 vols. (Cambridge, MA: Harvard University Press, 1927-1930); R. T. Herford, *The Pharisees* (London: George Allen & Unwin Ltd., 1924); E. P. Sanders, *Paul and Palestinian Judaism: A Comparison of Patterns of Religion* (London: SCM, 1977). Note the important critique of the deficiencies of Sander's understanding of grace in Barclay, *Paul and the Gift*, 151–58.

out as the raison d'être of the operation of divine grace in salvation history, with reprobation being its dark-sided corollary.[31] The theological legacy of each development still continues to influence modern scholarly discussion of Paul's understanding of grace.[32]

Closer to our era, Karl Barth struggled with the legacy of the post-war crisis of 1918 and challenged the optimistic, anthropocentric theologies of Adolf Harnack and Friedrich Schleiermacher.[33] Barth's theology of grace stands out for its richness throughout his *Church Dogmatics*.[34] According to Barth, the Bible is a miracle of grace to its readers (*CD* I.2 528–530); grace represents the supreme expression of God's love (*CD* II.1 353–68);[35] the election of divine grace is fully revealed in Christ, the electing and

31. While Calvin emphasises the freedom and sovereignty of divine grace in election (*Inst.* 3.21–24), he also strongly underscores the merit of Christ imputed to believers as the grounds of all grace (*ibid.*, 2.17): "Christ, by his obedience, truly purchased and merited grace for us with the Father" (*ibid.*, 2.17.3). The entirety of Book 3 of Calvin's *Institutes* is devoted to the mode of obtaining the grace of Christ, temporal and pretemporal. In sum, Calvin gives to his presentation of divine grace a sharp Christocentric focus. We should not discount the important Reformed work of Peter Martyr Vermigli (1499–1562) on divine election (*Predestination and Justification: Two Theological Loci*, trans. Frank A. James [Kirksville: Truman State University Press, 2003]).

32. For discussion, see G. C. Berkouwer, *Divine Election* (Grand Rapids: Eerdmans, 1960); H. Bavinck, *Reformed Dogmatics: God and Creation. Volume 2* (Grand Rapids: Baker Academic, 2004), Subject Index: *s.v.* "election, divine," "grace"; G. J. Spykman, *Reformational Theology: A New Paradigm for Doing Dogmatics* (Grand Rapids: Eerdmans, 1992), 507–12. For criticism of Berkouwer's position, see A. L. Baker, *Berkouwer's Doctrine of Election: Balance or Imbalance?* (Phillipsburg: Presbyterian and Reformed Publishing Co., 1981).

33. F. Schleiermacher (*The Christian Faith* [Edinburgh: T&T Clark, 1928], 366–67) argued that the power of Christ's God–consciousness brought about an increasing perfection in humanity as it assimilated the human consciousness of sin to itself. This communication of the God–consciousness on the part of Christ the Redeemer to humanity is what Scheiermacher perceived divine grace to be (*ibid.*, 262–64).

34. For an excellent discussion of grace in Barth's theology, see the older work of G. C. Berkouwer, *The Triumph of Grace in the Theology of Karl Barth* (Grand Rapids: Eerdmans, 1956). Grace is given considerably less attention in Barth's earlier lectures at Göttingen (*The Göttingen Dogmatics: Instruction in the Christian Religion Vol. 1* [Grand Rapids: Eerdmans, 1991], Index of Subjects *s.v.* "Grace"), though divine election is covered more expansively (*ibid.*, Index of Subjects *s.v.* "Election"). Barclay confines his assessment of Barth's understanding of grace to the theologian's famous epistle to the Romans (*Paul and the Gift*, 130–35).

35. Emil Brunner—Barth's famous neo-orthodox contemporary—omits grace from his discussion of God's attributes (*The Christian Doctrine of God. Dogmatics Vol. I* [London: Lutterworth Press, 1949]), reserving his discussion of divine grace for his third volume (*The Christian Doctrine of the Church, Faith and the Consummation Dogmatics Vol. III* [London: Lutterworth Press, 1962], Index of Subjects *s.v.* "God: grace").

elected one (*CD* II.2 3–194); and, finally, the triumphant grace of God is demonstrated in the atonement as the fulfilment of the covenant and is the underlying dynamic animating justification by faith (*CD* IV.1 69, 514–642). In Barth's presentation of the objective character of God's work in Christ the "objectivism of grace" is continuously underscored.[36] As Barth states,

> When Christ appeared and died and rose again, the grace of God became an event for all men, and all men are made liable for their being and activity, for their being and activity as it is revealed in the light of this event. For as the ultimate and profoundest reality, this event is the self-revelation of the truth, and therefore the truth about man.[37]

Although Barth is not writing a theology of Paul, the meticulous attention that he gives to the role of grace in the apostle's thought stands in marked contrast, inexplicably, to many contemporary theologies of Paul.

Another important theological work highlighting the centrality of grace, published in 1937 prior to the outbreak of the Second World War, was Dietrich Bonhoeffer's *The Cost of Discipleship*. This study highlighted how the Lutheran understanding of justification by grace had been progressively cheapened as the Christian West played down the call to costly discipleship:

> Judged by the standard of Luther's doctrine, that of his followers was unassailable, and yet their orthodoxy spelt the end and destruction of the Reformation as the revelation on earth of the costly grace of God. The justification of the sinner in the world degenerated into the justification of sin and the world. Costly grace was turned into cheap grace without discipleship.[38]

Although Bonhoeffer concentrated on the call to discipleship as expressed in the Sermon on the Mount, his insights captured well the corporate and participationsist transformation demanded by Paul of those living under the reign of grace (Rom 3:8; 6:1, 15; cf. 5:21b).[39]

In the second half of the twentieth century, several systematic theologians comment on divine grace in their works. Otto Weber's two-volumed

---

36. See the discussion of K. Runia, *Karl Barth's Doctrine of Holy Scripture* (Grand Rapids: Eerdmans, 1968), 213–16.

37. *CD* I.2 305.

38. D. Bonhoeffer, *The Cost of Discipleship* (London: SCM Press, 1959, Gmn. orig. 1937), 41.

39. See Bonhoeffer, *The Cost of Discipleship*, 201–75.

dogmatics devotes considerable attention to grace as a divine attribute and to its relation to justification and election.[40] Wolfhart Pannenberg ranges more widely on grace than most modern theologians, though within traditional systematic categories and without detailed attention to Paul.[41] The evangelical systematic theology of Millard Erickson touches on grace intermittently, though his concentration on Paul in this regard is surprisingly minimal, congregating around the twin foci of justification and election.[42] In the 1990's Thomas Oden's *The Transforming Power of Grace* was the first systematic study of divine grace in decades, incisive in its theological insight, and challenging in its cultural analysis and application.[43] Last, Rowan William's *Grace and Necessity: Reflections on Art and Love* unexpectedly explores the non–benefaction semantic domain of χάρις ("charm," "loveliness", "delight") in his discussion of aesthetics, the ancient philosophical study of Beauty.[44]

Several comments on the understanding of grace evinced by systematic theologians are apposite at this juncture. Not unexpectedly, the theological construct that emerges is generally "timeless," with little if any reference to the historical situation that Paul was facing. Where the Jewish context is briefly referred to in dogmatic theologies, the Reformation paradigm of first-century Judaism as being a Torah and merit-based faith has been too often perpetuated without any qualification.

No consideration is given to the Graeco-Roman context of grace, even though Paul as the apostle to the Gentiles would have been forced by the pressures of his converts' social world to address the theological and social dynamics of χάρις, within both the reciprocity system and the cult of the imperial benefactors in the Greek East and Roman West.[45] Surprisingly, no attention is given to the explosion of grace language in 2 Corinthians 8–9

---

40. Respectively, O. Weber, *Foundation of Dogmatics. Volume 1* (Grand Rapids: Eerdmans, 1983), 424–28; idem, *Foundation of Dogmatics Volume 2* (Grand Rapids: Eerdmans, 1983), 280–314, 411–48, 487–92.

41. W. Pannenberg, *Systematic Theology. Volume 3* (Grand Rapids: Eerdmans, 1993), Index of Subjects *s.v.* "Grace".

42. M. Erickson, *Christian Theology* (Grand Rapids: Baker, 1990), Name and Subject Index *s.v.* "Grace". The same could be said about W. Grudem, *Systematic Theology: An Introduction to Biblical Doctrine* (Leicester: IVP, 1994).

43. T. Oden, *The Transforming Power of Grace* (Nashville: Abingdon Press, 1993).

44. R. Williams, *Grace and Necessity: Reflections on Art and Love* (London: Continuum, 2005).

45. Harrison, *Paul's Language of Grace, passim.*

regarding the Jerusalem collection.[46] The "unofficial" brief of systematic theologians seems to be that once grace as an attribute of God, justification by faith, divine election, and the means and rewards of grace have been aired,[47] no additional theological comment is required. Consequentially, a truncated understanding of the intersection of divine and human grace emerges.

Furthermore, where divine election is extensively discussed in Romans, systematic theologians overlook the fact that Paul is writing to Gentile converts (Rom 1:13; 11:13; 15:15–16) who are living in the capital where the imperial ruler resided. The imperial propaganda promoted a symbolic universe in which Augustus—the iconic Roman ruler who, in the view of posterity, had dispensed overflowing grace[48]—was installed as the divinely elected vice regent of the gods.[49] The Priene inscription depicted Augustus as the *telos* of world history, whereas, by contrast, Paul's rhetoric portrayed Christ as the *telos* of the Jewish quest for Torah righteousness (Rom 10:4).[50] We are witnessing here a collision of symbolic universes that lifts divine election from "timeless" theology to something more germane for first-century Romans.[51] Through the grace of Christ they could be immediately incorporated as siblings into the household of Abraham as opposed to being, only in select cases, clients of the household of Caesar and of his freedmen (Phil 4:22; Rom 16:11b). The political implications of Paul's theology have been extensively explored, but the first-century imperial context of grace has been overlooked in discussing God's electing grace and the social values undergirding mid-fifties Rome.[52]

46. Ibid., 314–21.

47. E.g. H. Hoeksema, *Reformed Dogmatics. Volume 2* (Grandville: Reformed Free Publishing Association, 1966), 112–19, 280–85.

48. Harrison, *Paul's Language of Grace*, 226–42.

49. See J. R. Fears, PRINCEPS A DIIS ELECTUS: *The Divine Election of the Emperor as a Political Concept at Rome* (Rome: American Academy in Rome, 1977).

50. Harrison, *Paul's Language of Grace*, 228–31.

51. For criticism of my stance on the abstraction of timeless theology and exegesis, see McFarland, see *God and Grace in Philo and Paul*, 18.

52. For a brief coverage of the first-century imperial context of "electing" grace and its relation to Pauline theology, see Harrison, "Paul, Theologian of Electing Grace," 101–107. On the social values of Augustan Rome and its ethical legacy for Roman believers, see J. R. Harrison, "Augustan Rome and the Body of Christ: A Comparison of the Social Vision of the *Res Gestae* and Paul's Letter to the Romans," *HTR* 106.1 (2013): 1–36. See also R. Jewett, *Romans* (Hermeneia; Minneapolis: Fortress Press, 2007), *passim*. N. Elliott, *The Arrogance of Nations: Reading Romans in the Shadow of Empire* (Minneapolis: Fortress, 2008).

Finally, systematic theologians misconstrue to some extent the way in which Paul theologically operates. The hurly-burly of the ecclesiastical and social context in which Paul pastors and evangelises (e.g. Romans 3:8; 15:23-33; 1 Cor 1:10-17; 5:1, 9-11; 7:1; 8:1; 12:1; 2 Cor 11:28-29; 12:14-21; Gal 1:6-10) provided the stimulus for the apostle's creative application of his cruciform gospel to the pressing demands of his culture and his missionary outreach to the Gentiles. It might be concluded from this that Paul's approach as a theologian of grace is diametrically opposed to the approach of systematic dogmatics. However, this would overplay the role of contextual issues in the development of Paul's theology. Paul's theological framework regarding the reign of grace and divine election was firmly in place from the outset of his missionary career (e.g. Gal 2:11-14; cf. 1:13-17; 1 Thess 1:4; 2:12; 5:9, 24; cf. Acts 9:15; 22:14-16; 26:15-17).[53] Notwithstanding, the collision of *first-century* symbolic universes regarding election—Jewish and Roman—probably contributed in some way to Paul creating the meta-narrative of electing grace that has been so thoroughly combed over by systematic theologians.

We turn now to a survey of New Testament and Pauline theologians: do they adopt a more contextual approach to Paul's theology of grace or is their *modus operandi* consonant with traditional systematic approaches? Do they perceive Paul's understanding of divine grace to be the thematic lynchpin of his theology or is it more peripheral in comparison to other motifs?

The Understanding of Grace in New Testament Theologies and in Paul

Issues Arising from the Discussion of Grace in New Testament Theologies

When Johann Philipp Gabler argued for the separation of biblical theology from dogmatic theology in 1787,[54] the historical analysis of biblical texts became increasingly the focus of a new generation of scholars over against theological dogmatics. Consequently, Old Testament and New Testament theology began to emerge as separate disciplines, and within these disci-

---

53. F. Thielman, *Theology of the New Testament* (Grand Rapids: Zondervan, 2005), 227. For a discussion of grace in 1 Thessalonians, see Kim, *Paul and the New Perspective*, 85-100.

54. For discussion, see Esler, *New Testament Theology*, 11-37; Thielman, *Theology of the New Testament*, 23-24.

plines, specialist areas of study such as Pauline theology. What contribution has the biblical theology movement made to our understanding of Paul's theology of grace? Has it really advanced beyond the methodological impasse of systematic theology outlined above?

Only the most recent theologies of the New Testament are sensitive to the impact of the "New Perspective" upon the Paul's understanding of justification by grace. H. Marshall, for example, while not endorsing the "New Perspective", discusses the legitimacy of using "merit" terminology for Jewish boundary markers in Galatians.[55] He acknowledges the (alleged) ambiguity of understanding of grace in the Qumran literature[56] and also interacts incisively with the "covenantal nomism" of E. P. Sanders.[57] Marshall's discussion alerts readers of systematic theology to the potential stereotypes of first-century Judaism contained in New Testament theologies of the past. For example, R. Bultmann's heavy emphasis on Jewish "works" righteousness[58] and A. Richardson's dismissal of the Judaism of the rabbis as graceless are cases in point.[59]

Other scholars are frustratingly imprecise. G. B. Caird, for example, correctly claims that Paul highlights the sovereignty of grace over against the "Judaizers", but he never specifies their provenance and the type of sectarian Judaism that they embraced.[60] Other theologies of the New Testament do not pause at all to consider the nature of the Judaism that Paul's theology of grace might be addressing.[61] It is essential, therefore, for New

---

55. I. H. Marshall, *New Testament Theology* (Downers Grove: IVP, 2004), 212, n. 8. See also the critique of the "New Perspective" in F. S. Thielman, *Theology of the New Testament: A Canonical and Synthetic Approach* (Grand Rapids: Zondervan, 2005), 272-74.

56. Thielman, *Theology of the New Testament*, 227 n. 39.

57. Thielman, *Theology of the New Testament*, 227-29.

58. R. Bultmann, *Theology of the New Testament*, Volume 1 (London: SCM Press, 1952), 281-292. Similarly, H. Conzelmann, *An Outline of the Theology of the New Testament* (London: SCM Press, 1969), 214.

59. A. Richardson, *An Introduction to the Theology of the New Testament* (London: SCM Press, 1958), 283. G. E. Ladd (*A Theology of the New Testament* [Guildford and London: Lutterworth Press, 1974], 496-501) argues that obedience to the law became the condition of covenantal membership in the intertestamental period and replaced the grace-centered faith of the Old Testament. W. G. Kümmel (*Theology of the New Testament* [London: SCM Press, 1973], 195-96) proposes that the Qumran covenanters more emphasised obedience to the law than justification by grace.

60. G. B. Caird, *New Testament Theology*, ed. L. D. Hurst (Oxford: Clarendon Press, 1994), 184-88.

61. E.g. A. Schlatter, *The Theology of the Apostles: The Development of New Testament*

Testament theologies to appreciate the variegated understandings of divine grace and election present in first-century Judaism if we are to avoid injudiciously imposing "Reformation" or "New Perspective" paradigms upon the Pauline evidence.

As regards the Graeco-Roman context of grace, C. Spicq employs a wealth of inscriptional and papyrological evidence in order to illustrate the operation of grace in the honorific system of the eastern Mediterranean basin.[62] However, the imperial context of grace is frustratingly overlooked.

Finally, three New Testament theologians identify divine grace as the motif undergirding Paul's gospel of Christ crucified. W. Kümmel endorses H. D. Wendland's view that justification by grace through faith is "the center of the Pauline message".[63] D. Guthrie, identifying grace as a dominant feature of Paul's theology,[64] sums up his position thus:

> If there was one characteristic of God which captured the imagination of Paul more than another, it was the grace of God.[65]

F. Thielman repeatedly drives home that divine grace is the center of Paul's theology:

> If one theological theme is more basic than others in Paul's letters, therefore, it is this notion that God is a gracious God and that he has shown his grace preeminently in his arrangement of history to answer the problem of human sinfulness in the death and resurrection of his Son, Jesus Christ.[66]

Theology (Grand Rapids: Baker Books, 1998, Gmn. orig. 1922); J. Bonsirven, *Theology of the New Testament* (Westminster: Newman Press, 1963); L. Goppelt, *Theology of the New Testament. Volume 2: The Variety and Unity of the Apostolic Witness to Christ* (Grand Rapids: Eerdmans, 1982); F. Vouga, *Une théologie du nouveau testament* (Genève: Labor et Fides, 2001).

62. C. Spicq, *Théologie morale du nouveau testament* Tome 1 (Paris: Librairie Lecroffre, 1965), 110–45. His appendix ('Qu'est-ce que la grâce?', ibid., 451–61) is partially translated in C. Spicq, *Theological Lexicon of the New Testament* Vol.3 (Peabody: Hendrickson, 1994: Fr. orig. 1978), 500–06.

63. W. G. Kümmel, *Theology of the New Testament* (London: SCM Press, 1976), 142.

64. D. Guthrie, *New Testament Theology* (London: IVP, 1981) 620.

65. *Ibid.*, 106.

66. Thielman, *Theology of the New Testament*, 479; also 230–33. Note that T. R. Schreiner (*New Testament Theology: Magnifying God in Christ* [Grand Rapids: Baker Academic, 2008], 347–50) also touches on grace in Paul's thought, but we confine our discussion of Schreiner's views to his Pauline theology.

Thielman highlights the role of grace in the Jerusalem collection,[67] in human suffering,[68] in the eschatological reversal of the gospel,[69] in relation to the Mosaic law,[70] and in divine election.[71] The graciousness of God, he asserts, is "the most characteristic element of Paul's understanding of God".[72] Singular among recent New Testament theologians in this regard, Thielman has emphasised with Barthian relentlessness the pervasive structure of grace holding together Paul's theology.

Do we see the emphasis on divine grace so characteristic of Thielman's work reflected in Pauline theologies?

Issues Arising from the Discussion of Grace in Pauline Theologies

Since the 1950's theologies of Paul have devoted little space to an investigation of the role of grace in Paul's thought.[73] This oversight may well

67. Thielman, *Theology of the New Testament*, 338–40,

68. Ibid., 340–41.

69. Ibid., 281–82.

70. Ibid., 274–75.

71. Ibid., 450.

72. Ibid., 477–79.

73. J. C. Beker, *Paul the Apostle: The Triumph of God in Life and Thought* (Edinburgh: T&T Clark, 1980); Campbell, *The Deliverance of God*; W. S. Campbell, *Paul and the Creation of Christian Identity* (London: T&T Clark, 2008); L. Cerfaux, *The Church in the Theology of Paul, Christ in the Theology of Paul, The Christian in the Theology of Paul* (New York: Herder and Herder, respectively, 1959, 1959, 1967); C. A. Davis, *The Structure of Paul's Theology: "The Truth Which is the Gospel"* (Lewiston/Lampeter/Queenston: Edwin Mellen Press, 1995); T. Holland, *Contours of Pauline Theology: A Radical New Survey of the Influences on Paul's Biblical Writings* (Fearn: Mentor, 2004); R. P. Martin, *Reconciliation: A Study of Paul's Theology* (London: Marshall, Morgans & Scott, 1981); C. M. Pate, *The End of the Ages Has Come: The Theology of Paul* (Grand Rapids: Zondervan Publishing House, 1995); H. Ridderbos, *Paul: An Outline of His Theology* (Grand Rapids: Eerdmans, 1975); B. Witherington III, *Paul's Narrative Thought World: The Tapestry of Tragedy and Triumph* (Louisville: Westminster/John Knox Press, 1994); U. Schnelle, *Apostle Paul: His Life and Theology* (Grand Rapids: Baker Academic, 2003); D. E. H. Whitely, *The Theology of Saint Paul* (Oxford: Basil Blackwell, 1983); M. Wolter, *Paul: An Outline of His Theology* (Waco: Baylor University Press, 2015); Wright. *Paul and the Faithfulness of God*; J. Ziesler, *Pauline Theology* (Oxford: Oxford University Press, 1983). Similarly, late nineteenth and early twentieth–century interpreters of Paul's theology (e.g. A. Deissmann; P. Feine; O. Pfleiderer; F. Pratt; A. Sabatier; C. A. A. Scott; G. B. Stevens) either discuss grace in traditional dogmatic categories or treat it very briefly. For other significant Pauline interpreters (e.g. R. Bultmann, J. Louis Martyn, E. Käsemann, A. Badiou) not covered in this summary, see Barclay, *Paul and the Gift*, 135–50, 175–79.

have arisen because grace, in our post-Reformation and post-Barthian era, has almost attained an *axiomatic* status: if justification by faith and divine election are thoroughly discussed, then grace in the view of the Pauline interpreter has been effectively dealt with. This, of course, overlooks the vital fact that divine grace is not only favor granted but also power unleashed.[74] To ignore this plunges us into the morass of Bonhoeffer's "cheap grace" and robs Paul's thought of its socially transformative impetus.

However, the two Pauline theologians, J. D. G. Dunn and T. R. Schreiner, have exerted great care in showing how grace unites key aspects of Paul's theology in a more comprehensive manner than before.[75] As T. R. Schreiner astutely notes, many of the proposed centers of Paul's theology (e.g. justification, reconciliation, "in Christ" etc.) "exalt the gift above the giver."[76] What is required is a Pauline theme that unites the Father's soteriological and pneumatic gifts in their personal, ecclesiastical, and social expression. Certainly grace, the liberating and empowering characteristic of God's electing love, is a prime candidate.[77]

Finally, a recent work on grace in Pauline theology is Frank Matera's *God's Saving Grace: A Pauline Theology*.[78] Matera grounds Paul's Christology, eschatology, soteriology, and ecclesiology in Paul's Damascus road Christophany. Thus Paul's conversion leads Matera, in a letter-by-letter approach, to discuss Christ as the embodiment of divine grace, his soteriological demonstration of grace, the ecclesiology of grace, the experience of grace in the Christian life, and, in a focus often overlooked in traditional

---

74. T. R. Schreiner, *Paul: Apostle of God's Glory in Christ. A Pauline Theology* (Downers Grove: IVP, 2001), 246.

75. J. D. G. Dunn (*The Theology of Paul the Apostle* [Grand Rapids: Eerdmans, 1998], Index of Subjects *s.v.* "Grace", "Charism") brings a discussion of the *charismata* into his coverage of grace, while T. R. Schriener (*Pauline Theology*, Subject Index *s.v.* "Grace") expends considerable effort in demonstrating how grace is the dynamic behind the diverse elements of Paul's theology. Dunn (*The Theology of Paul* 499–532) also provides of an outstanding coverage of electing grace in Romans 9–11.

76. Schreiner, *Pauline Theology*, 18.

77. However, the most recent Pauline theology (Wolter, *Paul: An Outline of His Theology*) conducts an excellent chapter–by–chapter examination of a wide array of theological motifs in the apostle's thought but ineplicably consigns grace to a brief discussion towards the book's end (ibid., 384–88). This again demonstrates that, in contrast to the theological greats of the past, there still is little consensus among modern Pauline scholars that grace is the central theological motif unifying the apostle's thought.

78. F. J. Matera, *God's Saving Grace: A Pauline Theology* (Grand Rapids: Eerdmans, 2012).

theologies of grace, the parousia appearance of God's saving grace.[79] Also very refreshing is the way that Matera unveils in his final chapter the character of the God revealed through the saving grace of Christ, another frequently unobserved emphasis.[80] But, disappointingly, the social dimension of grace, revealed in the explosion of χάρις and its cognates in the description of the Jerusalem collection, is bypassed.

Summing Up

All books have a "shelf life," and it is certainly worth pondering what *Paul's Language of Grace* still has to offer amidst the avalanche of scholarly riches now available on the study of χάρις. I think that my book remains the most extensive coverage of the Graeco-Roman benefaction context of χάρις. Beyond that, however, the reader will have to judge what contribution that the book still makes to the study of the theology, ecclesiology, and social thought of the apostle Paul. I am deeply honoured in being approached by Wipf and Stock to republish this volume and it is my hope that the book will continue to bless its readers to the glory of God.

25 October, 2016

---

79. Ibid., 186–214.
80. Ibid., 215–49.

Chapter 1

Paul and the Reign of Grace

This thesis will argue that the Graeco-Roman *benefaction* context of χάρις is the backdrop for Paul's understanding of divine and human grace. Paul's language of grace would have been assessed by his auditors against the hellenistic reciprocity system that shaped the rituals of giving and receiving throughout the eastern Mediterranean basin.[1] This was, after all, the area in which Paul founded and pastored his fledgling house churches. Paul's Gentile converts were intimately familiar with the operations of hellenistic beneficence. To be sure, the Roman patronal system was well known in the Greek East, initially through the benefactions of the republican luminaries, and later through the munificence of the Caesars. But the traditional benefaction system of the Greek city-states continued to flourish well into the imperial period, along with its reciprocity conventions and terminology. This is illustrated by the numerous honorific inscriptions scattered throughout the entire region of the eastern Mediterranean.

To honour a benefactor the Council of a Greek city-state would usually inscribe a decree on a stone slab or bronze plaque and erect it in a conspicuous public place. Typically, the inscription eulogised the merit of a civic benefactor, detailed the benefits that he had conferred on the citizens, and specified what honours had been decreed to him by the Council. The city-state thereby ensured that the moral and social status of the benefactor was enhanced, in the hope that it would elicit further benefits from him and/or his peers.

An ethos of reciprocity governed the relations between the benefactor and his beneficiaries. Reciprocity — or the return of favour for acts of generosity by benefactors — created networks of obligation that were a matter of honour for benefactor and beneficiary alike. In conferring a range of public honours, the Council recompensed the benefactor's quest for honour (φιλοτιμία). Simultaneously, by means of the return of honour to its benefactor, the

---

[1] S.C. Mott (*The Greek Benefactor and Deliverance from Moral Distress* [unpub. Ph.D. diss. Harvard University 1971], 75) comments: 'The relationship with the gods as benefactors has the same reciprocal character as with human benefactors'.

Council maintained its own reputation of gratitude in front of the other Greek city-states. It is important to realise that by the first century AD χάρις had become the central leitmotiv of the hellenistic reciprocity system. By making this terminology the touchstone of his theology of grace, it would seem that Paul *deliberately* chose to articulate his understanding of χάρις over against the theological and social beliefs of the eastern Mediterranean city-states regarding beneficence.

It should be observed in this regard that Paul's Jewishness would not have insulated him against the impact of hellenistic reciprocity ideology. The very fact that Paul, in sharp contrast to the LXX, chose χάρις ('grace') over against ἔλεος ('mercy') as his central description of beneficence (divine and human) should alert us to this. Whereas *ḥesed* ('mercy') was the most frequently used Hebrew word for covenantal beneficence in the Old Testament, Paul rarely employs its LXX equivalents (ἔλεος, ἐλεεῖν). Instead, unexpectedly, he magnifies χάρις and its cognates.[2]

Moreover, the Jewish communities of Palestine and the diaspora had sought legitimation for the reciprocity ideology of their milieu in the Mosaic law and in the LXX narratives, domesticating its more socially congenial practices, and critiquing many of the same benefaction *topoi* as the popular philosophers. As Chapter 4 will demonstrate, χάρις retained its hellenistic reciprocal aspect even in a Jewish context.

Why, then, was χάρις so advantageous a term for Paul as he sought to unveil his gospel of grace for his Gentile converts?

First, the semantic versatility of χάρις in its hellenistic context meant that the word was ideally suited for reciprocity rituals. It designated the 'favour', 'good-will', or 'grace' conferred by the benefactor on the beneficiary. Equally, it could refer to the return of 'favour' or 'thanks' by the beneficiary to the benefactor, whether human or divine. Almost universally, Paul uses χάρις and its cognates in a benefaction context, but at times with reserve as far as reciprocity is concerned. The familiarity of χάρις and its associated reciprocity conventions ensured its ready recognition by Paul's first-century auditors and would probably have captured their attention as the apostle began to invest the word with new theological content.

Second, χάρις allowed Paul the opportunity to interact theologically and socially with the benefaction culture of his times. The emperor Augustus, for example, had ushered in an 'age of grace' that eclipsed all his rivals by virtue

---

[2] In the undisputed and disputed letters, Paul uses ἔλεος 10 times; ἐλεεῖν 12 times. By contrast, Paul uses χάρις 97 times; χάρισμα 16 times; χαρίζεσθαι 13 times; χαριτᾶν once; εὐχαριστία 12 times; εὐχαριστεῖν 24 times; εὐχάριστος once; ἀχάριστος once.

of the (seemingly endless) χάριτες he was able to marshal for his beneficiaries. As we will argue, this unilateral display of Augustan beneficence may well have provided the cue for one of Paul's central theological forays: the reign of eschatological grace. Again, the numerous honorific inscriptions celebrating the χάριτες of civic benefactors may have prompted the question: what differentiates the Christian views of generosity and gratitude from their hellenistic counterparts? Χάρις, nevertheless, became the primary vehicle for Paul's theological and social response.

Furthermore, this interaction with contemporary benefaction culture was not necessarily initiated by Paul himself. There were, undoubtedly, occasions when Gentile converts and interested outsiders would have enquired about the relationship of the gospel to various hellenistic perceptions of divine and human beneficence. The ethics of beneficence were widely discussed in the works of the popular philosophers on χάρις, as the conventions of reciprocity system reached down to the base of the social pyramid. The likelihood that some of Paul's converts understood gift-giving as a social exchange may well have forced the apostle's hand theologically on several occasions. Thus the central leitmotiv of eastern Mediterranean reciprocity, χάρις, was re-defined by Paul for believers in the light of the sacrifice of the crucified Christ.

Additionally, the debate between the Stoics and the Epicureans over divine beneficence and divine wrath continued to rage into the first-century AD and well beyond. It is hard to believe that Paul's teaching concerning justification by grace through faith was not somehow related to the wider theological questions of Graeco-Roman society.

At the outset, three questions should be posed regarding previous scholarship in our area. First, how far have modern studies of Graeco-Roman benefaction enabled us to unearth the first-century social strata in which χάρις lies embedded? Second, to what extent have modern studies on the Pauline theology of grace shown an interest in the Graeco-Roman benefaction context and its impact on the apostle's message? Third, what has been the contribution of modern social-scientific studies of patronage and grace in helping us to understand Paul's view of divine and human beneficence?

1.1. Modern Scholarship on Benefaction: The Clue to the First-Century Context of Charis?

There is no modern study of the Graeco-Roman benefaction system which devotes significant attention to χάρις, whether it be in the documentary or literary evidence. This omission is hardly surprising. Scholars writing on benefaction prior to World War 2 — with the exception of W.P. Clark — largely ignored the evidence of honorific inscriptions of the eastern Mediterranean city-states. Thus the civic context of hellenistic reciprocity rituals was overlooked, with the result that the language of moral obligation was cut loose from its referential moorings: that is, the *polis* or the Greek city-state.[3] Inevitably, the role that χάρις played in promoting the ethics of civic beneficence in the Greek *poleis* failed to capture the interest of historians.

What do we learn from these early studies of benefaction? The dissertation of W.P. Clark is a wide-ranging account of gift-giving among the Greeks in antiquity, with a wealth of epigraphic evidence detailing the donations of local benefactors to their *poleis*.[4] In the view of Clark, Christianity added nothing new to Greek beneficence because the Stoic idea of a common humanity had sufficiently generated an ethos of mutual helpfulness by the first century AD. Ultimately, Clark concludes, the Christian vision of charity was exclusivist, confined as it was to the relief of Christian communities.[5] The only real distinctive of Jewish-Christian charity was its imperatival framework ('Thus says the Lord'; 'I say unto you') over against the deliberative tradition of the Greek moralists.[6] Unfortunately, Clark does not ground his views concerning Christian beneficence in a serious, socially nuanced analysis of the relevant New Testament texts. He also misses the point that ancient observers like Julian complained precisely of the fact that Christians *did* extend financial aid to others.[7] Clark prefers the luxury of large interpretative brush strokes over against the rigour of historical detail.

E. Skard's pioneering study of rulers who were called 'benefactors' (εὐεργέται) in antiquity includes a useful analysis of a range of benefaction terminology.[8] Helpfully, he argues that the classical writers were heavily indebted to the stable, stereotyped formulae of the honorific inscriptions.[9] If

---

[3] See especially W.A. Meeks, *The Origins of Christian Morality: The First Two Centuries* (New Haven and London 1993), 12-13, 37-51.

[4] W.P. Clark, *Benefactions and Endowments in Greek Antiquity* (unpub. Ph.D. diss. Chicago University 1928).

[5] *Ibid.*, 72-73, 80.

[6] *Ibid.*, 75.

[7] See S. Davis, 'Philanthropy as a Virtue in Late Antiquity and the Middle Ages', in J.B. Schneewind (ed.), *Giving: Western Ideas of Philanthropy* (Bloomington and Indianapolis 1996), 1-23, esp. 8-13.

[8] E. Skard, *Zwei religiös-politische Begriffe: Euergetes-Concordia* (Oslo 1932), 6-66. The later article of B. Kötting ('Euergetes', *RAC* 6 [1965], 846-860) largely covers the same ground as Skard.

[9] E. Skard, *op. cit.*, 14-15.

Skard is correct in this regard, the honorific inscriptions represent — over against the literary evidence — a superior historical source for the ethical terminology of beneficence. But, unfortunately for us, Skard does not touch on χάρις at all.

H. Bolkestein investigates charity and poor relief in Egypt, Palestine, Greece and Rome in pre-Christian antiquity.[10] His thesis is that the extension of the meaning of mercy (ἔλεος) to include compassion to the poor and almsgiving (ἐλεημοσύνη) arose from the traditions of the Greek-speaking Orient rather than from the conventions of the Graeco-Roman benefaction system. Although Bolkestein misrepresents Graeco-Roman beneficence in this regard (§7.1 n.4), he also examines a spread of benefaction terminology, including χάρις. Bolkestein notes that beneficence was normally extended to good men, not to the poor, because only the good were able to reciprocate with commensurate thanksgiving (χάρις) and favour (χάρις).[11] Finally, after listing the reciprocity terminology found in Xenophon's *Memorabilia* — consisting of a series of ἀντί-compounds — Bolkestein observes that χάρις, like ξένος ('host', 'guest'), embodies the bilateralness of reciprocity rituals in its meaning.[12]

Since 1968 this trickle of interest in benefaction studies has swollen into a torrent of publication. Four fundamental studies demonstrate this. First, A.R. Hands ranges widely across the terrain of the Graeco-Roman benefaction system, including a section on reciprocity rituals and (usefully for the average reader) a selection of translated honorific inscriptions.[13]

Second, S.C. Mott's unpublished dissertation studies the use of σωτήρ ('saviour', 'deliverer') — along with its allied benefaction terminology — as a description of hellenistic benefactors.[14] In seeking to apply his results to the study of the Pastorals, Mott pays meticulous attention to the evidence of the honorific inscriptions, is sensitive to the hellenistic ethos of reciprocity, and frequently draws attention to the important role of χάρις in Jewish and Graeco-Roman benefaction contexts.[15] While conceding that from the first

---

[10] H. Bolkestein, *Wohltätigkeit und Armenpflege im vorchristlichen Altertum* (rpt. New York 1979: Gmn. orig. 1939).

[11] *Ibid.*, 107.

[12] *Ibid.*, 159-160.

[13] A.R. Hands, *Charities and Social Aid in Greece and Rome* (London and Southampton 1968). Hands (*ibid.*, 35) draws attention to a series of bilateral terms, including χάρις.

[14] S.C. Mott, *op. cit.* See also the 1951 essay of A.D. Nock, 'Soter and *Euergetes*', in *id.*, *Essays on Religion and the Ancient World* Vol.2 (Oxford 1972), 720-735.

[15] On reciprocity, see S.C. Mott, *op. cit.*, 41, 66-74, 79-80, 102-109, 157-158; *id.*, 'The Power of Giving and Receiving: Reciprocity in Hellenistic Benevolence', in G.F. Hawthorne (ed.), *Current Issues in Biblical and Patristic Interpretation: Studies in Honor of Merril C.*

century AD onwards the Stoics argued for an increased dependence on divine grace, Mott still considers the Jewish emphasis on the unilateral nature of God's grace to be distinctive in antiquity.[16]

Third, in a fine coverage of the Graeco-Roman benefaction system, P. Veyne argues that traditional euergetism had no direct link with the gods, and thus differed markedly from the ethical religiosity of Christian charity.[17] But, like W.P. Clark before him, Veyne weakens his case by ignoring the evidence of the Pauline epistles.

Fourth, F.W. Danker has performed an invaluable service for ancient historians by exploring the benefaction phenomenon in the honorific inscriptions, including its conventions and semantic fields.[18] Like A.R. Hands, he provided a wide selection of translated texts, with rich historical and philological commentary. Further, he has drawn attention to the presence of benefaction terminology and motifs throughout the entire New Testament.

Since Danker, ancient historians are continuing to research aspects of the Graeco-Roman benefaction system,[19] but, more recently, New Testament scholars have gained the ascendancy in publication on the topic. H.L. Hendrix has written a regional study of Roman benefactors at Thessalonica, providing the kind of detailed analysis required for a meaningful comparison of Greek euergetism and Roman patronage in the eastern Mediterranean basin.[20] A similar epigraphic and literary trail could profitably be followed in the case of the other New Testament urban centres. Elsewhere, Hendrix insightfully argues that the letter to the Ephesians reflects the structure of the honorific decrees and the Caesarian loyalty oaths.[21]

The issue of patronal relations within the Pauline house-churches and their interaction with Graeco-Roman social conventions has been a constant focus

---

Tenney (Grand Rapids 1975), 60-72. On χάρις, see id., op. cit., 48-49, 83, 106, 114-115, 302, 361; id., Biblical Ethics and Social Change (Oxford 1982), 22-38.

[16] Id., op. cit. (1971), 305-306.

[17] P. Veyne, Bread and Circuses: Historical Sociology and Political Pluralism (London 1990: Fr. orig. 1976), 19-34.

[18] F.W. Danker, Benefactor: Epigraphic Study of a Graeco-Roman and New Testament Field (St. Louis 1982). Danker (ibid., 245, 441) makes brief reference to the role of χάρις as regards the appropriateness of gratitude.

[19] G. Herman, Ritualised Friendship and the Greek City (Cambridge 1987); A. Wallace-Hadrill (ed.), Patronage in Ancient Society (London and New York 1990).

[20] H.L. Hendrix, Thessalonicans Honor Romans (unpub. Th.D. diss. Harvard University 1984). See also id., 'Beyond "Imperial Cult" and "Cults of Magistrates"' in H.R. Kent (ed.), Society of Biblical Literature 1986 Seminar Papers (Atlanta 1986), 301-308; id., 'Benefactor/Patron Networks in the Urban Environment: Evidence from Thessalonica', Semeia 56 (1992), 39-58.

[21] Id., 'On the Form and Ethos of Ephesians', USQR 42/4 (1988), 3-15.

of the writings of E.A. Judge.²² The momentum of Judge's pioneering research in this area has been maintained by scholars such as P. Marshall, R.M. Kidd, J.K. Chow, A.D. Clarke, B.W. Winter, and S. Joubert.²³ But, of all these authors, only Marshall and Joubert touch on the role of χάρις and *gratia* in benefaction ideology.²⁴

Finally, G.W. Peterman argues that while Paul endorses certain Graeco-Roman reciprocity conventions, he gives priority to the demands of the gospel in social relations.²⁵ The strength of Peterman's discussion lies in its theological insight. Importantly, he draws attention to the role of χάρις and its cognates in the return of gratitude, as well as its accompanying language of commensurability (ἄξιος, 'of like value', 'worthy'; κατάξιος, 'very worthy') in antiquity.²⁶ However, Peterman's dissertation is so focused on the evidence of Philippians — especially Paul's phrase δόσις καὶ λῆμψις (Phil 4:15)²⁷ — that inevitably his treatment of Graeco-Roman reciprocity is truncated. Unfortunately, Peterman underestimates the extent to which reciprocity governed both divine and human relationships in antiquity. As we will see, the gods, as much as human beings, could be put under counter-obligation.²⁸ Peterman is often overly reliant on the Roman evidence of Seneca at the expense of the Greek popular philosophers. Whereas Peterman

---

²² See our discussion of the work of E.A. Judge in §7.1 for pertinent references.

²³ P. Marshall, *Enmity in Corinth: Social Conventions in Paul's Relations with the Corinthians* (Tübingen 1987); R.M. Kidd, *Wealth and Beneficence in the Pastoral Epistles: A 'Bourgeois' Form of Early Christianity?* (Atlanta 1990); J.K. Chow, *Patronage and Power: A Study of Social Networks* (Sheffield 1992); A.D. Clarke, *Secular and Christian Leadership in Corinth: A Socio-Historical and Exegetical Study of 1 Corinthians 1-6* (Leiden-New York-Köln 1993); B.W. Winter, *Seek the Welfare of the City: Christians as Benefactors and Citizens* (Grand Rapids 1994); S. Joubert, *Paul as Benefactor: Reciprocity, Strategy and Theological Reflection in Paul's Collection* (Tübingen 2000).

²⁴ P. Marshall, *op. cit.*, 23-24; S. Joubert, *op. cit.*, 74 n.4, 101-102 n.98, 135-136, 153, 196, 199, 201-202, 216.

²⁵ G.W. Peterman, *Paul's Gift from Philippi: Conventions of Gift-Exchange and Christian Giving* [Cambridge 1997], 8): 'the demands of social reciprocity did not have the power to usurp the supreme place of the gospel in the apostle's life'. See, too, the helpful chapter of D.A. deSilva (entitled 'Patronage and Reciprocity: The Social Context of Grace') in *id.*, *Honor, Patronage, Kinship and Purity: Unlocking New Testament Culture* (Downers Grove 2000), 95-119.

²⁶ G.W. Peterman, *op. cit.*, 71ff, 83.

²⁷ *Ibid.*, 53-65.

²⁸ G.W. Peterman (*ibid.*, 89) overdraws the contrast between the LXX and hellenistic reciprocity when he writes: 'Divine reward does not enter into Greco-Roman reciprocity'. For support, Peterman cites G. Herman (*op. cit.*, 48-49). But, like Peterman in this instance, Herman has made a sweeping judgement unsupported by the wider evidence. On the gods reciprocating human piety, see our summary in §6.5.

extensively discusses reciprocity in several important papyri, his treatment of the honorific inscriptions is brief and unsatisfactory.[29] As a result, he does not sufficiently appreciate the civic and international scope of the hellenistic reciprocity system.[30] In sum, it would be unwise to assume that Peterman's study represents a balanced, definitive treatment of ancient reciprocity ideology.

Overall, very little attention has been paid to χάρις by modern writers on benefaction in antiquity. The time is opportune for a major investigation of divine and human grace in its Graeco-Roman benefaction context.

1.2. Modern Scholarship on Charis: A Timeless Construct?

Twentieth-century scholars who have written on χάρις largely ignore its Graeco-Roman context. One typical approach is to concentrate on the role of χάρις in the Greek epic poetry ranging from Homer to Pindar.[31] Such studies adeptly unfold for us the Homeric world of the counter-gift. However, the hellenistic reciprocity system of the first century AD is a complex social

---

[29] For the respective coverages, see G.W. Peterman, *op. cit.*, 73-83, 84-86. A similar comment might be made about S. Joubert's excellent book on the Jerusalem collection. Joubert confines himself to the literary evidence in discussing Roman patronage (e.g. Pliny the Younger, Martial, Juvenal and Seneca: *op. cit.*, 28-37, 40-51) and — less extensively — Greek euergetism (Aristotle, Dio Chrysostom: *op. cit.*, 38-40, 55-56). In an insightful coverage, Joubert devotes the most attention to Seneca. But Joubert's discussion of the honorific inscriptions, apart from the six decrees lightly touched on (*op. cit.*, 51-55), is largely dependent on the work of others. In sum, in spite of the fact that Paul's organisation of the Jerusalem collection took place in the eastern Mediterranean basin, Joubert presents us with a (predominantly) *literary* portrait of *Roman* imperial patronage for the conceptual background to ancient reciprocity. To some extent, Joubert redresses this imbalance with a fine discussion of Jewish benefaction and the Romanisation of Greek euergetism (*op. cit.*, 58-69, 93-98). But what is demanded is a thorough investigation of the eastern Mediterranean documentary evidence if the beneficence practised in Paul's house churches is to be accurately assessed in its proper context. For analysis of this material, see Chapters 2 and 3 *infra*. A more detailed response to Joubert's stimulating case regarding the Jerusalem collection is found in §7.2.2.3.

[30] See our summary at the beginning of §7.3.2.

[31] See J.W. Franzmann, *The Early Development of the Greek Concept of Charis* (unpub. Ph.D. diss. Wisconsin University 1972); M. Scott, '*Charis* in Homer and the Homeric Hymns', *AClass* 26 (1983), 1-13; *id.*, '*Charis* from Hesiod to Pindar', *AClass* 27 (1984), 1-13; B. MacLachlan, *The Age of Grace: Charis in Early Greek Poetry* (Princeton 1993). Mention might be made here of P. Hummel's study of χάρις in Pindar's poetry: *id.*, 'Le labeur et la grâce: Étude d'une constellation lexicale. δαπάνη, πόνος et χάρις dans Pindare', *Revue de philologie* 70/2 (1996), 247-254.

phenomenon which, if it is to be properly understood, requires a wide-ranging investigation of the literary and documentary sources. Certainly, the Homeric evidence may well throw light on hellenistic reciprocity conventions, but this can only be determined after a detailed study of the first-century Graeco-Roman benefaction context.

Various studies have also been written on the *Charites*, the daughters of Zeus, who personified grace, charm, and beauty.[32] O. Loew has also argued that the *Charites* conveyed pleasure, drawing his support from the etymological link of χάρις with χάρα ('joy').[33] However, the relevance of this material for the New Testament social historian is limited, precisely because Paul eschews the plural χάριτες when describing divine and human beneficence. At best, studies on the *Charites* belong to the wider cultural tapestry of Graeco-Roman society and only partially explain why Paul avoided the plural form of χάρις.

Several Christian scholars have touched on the topic of Pauline grace as a precursor to the later theological debates of the Church Fathers.[34] Needless to say, such studies labour under the weight of historical generalisation. Furthermore, in studies where the New Testament use of χάρις is the exclusive focus,[35] grace is usually treated as a timeless construct with minimal

---

[32] See T. Zielinski, '*Charis* and *Charites*', *CQ* 18 (1924), 158-163; K. Deichgräber, *Charis und Chariten: Grazie und Grazien* (München 1971).

[33] O. Loew, ΧΑΡΙΣ (diss. Marburg 1908). Loew (*ibid.*, 46) describes the *Charites* as 'deae laetificatrices'.

[34] E. Jauncey, *The Doctrine of Grace up to the End of the Pelagian Controversy* (London 1925); T.F. Torrance, *The Doctrine of Grace in the Apostolic Fathers* (Edinburgh 1948); R.F.G. Burnish, *The Doctrine of Grace from Paul to Irenaeus* (unpub. Ph.D. diss. Glasgow University 1971). However, A McGrath (*Thomas F. Torrance: An Intellectual Biography* [Edinburgh 1999], 59) notes that T.F. Torrance worked on the inscriptions documenting χάρις with M.N. Tod as part of his Basil thesis on grace, written under the supervision of Karl Barth. Unfortunately, this valuable research was largely omitted from his subsequently published work (*op. cit.*).

[35] See J. Moffatt, *Grace in the New Testament* (London 1931); W. Manson, 'Grace in the New Testament', in W.T. Whitely (ed.), *The Doctrine of Grace* (London 1932), 33-60; J. Wobbe, *Der Charis-Gedanke bei Paulus: Ein Beitrag zur neutestamentlichen Theologie* (Münster 1932); R. Winkler, 'Die Gnade im Neuen Testament', *ZST* 10 (1933), 642-680; L. Cerfaux, 'La théologie de la grâce selon Saint Paul', *VSpir* 83 (1950), 5-19; C. Ryder Smith, *The Bible Doctrine of Grace* (London 1956); W. Grundmann, 'Die Übermacht der Gnade: Ein Studie zur Theologie des Paulus', *NovT* 2/1 (1957), 50-72; R.F. Surburg, 'Pauline *Charis*: A Philological, Exegetical, and Dogmatical Study', *CTM* 29/10 (1958), 721-741; E.E. Flack, 'The Concept of Grace in Biblical Thought', in J.M. Myers (ed.), *Biblical Studies in Memory of H.C. Alleman* (Locust Valley 1960), 137-154; T.N. Schulz, *The Meaning of Charis in the New Testament* (Genova 1971); D.J. Doughty, 'The Priority of ΧΑΡΙΣ: An Investigation of the Theological Language of Paul', *NTS* 19 (1973), 163-180; H. Conzelmann and W. Zimmerli, 'χάρις, χαρίζομαι, χαριτόω, ἀχάριστος, χάρισμα,

relevance to the social and theological framework of Graeco-Roman society. The result is that the apostle of grace, who struggled to see his Gentile converts grow into maturity in Christ, vanishes into theological abstraction. Admittedly, several of these writers (e.g. J. Moffatt; W. Manson; H. Conzelmann and W. Zimmerli; H. Dörrie *et al.*) seek to locate χάρις in its wider Graeco-Roman context. But, in each case, their coverage is broad, with little attempt made to sift through the evidence chronologically, thematically, or according to its genre. It is simply assumed that this amorphous collection of ancient texts is somehow relevant to Paul's first-century social context.[36]

εὐχαριστέω', *TDNT* 9 (1974), 372-402; H. Dörrie *et al.*, 'Gnade', *RAC* 2 (1981), 314-446; M. Theobald, *Die überströmende Gnade: Studien zu einem paulinischen Motivfeld* (Würzburg 1982); K. Berger, 'χάρις', in H. Balz and G. Schneider (eds), *Exegetical Dictionary of the New Testament* Vol.3 (Grand Rapids 1993), 457-460; H. Boers, '' Αγάπη and Χάρις in Paul's Thought', *CBQ* 59/4 (1997), 693-713; M. Winger, 'From Grace to Sin: Names and Abstractions in Paul's Letters', *NovT* 41/2 (1999), 145-175.

[36] The recent article of H. Boers (*art. cit*) illustrates how deeply the paradigms of past scholarship remain entrenched. Boers asserts that Paul's use of χάρις does not move 'beyond anything expressed by that word in his Greek and Hebrew-Jewish background' prior to the writing of Galatians and Romans (*art. cit.*, 705). This sweeping statement is based on the analysis of a single Graeco-Roman text (Aristotle, *Rhetoric* 2.7.2: *art.cit.*, 703) and two paragraphs on select LXX texts (*art. cit.*, 704-705). This is accompanied by the obligatory (but uncritical) appeal to the works of G.P. Wetter and J. Moffatt (*art. cit.*, 704 n.17) as confirmation. However, Boer's assumption that Paul's use of χάρις is entirely conventional before Galatians and Romans is facile. Why does Paul, in contrast to the honorific inscriptions, resort to such profuse 'grace' language in 2 Corinthians 8-9 (χάρις 10 times; εὐχαριστία twice) if the Jerusalem collection is just another example of Graeco-Roman reciprocity? For our discussion, see §7.2.2.3. Boer — resurrecting the thesis of W. Wrede (*Paul* [Boston 1908], 122-137) — then proceeds to argue that Paul's doctrine of justification by faith in Galatians and Romans is polemical because it is aimed at the judaizing circumcision party (*art. cit.*, 709-710). Once again, the understanding of grace in Judaism and in early Christianity is reduced to timeless dogmatics and divorced from a detailed analysis of the Graeco-Roman reciprocity system. Precisely because Boer reads the Romans evidence through Galatian spectacles, he never pauses to ask whether Paul might be saying something distinctive about χάρις to the believers in Rome, the home of the imperial benefactors. For example, see the stimulating comments of D. Georgi (*Theocracy in Paul's Praxis and Theology* [Minneapolis 1991: Gmn. orig. 1987], 79-104) and J.L. White (*The Apostle of God: Paul and the Promise of Abraham* [Peabody 1999], 110-135, 173-206) regarding Augustus as divine benefactor. Also see our discussion in §6.1.2.4–§6.1.2.5. Boer concludes that Paul's use of χάρις acquires 'a certain technical status' in Galatians and Romans (*art. cit.*, 709) and this prevents us from clarifying the meaning of χάρις in the apostle's earlier letters. Note the telling comment of B. Eastman (*The Significance of Grace in the Letters of Paul* [New York 1999], 10) regarding such approaches: 'Focusing on grace with reference only to Paul's view of the law yields an incomplete picture of the role of grace in Paul's thought. Paul uses the concept of grace in *other than polemical* contexts, and it may be that in ignoring those occurrences has led to a diminished appreciation of the role of grace in Paul' (my emphasis). Finally, Boer fails to recognise the formative theological

As noted above, most Christian writers write as if grace is a timeless construct. M. Theobald, who investigates Paul's use of the language of abundance (περισσεύειν and cognates) in conjunction with χάρις, is a case in point. This fine theological work is partially weakened by the author's failure to address important historical questions. Why does Paul opt for the language of abundance over against the language of commensurability that so dominated his own culture? What do we make of the appearance of the language of abundance in the Caesar cult? What were the pitfalls and attractions for Paul of the varying types of language that accompanied χάρις in the first century AD? How would Paul's original audience have perceived his changes to (seemingly immutable) semantic conventions?

Similarly, the recent book of B. Eastman traces the theological lineaments of grace in Paul's thought with exegetical skill.[37] A particular strength of the work is that Eastman does not rigidly confine himself to an examination of χάρις and its cognates.[38] Instead the author ranges widely, focusing on the need for divine grace and the human dependence that flows from it. The result is a balanced thematic discussion. Notwithstanding, the work is sometimes theologically disappointing. We do not gain a strong impression of how grace operated socially in Paul's house churches as believers ministered to each other and to outsiders. One example is the scant attention devoted the Jerusalem collection.[39] It underlines the truth of S. Joubert's observation: 'A more encompassing approach that focuses on the consistent interplay of all the relevant social and theological factors related to the collection is long overdue'.[40]

The most recent book on Paul's language of grace is D.W. Pao's theological study of εὐχαριστία.[41] In Pao's view, Paul's emphasis on thanksgiving flows from a call to remember covenantal traditions, anti-idol polemic, and an

---

impact which Paul's experience of grace on the Damascus road had upon his subsequent apostolic teaching and ministry, whether that be evaluated in a Jewish or Graeco-Roman context. On this, see S. Kim, *The Origin of Paul's Gospel* (Tübingen 1981), 288-296; A.B. du Toit, 'Encountering Grace: Towards Understanding the Essence of Paul's Damascus Experience', *Neot* 30/1 (1996), 71-87; M. Hengel, *The Pre-Christian Paul* (London 1991), 85-86; M. Hengel and A.M. Schwemer, *Paul Between Damascus and Antioch: The Unknown Years* (London 1997), 98-101.

[37] B. Eastman, *op. cit.*

[38] As Eastman correctly observes (*op. cit.*, 10), 'grace is often implied where the word is absent'.

[39] *Ibid.*, 44-45, 55.

[40] S. Joubert, *op. cit.*, 5.

[41] D.W. Pao, *Thanksgiving: An Investigation of a Pauline Theme* (Downers Grove 2002).

eschatological focus on God's promises. Particularly gratifying is Pao's discussion of Paul's thanksgiving in relation to the Graeco-Roman reciprocity system.[42] He insightfully highlights several distinctive aspects of Paul's thought over against first-century patronage models. Perhaps this fine work signals that theological writers are starting to realise the inadequacy of treating grace as a timeless construct.

Finally, we will conclude by drawing attention to several scholars who take seriously the eastern Mediterranean benefaction context of χάρις. First, G.P. Wetter's seminal work of 1913 highlights the important contribution that the imperial inscriptions and the magical papyri make to our understanding of the historical context of first-century χάρις.[43] But subsequent scholars — with the sole exception of C. Spicq — merely endorse Wetter's conclusions regarding imperial χάρις in the inscriptions of Caligula and Nero, adding nothing new or insightful by way of research into the ever-burgeoning epigraphic corpus. Second, although P. Schubert focuses on the Pauline thanksgivings, he meticulously combs through the inscriptions and papyri, commenting on the social milieu and literary genre of the Pauline epistles.[44] Third, C. Spicq's general discussion of grace and glory is methodologically the best example of the approach that my study will advocate.[45] Spicq's footnotes are studded with valuable references to and extracts from the inscriptions and papyri that throw light on the social context of χάρις. Fourth, although D. Zeller does not locate Philo and Paul in their Graeco-Roman benefaction context, his comparative study of these two leading figures

---

[42] *Ibid.*, 165-173.

[43] G.P. Wetter, *Charis: Ein Beitrag zur Geschichte des ältesten Christentums* (Leipzig 1913). See our discussion of G.P. Wetter's contribution in §2.2, §3.1.1 and §3.6.

[44] P. Schubert, *Form and Function of the Pauline Thanksgivings* (Berlin 1939). Note especially Schubert's comment (*ibid.*, 142) on the superior value of the documentary over against the literary evidence: 'As contrasted with purely literary sources both inscriptions and papyri have the important qualification that they are direct data on the life of the society which "literature" merely describes'. Later Schubert (*ibid.*, 182) draws the important conclusion that 'the Pauline letters — functionally as well as formally — occupy a position between the epigraphic documents (which were intended for publication) and the humble though formal and intimate private letters (which were intended merely for the addressee)'. The earlier article of T. Schermann ('Εὐχαριστία und εὐχαριστεῖν in ihrem Bedeutungswandel bis 200 n. Chr.', *Philologus* 69 [1910], 375-410) largely concentrates on the patristic evidence.

[45] C. Spicq, *Théologie morale du nouveau testament* Tome 1 (Paris 1965), 110-145. His appendix ('Qu'est-ce que la grâce?', *ibid.*, 451-461) is partially translated in C. Spicq, *Theological Lexicon of the New Testament* Vol.3 (Peabody 1994: Fr. orig. 1978), 500-506. Another positive study of the New Testament understanding of grace in its Graeco-Roman context, utilising the evidence of the popular philosophers, is D.A. deSilva, *op. cit.*, 121-156.

of first-century diaspora Judaism is a model of the way that theological and historical studies should profitably interact.[46] Last, D.A. deSilva insightfully discusses the relationhip between reciprocity and the patronal context of χάρις. Although he draws largely on the evidence of the popular philosophers and modern sociological studies, his approach is an advance on much New Testament scholarship in the area.[47]

In conclusion, the time has come to proceed further down the trails pioneered by Wetter, Schubert, and Spicq. Only then will we perhaps gain a clearer view of the object of our quest: the apostle of grace who brought the gospel to eastern Mediterranean Gentiles. As a result, we will not be as easily beguiled by the many fleeting spectres of Paul which either disappear or reappear with each new generation of scholars.

1.3. Patronage and the Social-Scientific Approach: The Way Ahead for New Testament Social Research?

The social-scientific approach is now regarded by many scholars as a necessary adjunct to the literary and historical disciplines that traditionally characterise New Testament criticism.[48] Cross-cultural studies are increasingly plundered by New Testament scholars for comparative materials that might throw light on the social practices of the first-century Pauline churches.[49]

---

[46] D. Zeller, *Charis bei Philon und Paulus* (Stuttgart 1992).

[47] D.A. deSilva, *op. cit.*, 121-156.

[48] For general discussion, see J.G. Gager, *Kingdom and Community: The Social World of Early Christianity* (Englewood Cliffs 1975); B.J. Malina, *The New Testament World: Insights from Cultural Anthropology* (Atlanta 1981); id., *Christian Origins and Cultural Anthropology: Practical Models for Biblical Interpretation* (Atlanta 1986); B. Holmberg, *Sociology and the New Testament: An Appraisal* (Minneapolis 1990); G. Theissen, *Social Reality and the Early Christians: Theology, Ethics, and the World of the New Testament* (Edinburgh 1992), 1-29; P.F. Esler, *The First Christians in Their Social Worlds: Social-Scientific Approaches to New Testament Interpretation* (London 1994); J.H. Elliott, *Social-Scientific Criticism of the New Testament* (London 1995); D.G. Horrell, *Social Scientific Approaches to New Testament Interpretation* (Edinburgh 1999).

[49] In recent Pauline studies, there has been considerable interaction with sociological and anthropological literature. A few examples will suffice. Max Weber's sociology of authority: J.H. Schütz, *Paul and the Anatomy of Apostolic Authority* (Cambridge 1975); B. Holmberg, *Paul and Power: The Structure of Authority in the Primitive Church as Reflected in the Pauline Epistles* (Philadelphia 1980). The anthropologies of V. Turner and C. Lévi-Strauss: N.R. Petersen, *Philemon and the Sociology of Paul's Narrative World* (Philadelphia 1985). The sociology of sects: F. Watson, *Paul, Judaism and the Gentiles* (Cambridge 1986). M.T. Douglas' anthropology of purity concerns: J.H. Neyrey, *Paul in Other Words* (Louisville 1990). The sociology of patronage: S. Joubert, *op. cit.*

Importantly for us, the practice of patronage has been intensively studied from a cross-cultural perspective, with a view to devising sociological models that would explain the subtle social conventions behind the patron-client relationship in many cultures.[50] In particular, the theme of reciprocity has grabbed the attention of many sociologists and anthropologists. Their research may well suggest several profitable historical questions that could be directed at the documentary evidence from the eastern Mediterranean basin.[51] But, so far as I know, J-M. Laporte and D.A. deSilva remain the only New Testament scholars who have extensively applied insights from sociological literature (e.g. M. Mauss; E. Benveniste; P. Slater) to the theological study of grace.[52] Conversely, the recent postscript of J. Pitt-Rivers is the only extended anthropological discussion of grace.[53]

So far, few dissenting voices have been raised against (in the eyes of some) the indiscriminate and anachronistic transference of such materials across the centuries to vastly different cultures. E.A. Judge, to cite one prominent example, has summed up the pitfalls for the unwary in using modern sociological theories to explain New Testament social relations:

> Even if one accepts the assumptions of social determinism, the problem with this kind of explanation is that we simply do not know enough about the day-to-day workings of rank and status in the Roman world of the Caesars and St. Paul. The theories have usually been hammered out in the laboratory of a South-Seas-island anthropologist, and then transported half-way around the world, and across two millennia, without adequate testing for applicability in a new setting: so powerful is the assumption of the indelible pattern of human social behaviour.[54]

---

[50] See the helpful summary of J.H. Elliott, 'Patronage and Clientism in Early Christian Society: A Short Reading Guide', *Forum* 3/4 (1987), 39-48. In particular, see the excellent coverage in S. Joubert, *op. cit.*, 17-37.

[51] In addition to the literature cited in §1.3.1, see A.W. Gardiner, 'The Norm of Reciprocity: A Preliminary Statement', *American Sociological Review* 25/2 (1960), 161-178; M.S. Greenberg and S.P. Shapiro, 'Indebtedness: An Adverse Aspect of Asking for and Receiving Help', *Sociometry* 34/2 (1971), 290-301; J. Van Baal, *Reciprocity and the Position of Women: Anthropological Papers* (Assen-Amsterdam 1975), esp. 11-69. On reciprocity and the Jerusalem collection, see S. Joubert, *op. cit.*

[52] J.-M. Laporte, 'The Mystery of God's Abundance', in J. Plevnik (ed.), *Word and Spirit: Essays in Honor of David Michael Stanley on His 60th Birthday* (Willowdale 1975), 371-409; D.A. deSilva, *op. cit.* More recently, however, D.W. Pao, *op. cit.*, 165ff.

[53] J. Pitt-Rivers, 'Postscript: The Place of Grace in Anthropology', in J.G. Peristiany and J. Pitt-Rivers (eds), *Honour and Grace in Anthropology* (Cambridge 1992), 215-246.

[54] E.A. Judge, *Rank and Status in the World of the Caesars and St. Paul* (University of Canterbury 1982), 10. A similar opinion of E.A. Judge ('The Social Identity of the First Christians: A Question of Method in Religious History', *JRH* 11 [1980], 210) is endorsed by G.W. Peterman, *op. cit.*, 21. For positions similar to E.A. Judge, see S.K. Stowers, 'The Social Sciences and the Study of Early Christianity', in W.S. Green (ed.), *Approaches to*

The cautionary comments of E.A. Judge are well founded. To be sure, the Roman republican and imperial patronal system has been extensively studied,[55] and both Roman historians and modern sociologists have profitably engaged in an inter-disciplinary dialogue regarding patronage.[56] But the *Greek* ethos of reciprocity — which was the fundamental dynamic of the benefaction system in the eastern Mediterranean basin — has only recently been explored in depth by ancient and New Testament historians.[57] As we have noted, it was in the area of the Greek East, with its own distinctive understanding of social obligation, that Paul established his house churches. As a result, New Testament social historians who are sympathetic to the (more Roman-sounding) client-patron model espoused by the social-sciences are confronted with series of methodological problems.

Ancient Judaism: Studies in Judaism and its Greco-Roman Context Vol.5 (Atlanta 1985), 149-181; P.F. Craffert, 'More on Models and Muddles in the Social-Scientific Interpretation of the New Testament: The *Sociological Fallacy* Reconsidered', *Neot* 26/1 (1992), 217-239.

[55] For general coverage of Roman patronage, see M. Gelzer, *The Roman Nobility* (Oxford 1969: Gmn. orig. 1912); H. Bolkestein, *op. cit.*, 287-379; R. Syme, *The Roman Revolution* (Oxford 1939); L.R. Taylor, *Party Politics in the Age of Caesar* (Berkeley 1971: orig. 1948); G.E.M. de St. Croix, '*Suffragium*: From Vote to Patronage', *British Journal of Sociology* 5 (1954), 33-48; E. Badian, *Foreign Clientelae (264—70 BC)* (Oxford 1958); R.P. Saller, *Personal Patronage under the Early Empire* (Cambridge 1982); A. Wallace-Hadrill (ed.), *op. cit.*; A. Erskine, 'The Romans as Common Benefactors', *Historia* 43 (1994), 70-87. On the Roman language of patronage, see J. Hellegouarc'h, *Le vocabulaire latin des relations et des partis politiques sous la république* (Paris 1963). On patronage and the Caesars, see H. Mattingly, 'The Emperor and His Clients', in A.J. Dunston (ed.), *Essays on Roman Culture* (Toronto and Sarasota 1976), 159-186; P. Veyne, *op. cit.*, 347-377; F. Millar, *The Emperor in the Roman World (31 BC—AD 337)* (New York 1977), 133-201; R.P. Saller, *op. cit.*, 41-78.

[56] See R.P. Saller, *op. cit.*; L. Roniger, 'Modern Patron-Client Relations and Historical Clientelism: Some Clues from Ancient Republican Rome', *Archives européennes de sociologie* 24/1 (1983), 63-95; A. Wallace-Hadrill (ed.), *op. cit.*

[57] A. Dihle, *Die goldene Regel: Eine Einführung in die Geschichte der antiken und frühchristlichen Vulgärethik* (Göttingen 1962); A.R. Hands, *op. cit.*, 26-48; J.W. Franzmann, *op. cit.*, *passim*; S.C. Mott, *art. cit.*; W. Donlan, 'Reciprocities in Homer', *CW* 75 (1982), 137-176; F.W. Danker, 'Reciprocity in the Ancient World and in Acts 15:23-29', in R.J. Cassidy and P.J. Sharper (eds), *Political Issues in Luke-Acts* (New York 1983), 49-58; *id.*, 'Bridging St. Paul and the Apostolic Fathers: A Study in Reciprocity', *CurTM* 15/1 (1984), 84-94; *id.*, 'Paul's Debt to the *De Corona* of Demosthenes: A Study of Rhetorical Techniques in Second Corinthians', in D.A. Watson (ed.), *Persuasive Artistry: Studies in New Testament Rhetoric in Honour of George A. Kennedy* (Sheffield 1991), 262-280; G. Herman, *op. cit.*, Index s.v. 'Reciprocity'; G.W. Peterman, *op. cit.*; S. Joubert, *op. cit.*; B. MacLachlan, *op. cit.*, Index s.v. 'Reciprocity'; R. Seaford, *Reciprocity and Ritual: Homer and Tragedy in the Developing City-State* (Oxford 1994); C. Gill (*et al.*, ed.), *Reciprocity in Ancient Greece* (New York 1998).

First, as J.H. Elliott notes, the specific terminology of the Roman patronal system is largely absent from the eastern Mediterranean basin. But, equally, it would be unwise to downplay the existence of Roman patronal conventions and terminology in the Roman colonies of Corinth and Philippi. S.C. Mott, for example, has pointed to several clear occurrences of εὐεργέτης and πάτρων together in the Greek inscriptions, along with a case of πάτρων translating εὐεργέτης.[58]

Second, it is a moot point whether Roman conventions of patronage had either supplanted or (more likely) converged with Greek civic euergetism at a local level. Although Elliott is confident that 'several points of convergence with patronage and clientism' did exist,[59] F.W. Danker is far less convinced:

> It is unfortunate that the narrow term 'patron-client relationship' should have entered the discussion rather than the more comprehensive term 'reciprocity system' of which 'patron-client' more accurately describes an ancient Roman subset. Some of the current application of patron-client theory to Hellenic texts would have caused a shaking of heads in the ancient Greek-speaking world.[60]

But, again, caution is required. While the Roman patronal system had its own specific terminology, its reciprocity conventions increasingly impacted on the Greek East through the Caesars and various Roman benefactors.[61]

Third, the fundamental problem is that we will never know how far such modern sociological constructs are applicable to the Greek East until we have — as E.A. Judge has rightly insisted[62] — painstakingly researched the first-century world 'city by city, institution by institution', and (I would add) social convention by social convention.[63] The interaction of the Greek and

---

[58] S.C. Mott, *op. cit.* (1971), 90.

[59] J.H. Elliott, *art. cit.*, 45.

[60] F.W. Danker, *art. cit.* (1991), 278 n.1.

[61] On the Roman terminology of reciprocity and the sponsorship of its conventions through the Caesars, see R.P. Saller, *op. cit.*, 8-39, 69-78. H.L. Hendrix, *art. cit.* (1992), argues that at Thessalonica there was an increasing shift to the Romans as sources of benefaction over against the Greek locals in the early empire. Concomitantly, 'in the process "the gods" of Thessalonica were increasingly less active divine personae in the patronage of the city' (*ibid.*, 56). See also, *id.*, *op. cit.*, *passim*. For a first-rate discussion as to whether Roman patronage and hellenistic euergetism eventually coincide in the Greek East, see S. Joubert, *op. cit.*, 58-69; *id.*, 'One Form of Social Exchange or Two? "Euergetism," Patronage, and Testament Studies', *BTB* 31/1 (2001), 17-25.

[62] E.A. Judge, *art. cit.* (1980), 216.

[63] In recent New Testament scholarship, we are starting to witness the flowering of the 'city by city' approach that E.A. Judge advocated in regard to benefaction and epigraphic studies. On benefaction at Corinth, see J.K. Chow, *op. cit.*, *passim*; A.D. Clarke, *op. cit.*, 13-21, 31-36, 46-56; B.W. Winter, 'Secular and Christian Responses to Corinthian Famines', *TynBul* 40 (1989), 86-106; *id.*, *op. cit.*, 105-121, 145-164, 165-177. On benefaction at Philippi, see L. Bormann, *Philippi: Stadt und Christengemeinde zur Zeit des*

Roman benefaction systems, at the level of local *poleis* and more generally throughout the Eastern Mediterranean, still awaits the detailed regional study of ancient historians, especially as regards the ethos of reciprocity.⁶⁴ Only then can we assess the legitimacy of using the social-scientific construal of patronage in order to understand ancient benefaction.

Leaving aside temporarily the vexed issue of the appropriateness of applying social-scientific models to Paul's view of beneficence, we turn to the writings of modern sociologists to see whether they can (at the very least) help us in reading the ancient texts more critically.

1.3.1. Valuable insights from the social sciences for our understanding of first-century grace

Modern sociologists touch on several issues pertinent to the first-century benefaction context which Paul engaged theologically and socially.⁶⁵

1. *How much is Paul's doctrine of grace directed against a 'do ut des' ('I give that you may give') mentality?* On the basis of Vedic literature, H. Hubert and M. Mauss have argued that sacrifice to the gods compels the deity to reciprocate with blessing.⁶⁶ G.W. Trompf has also reminded us that in Melanesian society 'spirit-beings were not adored for their own sake but pleased in the hope of gift, concession, or reconciliation'.⁶⁷ As we will argue,

---

Paulus (Leiden–New York–Köln 1995), 178-205. On Ephesus and the inscriptions, see G.H.R. Horsley, 'The Inscriptions of Ephesos and the New Testament', *NovT* 34/2 (1992), 106-168. On benefaction at Thessalonica, see H.L. Hendrix, *op. cit.*; *id.*, *art. cit.* (1992), 39-58; B.W. Winter, *op. cit.*, 41-60. More recently, C. vom Brocke, *Thessaloniki — Stadt des Kassander und Gemeinde des Paulus. Eine frühe christliche Gemeinde des Paulus* (Tübingen 2001). Finally, as F.F. Bruce ('The New Testament and Classical Studies', *NTS* 22 [1976], 239) reminds us, it is particularly the inscriptions that reveal the legal and social institutions of the first-century city-states.

⁶⁴ F.W. Danker (*op. cit.* [1982], 49 n.1) comments: 'A history of Graeco-Roman reciprocity phenomena, with special reference to recognition in honorific pronouncement, remains to be written, but it will require the resources of an international team of scholars'.

⁶⁵ For a useful update on recent sociological research on gift giving, see G. Stansell, 'The Gift in Ancient Israel', *Semeia* 87 (1999), 65-70.

⁶⁶ H. Hubert and M. Mauss, 'Essai sur la nature et la fonction du sacrifice', *Année Sociologique* 2 (1899), 29-138. See also M. Mauss, *The Gift: The Form and Reason for Exchange in Archaic Societies* (London 1990: Fr. orig. 1950), 17.

⁶⁷ G.W. Trompf, *Payback: The Logic of Retribution in Melanesian Religions* (Cambridge 1994), 119. Note the helpful distinction that M. Mauss (*A General Theory of Magic* [London and Boston 1972: Fr. orig. 1950], 24) makes between traditional religion and magical rites outside of the mainstream benefaction system: 'Religious practices, on the contrary, even fortuitous and voluntary ones, are always predictable, prescribed and official. They *do* form part of a cult. Gifts presented to gods on the occasion of a vow, or an expiatory sacrifice offered during illness, are regular kinds of homage. Although performed in each case

Paul's emphasis on the unilateral nature of divine grace was directed against the idea that God was compelled by acts of human piety to reciprocate beneficently, as was the traditional belief in antiquity regarding the Graeco-Roman pantheon and the underworld deities of the magical papyri.[68]

2. *What are the consequences when the divine benefactor is not accorded supreme honour by His dependants within the hierarchy of honour?* In this regard, J. Pitt-Rivers describes Thomas Hobbes' hierarchy of honour in sixteenth-century Europe thus: 'We can see the hierarchy of honour stretching from its source in God, through a king whose legitimacy depends on divine sanction, through the ranks of the social structure down to those who had no honour at all'.[69] How relevant is such a model to Paul's portrait of God as a dishonoured Benefactor (Rom 1:21-22) and, concomitantly, to the rendering of honour to others lower in the pecking-order (12:10; 13:7; cf. 1 Cor 12:24-26)? If God is not accorded appropriate honour, what consequence does this have for the social fabric (cf. Rom 1:24-32)? By contrast, how do the honorific inscriptions understand the honouring and the (potential) dishonouring of the divine benefactor? To what extent did Paul embark on a radical re-definition of the Graeco-Roman honour system?

Conversely, we might dwell briefly on the issue of deflected honour in the patronal system. As J. Pitt-Rivers observes of the feudal system:

... the inferior in such a relationship participated in the honour of his chief and was therefore interested in defending it. Yet the principle holds beyond the ties of the feudal system; the system of patronage depends upon it, also. Hence the hubris of the tyrant's minion; the vicarious glory of the noble's servant.[70]

How would contemporary auditors have heard Paul's description of himself as a slave of God in the eschatological reign of grace (Rom 6:14-23)? How would this have been understood in a benefaction context? Was it an image of humiliation or, alternatively, one of deflected honour? Or, paradoxically, perhaps both?

---

voluntarily, they are really obligatory and inevitable actions. Magical rites, on the other hand, while they may occur regularly (as in the case of agricultural magic) and fulfil a need when they are performed for specific ends (such as a cure), are always considered unauthorised, abnormal and, at the very least, not highly estimable' (original emphasis).

[68] S.C. Mott (*op. cit.* [1971], 74) writes: 'Gods were beings or powers who, if treated properly, brought you blessings and gave you benefits'. By contrast, note the comment of the social-scientist J. Pitt-Rivers, *art. cit.*, in J.G. Peristiany and J. Pitt-Rivers (eds), *op. cit.*, 223: 'grace is a free gift of God, unpredictable, arbitrary and mysterious'.

[69] J. Pitt-Rivers, 'Honor and Social Status', in J.G. Peristiany (ed.), *Honour and Shame: The Values of Mediterranean Society* (Chicago 1966), 24.

[70] *Ibid.*, 36.

3. *What are the social consequences when a benefactor does not fulfil his commitment to act beneficently towards his dependants?* This was the situation that Paul faced with the recalcitrant Corinthians who had not been forthcoming with their promised contribution to the Jerusalem collection (2 Cor 8:6-8, 10-12; 9:3-5). Marc Bloch notes that in feudal society 'the obedience of the vassal was conditional upon the scrupulous fulfilment of his engagements by the lord'.[71] Likewise, in Maori culture, as M. Mauss observes, 'To refuse to give, and to fail to invite, just as to refuse to accept, is tantamount to declaring war; it is to reject the bond of alliance and commonality'.[72] In light of these comparative materials, we must ask how the delay of the Corinthians in benefiting the Jerusalem Christians would have been perceived in antiquity.[73] What unseen pressures did the situation impose upon Paul and the Corinthians? How did Paul shape his theological and social argument to meet its challenge?

4. *What are the social dangers of so overwhelming a beneficiary with benefits that they cannot possibly reciprocate?* Inadvertently, this may have been precisely the situation that the Jerusalem Christians faced in having to submit to a collection put together by Paul's Gentile churches. To be sure, the initiative for the almsgiving to the Jerusalem poor had come from the 'pillar' apostles, Cephas and John (Gal 2:9-10). But, as we will see, the tentacles of Graeco-Roman reciprocity system had as much gripped Palestine as the wider eastern Mediterranean basin. Everyone knew the social consequences of accepting extravagant gifts. P.M. Blau sums up the dilemma this way: 'A person can establish superiority over others by overwhelming them with benefits they cannot properly repay and thus subduing them with the weight of their obligation to him'.[74]

---

[71] M. Bloch, 'Feudal Society', in S.W. Schmidt (*et al.*, ed.), *Friends, Followers, and Factions* (Berkeley and Los Angeles 1977), 205.

[72] M. Mauss, *op. cit.* (1990: Fr. orig. 1950), 13. See also P.M. Blau, *Exchange and Power in Social Life* (New York 1964), 107. Note, however, the criticism made of Mauss in J. Pitt-Rivers (*art. cit.*, 217), in J.G. Peristiany and J. Pitt-Rivers (eds), *op. cit.*: 'the etiquette concerning the return of gifts contains more subtleties than Mauss explained'. This is especially so when one concentrates on the ancient evidence over against the anthropological case studies.

[73] See C.A. Gregory (*Gifts and Commodities* [London 1982], 183) for a fascinating discussion of how the manipulation of pig stocks at the triennial Pig Feasts in Papua New Guinea can lead to significant delays in the repayment of debts between clans.

[74] P.M. Blau, *op. cit.*, 113. C. Lévi-Strauss (*The Elementary Structures of Kinship* [Boston 1969: Fr. orig. 1949], 53) describes one of the aims of the *potlatch* ceremonies, where gifts are exchanged for equivalent gifts, among the Indians of Alaska and the Vancouver region as follows: '... to surpass a rival in generosity, to crush him if possible with future obligations which it is hoped he cannot meet, so as to take from him his

Conversely, there was also the potential danger that the Gentile churches involved in the Jerusalem collection might assume airs of superiority over their Jerusalem brethren (cf. Rom 11:13-24) or unfairly expect a commensurate counter-gift in the future (cf. 2 Cor 8:13-15). A lingering hostility over the issue of counter-gifts was a real possibility, as B. Malinowski reminds us of Melanesian society.[75] Presumably, Paul had to frame his theological arguments for the Jerusalem collection with great sensitivity, given the social intricacies of the reciprocity system.

5. *How far did Paul's understanding of grace differentiate itself from traditional Graeco-Roman reciprocity ideology? Was Paul — whether implicitly or explicitly — critiquing this prominent social convention, in the hope of transforming the ethos of commensurability that was axiomatic in the world-view and social practice of his converts?* These important questions arise out of recent studies regarding the impact that the Christian gospel has made on the Melanesian reciprocity system. As G.W. Trompf explains,

> Collisions between Christianity and indigenous traditions are thus inevitable, and sometimes the superficial affinities between the two in terms of reciprocity, generosity, hospitality, and the like, are not enough to prevent them. In certain cases complex reciprocations are based on a caste-looking or unjust social system. We have already seen how cargoist Irakau was influenced enough by Christian (and other non-traditional) notions that he tried to undermine Manam Island's rigid *tanepoa* aristocracy ...[76]

Therefore we have to reckon with the possibility that Paul's doctrine of grace contained not only a theological but also a social polemic.

Furthermore, we may also wonder whether Paul's avoidance of the inscriptional language of commensurability (ἄξιος, κατάξιος) in conjunction with the language of grace — notwithstanding 2 Thess 1:3 — is somehow related to the notion of the 'worthiness' of the recipient. In this regard, M.P. Di Bella refers to the Sicilian Catholic belief that 'the faithful are considered 'worthy' of the benefits that the saint bestows'.[77] Does this provide insight into Paul's unease about this type of language? Ultimately, did the

---

prerogatives, titles, rank, authority, and prestige'.

[75] B. Malinowski, *Argonauts of the Western Pacific* (London 1922), 96: 'If the article given as a counter-gift is not equivalent, the recipient will be disappointed and angry, but he has no direct means of redress, no means of coercing his partner, or of putting an end to the whole transaction'.

[76] G.W. Trompf, *op. cit.*, 400.

[77] M.P. Di Bella, 'Name, Blood and Miracles: The Claims to Renown in Traditional Sicily', in J.G. Peristiany and J. Pitt-Rivers (eds), *op. cit.*, 158. As Di Bella (*ibid.*) elaborates, 'the circumstances in which a person obtained grace is a way of making himself known as "worthy" of a miracle, "worthy" of receiving the saint's grace, and therefore "worthy" of renown'.

inscriptional language of commensurability imply for Paul a theology of civic merit which was at loggerheads with the gospel of grace?

6. *Conversely, to what extent does Paul endorse and transform traditional norms of Graeco-Roman reciprocity?* In the village of Poreporena — located in the heart of Port Moresby, the national capital of Papua New Guinea — the United Church became a pivotal force in ensuring the perpetuation of gift exchange as a social convention. In the words of C.A. Gregory,

> In spite of the tremendous changes that have occurred in the village, the clan structure has been fortified. This has been largely due to the influence of the United Church (formerly London Missionary Society). They suppressed the traditional gift exchange system and usurped the power of the traditional big-men. Nowadays big-men are no longer. They have been replaced by church deacons, the 'neo big-men' of the new gift exchange system that has been established by the church in order to raise money. It was the rise of these men that saved the clan (*iduhu*) system from collapsing.[78]

It is clear that whatever reservations Paul might have had about the Graeco-Roman reciprocity system, he still endorsed the traditional conventions of clientage (Rom 15:24; 16:1-2), employed reciprocity terminology (2 Cor 6:13; Phil 4:15; 1 Tim 5:4), and argued for the social expression of reciprocity within his churches (Rom 13:8-10; 15:27; 2 Cor 8:13-15; Phil 4:10-20; Phlm).

The importance of reciprocity conventions for Paul and how they operated within his house churches must therefore be examined. In this regard, recent sociological studies of charitable organisations have underscored the importance of the reciprocation of honour for continued beneficence.[79] For example, universities facilitate the potential benefactor's quest for social status by inviting their leading donors to participate on advisory councils or to attend the annual 'charity ball'. Another highly attractive ploy, with ancient precedent, is 'to recognise donors by attaching their names to facilities, positions, or projects, as when a university creates an endowed professorship in a donor's name'.[80] In view of this, it would be profitable to ask how Paul's insistence upon the return of honour (Rom 12:10; 13:8-10; 16:2; cf. 1 Tim 5:17) functions in the community of grace where the least is now honoured above all (1 Cor 12:24).

In short, the social-science perspective can be a useful methodological tool for historical research into the ancient reciprocity system. It enables the New Testament researcher to address fresh and pertinent social questions to our

---

[78] C.A. Gregory, *op. cit.*, 206.
[79] R. Frank, 'Motivation, Cognition, and Charitable Giving', in J.B. Schneewind (ed.), *op. cit.*, 130-152.
[80] *Ibid.*, 146.

texts,[81] without the straitjacket of the 'assured results' of critical scholarship or the constraints of theological assumption and historical selectivity.

But the same can equally be said of ancient historians who, by immersing themselves in a wide range of social evidence (documentary, literary, numismatic, and archaeological), acquire a sense of what is typical and distinctive as regards eastern Mediterranean beneficence, and then sensitively seek to locate Paul's view of grace somewhere within that grid.[82] The above questions, while finding a home in the modern sociological literature, initially arose out of my study of the ancient texts.

1.3.2. Deficiencies in the social-scientific approach for a historically nuanced understanding of first-century grace

We have spoken positively of the contribution that the social-scientific perspective can make to benefaction studies, notwithstanding the methodological reservations noted above. But, in our view, there still remain limitations to the usefulness of sociological and anthropological perspectives in regard to Paul's view of grace.

First, if we neglect the ancient evidence from the Greek East, we miss out on the terminology of reciprocity and commensurability that regularly accompanies the language of grace in antiquity. As R.P. Saller states of the (Latin) evidence, 'the words which describe the exchange are perhaps the best pointers to patronage'.[83] Why does Paul (almost universally) ignore the traditional range of terminology found with χάρις in the inscriptions? Why does he so often replace it with the language of abundance in his epistles? Or, more specifically, in the case of Romans, with regnal language? Or, in the case of Ephesians, with the language of power, glory, wealth, and mystery? What were the local conditions of the house churches that spawned these language shifts when Paul described grace? Are we witnessing here not only a local critique of benefaction ideology — as with Rome and Ephesus — but also a frontal assault on the Graeco-Roman reciprocity system per se?

Second, without a full-orbed examination of the ancient evidence, we will be deaf to dissenting voices in antiquity regarding divine beneficence and the

---

[81] Note the comment of P.F. Craffert (*art. cit.*, 232): 'The value of heuristic models lies not in their explanatory power but in their capacity to raise interesting questions'.

[82] Note the perceptive comment of E.A. Judge, *art. cit.* (1980), 216: 'History walks a tightrope between the unique and the typical. If we explain everything by analogy, we deny to our forebears the individuality we take as a basic feature of our own humanity ... we will never get the true measure of that until we can map out adequately the relationships of similarity and difference between the first churches and other group phenomena of their time'.

[83] R.P. Saller, *op. cit.*, 15.

reciprocity system. As a result, we will be unable to determine with any certainty the extent to which Paul is radical or typical of his age. Inevitably, the contours of Paul as a social and theological critic become blurred. The same can be said when Paul's corporate language of grace is not viewed against the practices and beliefs of the informal first-century associations.

Third, without the benefit of the ancient evidence from the eastern Mediterranean basin, we will automatically assume that Paul's theology of grace is merely countering Judaizers or some type of debased hellenised Judaism (if such an entity existed).[84] But, more likely, the apostle of the Gentiles is addressing two fronts, correcting both Jewish *and* Graeco-Roman misunderstandings of grace.

Fourth, as observed, the 'sociological fallacy' — to borrow the term of E.A. Judge[85] — imposes an exclusively Roman patronal understanding on the Greek *poleis* of the eastern Mediterranean basin. But even the recently founded Roman colonies of Corinth and Philippi retained a strong indigenous Greek culture that made its own contribution to benefaction conventions.

Last, by introducing comparative materials from other cultures into an historical vacuum, we risk simplifying the complexity of the hellenistic reciprocity system and thereby underestimate the subtlety of the cultural pressures that Paul faced as a theologian of grace.[86] In sum, the difficult work of unearthing first-century models of social organisation and practice within the eastern Mediterranean basin must be undertaken rather than naively assuming commensurability between vastly different cultures.

---

[84] This mindset is especially evident in an article of C.A. Wanamaker ('A Case against Justification by Faith', *Journal of Theology for Southern Africa* 42 [1983], 37-49). Wanamaker (*ibid.*, 48) argues that 'justification by faith has its principal role in interpreting the gospel to Jews and Jewish Christians'. By contrast, Paul's 'language about being-in-Christ' communicated more effectively to Gentiles (*ibid.*). Such statements reveal a total ignorance of the the pivotal role that χάρις played in the hellenistic reciprocity system and in the Caesar cult. The *real* challenge for Paul was how to speak to Gentiles about divine and human χάρις in a way that was fresh and striking, given the widespead use of χάρις and its cognates throughout the eastern Mediterranean basin.

[85] E.A. Judge, *art. cit.* (1980), 210.

[86] P.F. Craffert (*art. cit.*, 226) astutely observes: 'the explicit and conscious use of models, even so-called cross-cultural models, does not necessarily prevent anachronistic or ethnocentric interpretations, since the way models function is determined by preferences which are not implicit in the models themselves. Models are merely the tools used to achieve certain results and the instruments used within particular philosophy-of-science paradigms to serve the scientific needs of interpretative communities'.

1.4. Purpose and Plan of Study

The purpose of this study is to investigate the extent to which Paul interacts with Graeco-Roman benefaction ideology in choosing χάρις as his central description of divine and human beneficence. At a theological level, to what degree is Paul engaging notions of divine grace found in the Gentile cults, in the spiritual underworld of the practitioners of magic, and in the popular philosophers? How would Graeco-Roman auditors have responded to Paul's proclamation of the reign of divine grace?

At a social level, what aspects of the hellenistic reciprocity system does Paul endorse, treat with reserve, up-end by means of a radical critique, or reject outright? What determines his response in each case? How would the Jerusalem collection have been regarded by his Graeco-Roman contemporaries? How did Paul handle tensions and misunderstandings concerning giving and receiving in his churches?

In sum, does Pauline χάρις become a distinctive motif, theologically and socially, in its eastern Mediterranean benefaction context?

For a balanced presentation of the role of χάρις in the Graeco-Roman benefaction system our selection of ancient evidence is critical. In this respect, we are reminded of P. Schubert's comment that the genre of the Pauline epistles falls somewhere between the inscriptions and the papyri (§1.2 n.35). Therefore, in Chapter 2, it is argued that the Greek honorific inscriptions unveil the operations of the hellenistic reciprocity system and best approximate the public context of the New Testament documents.

In Chapter 3 we argue that the Greek papyri help us gauge how far benefaction terminology had spread beyond the large hellenistic urban centres into the villages of the surrounding countryside. In the case of the papyri, a private world of benefaction relationships — comparable to that of the Pauline house churches — is opened up for us. There we are able to see the darker social realities of the benefaction system masked by the positive tone of the honorific inscriptions.

In Chapter 4 we investigate whether the literary and documentary evidence of Greek-speaking Judaism had been substantially affected by Graeco-Roman benefaction ideology. However, because our primary focus is on the reaction of Greek-speaking Jews such as Josephus and Philo to hellenistic beneficence, the lively debate generated by E.P. Sanders regarding the place of grace in Tannaitic Judaism and its relation to Paul's portrayal of first-century Judaism cannot be given the detailed response that it deserves. Nonetheless, for the sake of completeness, we will examine the role that grace plays in the rabbinic literature.[87]

In Chapter 5 the role of χάρις and *gratia* in the Greek and Roman moral philosophers is examined in the belief that discussions of divine and human beneficence spread from the confines of the philosophical schools to more popular settings.

In discussing χάρις in its Graeco-Roman benefaction context in Chapters 2 to 5, we will concentrate on a series of recurring themes: the ethos of reciprocity, the disposal of χαρίτες by various benefactors (the gods, the Caesars, and civic luminaries), and the rare critiques of benefaction ideology in antiquity. From there we will be well placed to assess Paul's portrayal of divine and human χάρις in Chapters 6 and 7 respectively.

Finally, for the purposes of discussion, I will assume the authenticity of the traditional Pauline epistles, with the exception of the Pastorals.[88] (Where I do cite references from the Pastorals, this is by way of illustrating the perspective of the writer of these epistles — whether that be Paul, his secretary, or a pseudonymous author).[89] The standard conventions of abbreviation are used throughout.[90]

---

[87] For a discussion of grace in the Dead Sea Scrolls, see the original unpublished version of the thesis (Macquarie University 1996), §4.4 (103-108).

[88] The consensus among New Testament scholars concerning Pauline authorship is as follows: indisputably Pauline (Rom, 1 and 2 Cor, Gal, Phil, Phlm, 1 Thess); usually accepted (Col, 2 Thess); strongly disputed (Eph); rejected (Pastorals).

[89] I.H. Marshall ('Salvation, Grace and Works in the Later Writings in the Pauline Corpus', *NTS* 42/3 [1996], 339-358) argues that Paul's faith/works antithesis is as central to Ephesians and the Pastorals as the other undisputed letters.

[90] Abbreviations for the inscriptions follow *Supplementum Epigraphicum Graecum*. Note the very helpful attempt of G.H.R. Horsley and J.A.L. Lee at standardising epigraphic abbreviations: *id.*, 'A Preliminary Checklist of Abbreviations of Greek Epigraphic Volumes', *Epigraphica* 66 (1994), 136ff. Abbreviations for the papyri follow S.R. Pickering, *Papyrus Editions* (Macquarie University 1984). Abbreviations for the classical, biblical, and Jewish authors conform to those in the 'Instructions for Contributors' found in *JBL* 107 (1988) 579-596 and in N.G.L. Hammond and H.H. Scullard (eds), *The Oxford Classical Dictionary* (Oxford 1972). In the case of Philo, the Loeb Classical Library abbreviations are used. Abbreviations for periodicals, reference works, and serials conform to those in *JBL* 107 (1988) 579-596 and *L'Année Philologique*. Any additions to the *JBL* conventions can be found in *CBQ* 46/2 (1984), 393-408 and *Bib* 70/4 (1989), 577-594. Where there exist translations of the Greek inscriptions and papyri, these have been gratefully borrowed. The remaining translations are my own. The Loeb Classical Library is the translation adopted for the Greek and Latin literature. The RSV translation of the Bible is employed throughout. The standard English translations of the non-canonical Jewish literature (R.H. Charles, J.H. Charlesworth, H. Danby, J. Neusner) have been used.

Chapter 2

The Role of *Charis* in the Inscriptions

2.1. The Inscriptions and New Testament Benefaction Terminology

New Testament scholars have recently begun to explore how far our predominantly aristocratic literary remains reflect the social concerns of the ninety-five percent below the apex of the social pyramid.[1] Given the public nature of the gospel proclamation and the New Testament documents themselves,[2] we should not assume that Graeco-Roman auditors would have interpreted Paul's use of χάρις within an aristocratic literary grid. Even the papyri, while emanating from a wider social milieu, retained 'a measure of privacy' and would not necessarily have captured the public focus of the early Christian theology of grace.[3]

In contrast, the inscriptions provide us with a rich semantic domain that was accessible to the wider Graeco-Roman public. First-century auditors would have more readily recognised the Christian vocabulary of giving and

---

[1] See especially F.G. Downing, 'A Bas Les Aristos: The Relevance of Higher Literature for the Understanding of the Earliest Christian Writings', *NovT* 30/3 (1988), 212-230. Downing argues that our aristocratic sources can still be used to filter out the social world of the 'bottom ninety five percent'. By contrast, E.A. Judge ('The Rhetoric of Inscriptions', in S.E. Porter [ed.], *Handbook of Classical Rhetoric in the Hellenistic Period 330 BC—AD 400* [Leiden-New York-Köln 1997], 807-808) argues for the artificiality of the literary record in comparison to the inscriptions: 'The literary record has not only lost the living voice and its audience. For where it preserves the work of a great orator (Demosthenes, Cicero), it has been kept only to cultivate a refined discipline enshrined now in higher education. True, all literary work was still declaimed, but only to the artificial audience of school or salon ... What is inscribed must capture the vital essence of the moment ... precisely because they are being incised, we know that we have the words at the very point of utterance, immune from improving afterthoughts (the modern epigrapher can readily detect additions, and — with technical aid — even erasures)'.

[2] For evidence of the public reading aloud of Paul's epistles in the house churches, see 1 Thess 5:27 and Col 4:16. Also, cf. Acts 15:31.

[3] F.W. Danker, *Benefactor: Epigraphic Study of a Graeco-Roman and New Testament Semantic Field* (St. Louis 1982), 28. G.H.R. Horsley ('*Koine* or Atticism — A Misleading Dichotomy', *New Docs* 5 [1989], 45) helpfully observes that Paul's letters were addressed to groups, unlike the private letters.

receiving against this background rather than the polished products of the Graeco-Roman literary world. There are several reasons for this.

First, as Paul Veyne observes concerning ancient benefaction, the real motivation of the εὐεργέτης 'was not so much the honour itself as the engraving of the decree which awarded it and which posterity would be able to read'.[4] For five centuries prior to the Christian era, acts of munificence by heads of state and public officials had been celebrated in the stereotyped language of the honorific inscriptions.[5] Readers of Paul's epistles could not have missed the eulogistic vocabulary of the inscriptions, erected as they were in prominent locations for the appreciation of posterity.[6]

Often the honorific decrees were explicit in their instructions regarding where the eulogy of the benefactor was to be displayed. Accordingly, numerous decrees were set up as votive gifts in the temples of the deities,[7] the gymnasia,[8] the sacred place of the Assembly,[9] or at the sacred stoa.[10] They were also recorded on the wall at the front of the benefactor's house,[11] or

---

[4] P. Veyne, *Bread and Circuses* (London 1990: Fr. orig 1976), 127.

[5] Our examination of inscriptional uses of χάρις will be confined to 200 BC—AD 200. The following sample of inscriptions using χάρις predate 200 BC and demonstrate a use consistent with that of the later hellenistic and imperial period:

(a) *V cent. BC*: *SIG*³ 22. *SEG* X 131; XXX 30; XXXVI 139. E.S. Roberts, *An Introduction to Greek Epigraphy. Pt.1: The Archaic Inscriptions and the Greek Alphabet* (Cambridge 1887), §180, §181.

(b) *IV cent. BC*: *SIG*³ 204, 226, 227, 249, 285, 330, 336, 346. *SEG* IV 663; XXX 65, 140; XXXIII 276; XXXV 80, 104; XXXVI 155; XXXVII 70. L'Institut Fernand-Courby, *Nouveau choix d'inscriptions grecques: textes, traductions, commentaires pour l'Institut Fernand-Courby* (Paris, 1971), §9.

(c) *III cent. BC*: *SIG*³ 374, 391, 475, 485, 540, 547, 559, 912. *SEG* I 358; VII 11; VIII 496; XI 435; XII 390, 472; XIV 461; XV 111, 113, 877; XVI 73; XVII 120; XVIII 33, 197, 333; XXI 525; XXII 128; XXIV 1094; XXVII 71; XXVIII 964; XXXVIII 127, 1476. *Nouveau choix d'inscriptions grecques*, §11; C.B. Welles, *Royal Correspondence in the Hellenistic Period* (London 1934), §35.

[6] P. Veyne (*op. cit.*, 128) sums up the situation well: 'there was no shortage of readers. When a Greek or a Roman wanted to read a little, he could either go to a library or walk around a sanctuary or a public square, or along a road whose shoulders served as a cemetery, where he could read the votive offerings, the decrees, the pedestals of statues or the epitaphs'. See also E.A. Judge, *art. cit.*, in S.E. Porter (ed.), *op. cit.*, 808.

[7] Temples of Apollo: *SIG*³ 721, 814; *Michel* 235; *SEG* XVI 255. Temples of Asklepios: *Michel* 64; *SEG* XVIII 20, 27. Temples of Persephone, Zeus, Parthenos, Caesar, Artemis: respectively, *SIG*³ 800, 814; *Michel* 372; *SEG* XIII 258; *BMI* (Ephesos) 455. Unspecified temple, *Michel* 985.

[8] *SEG* XI 948; XIII 258; XXVI 1021; *I. Ephesos* 6.

[9] *SEG* XII 306.

[10] *I. Priene* 114.

[11] *SEG* XIII 258.

placed in the most conspicuous place of the unwalled village,[12] city,[13] and community.[14] It was not unusual for eulogistic decrees to be erected at multiple sites.[15] A copy of the decree was kept for the public archives.[16] Sometimes the object to be inscribed at the site was stipulated, including bases of statues[17] and pieces of gold-plated armour at the gymnasia.[18] Occasionally, the motivation behind the choice of site for the decree was explained. We can see this in the mid-first century AD decree, erected in honour of the prefect of Egypt at Bouseiris, which directs:

> it has been decided by the People from the village of Bouseiris of the Leopolite (nome) who live near the pyramids and by the district secretaries and village secretaries who dwell in (the nome) to pass a decree and to erect a stone stele near [the greatest god,] the Sun Hamarchis, from the good deeds engraved on it [showing] his benefactions and letting [everyone] know that his god-like favours (τὰς ισοθέους χάριτας αὐτοῦ) recorded by sacred writings, forever be remembered.[19]

In sum, the widespread accessibility of benefaction terminology to the Graeco-Roman public would have been a factor in its use by the early Christians.

Second, the geographical spread of the eulogistic inscriptions throughout the eastern Mediterranean basin would have secured a ready recognition of Paul's use of benefaction terminology.[20] By contrast, the extant papyri are 'geographically very focused', surviving only in the favourable climatic conditions of Egypt and Palestine.[21] Therefore, as evidence for the ancient historian, the inscriptions chart the progress of benefaction ideology throughout the eastern Mediterranean basin in a more comprehensive fashion than do the papyri.

---

[12] *SEG* VIII 527.

[13] *I. Priene* 114.

[14] R.K. Sherk, *Roman Documents from the Greek East* (Baltimore 1969), §49.

[15] Two sites (temples): *SIG*^{3} 814, *supra*. Three sites (temple, wall, gymnasium): *SEG* XIII 255, *supra*.

[16] *SIG*^{3} 800; *Michel* 372.

[17] *I. Ephesos* 6.

[18] *SEG* IX 4.

[19] *OGIS* 666. See also *SIG*^{3} 800 for another example.

[20] In the Latin West, the equivalent of χάρις — *gratia* and its cognates — was also used in the honorific inscriptions. See B. Laum, *Stiftungen in der griechischen und römischen Antike: Ein Beitrag zur antiken Kulturgeschichte* Vol.II (Berlin 1914), §50 (Italy, AD 18: 'gratia') and §104 (Narbo, undated: 'gratia', 'gratissimus', 'gratius'). For discussions of *gratia*, see J. Hellegouarc'h, *Le vocabulaire latin des relations et des partis politiques sous la république* (Paris 1963), 202-208; C. Moussy, *Gratia et sa famille* (Paris 1966), *passim*; H. Drexler, *Politische Grundbegriffe der Römer* (Darmstadt 1988), 159-187.

[21] See G.H.R. Horsley, 'The Inscriptions of Ephesos and the New Testament', *NovT* 34/2 (1992), 112, 114.

A third reason for the familiarity of inscriptional benefaction terminology stems from the social diversity of both its propagators and intended audience. Not all inscriptions emanated from the royal chancery, which employed secretaries of the highest professional standard to write up the various resolutions.[22] And even the chancery productions, in the case of the Caesars, were expected to be read or heard by all subjects.[23] Many decrees were erected in honour of benefactors by small clubs or associations that offered fellowship and feasting under the patronage of various deities or heroes. These provided mutual assistance in difficult times, as well as funerary services. F.W. Danker elaborates on the significance of the club or association for the pervasiveness of benefaction terminology in Graeco-Roman culture:

> In a world in which ordinary individuals had little contribution to make in the formation of their political destiny, the small groups offered some semblance of corporate dynamics. And like the United Kingdom, which endeavours through pomp and pageant to suggest a political reality that is no more, these clubs and associations affected the diction and syntax of city-states or of the chanceries of the Ptolemies or of the Seleucids. This diction and syntax brought to verbal expression deeply imbedded cultural values. For a brief moment ... their members could play the role of esteemed civil service officials, of members of councils and planning committees.[24]

---

[22] For an insightful discussion of the inscriptional chancery prose, see C.B. Welles, *op.cit.*, xxxvii-l.

[23] F.W. Danker ('On Stones and Benefactors', *CurTM* 8/6 [1981], 352) states the case succinctly: 'when such a communication appears on stone, everyone knows that Rome means business. An inscription is meant to be read or heard — there's always someone around to clue illiterate folk on the latest — by every citizen, temporary resident, slave, or tradesperson'. Plutarch (*Mor.*, 395A) mentions the professional guides of Corinth expounding the inscriptions. On literacy in antiquity, see W.V. Harris, 'Literacy and Epigraphy, I', *ZPE* 52 (1983), 87-111; P.J.J. Botha, 'Greco-Roman Literacy as Setting for the New Testament Writings', *Neot* 26/1 (1992), 195-215.

[24] F.W. Danker, *art. cit.*, 352. See also R. MacMullen, *Roman Social Relations* (New Haven 1974), 76. For inscriptions which use χάρις (and its cognates) in honour of the benefactors of clubs and associations, see P. Foucart, *Des associations religieuses chez les Grecs: thiases, éranes, orgéons* (Paris 1873), §6, §7, §8, §10, §30, §43; *Michel* 984, 998, 1011; *SEG* IV 598; XXV 564; *IG* V(1) 1175; XI(4) 1061; XII(9) 239; *I. Délos* IV 1520; J.-P. Waltzing, *Étude historique sur les corporations professionnelles chez les romains* Vol.III (rpt. New York 1970: 1895 Fr. orig.), §106, §114, §141. For a senatorial decree concerning the association of Greek artists, *SIG*³ 705. For discussions of the clubs in antiquity, see P. Foucart, *op. cit.*; J.-P. Waltzing, *op. cit.*, Vols I-IV; A.D. Nock, 'The Historical Importance of Cult Associations', *CR* 38 (1924), 105-109; M.N. Tod, 'Clubs and Societies in the Greek World', in *id., Ancient Inscriptions: Sidelights on Greek History* (Chicago 1932), 71-96; C.A. Forbes, *Neoi: A Contribution to the Study of Greek Associations* (Middletown 1933); *id.*, 'Ancient Athletic Guilds', *CPh* 50 (1955), 238-252; A.E.R. Boak, 'The Organisation of Gilds in Greco-Roman Egypt', *TAPhA* 68 (1937), 212-220; M. Ginsburg, 'Roman Military Clubs and Their Social Functions', *TAPhA* 71 (1940), 149-156; F.W. Danker,

Moreover, the associations drew their members from the various strata of society, providing the types of social exchange which would allow benefaction terminology to spread from the higher echelons of the social pyramid to its base.[25]

Additionally, the crafts associations pursued φιλοτιμία ('love of honour') with the same zeal as the municipal aristocracy, courting the patronage of the civic luminaries and basking in the privileges that their benefactions spawned for the association.[26] As R. MacMullen observes, 'Associations thus resembled the whole social context they found themselves in and imitated it as best they could'.[27] An honorific decree from Delos, erected at the beginning of the second century BC by a corporation of merchants, provides a fine example of the interplay between the benefactor and the association in the quest for φιλοτιμία. The benefactor Patron is praised for his 'useful' (συμφέροντα) and 'benevolent' (εὔνους) acts towards the guild (σύνοδος) and corporation (κοινόν) of merchants and ship owners, and for his embassy to the Athenians to establish a site for the temple precincts of Heracles. The decree continues:

> ... and (as) the elected ambassador to both the Council and the Athenian People, undertaking (the embassy) readily (προθύμως) he went by sea from his own expenses, and having displayed the good will of the guild towards the People he encouraged (the People) and on account of this responsibility he brought the wish of the members of the religious guilds to completion (ἐπετελέσατο) and he <increased> the honour of the gods just as was fitting for (the People); and having done the majority a kindness in the appropriate times, he also announced just deeds on behalf of the guild in the most pressing time with all earnestness (προθυμίας) and love of honour (φιλοτιμίας) and also he entertained the religious guild for two days on behalf of [...]; therefore in order that for the remaining time he may also render himself (to be one who does not need to be) summoned (in regard to beneficence) and that the

---

'Associations, Clubs, Thiasoi', in D.N. Freedman (ed.), *Anchor Bible Dictionary* Vol.1 (New York 1992), 501-503.

[25] On the mixed social composition of clubs and associations, see J.E. Stambaugh, 'Social Relations in the City of the Early Principate: State of Research', in P.J. Achtemeier (ed.), *Society of Biblical Literature 1980 Seminar Papers* (Chico 1980), 93-94, and the literature there cited. This is not to deny the greater exclusivity of Greek clubs in contrast to the Roman collegia, or the fact that clubs could be socially homogenous, or their fundamental drawing base from craftsmen and artisans, merchants and shopkeepers. For each position respectively, see L.Wm. Countryman, 'Patrons and Officers in Club and Church', in P.J. Achtemeier (ed.), *Society of Biblical Literature 1977 Seminar Papers* (Missoula 1977), 136; W.A. Meeks, *The First Urban Christians* (New Haven 1983), 79, 222 n.20 and E.A. Judge, *The Social Pattern of Christian Groups in the First Century* (London 1960), 44, 60; R.L. Wilken, *The Christians as the Romans Saw Them* (New Haven 1984), 35. However the immense variety of clubs and associations, their broad social and religious functions, and their contact with wealthy benefactors who sponsored their activities, would have ensured their social diversity.

[26] See the discussion of R. MacMullen, *op. cit.*, 75-77.

[27] *Ibid.*, 77.

guild may manifestly take thought of the men who are benevolently disposed to itself and that it may return worthy favours (χάριτας) to the benefactors and that more (of) the other (members) from the guild may be zealous imitators (ζηλωταί) on account of the (guild's) thankfulness (εὐχαριστίαν) for this (generosity of Paron) and that those who love honour (φιλοτιμούμενοι) may outdo (each other) to achieve something for the guild; with good fortune; it was resolved by the corporation of the merchants and of the owners of ships of Turioi Herakleistoi; that (the corporation) praise Patron the son of Dorotheos and crown him yearly with a gold crown in the sacrifices celebrated for Poseidon, on account of (his) merit (ἀρετῆς) and goodness (καλοκαγαθίας), which he continues holding towards the corporation of the merchants and the owners of ships of Turoi Herakleistoi ...[28]

The community of the early Christians — whose mixed social composition included artisans, small traders, and wealthy patrons[29] — would have had

---

[28] *I. Délos* IV 1519, *ll.*16-41. The text is also found in *Michel* 998. There are differences between *Michel* and the *I. Délos* editor in textual reconstruction of the decree, my own translation being based on the latter. Compare respectively, *ll.*17, 21-23, 26. For further association decrees employing χάρις, see P. Foucart, *op. cit.*, §6, §7, §8, §10, §30, §43.

[29] For Christians of artisan status: Aquila and Priscilla (Acts 18:2-3); Paul (Acts 18:3; 20:34-35; 1 Thess 2:9; and 2 Thess 3:7-9, if Pauline); Barnabas (1 Cor 6:9). The case is not affected by the fact that Paul and Barnabas had renounced their higher social status for an artisan role. On the latter, see E.A. Judge, 'The Social Identity of the First Christians: A Question of Method in Religious History', *JRH* 11 (1980), 213-214 and W.A. Meeks, *op. cit.*, 61. On Aquila and Priscilla, see J. Murphy-O'Connor, 'Prisca and Aquila', *Bible Review* 8/6 (1992), 40-51, 62. More generally, see R. Hock, *The Social Context of Paul's Ministry: Tentmaking and Apostleship* (Philadelphia 1980), *passim*; A. Deissmann, 'Primitive Christianity and the Lower Classes', *Expositor* 7 (1909), 216-218. For Christians of small trader status: Lydia (Acts 16:14ff). See W.A. Meeks, *op. cit.*, 62 and E.A. Judge, 'The Early Christians as a Scholastic Community', *JRH* 1/3 (1961), 128. For Christians of patronal status: Phoebe (Rom 16:1-2); Erastus (Rom 16:23); Gaius (Rom 16:23); Stephanus (1 Cor 16:15b); Philemon (Phlm 1-2, 22); Jason (Acts 17:1-9). On Phoebe, see E.A. Judge, 'Cultural Conformity and Innovation in Paul: Some Clues from Contemporary Documents', *TynBul* 35 (1984), 17-21; R. Jewett, 'Paul, Phoebe, and the Spanish Mission', in J. Neusner (*et al.*, ed.), *The Social World of Formative Christianity and Judaism: Essays in Tribute to Howard Kee* (Philadelphia 1988), 142-161; M. Zappella, 'A proposito di Febe ΠΡΟΣΤΑΤΙΣ (Rm 16, 2)', *RivB* 37/2 (1989), 167-171; M. Ernst, 'Die Funktionen der Phöbe (Röm 16, 1f) in der Gemeinde von Kenchreai', *Proto Bib* 1/2 (1992), 135-147; B. Brooten, 'Iael προστάτης in the Jewish Donative Inscription from Aphrodisias', in B.A. Pearson (ed.), *The Future of Early Christianity: Essays in Honour of Helmut Koester* (Minneapolis 1991), 149-162; C.F. Whelan, 'Amica Pauli: The Role of Phoebe in the Early Church', *JSNT* 49 (1993), 67-85; R.A. Kearsley, 'Women in Public Life in the Roman East: Iunia Theodora, Claudia Metrodora and Phoibe, Benefactress of Paul', *TynBul* 50/2 (1999), 189-211. On Erastus as benefactor, G. Theissen, *The Social Setting of Pauline Christianity: Essays on Corinth* (Philadelphia 1982), 75-83; D.W.J. Gill, 'Erastus the Aedile', *TynBul* 40 (1989), 294-301; A.D. Clarke, *Secular and Christian Leadership in Corinth: A Socio-Historical and Exegetical Study of 1 Corinthians 1-6* (Leiden-New York-Köln 1993), 46-56; B.W. Winter, *Seek the Welfare of the City: Christians as Benefactors and Citizens* (Grand Rapids 1994), 179-197. This assumes, of course, that Erastus is not a slave: see H.J. Cadbury, 'Erastus of Corinth', *JBL* 50 (1931), 42-58. J.J. Meggitt ('The Social Status of Erastus

members sensitive to the eulogistic conventions found in the association decrees.[30] Presumably, Paul would have been exposed to χάρις and its associated benefaction terminology through his work contacts with the local tradespeople and their patrons in the trade associations of Thessalonica, Corinth, and Ephesus.[31] Finally, in their role as burial societies, the associations furnished a tombstone for the deceased member from their own funds and may have inscribed it with the type of funerary hymn or epigram in

---

[Rom 16:3]', *NovT* 38/3 [1996], 218-223) argues that Erastus' socio-economic status was no greater than that of his Christian brethren. On Jason as benefactor, A.J. Malherbe, *Paul and the Thessalonians* (Philadelphia 1987), 12-17. On the prosopography of Early Christianity, see E.A. Judge, *op. cit.* (1960), 49-61; *id.*, *op. cit.* (1961), 125-137; G. Theissen, *op. cit.*, 69-119; A.J. Malherbe, *Social Aspects of Early Christianity* (Philadelphia 1983: 2nd ed.), 60-91; W.A. Meeks, *op. cit.*, 51-73; V.P. Branick, *The House Church in the Writings of Paul* (Wilmington 1989), 58-77; R. M Kidd, *Wealth and Beneficence in the Pastoral Epistles* (Atlanta 1990), 35-109; D.G. Horrell, *The Social Ethos of the Corinthian Correspondence: Interests and Ideology from 1 Corinthians to 1 Clement* (Edinburgh 1996), 91-101; J.J. Meggitt, *Paul, Poverty and Survival* (Edinburgh 1998), 127-149. For a sociological approach, R.L. Rohrbaugh, 'Methodological Considerations in the Debate Over the Social Class Status of Early Christians', *JAAR* 52/3 (1984), 519-546 and the literature there cited.

[30] On the relationship of Christianity to the associations, see E. Hatch, *The Organisation of the Early Christian Churches* (Oxford and Cambridge 1881), 26-54; E.A. Judge, *op. cit.* (1960), 40-48; L.Wm. Countryman, *The Rich Christian in the Church of the Early Empire: Contradictions and Accommodations* (New York and Toronto 1980), 162-171; *id.*, *art. cit.*, 136-141; R.L. Wilken, *op. cit.*, 31-47; *id.*, 'Collegia, Philosophical Schools, and Theology', in S. Benko and J.J. O'Rourke (eds), *The Catacombs and the Colosseum: The Roman Empire as the Setting of Primitive Christianity* (Valley Forge 1971), 279-286; V.P. Branick, *op. cit.*, 46-49; E.E. Ellis, *Pauline Theology: Ministry and Society* (Grand Rapids 1989), 123-147; J.S. Kloppenborg, 'Edwin Hatch, Churches, and Collegia', in B.H. McLean (ed.), *Origins and Method: Towards a New Understanding of Judaism and Christianity* (Sheffield 1993), 212-237; J. Kloppenborg and S. Wilson (eds), *Voluntary Associations in the Graeco-Roman World* (London 1996); R.S. Ascough, 'Translocal Relationships Among Voluntary Associations and Early Christianity', *Journal of Early Christian Studies* 5/2 (1997), 223-241; *id.*, *What Are They Saying About the Formation of Pauline Churches?* (New York 1998), 71-94; *id.*, 'The Thessalonian Christian Community as a Professional Voluntary Association', *JBL* 119/2 (2000), 311-328; J.R. Harrison, 'Paul's House Churches and the Cultic Associations', *Reformed Theological Review* 58/1 (1999), 31-47. For a fine discussion of the Ephesus inscription of the association of fishermen and fishermongers (*I. Ephesos* Ia. 20: Nero's reign), and its relevance for NT social historians, see G.H.R. Horsley, *op. cit.*, 95-114 and *art. cit.*, 127-135. For a similar discussion of a Dionysiac association inscription (Torre Nova: AD 150), see B.H. McLean, 'The Agrippinilla Inscription: Religious Associations and Early Church Formation', in *id.*, (ed.), *op. cit.*, 239-270.

[31] According to Acts 17:23, Paul used an inscription evangelistically at Athens. For helpful insights on the workshop and association, see A.J. Malherbe, *op. cit.* (1987), 17-20; *id.*, *op. cit.* (1983), 89-91.

which χάρις regularly appeared.³² Again, Graeco-Roman readers of epitaphs would not have missed a distinctive use of χάρις by the early Christians.

Having established the pervasiveness of benefaction rituals and terminology in the first century AD, we are confronted with a paradox. As we will see, the ground-breaking attempt of the early twentieth-century German scholar, G.P. Wetter, to situate χάρις in the context of the honorific inscriptions has not been expanded on by New Testament scholarship in any meaningful way. In our next section, we seek to determine what should be the future direction of studies in the area.

2.2. The Inscriptions, Charis, and New Testament Benefaction Studies

Surprisingly, little ink has been spilt by New Testament scholars on the role of χάρις in the inscriptions. The pioneering investigation of the use of χάρις in the imperial inscriptions was carried out by G.P. Wetter in 1913.³³ Subsequent scholarship leans heavily upon his work, and it still remains (with the exception of C. Spicq) the most extensive treatment of the topic available.³⁴ Wetter argued that the use of χάρις in the imperial inscriptions, especially those of Nero and Caligula, provided the linguistic springboard for understanding χάρις in the New Testament. He further pointed out that imperial 'favour' was often coupled with adjectives such as 'divine', 'immortal', 'godlike', and 'eternal'. In his discussion of the non-religious meaning of χάρις, Wetter cites inscriptional parallels for secular uses of χάρις in the New Testament ('thanks', 'credit', 'favour', and 'gift').³⁵ Wetter's achievement is singularly impressive, given the time of his work's publication and the wealth of inscriptional data that he assembles: some 53

---

[32] *Michel* 984 (178/177 BC): 'and when the Association on occasion lacked the necessary funds (Hermaios) gave liberally so that the departed could receive a decent burial'. For sepulchral hymns using χάρις, see *SEG* XI 334; XVIII 365; XIX 728; XXVIII 721; B.D. Meritt, *Corinth. Vol.VIII. Pt.1: Greek Inscriptions 1889—1927* (Cambridge Mass. 1931), §130; W. Peek, 'Grabepigramm aus Aegypten', *ZPE* 21 (1976), 133-134. See our discussion of χάρις in the Jewish funerary inscriptions in §4.6.2.

[33] G.P. Wetter, *Charis: Ein Beitrag zur Geschichte des ältesten Christentums* (Leipzig 1913), 12-20. Studies by classicists on χάρις in the honorific decrees are extremely rare. See C. Veligianni, 'Χάρις in den attischen Ehrendekreten der klassischen Zeit und die Ergänzung in *IG* I. 3(101), Z. 35-37, 51-52', *The Ancient History Bulletin* 3/2 (1989), 36-39. For a study of εὐχαριστία and its cognates in the inscriptions, see P. Schubert, *Form and Function of the Pauline Thanksgivings* (Berlin 1939), 143-158.

[34] On the work of C. Spicq, see §1.2.

[35] G.P. Wetter, *op. cit.*, 206-212.

inscriptions — and among these the three important inscriptions of Zosimos of Priene, strangely ignored by New Testament scholarship ever since.[36]

The next significant foray into the area came from W. Manson and J. Moffatt.[37] Manson gave Wetter's views a wide and sympathetic airing in the English-speaking world, but added little else which was original as far as his discussion of the inscriptional data. His conclusions are nicely encapsulated in the following quote from his 1932 article:

> Indeed the language of such inscriptions often bears an extraordinarily close resemblance to that in which St. Paul praises the riches of the Divine 'grace' ... It would seem reasonable, therefore, with Wetter to regard this style — a style which merely extends a current Greek signification of the term — as supplying the linguistic starting point for the Christian use of *charis*. 'Grace' on Christian lips will be primarily the 'gift' or 'benefaction' of God to man, the generous favour by which the Supreme Being makes men recipients of His salvation. The expression registers not simply a will to give but a deed of gift, not only an attitude of favour but an outflowing of favour in largess, not a mere benevolence towards men or cities or states, but an enriching of them with real blessings. For St. Paul it means the whole self-giving of God to men in Jesus Christ.[38]

In the year prior to Manson's article, Moffatt had briefly mentioned the inscriptional data in his discussion of χάρις. He aired the idea that in pre-Christian antiquity a dynamic sense of supernatural χάρις was already operative as a belief system.[39] This subterranean χάρις, emanating from a dead hero, was mediated by the underworld powers to his worshippers above ground. For evidence, Moffatt appeals to a second-century BC Euboean sepulchral inscription in which the tomb attendants are entrusted to the care of Χάρις and Ὑγίεια.[40] Moffatt also discusses the inscriptions of Caligula

---

[36] *Ibid.*, 47 n.1. The originality of G.P. Wetter's approach can be gauged by a comparison with the unpublished dissertation of O. Loew, ΧΑΡΙΣ (Marburg 1908), written 5 years before. However, Loew's work (*ibid.*, 81, 86) mentions only one inscription (*I. Priene* 287).

[37] W. Manson, 'Grace in the New Testament', in W.T. Whitley (ed.), *The Doctrine of Grace* (London 1932), 33-60; J. Moffatt, *Grace in the New Testament* (London 1931).

[38] *Ibid.*, 38-39.

[39] J. Moffatt, *op. cit.*, 29.

[40] For the inscription, *SIG*³ 1240. Note the comment of T. Zielinski, 'Charis and Charites', *CQ* 18 (1924), 161: 'the grave has become, so to say, a store room for that grace or mercy'. On χάρις and the Χάριτες see J.H. Oliver, *Demokratia, the Gods, and the Free World* (New York 1972), 91-117; K. Deichgräber, *Charis und Chariten und Grazien* (München 1971). I remain unconvinced about the applicability of *SIG*³ 1240 to the New Testament background: I can find no evidence in any New Testament writer for the hypostatisation — or divinisation — of χάρις nor its linkage to chthonic powers. See also our comments in §6.5 n.271. The sole example (so far as I know) of the hypostasis of 'Grace' in Christian literature is found in the late first- to early second-century AD (Syriac) *Odes of Solomon* 33.1:

> But again Grace was swift and repudiated the Corruptor,

and Nero. He draws attention to Paul's preference of χάρις to the LXX ἔλεος, especially in view of the negative connotation attached to ἔλεος in the Nero inscription. More generally, Moffatt notes the absence in Paul of the εὐ-compounds so numerous in the honorific inscriptions.[41]

Subsequently, scholars make fleeting references to the inscriptions in discussing χάρις, but do little else than duplicate the discussions of Wetter and Manson.[42] More recently, F.W. Danker makes several significant references to the inscriptional use of χάρις in two publications.[43] However, Danker earns both the praise and frustration of D.E. Smith in his 1984 review of *Benefactor*.[44] Danker, as Smith notes, tends to be suggestive in his coverage. He neither develops his arguments in analytical fashion nor (I would add) devotes sufficient attention to χάρις in view of the pivotal role that the word played in the hellenistic reciprocity system.

The time is long overdue for a major reinvestigation of the use of χάρις in the inscriptions. There are several compelling reasons for this.

1. The fundamental reason is that little work has been done since Wetter's limited incursion into the area, and most New Testament scholars have done little else than uncritically reiterate his conclusions. Further, as original as Wetter's contribution was, he neglected the wider conceptual terrain in which χάρις operated. Why did Paul choose χάρις, the leitmotiv of the hellenistic reciprocity system, to describe divine and human beneficence? Would not Paul have run the risk — certainly in the minds of his Graeco-Roman auditors — of misrepresenting God's unilateral grace as some type of reciprocal contract? To what extent does Paul incorporate and endorse aspects of reciprocity in his understanding of the Jerusalem collection? How does his overall approach compare with the honorific inscriptions?[45]

---

and descended upon him to renounce him.

[41] J. Moffatt, *op. cit.*, 118, 127-8, 229.

[42] See especially J.H. Moulton and G. Milligan, *The Vocabulary of the Greek New Testament* (London 1930), 685; T.F. Torrance, *The Doctrine of Grace in the Apostolic Fathers* (Edinburgh 1948), 4-5; R.F. Surburg, 'Pauline *Charis*: A Philogical, Exegetical, and Dogmatical Study', *CTM* 29/10 (1958), 728-729; T.N. Schulz, *The Meaning of Charis in the New Testament* (Genova 1971), 34-35; H. Conzelmann, 'χάρις', *TDNT* 9 (1974), 375-376.

[43] F.W. Danker, *op. cit.* (1982), 334, 437-38, 453, 472; *id.*, *2 Corinthians* (Minneapolis 1989), *passim*.

[44] D.E. Smith, 'Frederick W. Danker, *Benefactor*', *CBQ* 46/1 (1984), 150-152.

[45] There has been no detailed examination of reciprocity in the inscriptions. For works which deal with the issue, see J.W. Hewitt, 'The Development of Political Gratitude', *TAPhA* 55 (1924), 35-51; *id.*, 'The Terminology of "Gratitude" in Greek', *CPh* 22 (1927), 142-161; J.B. Mathews, *Hospitality and the New Testament Church: An Historical and*

2. The corpus of newly published and revised inscriptions has burgeoned dramatically since Wetter's contribution in 1913, as the *Supplementum Epigraphicum Graecum* and the *New Documents Illustrating Early Christianity* projects amply testify. At the very least, some recognition of their potential contribution to our understanding of χάρις is demanded. Moreover, in light of the wealth of inscriptional evidence now available, we are in a stronger position to determine with precision what the Graeco-Roman public use of χάρις was in the period spanning 200 BC—AD 200. This provides a highly instructive data base for assessing how the early Christian preaching of God's χάρις would have been perceived by its audience.
3. Another important reason for research in this area is the neglect of New Testament scholarship to explore the wider value system underlying the inscriptional data. Such an exploration could open up some tantalising questions. Was Paul's insistence on the priority of divine χάρις provoked (to some degree) by the Graeco-Roman preoccupation with civic merit (ἀρετή)? Certainly, in honouring its benefactors, Graeco-Roman society was promoting its own version of δικαιοσύνη as aggressively as Paul's Jewish opponents. Was Paul critiquing the quest of his eastern Mediterranean contemporaries for ἀρετή and φιλοτιμία? And even if this was not Paul's intention, would it have been apparent to his Graeco-Roman auditors that he was *not* criticising Graeco-Roman ideas of merit?
4. Relatedly, what other semantic domains occur with χάρις in the honorific inscriptions? Are they found in the Pauline vocabulary and how are they used? If not, should we attach any significance to their omission?
5. Finally, a fundamental methodological question needs canvassing. Does New Testament word usage generally bear a closer relation to the inscriptional data than that of the literary texts (which up to now have largely been the focus of New Testament scholarship)? A thorough examination of χάρις in the inscriptional and literary data would provide an interesting test case for some tentative conclusions. Therefore, in Chapter 5, we will examine whether the inscriptional use of χάρις is

---

Exegetical Study (unpub. Ph.D. diss. Princeton 1965), *passim*; A.R. Hands, *Charities and Social Aid in Greece and Rome* (London 1968), 26-48; S.C. Mott, *op. cit.*, 102-109; *id.*, 'The Power of Giving and Receiving: Reciprocity in Hellenistic Benevolence', in G.F. Hawthorne (ed.), *Current Issues in Biblical and Patristic Interpretation: Studies in Honour of Merril C. Tenney* (Grand Rapids 1975), 60-72; P. Marshall, *Enmity in Corinth: Social Conventions in Paul's Relations with the Corinthians* (Tübingen 1987), *passim*; B.W. Winter, 'The Public Honouring of Christian Benefactors: Romans 13:3-4 and 1 Peter 2:14-15', *JSNT* 34 (1988), 87-103. See alslo §1.3 n.55.

replicated in the discussions of beneficence found in the Greek popular philosophers. Two penetrating questions posed by D.E. Smith sum up the issue well:

> Are there examples other than in the NT where terms and concepts from the benefactor inscriptions are used in a context and genre different from that of the inscriptions themselves? How might these examples compare with the usage in the NT and perhaps explain it?[46]

We now turn to the study of the honorific inscriptions *per se* and the role of χάρις in the world-view of the Graeco-Roman benefaction system.

2.3. The Nature and Structure of Honorific Decrees

Before we survey a selection of inscriptions using χάρις from 200 BC—AD 200, the nature and structure of the honorific decree should be examined. As regards the nature of the honorific inscriptions, their eulogistic vocabulary is universally positive, couched as they are in the convention of politeness towards the honorand. To find any negative connotation attached to the inscriptional use of χάρις is rare, and such cases are universally from the non-honorific inscriptions.[47] Although the language is formulaic and (at times) verbose in its rhetoric, the *topoi* embedded in the decrees reflect the social realities underlying benefaction relationships better than the aristocratic literature.[48]

---

[46] D.E. Smith, *art. cit.*, 152. For good examples of this approach using the *Moralia* of Plutarch and Dio Chrysostom, see C. Panagopoulos, 'Vocabulaire et mentalité dans les *Moralia* de Plutarche', *DHA* 3 (1977), 197-235; M.-H. Quet, 'Rhétorique, culture et politique: le fonctionnement du discours idéologique chez Dion de Pruse et dans les *Moralia* de Plutarque', *DHA* 4 (1978), 51-119.

[47] In a senatorial decree of Delphi (117—116 BC), the Amphictyons make an oath concerning money and Apollo's marking stones: 'I will not give in any way false judgement neither on account of favour (χάριτας) nor friendship nor hatred' (*SIG*^{3} 826). A first-century AD epitaph to eighteen year old Aule has this dedication: 'To Aule: [his] parents who begot [him] raised up [this stone]; and he — among those no longer living — is [turned to] dust long ago, but the toils of parents have run into empty gratitude (χάριτα[ν])' (*SEG* XI 344). Last, a mid second-century BC gymnasiarchal law commands the following: 'let the gymnasiarch write out the good behaviour of those enrolled from among the seven men in the place and let him choose these by lot and bind by Hermes the three on whom the lot falls to judge justly, whosoever should seem to him the best disposed in body, neither on account of favour (χάρι[τ]ος) nor on account of any enmity' (*SEG* XXVII 261).

[48] It is unwise to attribute objectivity to an honorific decree. Note especially the comment of A.G. Woodhead (*The Study of Greek Inscriptions* [Oxford 1959], 4): 'An "honorary decree" may have been drafted while the proposer's tongue was in his cheek; it is no proof of the merits of the person honoured'.

Several factors account for this.[49] First, the homogeneity of the honorific decrees over five centuries and their wide geographical distribution underscores the pervasiveness of these social conventions throughout the eastern Mediterranean basin.

Second, the eulogistic terminology of a decree has an historical particularity in its public praise of a specific benefactor by a known community, with the view to calling forth additional gifts either from him or his peers. This differentiates the concrete social terminology of the decrees from the more artificial literary productions. Panagopoulos sums up succinctly the reason for interpreting the literary texts via an epigraphic grid and, only then, vice versa:

...on peut lire les textes littéraires contemporains et y repérer le vocabulaire des qualités sociales sans se perdre dans les dédales du style individuel et de l'intentionnalité adventice. Réciproquement, la lecture des textes littéraires permet de compléter et de préciser la grille, soit par l'apport de mots nouveaux, soit par la cnfirmation de l'emploi des mots du formulaire épigraphique, soit au contraire par l'écart de l'emploi singulier par rapport aux emplois de série, soit enfin par des enchaînements et des développements de connotations qui permettent de mieux situer le mot dans l'idéologie.[50]

Last, and significantly for the New Testament context, the honorific decrees occasionally abandon their stereotyped conventions and gravitate towards more genuine expressions of feeling in their reciprocation of honours to the benefactor.[51] Here the abstract attributes normally credited to the benefactor in the honorific decrees are abandoned for more intense expressions of affection. One such example comes in an inscription of Olbia, datable to the late Republic or early Principate, which describes the benefactor Theokles as follows:

...by his moderation (μέτριον), and his affection (φιλόστοργον) in regard to his country, and his hospitality (φιλόξενον) towards all the Greeks, he has surpassed all his ancestors, ... not ceasing to serve the concord in his public activities, becoming as a brother (ἀδελφός) in regard to the men of his own age, as a son (υἱός) in regard to the more aged, as a father (πατήρ) in regard to the more young, adorned with all merit (πάσῃ ἀρετῇ) ...[52]

Similarly, in the 84 BC inscription of Zosimos of Priene, we hear of the benefactor providing the equipment for the association (κ[οινων]ίαν) of the

---

[49] In what follows see C. Panagopoulos, *art. cit.*, 197-199.

[50] *Ibid.*, 199.

[51] W.P. Clark, *Benefactions and Endowments in Greek Antiquity* (unpub. Ph.D. diss. Chicago University 1928), 261.

[52] *CIG* II 2059. W.P. Clark (*op. cit.*, 261) comments regarding this inscription: 'Occasionally a bit of genuine feeling shines out from the records which are for the most part quite matter of fact, revealing a sort of game between givers and recipients, the latter voting honours, thanks, crowns, and the like in order to induce the former to continue their good works or to increase them and to move others to do likewise'.

athletes, as well as a teacher-supervisor for the *epheboi*, because of his own love of learning and literature. Such an undertaking on behalf of the *epheboi* stems from Zosimos not only 'wishing (them) to obtain a resolute body, but (also wishing) to advance (their) souls towards merit and human passion'.[53] Later, as gymnasiarch of the *neoi*, he is described as giving 'heed to good conduct, esteeming the instructors (as) colleagues of himself, and sharing in common (κοιν[οπο]ησάμενος) his own refinement with those men'.[54] The social levelling and familial imagery implicit in these portraits provide an interesting backdrop to the Pauline communities and their role as benefactors.

But what was the structure of the honorific decree and how did χάρις fit into its stylised format?[55] The honorific decree often began with a preamble naming the magistrate under whom the resolution was proposed, the date of its proposal, and any additional information relevant the resolution's identification. Next came the announcement that a resolution had been passed, signalled by the formula Ἔδοξεν τῇ βουλῇ καὶ τῇ δήμῳ ('Resolved by the council and the people'). After this the proposer of the resolution was named, identified by the verb εἶπεν ('he moved [the motion]'). The resolution itself was introduced by ἐπειδή ('whereas'), and followed up with a series of clauses which articulated the reasons for the benefactor's honours. At the end of this eulogy of the benefactor, a 'manifesto clause' was inserted, introduced by ὅπως or ἵνα ('in order that') along with the use of φαίνηται ('it may be manifest') and the participle.[56] After a wish of 'good fortune' (ἀγαθῇ τύχῃ) for the resolution's implementation, the inscription was concluded with the resolution proper and the honours apportioned to the benefactor. The format of an honorific decree could vary within this grid: either by the omission of the preamble (often along with the ἔδοξεν clause, or εἶπεν), or by the relocation of the expression of good fortune to the beginning of the decree, or by some other stylistic variation.[57]

---

[53] *I. Priene* 112. W.P. Clark (*op. cit.*, 261 n.1) pithily sums up the portrait of Zosimos in *I. Priene* 112-114: 'a kindly, formal, universally approved (Dean of Boys)'.

[54] *I. Priene* 113.

[55] The following is dependent on A.G. Woodhead, *op. cit.*, 38-39; D. Woodhead, 'Competitive Outlay and Community Profit: φιλοτιμία in Democratic Athens', *C&M* 34 (1983), 55-74; B.W. Winter, *art. cit.*, 88-89.

[56] The term is used by D. Woodhead, *art. cit.*, 63.

[57] For the omission of the preamble and/or εἶπεν, see *SIG*³ 587; 721; *Michel* 64; 475; 1007; *SEG* II 663; IX 4. For the relocation of ἀγαθῇ τύχῃ, see *OGIS* 666; *Michel* 297; 985. For stylistic variations to the preamble, see the uses of Θεοί (*Michel* 1561) and [Γ]νώμη (*Michel* 541).

The following decree of the priests at the Piraeus, outside our time range at 217/16 BC, is interesting for its occasional modifications to the typical format outlined above:

> Gods. With good fortune. In the archonship of Aischon; in the ordinary assembly of Mounichon. Dionusodoros Alopekethen the son of Zopuros moved [the motion]; that whereas Krateia, having obtained (the office) of priestess for the (archonship) year of Aischon, she both offered the sacrifice at the beginning (of the year) and came to offer the remaining sacrifices on behalf of the guild, — and also she spread out a bier for both days (of) the festival of Attis, and she provided the rest fairly and reverently, omitting nothing (by way of) love of honour (φιλοτιμίας) and she continued doing service fairly and piously to the goddesses and opening the temple on the days which were her duty. Therefore in order that the priests may also manifestly return favour (χάριν ἀποδιδόντες) to those who contribute liberally (φιλοτ[ι]μουμένοις) both towards the goddesses and themselves; with good fortune, it was resolved by the priests; to praise Krateia and crown (her) with an olive branch crown, on account of piety towards the goddesses and love of honour (φιλοτιμίας) towards (the goddesses) for themselves; and also to crown (her) at the time to come for the sacrifices and to proclaim publicly her crown. And (it was resolved) that the priests engrave and set up publicly this decree on a monument made of stone and erect (it) in front of the inmost part of the temple. The priests (honour) the priestess Krateia. The priestess Krateia (honours) the One of hallowed name.[58]

However, since the majority of the uses of χάρις in the honorific inscriptions occur in the manifesto clause, the function and meaning of χάρις within the clause itself and its overall relation to the decree must be discussed.[59]

2.4. Charis *in the Manifesto Clause: Return of 'Favour' or 'Thanks'?*

The manifesto clause in the honorific inscription sums up the response of the people, council, or association to the generosity of the ἀνὴρ ἀγαθός, previously eulogised in the ἐπειδή clauses. It sets the official seal of approval on the benefactor's quest for φιλοτιμία in the public interest, encourages its continuance either by himself or his peers, and promises rewards commensurate with his beneficence — rewards which would be eternally commemorated in stone for posterity to see. The dynamic behind the manifesto clause is more than the gratitude of the beneficiary (although that is present): it also involves the ethos of reciprocity — the return of favours for favours done. Thus the automatic rendering of χάρις — especially in conjunction with ἀποδιδόναι ('to return') or ἀπόδοσις ('return') — as

---

[58] *Michel* 982.

[59] J.W. Hewitt (*art. cit.* [1927], 149) comments: 'In many phrases, χάριν as the object of the verb is ambiguous, for it may denote either favour or gratitude'.

'thanks' masks the complexity of the social interchange occurring.[60] Several factors point to χάρις being here understood as a 'favour' that is returned to the benefactor.

First, we see the motif of reciprocation present through the preposition ἀπό ('from', 'away from') that prefaces the verb ἀποδιδόναι.[61] A range of terminology, normally occurring with χάρις outside the manifesto clause, also underscores the reciprocity motif: ἀμείβειν ('to repay', 'to return'), ἀμοιβή ('repayment', 'return'), ἀντάμειψις ('an exchanging'), ἐν μέρει ('in turn').[62] Sometimes this reciprocity terminology surfaces alongside χάρις in the manifesto clause proper. A second-century BC association decree from Delos rewards a father and his son with the honoured place at the guild banquet and with freedom from the public services. The manifesto clause provides the rationale for these honours:

> In order, therefore, that the rest who contemplate the everlasting (ἀειμνηστον) honour distributed to good men may be zealous imitators (ζηλωταί) of (their) peers and also that they may enlarge much more readily (προθ[υμ]ότερον) the temple, having made known the zeal (σπουδήν) of the guild in regard to an exchanging of favour (ἀντάμειψιν χάριτος) ...[63]

Second, the use of χάρις in the manifesto clause sometimes acquires a reciprocal aspect from earlier occurrences of χάρις in the preceding eulogy of the benefactor. In the 175/4 BC decree from Pergamon, Eumenes II and his brother Attalos are described as 'observing that the moment offered [an occasion] for doing a favour (χάριν) and a good deed (εὐεργεσίαν)'. The manifesto clause makes plain the understanding of reciprocity behind χάρις:

> In order, therefore, that the People may appear foremost in the returning of a favour (ἐγ χάριτος ἀποδόσει) and be conspicuous in honouring those benefiting (εὐεργετοῦντας) the People and its friends voluntarily and in committing the goodness of their deeds to eternal memory (ἀΐδιομ μνήμην)...[64]

---

[60] Translators are divided whether χάρις with ἀποδιδόναι should be translated 'favour' or 'thanks'. E.g. F.W. Danker (*op. cit.*, §20) and M.M. Austin (*The Hellenistic World from Alexander to the Roman Conquest* [Cambridge 1981], §72) translate 'thanks'. B.W. Winter (*art. cit.*, 88) and D. Whitehead (*art. cit.*, 63) opt for 'favours'. Note in this regard the comment of H. Bolkestein, *Wohltätigkeit und Armenpflege im vorchristlichen Altertum* (rpt. New York 1979: Gmn. orig. 1939), 160: 'häufig kann man zweifeln, was gerade mit χάριν ἀποδιδόναι gemeint wird: einen Gegendienst erweisen oder dank bezeigen'.

[61] G.B. Philipp, 'Kritzeleien eines erleichterten Lehrers auf einem hölzernen Buchdeckel', *Gymnasium* 85 (1978), 157: 'das Motiv der Erwiderung durch die Präposition ἀπό'.

[62] For our discussion of reciprocity terminology, see §2.6.

[63] *I. Délos* IV 1521.

[64] *OGIS* 248. Similarly, in *SIG*³ 800: 'and when during the next year a dearth of fruit occurred, (Nikasippos) performed conspicuously the priesthood with his wife Timasistrata, having regarded (as the utmost importance) the favour (χάριν) of (providing) the expenses of life on behalf of the majority of the Lykourasioi, ... it was resolved by the city of the

Third, χάρις — when used with ἀποδιδόναι or ἀπόδοσις — is often distinguished from εὐχάριστος ('thankful'), εὐχαριστία ('thankfulness'), or εὐχαριστεῖν ('to return thanks') within the manifesto clause itself, thereby diminishing the likelihood that the word is to be again rendered 'gratitude' or 'thanks'. This is apparent in the second-century BC proxeny decree of a doctor from Histria. There the manifesto clause says:

> In order, therefore, that the People may manifestly return thanks ([εὐ]χαρι[στῶν]) to both those who have good will towards it and those who have good will among men and behave in similar manner and that (the People) may not be wanting in the return of favour ([ἐγ χά]ριτος ἀποδόσει) ...[65]

Or, again, the second-century BC decree of Chalkis in honour of Archenus:

> In order, therefore, that the People may manifestly return the appropriate favours (τὰς καταξίας ἀποδιδοὺς χάριτας) to men who are fair and good and the rest, seeing the gratitude (εὐχαριστίαν) of the city to the benefactors, may be zealous imitators (ζηλωταί) of the good men ...[66]

Admittedly, it is possible that χάρις and εὐχαριστία in the Chalkis decree above are just stylistic variations, each meaning 'thankfulness'. However, the epithets ἀξίας ('worthy') and καταξίας ('appropriate', 'very worthy') which usually accompany χάριτας in the manifesto clause imply that the honours are 'commensurate with the value of the benefaction'.[67] With such notions we enter the Homeric world of gifts and counter-gifts.[68] Not that the Homeric world was remote from the Graeco-Roman reciprocity system of the first century AD. Seneca perfectly understood the reciprocity conventions behind the eulogistic inscriptions, to gauge by his comment that endorses

---

Lykourasioi to set up in the temple painted images of him and of Timasistrata his wife ... knowing that the city being thankful (εὐχάριστος) may not be left behind at any time in the return of favour (ἐν χάριτος ἀποδόσει)'. See also *IG* V(1) 931: χάριζεσθαι, χάρις.

[65] *SEG* XXIV 1100. For εὐχάριστος, *SIG*³ 721; *I. Magnesia* 92a.

[66] *IG* XII(9) 899. See also *Michel* 235; *I. Assos* 7; *IG* XI(4) 1061; XII(9) 239.

[67] B.W. Winter, *art. cit.*, 90. The bequest of C. Vibius Salutaris (*I. Ephesos* 1a. 27: AD 104), while not using χάρις, makes the same point with traditional reciprocity terminology: 'Since men who are munificent in the case of the city, and on every occasion show the affection of genuine citizens, should have honours corresponding to ([ἀ]μοιβαί[ων]) the enjoyment of those who have done well to the city in the past, and is laid up for those who are wishing to rival them about similar things ...' (*ll.*8-12). More generally, see G.M. Rogers, *The Sacred Identity of Ephesos: Foundation Myths of a Roman City* (London 1991).

[68] On this see M.I. Finley, *The World of Odysseus* (Harmondsworth 1954), Index s.v. 'Gifts'; *id.*, 'Marriage, Sale and Gift in the Homeric World', *RIDA* III Vol.2 (1955), 167-194; P. Marshall, *op. cit.*, Index s.v. 'Gift Giving'; R. Seaford, *Reciprocity and Ritual: Homer and Tragedy in the Developing City-State* (Oxford 1994). On χάρις in Homer, see §1.1 n.31.

'honourable rivalry in outdoing benefits by benefits'.⁶⁹ As he pithily remarks, 'he who has a debt of gratitude to pay (*gratiam debet*) never catches up with the favour unless he outstrips it'.⁷⁰ In contrast, the inscriptions are circumscribed by the convention of politeness. A first-century AD inscription from Cardamylae, in deference to the benefactor, describes the return of honour to Poseidippos for his many benefits as the 'lesser favour' (ἐλάττονος χάριτος).⁷¹

Fourth, a wide range of vocabulary — alternative to ἀποδιδόναι and ἀπόδοσις — could be used in conjunction with χάρις to express gratitude without the connotation of reciprocation of 'favour'. Hence it is safe to translate χάρις as 'thanks' in the manifesto clause when it is used with ἀπονέμειν or διανέμειν ('to distribute'), διαφυλάσσειν ('to preserve'), ἐναποδεικνύναι ('to display'), or κομίζειν ('to receive').⁷² Outside the manifesto clause, additional vocabulary was used for the extension of gratitude to the benefactor: προστιθέναι ('to bestow'), or κατατιθέναι ('to register').⁷³

In sum, χάρις in the manifesto clause was the standard term for expressing gratitude to the benefactor. However, when used with ἀποδιδόναι or ἀπόδοσις, χάρις denoted a more complex social interchange — Homeric in its antiquity — in which the beneficiary returned 'favour' to the benefactor. Admittedly, it was the 'lesser favour' that was returned, as the Cardamylae inscription reminds us, but it was still potent enough to elicit additional favours from those who competed against their peers for φιλοτιμία.

In the next section (§2.5), a survey of χάρις in the eastern Mediterranean inscriptions will be undertaken. There we will examine the use of χάρις in honorific and non-honorific contexts, as well as in a variety of inscriptional genres (decrees, letters, hymns, laws, catalogues, oracular responses, graffiti, apotropaic inscriptions etc). In subsequent sections, the finer detail of the inscriptional portrait of χάρις will be etched in, including the ethos of reciprocity (§2.6), the beneficence of the gods (§2.7), and a profile of five benefactors from the first century BC and AD (§2.8).

---

⁶⁹ Seneca, *Ben.*, 1.4.4.
⁷⁰ *Ibid.*, 1.4.3.
⁷¹ *SEG* XI 948.
⁷² ἀπονέμειν: *SIG*³ 587, 590, 708; *Michel* 372, 475; 1007; 1561; *SEG* II 564; XII 94; XVI 255; *I. Mylasa* 106, 110; *FD* III(4) 77; *IG* IX(2) 11; XII(9) 239. διανέμειν: *Michel* 1011. διαφυλάσσειν: *SEG* XXIX 121. ἐναποδεικνύναι: *IG* VII(2) 4133. κομίζειν: *Michel* 985; *SEG* XI 948; XVI 94; XXI 419; XXI 452.
⁷³ προστιθέναι: *SEG* XIX 4. κατατιθέναι: *I. Ephesos* 6.

2.5. A Survey of Charis in the Inscriptions

χάρις could be used in a variety of non-honorific contexts. This can be observed from the way that χάρις served the needs of Roman diplomatic parlance. It was the Greek equivalent of the Latin word *'gratia'* and was employed in the stereotyped formulae of the Senatus Consulta. Hence the common phrase *'gratiam amicitiam societatemque renovare'*, rendered χάριτα φιλίαν συμμαχίαν ἀνανεώσασθαι, meant in a diplomatic context: 'we shall reaffirm (the relationship of) favour, friendship, and alliance'.[74]

Further non-honorific uses of χάρις can easily be cited. One inscription post-dating the first century AD — an oracular response from the cult of Apollo at Didyma — sounds a strong note of optimism for its recipient:

Grace (χάρις) will always be unblaming of such cheerfulness, since when I first drove out grievous sickness, having put to shame [the] troublesome threads of the fates.[75]

In a poem from Stratonikeia, Menippos dedicates his writing to the gods in appreciation of their 'year long favour' (τὴν ἐτησίαν χάριν) towards himself.[76] Two stamps, datable to either the first century BC or AD, carry the word χάρις.[77] A gymnasiarchal law, already mentioned, also employs χάρις, as does a late first-century AD Epicurean meditation from Pompeii.[78] Finally, an ephebic catalogue, inscribed in Macedonia (c. AD 41—48), concludes with an epigram in which the final lines underline the importance of gratitude to the young athletes. As the epigram says,

For (the) bulk of (the) monument is set up with a little hard work but (the) gratitude (χάρις) of the men of the gymnasium (is) more desirable to the athletes.[79]

---

[74] *OGIS* 441; *SIG*³ 674, 705, 764; R.K. Sherk, *op. cit.* (1969), §12, §20, §21.

[75] *SEG* XV 670 (II—III cent. AD).

[76] *I. Stratonikeia* 1044 (9 BC).

[77] *SEG* XXXVIII 1270. See also the (undated) graffito of χάρις from Priene: *I. Priene* 355. Furthermore, in an (undated) inscription from Smyrna on a votive replica of a leg, Epikratos offers a prayer of favour (ἐπὶ χάριτος εὐχήν) to the Anatolian divinity Men for a cure. See H.S. Versnal, 'Religious Mentality in Ancient Prayer', in *id.* (ed.), *Faith, Hope, and Worship* (Leiden 1981), 136 (Appendix Catalogue No.43.1). We might also mention here the use of Χάρις as a personal name in the inscriptions and the papyri. For details, see O. Masson, 'Pape-Benseleriana VII. Le nom *Charis*, feminin et masculin', *ZPE* 37 (1980), 109-113.

[78] For the gymnasiarchal law, see §2.3 n.47. For the Epicurean meditation, see *SEG* XXIX 977.

[79] *SEG* XXXVIII 675. The ethics of beneficence were taught at the gymnasia. From Sosiades' collection of the maxims of the famous seven sages — cited *in extenso* by Stobaeus (Σωσιάδου τῶν ἑπτὰ σοφῶν ὑοθῆκαι, from Stobaeus, *Eclogae* 3.1.173) — we

The non-honorific uses of χάρις, therefore, demonstrate that the word had gained popular currency outside the formal literary or epigraphic texts, as evidenced by its appearance on stamps, votive offerings, or as a graffito. The traditional uses of 'gratitude' and 'favour' recur, but in the latter case χάρις is widened in its application to inter-state relations. The uses are universally positive — except for the connotation of unfair favour in the gymnasiarchical law — and are equally at home in an Epicurean or cultic context.

In the case of the sepulchral hymns, we have a highly literary use of χάρις that still captures the eulogistic dimension of the honorific inscriptions. A late hellenistic funerary epigram from Egypt positively sums up the life of its anonymous honorand:

To Hades I have gone free from care [...]
having completed three joyous decades of years,
and I possessed much favour (χάριν) in respect of the shroud;
for I was doing no one harm, and I was conspicuous
(as) best friend (βέλτιστος φί[λ]ος) to all.[80]

---

know that beneficence formed part of Greek ethical theory. These maxims, better known to us as the Delphic canon, had been inscribed for all to see at Delphi (Plato, *Prt.* 343A-B; Plutarch, *Mor.* 385D-E). Several maxims which have come down to us in Sosiades' collection employ the language of grace to underscore the importance of munificence: φίλωι χαρίζου ('Favour a friend'); ἔχων χαρίζου ('Do a favour when you can'); χάριν ἐκτέλει ('Return a favour'); χαρίζου ἀβλαβῶς ('Favour without harming'). Significantly, many of the Delphic maxims have been found inscribed — with minor variations — at the gymnasium(?) at Miletopolis in the Hellespont (*I. Kyzikos* II 2 col.1 [IV—III cent. BC]), including φίλωι χαρίζου ('Favour a friend') and χάριν ἀπόδος ('Return a favour'). Another version of the Delphic canon has also been found inscribed at the gymnasium of the ephebes at Thera (*IG* XII[3] 1020: IV cent. BC). However, the more fragmentary Therean version of the Delphic maxims does not contain any examples of the language of grace. It would seem that the ethics of grace, as found in the Delphic canon, had spread throughout the eastern Mediterranean gymnasia. The widespread dissemination of the Delphic maxims and the care taken in their transmission can also be gauged from their presence at Egypt (*P. Ath. Univ. Inv.* 2782 [I/II cent. AD]) and at Aï-Khanum on the Oxus (Afghanistan). On Egypt, see A.N. Oikonomides, 'The Lost Delphic Inscription with the Commandments of the Seven and *P. Univ. Athen* 2782', *ZPE* 37 (1980), 179-183. In the case of Aï-Khanum, the Delphic maxims were inscribed on a III cent. BC stele erected by Clearchus (of Soli?) in the sanctuary of Cineas, the founder of the city. Significantly, in the epigram on the front base of the stele, Clearchus says that the maxims on the stele came from a copy that he had *personally* transcribed while at Delphi. See L. Robert, 'De Delphes a l'Oxus: inscriptions grecques nouvelles de la Bactriane', *Comptes Rendues de l'Académie des Inscriptions et Belles Lettres*, (1968), 416-457; *Nouveau choix d'inscriptions grecques*, §37. I am indebted to E.A. Judge, ('Ancient Beginnings of the Modern World', in T.W. Hillard [*et al.*, ed.], *Ancient History in a Modern University. Volume II: Early Christianity, Late Antiquity, and Beyond* [Grand Rapids 1998], 468-482) for the above references.

[80] W. Peek, *art. cit.*, 133-134. In my translation, I have followed Peek's reconstruction of the second verse.

A hymn from Megalopolis, honouring the priestess Isidis Dionysia for her 'holy life (βίον σε[μ]νόν)', promises that divine blessings would flow from her religious service:

> ...and if you would seek a name, (it is) Dionysia, which blesses anyone who knows the sacred favours (θείας χάριτας) which she received.[81]

A hymn from Thasos praises Elpis for showing selfless devotion to her children (φιλότεκνε), inspiring one of them to dedicate a tomb to her: 'O tomb, cared for by the pious favours ([εὐσεβ]έσιν χάρισιν) of a child'.[82] If this inscription is sufficiently representative, the hellenistic reciprocity system expected that children would continue to extend piety towards parents even after their death.

An undated funerary epigram from Stratonikeia portrays the Evil Eye of Hades as being consumed with jealousy over the beauty of the deceased (Kallinikos): 'Hades is jealous and makes the good people's eyes melt away when they see so much grace (or 'beauty': χάρις)'.[83] Here we gain our first glimpse into the important role that χάρις played in the world of magical practice (§3.6; §6.1.3.1).

Finally, in reply to those enquiring who was the tomb's owner, a sepulchral inscription of Corinth gives this answer: 'Preimas finished life while a pure young girl, having begotten delights (χάριτας), she weds a spouse'.[84]

The use of χάρις in the literary sepulchral hymns, therefore, conveys a strong sense of the disposal, reciprocation, and possession of 'favour', whether human or divine. Only in the hymns from Corinth and Stratonikeia,

---

[81] *IG* V(2) 472: III—II cent. AD. The *Inscriptiones Graecae* edition is to be preferred to L. Vidman (*Sylloge Inscriptionum Religiosae Isiacae et Sarapiacae* [Berlin 1969], §42) who restores λείπουσαν instead of λείπουσα in *l*.2.

[82] *SEG* XVIII 365 (I—II cent. AD). See the requirement of filial duty to parents by the Egyptian goddess Isis in G.H.R. Horsley, 'A Personalised Aretalogy of Isis', *New Docs* 1 (1981), §2 *ll*.31-34 (ἡ χάρις).

[83] *SEG* XXXVIII 1103. See the slightly different interpretation of M.W. Dickie, 'An Epitaph from Stratonikeia in Caria', *ZPE* 100 (1994), 109-118, esp. 113ff. In antiquity, apotropaic inscriptions — often found in the mosaics at the baths — protect χάρις ('beauty') from the Evil Eye. For example, note the mosaic inscription from Sheikh Zuweid: 'Friend, observe with pleasure the charming things (τὰς χάριτας) which art has placed in the mosaic cubes petrifying and repelling the jealousy and the eyes of envy. You are the one who is often proud of the enjoyable art' (*SEG* XL 1672). On the χάρις of the baths, see L. Robert, 'Épigrammes relatives à des gouverneurs', *Hellenica* IV (1948), 78-84. On the Evil Eye generally, see J.H. Elliott, 'The Fear of the Leer: The Evil Eye from the Bible to Li'l Abner', *Forum* 4/4 (1988), 42-71.

[84] B.D. Meritt, *op. cit.*, §120. For futher examples of sepulchral inscriptions, see *SEG* XI 344 (discussed in §2.3 n.47); XXVIII 721.

cited above, is there a use of χάρις that is not paralleled in the New Testament.

As noted in §2.4, χάρις regularly occurs in the manifesto clause of the inscriptions — coupled with ἀποδιδόναι and its cognates — and conveys the idea of reciprocation of 'favour'.[85] But elsewhere in the honorific decrees and inscriptional letters there are many examples of χάρις carrying the meaning of 'favour', 'goodwill', or 'benevolence'. In 71 BC the Roman benefactors of Gytheion, Numerius and Marcus Cloatius, had demonstrated their 'favour' and 'good will' by releasing the city from its repayment of two loans.[86] In the late second century BC, Xenocleas of Akraephiae had 'performed not a few favours (χάριτας) for the people' in providing corn when there was a scarcity in pressing times.[87] Two centuries later, the town clerk of Oenoanda would provide corn in a similar time of emergency. But he also 'contributed to a public subscription for a distribution of money, ten denarii to each citizen, so that all who dwell in the city share this benevolence (χάριτος)'.[88] The letter of the consul Titus Quinctius Flamininus (194 BC) resorts to platitudes when explaining the Roman policy of returning confiscated properties to Chyretiae: 'we are determined to seek absolutely no financial profit, esteeming good will (χάριτα) and reputation above all else'.[89] One more example will suffice. Antonia Truphaina, who had dedicated the restoration of Cyzicus in thanksgiving of Augustus (χαριστηρίον τοῦ Σεβαστοῦ), is eulogised for 'not observing us as an ancient colony of Cyzicus, but (instead) recognising the recent favour (χάριν) of Agrippa'.[90]

The above examples demonstrate that χάρις functioned as the central term for the 'favour' of benefactors towards their dependants. However, as we will see, χάρις reveals the reverse side of the benefaction ritual, in which the beneficiary returns 'thanks' to his benefactor.

---

[85] ἀποδιδόναι: *OGIS* 248; *SIG*³ 613(A), 615, 709, 711(L), 721, 800; *Michel* 163, 235, 297, 334, 477, 515, 542, 998; *IGRR* I 864; *SEG* II 564, 663; IV 598; XVIII 20, 27, 143; XXIV 1100; *I. Priene* 53, 112; *I. Assos* 7, 8; *I. Stratonikeia* 15; L. Vidman, *op. cit.*, §165; *I. Magnesia* 31, 61, 92a; *I. Kalchedon* 1; J. Benedum, 'Griechische Arztinschriften aus Kos', *ZPE* 25 (1977), 265-276 Nos.2 and 4; *I. Délos* IV 1504, 1507, 1518, 1520; *IG* IV 2; V(1) 1, 14; V(1) 931, 1175; VII(1) 18, 21, 412; VII(2) 4132, 4262; IX(2) 66a, 512, 639, 1230; XI(4) 1061; XII(9) 899. For ἀπόδοσις *OGIS* 248; *SIG*³ 618, 800; *Michel* 542; *SEG* II 564; IV 598; XII 306; XXIV 1100; *I. Délos* IV 1540; *IG* V(1) 14.

[86] *SIG*³ 748.
[87] *Michel* 236.
[88] *IGRR* III 493.
[89] *SIG*³ 593 (AD 38).
[90] *SIG*³ 799. For further examples, *SIG*³ 876; *IGRR* IV 351, 1156b; *SEG* XXVI 1021; *I. Priene* 118; *IG* V(1) 1361; VII(2) 2712; *FD* III(4) 287, 313.

We have already examined the considerable range of vocabulary available for expressing 'gratitude' or 'thanks' for beneficence in the manifesto clause.[91] The same contours of meaning appear in the wider inscriptional landscape. Plotina, the wife of the emperor Trajan, in a letter (AD 121) regarding the succession of Epicurus at Athens, comments that 'we ought to evince fitting gratitude (ἀξίαν χάριν) to the one who is truly the benefactor and provider of all education'.[92] Earlier in the first century AD, the city Hadrianopolis had honoured the emperor Nerva in typical fashion:

To the god Nerva, from the inhabitants of the added land belonging to the Caesars, the Council and the People [offer] thanks (χάριν).[93]

Or again, to cite another first century example (this time from Chios), an epigram in honour of Megakles the president of the Presbyteroi:

The elders (honoured) Megakles the (adopted) son of Theogeiton but by birth (the son) of Damonikos, having been the leader of the Council on account of (his) piety (εὐσέβειας) towards the gods and (his) merit (ἀρετῆς) and love of honour (φιλοτιμίας) towards themselves. For you glory (δόξα) shines forth, but to noble men (such as you) the illustrious assembly of the elders bestowed faithful gratitude (ἐσθλὰν χάριν) for (your) works, having set up an image of you, breathing into (it) an impression of appearance...[94]

χάρις, therefore, captures the attitudinal aspects behind the reciprocity system, spotlighting not only the conventional return of favour but also the importance of a genuine and commensurate gratitude on the part of the beneficiary.

Finally, as G.P. Wetter observed many years ago, the role of the Caesars as bestowers of divine χάρις is a fundamental feature of the inscriptions. In the AD 68 edict of Tiberius Julius Alexander from Girgeh in Egypt, reference is made to the privileges of immunity and abatement of taxation for Egyptians 'in accord with the dispensation of the divine Claudius (τοῦ Θεοῦ Κλαυδίου χάριτι)'.[95] The fishing rights of the people of Istria are secured 'by the grace of the Augusti ([τῇ] χάριτι τῶν [Σεβαστῶ]ν)'.[96] Another inscription speaks of an imperial benefaction made to Ephesus sometime after AD 14:

---

[91] See §2.4. For εὐχάριστος SIG³ 587, 590, 721, 800; SEG XVIII 143; I. Priene 108; I. Magnesia 92a; IG VII(2) 2712. For εὐχαριστία SIG³ 800; Michel 235, 372, 477, 998; SEG IV 598; XI 948; XVIII 143; XXVI 564; I. Priene 53; I. Assos 7, 8; IG XI(4) 1061; XII(9) 239, 899. For εὐχαριστεῖν: SIG³ 709, 748, 814; Michel 475; IGRR IV 598; SEG XIII 526; FD III(4) 313.
[92] SIG³ 834.
[93] IGRR III 148.
[94] SEG XXVI 1021. For other examples, see SEG XXXII 1243; I. Priene 108.
[95] OGIS 669.
[96] SEG XXIV 1108 (I—II cent. AD).

By the favour ([χάρι]τι) of Caesar Augustus God (θεοῦ) from the holy revenues which he himself gave to the goddess the road was made level in the proconsulship of Sextus Appuleius.[97]

In a letter to Hadrian, those officiating at the cult of Apollo at Delphi rendered honours along with public prayers in return for ([ἀντιτετει]μημένοι κοι[ναῖς εὐχαῖ]ς) 'the unsurpassable favours ([χάριτας]) of your divine (nature)'.[98]

The attribution of divine favours to benefactors, however, was not confined to the house of the Caesars alone. The people of the village of Bouseiris in Egypt erected a stone stele in the mid first century AD in honour of the Prefect Tiberius Claudius Balbillus with the inscription:

For it is [fitting] that his god-like favours (τὰς ἰσοθέους αὐτοῦ χάριτας), recorded by sacred writings, forever be remembered. He came into our nome and performed an act of adoration of the Sun Hamarchis, overseer and saviour, having enjoyed the pyramids' greatness and magnificence.[99]

Finally, G.P. Wetter was probably correct in isolating the χάρις of the Caesars as an important parallel to the early Christian use, over against the many other contexts in which χάρις is found in the inscriptions, outlined above. During the first century AD, the *imperatores* of the Julio-Claudian dynasty progressively eclipsed all the competitors from the old houses of the Roman *nobiles*. The triumph of the Julio-Claudians was largely accomplished by their unprecedented display of beneficence and by their establishment of numerous *clientes* throughout the empire.[100] The burden of gratitude for such a unilateral demonstration of favour by the Julio-Claudians was expressed semantically in the divine honours of the ruler cults. The very one-sidedness of the Julio-Claudian disposal of χάριτες must have been striking to the contemporary observer. Rivals were simply not able to compete on the same scale. The early Christians, therefore, could hardly have missed the parallel in their choice of χάρις for the unlimited beneficence of the Covenantal God and his Son.

---

[97] J and L. Robert, *Bulletin epigraphique* 5 (1964-1967), §340.
[98] *FD* III(4) 308.
[99] *OGIS* 666.
[100] See P. Veyne, *op. cit.*, 347-377; F. Millar, *The Emperor in the Roman World 31 BC—AD 337* (New York 1977), 133-201; R.P. Saller, *Personal Patronage under the Early Empire* (Cambridge 1982), 41-78. For the period leading to the later empire, see V. Nutton, 'The Beneficial Ideology', in P.D.A. Garnsey and C.R. Whittaker (eds), *Imperialism in the Ancient World* (Cambridge 1978), 209-221. The magnitude of imperial largesse can be seen from *Res Gestae* 15-24.

2.6. Charis *and the Ethos of Reciprocity*

The ethos of reciprocity, as found in the manifesto clauses of the honorific decrees, has been briefly referred to in §2.4. However, to appreciate more fully the hellenistic reciprocity system, we must investigate the additional reciprocity terminology (ἀμείβειν, ἀμοιβή, ἐν μέρει) that often accompanies χάρις in the inscriptions. It would also be helpful to examine any instances of the multiple use of χάρις, within the same inscription, that bear reciprocity of meaning. Last, inscriptions from Cardamylae and Ephesus provide strong evidence that the Homeric ritual of the counter-gift still animated a variety of benefaction relationships in the first century AD.

First, in the AD 37 inscription of Gaius Caligula, it is stated that the sons of Kotys, each of whom had been sponsored by the emperor in their respective kingdoms, 'put a great amount of thought into discovering appropriate recompense (ἴσας ἀμοιβάς) to show their good feeling for the gracious act of such a great god'.[101] In the early first century AD the People of Busiris, 'desiring to reciprocate with favours (ἀμείβεσθαι χά[ρισιν])' their general Gnaius Pompeius, set up a stone stele in praise of his building of dykes and the fair distribution of the crop.[102] A second-century BC decree from Teos was written up in order that the proposers would 'not be left behind in turn of favour (ἐν μέρει χάριτος) to those who are benevolently disposed to us'.[103] In each case above, the inference is plain: honours are favours reciprocated, in recompense for favours done. This is clearly signalled by the accompanying reciprocity terminology.

Second, in the AD 43 inscription of Iunia Theodora of Solomos (Corinth), the benefactress is spoken of as continuing 'to act on behalf of our citizens in regard to any favour (τὰς χάριτας) asked'.[104] Owing to the favourable testimony concerning Iunia's generosity, the decree elaborates that

...the People in gratitude (εὐχάριστον ὄντα) agreed to vote to commend Iunia ... and to invite her to extend her loyalty to the people in the certainty that in its turn our people will not show any negligence in its devotion and gratitude (χάριτος) to her.

Here the element of exchange is conventionally stated: the favours (χάριτες) of Iunia Theodora spawn the gratitude (χάρις) of the citizens of

---

[101] *SIG*³ 798. See also *I. Priene* 113, 117 which use ἀμοιβή for the 'recompense' of the city or country to the benefactor.

[102] *SEG* VIII 527. See also *I. Priene* 117: 'to repay with honours and favours (ἀμείψασθαι τιμαῖς καὶ χάρισιν)'.

[103] *Michel* 64.

[104] *SEG* XVIII 143.

Solomos. Similarly, in the manifesto clause of a decree honouring the priest Phaedros Parembordea, we see another reciprocal use of χάρις:

In order, therefore, that the People of Olymni, being left behind in no respect of return of favour (ἐν χάριτος ἀποδόσει), but remembering fine and good men, manifestly distributes appropriate gratitude (τὴν καταξίαν χάριτα) and honour to all ...[105]

Thus, from the foregoing uses of χάρις, we observe a subtle interplay of meaning that shifts from benefactor to the beneficiary, with χάρις in each case spelling out the appropriate behaviour and responsibilities of each party. Thus the semantic versatility of χάρις ensured that the word became intimately identified with hellenistic reciprocity rituals.

Third, we now come to two honorific decrees which eloquently articulate the nuances of obligation involved in benefactor-beneficiary relationships. Importantly, each decree operates at a different consensual level: on the one hand, the level of civic obligation between the benefactor Poseidippos and the city of Cardamylae; and, on the other hand, the level of interstate relations between Rome and the cities of Aphrodisias and Ephesus. Each decree throws light on the ethos of reciprocity in the first century AD.

The honorific decree from Cardamylae praises its benefactor in this fashion:

... it was resolved by the People and the City and the ephors to praise Poseidippos the son of Attalos on account of the aforesaid kindnesses and also to return (καταστῆ[σαι]) never-ending gratitude (ἀτελῆ χάριν) in recompense of ([ἀμοι]βῆς) (his bestowal) of benefits; and also to give to him the front seats at the theatre and the first place in a procession and (the privilege of) eating in the public festivals which are celebrated amongst us and to offer willingly (χαρ[ιζομέ]νους) all (the) honour (τειμήν) given to a good and fine man in return for (ἀντί) the many (kindnesses) which he provided, while giving a share of the lesser favour (ἐλάττονος χάριτος), (nevertheless) offering thankfulness (εὐχαριστίας) to the benefactors of ourselves as an incentive to the others, so that choosing the same favour (χάριν) some of them may win (the same) honours (τειμῶν). And (it was resolved) to set up this decree on a stone stele in the most conspicuous place in the gymnasium, while the ephors make the solemn procession to the building without hindrance, in order that those who confer benefits may receive favour (χάριν) in return for (ἀντί) love of honour (φολοτειμίας), and that those who have been benefited, returning honours (ἀποδιδόντες τειμάς), may have a reputation of thankfulness (εὐχαριστίας) before all people, never coming too late for the sake of recompense (ἀμοιβήν) of those who wish to do kindly (acts).[106]

This decree is replete with the terminology of exchange: ἀμοιβή, ἀντί, καθιστάναι, and ἀποδιδόναι. χάρις, too, bears reciprocity in its subtle shifts of meaning. It initially signifies the eternal 'gratitude' of the city of Cardamylae for benefactions; but then, with characteristic deference to

---

[105] *SEG* II 564. I cent. BC or AD.
[106] *SEG* XI 948.

Poseidippos, gratitude is viewed as the return of 'the lesser favour' to the benefactor; and this, in turn, stimulates counter-favours from rival benefactors. The cognates of χάρις — χαρίζεσθαι and εὐχαριστία — are also employed with reciprocity of meaning: Cardamylae offers willingly (χαρ[ιζομέ]νους) honours to the ἀνὴρ ἀγαθός, in order that it may have a reputation for gratitude ([εὐ]χαριστίας) before all people. φιλοτιμία is given pride of place in this tabulation of the incentives for the benefactor and beneficiary. The equation is defined with precision: Poseidippos receives favours from Cardamylae in exchange for his love of honour, while Cardamylae receives the coveted reputation of gratitude in its return of honour to Poseidippos. The ethos of reciprocity, as formulated in the Cardamylae inscription, is striking for its calculation of the benefits to both parties. The early Christians could hardly have been unaware of this wider conceptual framework behind the first century use of χάρις, including (presumably) both the advantages and disadvantages posed by χάρις as the central Christian description of human and divine beneficence.

In AD 89/90 the People of Aphrodisias in Caria honoured the emperor Domitian with this decree from Ephesus:

To Imperator [[Domitian]] Caesar Augustus [[Germanicus]] when the proconsul was Marcus Fulvius Gillo. The People of Aphrodisias, loyal to Caesar (φιλοκαῖσαρ), being free (ἐλεύθερος) and autonomous (αὐτόνομος) from the beginning by the grace of the Augusti (τῆι τῶν Σε[βασ]τῶν χάριτι), set up (this statue) by a private (act of) grace (ἰδίᾳ χάριτι) because of its reverence (εὐσέβειαν) toward the Augusti and its goodwill (εὔνοιαν) toward the neokorate city of the Ephesians, (because of) Asia's common temple of the Augusti in Ephesus. (This was) accomplished by Aristo [the son] of Artemidorus of Kalli[...]os, priest of Pluto and Kore, and neopoios of the goddess Aphrodite, when the high priest of Asia was Tiberius Claudius Pheseinus [[...]] [[...]] [[...]].[107]

In contrast to the Cardamylae decree, any hint of reciprocity seems strangely muted here. The decision of Aphrodisias to benefit Ephesus with a neocorate is a unilateral one. No return of favour is envisaged on the part of Ephesus, and Aphrodisias is seemingly not under any compulsion from Rome to offer a benefaction. The People of Aphrodisias are at pains to emphasise the unconstrained nature of their act from the outset: they are free, independent of Roman rule, and their act of beneficence is a private decision. The reason for

---

[107] *I. Ephesos* II. 233. For discussion of the grace of the Flavian emperors in the province of Asia, see S.J. Friesen, *Twice Neokoros: Ephesus, Asia, and the Cult of the Flavian Imperial Family* (Leiden-New York- Köln 1993), 158-160. More generally, E.E. Judge, *art. cit.*, in S.E. Porter, *op. cit.*, 815-817. In an unpublished paper, 'Benefactors at Ephesus', E.A. Judge (Macquarie University 1993) has dated 50 inscriptions from the Ephesus corpus 'to the first 250 years of the Roman hegemony'. Only two uses of χάρις fall in our time range: *I. Ephesos* Ia. 6 (II cent. BC) and *I. Ephesos* II. 233 (AD 80/90).

the heavy emphasis of Aphrodisias upon this point is plain. The second-century BC treaty between Aphrodisias and her two neighbouring towns not to adopt a hostile profile towards Rome, and to embrace the cult of Roma, had ensured her status as φιλοκαῖσαρ.[108]

However, 'although Aphrodisias had full exemption from the control of the governor', as S.R.F. Price reminds us, 'there was in the city an imperial temple, probably of considerable grandeur'.[109] Again, reciprocity re-enters the arena in the guise of εὐσέβεια. Aphrodisias' gift of a statue at Ephesus was a calculated act of piety towards the Augusti, as the decree itself concedes. It is therefore to be viewed as the return of favour to the Roman *imperatores* who had guaranteed her continuing independence through the cult of Roma. Aphrodisias was well aware of the importance of the public acknowledgment of the χάριτες Σεβαστῶν — as the important phrase τῆι τῶν Σε[βασ]τῶν χάριτι demonstrates.

2.7. Charis *and the Gods*

In the inscriptions, χάρις orchestrates the way that a relationship between human beings and the gods should be established and maintained. People initiated a relationship with the gods in the hope of reciprocal favour.[110] By observing the proper cultic rites in honour of the gods, human beings might secure the gods' favour. A bond of mutual obligation — initially founded on the gods' acceptance of the rites — ensued, with the suppliant adopting a grateful disposition towards the gods, and the gods reciprocating with favours and gratitude to those who had demonstrated the requisite piety. However, as W. Burkert observes regarding the gratitude of the gods, 'it is never possible to count on this with certainty'.[111] Ingratitude on the part of the suppliants towards their human benefactors, as we will soon see, may well provoke divine wrath.

---

[108] For the treaty, see J.M. Reynolds, *Aphrodisias and Rome* (London 1982), §1.

[109] S.R.F. Price, *Rituals and Power: The Roman Imperial Cult in Asia Minor* (Cambridge 1984), 83. Index s.v. 'Aphrodisias'.

[110] See the perceptive discussions of W. Burkert, *Greek Religion: Archaic and Classical* (Cambridge, Mass. 1985: Gmn. orig. 1977), Index s.v. χάρις J.W. Franzmann, *The Early Development of the Greek Concept of Charis* (unpub. Ph.D. diss. Wisconsin University 1972), 46-55; H.S. Versnal, *art. cit.*, in *id.* (ed.), *op. cit.*, 1-64, esp. 42ff on 'Prayers of gratitude'.

[111] W. Burkert, *op. cit.*, 189.

First, how do the inscriptions view the establishment of a bond of favour with the gods? In four hymns to Isis-Hermouthis from first-century AD Egypt, Isidorus lavishes praise on the goddess for her benefits to mankind. In Hymn II (*ll*.1-8, 15-16), Isidorus nominates prayer (presumably ritualistic) as the chief means by which the gods' favour is secured:

Hail, Agathetyche, greatly renowned Isis, mightiest
   Hermouthis, in you every city rejoices;
O Discoverer of life and Cereal food wherein all
   mortals delight because of your blessing(s) (χαρίτων),
All who pray to you to assist their commerce
   prosper in their piety (εὐσεβέες) forever;
all who are bound in mortal illness in the grip of death,
   if they (but) pray to you, quickly ...
All indeed who wish to beget offspring,
   if they (but) pray to you, attain fruitfulness.[112]

Isidorus meticulously charts the path of piety if favour from Isis-Hermouthis is to be maintained. As an annual act of remembrance for the beneficence of the goddess — seen in the fertility of the crops watered by the Nile (*ll*.17-20) — the farmers are to observe a Thanksgiving festival in her honour, as well as pay their annual Temple tax from the harvest. The next year, the goddess reciprocates with further harvest blessings and the farmers again respond in gratitude with another festival. This cycle of the gods' beneficence and the human response of cultic gratitude is seen in *ll*.21-28:

Remembering your gifts, men to whom you have granted wealth
   and great blessings (χάριτας) (which you give them to possess all their lives)
all duly set aside for you one tenth of these blessings
   rejoicing each year at the time of your Panegyrie.
Thereafter you allow them, as the year rolls round (again),
   everyone to rejoice in the month of Pachon.
Joyful after your festival, they return home
   reverently (and are) filled with a sense of blessedness that comes only from you.[113]

Isidorus himself experiences this cycle of divine reciprocity when his prayers for the 'blessings of children' are positively answered: 'Hearing my prayers and hymns, the gods have rewarded me with the blessings (χάριτα) of great happiness'.[114] Finally, while there is a universality about the benefactions of Isis-Hermouthis, Hymn III makes it plain that those who experience her grace

---

[112] *SEG* VIII 549. For translation and discussion, see V.F Vanderlip, *The Four Greek Hymns of Isidorus and the Cult of Isis* (American Studies in Papyrology: Vol.12 Toronto 1972). Note the astute comment of W. Burkert (*op. cit.*, 73) in regard to the ancients' prayers: 'There is rarely a ritual without prayer, and no important prayer without ritual'.

[113] *SEG* VIII 549.

[114] *Ibid.* (*ll*.33-34). On Paul's 'cycle of grace' (2 Cor 9:11-15), see §6.4.1.

are precisely the pious: 'O most hallowed Bestower of good things, to all men who are righteous (ἅπασι εὐσεβέσιν), You grant great blessings (χάριτας)'.[115]

Other inscriptions confirm the belief that the sacrifices and piety towards the *mos maiorum* are of crucial importance if the gods are to reciprocate favours. The manifesto clause of an inscription of the cult of Apollo makes the connection absolutely clear:

> In order, therefore, that both the Council and the People may also manifestly watch closely not only the institutions of the ancestors, but also increase further both the sacrifices and honours well and piously (εὐσεβῶς), in order that they also may gain the appropriate favours (τὰς καταξίας χάριτας) proceeding from the gods ...[116]

Last, in the dedication of Hadrian, we see the Emperor petitioning grace from Aphrodite, the purveyor of wisdom — mediated through her son Eros — in the familiar strains of reciprocity:

> Child with the bow of Cyprus and the melodious voice, you who live in Thespiae on Helicon, near the flowery garden of Narcissus, grant me your favours. What Hadrian offers you, receive it as the first fruits of a she-bear which he has killed in striking it from the top of his horse. But you, in return (ἀντί), O Sage, breathe to him the grace (χάριν: alternatively, 'beauty') of Aphrodite Ourania.[117]

Thus, when the early Christians spoke of the mediation of God's grace through his Son Jesus, such a concept would not have been totally alien to a Graeco-Roman audience.

Second, how do the inscriptions depict human gratitude to the gods for their beneficence? In the second-century AD decree of Tomi, we hear of the people returning thanks to the gods (ἀποδιδόναι τὰς ἀξίας χάριτας) for their protection from the recent attacks of the Karoi, because of the creation of a forty-strong citizen guard.[118] Alternatively, Plancius Piso thanks (εὐχαριστεῖν) Asclepius and his Nymphs, along with the official physician, for health after being treated for his ailment in a dream.[119] Two dice oracles

---

[115] *SEG* VIII 550 (*ll*.3-4). In a late Hellenistic dedication to Apollo (*I. Smyrna* 750), Asklepiades makes this request: 'May you be gracious, O Phoibos, with your son and may you give health to the one who hymns your favour (χάριν)'. See also *I. Priene* 109: [τῆς τ]ῶν θεῶν χάριτας.

[116] *SEG* XXI 469 (129/8 BC).

[117] J. Pouilloux, *Choix d'inscriptions grecques: textes, traductions et notes* (Paris 1960), §48. As far as I know, C. Spicq (*Théology morale du nouveau testament* Tome 1 [Paris 1965], 116 n.1) has been the only New Testament scholar to draw attention to this important inscription.

[118] *Michel* 334(I.). In this case of ἀποδιδόναι with χάρις, 'thanks' is preferred to 'favour'.

[119] *SEG* XIII 526 (II cent. AD).

from Central Pisidia affirm Zeus' intention to grant 'happiness to your tasks, for which you will give thanks'.[120] Conversely, ingratitude, merits the wrath of the gods. In the first century AD, an unidentified benefactor speaks of the gods' anger at the 'accursed' and 'lawless' who were 'forgetful of my favour (τῆς ἐμῆς χάριτος)'.[121]

Third, how do the inscriptions depict the reaction of the gods to human acts of beneficence in their honour? According to the Graeco-Roman reciprocity system, not only did the benefactor appropriate the 'favour' of the gods, but he also earned their 'gratitude'. The 100 BC decree in honour of Aristagoras of Istropolis attributes a growing reverence for the gods to the benefactor. Aristagoras had assumed the crown of Zeus and commendably exercised the priesthood; after this he also voluntarily accepted the official crown established by the city for Apollo. Again this priesthood was carried out with distinction:

...he honoured the city and the gods with festal gatherings to which all were invited and by sacred processions and by donations to the tribes, wishing to make this clear, that there is gratitude (χάρις) alike from gods and from men who receive benefits for those who conduct themselves in the life of the city with reverence (τοῖς εὐσεβέστατα) and with noble purpose...[122]

A singular honour was still to come:

...again, three years later, when the people...were seeking a priest of Apollo, the Healer, men's private resources being under severe pressure, he made offer of himself and coming forward before the assembly he assumed the same crown, so obtaining double gratitude (χάριτας) for himself both from the gods and from those he benefited.[123]

Aristagoras went on to exercise this office as priest with equal distinction by spending his own money lavishly on life's expenses for the citizens, 'wishing to distribute the gratitude of piety (τὰς τῆς εὐσεβήας χάριτας) to the gods'.[124]

Thus, with the return of gratitude to the benefactor by the gods, reciprocity had come full circle: ritual had prepared the initial ground for the gods' favour; the gods then dispensed benefactions; the recipient returned gratitude and exhibited appropriate reverence in the gods' service; the gods, with consummate fairness, reciprocated with gratitude. Again, the unilateral understanding of God's grace in early Christianity — where God was not

---

[120] G.H.R. Horsley and S. Mitchell (eds), *The Inscriptions of Central Pisidia* (Bonn 2000), §5A.I ([χαρ]ήσ[σεις]), §5B.XXVII (χαρήσῃ).
[121] B. Laum, *op. cit.*, §78a.
[122] A.R. Hands, *op. cit.*, §D.9 (*SIG*^{3} 708).
[123] *Ibid.*
[124] *Ibid.*

obligated to anyone by way of gratitude or favour (Rom 11:25; 1 Cor 4:7) — must have fallen on many uncomprehending ears in view of the prevailing ethos of reciprocity.[125]

2.8. A Profile of Benefactors and their Communities

How important was χάρις in the self-understanding of the benefactor? Do we possess any inscriptions in which the benefactor comments on the nature of his χάριτες and elaborates on the obligations of his beneficiaries? In this regard, the inscriptions of Antiochus I of Kommagene, Phainios of Gytheum, and the emperors Caligula and Nero are especially instructive. χάρις occurs several times in each inscription and there is no appearance of the word in the stereotyped manifesto clauses. Here we are freed from the typical rituals of thanksgiving. Instead, we gain a rare glimpse into the way that benefactors themselves viewed the hellenistic reciprocity system, as each man portrays his exalted status as a civic luminary and explains for posterity the motivation impelling his munificence.[126]

By contrast, the three honorific decrees of Zosimos of Priene are representative of many such inscriptions that speak eloquently of the honours which the hellenistic city-states accorded to their benefactors. However, two features grab our attention. First, in explaining the ideology of the reciprocity system, the first inscription of Zosimos links χάρις with ἀρετή in a highly unusual and arresting way. Second, as noted (§2.3), the Council and People of Priene display an affection towards Zosimos that goes well beyond mere honorifics.

In discussing the inscriptions of our five benefactors, we will proceed chronologically.

---

[125] Note the perceptive remark of B. Witherington III (*Conflict and Community in Corinth: A Socio-Rhetorical Commentary on 1 and 2 Corinthians* [Carlisle 1995], 420 n.28): 'the relationship between a human being and a god in Greco-Roman religion was perceived to involve reciprocity. The god gave blessings and the human being responded or petitioned with prayers, sacrifices, verbal or written praise (gratitude), and the like. With such a background, the concept of grace must itself have been quite difficult for the Gentile Corinthians to grasp, but the idea of God as benefactor to whom one was obligated to respond would not be difficult to grasp'.

[126] In the case of Antiochus 1 and the Caesars (Caligula and Nero), the chancery secretaries undoubtedly wrote up the contents of the decrees. Nonetheless, the propaganda of the ruler regarding his public beneficence would have been strictly adhered to.

2.8.1. Zosimos of Priene (84 BC)

Zosimos of Priene is known to us through three honorific inscriptions (*I. Priene* 112-114) which, though fragmentary at places, comprise some 309 lines. Χάρις is used six times in all, along with a wide variety of traditional benefaction terminology. After a brief catalogue of the honours awarded Zosimos as gymnasiarch of the *neoi*, the ἐπειδή clause of the first honorific decree unfolds the ethics of beneficence that animated the civic life of Zosimos:

> Whereas Aulos Aimilios Zosimos the son of Sextos, being a fair and good man, not lacking in ambition for glory (δόξ[αν]) in (his) manner of living, but having striven (ἐ[ζη]λωκώς) for both liberality (ἁπλότη[τά]) and noble character in (his) worthy judgement of honour, and not M[...]ISDT[......] of those who will be and [......] — — — 14 — — — good, and he — rashly seeking after his own pleasure in nothing, and understanding that merit (ἀρετῆι) alone returns (ἀποδίδωσιν) the greatest fruits (καρπούς) and favours (χάριτας) to those who treasure virtue in honour (ἐν τιμῇ) before (the) foreigners and citizens — laid up in store for himself commendation from the living, and remembrance from those still to be born; for he, having behaved favourably towards our city, and being by decree a citizen, has not displayed the fruitless (ἄ[καρπον]) return (ἀμοιβήν) of honour (τιμῆς) — (that is, just) being content with the city as (his) fatherland, and offering (the) care of a genuine citizen, as it were when favour (χάριτος) is maintained towards one up to the lifetime as far as the (person) affected (is concerned) — because (his) beneficence was bestowed towards the People for eternal fame...[127]

Here we are confronted with a highly individual perspective on Graeco-Roman reciprocity, seen in the way that the inscription forges a direct link between ἀρετή and χάρις.[128] Those who, like Zosimos, would achieve glory and honour should not seek their own ends. Instead, they should display liberality in the public arena. Such people, being paragons of ἀρετή, understand well the principle of reciprocity. They know that they will acquire 'favours' and 'honours' in return because — as the inscription asserts — ἀρετή always provides substantial rewards for civic benefactors. So, the more benefactors seek ἀρετή on its own terms, the more fruitful will be their return in commendation and, commensurately, the more glorious will be the eternal report of their beneficence.

The civic life of Zosimos was the embodiment of the above value system. Zosimos, who manifested willingness (προθυμία) as secretary of the council,

---

[127] *I. Priene* 112.

[128] For a discussion of the reciprocity underlying the use of ἀρετή with χάρις in Thucydides (2.40.4), see J.T. Hooker, 'Χάρις and ἀρετή in Thucydides', *Hermes* 102 (1974), 164-169.

'made a beginning of favour (χάριτος) towards the city' by managing the public service (λειτουργία).[129] Also, as a *theoros*, Zosimos

...made the festivals — (which were) at the public expense and shared in common — even more remarkable for the people by (his) favours (χάρισι), and he doubled those who used these beneficences, supplying a bath as a free gift (δωρεάν) both among them and all the citizens and (among) the foreigners and inhabitants and aliens and the Romans and (their) women and children, and ordering olive oil and assigning salve for the bathing room...[130]

When elected to the first secretaryship, he 'has unrepentantly given away favours (χάριτας)' to the city and its people, securing the preservation and faithfulness of the city records by handing over a double copy of them on skin and papyrus rolls.[131] Finally, as the appointed gymnasiarch of the *neoi*, he increased his zeal ([ζῆλον]) for the association ([κοινω]νίαν) of the athletes, making common (κοινοποησάμενος) the gift of oil from sunrise until sunset, for which he received the thanks (χάριτας) of the people and young men.[132]

2.8.2. Antiochus I of Kommagene (Mid first century BC)

Only two inscriptions of Antiochus I of Kommagene are extant. First, there is an autobiographical declaration from Antiochus' mausoleum which establishes the cultic rituals to be observed at the site. Second, another declaration outlines the same rituals for the mausoleum site of Antiochus' father, Mithridates Kallinikos.[133]

In the declaration from Antiochus' mausoleum there are six uses of χάρις. Antiochus adopts χάρις as the catch word which sums up the subject-matter of his inscription: namely, 'his own gracious deeds' (*l*.9: ἔργα χάριτος ἰδίας). χάρις is employed to designate the 'favour' of Antiochus in providing the priests — who served at the statues of the gods and Heroes — with the requisite Persian garments for the monthly and annual feasts (*ll*.136-7: [χ]άρις ἐμή). Again, Antiochus uses χάρις in a sacrificial context when he outlines all the produce for the sacrifices and sacred feast. This produce, according to Antiochus, was sanctified by 'the sacred grace of (his) Heroic nature' (*l*.141: χάρισιν). Moreover, the universality of Antiochus' grace is emphasised in his description of the sacred feast. The entire populace (including natives and strangers) participates in the meal, with extra food —

---

[129] *I. Priene* 113.
[130] *Ibid.*
[131] *I. Priene* 114.
[132] *Ibid.*
[133] The Greek text of each inscription: respectively, *OGIS* 383 and H. Waldmann, *Die kommagenischen Kultreformen unter König Mithridates I. Kallinikos und seinem Sohne Antiochus I* (Leiden 1973), 62-71, 82-87. See also F.W. Danker, *op. cit.*, §41, §42.

designated 'my grace' (*l*.154: χάριν ἐμήν) — being apportioned to anyone in receipt of Antiochus' benefits. The two final uses of χάρις relate to the gods. Antiochus reminds his audience that the 'gratitude of the gods and the Heroes' (*l*.190: χάρις) is aroused by piety (*l*.191: εὐσέβεια). Therefore, one shows εὐσέβεια by refusing either to exploit the sacred slaves or appropriate the village produce dedicated to the Divinities. In the view of Antiochus, ancestral piety towards the gods and the ancestors ensured that the gods would remain propitious and continue to dispense 'every favour' (*l*.227: πᾶσαν χάριν).

In the declaration concerning the mausoleum site of Antiochus' father, there are eight uses of χάρις. Since the law concerning the cultic rituals is replicated in each inscription, several occurrences of χάρις are the same: the grace of Antiochus in clothing the priests, his distribution of food during the feasts (*ll*.114, 134), the gratitude of the gods, and the maintenance of their favour are all reiterated (*ll*.164, 184). However, it is also mentioned that the priest must dispense the 'sacred honours' due the Heroes (*l*.120: χάρισιν ἱεραῖς) in the sacrifices and feasts. Elsewhere, Mithridates Kallinikos is said to have named Arsameia 'in recognition of his own grace' (*l*.23: χάριτας ἰδίας). Similarly, 'royal grace' (*l*.67-68: βα[σι]λικαῖς χάρισιν) is the term that Antiochus chooses for his establishment of an hereditary priesthood and an hierodulic service in honour of his father.[134] Finally, and importantly in view of 2 Corinthians 8:4, χάρις is linked wth κοινωνία.[135] But the meaning here is fundamentally different from that in 2 Corinthians (§7.2.1.1). Antiochus is referring to his opportunity 'to share in (κοινωνίαν) the meet and due thanksgiving (χάριτος)' at his father's mausoleum (*ll*.102-3).

It is clear that Antiochus employs χάρις as a leitmotiv to sum up his beneficence and clarify his piety towards his father's memory and the ancestral gods. Antiochus uses epithets such as 'kingly' and 'sacred' to enhance the quality, scope, and authority of his favour. He also places strong emphasis on its universality. Reciprocity exists in his understanding of the gods: they dispense favours to the ritually pious, and convey their gratitude to those who, like himself, maintain the ancestral cults.

2.8.3. *Phainios of Gytheion (AD 41/42)*

Five uses of χάρις are found in the public bequest of Phainios, son of Aromatios, to the city of Gytheion. Phainios had left a sum of 8,000 *denarii*

---

[134] For the contribution that Antiochus' inscription potentially makes to Paul's imagery of 'the reign' of grace, see §6.1.2.4 n.62.

[135] The only other conjunction of a cognate of χάρις (κεχαρισμένος) with κοινωνία in the inscriptions occurs in *I. Stratonikeia* 29.

for the city magistrates to lend out as needs arose. There was the strict proviso that adequate security in land had to be guaranteed from the borrower. Moreover, the interest accruing from the capital sum also had to be used for the provision of oil at the gymnasium for citizen and non-citizen alike.[136]

As a result, Phainios was very explicit in his stipulations regarding all loans from the bequest. His overriding desire was that 'out of my favour ([τῆς ἐ]μῆς χάριτος) and gift (δωρεᾶς) everlasting profits may accrue of the money which is given out'. Not under any circumstance was there to be a diminution of the everlasting gift of olive oil made to the gymnasium or city. To take that path, in Phainios' view, was 'to neglect utterly my grace (τῆς ἐμῆς χάριτος)'. Furthermore, if mismanagement of the bequest by the magistrates was proven by an accuser, the accuser would gain one quarter of the bequest while the Spartans inherited the remaining 6,000 *denarii*. The Spartans, therefore, were again reminded not to neglect 'my grace ([τῆς ἐμ]ῆς χάριτος)'. Any breach of the contract meant that the money would belong to Augusta the goddess. Finally, to ensure absolute clarity concerning the provisions of the bequest, Phainios requested that his 'gift and favour (τῆς ἐμῆς [χάριτος]) bestowed upon the gymnasium on the stated conditions ... be published on three marble pillars'. In that way his 'philanthropic and kindly act ([τῆς εμ]ῆς χάριτος φιλανθρωπία)' would be known to all.

Several remarkable features characterise the bequest of Phainios. First, slaves were to share in Phainios' gift of oil for six days each year. Second, Phainios is unabashed about his overall aim in providing the bequest: 'My idea is to achieve immortality in making such a just and kindly disposal [of my property] and, in entrusting it to the city, I shall surely not fail in my aim'. Third, the bequest of Phainios is eloquent testimony to the exalted status given to χάρις in the first century AD. To ignore the grace of a benefactor, as Phainios reminds the Spartans, was no minor matter in the hellenistic reciprocity system.

2.8.4. *Caligula (AD 37) and Nero (AD 67)*

We will not linger long over these two inscriptions, because they have been regularly cited by New Testament scholars in discussions of the inscriptional use of χάρις. There are three uses of χάρις in the Caligula inscription, while in Nero's there are only two, coupled with one use of the verb χαρίζεσθαι.

In the case of the first inscription, the status of Caligula as the New Sun lends a numinous quality to his beneficence. Two client-kings of Caligula, Rhoimetalkes and Polemon, are described as 'reaping the abundance of his

---

[136] *SEG* XIII 258.

immortal favour (ἀθανάτου χάριτος)'. The invidious comparison between the royal power which they inherited from their father, Kotys, and the superiority of the divine favour procured from Caligula, is very pointed:

> ... although they held (the royal power) from their fathers, they became kings in the joint rule of such great gods as a consequence of the favour (χάριτος) of Gaius Caesar, and the favours (χάριτες) of gods differ from human successions (of power) as sunlight from night and as the immortal from mortal nature ...[137]

Thus we see that the χάριτες of the exalted Caligula are not easily reciprocated, as the inscription had earlier conceded:

> ... the kings had put a great amount of thought into discovering appropriate recompense (ἴσας ἀμοιβάς) to show their gratitude (εὐχαριστίαν) for the gracious act of such a great god, but failed to discover one ...[138]

The Nero inscription, celebrating the short-lived liberation of the province of Greece in AD 67, indicates a desire on the emperor's part for the expansion of the scope of his favour, had circumstances been otherwise (ll.18-19: τῆς χάριτος, μου τὸ μέγαθος τῆς χάριτος). While the initial grounds of the gift (χαρίζεσθαι) originated, according to Nero, in his generous nature (l.11: μεγαλοφροσύνης), reciprocity is the real dynamic behind his actions. Nero's liberation of Greece is given in exchange for the past beneficence of the Greek gods (l.21: ἀμείβομαι τοὺς θεοὺς ὑμῶν) to the emperor on land and sea.[139]

2.8.5. Conclusion: Charis *in the first century AD*

To conclude, what is the overall panorama of χάρις in the first century AD from the foregoing inscriptions? Benefactors had heightened the dependence of the beneficiary upon their grace. Threats of the withdrawal of grace were real, and no doubt intensely felt. This was reinforced at a semantic level by the addition of lofty epithets such as 'immortal', 'royal', or 'sacred', which accentuated the suppliant position of the community or person who had been benefited. Or, more simply, the addition of ἐμή to χάρις would remind the beneficiary of the obligation of gratitude. Reciprocity from the gods was a commonplace, with the cultic observance of piety towards ancestors being the standard means to secure favours or gratitude. Also, a strong conceptual link had been forged between χάρις and ἀρετή, in which ἀρετή rewarded its benefactors with the eternal gratitude of posterity. Last, if the inscriptions of Antiochus I and Phainios of Gytheum are representative (§7.1 n.4), χάρις

---

[137] *SIG*³ 798.
[138] *Ibid.*
[139] *SIG*³ 814.

exhibited a surprising universalism in regard to those who received the favours of a benefactor.

2.9. Conclusion

Graeco-Roman culture was keenly attuned to the eulogistic conventions underlying the honorific inscriptions. Their wide geographical distribution and prominence of location throughout the Greek East would have ensured their familiarity. Early Christians would also have encountered benefaction terminology in the association decrees, either through their work contacts as artisan-traders or, in a few cases, as members of the patronal class.

By the first-century AD χάρις had become the fundamental leitmotiv of the hellenistic reciprocity system. It was equally applied to each party involved in the benefaction ritual, referring either to the disposal of 'favour' by the benefactor, or the return of 'favour' or 'gratitude' by the beneficiary.

In the honorific inscriptions, χάρις appears mainly in the manifesto clause, but its general use and appearance in the inscriptions was both extensive and varied. G.P. Wetter was correct in seeing the bestowal of χάρις by the Caesars as the linguistic springboard for the New Testament. But the dominant use of the word was subsumed under the ethos of reciprocity — whether human or divine. In this respect, as a semantic starting point for the New Testament understanding of grace, χάρις — unless carefully defined — carried as many dangers as advantages.

Chapter 3

The Role of *Charis* in the Papyri

3.1. Charis *and the Ancient Epistolary Theorists*

3.1.1. Charis, *the papyri, and benefaction studies*

There has been little investigation of the role of χάρις in the papyri since G.P. Wetter's limited foray earlier this century.[1] Wetter narrowly focused on the understanding of grace found in the papyrological thanksgiving formulae and in the magical papyri, bypassing the interpretation of χάρις in its ancient benefaction context. Later contributions of scholars on χάρις and its cognates in the papyri were just as circumscribed. An important advance in papyrological and New Testament research occurred through P. Schubert. He proposed that Paul had adopted the traditional hellenistic epistolary convention of opening a letter with a thanksgiving to the gods or the divinity (χάρις τοῖς θεοῖς, εὐχαριστῶ [εὐχαριστοῦμεν] τοῖς θεοῖς [τῷ θεῷ]).[2] Subsequent works on the Pauline thanksgivings, however, have typically either endorsed Schubert's analysis without addition, or entirely eschewed any further examination of the papyrological evidence.[3] Moreover, other promising trails for research have been generally left unexplored. An instance of this is the suggestion of A. Deissmann that Paul's apologetic of grace — along with his rejection of justification by works — was aimed as much at the Gentile cults as at Judaism.[4]

Only recently has S.K. Stowers pointed to the evidence of the epistolary handbooks for the social interaction between benefactors and their beneficiaries.[5] But, again, the pervasive role which χάρις and its cognates

---

[1] See G.P. Wetter, *Charis: Ein Beitrag zur Geschichte des ältesten Christentums* (Leipzig 1913), esp. 130-137, 206-11. A glance at Wetter's Index (*ibid.* 221-222) reveals a remarkable collection of papyrological evidence, given the date of publication.

[2] P. Schubert, *Form and Function of the Pauline Thanksgivings* (Berlin 1939), 158-179.

[3] See G.P. Wiles, *Paul's Intercessory Prayers: The Significance of the Intercessory Prayer Passages in the Letters of Paul* (Cambridge 1974), 28-29, 158-159; P.T. O'Brien, *Introductory Thanksgivings in the Letters of Paul* (Leiden 1977), 6ff.

[4] A. Deissmann, *Light from the Ancient East* (2nd ed. 1927: rpt. Grand Rapids 1978), 161. Deissmann refers to the letter of Zoilus, a servant of Sarapis at Alexandria (*PSI* IV 435: 258—257 BC).

[5] S.K. Stowers, 'Social Typification and the Classification of Ancient Letters', in J.

played in informing social dynamics at an epistolary level was not touched on. Finally, in an insightful discussion of *philophronesis* in the papyri, H. Koskenniemi drew attention to the use of χάρις cognates in relationships of friendship between correspondents in letter-writing.[6] There the social dynamic moved from the hierarchical patron-client relationship towards a genuine warmth among equals, well encapsulated in the directive of Julius Victor: 'A letter written to a superior should not be droll; to an equal, not cold (*ne inhumana*); to an inferior, not haughty'.[7]

Overall, as Stowers notes, New Testament epistolary scholarship has been beguiled by form-critical issues, at the expense of the 'socially oriented perspective of the handbooks'.[8] In the evidence of epistolary handbooks we are afforded the rare opportunity of correcting a blindspot that impairs the social world-view of the inscriptions. In the quest for continuing munificence, local communities rendered praise to benefactors through the public

---

Neusner (*et. al.*, eds), *The Social World of Formative Christianity and Judaism* (Philadelphia 1988), 78-90.

[6] On *philophronesis*, see H. Koskenniemi, *Studien zur Idee und Phraseologie des griechischen Briefes bis 400 n. Chr.* (Helsinki 1956), 35-37, 115-127. On p.123 he cites *P. Mert.* I. 12, discussed below (§3.3).

[7] Julius Victor, *Ars Rhetorica* 27 (*De Epistolis*), tr. A.J. Malherbe, *Ancient Epistolary Theorists* (Atlanta 1988). Cf. Pseudo-Demetrius, Τύποι Επιστολικοί 1 and Pseudo-Libanius Ἐπιστολιμαῖοι Χαρακτῆρες 11, 58 on the φιλική style of epistle.

[8] S.K. Stowers, art. cit., 78. The literature is voluminous: O. Roller, *Das Formular der paulinischen Briefe: Ein Beitrag zur Lehre vom antiken Briefe* (Stuttgart 1933), esp. 111ff; P. Schubert, 'Form and Function of the Pauline Letters', *JR* 19 (1939), 365-377; K. Berger, 'Hellenistische Gattungen im Neuen Testament', *ANRW* II 25/2 (1984), 1327-1363; W.G. Doty, 'The Classification of Epistolary Literature', *CBQ* 31/2 (1969), 183-199; *id.*, *Letters in Primitive Christianity* (Philadelphia 1973); R.W. Funk, *Language, Hermeneutic, and Word of God: The Problem of Language in the New Testament and Contemporary Theology* (New York 1966), 251-274; C-H. Kim, 'The Papyrus Invitation', *JBL* 94/3 (1975), 391-402; *id.*, *Form and Structure of the Familiar Greek Letter of Recommendation* (Missoula 1972); T.Y. Mullins, 'Petition as a Literary Form', *NovT* 5 (1962), 46-54; *id.*, 'Disclosure: A Literary Form in the New Testament', *NovT* 7 (1964), 44-50; *id.*, 'Greeting as a New Testament Form', *JBL* 87 (1968), 418-426; *id.*, 'Formulas in the New Testament Epistles', *JBL* 91 (1972), 380-390; B. Rigaux, *The Letters of St Paul: Modern Studies* (Chicago 1968: Fr. orig. 1962), 115-122; J.L. White, 'Introductory Formulae in the Body of the Pauline Letter', *JBL* 90 (1971), 91-97; *id.*, *The Form and Structure of the Official Petition: A Study in Greek Epistolography* (Missoula 1972); *id.*, *The Body of the Greek Letter* (Missoula 1972); *id.* and K.A. Kensinger, 'Categories of Greek Papyrus', in G. MacRae (ed.), *Society of Biblical Literature 1976 Seminar Papers* (Cambridge, Mass. 1976), 79-91; *id.*, 'The Greek Documentary Letter Tradition Third Century BCE to Third Century CE', *Semeia* 22 (1981), 89-106; *id.*, 'Saint Paul and the Apostolic Letter Tradition', *CBQ* 45/3 (1983), 433-444; *id.*, 'New Testament Epistolary Literature in the Framework of Ancient Epistolography', *ANRW* II 25/2 (1984), 1730-1756; *id.*, *Light from Ancient Letters* (Philadelphia 1986); H. Probst, *Paulus und der Brief: Die Rhetorik des antiken Briefes als Form der paulinischen Korintherkorrespondenz (1 Cor 8-10)* (Tübingen 1992), 29-107; P. Arzt, 'The "Epistolary Introductory Thanksgiving" in the Papyri and in St. Paul', *NovT* 36/1 (1994), 29-46.

inscriptions and of necessity minimised any hostilities or social humiliation implicit in the benefaction system.⁹ In contrast, the ancient epistolary theorists adhered to the benefaction ethos, but stripped away the veneer of deferential politeness which marked the inscriptions.

In an attempt to redress the imbalances of previous scholarship, we will make several comments on the methodological pitfalls involved in handling the papyrological evidence (§3.1.2). We will then turn to the evidence of the epistolary theorists concerning benefaction (§3.1.3). In subsequent sections, after a survey of χάρις and its cognates in the Jewish and Greek papyri (§3.2), a series of traditional benefaction motifs will be investigated: the ethos of reciprocity (§3.3), the beneficence of the gods (§3.4), the munificence of the Caesars (§3.5). Last, from the evidence of magical papyri (§3.6), we will gain some insight into the χάριτες which the hellenistic practitioners of the spiritual underworld promised to dispense.

3.1.2. Papyrological methodology and benefaction studies

There are several methodological cautions for the New Testament scholar who would adduce parallels from the papyri for the early Christian use of benefaction terminology, whether in a congregational or evangelistic setting.¹⁰ First, the distribution of the extant papyri is geographically confined to Egypt and Palestine.¹¹ As S.K. Stowers has observed, the cultural minutiae of Egyptian provincial life found in the papyri are far removed from those of the sophisticated urban centres of hellenistic culture which Paul visited.¹² Nevertheless, the papyri may help us gauge how far benefaction terminology had spread beyond such urban centres into the surrounding countryside.¹³

---

⁹ Some inscriptions drop hints of a 'darker' side to the benefaction ritual in their trenchant comments concerning ungrateful recipients: for examples, see *SEG* XIII 258; B. Laum, *Stiftungen in der griechischen und römischen Antike: Ein Beitrag zur antiken Kulturgeschichte* Vol.II (Leipzig-Berlin 1914), §78a.

¹⁰ On the public nature of the Pauline epistles and the inscriptions, see §2.1.

¹¹ G.H.R. Horsley, 'The Inscriptions of Ephesos and the New Testament', *NovT* 34/2 (1992), 112.

¹² S.K. Stowers, *Letter Writing in Greco-Roman Antiquity* (Philadelphia 1986), 19. On life and culture in the papyri, see R.C. Horn, 'Life and Letters in the Papyri', *Classical Journal* 17 (1922), 487-502; J.G. Winter, *Life and Letters in the Papyri* (Ann Arbor 1933). Note, too, H.A. Steen's comment ('Les clichés épistolaires dans les lettres sur papyrus grecques', *C & M* 1 [1938], 123) on the subject bias of the surviving papyri: 'La plupart des lettres sur papyrus sont des lettres commerciales de toute sorte; aussi les expressions le plus ordinaires sont des ordres et des demandes'.

¹³ In regard to the inscriptions, W.A. Meeks (*The Moral World of the First Christians* [Philadelphia 1986], 39) has argued that moral values flowed from the *polis* to the village: 'Rural tombstones are rarer than those found around cities, naturally, but wherever they are found, they echo the style of the urban epitaphs, with however many misspellings, and praise similar virtues of the deceased'.

Second, A. Deissmann's distinction between the non-literary *letter* (the occasional products of Paul and the wider corpus of papyri) and the literary *epistle* (the polished productions of a Cicero, Pliny, or Seneca) has been rightly jettisoned as artificial.[14] Concomitant with this, Deissmann had proposed different epistolary audiences: letters were essentially private, epistles public in domain.[15] However, Deissmann's contrast is strained. Both polished and unpolished letters qualified as epistolary literature; indeed, each type may have been read — as occasion demanded — to either individuals or communities, ensuring a widespread distribution of benefaction terminology.[16]

Third, the descriptions of letter types by the epistolary theorists outlined a wide range of rhetorical conventions for writers to use.[17] A writer of such rhetorical power as Paul was undoubtedly aware of conventional epistolary praxis, but was not necessarily constrained by its strictures or epistolary clichés.[18] This is observed in the way that Paul incorporated and modified the letter of recommendation (συστατική) — an epistolary genre which employs χάρις cognates — in his own writings.[19] Presumably he was also au fait with the delicately nuanced range of epistolary conventions concerning benefaction.

---

[14] See A. Deissmann, 'Prolegomena to the Biblical Letters and Epistles', in *id.*, *Bible Studies* (Winona Lake 1979: orig. Edinburgh 1923), 1-59; *id.*, 'Epistolary Literature', *Encyclopaedia Biblica* Vol.2 (London 1901), cols. 1322-1329; *id.*, *op. cit.* (1978), 148-251. For a major critique of Deissmann, see W.G. Doty, *art. cit.* and *op. cit.*, 1ff. See also H.D. Betz, *2 Corinthians 8 and 9* (Philadelphia 1985), 133; S.K. Stowers, *op. cit.*, 19-20.

[15] A. Deissmann, *op. cit.* 1978, 148.

[16] F.X. Exler, *The Form of the Ancient Greek Letter: A Study in Greek Epistolography* (Diss. Catholic University of America 1923), 16-17. Claudius' letter to the Alexandrians (*P. Lond.* VI 1912) is clearly intended for the entire *polis*, as were the letters of Claudius and Vespasian to the Travelling Athletic Association (*Pap. Agon.* 6).

[17] For letter types employing χάρις and its cognates, see §3.1.3.

[18] H.D. Betz, *op. cit.*, 130. On Paul's rhetorical skill, see E.A. Judge, 'Paul's Boasting in Relation to Contemporary Professional Practice', *Australian Biblical Review* 16 (1968), 37-50; C. Forbes, '"Unaccustomed As I Am": St. Paul the Public Speaker in Corinth', *Buried History* 19/1 (1983), 11-16; *id.*, 'Comparison, Self-Praise and Irony: Paul's Boasting and the Conventions of Hellenistic Rhetoric', *NTS* 32/1 (1986), 1-30; J.P. Sampley, 'Paul, His Opponents in 2 Corinthians 10-13 and the Rhetorical Handbooks', in J. Neusner (*et. al.*, eds), *The Social World of Formative Christianity and Judaism* (Philadelphia 1988), 162-177. Certainly Paul's opponents conceded that his letters demonstrated substantial rhetorical power (2 Cor 10:10).

[19] On genuine cases of συστατική in Paul, see 2 Cor 3:1-3 (v.1: συστατικῶν ἐπιστολῶν); Rom 16; Phlm. For further recommendatory material, see 1 Cor 4:17; 16:10ff; 2 Cor 8:16ff. For modern discussion, see C.W. Keyes, 'The Greek Letter of Introduction', *AJP* 56 (1935), 28-44; E.J. Goodspeed, 'Phoebe's Letter of Introduction', *HTR* 44 (1951), 55-57; W. Baird, 'Letters of Recommendation: A Study of 2 Cor 3:1-3', *JBL* 80/2 (1961), 166-172; C.-H. Kim, *art. cit.* and *op. cit.*; H.D. Betz, *op. cit.*, 132ff. On χάρις cognates in ἐπιστολὴ συστατική, see J.L. White, *art. cit.* (1984), 1736-1737 and *op. cit.* (1986), 204-205.

This would have been especially the case when Paul was either urging the recalcitrant Corinthians in their role as benefactors of the Jerusalem church, or countering deep-seated resentments over his role as their Father-benefactor (§7.4.1).

3.1.3. The social world of benefaction in the epistolary theorists

The aim of the epistolary theorist was to provide a rhetorically elegant model for people of differing or similar social status who had to frame a written response for various social situations.[20] While the epistolary handbooks were largely the domain of professional letter writers, the authors of the handbooks envisaged varying social transactions involving hierarchical relations (the εὐεργέτης and his dependants), relations between equals (φιλία amongst various φίλοι), and the complex web of relationships of the household (οἶκος).[21] As S.K. Stowers observes,

The ancient approach to classification reflected in the handbooks, student exercises, and comments by theorists allows us to see how the same kinds of language acts and social transactions were attempted by people of different social and educational levels.[22]

Within this range of social transactions, the epistolary theorists enable us to see better than the inscriptions how praise and blame (with its consequent shame and social dishonour) could be assigned to the participants in the benefaction system. Significantly, χάρις and its cognates functioned as a useful terminological bridge in this whole process of assigning and retracting honour.

A variety of letter types — the πρεσβευτική ('diplomatic'), ἐρωτηματική ('enquiry'), ἀπευχαριστικός or εὐχαριστική ('thankful'), παραίτησις ('petition') and συστατική ('commendation') — existed for establishing, maintaining, and extending relationships with social superiors (benefactors) and equals (friends).

Pseudo-Libanius' model of the 'diplomatic' letter resonates with inscriptional benefaction terminology. It is designed to remind the καλοκἀγαθός that he was constrained by honour to maintain munificence:

We continue to enjoy the gifts (δωρεαί) your solicitude bestows on us. Hence, now too, gentlemen, through these appeals do we make the following request which you have customarily granted (ἐχαρίσασθε) to those who make it. Be constrained, then, to show in this matter how magnificently excellent you are (τὸ μεγαλόψυχον τῆς ὑμετέρας ἀρετῆς).[23]

---

[20] On epistolary theory, see J. Sykutris, 'Epistolographie', *PWSup* V (1931), cols. 189ff; J. Schneider, 'Brief', *RAC* II 1954, cols. 569ff; H. Koskenniemi, *op. cit.*, 18ff; K. Thraede, *Grundzüge griechisch-römischer Brieftopik* (München 1970), 17ff; W.G. Doty, *op. cit.*, 8ff; S.K. Stowers, *op. cit.*, 32ff; J.L. White, *op. cit.*, 190ff; A.J. Malherbe, *op. cit.*, *passim*.

[21] See the helpful discussion of S.K. Stowers, *op. cit.*, 27-31.

[22] S.K. Stowers, *art. cit.*, 87.

[23] Pseudo-Libanius,'Επιστολιμαῖοι Χαρακτῆρες 76. Note the advice of Seneca, *Ben.*

Similarly, in a letter of 'enquiry' regarding a rhetorical topos, the correspondent flatters the respondent's 'technical knowledge of the subject', in the hope that he would be granted the favour (τὴν χάριν) he was asking.[24]

The 'thankful' letter, as Pseudo-Demetrius informs us, was designed to 'call to mind the gratitude (χάριν) that is due (the reader)'. In the example cited below, Pseudo-Demetrius inculcates the same deference on the part of the beneficiary that the city Cardamylae had displayed towards its benefactor, Poseidippos, in a first-century AD inscription:

I hasten to show in my actions how grateful I am to you for the kindness you showed (εὐεργέτησάς) me in your words. For I know that what I am doing for you is less (ἔλαττον) than I should, for even if I gave my life for you, I should not be giving adequate thanks (ἀξίαν ἀποδώσειν χάριν) for the benefits I have received. If you wish anything that is mine, do not write and request it, but demand a return (χάριν). For I am in your debt.[25]

As with the Cardamylae decree, χάρις exhibits a reciprocal aspect as it shifts meaning from 'thanks' to 'return'. Further, the writer's final exhortation to 'demand a return' imbibes the spirit of Homeric society where the counter-favour was the code of practice. The strong emphasis on the recipient's inability to render his benefactor adequate gratitude in recompense of benefits received — underlined by his use of ἔλαττον — captures well the ethos and terminology of the Cardamylae decree. There the city admits that in 'offering thankfulness (εὐχαριστίας) to the benefactors of ourselves', it was nevertheless 'giving a share of the lesser favour (ἐλάττονος χάριτος)'.[26]

By contrast, Pseudo-Libanius advises writers of the εὐχαριστική letter type to focus on the ἀρετή of the benefactor when assigning him thanks:

For many other good gifts am I grateful (χάριν) to your excellent character (τῇ σῇ καλοκἀγαθίᾳ), but especially for that matter in which you benefited me above all others.[27]

Last, in letters of 'petition' or 'commendation', cognates of χάρις were used to express the writer's confidence that not only would the request be acceded to, but it would be carried out as an obligation of friendship on the part of the respondent. Thus, in Pseudo-Demetrius' petition for forgiveness over the unnecessarily harsh discipline of a mutual friend, the writer is confident that

---

1.2.4: 'complete the role of a good man (boni viri)'.

[24] Pseudo-Libanius, op. cit., 82.

[25] Pseudo-Demetrius, Τύποι Ἐπιστολικοί 21. For discussion, see G.W. Peterman, *Paul's Gift from Philippi: Conventions of Gift Exchange and Christian Giving* (Cambridge 1997), 82-83. See our translation and discussion of *SEG* XI 948 in §2.6.

[26] See also our discussion of *P. Brem.* 49 (cf. μικρὸς μὲν ἐγώ) in §3.3 below. Seneca, too, has similar sentiments: 'So we declare that he who receives a benefit in a kindly spirit has repaid it by gratitude, yet, nevertheless, we leave him in debt — still bound to repay gratitude even after he has repaid it' (*Ben.* 2.35.3).

[27] Pseudo-Libanius, op. cit. 57.

this action would be overlooked because the respondent was good and gracious (χαριζομένος) to his friends.[28] Pseudo-Libanius' letter of commendation accentuates the ἀρετή of a prospective guest, and posits the mutual obligation of friends as the rationale for extending hospitality to this stranger:

> Receive this highly honoured (τιμιώτατον) and much sought-after man, and do not hesitate to treat him hospitably, thus doing what behoves you and pleases (κεχαρισμένα) me.[29]

Notwithstanding the positive tone of the foregoing examples, a darker aspect to benefaction and friendship rituals is imaged in the μεμπτική ('blaming'), ὀνειδιστική ('reproachful'), and διαβλητική ('maligning') letter types of the handbooks.

Although the 'blaming' letter type of Pseudo-Libanius does not employ χάρις or its cognates, it captures succinctly the fear of the ancients that the social fabric was exposed to real danger when benefactors were not rendered appropriate honour:

> You did not act well when you wronged those who do good to you. For by insulting your benefactors (εὐεργέτας) you provided an example of evil (κακίας) to others.[30]

In contrast, Pseudo-Demetrius places this social transaction in a more personal context when he advises the μεμπτική letter writer 'not to seem harsh' in allocating blame. Initially, the benefactor should attempt to effect reconciliation. This could be achieved by construing the beneficiary's ingratitude as simply a case of tardiness in reciprocating gratitude. Even the public vilification of the benefactor by the recipient, while blameworthy, is relativised: perhaps the benefactor himself has to accept some responsibility as a bad judge of character.[31] Nonetheless, the tone is very strained:

> Since you have not yet had time to express your thanks for the favours (χάριτας) you have received, for that reason I thought it well not to mention what you have received. And yet you are annoyed with us, and impute words (to us). We do, then, blame you for having such a character, and we blame ourselves for not knowing that you were such a man.[32]

According to Pseudo-Demetrius, the occasion for the 'reproachful' letter type arises 'when we once more reproach, with accusation, someone whom we had earlier benefited (προευεργετημένον), for what he has done'.[33] We sense in

---

[28] Pseudo-Demetrius, *op. cit.* 12.
[29] Pseudo-Libanius, *op. cit.* 55.
[30] *Ibid.*, 53.
[31] Seneca (*Ben.* 1.10.5) says: '... we ought to be careful to confer benefits by preference upon those who will be likely to respond with gratitude'. However, see his more detailed discussion in *ibid.*, 4.9-10.
[32] Pseudo-Demetrius, *op. cit.*, 3.
[33] *Ibid.*, 4.

Pseudo-Libanius' letter type the amazement which the ancients felt over the cardinal sin of ingratitude.[34] It violated the principle of reciprocity where the benefactor as καλοκἀγαθός was publicly recompensed with honours. More fundamentally, this negligence on the part of the beneficiary was an act of enmity since it deprived the benefactor of his prized status as a man of ἀρετή:

> You have received many favours (καλά) from us, and I am exceedingly amazed that you remember none of them but speak badly of us. That is characteristic of a person with an ungrateful disposition (ἀχαρίστου). For the ungrateful (ἀχάριστοι) forget noble men (καλούς), and in addition ill-treat their benefactors (εὐεργέτας) as though they were enemies.[35]

Bologna Papyrus 5, a series of sample letters from the 3rd—4th century AD, affords us insight into the antipathy which the ancients felt towards those who were ungrateful. The public perception of oneself as an ingrate aroused a sense of profound unease, as this revealing snippet illustrates: 'He will see it as ungrateful (ἀχάριστον), or would prove us to be idlers'.[36] In a letter of advice about the small size of a legacy, the writer voices dismay over the injustice which Publius, the deceased, perpetrated when he did not adequately requite in his legacy those who had previously been generous to him:

> We know that [your] gifts were not matched by Publius, which is not at all what you deserved. The documents (only) describe the deceased. Do not, then, let so ungracious (ἀχάριστος) an omission take away anything from what is yours. Indeed, all of us men are unequal.[37]

Finally, the 'maligning' letter of Pseudo-Libanius, which employs reciprocity terminology, attributes the failure of a beneficiary to return favours to the meanness of his birth, and hints at the outbreak of social evil:

> So-and-so, who has a very bad character, has caused me much harm. For, after having acted as though he were my friend, and having received many favours (καλά) from me when he was not able to repay me measure for measure (τοῖς ἴσοις ἀμείψασθαι) because he possessed no noble qualities, he brought the greatest evils down upon me (μεγίστοις περιέβαλε κακοῖς). Be on your guard (φυλάττου), therefore, against this man, lest you, too, experience terrible trials at his hands.[38]

---

[34] Seneca (*Ben.* 4.18.1) says: '... ingratitude is something to be avoided in itself because there is nothing that so effectively disrupts and destroys the harmony of the human race as this vice'. Also, *ibid.*, 3.1.1.

[35] Pseudo-Libanius, *op. cit.*, 64.

[36] *Bologna Papyrus 5* II.1-4. Seneca (*Ben.* 2.23.3) captures well the shame attached to ingratitude in the ancient world when he says: '... while they fear the reputation of being a dependant, they incur the more painful one of being an ingrate'.

[37] *Bologna Papyrus 5* IV.14-25.

[38] Pseudo-Libanius, *op. cit.*, 80. Paul — or the pseudonymous author of 2 Timothy — reflects the 'maligning' epistolary style when he writes: 'Alexander the coppersmith did me great harm (πολλά μοι κακὰ ἐνεδείξατο); the Lord will requite him (ἀποδώσει αὐτῷ) for

In conclusion, the epistolary theorist ushers us past the polished rhetoric of the eulogistic inscriptions — which he was also sensitive to — into a more complex and threatening web of benefaction relationships. Should the benefactor cease being munificent, the social fabric was at substantial risk; the benefactor himself had to choose his dependants carefully, lest they prove ungrateful and deny him his coveted prize of ἀρετή. The invective behind a word such as ἀχάριστος carried more than social opprobrium when applied to an individual: it could be an outright declaration of enmity. Undeniably, at a cultural level, Paul faced a situation of some delicacy with the Corinthians' intransigence in their role as benefactors to the Jerusalem church and as (attempted) benefactors of himself.

3.2. A Survey of Charis and Its Cognates

In this section we will argue that χάρις (and its cognates) is as versatile in the papyri as the inscriptions. While the basic rituals of the benefaction system are endorsed — the bestowal of favour (χάρις, χαρίζεσθαι, εὐχαριστεῖν) and the rendering of gratitude (χάρις, εὐχαριστία) — the papyri also extend the semantic range of χάρις into the realms of administration, commerce and the family. As noted above, the various letter types (e.g. the συστατική) consistently used χάρις cognates to underscore the obligation of the respondent as a φίλος to accede to the letter's request. Last, as a preface to our discussion of χάρις in first-century Judaism,[39] we will examine the evidence of the Jewish papyri. All the papyri discussed range from 200 BC—AD 200.

3.2.1. The bestowal of a favour or a gift

In the papyri χάρις often occurs in administrative contexts where a superior either promises to benefit his client or seeks the client's co-operation for his own purposes. An example of the latter situation appears in a letter (AD 160) concerning the reading of a will. There the official, Heraklas, introduces himself to his unknown addressee in an accommodating manner: 'Heraklas

---

his deeds. Beware of him yourself (σὺ φυλάσσου), for he strongly opposed our message' (2 Tim 4:14-16). Note how Seneca (*Ben.* 1.9.4) relates ingratitude to other social evils: 'Homicides, tyrants, thieves, adulterers, robbers, sacrilegious men, and traitors there always will be; but worse than all is the crime of ingratitude, unless it be that all these spring from ingratitude, without which hardly any sin has grown to great size'.

[39] See Chapter 4.

your fellow-freedman in greater honour, O most honourable brother, (wishes) with your gracious help (χάριτι) to be there'.[40]

χάρις also appears in family contexts where a relative undertakes to carry out various kindnesses on behalf of his next-of-kin. A letter regarding the sale of a house (AD 194) stipulates that 500 drachmae be withdrawn for Pakusis, a minor, through the 'unalterable favour of Tanephremmis (χάριτι ἀναφαιρέτῳ)', his guardian.[41] Julia Herakla, in conjunction with her guardian, agrees with Theon to cede to her daughter Gaia 'as an unalterable deed of gift (χάριν ἀναφαίρετον)' five arourae of catoecic land.[42] In this regard, the idea that 'unalterable' χάρις could be conveyed to family members may well have appealed to Paul. But Paul's emphasis was on the permanent extension of God's grace to brothers who had acquired family status on the basis of the new covenant of Christ.[43]

A novel use of χάρις is encountered in the commercial papyri. The ἀναγραφὴ γραφείου, datable to the sixth year of Tiberius (AD 45—46), is a chronological list of documents (contracts, petitions, guild ordinances, etc) written in the public record office. The sum (γραμματικά) paid to professional scribes for the writing of these documents was usually entered after the record of each document. On occasion, the sum was omitted for an unspecified reason and the substitution of the phrase ὀφείλει τὸ γραμματικόν signalled payment. In twenty-five entries, however, the word χάρις is used instead of the usual γραμματικόν and carries the meaning of 'no charge', 'gratis' or 'free'.[44] Each document in question had been prepared free of charge by a grapheion official, and was frequently accompanied by his name or by that of a benefactor to the grapheion staff.[45] Another ἀναγραφὴ γραφείου, datable to AD 46—49, records 'a free law of the association of

---

[40] *P. Ross. Georg.* II 26.

[41] *SB* X 15071. In a registration of a contract of sale (*P. Gr.* 1236: post AD 175), the letter writer says: 'by the means of the unalterable favour (χάριτι ἀναφαιρέτῳ) of (my) father I will also establish free from all public debt until the present day with all (legal) warranty [...]'.

[42] *P. Oxy.* II 273 (AD 95).

[43] While Paul does not use ἀναφαίρετος of grace, he nevertheless spotlights the abundance of God's grace through the verb περισσεύειν. See M. Theobald, *Die überströmende Gnade: Studien zu einem paulinischen Motivfeld* (Würzburg 1982), *passim*. For examples of Paul's linkage of χάρις to the Christian's family status: Abraham's offspring (παντὶ τῷ σπέρματι: Rom 4:16); sons (υἱοθεσίαν: Eph 1:5-6); brothers (ἀδελφοί ἐν Χριστῷ: 2 Cor 8:1; Col 1:2).

[44] *P. Mich.* II 123. Cols 2. 32, 36, 37; 4. 15, 26, 44; 5. 33; 6. 4, 11, 21; 7. 3; 8. 7, 26, 34; 12. 4, 18; 13. 17; 14. 8, 27; 15. 4, 27, 16. 16, 19; 20. 25; 21. 32. See also *P. Mich.* II 128. Col. 1. 6, 7 (AD 46—47).

[45] Names of officials (Kronion, Eutuchas, Heraklas); officials (ἀμφοτέρων); benefactor to the grapheion staff ('gratis to Heron the doctor': χάρις Ἥρωνι εἰατρῷ).

[the] god' (χάρις νόμος συνώδο[υ] θεοῦ).⁴⁶ This novel meaning of χάρις in the commercial papyri may well have been familiar to Paul. This is evident in Rom 4:4 where Paul uses similar commercial terminology — οὐ λογίζεται κατὰ χάριν ἀλλὰ κατὰ ὀφείλημα — when contrasting justification by works with justification by faith.

The verbs χαρίζεσθαι and εὐχαριστεῖν are used for the disposal of a variety of favours, commercial obligations, and gifts. In a letter of Terentianus to his father, which sought to win the father's approval for his plan of bringing a woman into the household, we come across this piece of special pleading:

> If perchance the woman whom I decide to bring down is one able to be the more kindly disposed (εὐνοεῖν) toward you for my sake (?) and to take more thought for you than for me, the outcome is that I do you a favour (εὐχαρ[ι]στεῖν) rather than that you blame me. On this account, lacking your approval, until today no woman has come into my house.⁴⁷

χαρίζεσθαι, too, was standard fare in the commercial papyri. Two examples will suffice. A second-century AD order for payment commands the recipient thus: 'accept from Didymos (the son) of Sarapion 112 drachma, but you offer as a free gift (χάρισαι) the drink offering'.⁴⁸ Also, in a bank-*diagraphe* regarding the incomplete repayment of loans, Thais willingly offered (ἐχαρίσατο) 300 drachmae to Isidora as payment for an outstanding IOU.⁴⁹

A highly unusual use of χαρίζεσθαι, with Pauline parallel, occurs in a second-century AD letter of Ammonius to Sabinus.⁵⁰ Apollinarius had been assigned as *secutor* to the staff of Valerius Pius. Accordingly, Apollinarius had then urged his son (also named Valerius) to accept a post offered him by Pius on the same staff or corps as himself. The author of the letter, Ammonius, acting as an intermediary between Apollinarius and his son, secured the assistance of Sabinus and urged him

> ... to act again in my place and urge Valerius to write to Pius, relying on my good faith (πίστει) and assurance, so that in every way you may be not only a helper in the affair but also a good pilot, restoring (χαρ[ι]ζόμενος) a son to his father.

As the editor of the text observes, the restoration envisaged by the letter is the ending of the physical separation current between the father and his son. This, of course, would happen when the son, Valerius, accepted the proffered

---

⁴⁶ *P. Mich.* II 124. Col. 2. 21. For an additional uses of χάρις in the Michigan papyri, *P. Mich.* VIII 477 (χάρις early II cent. AD); *P. Mich.* VIII 478 (χάριτος, [χ]άριν: early II cent. AD).
⁴⁷ *P. Mich.* VIII 476 (early II cent. AD).
⁴⁸ *P. Oxy.* III 610.
⁴⁹ *P. Soter.* 24. (18 September 106 AD). See also *P. Bon.* 17 (χαρίσασθ[αι]: AD 121/122); *P. Wisc.* II 48 (χαρισθέντες: II cent. AD).
⁵⁰ *P. Mich.* VIII 485.

posting of Pius. The editor also points to the parallel in Phlm 22. There Paul requests a guest room for himself in the anticipation that he 'would be restored (χαρισθήσομαι) to (Philemon) in answer to (his) prayers'.

Last we come to a series of letters which, like their inscriptional counterparts, depart from the uniformly positive valuation of χάρις.[51] In official correspondence concerning the proposed sale of persea and acacia-wood, this directive is given:

... see whether (the persea and acacia-branches) are dry and ought to be appropriated by the privy purse in accordance with the tariff, add the true value with a signed declaration and report clearly, making it your aim that nothing be concealed or done by favour (πρὸς χάρ[ιν] οἰκονομηθ[ῆναι]), knowing that you will be held accountable in any inquiry concerning the facts that remain unknown.[52]

The wider implication is plain: the disposal of χάριτες is necessarily altruistic and not open to bribery.

3.2.2. The return of gratitude

A prominent meaning of χάρις in the papyri is the return of gratitude by the beneficiary for favours dispensed. At the outset, a word of caution is apposite: many expressions of thanks employing χάρις in the papyri are little more than epistolary clichés.[53] But the intricate network of benefaction relationships in ancient society provided occasion for letter writers to express genuine thankfulness: for instance, the generous help given by a doctor to Herakleos;[54] the warm reception accorded Kastor in his negotiations with the general Apollonius;[55] or, finally, the payment of a mother's public dues, thanks to her son's generosity.[56]

Sometimes χάρις and its cognates captures the obligation of reciprocity that existed between various military officials of differing rank. In a letter to Apollonius (156 BC), the officials Barkaios and Ammonius evince gratitude (χάριν μεγάλην) for Apollonius' report regarding the 'evil-doers' who had escaped from the military guard and found asylum in the temple precincts of Sarapis. Barkaios suggests that Apollonius would do him a favour (χαριεῖ) if he continued to watch the escapees and reported any of their subsequent

---

[51] For less than positive uses of χάρις in the inscriptions, see §2.3 n.47.

[52] *P. Oxy.* IX 1188 (AD 13). Similarly, *P. Oxy.* XX 2277 (AD 13); *P. Tebt.* IV 1101 (113 BC).

[53] Examples of thanksgiving clichés: Χάριν θεοῖς (*P. Oxy.* I 113; *P. Oslo* III 155; *P. Fay.* III 124: II cent. AD). Μετὰ χάριτος (*P. Oxy.* XIV 1672: AD 37—41).

[54] *P. Ross. Georg.* V 4 (χάριταν: II cent. AD).

[55] *P. Brem.* 54 (χάριν: I cent. AD). See also *P. Brem.* 52 (χάριν: II cent. AD).

[56] *P. Mich.* VIII 510 (τῇ σῇ χάριτι: II—III cent. AD).

movements outside the right of sanctuary.⁵⁷ He promises to give to Apollonius the reward of three copper talents as an incentive. Here we see that Barkaios' discharge of gratitude affords him the opportunity to request a counter-favour from the subordinate official, Apollonius, coupled with the promise of recompense for his continuing cooperation as regards the escapees.

εὐχαριστία and its cognates feature prominently in the papyri. Thanksgiving forms part of the diplomatic parlance employed in letters of petition to superiors. In a letter of petition (AD 182) to a nomarch concerning the non-repayment of a loan, the writer concludes obsequiously in order to force the nomarch's hand: 'I shall be able through your assistance to get back my own property and to remain thankful (εὐχαριστεῖν) for ever to your fortune (τῇ τύχῃ), and that I shall obtain relief (εὐεργετη[μένος])'.⁵⁸ Babatha, in a protest-statement over the non-payment of her son's interest by his guardians, had approached Ioios Iouianos the *hegemon* for a resolution of her claim. In adopting this approach she had hoped that her 'son may manifestly come through safe (as) one giving thanks (εὐχ[αρι]στοῦντα) for the most fortunate times of the office of Ioios Iouianos *hegemon*'.⁵⁹ The suppliant role adopted by Babatha towards this official from Petra is aimed at securing his legal aid, with the extra inducement of her son's public gratitude to him.

A commonplace of the papyri is the use of εὐχαριστία for thanksgiving to the god(s) and Sarapis.⁶⁰ Most of the occurrences are epistolary clichés and tell us little about the individual piety of the letter writer. One status-conscious writer, however, displays a keen sense of gratitude and a touch of humour:

I give thanks to Sarapis and Good Fortune (εὐχαρισ[τῶ δὲ] τῷ Σαραπιδί καὶ ['Αγαθῇ] Τύχῃ) that while all are labouring the whole day through at cutting stones I as an officer move about doing nothing.⁶¹

The papyri are littered with thanksgivings — usually employing εὐχαριστεῖν — from various family members. Dionysia thanks her brother for his message that the builders had repaired her house;⁶² Teeus expresses gratitude to Aline for carrying out her father's instructions.⁶³ In the letter of

---

⁵⁷ *UPZ* I 64.

⁵⁸ *P. Fam. Tebt.* 43.

⁵⁹ *SB.* X 10288. (12 October 125 AD).

⁶⁰ τῷ θεῷ: *P. Mich.* VIII 478 (early II cent. AD). τοῖς θεοῖς: *P. Oxy.* XII 1481 (early II cent. AD); *P. Mich.* VIII 473 , 476 (early II cent. AD); *UPZ* I 59, 60 (168 BC); *SB.* XIV 11645 (I—II cent. AD), XVI 12589 (2 AD). τῷ (κυρίῳ) Σαράπιδι: *P. Mich.* VIII 492 (II cent. AD); *SB.* VI 9017 No.23 (I—II cent. AD).

⁶¹ *P. Mich.* VIII 465 (AD 107).

⁶²*P. Wash. Univ.* II 106 (13 January 18 BC): εὐχαριστῶ.

⁶³ *P. Brem.* 63: εὐχαριστ[οῦ]σα. In the same letter the father, Eudaimomis, thanks

Didyme to Apollonius, the thanksgiving is prefaced with a striking metaphor of affection:

Didyme to Apollonius her brother and sun, greetings. You know that I do not view the sun, because you are out of my view; for I have no sun but you. I am grateful (εὐχαριστῶ) to your brother Theonas.[64]

Finally, the papyri confirm the profound revulsion felt by the ancients towards the ἀχάριστοί, a feature noted in our discussion of the epistolary theorists (§3.1.3). Two letters from Dionysius to Nicanor and Pasion request the recipients to help his brother Demetrius in measuring out corn, because of his own illness. Dionysius highlights the fact that this imposition on his part merely recompenses his past generosity, and was done on behalf of one who had an appreciative character:

Dionysius to his dearest Nicanor, greetings. I request you, brother, to assist my brother Demetrius until he has measured out the corn, since I am still dangerously ill. You know that you do not give your help to an ungrateful person (ἀχαρίστῳ). I know your kindness. Good-bye, dearest. For I in my turn, when I was with you was attentive to your wishes.[65]

3.2.3. *The letter of recommendation and the disposal of favour*

In the συστατική (the letter of recommendation) the writer employed χάρις cognates to apply gentle pressure on the recipient concerning his obligation as a man of honour. The following letter of Theon (AD 25) to the *dioecetes*, Tyrannus, is typical of the approach:

Theon to his esteemed (τιμιωτάτωι) Tyrannus, many greetings. Heraclides, the bearer of this letter is my brother. I therefore entreat you with all my power to treat him as your protégé. I have also written to your brother Hermias asking him to communicate with you about him. You will confer upon me a very great favour (χαρίσαι) if Heraclides gains your notice. Before all else you have my good wishes for unbroken health and prosperity. Good-bye.[66]

(χάριν) his wife for being inseparable from their other daughter Aline. Other household examples: *P. Sarap.* 52 (εὐχαριστῶ: I cent. AD); *P. Würzb.* 21 (εὐχαριστῶ [sic]: II cent. AD). More generally, see *P. Brem* 57 (II cent. AD); *P. Oxy.* XI 396 (late I cent. AD); *P. Mich.* VIII 466 (26 March 107 AD).

[64] *P. Oxy.* XLII 3059 (II cent. AD).

[65] *P. Oxy. Hels.* 47a (II cent. AD). The letter to Pasion (47c) is almost identical: 'You know that not to an ungrateful ([ἀχαρίσ]τῳ) person ...'. In *UPZ* II 199 (20 November 131 BC), Dionysios castigates Diogenes as ungrateful (ἀχαρίστωι) for his part in the loss of 90 talents belonging to the God Amonrasonter, despite favours towards him in the past (ηὐεργετήκαμεν). See also the fragmentary reference in *P. Fouad.* 25 (ἀχαρίστων: II cent. AD).

[66] *P. Oxy.* II(2) 292. Note, too, the letter of Pellis to Antas (*SB.* XII 10790: II cent. BC): 'I also wrote to you in the first place returning thanks (εὐχαριστῶν) for Hermippos (in) that he does everything for me on your recommendation'.

The reciprocal obligation imposed by such a system is amply illustrated by the effusive terms of the second-century AD letter of Gemellus to his brother Apollinarius.[67] Both the intermediary role of the φίλος, Rullius, and the initiative of the brother are described in the standard benefaction vocabulary of the eulogistic inscriptions:

> Gemellus to Apollinarius, his most esteemed (τιμιωτάτωι) brother, greeting. Very many thanks (χάρις) to you, brother, for your care of me; your letter of recommendation (σύστασις) helped me greatly. And before that your very good friend (φίλῳ) Rullius, who knows the good will (εὔνοιαν) that you have for me, was concerned to make up for your absence; he introduced me without delay and with zeal (σπουδαίως) to Aemilianus as a kinsman of you whom he cherished. And I ask you brother, that you make acknowledgment to Rufus if you write to him ...

In similar vein, letters of request seek to exercise pressure on their recipients through the use of χάριτα and κεχαρισμένος.[68] Although this process was normally cordial, relations between the correspondent and recipient could become quite sarcastic as parties of differing social status attempted to manipulate the situation in their own favour. A letter from an unknown superior to Dorion, concerning the substitution of 25 artabas of barley for the specified grain repayment, is a case in point.[69]

> Dorion, since we could not get in touch with you because of the bombast and fear which surround you — from the start I have prayed to all the gods that in these respects you may progress further — I have been brought to the point to propose to you in writing, that if it seems good to you, you order that it be written to Ptolemaios, the scribe of the farmers, that instead of grain he accepts 25 art(abas) of barley from me because of the pressure which surrounds me this year. If you act accordingly you will be pleasing (κεχαρισμένος) to both gods and men.

The superior, acerbic tone adopted in the conventional aside — 'I have prayed to all the gods that in these respects you may progress further' — is wielded with humiliating effect in the writer's conclusion. For in acceding to the letter's request, the recipient — undoubtedly an intimidating official with an inflated sense of his own importance — acknowledges the fundamental piety of the writer's cause and prayers, in front of the gods and men alike. Here, in this papyrus, the raw nerve of the benefaction system lies exposed for all to see.

---

[67] *P. Mich.* VIII 498.

[68] κεχαρισμένος: *P. Oxy.* VII 1061 (22 BC); *P. Tebt.* III(1) 766 (136? BC); *UPZ* I 64 (156 BC); *P. Mert.* II 62 (AD 6). χάριτα: *P. Princ.* 162 (AD 89—90); *P. Bon.* 43 (I cent. AD); *P. Stras.* II 117 (I cent. AD).

[69] *P. Erasm.* I 6 (mid II cent. BC). The editor (correctly) posits that the writer is the social or professional superior of the recipient: 'the peremptory, not to say sarcastic tone points in the same direction, as do the literary echoes'. He concludes that the provocative omission of χαίρειν and the closing formula was designed to be deliberately rude.

3.2.4. Charis *and its cognates in the Jewish papyri*

Although sparse, the occurrence of χάρις and its cognates in the Jewish papyri is nonetheless revealing in that they cluster around the cult of the Caesars.[70] The letter of Claudius to the Alexandrians, which touches on hostilities between Greeks and Jews, is prefaced with this proclamation of the Caesar's beneficence:

> Since, because of its numbers, not all the populace was able to be present at the reading of the most sacred letter which is so beneficent (εὐεργετικωτάτης) to the city, I have thought it necessary to publish the letter so that each one of you may read it and wonder at the greatness of our god Caesar and be thankful (χάριν) for his goodwill (εὐνοίᾳ) towards the city.[71]

Later, Claudius personally reaffirms the traditional munificence of the Caesars towards the Alexandrians:

> ... it is also my will that all privileges which were granted (ἐχαρίσθη) to you by emperors, kings, and prefects before my time shall be confirmed, in the same way that the god Augustus confirmed them.

In a fragmentary papyrus, whose occasion is either Vespasian's acclamation of 1 July 69 AD or his visit to Alexandria, the prefect of Egypt, Tiberius Julius Alexander, praises the emperor as σωτὴρ καὶ ε[ὐεργέτης] in a speech where the protection of Augustus and the Egyptian deities is (seemingly) invoked.[72] The prefect himself is subsequently thanked ([εὐ]χαριστοῦμεν), presumably by the enthusiastic crowds. In a badly damaged speech from the 'Acts of the Alexandrian Martyrs' (AD 119–120), the Jews appeal to the beneficence of the emperor Hadrian ([αὐτο]κράτωρ, χάρις σου).[73] Last, in a papyrus from the reign of Commodus (AD 180–192), Appian asks the emperor to grant him the right of execution in his noble insignia.[74]

If these Alexandrian-based papyri are in any way representative, diaspora Judaism in imperial times was exposed to benefaction terminology through the Caesar cult. Again, as in the inscriptions, χάρις was an important

---

[70] V. Tcherikover (*CPJ* Vol.1 [Cambridge 1957], xvii-xx) points to four criteria for assigning Jewish provenance to any papyrus. See the insightful critique of P.W. van der Horst, *Ancient Jewish Epitaphs: An Introductory Survey of a Millennium of Jewish Funerary Epigraphy 300 BCE—700 CE* (Kampen 1991), 16-18. Reference has already been made to a Jewish papyrus in *P. Brem.* 63 above. Outside our time range, *CPJ* I 4 (χάρις τοῖς θεοῖς: 257 BC). For discussion of Aramaic and Hebrew epistolography, see J.A. Fitzmyer ('Some Notes on Aramaic Epistolography', *JBL* 93 [1974], 201-225) and D. Pardee ('An Overview of Ancient Hebrew Epistolography', *JBL* 97/3 [1978], 321-346).

[71] *P. Lond.* VI 1912 (*CPJ* II 153: 10 November 41 AD). For discussion, see H.I. Bell (ed.), *Jews and Christians in Egypt: The Jewish Troubles in Alexandria and the Athanasian Controversy* (London 1924).

[72] *P. Fouad.* 8 (*CPJ* II 418: end of I cent. AD).

[73] *P. Louvre* (*CPJ* II 158a).

[74] *P. Yale I.* 1536 (χάρ[ισ]αι: *CPJ* II 159b: late II cent. AD).

3.2.5. Conclusion

From this survey, how do the papyri add to our understanding of χάρις and beneficence in the period of the New Testament? First, we gain deeper insight into the role which χάρις played in the relationships of the οἶκος: for in the benefaction system the conferral of favour and the reciprocation of gratitude extended as much to the family as the *polis*. Second, two unusual occurrences of χάρις provide parallels to Paul. In the commercial papyri the free nature of grace was heavily accented, while χάρις cognates could also be applied to the restoration of people separated by distance. Third, the papyri unfold for us better than the inscriptions the great unease felt by the ancients over ingratitude. Fourth, letters of recommendation employ χάρις and its cognates to heighten the obligation of the recipient to acquiesce to the request. In contrast, letters of petition couch their requests in diplomatic parlance using εὐχαριστεῖν. However, one particular letter of request reveals the antagonism generated when people of differing social status sought to manipulate a situation in their favour. Finally, the Jewish papyri confirm the all-pervasive presence of benefaction ideology throughout diaspora Judaism by way of the Caesar cult.

We now pursue the evidence of the papyri to see whether the ethos of reciprocity not only shaped the civic life of the hellenistic *poleis* but also directed the daily routines of remote provincial village life.

3.3. Charis *and the Ethos of Reciprocity in the Papyri*

Whereas the eulogistic inscriptions publicly display in stone the return of favour required of the *polis* for its benefactors, the papyri unfold a personal dimension to ancient reciprocity not generally present in the inscriptions. To be sure, the official missives among the corpus of papyri range over familiar terrain in their careful reciprocation of benefits, as subsequent examples will demonstrate. Nevertheless, the papyri also alert us to the fact that the benefaction ethos — as expressed in reciprocity — informed both hierarchical and non-hierarchical relationships among family and friends.[75]

---

[75] In discussing household relationships, Seneca (*Ben.* 3.18-38) occasionally pictures the obligation of beneficence non-hierarchically. Whereas parents 'almost always outdo' their children in benefaction (*ibid.*, 5.5.2; cf., 6.24.1-2), children 'can sometimes bestow on their parents greater benefits than they have received from them' (3.29.1). Similarly, slaves can

In the official missives there are many echoes of the inscriptional benefaction terminology and reciprocation motifs when honour is returned to benefactors. Three examples will establish the point. A person whose name is lost requested Apollonios, *strategos* of the nome Apollonopolites Heptakomias, to accord a visiting protégé attention commensurate with his bearing in the nome. In performing this favour for (presumably) a superior in the Egyptian hierarchy, Apollonios would place both the protégé and the letter writer under the counter-obligation of thankfulness:

I ask you, (my) brother, both to deal with him generously (φι[λανθρώπως]) overall and to strive (σπουδάσαι) to see that he — having obtained the befitting recompense (τῆς προσηκούσης ἀμοιβῆς) corresponding to the example he sets in the nome under your control — might be thankful (εὐχαριστήσῃ) for his visit to you. For I will acknowledge to you the greatest thanks (χάριν) for this.[76]

In an obsequious letter to the gymnasiarch Aelius Apollonius, Hermaios tacitly acknowledges that he is unable to requite adequately his benefactor due to his inferior social status (μικρὸς μὲν ἐγώ). Faced with this very real dilemma, Hermaios leaves his benefactor's requital with the gods:

Hermaios greets the most esteemed Aelius Apollonius. Both in this and in all the rest, Lord, you supply to me the good will (εὔνοιαν) fitting for you and friendship (φιλίαν) and while I am small (μικρὸς μὲν ἐγώ) to render gratitude (χάριν) to you, the Gods will requite you (ἀμείψονται).[77]

In a fitting conclusion to the letter, Hermaios adds that he would continue to intercede for the benefactor and his family because Apollonius had secured him favour from the god (τῶι θεῶι με ἐχαρίσω) by means of a dedication ceremony.

In a fragment of another official missive, there is mention of the receipt of worthy gratitude (ἀξίαν χάριν) and the return of honour (ἀποδοῦναι τὴν τιμήν) to a benefactor by means of some appropriate memorial.[78]

Above all, in a letter from Ammonius to Apollonius (I—II cent. AD) we see most clearly the strained operation of reciprocity within the Egyptian bureaucracy and the sensitivities aroused in professional relations as individuals and groups of differing status interact with each other. Ammonius is writing to his patron (δέσποτα) and his patron's wider retinue (τοὺς ἀδελφούς) within the bureaucracy. The patron, Apollonius, has recently sent Ammonius some gifts of poor quality: inferior reeds (οὐ καλάς) and old cloaks. This has surely rankled Ammonius. The problem is further

---

benefit their masters (3.18-28).

[76] *P. Brem.* 8 (II cent. AD). Note the comment of Seneca (*Ben.* 2.22): 'He who receives a benefit with gratitude repays the first instalment on his debt'.

[77] *P. Brem.* 49 (II cent. AD).

[78] *BGU* VIII 1787 (I cent. AD).

complicated by the recent fracas among his patron's retinue. In some unspecified manner, Ammonius — or his representative(s) — had provoked internal division within the bureaucracy of the Oxyrhynchus nome over the issue of a key to the single room. Moreover, Ammonius admits that his previous letter to his patron was inelegantly worded (over the issue of the wool from Salvius or perhaps something else?) and this blunder too needed to be overlooked by his patron. Given the tense situation, the letter — reproduced in full below — affords us an intriguing insight into how a social inferior construes his obligations within the reciprocity system.

> Ammonius to Apollonius his brother, greetings. I received the crossed letter and the portmanteau and the cloaks and the reeds, not good ones — the cloaks I received not as old ones, but as better than new if that's possible, because of the spirit (in which they were given). But I don't want you, brother (ἄδελφε), to load me (βαρύνειν με) with these continual kindnesses (φιλανθρωπίαις), since I can't repay them (ἀμείψασθαι) — the only thing we suppose ourselves to have offered you is (our) feelings of friendship (προαίρεσιν φιλικῆς διαθέσεως). Please, brother (ἄδελφε), don't concern yourself further with the key of the single room: I don't want you, my brothers (τοὺς ἀδελφούς), to quarrel for my sake or for anyone else's; indeed I pray for concord (ὁμόνοιαν) and mutual affection (φιλαλλη[λ]ίαν) to maintain itself in you, so that you can be beyond the reach of gossip and not be like us: experience leads me to urge you to live at peace and not to give others a handle against you. So try and do this for my sake too — a favour to me (χαρισαμενός μοι), which in the interim you'll come to recognise as advantageous to you as well. If you've received the wool from Salvius to the full amount, and if it's satisfactory, write back to me. I wrote you silly things in my previous letter, which you'll discount: the fact is my spirit relaxes when your name is there — and this though it has no habit of tranquillity, because of its pressing troubles. Well, Leonas bears up (?). My best wishes to you, master (δέσποτα), and all your people. Good health, most honoured friend.
>
> (Address) To Apollonius ..., surveyor, his brother. [79]

How does Ammonius chart a path through this diplomatic Scylla and Charybdis? First, as regards the acceptance of inferior gifts from a patron, Ammonius construes the 'old' cloaks as 'better than new' because of the beneficent spirit in which Apollonius had given them. Clearly it is not worth insulting one's social superior. Ammonius tactfully airs the burden of being overloaded with kindnesses which he cannot repay — not only because of the inherent difficulties of the reciprocity system itself, but also perhaps to forestall any further gifts of an inferior kind from his patron. Instead, Ammonius asserts that his ethical 'choice' (προαίρεσιν) is one of 'friendly disposition' (φιλικῆς διαθέσεως). Thus, in Ammonius' view,

---

[79] *P. Oxy.* XLII 3057. For discussion, see G.W. Peterman, *op. cit.*, 80-82. The possibility that this is a Christian letter — for discussion in the scholarly literature, see *ibid.*, 81 n.91 — is highly unlikely. There are no clearly identifiable Christian papyrus letters until the III cent. AD. Moreover, the terminology used in the letter is in any case not (as has been suggested) favoured by the Christians. See also our discussion of βαρύνειν in §7.4.1 n.153.

notwithstanding the demands of the reciprocity system, a relationship of friendship (φιλία) among nominal equals would better facilitate relations in the bureaucracy.

Second, Ammonius is not backward in asking an additional favour (χαρισάμενος) of his patron. Apollonius should maintain concord (ὁμόνοιαν) and mutual affection (φιλαλλη[λ]ίαν) among his retinue in the Egyptian bureaucracy. Only in this way can Ammonius extricate himself, through his patron's favour, from the fracas which his recent actions have caused. Ammonius also cleverly appeals to the personal advantage to Apollonius in doing this.

Third, Ammonius unashamedly flatters Apollonius. Why is Ammonius so confident that he will not be held accountable for his imprudent remarks? His answer glides as smoothly as the ink over his papyrus: the very presence of his patron's name on the letter brings tranquillity to his troubled spirit. In sum, we are witnessing here the complex social tensions which the reciprocity system, as it found expression in the Egyptian bureaucracy, spawned. It is clear that Ammonius is an adept player of the system. Ammonius trades on his patron's good-will in order to extricate himself from various blunders, cajoling his patron with flattery and obsequiousness, while at the same time trying to distance himself from some of the implications of social inferiority.

Family relationships were another arena in which the conventions of reciprocity were unconsciously assumed and (no doubt) intensely felt. The letter of the soldier, Petronius Valens, to his father Ptolemaios offers us a glimpse of the pressure imposed by the reciprocity ethos within the οἶκος. Of his worthy (ἄξιος) father, Petronius prays to Sarapis 'that you live for many years until having grown up I return your kindnesses (ἀποδώσω τὰς χάριτας)'.[80] Thus the expectation within the ancient household was that the beneficence of family members ought to be acknowledged with gratitude, as the down-payment of fuller requital in the future.

Finally, H. Koskenniemi has observed that scarcely a single letter from the first century counts among the 'Freundschaftsbriefen'.[81] Admittedly, the typical φιλία motifs of care and obligation regularly occur. However, the overall quality of relationships revealed in these mundane papyri — concerned as they are with the practical issues of life — is meaningful but

---

[80] *P. Turner* 18 (AD 96—105). Note the astute observation of S.R. Llewelyn ('A Soldier's Letter Home', *New Docs* Vol.6 [1992], 157 n.176): '... it should be borne in mind that ἀποδίδωι (*sic.*) describes the reciprocal obligation required by a giver of the receiver. This is so not only in commercial transactions such as the making of loans or the giving of dowries but also in personal relationships such as in the family, as here, or among friends'.

[81] H. Koskenniemi, *op. cit.*, 120.

more or less superficial.[82] In light of this, J.L. White is accurate in classing *P. Mert.* I. 12 as a striking example of a 'literate, almost philosophical, expression of cordiality and friendship'.[83] The letter itself, addressed to Dionysios the physician, comes from a professional colleague and is datable to 29 August AD 58. The introduction moves beyond the customary epistolary clichés into an extended expression of intimate friendship:

> Chairas to his dearest (φιλτάτωι) Dionysios: many greetings and continual good health. When I received your letter, I was exceedingly joyous as if I had actually been in my own native place; for without (the joy of) that there is nothing. And I can disregard writing to you with great gratitude (εὐχαριστίας), for it is (only) required that one express thankfulness (εὐχαριστεῖν) with words to those who are not friends (φίλοις). I am confident that I can persevere with sufficient tranquillity, and if not able to render something equivalent (τὰ ἴσα), I will be able to render some humble return for your warm affection (φιλοστοργίᾳ) toward me.

This highly individual perspective, not easily assignable to any Greek theory of friendship, is remarkable for the dismissive attitude it adopts towards the expression of gratitude. The dynamics of reciprocity now makes thankfulness inappropriate among φίλοι: what matters is that they *will* somehow be recompensed, whether commensurately or not. Here φιλοστοργία amongst equals modifies two axiomatic cultural expectations built into the benefaction system. No longer is gratitude to the benefactor the first obligatory instalment on a debt; nor is it obligatory — or even necessarily desirable — to outdo the original benefit of the benefactor by way of recompense. Seneca, by contrast, says the opposite:

> ... even after I have paid my debt of gratitude, the bond between us still holds; for, just when I have finished paying it, I am obliged to begin again, and friendship endures.[84]

P. Mert. I. 12 is the closest the papyri come to a critique of the benefaction system. Whereas the benefaction system was openly appraised within first-century Judaism, Chairas' new perspective on reciprocity is implicit rather than explicit, flowing as it does from a markedly individual view of φιλία.

In our next section, we will look at how the papyri portray the beneficence of the gods and the reciprocal obligations that resulted for the divine and human realms alike.

---

[82] *Ibid.*

[83] J.L. White, *op. cit.* (1986), 145. H. Koskenniemi (*op. cit.*) points to the 'aufrichtige Freundschaft' expressed in the papyrus. For additional discussion, see G.W. Peterman, *op. cit.*, 95-97.

[84] Seneca, *Ben.* 2.18.5. Again, contrary to the letter of Chairas, Seneca (*Ben.* 6.34.5) sees the repayment of gratitude expressed in affection: 'We must look for a friend, not in a reception hall, but in the heart; there must he be admitted, there retained, and enshrined in affection. Teach a man this — and you show gratitude'.

3.4. Charis *and the Gods in the Papyri*

In a perceptive discussion of *PSI* IV 435 (258—257 BC), A. Deissmann looked at the wider conceptual grid governing relations between men and Sarapis. According to Deissmann, hellenistic religion was at heart 'a business transaction, *do ut des*, between man and a fetish'.[85] In our papyrus, Deissmann pointed out that Zoilos, a priest of the Sarapis cult, had obscured any understanding of grace by adopting precisely this approach. In this context, Deissmann argued, Paul's theological attack on works-righteousness would have been directed as much against the Gentile cults as the Judaism of his day.

Whilst Deissmann passed over clear indications elsewhere of Sarapis imparting unsolicited grace, his approach was nevertheless methodologically sound.[86] There is always the danger that in being so semantically focused we forget to ask obvious questions of the papyri. On what basis did the ancients establish and maintain a relationship with the gods? Do elements of grace still appear when χάρις terminology is either absent or (if present) purely conventional?

In a second-century AD papyrus, the writer notes that Harpebekis (the Egyptian deity, Horus-the-Hawk) had received with pleasure an offering of κῦφι, a perfume, from the addressee. After burning the perfume in the presence of the Harpebekis, the writer thanked (χάριν ἔχω) the god for

---

[85] A. Deissmann, *op. cit.*, 161. Deissmann interprets Zoilos' request of Apollonios for a Sarapeion as follows: 'Build a temple, and your influence with the king increases; if you do not build, you fall ill!'

[86] *IG* XI(4) 1299 (Delos: III—II cent. BC) affords a striking vignette of the grace of Sarapis. Demetrios, a priest of Sarapis, had received an unsolicited dream-revelation from the god to the effect that he should establish a Sarapeion. In view of the hostility of local residents and a pending civil suit, Sarapis assured Demetrios of victory in another dream. In the 'God-guided proceedings' (δίκης θεομήτιδος), Sarapis immobilised those bringing the suit by depriving them of speech. The following paean is testimony of the grace of Sarapis: '... since we have emerged as victors in the struggle in a manner worthy of God, we offer appropriate thanks (ἀξίαν χάριν ἀποδιδόντες) in our praise to the gods'. For discussion, see F.W. Danker, *Benefactor: Epigraphic Study of a Graeco-Roman and New Testament Semantic Field* (St. Louis 1982), §27. See also H. Engelmann, *The Delian Aretalogy of Sarapis* (Leiden 1975). Important too are the letters concerning the κάτοχος Hephaiston (*UPZ* I 59-60: 168 BC). He had assumed religious bondage to Sarapis in the temple at Memphis because he was grateful for his preservation from great dangers. On the κάτοχοι, see T.A. Brady, *Sarapis and Isis: Collected Essays* (Chicago 1978), 27-29; H.C. Youtie, 'The *Kline* of Sarapis', *HTR* 41 (1948), 26-27. Sometimes the inscriptions attribute human faithfulness in observing the cults to the grace of the gods. Thus Antiochus 1 of Kommagene (F.W. Danker, *op. cit.*, §42 *ll*.248-250) exhorts those who would participate in the continuing rites and ceremonies at his father's mausoleum: '... let them be assured that Zeus Oromasdes is attentive to holy petitions and graciously supports them in their contest of good works'.

confirming that the addressee would live a long time.⁸⁷ This is a case of technical divination where the smoke ascending from the altar signified the god's promise of longevity. By contrast, the Christian rendering of εὐχαριστία is a response to God's unilateral act of grace, not a manipulation of the divine favour by cultic or divinatory means.

In *P. Mich.* VIII 502 (II cent. AD) Valerius Gemellus thanks his sister Thermoutharion in the presence of the gods (εὐχαριστῶ παρὰ θεοῖς). Considerably more interesting than the routine thanksgiving formula is the way that Gemellus enlists the authority of the gods in pressing his case over his brother's absence of mail contact. At the outset, the stereotyped προσκύνημα formula is given extra force by a unique addition of Gemellus. He makes obeisance for his brother 'in the presence of the hair at Koptus'.⁸⁸ The mention of this revered relic of the goddess Isis authenticates Gemellus' piety and lifts the introduction above the level of epistolary cliché.⁸⁹ As a result, Gemellus could afford to be uncompromisingly blunt: 'I ask you to write to me, and the gods ask the same thing of you'.

Further, Gemellus contrasts his brother's singular lack of regard with his own divinely motivated concern: 'But I regard you, in the manner of a pious (δίκην) brother, as I do Sarapis'. The weight of divine authority appealed to enables Gemellus to end on a less authoritarian note. According to him, the 'candid intercourse of brothers (παρρησία τῶν ἀδελφῶν) and one's own people' was a central facet of human existence not to be spurned. In this papyrus the writer wields the authority of Sarapis and his own cultic piety in order to manipulate a sense of guilt in his brother and thereby enforce a change of attitude on his part. Any sense of the dynamics of God's grace ameliorating the situation, or effecting the mutual reconciliation of the brothers through a change of character, is conspicuously absent.

In a series of papyri (168—162/161 BC) about the sesame and kiki oil necessary for the drink offerings to Sarapis, we gain insight into the cultivation of the gods' favour. The twins, Thaues and Gaous, who served in the Sarapeion near Memphis, had written a petition to King Ptolemaios and Queen Kleopatra concerning the withholding of their oil entitlement for the Years 20 and 21.⁹⁰ The King and Queen, in an act of piety (εὐσέβεια) towards the grateful gods (οἱ εὐχάριστοι θεοί) and of care (πρόνοια) towards the twins, intervened on their behalf by restoring the oil still owing

---

⁸⁷ *P. Warren* 13.

⁸⁸ See H. Koskenniemi, *op. cit.*, 104-114 for a discussion of these formulae.

⁸⁹ Isis upon hearing of Osiris' death was said to have 'cut off one of her tresses and put on a garment of mourning in a place where the city still bears the name of Kopto'. Plutarch, *Mor.*, 356D.

⁹⁰ *UPZ* I 41.

from Year 19. The remainder of the official correspondence praises the under-*dioketes* (the chief financial official) for his assiduity in returning the outstanding oil from Years 18 and 19.[91] Each letter assures the recipient of the divine grace which flows from the fulfilment of this cultic obligation : 'For this Sarapis and Isis Anmut may now give to you favour (χάρειν) and satisfaction in regard to the King and the Queen, on account of your holy relations to the divinity'. Moreover, the official was to write Mennides the manager and secure the remaining oil for Years 20 and 21. Again the benefits ensuing from this are baldly put:

But then you should accept elegance (and) favour (χάρις) (because of the fact) that you are piously disposed towards the divinity and of the temple slaves and of the rest who are in the temple.

What picture of the grace of Sarapis emerges from this correspondence? It is singularly cultic. The gods dispense χάριτες to those who ensure that the correct drink offerings are regularly provided. Furthermore, the gods themselves are placed under obligation by correct ritual: they reciprocate with gratitude. As we saw in our discussion of the inscriptions (§2.7), this understanding of divine grace was at odds with the Christian understanding that emphasised that God exercised genuine χάρις precisely because He was *not* under obligation.

To what extent did the benefaction ideology of the Caesars impact upon traditional provincial village life as opposed to the larger urban centres of the eastern Mediterranean basin? We turn to this question in our next section.

3.5. Charis *and the Caesar Cult in the Papyri*

Three papyri from the reign of Nero contain occurrences of χάρις and its cognates, one of which is instructive for the Pauline context. In a papyrus which is (seemingly) a rough draft for an official circular or public proclamation for Nero's accession, thanks are given to the gods both for Claudius' deification and Nero's assumption of the imperial *potestas*:

The Caesar who had to pay his debt to his ancestors, god manifest, has joined them, and the expectation and hope of the world has been declared Emperor, the good genius of the world and the source of all good things, Nero, has been declared Caesar. Therefore ought we all wearing garlands and with sacrifices of oxen to give thanks (χάριτας) to all the gods.[92]

---

[91] *UPZ* I 34, 35, 36.
[92] *P. Oxy.* VII 1021 (AD 51).

In a letter to the Arsinoite nome, Egypt, the emperor Nero explains why he had refused divine honours:

(Col. 1) [---] of the remaining two (honours), your temple I decline because to the gods alone is this honour (τειμήν) to be granted rightly by men, and the gold crown I granted (χαρισθή[σεσ]θε: sic.) to be sent back to you, not wishing to burden you (ἐπειβαρε[ῖν ὑ]μᾶς) at the beginning of (my reign as) Princeps.[93]

The two foregoing papyri are typical of the benefaction rituals of the Caesar cult. In the former the gods are ritually thanked in anticipation of Nero's future benefactions whereas, in the latter, Nero demonstrates his εὐσέβεια towards the gods.

More important for our purposes is a verbal proceedings, cited below, concerning the πολιτεία of discharged soldiers (μισσικίων). There a magistrate (probably the prefect) apportions the imperial favour to the soldiers on behalf of Nero:

I have said to you before that your situation is not identical, nor similar. For certain (individuals) among you are veterans of the legions, others of the troops, others of the cavalry, others of the crews of rowers: you do not all have the same right! I will occupy myself with the question. I have written to the generals of the nome in order that the complete favour (ἡ χάρις ὁλόκληρος) may be applied to you in full, according to the right of each.[94]

What constitutes χάρις ὁλόκληρος is not precisely defined here, but it certainly included the right of the city and various other prerogatives (including honours, exemptions from liturgies, plots of land, etc). Significantly, the Christian understanding of χάρις stands in marked contrast to the approach of the imperial prefect. Whilst God's grace in Christ does not discriminate concerning the worth of its recipient, imperial χάρις observes hard and fast distinctions — 'you do not all have the same right (τὸ αὐτὸ δείκαιον)!'. As the prefect explains, the χάριτες of the veterans would be determined 'according to the right of each (κατὰ τὸ ἑκάστου δί[κα]ιον)'. Certainty of interpretation concerning the selection criteria is not possible here. But, seemingly, the status amongst the veterans differed (were they discharged or not?), and some hierarchy must have existed among the various

---

[93] SB XII 11012 (AD 55). For a discussion of ἐπιβαρεῖν and its cognates, see §7.4.1 n.153.

[94] P. Fouad. 21 (AD 63). See, too, the other papyrus record of the same event in R.K. Sherk (ed.), The Roman Empire: Augustus to Hadrian (Cambridge 1988), §67B. I have departed from the editor's translation of χάρις ὁλόκληρος ('la constitution impériale'), since it imports an unwarranted constitutional understanding into the text. The editor of SB VIII 9668 restores the same text as ἡ χάρις τοῦ κυρίου. This, of course, would provide an interesting parallel to the (almost) exclusive use of the phrase by Paul in the New Testament: Rom 16:20; 1 Cor 16:23; 2 Cor 13:13; Gal 6:18; Phil 4:23; 1 Thess 5:28; Phlm 25. If Pauline, 2 Thess 3:18; 1 Tim 1:14. Elsewhere, Rev 22:21.

forces (legions, troops, cavalry, rowers). Only those with the requisite qualifications would experience Nero's grace.

Other papyri are equally revealing. A certificate of membership for the Travelling Athletic Association, which admits the boxer Herminos, is prefaced by the texts of three imperial rescripts, including this letter of Claudius:

Letter of Claudius. [Tiberius] Claudius Caesar Augustus Germanicus Sarmaticus, Pontifex [Maximus], possessor of Tribunician authority (7th time), Consul (6th time), Imperator (18th time), Father of the Fatherland, greets the Travelling Athletic Association, which honours Herakles: in the two decrees presented simultaneously to me you testified [— —] in front of me that Gaius Iulius Antiochus, King of [Kommagene], and Iulius Polemon, King of Pontus, men (who are) my esteemed friends (τειμίοι φίλοι), were treated by you with all eagerness (σπουδῇ) and kindliness (φιλανθρωπίᾳ), at the time when they celebrating the games held by them in my name. I was pleased with you on account of your thankfulness (εὐχαριστίας) with regard to them, and I acknowledged more than wondered at the good will (εὔνοιαν) of those (men) towards myself, and (their) kindliness (φιλανθρωπίαν) in relation to you. Those who were engraving for the decrees were Diogenes, son of Mikkalos, from Antiocheia, who has only recently become the high priest of the Association, whom I (also), together with his two daughters, regarded to be worthy (ἄξιον) of the Roman citizenship, as well as Sandogenes [— — and Dion?], the son of Mikkalos, from Antiocheia. Farewell![95]

The games held in honour of the Caesars were another avenue for the dissemination of benefaction terminology, either through the imperial φίλοι who as benefactors hosted them, or through the associations of athletes who were involved in them. The standard vocabulary of the eulogistic inscriptions marks the letter of Claudius to the Travelling Athletic Association, cited above. Reciprocity occurs in the exchange between the imperial φίλοι and the association. The imperial φίλοι had exercised φιλανθρωπία towards the association; conversely, the Travelling Athletic Association had responded with appropriate σπουδή, φιλανθρωπία, and εὐχαριστία to their host benefactors. Moreover, as φίλοι of the Caesars, Antiochus and Polemon — client-kings of Kommagene and Pontus — were well aware that they owed their independent states to the provincial policy of Claudius.[96] Thus the games themselves were an act of reciprocation on the part of both client-kings to Claudius, designed to cultivate εὔνοια between Rome and their own kingdoms. This was not without the desired effect, as gauged by Claudius' measured response: 'I acknowledged more than wondered at the good will (εὔνοιαν) of those (men) towards myself'.

Last, in two petitions to Septimius Severus and Caracalla, several villages from the Oxyrhynchite nome had requested benefaction of each of the emperors, because of the burdensome nature of the annual λειτουργίαι.

---

[95] *Pap. Agon.* 6 (22 September 194 AD).
[96] See B. Levick, *Claudius* (London 1990), 165-166.

Their proposal was that a benefaction should be made to each village for the purchase of hay, the revenue of which could maintain those subject to λειτουργίαι. The emperors responded in typical benefaction parlance:

> We approve of this benefaction (ἐπιδόσεως) also which you request leave to confer upon the villages of the Oxyrhynchite nome, giving (to different persons) a succession in the enjoyment of it (?) (ἀποδιδοὺς ἀμοιβὴν ἐνκτήσεως). The same rule shall be observed in this case also, and, as you wish, no change shall be introduced which would divert the gift (χάριν) to any other purpose.[97]

In conclusion, the papyri — and the isolated provincial villages they individually represent — exhibit considerable familiarity with benefaction terminology and its motifs. Further, the occasions for the dissemination of benefaction terminology are varied: the accession of a new emperor; the games in honour of the Caesars; various imperial gifts to temples; questions concerning πολιτεία or λειτουργίαι; the interaction of the associations with the Caesars or client kings. There is a surprising complexity in all of these relationships, in spite of the provincial status of the papyrological evidence. Most significantly, χάρις continues to be the central description of imperial beneficence and in one instance afforded a telling contrast to the non-discriminatory approach of the early Christians.

Finally, we turn to the practitioners in the spiritual underworld of antiquity to see how χάριτες were mediated to the interested enquirer.

3.6. Charis *in the Magical Papyri*

Given that the magical papyri largely postdate the third century AD, some justification is perhaps required for proceeding to an investigation of the role of χάρις in this shadowy subculture of the ancient world. First, as D.E. Aune and A.D. Nock argue, the essential formulae of Graeco-Egyptian magic had started to take shape by the New Testament era.[98] This is confirmed by Luke's strong anti-magical polemic in Acts.[99] Undoubtedly, there existed in

---

[97] *P. Oxy.* IV 705 (AD 200—202).

[98] D.E. Aune, 'The Apocalypse of John and Graeco-Roman Revelatory Magic', *NTS* 33/4 (1987), 483; A.D. Nock, 'Greek Magical Papyri', in *id.*, *Essays on Religion and the Ancient World* Vol.1 (Oxford, 1972), 187. On the concern of magicians to preserve their traditions, see H.D. Betz, 'The Formation of Authoritative Tradition in the Greek Magical Papyri', in B.F. Meyer and E.P. Sanders (eds), *Jewish and Christian Self-Definition. Vol.3. Self-Definition in the Graeco-Roman World* (London 1982), 161-170.

[99] For Luke's anti-magical polemic, see Acts 8:14ff; 13:4ff; 19:19. For discussion, S.R. Garrett, *The Demise of the Devil: Magic and the Demonic in Luke's Writings* (Minneapolis 1989). For excellent discussions of magic and early Christianity, see D.E. Aune, 'Magic in Early Christianity', *ANRW* II 23/2 (1980), 1507-1557; S. Benko, *Pagan Rome and the Early*

the Pauline house-churches converts who had dabbled in the magical arts prior to their conversion, and who needed substantial reorientation as to the nature of the χάρις that Christ dispensed.[100]

Second, G.P. Wetter has pointed out that the magical papyri employed χάρις in conjunction with words such as δύναμις, πνεῦμα, νίκη, τύχη, and πρᾶξις.[101] Practitioners of magic, in summoning the help of supernatural or demonic forces, used this terminology to describe the powers available to the occult enquirer.

Modern scholars have legitimately criticised Wetter's contention that a *higher* religious and mystical sense of χάρις trickled from the magical circles into other first-century religious groups. In Wetter's view, the result was that a less debased view of χάρις eventually flowed into mainstream Christianity.[102] While Wetter's arguments were highly speculative at this juncture, he was nonetheless justified in drawing scholarly attention to the widespread dissemination of χάρις and its cognates among the devotees of magic in the early empire:

... die Amulette sich in der Kaiserzeit mit jedem Tag mehrten, und die Zauberbücher in diesen Zeiten zu Tausenden haben existieren müssen.[103]

Wetter may have come up with less controversial conclusions if he had paid greater attention to the traces of benefaction terminology and motifs found in the magical papyri. Intriguingly, in the eastern Mediterranean basin where magic was viewed as a shadowy and dangerous alternative to authorised religion,[104] the quest for χάρις continued unabated on all fronts — whether it be through the traditional sacrificial cults or via the unauthorised magical rites. Magic, therefore, represented an unabashed attempt to manipulate the underworld deities into providing far-ranging χάριτες, independent of the traditional benefaction system and its reciprocal obligations.[105] It will be

---

Christians (London 1985), 103-139.

[100] See the insightful discussion of C.E. Arnold, *Ephesians: Power and Magic. The Concept of Power in Ephesians in Light of its Historical Setting* (Grand Rapids 1992).

[101] G.P. Wetter, *op. cit.*, 130-137. For examples, see *PGM* IV 197 (δυνάμωσον, χάριν), 1615-1616 (δοξάν, τιμήν, χάριν, τύχην, δύναμιν); XII 105 (χάριν, πρᾶξιν), 271 (χάριν, νίκην); XXV 26 (χάριν, νίκην, δύναμιν, πνεῦματον: cf. *ll*.16, 24); XXXVI 225 (δύναμιν, χάριν).

[102] See W. Manson, 'Grace in the New Testament', in W.T. Whitely (ed.), *The Doctrine of Grace* (London 1932), 39-40; R.F. Surburg, 'Pauline *Charis*: A Philological, Exegetical, and Dogmatical Study', *CTM* 29/10 (1958), 729.

[103] G.P. Wetter, *op. cit.*, 130.

[104] See in this regard the helpful observation of M. Mauss in §1.3.1 n.66.

[105] The technical term χαριτήσιον — a 'spell to gain favour' (e.g., *PGM* XXXVI 35, 275; LXX 1) — points to the benefaction ideology informing many of the magical papyri. For a discussion of the terms of classification in the magical papyri, see H.D. Betz, *art. cit.*, 168.

interesting in this regard to see whether Paul's use of χάρις in Ephesians was intended to counter the pervasive influence of magic throughout Asia Minor as well as in Ephesus itself (§6.1.3.1).

3.6.1. Charis *and beneficence in the magical papyri*

At several places in the magical papyri, the beneficent role of the underworld deities is presented in terms reminiscent of the eulogistic inscriptions. In a love spell of Astrapsoukos, Hermes is summoned as the cosmic Benefactor to make earthly benefactors unreservedly generous:

> ... serve well, benefactor (εὐεργέτησον) of the world. Open up for me the hands of everyone who [dispenses gifts] and compel them to give (χάρισόν) me what they have in their hands.[106]

Throughout this entire papyrus Hermes is regarded as the source of favour (χάριν) and of the trappings of social success.[107] Even Isis had invoked Hermes against her enemies ('gods, and men and daemons, creatures of water and earth') and subsequently experienced the victory of his favour (χάριν).

In the magical papyri many other underworld deities were eulogised in the traditional benefaction parlance. The epithets 'delight' (χάρις) or 'protector' (πρόστατις) were applied to the deities,[108] as were 'benefactors (εὐεργέται) of every race' and 'benevolent assistants in this rite'.[109] A lofty sample of this approach is found in a spell designed to establish a relationship with Helios:

> We give you thanks ([χ]άριν) with every soul and heart stretched out to [you], unutterable name honoured (τετιμημένον) with [the] appellation of god and blessed with the [appellation of father], for to everyone and to everything you have shown fatherly goodwill (πατρικὴν [εὔ]νοιαν) affection, friendship (φιλίαν) and sweetest power, granting (χαρισάμενος) us intellect, [speech], and knowledge.[110]

Further echoes of the eulogistic inscriptions occur when beneficence is requested of the underworld deities: 'safety' (σωτηρία), 'honour' (εὐδοξία), and 'grace' (χάρις) are provided,[111] as well as 'glory and favour' (δόξα καὶ χάρις).[112]

Inscriptional reciprocity terminology also appears in the magical papyri. In an untitled charm, Demetria conjures daemons to acquire power over her

---

[106] *PGM* VIII 16-20.

[107] *Ibid.*, 5, 26, 36.

[108] *PGM* VII 699.

[109] *PGM* XII 225, 226-227.

[110] *PGM* III 591-596. The syncretistic prayer of Jacob recalls God's generous grant of the kingdom of Israel to Abraham and his stock (*PGM* XXIIb 6, 20 [ἐχαρίσατο, χαριζομένων]).

[111] *PGM* III 580.

[112] *PGM* IV 1650.

lover, Nilos. The lover, it is claimed, would reciprocate the gods' favours (ἀποδώσεις τὰς χάριτας) by being eternally affectionate towards Demetria.[113]

Finally, H.D. Betz has summed up the widespread availability of χάριτες in the magical papyri thus:

> The underworld deities, the demons and the spirits of the dead, are constantly and unscrupulously invoked and exploited as the most important means for achieving the goals of human life on earth: the acquisition of love, wealth, health, fame, knowledge of the future, control over other persons, and so forth.[114]

A few examples will suffice to illustrate the tenor of the evidence. A victory charm promises 'success, charm, reputation (δόξαν), glory (χάριν) in the stadium'.[115] A spell for favour concludes with a strong sense of the daemon's presence and material blessing:

> Give me all favour, all success (πρᾶξιν), for the angel bringing good, who stands beside [the goddess] Tyche, is with you. Accordingly, give profit [and] success (πρᾶξιν) to this house. Please, Aion, ruler of hope, giver of wealth, O holy Agathos Daemon, bring to fulfilment all favours (χάριτας) and your divine oracles.[116]

Love spells of attraction, however, can often be uncompromisingly chauvinistic:

> ... attract her to me, beneath my feet, melting with passionate desire at every hour of the day and night, always remembering me while she is eating, drinking, working, conversing, sleeping, dreaming, having an orgasm in her dreams, until she is scourged by you and comes desiring me, with her hands full, with a generous soul and graciously giving (χαριζομένη) me both herself and her possessions and fulfilling what is appropriate for women in regard to men.[117]

More circumspectly, a stele of Aphrodite — to be engraved in triangular shape on a tin plate — offers 'friendship (φιλίαν), favour (χάριν), success, and friends (φίλους)'.[118] The spell belonging to a love charm, recited over olive oil, describes the oil as 'the mucus of Isis, the utterance of Helios, the power (δύναμις) of Osiris, the favour of the gods (χάρις τῶν [θεῶν])'.[119]

---

[113] *PGM* XV 8.

[114] H.D. Betz (ed.), *The Greek Magical Papyri in Translation, Including the Demotic Spells* Vol.1 (Chicago and London 1986), xlvii.

[115] *PGM* VII 391-392.

[116] *PGM* IV 3165-3170.

[117] *PGM* XVIIa 8-20.

[118] *PGM* VII 215-216. For other examples, see *PGM* XII 69; XXIIa 20; LII 17.

[119] *PGM* LXI 9. See the discussion of H.I. Bell and A.D. Nock (eds), *Magical Texts from a Bilingual Papyrus in the British Museum* (London 1932). See too R.W. Daniel and F. Maltimi (eds), *Supplementum Magicum* Vol. II (Opladen 1992), §63 (early III AD):

> If on account of you all beings fear your name, your great might, give me the good things: the strength of Akryskylos (?), the intelligence of Euonos, the radiance of Solomon, the voice of Abrasax, the grace (τὴν χάριν) of the god Adonis (?). Hither to

Of particular interest, too, is the fact that χάρις had acquired the status of *vox magica* in the magical papyri.[120] These often untranslatable and incomprehensible magical names were recited by magicians to effect their spell. This more than anything else highlights the 'pneumatic' power that had been accorded χάρις by practitioners in magic. It also illustrates the considerable care which Paul may have had to exercise in teaching recent converts about the liberation from magic effected by the grace of Christ. There could be no room for confusion between the two.

3.6.2. Thanksgiving in the magical papyri

The majority of thanksgivings in the magical papyri cluster around the appearance or the departure of the underworld deity. The appearance of the deity is (at times) greeted with a rapturous response that borders on the lyrical. In a spell to summon Apollonius of Tyana's old serving woman, the goddess — Nephthys, sister of Isis — appears in response to the *voces magicae*:

> ... you will behold sitting on an ass a woman of extraordinary loveliness, possessing a heavenly beauty, indescribably fair and youthful. As soon as you see her, make obeisance and say: 'I thank (εὐχαριστῶ) [you], lady for appearing to me. Judge me worthy (ἀξίον) of you. May your Majesty be well disposed to me. And accomplish whatever task I impose on you'.[121]

Again, in the following example, the emphasis falls simultaneously on the Otherness of the divine visitor and the worthiness of the grateful host:

> Now when the god comes in do not stare at his face, but look at his feet while beseeching him ... and giving thanks (εὐχαριστῶν) that he did not treat you contemptuously, but you were thought worthy of the things about to be said for your correction of your life.[122]

There was also room for thanksgiving for the knowledge imparted or for the fatherly benefactions of the deity.[123] In a magico-medical recipe for bloody flux, a pan of coals had to be thrown on the altar should the patient show ingratitude (ἀχαριστήσαντος).[124]

---

me, Kypris, every day of (my) life. If your hidden name has granted favour (ἐχάρισεν), *thoathoêthatoouthaethôystoaithithêthointhô*, give me victory, repute (δόξαν), beauty before all men and before all women'. Note, too, the (Jewish or syncretistic?) silver amulet (*ibid*, §64 [II-III AD]: '*aeêiouô iaô - - - Adônaie Sabaôth*, give favour (χάριν), love, success, charm to the wearer of this amulet.

[120] *PGM* VII 386.
[121] *PGM* XIa 12-16.
[122] *PGM* XIII 705-708.
[123] *PGM* III 601-602; III 591-596.
[124] *PGM* XXII 5-6.

Last, the departure of the god also occasioned thankfulness, as several examples in the magical papyri amply demonstrate.[125]

3.6.3. Conclusion

By the first century AD the magical papyri had appropriated a spread of benefaction terminology in the quest of its practitioners to secure χάριτες and δύναμις outside of the benefaction system. χάρις was a central term in this whole process, and had acquired the independent pneumatic status of *vox magica*. Early Christians competed against this shadowy subculture in their proclamation of God's χάρις and in the promise of the continuing endowment of Christ's pneumatic power.

3.7. Conclusion

The papyri have substantially contributed to our understanding of χάρις. At a literary level, the epistolary theorists stripped back the polite veneer of the eulogistic inscriptions, revealing a darker side to the social reality behind the benefaction system. This was later confirmed at a papyrological level in our discussion of one particularly acerbic letter of request, and in the profound sense of unease generated by the ἀχάριστοί throughout the papyri.

The papyri themselves unearthed several novel uses of χάρις and its cognates that may have contributed to the New Testament context. For instance, the bestowal of χάρις could be 'unalterable', or 'free' of charge; and the reconciliation of those separated by distance was embraced by the use of χαρίζεσθαι. The return of gratitude operates conventionally within the papyri. However, the papyri provide us with the salutary reminder that the obligation of reciprocity extended as much to the mundane relationships of the οἶκος as to the sphere of civic benefaction. A striking letter of friendship (*P. Mert.* I. 12) is the closest the papyri come to providing a critique of the ethos of reciprocity.

The Jewish papyri point to the pervasiveness of benefaction terminology and motifs within a Jewish milieu. Our next chapter on χάρις in its Jewish context will confirm this impression. The Greek papyri — and the provincial backwaters they represent — were deeply imbued with a strong understanding of benefaction ideology and its rituals through the Caesar cult. In one case, the Christian understanding of χάρις differed markedly from the discriminatory approach adopted by Nero's prefect.

---

[125] *PGM* III 195, 260; IV 1061-1062; LXII 37-39.

Last, the bestowal of grace by the deity Sarapis was singularly cultic, and the gods were placed under counter-obligation through correct ritual. A transfer of benefaction terminology and its allied status occurred in the magical papyri. Whereas χάριτες were normally dispensed through civic benefactors or the public cults, χάρις — a word of pneumatic power — was now also the preserve of magicians and their underworld deities.

Chapter 4

The Role of *Charis* in First-Century Judaism

4.1. Grace and First-Century Judaism Post E.P. Sanders

4.1.1. E.P. Sanders and the 'new perspective' on Paul: situating grace in its Jewish context

Any discussion of grace within first-century Judaism cannot ignore the Copernican revolution brought about at a theological and historical level by E.P. Sanders' *Paul and Palestinian Judaism*.[1] Sanders argues that 'covenantal nomism' was the soteriological pattern of Tannaitic Judaism, the Dead Sea Scrolls, and the Apocrypha and Pseudepigrapha.[2] In selecting the term 'covenantal nomism', Sanders is emphasising the priority of Israel's election and the centrality of the Covenant of grace. Israel's obedience to the Torah was not a merit-earning exercise but simply the way that the righteous responded to the salvation of a merciful God. In the view of Sanders, first-

---

[1] E.P. Sanders, *Paul and Palestinian Judaism: A Comparison of Patterns of Religion* (London 1977). See also *id.*, 'Patterns of Religion in Paul and Rabbinic Judaism: A Holistic Method of Comparison', *HTR* 66/4 (1973), 455-478; *id.*, 'The Covenant as a Soteriological Category and the Nature of Salvation in Palestinian and Hellenistic Judaism', in R. Hamerton-Kelly and R. Scroggs (eds), *Jews, Greeks and Christians: Cultures in Late Antiquity. Essays in Honour of William David Davies* (Leiden 1976), 11-44; *id.*, *Paul, the Law, and the Jewish People* (Philadelphia 1983); *id.*, *Judaism: Practice and Belief 63 BCE—66 CE* (Philadelphia 1992), 275-278. D.A. Hagner ('Paul and Judaism. The Jewish Matrix of Early Christianity: Issues in the Current Debate', *Bulletin for Biblical Research* 3 [1993], 111-112) correctly observes that an earlier generation of scholars (e.g. C.G. Montefiore, G.F. Moore, R.T. Herford, S. Schechter) had anticipated Sanders' thesis. For a revised version of Hagnar's essay, see P. Stuhlmacher, *A Challenge to the New Perspective: Revisiting Paul's Doctrine of Justification With an Essay by Donald Hagnar* (Downers Grove 2001), 75-105. In using the term 'Judaism', I am not denying the diversity of first-century Judaism. The use of the plural 'Judaisms' by modern scholars, while conceptually helpful, overlooks the fact that ’Ιουδαϊσμός never appears in the plural in antiquity (Gal 1:14; 2 Macc 2:21; 8:1; 14:38; 4 Macc 4:26). Clearly Jewish writers were convinced that — notwithstanding their differences of opinion over praxis and belief — there remained one Judaism. See W.D. Davies' critique ('Reflections on the Nature of Judaism', *RHPR* 75/1 [1995], 85-111) of J. Neusner's insistence on a multiplicity of Judaisms. Davies argues that the grace of God is at the centre of the heart of Judaism.

[2] *Id., op. cit.* (1977), 33-428.

century Judaism and Paul agreed that entrance into the covenantal community was inaugurated by grace and maintained by obedience to the Torah.[3] What differentiated Paul from the Judaism of his day were the specifics of how one entered the covenantal community.

In this regard, Sanders proposes that Paul's critique of Judaism and the Torah is christologically motivated. Paul focused on the shift of the covenant brought about by the coming of Christ. Consequently, although first-century Judaism acknowledged the historical priority of divine grace, it rejected Paul's emphasis on the primacy of Christ as the universal Lord and sole Saviour.[4] Thus the Lutheran stereotype of Judaism as a religion of legalistic works-righteousness is misconceived. The real point of contention for Judaism was the exclusivism of Paul's claims about Christ, not a concern over his (alleged) antinomianism (cf. Rom 3:8; 6:1-2; Gal 1:10). In the words of Sanders, 'the Judaism of before 70 kept grace and works in the right perspective, did not trivialise the commandments of God and was not especially marked by hypocrisy'.[5]

In a subsequent work, Sanders adds a further strut to the framework of his argument. He asserts that Jewish particularism — seen in the membership requirements of circumcision and acceptance of the Torah — socially isolated the Gentiles and placed the Jews in a position of privilege.[6] Thus Paul's debate about the law in Galatians 3 and Romans 3-4 was essentially 'an inner-Christian one', aimed at Jewish-Christian opponents who wanted to maintain 'Jewish exclusivism and privilege'.[7]

While J.D.G. Dunn is critical of Sanders' portrait of Paul, he expands upon the theme of the particularism of the Jewish Law.[8] In Dunn's view, Paul's

---

[3] *Ibid.*, 515-518. For our disagreement with Sanders on this issue, see §6.1.2.5 n.117.

[4] *Ibid.*, 442-447, 511-515, 549-552. Similarly, *id., op. cit.* (1983), 157. Similarly, W. Wrede (*Paul* [Boston 1908], 125): 'The real distinctive note was simply belief in Jesus Christ. Here we have the source of the formula, *not the Law with its works, but faith*'. Original emphasis.

[5] *Id., op. cit.* (1977), 427.

[6] *Id., op. cit.* (1983), 155: 'When (Paul) criticises Judaism, he does so in a sweeping manner, and the criticism has two focuses: the lack of faith in Christ and the lack of equality for the Gentiles'.

[7] *Id., op. cit.* (1983), 159-160.

[8] J.D.G. Dunn's series of articles ('The Incident at Antioch [Gal 2:1-18]'; 'The New Perspective on Paul'; 'Works of the Law and the Curse of the Law [Gal 3:10-14]') are collected in *id., Jesus, Paul, and the Law: Studies in Mark and Galatians* (Louisville 1990), Chapters 6-8 (129-241). Additionally, *id., The Partings of the Ways: Between Christianity and Judaism and Their Significance for the Character of Christianity* (London 1991), 117-139; *id.*, 'The Justice of God: A Renewed Perspective on Justification by Faith', *JTS* 43 (1992), 1-22. The earlier article of N.T. Wright ('The Paul of History and the Apostle of Faith', *TynBul* 29 [1978], 61-88) anticipates the views of Dunn. Similarly, K. Stendahl,

rejection of justification by the 'works of the law' was primarily directed against a nationalistic understanding of the Jewish identity and boundary makers (circumcision, food laws, observance of the Sabbath etc). The covenantal grace of God, extended to the Gentiles through justification by faith, was no longer confined to those who maintained an *exclusively* Jewish righteousness. The viewpoint of the Protestant Reformation that justification by 'works of the law' referred to 'meritorious good works' ignores Paul's first-century social context and misinterprets what he is arguing against.

In stating his position, Dunn does not restrict his understanding of the 'works of the law' entirely to the Jewish identity and boundary markers. The 'works of the law' includes the full-orbed obedience — moral and ceremonial — demanded by the entirety of the law, but with a *special* focus on those requirements that mark the distinctiveness of Israel's identity.[9] Furthermore, in response to Cranfield's criticisms,[10] Dunn argues that Paul is attacking *both* Jewish disobedience to the law and Jewish ethnocentrism regarding the law.[11] Ultimately, however, Paul's emphasis lies on the latter in his attack upon the law. Thus, in Dunn's view, Paul's critique of Judaism has a much greater depth and subtlety to it than merely (as Sanders argues) the covenantal shift brought about by Christ's advent.[12]

Historians of Judaism and New Testament theologians have reacted vigorously to (what is dubbed by J.D.G. Dunn) the 'New Perspective' on

---

Paul among Jews and Gentiles (London 1977). More recently, B.W. Longenecker (*Eschatology and the Covenant: A Comparison of 4 Ezra and Romans 1-11* [Sheffield 1991], *passim*) has argued that both Paul and the author of 4 Ezra oppose a Jewish ethnocentrism and re-evaluate the covenant from their respective eschatological viewpoints. For a presentation of N.T. Wright's views and a helpful critique of his position regarding grace, see G. Bray, 'Justification: The Reformers and Recent Scholarship', *Churchman* 109/2 (1995), 102-126; R. Smith, 'Justification in "The New Perspective on Paul"', *Reformed Theological Review* 58/1 (1999), 16-30, esp. 25-29; *id.*, 'A Critique of the "New Perspective" on Justification', *ibid.* 58/2 (1999), 98-113.

[9] J.D.G. Dunn, 'Works of the Law and the Curse of the Law (Gal 3:10-14)', in *id., op. cit.* (1990), 223.

[10] C.E.B. Cranfield, '"The Works of the Law" in the Epistle to the Romans', *JSNT* 43 (1991), 89-101.

[11] J.D.G. Dunn, 'Yet Once More — "The Works of the Law": A Response', *JSNT* 46 (1992), 108-109, 111, 116; *id., art. cit.* (1992), 11-12. For recent discussion of the issue, see B. Eastman, *The Significance of Grace in the Letters of Paul* (New York 1999), *passim*; J.C. de Roo, 'The Concept of "Works of the Law" in Jewish and Christian Literature', in S.E. Porter and B.W.R. Pearson (eds), *Christian-Jewish Relations through the Centuries* (Sheffield 2000), 116-147.

[12] J.D.G. Dunn ('The New Perspective on Paul', in *id., op. cit.* [1990], 187) memorably sums up his objection to Sanders' portrait of Paul in this way: 'The Lutheran Paul has been replaced by an idiosyncratic Paul who in arbitrary and irrational manner turns his face against the glory and greatness of Judaism's covenant theology and abandons Judaism simply because it is not Christianity'.

Paul.[13] Sanders' contention that Judaism was not 'legalistic' is widely accepted by most New Testament scholars today, as is his description of its soteriology as 'covenantal nomism'. But, as we will see, some scholars still claim that traces of a merit theology remain embedded in the strata of Judaism.[14]

Much ink has been spilt in rebutting Sanders' and Dunn's construction of Pauline theology. Positively, scholars readily acknowledge the contribution of Sanders and Dunn in opening up the social dimension of justification by faith. Negatively, there is unease whether the christological and social paradigms of the 'New Perspective' account for Paul's critique of the Torah, his view of human nature, and several of his central theological emphases. While I endorse some of these reservations, each side of the debate has unnecessarily polarised the portrayal of grace in Judaism and in Paul (§4.1.2). There were variegated understandings of grace within Palestinian and Diaspora Judaism. Paul himself approached the issue from several vantage points.

But my overall objection to the approach of Sanders and Dunn lies elsewhere. Any discussion of Pauline χάρις from a Jewish viewpoint should investigate the word in its first-century benefaction context. It is unwise to assume that the Hebraic background of grace was determinative for Greek-speaking Jews — let alone for Paul's Gentile converts. As J. Barr has perceptively commented in a much earlier context,

> It could be argued that this emphasis upon the Hebraic background of ideas may indeed have been present in the minds of instructed Jews like St. Paul, but that the words which had this series of associations for him would for the most part be *understood* by Gentile Christian readers, especially by the less instructed among them, in the normal hellenistic sense of the words.[15]

In this chapter, I will argue that the Old Testament understanding of covenantal grace as unilateral (§4.3 n.80) had been compromised in some

---

[13] For critical reviews of Sanders by scholars on Judaism, see J. Neusner, 'Comparing Judaisms', *HR* 18 (1978), 178-191; J.M. Charlesworth, *The Old Testament and the New Testament: Prolegomena for the Study of Christian Origins* (Cambridge 1985), 47-55. Among the many theological responses to Sanders and Dunn, see (along with the literature cited) R.H. Gundry, 'Grace, Works, and Staying Saved in Paul', *Bib* 66/1 (1985), 1-38; S. Westerholm, *Israel's Law and the Church's Faith: Paul and His Recent Interpreters* (Grand Rapids 1988); M. Silva, 'The Law and Christianity: Dunn's New Synthesis', *WTJ* 53/2 (1991), 339-353; T.R. Schreiner, *The Law and Its Fulfilment: A Pauline Theology of Law* (Grand Rapids 1993); R. Smith, *art. cit* (58/1, 58/2).

[14] See especially the recent collection of essays in D.A. Carson (*et al..* ed.), *Justification and Variegated Nomism. Volume 1 — The Complexities of Second Temple Judaism* (Tübingen 2001).

[15] J. Barr, *The Semantics of Biblical Language* (London 1961), 250. Original emphasis. Similarly, J.L. White, *The Apostle of God: Paul and the Promise of Abraham* (Peabody 1999), 57-59.

circles by hellenistic reciprocity ideology.[16] In responding evangelistically and pastorally to Jewish *and* Graeco-Roman views of grace (§1.3.2), Paul may well have encountered similar attitudes to beneficence. Paul's doctrine of grace, therefore, operated on more than one cultural front. It is overly simplistic to mirror-read the type of Judaism that Paul attacks from his letters and then look for a corresponding 'fall-guy' in the Jewish literature. Paul styles his Jewish-Christian opponents in his own way and for his own purposes. What we require is a full-orbed presentation of grace in the Greek literary and documentary evidence of Judaism. Then we will more accurately locate Paul's view of grace in its Jewish context without unfairly stereotyping Judaism or unnecessarily idealising it.

4.1.2. The 'new perspective': an adequate portrayal of Judaism and Paul?

The contention of Sanders that Judaism adhered to the priority of covenantal grace has by no means commanded the universal assent of New Testament scholars. D.A. Hagner, for example, argues that legalism still influenced the practises of Judaism in spite of its doctrinal commitment to grace. The reason, in his view, is that the overwhelming detail of rabbinic legal commentary tended to obscure its covenantal framework.[17] While such observations may well be true, I suspect that for some exegetes they acquire the status of dogmatic axioms. The New Testament historian, however, must demonstrate from the literature of Greek-speaking Judaism and the Tannaim that the Old Testament covenantal perspective *was* in fact partially or progressively abandoned.[18] Thus, in discussing χάρις in this chapter, we will highlight any departures from the Old Testament portrayal of God's grace as unilateral and covenantal.

---

[16] P. Spilsbury ('Josephus', in D.A. Carson [*et al.*, ed.], *op. cit.*, 249-252) argues that Josephus unveils a hellenistic portrait of God entering into a reciprocal client-patron relationship with Israel instead of (as Sanders alleges) 'covenantal nomism'. See also P. Spilbury's more extensive discussion of the issue in *id.*, 'God and Israel in Josephus: A Patron-Client Relationship', in S. Mason (ed.), *Understanding Josephus: Seven Perspectives* (Sheffield 1998), 172-191. For our discussion of Josephus' patronal portrait of God, see §4.5.1.

[17] See D.A. Hagnar, 'Salvation, Faith, Works', *The Reformed Journal* 29/4 (1979), 26; *id.*, *art. cit.*, 117-119. See also R.H. Gundry, *art. cit.*, 6-7; M.A. Seifrid, *Justification by Faith: The Origin and Development of a Central Pauline Theme* (Leiden-New York-Köln 1992), 56-57; T.R. Schreiner, *op. cit.*, 114-121.

[18] T. Laato (*Paul and Judaism: An Anthropological Approach* [Atlanta 1995]) is a sound example of the approach required. He charts from the intertestamental and rabbinic literature how Judaism embraced an optimistic anthropology in its concentration on human free will (*ibid.*, 67-75). The synergistic approach of Judaism, Laato argues, stands in contrast to Paul who, because of his pessimistic anthropology of human depravity (*ibid.*, 75-146), emphasised salvation by grace alone (*ibid.*, 147-168). Similarly, B. Eastman (*op. cit.*, 214).

Sanders' handling of the issue of merit in Judaism continues to provoke scholarly comment. D.A. Carson criticises Sanders for playing down the merit theology present in the literature of Judaism.[19] B. Byrne argues that the (so-called) 'works-righteousness' of 4 *Ezra* is replicated in 2 *Baruch*.[20] C.A. Evans observes that in the *Life of Adam and Eve* the forgiveness of sin was as much conditioned by vigorous repentance as divine grace.[21] According to M. Silva, the atoning value ascribed to almsgiving in Judaism represents 'a fairly blatant view of self-salvation'.[22] Again, while I agree to some degree with these comments, there remains the danger of historical overstatement because of the various theological agendas of each side of the debate.[23] To cite one

---

[19] D.A. Carson, *Divine Sovereignty and Human Responsibility: Biblical Perspectives in Tension* (Atlanta 1981), 50-54, 69, 71-72, 84-93, 111-112; *id.*, 'Divine Sovereignty and Human Responsibility in Philo', *NovT* 23/2 (1981), 162-163.

[20] B. Byrne, *'Sons of God' — 'Seed of Abraham'* (Rome 1979), 230. Scholars disagree as to whether a merit theology exists in these works and, if it does, what is its extent. For example, M.A. Seifrid (*op. cit.*, 133-135) is confident that 4 *Ezra* retains a covenantal framework. But R. Bauckham ('Apocalypses', in D.A. Carson [*et al.*, ed.], *op. cit.*, 174), like B. Byrne, posits the presence of a merit theology in 4 *Ezra*: 'the emphasis is overwhelmingly on meriting salvation by works of obedience to the Law, with the result that human achievement takes center-stage and God's grace, while presupposed, is effectively marginalised'. Similarly, in the case of 2 *Baruch*, Bauckham (*ibid.*, 182) argues that the writer encourages a 'renewed adherence to the Law which, along with God's mercy, would ensure salvation'. Alternatively, D.E. Gowan ('Wisdom', in D.A. Carson [*et al.*, ed.], *op. cit.*, 223-224) views this simply as a case of the Old Testament balance between divine initiative and human responsibility. It would seem, then, that for some scholars the presence of covenantal motifs is decisive in gauging the presence of a theology of grace in a writer's work, whereas for other scholars it is the overall emphasis of Law and covenantal motifs that is determinative. The issue is further complicated by the rhetorical aims of particular works. A Jewish writer may well place a heavy emphasis on obedience to the Law in order to persuade his fellow Jews to maintain their national identity, while still subscribing to God's gracious election of Israel as a 'holy people'.

[21] C.A. Evans, 'Scripture-Based Stories in the Pseudepigrapha', in D.A. Carson (*et al.*, ed.), *op. cit.*, 69.

[22] M. Silva, *art. cit.*, 349. Unfortunately, Silva confines his sweeping comment to Sir 3:3, 30. A comprehensive survey of the rabbinic literature would be fairer and more balanced.

[23] Again, what is required is the painstaking analysis of the rabbinic evidence found in the writings of R. Avemarie: *Tora und Leben: Untersuchungen zur Heilsbedeutung der Tora in der frühen rabbinischen Literatur* (Tübingen 1996); 'Bund als Gabe und Recht', in *id.* and H. Lichtenberger (Hrsg.), *Bund und Tora: Zur theologischen Begriffsgeschichte in alttestamentlicher, frühjüdischer und urchristlicher Tradition* (Tübingen 1996), 163-216; *id.*, 'Erwählung und Vergeltung: Zur optionalen Struktur rabbinischer Soteriologie', *NTS* 45/1 (1999), 108-126. E.P. Sanders' approach to the rabbinic evidence, in Avemarie's view, is ultimately one-sided. While it is clear that unconditional grace was the grounds of Israel's election (cf. §4.8.2), salvation was also sometimes seen as dependent upon human merit and obedience (*Midr. Deut.* 33.2; *Lev. Rab.* 1.11; *y. Pe'a* 1.1; cf. §4.8.2 n.334). Precisely because eternal life was the divine reward for keeping the law (*'Abot R. Nat B* 10), it was possible for righteous Gentiles to inherit the future heavenly kingdom (*t. Sanh.* 13.2; *b. 'Abod. Zar.* 10b). Thus the rabbis could emphasise salvation either by law or grace, depending on the context being addressed. See also the comprehensive critique of E.P.

example: the rabbinic doctrine of the 'Merits of the Fathers' must be interpreted fairly, with due attention being paid to any accompanying covenantal texts or grace motifs (§4.8.2). Otherwise we will automatically filter what the rabbinic literature said about human merit through a Lutheran lens.[24]

Finally, Dunn's view that the 'works of the law' primarily refer to the ethnic boundary markers of Judaism has been challenged. In reply, M.A. Seifrid argues that obedience to the law marked personal piety in Judaism[25] and — in the case of the *Psalms of Solomon* — was of salvific value to the pious.[26] Caution is again warranted. M. Abegg has recently claimed that two words from the Dead Sea Scroll text 4QMMT, *ma'ase ha-torah*, are the Hebrew equivalent of Paul's ἔργα νόμου ('works of the law': Rom 3:20, 28; Gal 2:16; 3:2, 5, 10).[27] Dunn has been quick to endorse Abegg's case in an exhaustive analysis of the points of connection between Galatians and 4QMMT.[28] Abegg asserts that 4QMMT is really documenting an *internal* community dispute over purity concerns rather than advocating the separation of the Qumran sect from mainstream Judaism. If Abegg is correct regarding the Hebrew terminology and the intra-communal focus of 4QMMT,[29] then Paul

---

Sanders by M. Hengel and R. Deines, 'E.P. Sanders' "Common Judaism", Jesus, and the Pharisees', *JTS* 46/1 (1995), 1-70; R. Deines, 'The Pharisees Between "Judaisms" and "Common Judaism"', in D.A. Carson (*et al.*, ed.), *op. cit.*, 443-504.

[24] For Sanders' discussion of the 'Merits of the Fathers', see *id., op. cit.* (1977), 87, 99-100. See also the interesting perspective of R.T. Herford, *The Pharisees* (London 1924), 128-135. Conversely, one suspects that the new perspective on Paul desires rapprochement with modern Judaism — as worthy a motivation as that may be (cf. Rom 9:1-5; 10:1). See L. Gaston, *Paul and the Torah* (Vancouver 1987), s.v. Index 'Anti-Judaism'; J.D. Dunn, *op. cit.* (1991), 248-251 and s.v. Index 'Anti-semitism'.

[25] M.A. Seifrid, 'Blind Alleys in the Controversy over the Paul of History', *TynBul* 45/1 (1994), 77-85.

[26] *Id., op. cit.*, 109-133. By contrast, D. Falk ('Psalms and Prayers', in D.A. Carson [*et al.*, ed.], *op. cit.*, 43, 49, 51) argues that the author of the *Psalms of Solomon* grounds righteous behaviour in God and His covenant, with a corresponding emphasis on a humble confession of sin.

[27] M. Abegg, 'Paul, "Works of the Law" and MTT', *BAR* 20/6 (1994), 52-61, 82. However, it should be noted that the two central struts of Abegg's argument, outlined above, are dependent in each case on the correctness of his proposed translation of the text. See, too, the earlier debate of C.E.B. Cranfield (*art. cit.* [1991], 89-101) and J.D.G. Dunn (*art. cit.* [1992], 99-117).

[28] J.D.G. Dunn, '4QMMT and Galatians', *NTS* 43/1 (1997), 147-153.

[29] The argument that the words *ma'ase ha-torah* in 4QMMT throw light on Paul's ἔργα νόμου of Galatians has not gone unchallenged. See J.A. Fitzmyer, 'Paul's Jewish Background and the Deeds of the Law', in *id., According to Paul: Studies in the Theology of the Apostle* (New York 1992), 18-35; T.R. Schreiner, *Romans* (Grand Rapids 1998), 171-174.

was either confronting a sectarian theology of Judaism or (more likely) a Jewish Christianity which emphasised Torah obedience as a boundary marker.

Notwithstanding, this does not preclude Paul from widening the focus of the Galatian debate on the continuing validity of the law so that he could highlight the primacy of grace (Gal 1:6; 2:21; 5:4). The Galatian opponents had tried to restrict the radical social impact of the gospel by imposing Jewish boundary markers on the emerging Gentile churches (Gal 2:3-5, 11-14; 5:1-12). This demonstrated that they did not fully understand the *continuing* role that grace plays in their salvation, both at an individual and a corporate level (Gal 2:4-5, 14). In reverting to the Torah rather than keeping in step with the Spirit (Gal 3:2-3, 5; 5:25), the Galatians ran the risk of introducing boastful and legalistic attitudes (3:3; 6:12-14) — arising from Jewish-Christian exclusivism — into the gospel of God's grace in Christ (cf. Rom 4:4-5; 11:6; Eph 2:8-10; Phil 3:9).[30] In so doing, Paul argues, the Galatians would imperil the entire dynamic of the new creation (Gal 1:6-9; 6:15 [cf.5:6]).[31]

Turning to the new perspective on Paul, it has been suggested that Paul is not criticising mainstream Judaism at all. Rather he is interacting with some type of *Christian* Judaism.[32] But, in my view, two pieces of Pauline polemic (Rom 10:2-3; Phil 3:5-6) indicate that the apostle was as much critiquing the rise of a merit theology within first-century Judaism (§4.8.1 n.311) as the exclusivism of certain Christian Jews in the early house-churches.

Other scholars argue that Paul's critique of the law in Galatians and Romans was more fundamental than Sanders and Dunn have suggested. There is certainly substance to this criticism in regard to Paul's portrayal of grace. First, over against Sanders, Paul's dispute with Judaism not only extends to the entrance requirements of the covenantal community but also to their

---

[30] See K.T. Cooper, 'Paul and Rabbinic Soteriology: A Review Article', *WTJ* 44/1 (1982), 130; R.H. Gundry, art. cit., 8-12, 19-20; T. Deidun, 'E.P. Sanders: An Assessment of Two Recent Works', *HeyJ* 27 (1986), 46-47.

[31] See also S. Kim's recent critique of Dunn as 'self-contradictory', including an assessment of Dunn's view of the 'works of the law' in *id.*, *Paul and the New Perspective: Second Thoughts on the Origin of Paul's Gospel* (Grand Rapids-Cambridge 2002), 1-84, esp. 57ff.

[32] B. Loader, 'Paul and Judaism — Is He Fighting Strawmen?', *Colloquium* 16/2 (1984), 11-20. However, S. Mason ('Paul, Classical Anti-Jewish Polemic, and the Letter to the Romans', in D.J. Hawkin and T. Robinson [eds], *Self-Definition and Self-Discovery in Early Christianity: A Study in Changing Horizons* [Lewiston-Queenston-Lampeter 1990], 181-223, esp. 195ff) argues that Paul does make several programmatic statements on Judaism as a whole (1 Thess 2:15-16; Phil 3:2-10; 2 Cor 3; Galatians) that put him at odds with his native religion. On Galatians, see the helpful discussion of C.G. Kruse (*Paul, the Law and Justification* [Leicester 1996], 54-113) and P.F. Esler ('Group Boundaries and Intergroup Conflict in Galatians: A New Reading of Galatians 5:13—6:10', in M.G. Brett [ed.], *Ethnicity and the Bible* [Leiden-New York-Köln 1996], 215-240).

maintenance through Torah-obedience.³³ As will be argued, for Paul divine grace undergirds the entire process (§6.1.2.5 n.117).

Second, several scholars also remain unconvinced that Paul *invariably* worked from a christological solution back to the inadequacy of the Torah, as Sanders has suggested.³⁴ It is more likely that Paul believed that *both* the reign of divine grace and the corruption of human nature disqualified the law as the means of justification in front of God (§4.8.1 n.311).³⁵

Finally, I would argue that both Sanders and Dunn overlook the apocalyptic framework of Paul's view of law and grace. According to the apostle, the law is recruited against its will by the reigning and enslaving powers — Sin, Death and (perhaps) Flesh — which are ranged against humanity.³⁶ Sin is aroused and empowered by the law (Rom 7:5, 7-11, 13; 1 Cor 15:56b). Although the law is holy and just and good (Rom 7:7, 12-14, 16, 22), it is impotent to effect righteousness due to the sinful flesh (Rom 8:3, 7; cf. Gal 3:21-22). Furthermore, the law is both inferior and outdated in comparison to the revelation of the gospel age (2 Cor 3:10-11, 15; Gal 3:19b-

---

³³ In addition to n.19 above, see C.F.D. Moule, 'A Christian Understanding of Law and Grace', *Christian Jewish Relations* 14 (1981), 52-61; *id.*, 'Jesus, Judaism, and Paul', in G.F. Hawthorne and O. Betz (eds), *Tradition and Interpretation in the New Testament: Essays in Honor of E. Earle Ellis for His 60th Birthday* (Grand Rapids 1987), 48-49; S. Westerholm, *op. cit.*, 147-148.

³⁴ See P. Garnet, 'Qumran Light on Pauline Soteriology', in D.A. Hagner and M.J. Harris (eds), *Pauline Studies: Essays Presented to F.F. Bruce* (Exeter 1980), 19-32; F. Thielman, *From Plight to Solution: A Jewish Framework for Understanding Paul's View of the Law in Galatians and Romans* (Leiden 1989). See also S.K. Stowers, *A Rereading of Romans: Justice, Jews, and Gentiles* (New Haven and London 1994), 329.

³⁵ D.J. Moo, '"Law", "Works of the Law", and Legalism in Paul', *WTJ* 45/1 (1983), 98; R.H. Gundry, *art. cit.*, 27. In this regard, several authors (S. Westerholm, *op. cit.*, 142, 169; T.R. Schreiner, *op. cit.*, 29, 85) argue that Paul has a more pessimistic view of human nature than the rest of first-century Judaism.

³⁶ On apocalyptic motifs in Paul's thought, see V.P. Furnish, *Theology and Ethics in Paul* (Nashville 1968), 115-143; R. Scroggs, *Paul for a New Day* (Philadelphia 1977); J. Christiaan Beker, *Paul the Apostle: The Triumph of God in Life and Thought* (Edinburgh 1980), 135-181. See, too, the helpful article of R.B. Sloan, 'Paul and the Law: Why the Law Cannot Save', *NovT* 33/1 (1991), 35-60. More recently, P. Stuhlmacher, *op. cit.*, 52-73. According to Paul, sin has entered the world (Rom 5:12), reigning over (βασιλεύειν: Rom 5:21; 6:12; κυριεύειν: Rom 6:14) and enslaving humanity (δουλεύειν, δοῦλος: Rom 6:6, 16-17, 20; ὑφ' ἁμαρτίαν: Rom 3:9; 7:14; Gal 3:22). In this regard, the law itself enslaves humanity (Gal 4:3, 8-9, 21-31). As a result, sin became the agent of death (Rom 5:12; 7:24; 8:10). Death therefore reigns (βασιλεύειν: Rom 5:14, 17, 21; κυριεύειν: Rom 6:9) and still remains the last enemy to be destroyed (Rom 8:38; 1 Cor 15:26). Finally, it is a matter of debate whether Paul sees 'flesh' as a power that influences humanity 'from outside' or is an impulse 'within'. On the apocalyptic dimension of 'flesh' in Paul's thought, see J.M.G. Barclay, *Obeying the Truth: Paul's Ethics in Galatians* (Minneapolis 1988), 116-117, 178-215; J. Louis Martyn, *Theological Issues in the Letters of Paul* (Edinburgh 1997), 111-123, 251-266. Note how Paul closely allies 'flesh' with 'works of the law' in Gal 3:2-3.

20; 6:15). The law, like the slave-attendant of antiquity, only controls the free-born sons of the Master's household until their coming of age in Christ (Gal 3:23-25; 4:1-7; cf. Rom 8:3-4). As a result, the law effects a ministry of death (Rom 7:11b; 2 Cor 3:7), calling down the divine wrath on humanity (Rom 4:15; Gal 3:10, 13; Col 2:14) and causing the creation to long for the liberty of the eschatological age (Rom 8:19-23). Only the reign of divine grace will bring delivery from its curse (§6.1.2.4). Seemingly, more is at stake here for Paul than just Jewish exclusivism or boundary markers.

In exploring the Jewish understanding of grace, we will examine the Septuagintal (LXX), Apocryphal, and Pseudepigraphical use of χάρις (§4.2—§4.3). The benefaction context of χάρις in Judaism is best illustrated by the writings of Philo and Josephus, as well as by the Jewish honorific and funerary inscriptions in Greek (§4.4—§4.6). An intriguing perspective on the unilateral view of grace is found in the synagogal sermons of Pseudo-Philo (§4.7).[37] Finally, the rabbinic exposition of the Old Testament *hen* texts may throw some light on first-century proto-rabbinic views of grace (§4.8). The Jewish papyri have already been discussed in Chapter 3.

4.2. *The Use of* Charis *in the LXX*

In confining our examination of grace in the Old Testament to the LXX use of χάρις, we concede at the outset that the understanding of grace in the Hebrew Old Testament text embraced a spread of terminology, not just a single word or expression.[38] However, since the LXX was the Bible of first-century Greek-speaking Jews, we must determine whether the LXX use of χάρις captures in nascent form any of the theological emphases that Paul subsequently developed in his letters. It could be argued that these theological developments may have partially arisen in reaction to the type of Judaism that produced the LXX. H.J. Schoeps, for example, has asserted that the piety of the LXX belonged to a brand of hellenistic Judaism which replaced 'the Old

---

[37] The unilateral view of grace in the Dead Sea Scrolls, omitted in my discussion here, is dealt with in Chapter 4 of the original thesis (Macquarie University 1996). A discussion of grace in the synagogal sermons of Pseudo-Philo has been included instead because it more closely approximates the diaspora setting of Paul and his converts. I am grateful to Professor Martin Hengel for drawing my attention to the theology of grace found in Pseudo-Philo's sermons.

[38] Fundamental to any Hebrew understanding of grace are *hen* ('grace'), *hesed* ('mercy'), *'ahabah* ('love'), *rachamin* ('compassion'). See W.R. Roehrs, 'The Grace of God in the Old Testament', *CTM* 23/12 (1952), 895-910.

Testament religion of grace by a human religion of virtuous works'.[39] In Schoeps' view, Paul's protest against a Jewish works-righteousness — and his affirmation of χάρις — was more aimed at the hellenistic Judaism of his childhood than the Judaism of his rabbinic training. Thus, a brief overview of the LXX use of χάρις will help us to determine how far Paul's understanding of beneficence fits into the LXX grid.

The Greek translators of the Old Testament Hebrew text rendered *ḥen* ('grace', 'favour') in the Greek χάρις. It is strange that the standard Hebrew term for covenantal grace — *ḥesed* (LXX ἔλεος: 'mercy', 'kindness') — is not translated as χάρις in the LXX.[40] Only on two occasions is χάρις used for *ḥesed*.[41] Briefly, the LXX use of χάρις can be summarised as follows.

---

[39] H.J. Schoeps, *Paul: The Theology of the Apostle in the Light of Jewish Religious History* (Philadelphia 1961: Gmn. orig. 1959), 31. Schoeps (*ibid.*) nominates the LXX translation of the Hebrew text of Proverbs as having Stoic overtones and a generally 'more friendly attitude towards Greek culture and thought'.

[40] E. Jacob (*Theology of the Old Testament* [London 1958: Fr. orig. 1955], 106) points out that in the Old Testament Hebrew text *ḥesed* belonged to the language of covenantal reciprocity, whereas *ḥen* was 'only used in a unilateral sense which excludes reciprocity'. Similarly, W.R. Roehrs, *art. cit.*, 903. However χάρις — the LXX translation of *ḥen* — was the dominant hellenistic leitmotiv for divine and human reciprocity. For suggestions why the LXX translators preferred ἔλεος to χάρις as a theological description of God's grace, see T.F. Torrance, *The Doctrine of Grace in the Apostolic Fathers* (Edinburgh 1948), 12; E.E. Flack, 'The Concept of Grace in Biblical Thought', in J.M. Myers (ed.), *Biblical Studies in Memory of H.C. Alleman* (New York 1960), 144-145. Occasionally, ἔλεος is found in close conjunction with χάρις (and its cognates) in the LXX and in later Jewish literature. See Gen 39:21; Wis 3:9, 4:15; Philo, *Jos.* 229-230, *Quod Deus* 74, *Spec. Leg.* II. 138; Josephus, *AJ* 2.151.

[41] LXX: Esth 2:9, 17. Conversely, there are only three occurrences of ἔλεος rendering *ḥen* (LXX: Gen 19:19; Num 11:15; Judg 6:17). A voluminous literature exists on χάρις (*ḥen*) and ἔλεος (*ḥesed*) in the LXX: E. Jauncey, *The Doctrine of Grace up to the End of the Pelagian Controversy* (London 1925), 17-30; J. Moffatt, *Grace in the New Testament* (London 1931), 37-44; W. Manson, 'Grace in the New Testament', in W.T. Whitley (ed.), *The Doctrine of Grace* (London 1932), 36-37; W.F. Lofthouse, '*Hen* and *Hesed* in the Old Testament', *ZAW* 51 (1933), 29-35; C.H. Dodd, *The Bible and the Greeks* (London 1935), 59-62; J.A. Montgomery, 'Hebrew *Hesed* and Greek *Charis*', *HTR* 32/2 (1939), 97-102; R.C. Trench, *Synonyms of the New Testament* (Grand Rapids 1948), 166-171; T.F. Torrance, *op. cit.*, 10-20; N.H. Snaith, *The Distinctive Ideas of the Old Testament* (London 1950), 94-130; W.L. Reed, 'Some Implications of *Hen* for Old Testament Religion', *JBL* 73/1 (1954), 36-41; C.R. Smith, *The Bible Doctrine of Grace* (London 1956), 33-39; R.F. Surburg, 'Pauline *Charis*: A Philological, Exegetical, and Dogmatical Study', *CTM* 29/10 (1958), 725-727; E.E. Flack, *art. cit.*, in J.M. Myers (ed.), *op. cit.*, 139-145; J. Roussillon, 'Les termes hébreux en théologie chrétienne: justification de leur choix', *RevThom* 38 (1960), 86-89; R.F.G. Burnish, *The Doctrine of Grace from Paul to Irenaeus* (unpub. Ph.D. diss. Glasgow University 1971), 1-13; H.J. Stoebe, '*haésaed*', in E. Jenni and C. Westermann (Hrsg.), *Theologisches Handwörterbuch zum Alten Testament Bd.I* (Zürich 1971), 600-621; T.N. Schulz, *The Meaning of* Charis *in the New Testament* (Genova 1971), 23-32; W. Zimmerli, 'χάρις', *TDNT* 9 (1974), 376-387; H. Dittmann, 'Gnade', *RAC* 11 (1981), 333-342.

1. The dominant meaning is 'to find favour' (εὑρεῖν χάριν, ἔχειν χάριν), whether in the eyes of God or a superior. δοῦναι χάριν ('to give favour') is also used of God giving His servants favour in the eyes of others.[42]
2. χάρις can also refer to the bestowal of a 'favour' or 'kindness'.[43]
3. The Classical use of χάρις, with meaning of attractiveness of speech[44] or physical beauty,[45] is relatively scarce in the LXX.

In light of the LXX use of χάρις outlined above, several observations are apposite. First, while *ḥen* in the Hebrew text denotes the condescension and unmerited favour of a superior, the Old Testament occurrences of the Hebrew word, when applied to God's gracious and merciful nature, are rarely rendered by χάρις in the LXX.[46] The clearest expression of χάρις as a reference to God's gracious and compassionate disposition in the LXX is found in Zech 12:10. There God promises that He will pour out a 'spirit of grace (πνεῦμα χάριτος) and compassion' upon the house of David. Some explanation as to why Paul adopted χάρις as his central description of God's salvation activity is therefore imperative.

Second, χάρις in the LXX does not embrace the Pauline understanding of salvation from sin or gratitude in response to grace (whether human or divine).[47] Moreover, Paul — in contrast to Philo — does not cite a single LXX text employing χάρις.[48]

Third, we need to ask why there was an increasing tendency for first-century Jewish writers like Paul to supplant the LXX ἔλεος with χάρις as the central description of divine beneficence. E.E. Flack has pointed to the

---

[42] εὑρεῖν χάριν [LXX]: Gen 6:9; 18:3; 30:27; 32:5; 33:8, 10, 15; 34:11; 39:4; 47:25, 29; 50:4; Exod 33:13, 16, 17; 34:9; Num 11:11; 32:5; Deut 24:3; Ruth 2:2, 10, 13; 1 Kgs 1:18; 16:22; 20:3, 29; 25:8; 27:5; 2 Kgs 14:22, 15:25; 16:4; Esth 2:9, 15, 17; 5:8; 7:3; 8:5; Prov 3:4; 12:2. ἔχειν χάριν [LXX]: Exod 33:12. δοῦναι χάριν [LXX]: Gen 39:21; 43:14; Exod 3:21; 11:3; 12:36.

[43] LXX: Ps 83(84):11; Prov 3:34; 11:27; 13:15; 15:7; 17:8; 18:22; 22:1; 25:10; 28:23; Eccl 9:11; Zech 6:14.

[44] LXX: Ps 44(45):2; Prov 7:5; 10:32; Eccl 10:12.

[45] LXX: Prov 1:9; 3:22; 4:9; 5:19.

[46] T.F. Torrance, *op. cit.*, 11-12. The translators of the LXX avoid χάρις and its cognates as a possible translation for *ḥannun* ('gracious') and *ḥanan* ('to be gracious', 'to be merciful') — both cognates of *ḥen* ('grace', 'favour') — where the Hebrew Old Testament text is referring to God's gracious character or actions. Alternatively, they opt for cognates of ἔλεος ('mercy', 'kindness').

[47] D.J. Doughty ('The Priority of ΧΑΡΙΣ: An Investigation of the Theological Language of Paul', *NTS* 19 [1973], 170-171) points out that χάρις was 'almost totally unknown in Jewish religious literature'. As a result, 'Paul himself seems to have been the first theologian to use this word in a technical way to interpret the salvation activity of God'.

[48] Philo (*Quod Deus* 71) discusses the concept of grace found in LXX Gen 6:9. For rabbinic discussions of the Hebrew 'grace' texts, see §4.8.

same tendency in Philo.⁴⁹ Was Paul reflecting the variety of Judaism which Philo represented, or was he merely absorbing late hellenistic philological trends?

Alternatively, R.C. Trench has argued regarding χάρις that the ethical terminology of the Greek philosophical schools had already sown in a Jewish context the conceptual seed of a favour freely done, without any expectation of return.⁵⁰ That possibility will be left open until our discussion of Philo (§4.4) and the philosophers more generally in Chapter 5.

Fourth, it is worth noting at this juncture that *hesed* in the Old Testament Hebrew text always had strong elements of reciprocity in its usage.⁵¹ A wide variety of mutually obligatory relationships between human beings are described by the word *hesed* (Gen 21:23; 40:14; Josh 2:12, 14; Judg 1:24; 8:35; 2 Sam 2:5-6; 9:1, 7; 10:2 [*par*. 1 Chr 19:2]; 1 Kgs 2:7). Moreover, a reciprocal relationship between God and Israel emerges when *hesed* is linked to divine grace and the mutual obligations of the covenant or *bᵉrît* (Gen 21:23, 27; 1 Sam 20:8, 14ff; Ps 89:28; 106:45). Similarly, a mutuality of obligation is seen in the relationship between God and the Davidic king (1 Kgs 3:6; 8:23-25; 2 Sam 7:14-15 [*par*. 1 Chr 17:13-14]; Ps 89:1-4, 28-29, 33).

Thus W.F. Lofthouse rightly notes that it is the establishment of a recognised tie which often distinguishes *hesed* ('mercy', 'kindness') from *hen* ('grace', 'favour') in the Hebrew Old Testament.⁵² To be sure, as R. Routledge observes of Psalm 89:28,⁵³ '*hesed* precedes ... and ... gives rise to the *bᵉrît*', but the mutuality of obligation for Israel and the Davidic king is strongly underscored'. Was Paul's preference for χάρις over the LXX ἔλεος, therefore, also partially occasioned by the idea of reciprocity attached to *hesed* in the Hebrew Old Testament? The irony is that in choosing the word

---

⁴⁹ E.E. Flack, *art. cit.*, in J.M. Myers (ed.), *op. cit.*, 145. C.H. Dodd (*op. cit.*, 61) points to three uses of χάρις — each rendering *hesed* — in Esther and Sirach as evidence for its growing popularity.

⁵⁰ R.C. Trench, *op. cit.*, 168.

⁵¹ For discussion, see N. Glueck, ḤESED *in the Bible* (Eng. trans. 1967 [orig. 1927]; repr. New York 1975); K.D. Sakenfield, *The Meaning of* HESED *in the Hebrew Bible: A New Inquiry* (Missoula 1978); H.-J. Zobel, '*hesed*', *TDOT* 5 (1986), 44-64; G.R. Clark, *The Word* Hesed *in the Hebrew Bible* (Sheffield 1993); R. Routledge, '*ḤESED* as Obligation: A Re-examination', *TynBul* 46/1 (1995), 179-196; H.M. Kamsler, '*HESED* — Mercy or Loyalty?', *Jewish Bible Quarterly* 27/3 (1999), 183-185. For recent discussions of reciprocity in gift giving in ancient Israel and Second Temple Judaism, see G. Stansell, 'The Gift in Ancient Israel', *Semeia* 87 (1999), 65-104; V.H. Matthews, 'The Unwanted Gift: Implications of Obligatory Gift Giving in Ancient Israel', *Semeia* 87 (1999), 91-104; S. Joubert, *Paul as Benefactor: Reciprocity, Strategy and Theological Reflection in Paul's Collection* (Tübingen 2000), 93-99.

⁵² W.F. Lofthouse, *art. cit.*, 32-33.

⁵³ R. Routledge, *art. cit.*, 187-188.

χάρις Paul opts for the central *leitmotiv* of the Graeco-Roman reciprocity system.

But, in anticipation of our future discussion, I will venture two brief observations. First, benefaction ideology dominated first-century Jewish and Graeco-Roman civic life, including the trade guilds and synagogues that Paul had contact with throughout the Eastern Mediterranean basin. The χάριτες of civic benefactors were regularly inscribed in stone in the public places and proclaimed in the local assemblies of the various *poleis*. Paul could hardly have been oblivious to the terminological opportunities that χάρις provided as a central leitmotiv of hellenistic beneficence. Second, we must not discount Paul's own theological originality and the continuing impact that his encounter with the risen Christ made to informing his view of χάρις.

4.3. The Use of Charis in the Apocrypha and Pseudepigrapha

The Greek Old Testament use of χάρις appears in the Apocryphal writings, either as a reference to the favour found in the eyes of God (or a human superior),[54] or the bestowal of favour by a benefactor (whether human or divine).[55] The standard Classical uses are found too.[56] There are hints of a more theological use when God extends χάρις and ἔλεος to His saints[57] and also provides them with the gift of faith (τῆς πίστεως χάρις).[58]

However, several changes to the Greek Old Testament use of χάρις point to an increasing hellenisation of the terminology in the Apocryphal literature.[59] The meaning of 'gratitude' attached to χάρις — omitted in the

---

[54] εὑρεῖν χάριν: 1 Esdr 8.4; Sir 1.13, 3.18, 42.1, 44.24; Bar 1.12; 1 Macc 10.60. See also 1 Esdr 8.80; Bar 2.14. For discussions of χάρις in the Apocrypha and Pseudepigrapha, see R.F.G. Burnish, *op. cit.*, 13-18; H. Dittmann, *art. cit.*, 342-344.

[55] 1 Esdr 6.5; Sir 8.19, 35.10, 35.21; Tob 1.13, 12.18; Jdt 10.8; Wis 3.9, 3.14, 4.15, 8.21, 14.26; 4 Macc 5.8, 11.2.

[56] Graciousness: Sir 7.19; 26.15. Grace of speech: Sir 20.13; 21.16. Grace of form or disposition: Sir 26.13, 15; 40.22. Joy: Sir 30.16; Tob 7.18. Pleasant savour: Sir 24.17.

[57] Wis 3.19; 4.15.

[58] Wis 3.14.

[59] I have artificially separated my discussion of χάρις in the LXX translation of the Hebrew scriptures (§4.2) from that of the LXX translation of the Old Testament Apocrypha (§4.3). However, it must be emphasised that the Old Testament Apocrypha, comprising (mainly Semitic language) works from c. 300 BC—AD 70, belonged to the LXX. Further, the formation of the LXX rendering of the Hebrew scriptures spanned the earliest attempts at translation in the III cent. BC (probably the Torah) to the completion of the final portions by the first part of the I cent. BC. Thus the combined LXX translation of the Hebrew scriptures and the Jewish Old Testament Apocrypha stretched over more than 300 years. This explains why we see a change in the use of the language of grace during that period. We have already

Greek Old Testament — surfaces for the first time,[60] as does reciprocity terminology.[61] Conversely, ingratitude for benefits received (χάριτος ἀμνησία) is castigated as a characteristic of the idolater.[62] Of particular interest is Ben-Sira's insightful exposé of the hostility implicit in benefaction rituals, engendered by the grudging hospitality of the benefactors, and by the ingratitude of their beneficiaries:

> The chief thing for life is water, and bread, and clothing, and a house to cover shame. Better is the life of a poor man in a mean cottage, than delicate fare in another man's house. Be it little or much, hold yourself contented, for it is a miserable life to go from house to house: for where you are a stranger, you dare not open your mouth. You shall entertain, and feast, and have no thanks (ἀχάριστα): moreover you shall hear bitter words: Come, stranger, and furnish a table, and feed me of that you have ready. Give place, stranger, to an honourable man; my brother comes to be lodged, and I have need of my house. These things are grievous to a man of understanding; the upbraiding of houseroom, and the reproaching of the lender.[63]

Here Ben-Sira's portrayal of the social humiliation implicit in the benefaction system stands in stark contrast to the positive inscriptional catalogues of honours, which were rendered to benefactors in recompense of their munificence to their local communities. Finally, while the presence of benefaction terminology alongside LXX occurrences of χάρις is very rare,[64] χάρις is linked to almsgiving (ἐλεημοσύνη) on two occasions.[65]

As far as the Pseudepigraphal literature, the standard Classical and Greek Old Testament uses recur, along with traces of benefaction terminology in χάρις contexts.[66] The flowering of a more theological use of χάρις in the Apocrypha continues into the Pseudepigrapha. A second-century BC work, *Testaments of the Twelve Patriarchs*, describes an eschatological priest who would reign eternally in the new Eden and distribute God's grace to the nations:

---

noted the tendency of first-century Jewish writers to supplant the LXX ἔλεος with χάρις as the central description of divine beneficence (§4.2) and will demonstrate the increasing hellenisation of χάρις in the Apocrypha.

[60] εὐχαριστεῖν: Wis 18.2. χάρις Sir 12.1; 1 Macc 14.25; 2 Macc 3.33, 9.20; 3 Macc 1.9, 5.20.
[61] ἀνταποδοῦνα χάριν: Sir 3.31, 30.6, 32.2.
[62] Wis 14.26.
[63] Sir 29.21-28.
[64] For δόξα and χάρις, see 1 Esdr 8.4; Sir. 24.16. For ἀτιμία and χάρις, see Jdt 8.23.
[65] Sir 17.22; 40.17.
[66] Classical uses: e.g. 'joy' (χάρις *1 Enoch* 5.7); 'graciousness of countenance' (χάρις *T. Jos.* 3.4); 'beauty' (χάρις *Sib. Or.* 5.59). LXX uses: εὑρεῖν χάριν, *T. Rub.* 4.8; *T. Sim.* 5.2. διδόναι χάριν ἐν ὀφθαλμοῖς *T. Jos.* 11.6. διδόναι χάριν πρὸς πάντας *Ep. Arist.* 249. Benefaction terminology: δόξα and χάρις *T. Sim.* 4.5; *Sib. Or.* 5.59. For a fine discussion of the Pseudepigrapha in relation to Judaism and the New Testament, see J.H. Charlesworth, *op. cit.*

And in his priesthood the nations shall be multiplied in knowledge on the earth,
and they shall be illumined by the grace (χάριτος) of the Lord,
but Israel shall be diminished by her ignorance
and darkened by her grief.[67]

In the same document, Judah praises God for His bestowal of grace (χάριν) on all his undertakings.[68] Judah also prophesies that an eschatological descendent from his house — the sinless Sun of Righteousness — would pour out the 'spirit of grace' (πνεῦμα χάριτος) upon his sons so that they would walk in truth and the Law.[69] Joseph, too, knew the blessing of God 'because grace from heaven (χάρις ἐκ τοῦ οὐρανοῦ) (was) with him'.[70]

Other pseudepigraphal works depict God's bestowal of grace to His people, as well as confirming its sufficiency for them at the last Judgement. The following examples will suffice. Joseph's wife, Aseneth, prays that God would preserve Joseph in the wisdom of His grace (χάριτος).[71] Daniel, who abstained from desirable food, was 'beautiful in the favour (χάριτι) of the Lord' in spite of his gaunt appearance.[72] In a non-canonical tradition, God exercised His favour (χάριν) towards Jeremiah, enabling him to seize the ark of the Law before the Temple's capture, and then to conceal it miraculously till the resurrection day. *Sibylline Oracles* 4, a hellenistic composition updated in the late first century AD, affirms God's favour (χάριν) to the pious at the last Judgement.[73] After a series of bitter oracles against Rome and the Gentiles, *Sibylline Oracles* 5 — a composite work (c. AD 80—132) — petitions God's grace for Judaea on the basis of her covenantal status:

Be gracious, begetter of all, to the fertile, luxurious,
great land of Judaea, so that we may behold your plans.
For you knew this one first, God, with favours (χάριτεσσιν),
so that she seemed to be your special gift (προχάρισμα) to all men
and to attend as God enjoined.[74]

The foregoing texts demonstrate that χάρις had acquired considerable theological versatility as a description of God's beneficence by the time of

---

[67] *T. Levi.* 18.9. I have used the dating found in J.H. Charlesworth (ed.), *The Old Testament Pseudepigrapha* 2 Vols (New York 1983, 1985).

[68] *T. Jud.* 2.1.

[69] *Ibid.*, 24.2.

[70] *T. Jos.* 12.3. According to *Asen.* 4.7, Joseph experiences the Spirit of God and His grace (χάρις).

[71] *Asen.* 13.15. (I cent. BC—II cent. AD).

[72] *LivPro.* 4.3. In this first-century AD work, Daniel's prayer-fasts are ascetic in nature rather than an expression of obedience to the Levitical food-laws — as was the case in the LXX narrative (Dan 1:8).

[73] *Sib. Or.* 4.46, 189.

[74] *Sib. Or.* 5.328-332.

Paul. χάρις appears in eschatological and covenantal contexts; the divine initiative is thrust to the forefront when χάρις describes either the bestowal of God's wisdom or His Spirit; and χάρις sums up God's reward to His faithful children. Last, the *Odes of Solomon* (late first to early second century AD) need not detain us because the work is clearly early Christian.[75]

Benefaction ideology and terminology has unquestionably impacted upon the author of the *Letter of Aristeas* (c. 170 BC). There the Egyptian king, Ptolemy II, conducts a series of interviews during a week-long banquet at Alexandria with the six translators whom he had commissioned to render the Old Testament into Greek. In view of the author's concentration on 'the educational ideal of the καλοκἀγαθία',[76] it is not surprising to find the inscriptional ideals of beneficence lauded in the letter. In answer to Ptolemy's question as to how one maintains his honour (δοξαζόμενος), one guest adopts traditional benefaction parlance: 'If by earnestness (προθυμίᾳ) and favours (χάρισι) he showed munificence (μεταδοτικός) and liberality (μεγαλομερής) toward others, he would never lack honour'.[77] Another guest flatters the glorious rule of Ptolemy, isolating as its chief strength the royal 'favours (χάριτας) which produce goodwill (εὔνοιαν)'.[78] The king himself questions his guests concerning the desirability of parents receiving appropriate gratitude (τὰς ἀξίας ἀποδῴη χάριτας).[79] These tantalising exchanges between Ptolemy and his guests highlight the inroads that benefaction ideology had made into first-century Judaism.

At a conceptual level, the appearance of a merit theology regarding almsgiving may call into question the extent to which a unilateral and covenantal understanding of grace dominated first-century Judaism.[80]

---

[75] God's gracious character: *Odes. Sol.* 5.3, 7.5, 7.10, 9.5, 20.9, 21.1, 29.3, 33.10. The Messiah (41.3), salvation (5.3, 21.2, 25.4, 33.10, 34.6), justification (29.5), liturgy (7.22, 7.26), and eschatology (15.8, 20.7, 31.7) are all related to God's bestowal of grace. There is also an instance of the hypostasis of grace (*Odes. Sol.* 33.1).

[76] M. Hengel, *Judaism and Hellenism: Studies in Their Encounter in Palestine during the Early Hellenistic Period* Vol.1 (London 1974: Gmn orig. 1973), 68.

[77] *Ep. Arist.* 226.

[78] *Ibid.*, 230.

[79] *Ibid.*, 238. See also the use of χάρις with τιμή and ἀρετή: *ibid.*, 278. For another use of χάρις in the Pseudepigrapha with inscriptional parallel: *Ps-Phoc.* 9.

[80] E. Frisch (*An Historical Survey of Jewish Philanthropy from the Earliest Times to the Nineteenth Century* [New York 1924], 29) argues that the development of a merit theology 'must have taken place in the wake of the wholesale suffering and slaughter that befell people in the Maccabean wars'. Whatever the truth of the matter, the Hebrew Old Testament conspicuously avoids any suggestion that Israel's election was due to her own merit. The election of Israel is viewed as a unilateral act of God (Exod 19:4-5; Amos 3:2; Hos 9:10; Ezek 16:1-52). In this regard, the gratuitous nature of God's love is heavily underscored in both Deuteronomy (Deut 4:37; 7:7-9; 9:6; 10:14-15; 32:10-11) and Hosea (Hos 2:14-23).

Almsgiving, it was believed, could atone for sin.[81] The same sentiment is echoed in *Tobit* 12.8, with the addition that almsgiving delivers its practitioners from death.[82] Further, W.L. Lane has recently argued that the theology of the *Psalms of Solomon* is ultimately performance-based, with mercy (ἔλεος) being the divine response to pious obedience.[83] There is perhaps warrant for D. Moo's observation that first-century Judaism may have been more diverse in its attitude to merit than E.P. Sanders has allowed.[84] Whether Moo or Sanders is ultimately correct on this issue in regard to Tannaitic Judaism, it will be argued in this chapter that Graeco-Roman conceptions of ἀρετή were impacting on Greek-speaking Judaism through the operation of the eastern Mediterranean benefaction system.

4.4. Charis, *Philo, and Beneficence*

Philo (20 BC—AD 50) is an invaluable source for the use and understanding of Graeco-Roman benefaction terminology (including χάρις) within first-century diaspora Judaism. This aspect of Philo's thought has rarely fired the interest of New Testament scholars, despite the fact that benefaction studies is a growth industry within their discipline.[85] Nonetheless, more general

---

God's Covenant with Israel is also labelled the 'Covenant of love' (1 Kgs 8:23; Neh 1:5; 9:32; Dan 9:4; 2 Chr 6:14). Moreover, precisely because God's love outlives the Covenant (Ps 136), the Covenant itself is confidently regarded as the basis for continuing grace (Pss 106:45; 111:5, 9). This is not to deny that there were aspects of reciprocity in the Covenant. God requires that He is to be honoured as the covenantal and cosmic Benefactor (Hag 1:8; Mal 1:6; Prov 14:31; 1 Chron 16:26-27; Pss 29:1-2; 96:5-6; 104:1). S.M. Olyan ('Honour, Shame, and Covenant Relations in Ancient Israel and Its Environment', *JBL* 115/2 [1996], 205) is entirely correct when he observes that God 'participates in reciprocal honour'. As 1 Sam 2:30 states of God, 'those who honour me I will honour, those who despise me shall be lightly esteemed' (cf. Ps 91:15; Prov 3:9-10; 14:31; Is 43:20). However, what must be realised here is that while God's grace imposes obligation upon His beneficiaries, it also extends to them the promise of recompense. God graciously maintains His covenantal loyalty to His dependants. For additional scholarly discussion, see n.27 above.

[81] Sir 3.30. The case for a merit theology is easily overstated in this instance. Is it legitimate to derive a systematic theology from wisdom literature such as Sirach? Do we thereby run the risk of misinterpreting or overinterpreting the literature?

[82] See also Tob 4.7ff, 14.10. However, note the cautionary comments of E. Frisch (*op. cit.*, 29) on constructing 'a precise relation between merit and reward' from Tobit. For rabbinic examples of the atoning power of ancestral merit, see C.G. Montefiore and H. Loewe, *A Rabbinic Anthology* (New York 1974), §587, §588.

[83] See W.L. Lane, 'Paul's Legacy from Pharisaism: Light from the Psalms of Solomon', *Concordia Journal* 8 (1982), 130-138.

[84] D. Moo, 'Paul and the Law in the Last Ten Tears', *SJT* 40 (1987), 298.

[85] See §1.1.

investigations of χάρις in Philo's works have proceeded apace this century. So far, no consensus has emerged among scholars.

In 1974 H. Conzelmann drew attention to the 'opposing judgements of scholars' on Philo's understanding of χάρις.[86] Three issues have provoked this polarisation of scholarly debate: namely,

1. the extent to which Philo's understanding of χάρις is fundamentally Jewish or hellenistic (or an amalgam of both);
2. the distinctiveness of Philo's doctrine of χάρις in comparison to Paul's justification by grace;
3. how the problem of merit is to be incorporated into Philo's concept of χάρις (whether by synergism or the outworking of a 'grace ethic', or by some other means).

Despite the value of this research, the methodological blindspot which has characterised New Testament scholarship on χάρις similarly vitiates studies on Philo: the abstraction of χάρις from its Graeco-Roman benefaction context. Little interest has been shown in viewing Philonic χάρις against the backdrop of the honorific inscriptions. This is a strange oversight, given Philo's wide use of benefaction terminology and reciprocity motifs. The audience of Philo would have been sensitive to the eulogistic vocabulary of the inscriptions, erected as they were in prominent locations for the appreciation of posterity. Moreover, there is the clear evidence that Philo critiques the Graeco-Roman understanding of χάρις in its benefaction context. Indeed, Paul himself may well have appropriated benefaction terminology through the very type of Judaism that Philo represents.

At the outset, we will survey modern scholarship on Philonic χάρις to gauge the limitations of previous scholarly approaches to Philo.

4.4.1. Modern scholars, Philo, and charis: a survey

G P. Wetter's contribution was the starting-point of twentieth-century scholarship on Philo and χάρις. He characterises Philo's thought on χάρις as an 'eigentümlichen Vermischung von echt jüdischen Gedanken und oberflächlich ergriffenen hellenistischen Ideen'.[87] Although Philo follows 'alten jüdischen Schultheologie',[88] 'griechische Einflüsse' underlie his

---

[86] H. Conzelmann, art. cit., 389 n.122.

[87] G.P. Wetter, Charis: Ein Beitrag zur Geschichte des ältesten Christentums (Leipzig 1913), 12. See also J. Daniélou, Philon D'Alexandrie (Paris 1958), 179: 'thèmes stoïciens, platoniciens, cyniques'.

[88] Ibid., 12. As one example of Philo's Jewish framework, Wetter (op. cit., 12-13) nominates his distinction between God as θεός and κύριος (Som. I. 163).

terminology.[89] This was a 'populären Stoizismus' which views the entire natural order — Earth, Water, Air, and Fire — as God's gift of grace to humankind.[90] Philo's 'Popularphilosophie' also surfaces in his view that God distributes the χάριτες of sight, hearing, and reason to the pious so that they may live uprightly.[91] Surprisingly, although Wetter was the first scholar to probe the benefaction context of χάρις,[92] he fails to consider Philo's view of grace against this backdrop, preferring to look elsewhere (e.g. Epictetus) for an explanation of Philo's Greek influences.[93]

New scholarly contributions continued along the trail pioneered by Wetter. H.A.A. Kennedy covers the same terrain, but occasionally ventures into new territory. He suggests that Philo came the closest to Paul in emphasising the priority of χάρις.[94] In the view of É. Bréhier, Philo's hypostasis of the Χάριτες is an example of an 'éxègese allégorique stoïcienne', similar to that of Cornutus.[95] Philo also underscores the 'universalité de la grâce divine'.[96] Importantly, Bréhier draws attention to a fundamental contradiction in Philo's theory of grace:

Philon, le premier, énonce, sans en avoir l'idée nette, la contradiction fondamentale dans laquelle se débattra plus tard la théorie de la Grâce: d'une part le mérite ou la capacité de recevoir des grâces dépend de la grâce et du don divin et, l'autre part, la grâce dépend du mérite et de la capacité de l'être. Quoi qu'il en soit, c'est le sage autodidacte qui montre le mieux que la grâce divine ne dépend d'aucune activité humaine.[97]

Another important contribution to this scholarly debate earlier this century was made by J. Moffatt.[98] In his view, Philo sees all creation and human nature as the arena of God's grace: the covenant, prayer, and every activity of the soul are all undergirded by grace.[99] In this emphasis, Philo is in line with

---

[89] G.P. Wetter, *op. cit.*, 15.
[90] Wetter (*ibid.*, 14) cites as examples *Leg. All.* III. 78; *Quaest in Gn.* III. 3-4; *Quod Deus* 104-108.
[91] G.P. Wetter, *op. cit.*, 14.
[92] *Ibid.*, 14-15.
[93] *Ibid.*, 15.
[94] H.A.A. Kennedy, *Philo's Contribution to Religion* (London 1919), 142-157, esp. 150-152.
[95] É. Bréhier, *Les idées philosophiques et religieuses de Philon d'Alexandrie* (Paris 1925: 2nd ed.), 147.
[96] *Ibid.*, 221.
[97] *Ibid.*, 278. H. Conzelmann (*art. cit.*, 390) sums up Philo's position as follows: 'some see in Philo a "Catholic" vacillation between grace and man's own work, while others speak of a Hell.-Jewish synergism to the degree that grace is in fact a help in the attainment of virtue'. In Conzelmann's view, a full-blooded synergism is excluded by Philo's strong emphasis on God's achievement.
[98] J. Moffatt, *op. cit.*, 45-51.
[99] *Ibid.*, 45-48.

Paul. However, Moffatt provides several telling qualifications.[100] First, Philo's transcendentalism precludes the possibility that God might give Himself more intimately to humankind. Second, despite some healthy protests against merit — e.g. *Sacr.*, 52-58 — Philo does not resolve the problem of merit as tidily as Paul. Third, Paul does not hypostasise grace, but keeps its focus both christological and soteriological. Fourth, nowhere in the New Testament is grace related to nature, as with Philo. Last, Moffatt (along with Manson) draws attention to Philo's preference for the plural χάριτες, in contrast to the Pauline singular use.[101]

Scholarship from the 1940s onwards demonstrates the difficulty of finding any consensus on Philo's view of grace. In contrast to G.P. Wetter — who allowed a blend of rabbinic and hellenistic elements in Philo — T.F. Torrance argues that '*charis* in Philo is in no sense different from *charis* in hellenistic Greek', albeit in a Jewish context.[102] The evidence adduced by Torrance to substantiate this position includes the tendencies of Philo to

1. abstract χάρις from all relation to sin,
2. reduce χάρις to a divine potency, instead of the LXX divine favour,
3. identify χάρις with human natural endowments,
4. import an unhebraic understanding of freedom into χάρις, and
5. hypostasise χάρις in typical hellenistic mythological fashion.

H.A. Wolfson explored the relation of χάρις to free will in Philo's thought.[103] According to Wolfson, Philo believed that God's grace is an aid to virtue on the part of those who, with God's help, strive to attain it. However, contrary to Torrance, Wolfson posits a Jewish background for Philo's views, and cites examples from the *Wisdom of Solomon*, the *Letter of Aristeas*, Pharisaic doctrine as interpreted by Josephus, and several rabbinic writings.[104]

More recent studies on grace in Philo have been stimulating and (occasionally) ground-breaking. In an insightful study, H. Thyen proposes that Philo possessed a strong sense of the negativity of sin and the need for redemption.[105] Redemption from sin's guilt originates in God's undeserved

---

[100] *Ibid.*, 45, 50-51.

[101] *Ibid.*, 48, 51; W. Manson, *art. cit.*, 37. For works reiterating the arguments of Moffatt and Manson, see R.F. Surburg, *art. cit.*, 727; T.N. Schulz, *op. cit.*, 32-34.

[102] T.F. Torrance, *op. cit.*, 6-10.

[103] H.A. Wolfson, *Philo: Foundations of Religious Philosophy in Judaism, Christianity, and Islam* Vol.1 (Cambridge Mass. 1962), 445-455. The discussion of χάρις in Philo by R.F.G. Burnish (*op. cit.*, 22-28) is largely dependent on Wolfson.

[104] H.A. Wolfson, *op. cit.*, 449-450.

[105] H. Thyen, *Studien zur Sündenvergebung im Neuen Testament und seinen alttestamentlichen und jüdischen Voraussetzungen* (Göttingen 1970), 98-130. Thyen's study is more a conceptual analysis of grace than a linguistic study of the word χάρις.

mercy, and is mediated through 'Gottes gnädige Gabe' of repentance (μετάνοια).[106]

S.C. Mott is the only scholar to examine the role that benefaction ideology plays in Philo's world-view. He suggests that a bridge exists between the benefaction terminology found in the Judaism of Philo and the same terminology found in the New Testament (e.g. Titus 2:10-14, 3:3-7).[107] In this respect, χάρις is part of a large semantic domain which congregates around the description of the benefactor as σωτήρ ('saviour'). Although Mott devotes no detailed analysis to Philo's use of χάρις in benefaction contexts,[108] the methodological implications of his approach are highly suggestive for New Testament studies. For example, how much of Paul's benefaction terminology was mediated through the type of Judaism which Philo represents? How widely had benefaction terminology permeated the variegated Judaism of the first century AD? What contrast can be observed between Paul and Philo in their adoption and critique of benefaction terminology? Some of these issues will be briefly referred to in later chapters (§6.5; §7.3.2).

The issue of merit and its relation to χάρις in Philo's thought continues to provoke animated debate. S. Sandmel canvasses the extent to which Philo regards ethics (i.e. good deeds) as a prerequisite to salvation.[109] At a philosophical level, Philo distinguishes in Platonic fashion between generic virtue and the specific virtues. Generic virtue is attained by reason, not deeds, and is its own reward. However, although in Philo's works deeds appear to be a reflection of virtue (not its means of attainment), Sandmel offers the caveat that there is 'nothing in Philo to obstruct a quite opposite conclusion that a man achieves virtue by his own deeds'.[110]

Alternatively, D.A. Carson argues that Philo abandons the Old Testament understanding of election by grace: the initiative lies with the suppliant (e.g.

---

[106] *Ibid.*, 119.

[107] S.C. Mott, *The Greek Benefactor and Deliverance from Moral Distress* (unpub. Ph.D. diss. Harvard University 1971), 359, 371. For discussions of benefaction terminology in Philo, see *ibid.*, 61-65, 179-257. For discussions of Philo's views on wealth in relation to the poor, see D.L. Mealand, 'Philo of Alexandria's Attitude to Riches', *ZNW* 69/3 (1978), 258-264; *id.*, 'The Paradox of Philo's Views of Wealth', *JSNT* 24 (1985), 111-115; T.E. Smith, 'Hostility to Wealth in Philo of Alexandria', *JSNT* 19 (1983), 85-97; F.G. Downing, 'Philo on Wealth and the Rights of the Poor', *JSOT* 24 (1985), 116-118.

[108] S.C. Mott (*op. cit.*, 251) argues that Philo used benefaction terminology to illustrate that grace is the dynamic behind God's actions.

[109] S. Sandmel, 'Virtue and Reward in Philo', in J.L. Crenshaw and J.T. Willis (eds), *Essays in Old Testament Ethics* (New York 1974), 217-223.

[110] *Ibid.*, 222. Sandmel, however, cites no evidence to substantiate his assertion of an underlying 'works ethic' in Philo.

Virt., 184-6), rather than with the unilateral decision of God. Individuals such as Noah or Abraham attract grace either through their righteousness, or by their status as 'the elect' (e.g. *Leg. All.* III 77ff.; *Gig.*, 63ff.).[111] In this respect, Carson justifiably criticises H.A.A. Kennedy's contention that Philo's doctrine of grace is substantially akin to Paul's.[112] Nevertheless, in the estimate of Carson, to attribute a full-blown 'merit theology' to Philo is misconceived.[113] The merits of the patriarchs provide an incentive for self-improvement rather than the means of acquittal or reward for their descendants.

Several familiar strains of previous scholarship are heard in H. Dittmann's discussion of Philo's use of χάρις, and need not be repeated here.[114] In sum, when Philo looks upon God as benevolent, he follows a 'griechischer Tradition' in which the gods and heroes dispense benefactions;[115] but, when Philo deals with the relationship of human and divine behaviour, Philo follows 'jüdischem Gedankengut'.[116]

The major work of J. LaPorte on Philo's use of εὐχαριστία makes an important contribution to the understanding of grace in first-century Judaism.[117] A central pillar of LaPorte's thesis stands out in the following extract:

Philo seems to be very concerned with the defence and the development of a theology of grace in the context of the inner life, because a real danger threatens those who are advanced in the way of virtue and close to perfection. This danger can be discerned only by those who have reached this point and by the spiritual writers who study the higher levels of religious life ... To take pleasure in one's good deeds, or to consider oneself as their only author without further distinction, is to deny the necessity of God and to introduce impiety at the summit of spiritual life, at the moment when perfection seems close at hand ... As a remedy to this perversion, Philo offers thanksgiving, since it is the antidote to self-love.[118]

In the opinion of LaPorte, a controversy over merit existed at the time of Philo — notwithstanding the strong Jewish antecedents of grace[119] — and

---

[111] D.A. Carson, *art. cit.*, 148-164.
[112] *Ibid.*, 161. Cf. H.A.A. Kennedy, *op. cit.*
[113] D.A. Carson, *art. cit.*, 162-163.
[114] H. Dittmann, *art. cit.*, 333-351. For Philo, see *ibid.*, 345-346.
[115] *Ibid.*, 345.
[116] *Ibid.*, 346.
[117] J. LaPorte, Eucharistia *in Philo* (New York and Toronto 1983). See also T. Schermann, 'Εὐχαριστία und εὐχαριστεῖν in ihrem Bedeutungswandel bis 200 n. Chr.', *Philologus* 69 (1910), 385-386; P. Schubert, *Form and Function of the Pauline Thanksgivings* (Berlin 1939), 122-131.
[118] J. LaPorte, *op. cit.*, 4-5. For a similar view, see J. Koenig, *art. cit.*, 574.
[119] J. LaPorte, *op. cit.*, 141-144.

both Philo and Paul responded to this with different apologias.[120] Also, to his credit, LaPorte makes some attempt at interpreting εὐχαριστία against its inscriptional background.[121]

Last, to assess D. Zeller's recent work, Charis bei Philon und Paulus, is beyond our scope.[122] Zeller covers more thoroughly than most the ethical and religious context of Philo's thought in Graeco-Roman antiquity and Greek-speaking Judaism. However, Zeller's discussion of divine and human benefaction barely touches on the inscriptions (and these typically culled from Wetter).[123] Nevertheless, his attention to beneficence in the philosophers is gratifying, along with his coverage of the mythological background.[124]

In conclusion, Philonic scholarship on χάρις has been so dominated by the (perceived) concerns of Pauline theology — or its implied contrasts — that the role which benefaction terminology played in first-century Judaism has simply been overlooked. The thought of both Philo and Paul on χάρις has been abstracted from its historical context and, as a result, we miss out on some of the surprise and delight which their original contributions must have produced among contemporaries. We turn first to Philo's use of χάρις in contexts of divine benefaction.

4.4.2. Grace and the beneficence of God in Philo

A cursory examination of Philo's works against the background of the honorific inscriptions reveals a man who was intimately acquainted with the terminology and ideology of benefaction. This can be observed in the broad spectrum of benefaction terminology which Philo employs to describe both the inexhaustible boons (χάριτες) of God as εὐεργέτης and acts of human beneficence. Apart from the fundamental terms — δωρέα, εὐεργέτης, λειτουργία, and χάρις — a range of benefaction words and phrases from the honorific inscriptions appear in Philo. These include not only the general honorifics regularly attributed to benefactors in the inscriptions (e.g. ἀρετή; εὔνοια; εὐσέβεια; ζῆλος; ἴσος; ἰσότης; καλοκἀγαθία; προθυμία; σπουδή; σωτήρ; τιμή; φιλανθρωπία; φιλία; φιλοτιμία), but also rarer words and phrases that appear in specific benefaction contexts (e.g. ἀθάνατος; ἀτελής; ἐν τοῖς ἀναγκαιοτάτοις καιροῖς; καρπός). Undoubtedly, Philo would have seen many such inscriptions erected in honour of the Caesars and the civic luminaries of first-century Alexandria.

---

[120] Ibid., 178.
[121] Ibid., 13-14. In this respect LaPorte is dependent on T. Schermann, art. cit.
[122] D. Zeller, Charis bei Philon und Paulus (Stuttgart 1990).
[123] Ibid., 14-32.
[124] Ibid., 16 n.19, 18 n.27.

Philo's familiarity with benefaction terminology can also be seen in other ways. He insists upon proper decorum on the part of the recipients in the benefaction ritual: only those who are the ἄξιοι — as opposed to the ἀχάριστοι — may experience God's beneficence by returning to Him appropriate εὐχαριστία and τιμή. Occasionally, in speeches where God clarifies the nature of His generosity, Philo adopts the eulogistic parlance of the honorific inscriptions to portray the divine beneficence. Concomitant with this, benefaction terminology is also used by Philo in the speeches of God's human servants who mediate His boons. A presentation of Philo's evidence will give flesh to this outline.

First, what is Philo's understanding of God as εὐεργέτης? In Philo's view, the impetus for God's beneficence stems from His dual Potencies (δυνάμεις). The θεός Potency, or the 'beneficent' (χαριστική), is the agency through which God created the world: the κύριος Potency, or the 'punitive', is the agency through which God rules the world.[125] God's entire creation is a eulogy to His grace: 'all things are the grace or gift of God (χάριν ὄντα θεοῦ) — earth, water, fire, sun, stars, heaven, all plants and animals'.[126] As the Creator, God determined 'to confer (εὐεργετεῖν) rich and unrestricted benefits (χάριτας)' upon His creation.[127] At Eden, therefore, God as the Giver of wealth rained down 'His virgin (παρθένους) and deathless boons (ἀθανάτους χάριτας)'.[128] As the Beginning and End of all things, God displayed His perfection in a special act of grace (χάρισι) by making the earth immensely fertile. Fruit (καρπός), Philo observes, is one of the many perfect gifts of God's grace (χάρις).[129]

---

[125] *Quis Her.* 166. See also *Som.* I.162-163, *Abr.* 143-146.

[126] *Quod Deus* 107. Cf. the 'rich boons' (πλουσίαι χάριτες) of nature, *Virt.* 94.

[127] *Op.* 23.

[128] *Post.* 32. In *Ebr.* 107, Philo again refers to God's 'undying acts of grace' (ἀθάνατοι αὐτοῦ χάριτες). The word ἀθάνατος was standard inscriptional fare. In an inscription outlining the management of his bequest to the city (*SEG* XIII 258 [AD 41/42]), Phainios of Gytheion refers to the undying (ἀθάνατα) profits which will accrue from his favour (χάριτος) and gift (δωρεᾶς). A decree of the Dionysiac craftsmen (*IG* XI[4] 1061: 172—167 BC) describes the craftsmen's immortal glory (ἀθάνατος δόξα) as remaining forever.

[129] *Agr.* 93. In *Spec. Leg.* II. 219, Philo also places great emphasis on the earth's fruits (καρποί) as evidence of God's boons (χάριτες) and gifts (δωρεαί). Similarly, in an inscriptional hymn to Isis-Hermouthis (*SEG* VIII 549), Isodorus points to the fertility of the crops (καρπός) as evidence for the beneficence of the goddess. Additionally, Philo allegorises the καρποί of God's grace as both 'virtues' (ἀρεταί: *Cher.* 84, *Ebr.* 224) and 'thanksgiving' (εὐχαριστία *Agr.* 126). The inscriptions, too, make similar statements. Precisely because Zosimos of Priene (*I. Priene* 112: 84 BC) understood 'that merit (ἀρετή) alone returns the greatest fruits (καρπούς) and favours (χάριτας)', he did not achieve a 'fruitless (ἄκαρπον) return of honour'. An epigram on a Jewish funerary inscription from Beth She'arim (first half of the III cent. AD) employs a metaphorical use:
I, the son of Leontios, lie dead, Justus, the son of Sappho,

The Divine bounty (δωρεάς), however, is always given in proportion to the capacities of His recipients (τὰς τῶν εὐεργετουμένον δυνάμεις) and stands in contrast to God's own limitless bounties (χαρίτες).[130] Elsewhere, in a brief commentary on Deut 15:8, Philo expands upon God's bestowal of His boons. He argues that 'we must not grant (χαριστέον) everything to everybody', but only what is appropriate to their need.[131] This policy is modelled on God's beneficence. As Philo elaborates, He 'causes His earliest gifts (χάριτας) to cease before their recipients are glutted and wax insolent'. These initial gifts of God are stored up for future benefactions, and are progressively re-introduced to replace existing gifts.[132]

The thorny issue of the relation between God's grace and His judgement is aired by Philo. God, whose nature is good and bountiful (φιλόδωρος), continually extends boons (χάριτας), gifts (δωρεάς), and benefits (εὐεργεσίας). But His punishments are meted out by those authorities sovereignly appointed for such services.[133]

Further, the era of the patriarchs testifies to the reality of God's continual beneficence.[134] God's gracious gifts (χάριτες), as evidenced in His promise of Isaac's birth, strengthen Abraham's piety (εὐσέβεια).[135] Joseph's brothers (unbeknownst to them) beg their long-lost brother, now God's vice-regent in Egypt, to spare their youngest brother Benjamin. They request this boon (χάρις) out of pity (ἔλεος) for their father, Israel, who was a man of virtue (ἀρετή), honour (τιμή), and nobility (καλοκἀγαθία).[136] Moses exudes confidence in God's generosity, 'magnifying God's love of giving gifts and granting favours (τὸ τοῦ θεοῦ φιλόδωρον καὶ χαριστικόν)'.[137] Prior to the Exodus, Moses urges the Israelites to make the Passover sacrifice, both as a sign of their unfailing eagerness (προθυμία) to struggle against the passions,

---

Who, having plucked the fruit (κ[αρπό]ν) of wisdom,
Left the light, my poor parents in endless mourning,
And my brothers too, alas, in my Beth She'arim.
See M. Schwabe and B. Lifshitz (eds), *Beth She'arim. Volume II: The Greek Inscriptions* (Jerusalem 1974), §127.

[130] *Op.* 23.
[131] *Post.* 142.
[132] *Ibid.*, 145. *Agr.* 89-90 presents a gracious God (χαριζόμενος) who dispenses His benefits, gifts, and boons (χάριτας) 'in ceaseless flow' and 'in unbroken cycle'. This inspires both loyalty (φιλία) and affection (εὔνοια) towards God as Benefactor. See also *Ebr.* 32.
[133] *Fug.* 66.
[134] The names of antediluvian figures such as Enoch embody grace terminology (χάρις *Conf.* 123, *Post.* 35-36, 41; κεχαρισμένος *Abr.* 17). Noah, too, found grace (LXX Gen. 6:8: χάριν) in contrast to the ungrateful (ἀχάριστοι: *Quod Deus* 70-71, 74).
[135] *Mut.* 155; cf. *ibid.*, 267. *Quis Her.* 30-31.
[136] *Jos.* 229-230.
[137] *Leg. All.* III. 106.

and as a thanksgiving (εὐχαριστία) to God the Saviour (σωτήρ).[138] Finally, the matriarchs feature in Philo's works as allegories of virtue.[139] Hanna, whose name is interpreted as 'her grace' (χάρις αὐτῆς), is blessed with the wisdom of God as a gift (δώρημα).[140]

Second, how does Philo incorporate the role of God as εὐεργέτης into the wider Old Testament covenantal framework? Philo expends considerable effort in explaining how the covenant is undergirded by God's grace. However, in the process, he allegorises the Old Testament text. As a result, his conception of the covenant of grace differs markedly to the Old Testament counterpart. Three examples will secure the point.

In his exposition of Deut 9:5, Philo argues that 'the covenant of God is an allegory of His gifts of grace' (χάριτες). Because of the perfection of God's gifts, only virtue (ἀρετή) and virtuous actions (αἱ κατ' ἀρετὴν πράξεις) can preserve God's people from vices such as ingratitude (ἀχαριστία).[141] Here Philo has moved the focus away from Deuteronomy's emphasis — the rejection of any merit on Israel's part as the condition of God's covenantal blessing — to a more Graeco-Roman concentration on merit.

Further, on the basis of Gen 17:2, Philo states that the 'covenants are drawn up for the benefit of those who are worthy of the gift' (τῶν δωρεᾶς ἀξίων). Certainly, the covenant is a symbol of grace (χάριτος). But, above all, it is 'virgin grace' (παρθένος χάρις) which is God's crowning benefaction in the human soul. For readers of Philo, this may have bordered on the mythological through Philo's addition of παρθένος, an epithet elsewhere applied by Philo to the 'virgin' Χάριτες, the daughters of Zeus. Whether Philo intended a mythological reference in this case is difficult to determine.[142]

---

[138] *Mig.* 25. The Old Testament nowhere presents mortification of the passions as a reason for the Passover institution (as Philo does). See Exod 12:1-13, 21-27, 43-49; Deut 16:1-8.

[139] See J. LaPorte, *op. cit.*, 147-155.

[140] *Quod Deus* 5-6; *Mut.* 144.

[141] *Sacr.* 57-58.

[142] *Mut.* 52-53. For the hypostasis of χάρις in Philo — and the related use of παρθένος (the 'virgin' Graces, daughters of Jupiter) — see *Post.* 32; *Abr.* 52-54; *Fug.* 140-141; *Mos.* II. 7; *Mig.* 31; *Leg.* 105. Also, Seneca, *Ben.*, 1.3.1-10 (*virgines*: 1.3.2). For the attribution of παρθένος to Greek deities, see G. Delling in *TDNT* 5 (1967), 827-829. I remain unconvinced by the suggestion of A. Jaubert (*La notion d'alliance dans le judaïsme aux abords de l'ère chrétienne* [Paris 1963], 431) that when Philo associates the grace of God with the epithet παρθένος, it has lost 'ses résonances païennes inquiétantes' and merely evokes 'la merveilleuse pureté de la grâce divine'. Philo's Greek audience may well have thought otherwise. Finally, we note in passing that archaeological excavation of the third-century AD synagogue at Dura-Europos has unearthed (arguably) a representation of the Χάριτες. This pictorial hypostatis of χάρις in the 'Infancy of Moses' underlines the continued hellenisation of the Jewish theology of grace incipient in Philo. See J. Neusner,

However, to dub grace παρθένος — even if Philo's use is symbolic — was bold on his part.

Last, in a complex allegory of Gen 9:11, Philo locates the bounties (χαρίτες) of the covenant in the soul of the just person (δίκαιος). God's covenant, a divine expression of the highest law and principle that rules over everything, is identical to justice (τὸ δίκαιον). Therefore,

... while the gifts bestowed (χαρίζονται) by others are not the same as the recipients, God gives not only the gifts but in them gives the recipients to themselves. For He has given myself to me and everything that is to itself, since "I will establish my covenant with thee" is the same as "I will give thyself to thee". And it is the earnest desire (σπουδάζουσι) of all the God-beloved to fly from the stormy waters of engrossing business with its perpetual turmoil of surge and billow, and anchor in the calm safe shelter of virtue's (ἀρετῆς) roadsteads.[143]

This process of giving the covenant to just individuals (οἱ δίκαιοι), characterised by Philo as the recipients receiving themselves, is directed towards the establishment of ἀρετή in the soul.

To conclude, Philo's view of the covenant gravitates more towards a Graeco-Roman conception of ἀρετή and mythological conceptions of χάρις, than to the Old Testament understanding of God's sovereign bestowal of grace to His chosen people in history.

Third, who are the recipients of God's grace in the perspective of Philo? χάρις is restricted to those who are ἄξιοι.[144] In an important discussion of LXX Gen 6:9, Philo canvasses the interpretative options for the statement that 'Noah found grace (χάριν) with the Lord.' Did the text mean that Noah 'obtained grace' or 'was thought worthy of grace' (χάριτος ἄξιος)? Philo dismisses the first option since God would be acting unfairly in the allocation of His 'divine grace' (χάριτος θείας) by arbitrarily distributing His favour to Noah. Philo's preferred exegetical position is that God judges those who are worthy of His gifts (δωρεῶν ἀξίους) to be the recipients of His grace.

Admittedly, Philo refocuses the whole debate by concentrating on the nature of God Himself. Because God bestows no gift of grace (κεχάρισται) on Himself, He prefers to be beneficent (τὸ εὐεργετεῖν) in accordance with His eternal goodness, rather than dispensing bounties to those who are worthy

---

Early Rabbinic Judaism (Leiden 1975), 193-196; W.G. Moon, 'Nudity and Narrative: Observations on the Frescoes from the Dura Synagogue', *JAAR* 60/4 (1992), 587-658.

[143] *Som.* II. 224.

[144] See S. Sandmel, 'Philo Judaeus: An Introduction to the Man, His Writings, and His Significence', *ANRW* II 21/1 (1983), 26: 'Grace can most readily come to the man whose virtue puts him into the position of receiving it'.

of His grace.¹⁴⁵ But, elsewhere, Philo reverts to his view that the recipients should be worthy of God's bounties.

Moses, therefore, 'is deemed worthy of the boon' (ἀξιοῦνται μέντοι τῆς χάριτος) due to his ἀρετή.¹⁴⁶ The brothers of Joseph praise his fairness (ἔπαινος ἰσότητος) and kind behaviour in treating them as worthy of his favour (χάριτος ἀξίοις).¹⁴⁷ In his discussion of Deut 30:9-10, Philo portrays God, like any human parent, being gladdened by His children who strive for virtue (ἀρετήν) and demonstrate 'an ardour for noble living' (καλοκἀγαθίας ζῆλον).¹⁴⁸ Abraham is praised for his practice of piety (εὐσέβεια), displayed in his mercy towards the poor (πένητας ἐλεῶν) and kindnesses towards friends (φίλους εὐεργετῶν). God regards such beneficence 'with special favour' (τὰ σπουδαῖα χάριτι).¹⁴⁹ Finally, on the basis of Gen 17:4, Philo draws the conclusion that the Abrahamic covenant assures bounties (χάριτας) and gifts (δωρεάς) to those who are worthy to receive them (ἀξίοις).¹⁵⁰

Overall, Philo's views on this issue are likely to have been influenced by Graeco-Roman ideas of beneficence. The honorific inscriptions insist that recipients of beneficence must return favours or register thanks that are worthy of the original benefits.¹⁵¹ The implication is clear: benefactors simply did not benefit those who were unworthy or who might respond unworthily. Philo's thought on χάρις and the ἄξιοι arises from the ideology of the inscriptions, not from the Old Testament. To be sure, the Old Testament demanded a proper response from the recipients of God's grace: but the idea that the ἄξιοι somehow attracted God's χάρις is eschewed there, and acts of piety were regarded as the consequence of being in a covenantal relationship with God.¹⁵²

---

¹⁴⁵ *Quod Deus* 104-108.
¹⁴⁶ *Leg. All.* III. 14. More generally, *ibid.*, III. 164.
¹⁴⁷ *Jos.* 249.
¹⁴⁸ *Som.* II. 176-178: ἄξιοι χάριτος, 177.
¹⁴⁹ *Mut.* 39-40.
¹⁵⁰ *Ibid.*, 52, 58.
¹⁵¹ E.g. *SIG*³ 587; *Michel* 515, 985, 1011; *I. Kalchedon* 1; *I. Délos* IV 1507; *IG* XI(4) 1061. See especially the discussion of S.C. Mott, *op. cit.*, 224 n.27. We should, however, be wary here of narrowly interpreting ἄξιος through the grid of the Reformed theological framework of grace versus merit. The issue in the first-century context is slightly different. The use of the epithet ἄξιος in conjunction with χάρις in the honorific inscriptions points not only to the obligation of reciprocity but also to the importance of commensurability of return (§2.4). The problem for Paul was probably that this traditional benefaction ideology, when employed in covenantal contexts similar to that of Philo, reverses the direction of our indebtedness to God (§6.5).
¹⁵² Philo (*Mig.* 73) comes closer to the LXX understanding when he says: 'God bestows

Fourth, how should the recipients of divine grace respond to God as εὐεργέτης, and to His human servants who dispense χάριτες? Undoubtedly, Philo was well aware of the shame often associated with ancient benefaction rituals.[153] One illustration from Philo will suffice. While God bestows gifts (χαρίσασθαι) easily, Philo concedes that 'it is no light matter to receive the proffered boons (δωρεάς)'.[154] Nevertheless, the priests who ministered in the temple should feel no shame in accepting their share of the first fruit offerings, since these gifts originated in the free beneficence (χαρίζεσθαι) of God — not men.[155] Overall, then, Philo assumes that thankfulness to the benefactor was the fitting response, along with the conferral of appropriate honours.[156]

Nor is Philo backward in highlighting the folly of people in ignoring this fundamental tenet of gratitude to benefactors. If God had not exercised pity, the human race would 'have been wiped out by reason of its ingratitude (ἀχαριστίαν) to God its benefactor (εὐεργέτην) and preserver (σωτῆρα)'.[157] Philo, reflecting on the chief butler's failure to remember Joseph's help, draws a telling conclusion: 'the ungrateful (ἀχάριστος) are always forgetful of their benefactors (εὐεργετῶν)'.[158] Anyone who shows ingratitude (ἀχαριστεῖν) falls from the state of virtue in which he received the benefits.[159] Finally, 'the thankful (εὐχάριστος) soul is the enemy of arrogance', whilst 'unthankfulness (ἀχαριστία) is akin to pride'.[160] By contrast, the generous person imitates God in freely bestowing boons (χαρίζεσθαι).[161]

Last, how do God's servants fit into the overall scheme of divine benefaction? In this respect, Philo uses speeches (human and divine) as a

---

(χαρίζεται) on those who obey Him no imperfect boon (ἀτελὲς οὐδέν)'. Note that ἀτελής was the word chosen by the citizens of Cardamylae (SEG XI [948]: I cent. AD) to describe their 'never-ending gratitude' (ἀτελῆ χάριν) to the city's benefactor, Poseidippos. In *Fug.* 141, Philo also mentions that our seach for God is never fruitless (ἀτελής), since He meets us with His pure and virgin graces (παρθένοις χάρισι).

[153] Note the comment of B.J. Malina (*The New Testament World: Insights from Cultural Anthropology* [London 1981], 79): 'Among equals, such "gratitude" is shameful, but with superiors it is honourable, provided that no more interactions with the same superior are foreseen or expected'.

[154] *Mut.* 218-219.

[155] *Spec. Leg.* I. 152.

[156] Philo links εὐχαριστία with τιμή on several occasions (*Sac.* 63; *Quod Deus* 7; *Agr.* 81), as do the inscriptions. E.g. *SIG*³ 748; *Michel* 372 (χάρις καὶ τιμή), 475; *SEG* XI 948.

[157] *Op.* 169.

[158] *Jos.* 99.

[159] *Spec. Leg.* I. 284.

[160] *Virt.* 165-166.

[161] *Ibid.*, 168-169. For further examples, see *Sac.* 58; *Quod Deus* 48, 74; *Quis Her.* 226, 302; *Mos.* I. 58; *Leg.* 118.

showcase for benefaction terminology and its underlying rationale. Two examples will establish the point. In reply to Moses' request for God to reveal Himself, God endorses the zeal (προθυμία) of Moses as praiseworthy (ἐπαινετή). Nevertheless, God does not accede to Moses' request, adding by way of explanation His own rationale of benefaction:

> I freely bestow (χαρίζομαι) what is in accordance with the recipient; for not all that I can give with ease is within man's power to take, and therefore to him that is worthy of My grace (τῷ χάριτος ἀξίῳ) I extend all the boons (δωρεάς) which he is capable of receiving.[162]

In sum, Moses had been reminded by God that all benefaction exclusively resided in His sovereign freedom and grace, and not in the initiative of His servants.

Elsewhere, in a dramatic speech replete with benefaction terminology, Joseph tells his (unknowing) brothers that he is both their benefactor and lost brother. Undoubtedly, Philo's audience would have recognised Joseph as the ἀνήρ καλὸς καὶ ἀγαθός of the honorific inscriptions by virtue of the benefaction terminology employed in the speech. Joseph's reverence (εὐσέβεια) for his father and humanity (φιλανθρωπία) towards mankind explained the favour (χάρις) which he was now displaying towards his faithless brothers.[163] As God's servant and viceroy in Egypt, he was in the position to administer boons (χάριτας) and gifts (δωρεάς) 'in the time of their greatest need (ἐν τοῖς ἀναγκαιοτάτοις καιροῖς)'.[164] Consequently, Joseph held the first place of honour (τιμή) with the king. Moreover, the honour given to Joseph by the king was not just positional, but personal: 'though I am young and he my elder (μὲ νέον ὄντα πρεσβύτερος ὤν), he honours me as a father (ὡς πατέρα τιμᾷ)'.[165] Further, as the Egyptian viceroy, Joseph was not only responsible for the inhabitants of Egypt —the international arena demanded his attention as well. In the words of Joseph, the other nations 'need me at the head'.[166] Thus, in this regard, Joseph's responsibilities included the distribution of silver, gold, and sustenance to foreign suppliants.[167]

What is remarkable about Joseph's speech is not just its widespread use of benefaction terminology, but (in view of the inscriptional evidence) the precision and rarity of its phraseology. The phrase, ἐν τοῖς ἀναγκαιοτάτοις

---

[162] *Spec. Leg.* I. 43-44.
[163] *Jos.* 239.
[164] *Ibid.*, 241.
[165] *Ibid.*, 242. Philo has interpreted the LXX ἐποίησέ με ὡς πατέρα Φαραώ (Gen 45:8) from a benefaction perspective.
[166] *Jos.* 242.
[167] *Ibid.*, 243.

καιροῖς, is found only twice in our sample of the honorific inscriptions using χάρις. Philo's audience would have measured the beneficence of Joseph against contemporary Graeco-Roman civic benefactors who delivered their suppliants from distress in times of acute need. For example, Xenokleas of Akraephiae was serviceable to the city 'in the most pressing times' (ἐν τοῖς ἀναγκαιοτάτοις καιροῖς) of corn shortage; Patron of Delos, benefactor of a corporation of merchants and ship owners, 'announced just deeds in the name of the guild in the most pressing time (ἐν τῶι ἀναγκαιοτάτωι καιρῶι)'.[168] Finally, the very personal honours accorded Joseph by the Egyptian king find close parallel in Theokles of Olbia, who became 'as a son (ὡς υἱός) in regard to the more aged (πρεσβυτέροις), as a father (ὡς πατήρ) in regard to the more young (παισίν)'.[169] Thus, in the view of Philo, some of God's servants in the Old Testament period best approximated the contemporary paragons of munificence known so well to Philo's audience through the inscriptions.

In our next section, we will examine the motif of reciprocity in Philo and assess its relevance to Philo's understanding of χάρις.

4.4.3. Philo and the ethos of reciprocity

As we have seen, reciprocity was an important leitmotiv in first century inscriptions, with the Homeric ritual of the counter-gift being applied to both divine and human relationships.[170] Philo's view of divine reciprocity is delicately poised.[171] Stated succinctly, Philo says that while it is impossible for any human to requite God's generosity, God nonetheless requites human piety with His own acts of mercy. Overall, Philo gives the strongest emphasis to the unilateral nature of God's benefits. However, reciprocity remains the basis for human relationships and for the Mosaic legislation.

The tension between our total indebtedness to God and His requital of human piety is easily demonstrated from Philo. The idea that we can somehow recompense (ἀμείψασθαι) or praise (ἐπαινέσαι) the infinite Creator God as He deserves (κατὰ τὴν ἀξίαν) is jettisoned by Philo. God is never honoured as He deserves (ἀξίως), just as we (humanly speaking) never requite our parents with boons equal to their original generosity (τοῖς

---

[168] Michel 236, 998. For additional inscriptional examples, see C.B. Welles, *Royal Correspondence in the Hellenistic Period: A Study in Greek Epigraphy* (London 1934), §63; *I. Délos* IV 1517 (154 BC); *IG* II(2) 971 (140—139 BC); *I. Iasos* 152; *I. Keramos* 6. For the papyri, see *UPZ* I 71 (152 BC).

[169] *CIG* II 2059.

[170] See our discussion of divine and human reciprocity in §2.6—§2.7.

[171] See the discussion of G.W. Peterman, *Paul's Gift from Philippi: Conventions of Gift Exchange and Christian Giving* (Cambridge 1997), 45-49.

γονεῦσιν ἴσας ἀποδοῦναι χάριτας).[172] However, when Abraham offered Isaac as a sacrifice, God Himself acts reciprocally. Isaac was spared 'since God returned (ἀντιχαρισαμένου) the gift (δῶρον) of him and used the offering which piety (εὐσεβεῖτο) rendered to Him to repay (ἀντιτιμήσαντος) the offerer'. Here God meets the reciprocal obligations implicit in benefaction rituals. He ensures that Abraham's gift (the presentation of Isaac for sacrifice) is recompensed with His own counter-gift (the preservation of Isaac's life). The entire transaction demonstrates that those who display the appropriate cultic piety will experience the reciprocation of divine favour.[173]

Furthermore, Philo urges that God should be requited with appropriate expressions of gratitude (ταῖς εὐχαριστίαις ἀμείβεσθαι).[174] Elsewhere, he elaborates on the reasons for this. God's characteristic work is the bestowal of boons (εὐεργετεῖν). All creation, by contrast, is to render thanks (εὐχαριστεῖν) because 'it has no power to render in return (ἀμοιβήν) anything beyond this'.[175] In this respect, Philo observes that whatever we attempt to give God by way of requital (ἀντιχαρίσασθαι) — apart from thanks — is already His property as Creator.

Reciprocity is also binding for any relationship that has been established through beneficence. In this regard, Joseph behaved admirably when he resisted the sexual advances of Potiphar's wife. Potiphar, as the εὐεργέτης of Joseph, would not have been given 'a suitable return (ἀντιπαρέχειν) for his preceding favours (ταῖς προϋπηργμέναις χάρισιν)', had Joseph succumbed to her charms.[176]

According to Philo, the fifth commandment of the Mosaic Decalogue must be understood within a reciprocity framework. All impiety (ἀσέβεια) towards parents is reprehensible when it is remembered that parental boons (δωρεαί) towards children exceed all possibility of repayment (ἀμοιβάς).[177] Although children are unable to make a complete return (ἀντιχαρίζεσθαι) to

---

[172] *Leg. All.* III. 10.
[173] *Abr.* 177.
[174] *Spec. Leg.* I. 224.
[175] *Plant.* 130.
[176] *Jos.* 46. Philo has enhanced the benefaction perspective present in the LXX story (Gen 39). Although Potiphar's patronage of Jacob is acknowledged in the LXX (Gen 39:4 [εὗρεν Ἰωσὴφ χάριν ἐναντίον τοῦ κυρίου αὐτοῦ]; Gen 39:8-9a), the ultimate source of Joseph's patronage remains God (Gen 39:2-3, 5, 21, 23). Therefore, in contrast to Philo, the LXX provides a different reason for Joseph's refusal to broach Potiphar's trust in him. According to the LXX, an adulterous affair with Potiphar's wife would have plunged Joseph into heinous sin against God (LXX Gen 39:9b), involving him in considerably more that just — as Philo asserts (*Jos.* 46-47) — the violation of the norms of reciprocity and divine justice.
[177] *Decal.* 111-112.

their parents, Philo says that they should ponder the faithfulness of animals in returning the kindnesses (ἐν χαρίτων ἀμοιβαῖς) of their human benefactors.[178] This emphasis upon the reciprocation of parental favour departs from the reason that the Mosaic Decalogue gives for honouring parents: God's promise of covenantal blessing (Exod 20:12; Deut 8:18). Philo, in this instance, has dressed the Mosaic legislation in benefaction garb.

In Philo's discussion of other sections of the Mosaic Law similar motifs recur. Philo, commenting on LXX passages prohibiting the loan of money on interest (Exod 22:5; Lev 25:35-37), points to the law's charity (φιλανθρωπία) when it demands repayment of the principal alone (i.e. without any additional interest). According to Philo, the rationale behind these particular Mosaic Laws was the opportunity that it gave to the borrowers for reciprocity in the future:

For later, as the proper occasion arise, they will make the same sacrifice to their present creditors and requite with equal assistance (ἀμειβόμενοι ταῖς ἴσαις ὠφελείαις) those who were the first to bestow the benefit (τοὺς χάριτος ἄρξαντας).[179]

Again, in another discussion of loans, Philo encourages his readers to show readiness (προθυμότατα) in generosity, with the assurance that their sacrificial giving would be reciprocated:

... to give free gifts (χαρίζεσθαι) to those who need, reflecting that a free gift (χάρις) is in a sense a loan that will be repaid (ἀποδοθησόμενον) by the recipient, when times are better, without compulsion (ἄνευ ἀνάγκης) and with a willing heart.[180]

Overall, Philo's reciprocity motif distorts the focus of the Mosaic Law in the cases cited above. The Mosaic Law points to God's redemptive love, not reciprocity, as the incentive for Israelite generosity to the impoverished (Lev 25:36, 38). However, an intriguing question remains: does Philo critique χάρις against its Graeco-Roman benefaction context?

4.4.4. Philo's critique of charis in its benefaction context

Philo interacts with the concept of χάρις as propagated in the honorific inscriptions on one occasion. In *Cher.* 122-123, cited below, Philo probes each side of the benefaction ritual, exposing (what he perceives to be) the

---

[178] *Ibid.*, 112-115.

[179] *Spec. Leg.* II. 78. On the aspect of equality (ταῖς ἴσαις ὠφελείαις), see §4.5.1 n.205 below.

[180] *Virt.* 83. Philo's emphasis upon the lack of compulsion (ἄνευ ἀνάγκης) in generosity may be derived from Deut 15:10 (similarly, Paul in 2 Cor 9:7: ἐξ ἀνάγκης). Nevertheless, caution is warranted here since the LXX does not employ ἀνάγκη on this occasion.

mercenary nature of the mutually advantageous relationship between benefactors and their beneficiaries:

> Look round you and you shall find that those who are said to bestow benefits (χαρίζεσθαι) sell rather than give (δωρουμένους), and those who seem to us to receive them (λαμβάνειν χάριτας) in truth buy. The givers are seeking praise (ἔπαινον) or honour (τιμήν) as their exchange (ἀμοιβήν) and look for the repayment of the benefit (χάριτος ἀντίδοσιν), and thus, under the specious name of gift (δωρεᾶς), they in real truth carry out a sale; for the seller's way is to take something for what he offers. The receivers of the gift (τὰς δωρεάς), too, study to make some return (ἀποδοῦναι), and do so (ἀποδιδόντες) as opportunity offers, and thus they act as buyers. For buyers know well that receiving and paying (ἀποδοῦναι) go hand in hand. But God is no salesman, hawking his goods in the market, but a free giver of all things, pouring forth fountains of free bounties (χαρίτων), and seeking no return (ἀμοιβῆς). For He has no needs Himself and no created being is able to repay His gift (ἀντιδοῦναι δωρεάν).

In Philo's view, benefaction is at heart a financial transaction, in spite of the specious nature of its terminology (δωρεά: 'gift'; χάρις: 'benefit'). In reality, benefactors 'sell' their benefits in exchange for praise and honour; conversely, the beneficiaries 'buy' their benefits, with deference, gratitude, and public honours for the benefactor being the currency of trade.[181] The motif of reciprocity is emphasised in Philo's choice of terminology for the benefaction ritual. Prepositions such as ἀπο and ἀντί, which preface verbs such as ἀποδιδόναι and ἀντιδιδόναι, sharpen our focus on the projected return in the transaction, as does reciprocation terminology like ἀμοιβή. In terms of its terminology and motifs, Philo's presentation of the whole benefaction process bears a strong stylistic resemblance to the Cardamylae inscription in honour of Poseidippos: it enshrines first-century cultural orthodoxy as far as beneficence and best represents the view Philo is caricaturing.[182]

Even more remarkable are the contrasts Philo draws between the inscriptional view of χάρις and the χάριτες of the Old Testament God. God does not operate like an ancient benefactor, who hawks his goods in a commercial enterprise. Rather, God's character is animated by an unconditional generosity, not by any sense of obligation — whether it be some personal need or expectation of return on God's part. We would be mistaken, however, if we think that a Jewish understanding of God exclusively informs Philo's views at this point. Seneca, too, can speak of divine beneficence in Stoic terms similar to Philo:

> It is our aim to live according to Nature, and to follow the example of the gods. Yet, in all their acts, what inducement have the gods other than the very principle of action? Unless

---

[181] For a similar criticism of the benefaction system, see Dio Chrysostom *Or.*, 7.89 (§5.5.2).

[182] *SEG* XI 948. See our discussion of the inscription in §2.6.

perchance you suppose that they obtain a reward for their deeds from the smoke of burnt offerings and the odour of incense! See the gigantic efforts they make every day, the great largesses they dispense ... They do all these things without any reward, without attaining any advantage for themselves.[183]

Nevertheless, Philo's approach to beneficence is unusual in ancient literature by virtue of his unabashed criticism of an institution which was viewed in a positive light. Admittedly, there was the inevitable grumbling of benefactors in antiquity over the burdensome nature of λειτουργίαι.[184] However, such complaints were usually overcome by the benefactors being designated 'free from λειτουργίαι' (ἀλειτούργητος) on account of their generosity, or by being induced with the irresistible bait of more public honours.[185] Certainly, nothing comparable appears in the inscriptions, and this underlines the stability of the cultural stereotype that Philo is attacking. In the case of the moralists — who present 'a darker side' to the social conventions underpinning the honorific inscriptions[186] — the various failures of the benefaction system are stated with appropriate moral censure.[187] However, the overall confidence of the moralists in the benefaction system is not undermined by that, nor is it subjected to theological re-evaluation (as with Philo).

Last, in *Fug.* 28-29, Philo adopts the censorious tone of the moralists in his contrast between the 'worthless man of wealth' and the truly beneficent man. The worthless man, a slavish creature in Philo's opinion, manifests a contradiction in lifestyle. He may be 'a skinflint and a splitpenny.' Alternatively, he could be trapped in 'a whirl of prodigality', seeking the company of courtesans, pimps, and other low life. True beneficence, Philo reminds us (*Fug.*, 29), is marked by its civic-mindedness and by φιλία towards those deserving of benefaction:

---

[183] Seneca, *Ben.*, 4.25.1-2. Cf. Cicero, *Nat. D.* 1.121; Plutarch, *Mor.*, 423D.

[184] For protests against nomination to a liturgy in the papyri, see N. Lewis, *Leitourgia Papyri: Documents on Compulsory Public Service in Egypt under Roman Rule*, (Philadelphia 1963: *TAPhA* 53/9), Nos. 4 (AD 161) and 5 (AD 180).

[185] An association decree from Delos (I. Délos IV 1521: II cent. BC), in praise of a father and his son, apportions the following honours: 'it was resolved to praise both together and to honour each of them with a gold crown and with a bronze image and to set up (the image) in whatever (place) they prefer; and that they receive in addition the fitting privilege of entrance to the guild, having an honoured place for reclining (at the guild banquets), being free (ἀλειτουρ[γήτ]ους) of all public service (λειτουργίας) and that in the course of each drinking-bout both be honoured in the guild with a proclamation'. For further uses of ἀλειτούργητος, see Michel 475, 998; *RDGE* 49; *I. Délos* IV 1520.

[186] R.M. Kidd, *Wealth and Beneficence in the Pastoral Epistles: A 'Bourgeois' Form of Early Christianity?* (Atlanta 1990), 88.

[187] *Ibid.*, 88-90.

You will contribute freely to needy friends, will make bountiful gifts (δωρεάς) to serve your country's wants, you will help parents without means to marry their daughters, and provide them with an ample dowry; you will all but throw your private property into the common stock and invite all deserving of kindness (τοὺς ἀξίους χάριτος) to take a share.

4.4.5. Conclusion

More could be said about the role of χάρις in Philo.[188] Notwithstanding, modern scholarship on Philo has laboured under the misconception that Philo's view of grace is better contrasted against the concerns of Paul's theology than its first-century benefaction context. The foregoing discussion has demonstrated the enrichment in our understanding of Philo which occurs when his benefaction terminology (including χάρις) is interpreted against the backdrop of the honorific inscriptions.

In contexts where χάρις is used, Philo employs words and phrases from the inscriptions to describe God's acts of beneficence and those of His servants. This would have secured a ready recognition of Philo's terminology, as his presentation of Joseph as the inscriptional ἀνήρ καλὸς καὶ ἀγαθός demonstrates. However, in reworking the LXX from a benefaction perspective, Philo is often tempted to diverge from the Old Testament understanding of covenantal grace.

At a theological level, Philo believes that God dispenses χάρις in accordance with His eternal goodness. Overall, Philo leans towards a Graeco-Roman understanding of merit and alludes to traditional mythological motifs in his presentation of covenantal χάρις. In a radical departure, Philo critiques the orthodox inscriptional view of χάρις by means of a familiar caricature of the benefaction system and by the use of Stoic theology. Finally, Philo's understanding of χάρις and the ethos of reciprocity is largely typical of his times, with the exception of his stronger emphasis on the unilateral nature of divine grace.[189] However, Philo's interest in the reciprocity motif leads him to distort the theological rationale of several items of Mosaic legislation.

4.5. Charis, *Josephus, and Beneficence*

A much-neglected source for the understanding of χάρις in its first-century context is the Jewish historian Josephus (AD 37/38—c. 100). Modern

---

[188] See Philo's conception of χάρις in relation to repentance (*Spec. Leg.* I. 187), prophetic inspiration (*Ebr.* 145-146), salvation (*Ebr.* 112), piety (*Mut.* 155), the use of the mind and senses (*Conf.* 127; cf. *Migr.* 70), and the thought-life (*Leg. All.* II. 32-33).

[189] See the discussion of S.C. Mott, *op. cit.*, 306-307.

scholarship has largely ignored Josephus' view of χάρις and his portrayal of beneficence in the Jewish and Graeco-Roman world more generally.[190] Josephus' citation of honorific inscriptions and royal correspondence should have alerted scholars to the importance of benefaction terminology and motifs in his writings.[191] But, apart from E.P. Sanders' (entirely conceptual) analysis of the Josephan view of grace, these tantalising clues have not been taken up.[192] Thus the methodological blindspot which has afflicted modern discussions of Philonic and Pauline grace — the abstraction of χάρις from its Graeco-Roman benefaction context — applies to modern Josephan scholarship as well.

We should not overlook the real possibility that Josephus' apologetic aims have influenced his presentation of divine and human χάρις. That Josephus' portrayal of Jewish history has a polemical edge is clear enough. The first-century Alexandrian author, Apion, had asserted that the Jewish nation spawned no-one as eminent as Socrates, Zeno or Cleanthes. In the *Antiquities* Josephus responds to Apion's charge with a cavalcade of Old Testament luminaries who (in his view) were as deserving of commendation (ἔπαινοῦ) as the ἄνδρες καλοὶ καὶ ἀγαθοί of the Greek city-states.[193] Josephus states in the preface of the *Antiquities* that he chose to write on Jewish origins and antiquities so that the Greeks would consider his own civilisation worthy of study.[194] He points to King Ptolemy Philadelphus, who set in motion the

---

[190] Note the fleeting references of A. Schlatter, *Wie sprach Josephus von Gott?* (Gütersloh 1910), 58, 63, 65; G.P. Wetter, *op. cit.*, 14 n.1; J. Moffatt, *op. cit.*, 33, 35, 51, 103, 127, 338. For a brief discussion of Josephus' use of benefaction terminology and his avoidance of covenantal theology, see H.W. Attridge, *The Interpretation of Biblical History in the* Antiquitates Judaicae *of Flavius Josephus* (Missoula 1976), 78ff.

[191] Respectively, *AJ* 14.149-155 (Attica: 106—105 BC); 12.48-57.

[192] E.P. Sanders, 'Judaism and the Grand "Christian" Abstractions: Love, Mercy, and Grace', *Int* 39/4 (1985), 357-372. Sanders (*ibid.*, 371) makes this comment regarding the Josephan view of grace (original emphasis): 'Josephus derived that elevated theology *from somewhere*. He shows no sign of being a creative theologian himself, and here he is passing on what he perceives to be the standard view of the relationship between grace and works'. In my opinion, E.P. Sanders' case is flawed in two respects. First, he has not considered the extent to which the Graeco-Roman benefaction system may have subverted traditional Jewish views of grace. Second, Sanders has underestimated the degree to which Josephus either reinterprets or mutes the covenantal framework of LXX χάρις On the latter, see B.H. Amaru, 'Land Theology in Josephus' Jewish Antiquities', *JQR* 71 (1980), 201-209; *id.*, 'Land Theology in Philo and Josephus', in L.A. Hoffman (ed.), *The Land of Israel: Jewish Perspectives* (Notre Dame 1986), 65-93. On Josephus' religious views, see J.A. Montgomery, 'The Religion of Flavius Josephus', *JQR* 1 (1920), 277-305; R.J.H. Shutt, 'The Concept of God in the Works of Flavius Josephus', *JJS* 31 (1981), 171-189; P. Bilde, *Flavius Josephus Between Jerusalem and Rome: His Life, His Works, and Their Importance* (Sheffield 1988), 182-191.

[193] *Ap.* 2.135-136.

[194] *AJ* 1.5.

translation of the LXX, as an example of the Greeks likely to be attracted by such an enterprise.[195]

Therefore it is entirely possible that Josephus, like Philo before him, would render events and characters of the LXX narrative in the familiar strains of the honorific inscriptions, as part of his apologetic hellenisation of the Old Testament.[196] This is confirmed by the wide range of benefaction terminology which accompanies χάρις in Josephus.[197] Two other apologetic motifs of Josephus provide him the opportunity of further interaction with Graeco-Roman benefaction perspectives. First, the pro-Roman stance of Josephus forces him to abandon the LXX emphasis on covenantal χάρις for the more general idea of God's providential care.[198] Second, Josephus is highly critical of the unpredictable nature of the pagan gods and the manipulation of divine beneficence by means of the cult.

In the following sections (§4.5.1—§4.5.3), we will explore the role of divine and human χάρις, the ethos of reciprocity, and the critique of benefaction ideology in Josephus' works.

4.5.1. Grace and divine beneficence in Josephus

Whereas Philo often has a cosmological and metaphysical perspective on divine grace,[199] Josephus apologetically transforms the LXX picture of God's *covenantal* grace for his Graeco-Roman audience. This is evident in the *Antiquities* where Josephus consistently avoids the LXX translation

---

[195] *AJ* 1.10-12.

[196] Note the series of articles by L.H. Feldman who persuasively argues that Josephus dresses various Old Testament characters in hellenistic garb for his Greek audience. A selection includes: *id.*, 'Abraham the Greek Philosopher in Josephus', *TAPA* 99 (1968), 143-156; *id.*, 'Hellenizations in Josephus' Version of Esther (Ant. Jud. 11, 185-295)', *TAPhA* 101 (1970), 143-170; *id.*, 'Josephus as an Apologist to the Greco-Roman World: His Portrait of Solomon', in E.S. Fiorenza (ed.), *Aspects of Religious Propaganda in Judaism and Early Christianity* (Notre Dame 1976), 69-99; *id.*, 'Josephus' Portrait of Saul', *HUCA* 53 (1982), 45-99; *id.*, 'Josephus' Portrait of Hezekiah', *JBL* 111/4 (1992), 597-610; *id.*, 'Josephus' Portrait of Ezra', *VT* 43/2 (1993), 190-214. Also, *id.*, 'Flavius Josephus Revisited: The Man, His Writings, and His Significance', *ANRW* II 21/2 (1983), 763-862. Many of these articles (and more) are found in revised form in L.H. Feldman, *Josephus's Interpretation of the Bible* (Berkeley-Los Angeles-London 1998).

[197] Josephus' benefaction terminology largely replicates that of Philo (§4.4.2). Additionally, δικαιοσύνη; δόξα; ἐκτενῶς, μεγαλοψύχος; ὁμόνοια; πίστις; προστάτης.

[198] See B.H. Amaru, *art. cit.* (1980), *passim*.

[199] The only place where Josephus approaches Philo's more metaphysical use of χάρις is at *AJ* 15.17. There Josephus links χάρις and τύχη to explain the development of royal hubris: 'favours (χάριτας) received by commoners are not returned (ἀποδίδοσθαι) by them in like manner when they become kings, since Fortune (τύχη) changes them in no small measure'.

(διαθήκη) of the Hebrew word for 'covenant' (*berit*).²⁰⁰ By contrast, Josephus emphasises how God *providentially* cares for the Israelites. As B.H. Amaru conjectures, the pro-Roman Josephus deletes all reference to covenantal land theology because he fears the resurgence of a new Davidic messianism in Judaea, given the tragic outcome for Jerusalem of the recent anti-Roman revolutionary fervour.²⁰¹ Moreover, not only does Josephus unravel the covenantal threads of the LXX fabric, he weaves in the new colours of benefaction ideology.

Josephus has little to say about the presence of divine χάρις in primeval history. The sole case involves Noah's prayer to God for His continuing clemency after the flood. There God explains that any decision on His part to inflict additional punishment on humanity would conflict with His role as the bestower of life (χαρίσασθαι).²⁰² Significantly, while God's cosmological benefits are underscored,²⁰³ Josephus carefully excises the LXX references to God's covenantal grace towards Noah and creation.²⁰⁴

Josephus largely confines the manifestation of divine χάρις to the patriarchal era. But, as noted above, the portrayal of salvation history is either played down or interpeted along benefaction lines. A brief coverage of the patriarchal evidence will establish the point. Reubel, the eldest of Joseph's brothers, warned his brothers against selling Joseph into slavery in order that they might acquire an equal share (τὸ ἴσον) of their brother's future prosperity.²⁰⁵ In Reubel's view, this action would merit God's wrath precisely because Joseph had been considered worthy (ἄξιος) of the divine favour (χαρίσεται).²⁰⁶ Needless to say, the benefaction motifs which Josephus has incorporated into his narrative are absent from the LXX text.²⁰⁷

Later, at the first camp of the Israelites after the Red Sea crossing, Moses prays for the provision of water and God responds with grace (τὴν χάριν) by sweetening the bitter waters at Marah.²⁰⁸ Moses reproves the Israelites for their continual grumbling and exhorts them not to be unmindful of God's

---

²⁰⁰ I am indebted to the discussion of B.H. Amaru, *art. cit.* (1980), 205ff.
²⁰¹ *Ibid.*, 229. See also the discussion of H.W. Attridge, *op. cit.*, 71-107.
²⁰² *AJ* 1.100.
²⁰³ On God's cosmic benefits, see also *Ap*. 2.190 (χάρισιν).
²⁰⁴ The LXX highlights God's covenantal grace in His dealings with Noah (Gen 6:18; 9:8, 11-13, 15-17). Josephus, in contrast to Philo (§4.4.2), ignores the LXX reference to Noah finding grace (Gen 6:9: χάριν) before God.
²⁰⁵ *AJ* 2.27-28. For a brief discussion of 'equality' in benefaction ideology, see our discussion of 2 Cor 8:13-15 in §7.3.2.2.
²⁰⁶ On the 'worthiness' of the recipients of benefaction in Philo and the inscriptions, see §4.4.2 n.151 above.
²⁰⁷ LXX Gen 37:21-22.
²⁰⁸ *AJ* 3.7.

favours (χάριτας) and bounties (δωρεάς).²⁰⁹ In a revealing aside to the manna episode of the Israelites' wilderness wanderings, Josephus mentions that in his own day the region was still well watered by God as a favour to Moses (Μωυσεῖ χαριζόμενος).²¹⁰ Clearly, in this instance, Josephus abandons the Old Testament understanding of the unilateral nature of God's grace (§4.3 n.80) in suggesting that the merits of the Fathers somehow provoked God's continuing generosity.

Subsequently, at Rephidim, Moses beseeches God to undergird His past generosity with a new boon (δωρεά) of water, in order that the gratitude (χάρις) of the Israelites would be maintained.²¹¹ Further, the conferral of the priesthood upon Aaron is credited to God's choice and not to any favouritism (χάρις) on Moses' part.²¹² Finally, Josephus incidentally mentions the possession of the promised land by the Israelites as a gift of God's grace (χάριτος) and bounty (δωρεᾶς).²¹³ Here Josephus is clearly at odds with the lyrical way that the LXX describes the promised land (Num 14:7; Deut 8:7-9; 11:12). Moreover, he fails to replicate the strong LXX emphasis upon the land as God's unilateral gift of grace (Deut 9:6).²¹⁴

After the patriarchal period, expressions of divine χάρις towards the Israelites are increasingly scarce in Josephus. In the period of the Judges, the visitation of an angel to the sterile wife of Manoah, announcing her future pregnancy with Samson, is an occasion for grace (χάρις τοῦ θεοῦ) and thankfulness (χάρις) on the part of the recipients.²¹⁵ In the reign of the King Ahab, God graciously intervenes to spare (χαρίσασθαι) Elijah from the bitter recrimination of the widow of Zarephath over her son's death. This is accomplished when God raises the boy from the dead through the agency of Elijah.²¹⁶ Much later, in the time of Israel's exile in Babylon, God gives Nehemiah grace (χάριν) and persuasiveness of speech when he approaches

---

²⁰⁹ *AJ* 3.14.

²¹⁰ *AJ* 3.31.

²¹¹ *AJ* 3.34-35.

²¹² On χάρις as favouritism in the inscriptions, see our references to *SIG*³ 826 and *SEG* XXVII 261 in §2.3 n.47.

²¹³ *AJ* 5.54.

²¹⁴ B.H. Amaru, *art. cit.* (1980), 212: 'In contrast to Josephus' description of the historical ordinariness of Israel's conquest of, and dominion over, Canaan, the Biblical text stresses the peculiar character of that dominion. Unlike any other land, this land belongs to God; its conquerors, even to those to whom the land is covenanted, are "strangers and sojourners with God on his land" (Lev 25:23)'.

²¹⁵ *AJ* 6.280.

²¹⁶ *AJ* 8.327.

the Persian king regarding the rebuilding of the Jerusalem temple and its walls.[217]

More generally, Josephus spells out God's favourable reaction towards His people's obedience. A favourite word of Josephus is the cognate of *charis*, κεχαρισμένος, which is used to designate behaviour that is gratifying to God. Examples of such behaviour include Abraham's willingness to sacrifice Isaac;[218] Saul's warning to the victorious Israelites not to feast on flesh sacrifices containing blood;[219] Ezra's encouragement of the Israelites to dismiss their foreign wives.[220] But, typically, in the case of Ezra's reforms Josephus removes the covenantal reference of the LXX (Ezra 10:3).

Finally, the temple and the cult are also included in the orbit of God's pleasure. According to Josephus, the temple sacrifices and prayers are common (κοινός) to everyone, because 'we are born for fellowship (κοινωνία)'. In this respect ritual acts of piety, which subordinate one's private interests to those of the wider community, are especially 'acceptable to God (κεχαρισμένος)'.[221]

In conclusion, Josephus' reticence in mentioning the covenant stands in vivid contrast to Paul who highlights the covenantal dimension of divine χάρις (Rom 4:16; 11:5-6; Gal 3:18 [κεχάρισται]; cf. ἔλεος: Rom 15:8-9). Rather than playing down the covenantal land theology of the LXX, Paul points to its eschatological fulfilment in God's justification of the ungodly (Rom 4:13ff) and in the outpouring of the Spirit on the Gentiles (Gal 3:14). How, then, does Josephus visualise the operation of human beneficence?

4.5.2. *Grace and human beneficence in Josephus*

In our discussion of Philo's view of beneficence (§4.4.2), we noted how he modelled the patriarch Joseph on the καλοκἀγαθοί of the honorific inscriptions. Does Josephus embark on a similar enterprise in his rendering of Jewish history? Earlier we endorsed G.P. Wetter's assertion that the Greek inscriptions of the Caesars were the linguistic springboard for New Testament χάρις (§2.2). As an additional test of Wetter's position, it would be profitable to trace Josephus' literary portrayal of imperial beneficence in first-century Palestine and in the empire more generally. To what extent were first-century Jews familiar with the benefits and obligations of imperial χάρις?

---

[217] *AJ* 11.165. God grants (χαρίζεται) the release of the Judaean king, Manasseh, in answer to prayer (*AJ* 10.41).
[218] *AJ* 1.224.
[219] *AJ* 6.121.
[220] *AJ* 11.149.
[221] *Ap.* 2.193-197. Cf. *AJ* 4.311.

Josephus often casts Old Testament characters as benefactors in his staging of the LXX narrative. The following examples illustrate the way that Josephus enhances any trace of benefaction motifs that may be implicit in the Old Testament text. A case in hand is Isaac who effects reconciliation with Abimelech because of the favour (χάρις) previously shown to his father's house.[222] Again, Judah's speech to the Egyptian vice-regent — and (unbeknownst to him) his brother — resonates with benefaction terminology as he flatters his benefactor in an attempt to elicit even further favours.[223] Finally, the struggle between David and King Saul for control of the kingdom involves competition for both clients and powerful benefactors. Therefore, David is dependent upon the χάριτες of the Moabite king and King Achish of Gath, whereas the men of Ziph, in order to secure the favour of King Saul, betray David.[224]

More importantly, Josephus is keenly attuned to the establishment and maintenance of benefaction relationships in the first century BC and AD. In an exchange — undoubtedly authentic — between the imperial patron and the official delegate of his client, Josephus adeptly sketches the delicately balanced set of expectations and obligations involved on both sides of the benefaction system.[225] In his address to Agrippa at Mytilene (14 BC), Nicolas of Damascus pleads the case for the continuance of the Roman protective edicts towards the Ionian Jews. He reminds Agrippa, Augustus' colleague, of his past favours (χάριτας) towards them and comments on the way that the Jewish recipients of the Roman favour have shown themselves to be deserving (ἀξίους) of imperial benefaction.[226] In reply, Agrippa acknowledges the obligation he is now under because of Herod's goodwill (ἔνοιάν) and friendship (φιλίαν) as a trustworthy client-king of Rome. Accordingly, Agrippa reciprocates with the imperial favour (χαρίζεσθαι) and preserves their Jewish rights.[227]

Finally, Josephus is an astute observer of how adeptly the Caesars exploited the benefaction system to maintain and reward valuable clients, both

---

[222] *AJ* 1.264.

[223] *AJ* 2.140-158. Benefaction terminology: χάρις and cognates: *ibid.*, 2.142, 143, 147, 151, 157. σωτηρία: 2.141, 142. δωρέα: 2.144, 152. ἀρετή: 2.145.

[224] *AJ* 6.248; 6.277; 6.321.

[225] The astute observation of M. Grant (*Herod the Great* [New York 1971], 182) is worth repeating: 'Most of the orations of Josephus, as in other ancient historians, are more or less fictitious ... But since Nicolaus was Josephus' principal source, and is specifically stated by him to have written about this whole occasion at length, the speech is probably authentic'.

[226] *AJ* 16.31-33.

[227] *AJ* 16.60. For a further grant (χάρις) of Caesar to Herod, see *AJ* 15.348.

within Judaea and inside the very corridors of the imperial house itself. Caesar makes a present (χαρίζεται) of the royal palace of Ascalon to Salome, King Herod's sister, upon her brother's death.[228] Josephus himself, a handy political turncoat, is rewarded with a gift of sacred books by the gracious favour of Titus (χαρισαμένου Τίτου).[229] Allegedly, the influential freedman of the Emperor Gaius, Callistus, paid secret court to Claudius, laying up in advance a store of favour (χάρις) so that he might subsequently retain his standing in the administration of Claudius.[230] Claudius himself returns the favour of the praetorian guards, who had supported his accession to imperial *potestas* when he subsequently grants them an honorarium (χάριτος αὐτοῖς ἀποδιδόντα τιμήν).[231]

In our next section, we address the important issue of Josephus' portrayal of the Graeco-Roman reciprocity system.

4.5.3. Josephus and the ethos of reciprocity

The inscriptional terminology of reciprocity (ἀμοιβή, ἀντί-compounds, and ἀποδιδόναι) regularly accompanies χάρις and εὐχαριστία in the writings of Josephus.[232] This is hardly surprising in view of Josephus' close attention to benefaction rituals. Josephus underlines the ethos of reciprocity when he is describing the patriarchal era and Davidic kingdom, various acts of international diplomacy, and the reigns of the Caesars and the Herods. Of considerable interest is the way that Josephus, like Philo, often abandons the theological emphasis of the LXX account for more contemporary benefaction perspectives. Finally, in traditional fashion, Josephus affirms the propriety of the return of gratitude in benefaction rituals.

Reciprocity, Josephus asserts, was the dynamic governing personal relationships in the patriarchal era and in the Davidic kingdom. Several examples will secure the point. First, Isaac gives Rebecca the counter-gift of a necklace and some ornaments as recompense (χάριτος ἀμοιβήν εἶναι) for her provision of a drink to him.[233] Second, in response to Moses' beneficence (εὐεργετηθεῖσαι) in protecting shepherdesses from outside interference, the father of the women, Raguel, urges that such charity should not 'go for naught or unrewarded (ἀμοιβῆς)'. He praises his daughters for their zeal for their benefactor (τῆς περὶ τὸν εὐεργετηκότα σπουδῆς) and requests that Moses

---

[228] *AJ* 17.321.
[229] *Vit.* 419.
[230] *AJ* 19.66.
[231] *AJ* 19.225.
[232] For discussion see G.W. Peterman, *op. cit.*, 42-45.
[233] *AJ* 1.249.

be brought to him to receive appropriate gratitude (χάριτος δικαίας).²³⁴ In a speech where Raguel honours Moses for his gallantry (ἀρετή), Josephus well captures the eulogistic conventions and reciprocation motifs of the inscriptions. Moses, as the priest Raguel explains,

> ... had not bestowed this service (εὐεργεσιῶν) upon those who had no sense of gratitude, but on persons well able to requite a favour (ἐκτίσαι χάριν), indeed to outdo by the amplitude of the reward (τῷ μεγέθει τῆς ἀμοιβῆς ὑπερβαλεῖν) the measure of the benefit.²³⁵

Third, David praises those who had buried King Saul, promising 'that he would repay them for their devotion (χάριτας ἀποδώσειν ἀντὶ τῆς σπουδῆς) to the dead'.²³⁶ Similarly, David repaid the debt (τὰς ἀμοιβάς ἀποδώσει) that he owed to Jonathan for his friendship (φιλίαν) and devotion (σπουδήν). Therefore David makes the surviving son of Jonathan the recipient of his kindness in return for his father's benefits (τὰς τῶν εὐεργεσιῶν χάριτας).²³⁷

Fourth, Josephus sometimes employs reciprocity terminology to enhance the merits of the Fathers. For example, Josephus observes that the 147 years old Jacob was a man of piety (εὐσέβεια) towards God and was recompensed (τυχὼν δὲ ἀμοιβῆς) at his death with honour equivalent to his forefathers.²³⁸ However, Josephus also inverts the traditional bonds of reciprocity which were established when a superior benefited an inferior. We see this when Joseph, as Pharaoh's vice-regent, eschews the opportunity to maintain any advantage over his faithless brothers upon his father's death. Joseph forsakes all opportunity of revenge, granting (ἐχαρίσατο) his brothers both his unconditional goodwill and gifts, thereby removing any

---

²³⁴ *AJ* 2.261-262. Compare the guild decree of the Dionysiac craftsmen (172—167 BC: *IG* XI[4] 1061) in which the guild 'at once honoured the benefactor (εὐεργέτην) Kraton himself returning just thanks (χάριτας τὰς δικαίας) (for) the kindnesses (εὐεργετημάτων)'.

²³⁵ *AJ* 2.262-263. The emphasis of Josephus on outdoing the original benefaction is also found in an association decree from Delos (*I. Délos* IV 1519: II cent. BC). There the guild returns favours (χάριτας) to its benefactor Patron so that 'those who love honour may outdo (each other) to achieve something for the guild'. For additional discussion of the inscriptional rivalry and competition motifs, see §7.3.1.2. For ὑπερβάλειν and ὑπερβολή in the Priene inscription of Augustus (9 BC), see §6.1.2.4. For further examples of Moses commanding reciprocity (ἀμοιβή) in thanksgiving (εὐχαριστία), see *AJ* 2.212.

²³⁶ *AJ* 7.8.

²³⁷ *AJ* 7.111-113. For further examples, see *AJ* 6.352; 7.387.

²³⁸ *AJ* 2.196. The Josephan emphasis on achieving honour commensurate with one's ancestors is found in the honorific inscriptions. Xenocleas of Akraephiae maintained for himself 'the reputation of being a fine and good man which was already in existence on account of (his) ancestors' (*Michel* 236: II cent. BC). In a II cent. BC inscription from Hieropolis (*Michel* 541), Queen Apollonis Eusebes of Pergamon is said to have made a conspicuous display of merit 'piously for the gods and most devoutly for (her) parents'.

obligation on their part to feign gratitude (χαρίζοιτο).²³⁹ Thus, in his presentation of Gen 50:15ff, Josephus has moved away from the LXX emphasis — namely, God's gracious overruling of the evil intentions of Joseph's brothers (50:19-20) — to a re-interpretation of the episode from a benefaction perspective.²⁴⁰

In the arena of international relations, Josephus cites royal correspondence which employs traditional reciprocity motifs.²⁴¹ For example, in a conciliatory letter to the Jewish nation, King Demetrius commends the high-priest Jonathan for the nation's friendship (φιλίαν) and loyalty (πίστιν), promising royal recompense and favour (ἀποληψομένους ἀμοιβάς καὶ χάριτας).²⁴² Similarly, the replies of various dignitaries to the royal correspondence are couched in reciprocity terminology. In reply to King Ptolemy's promise of beneficence (χαρίζεσθαι),²⁴³ the high-priest Eleazar thanks the king for the gifts brought by his emissaries:

> Andreas and Aristaeus, your most honoured friends, who are good men (ἄνδρες ἀγαθοί), eminent in learning and worthy of your own excellent qualities (ἀρετῆς ἄξιοι). Be assured that we shall submit to anything that is of benefit to you, even though it exceed our nature, for we ought to make a return (ἀμείβεσθαι) for the kindness (εὐεργεσίας) which you have shown our fellow-citizens in various ways.²⁴⁴

Josephus also bears witness to the role that reciprocity played in Judaea as a Roman tributary state during the reign of King Herod in the first century BC. First, when Herod desired the return of Hyrcanus II to Judaea from Parthia, he sent gifts (δῶρα) to King Phraates of Parthia with a message emphasising the bond of reciprocity that exists between patron and client. As Herod observed, 'this was the moment for the one (Herod) to repay and the other (Hyrcanus) to receive payment for the kindness (τὰς χάριτας) that Herod had received in being maintained and having his life saved by him'.²⁴⁵

Second, in a passage replete with benefaction terminology,²⁴⁶ Herod's solicitude (ἐπιμέλεια), generosity (χάρις), and munificence (φιλοτιμία) in

---

²³⁹ *AJ* 2.197.
²⁴⁰ The LXX episode mentions neither benefaction terminology nor merit theology, while the details about Joseph's gifts to his brothers are Josephan additions to the text.
²⁴¹ Josephus is aware of the role of χάρις in Roman diplomatic parlance: χάριτα φιλίαν συμμαχίαν (*AJ* 14.146, 148). For inscriptional references, see §2.5.
²⁴² *AJ* 13.48.
²⁴³ *AJ* 12.48.
²⁴⁴ *AJ* 12.53-54. The motif of the ἀνὴρ καλὸς καὶ ἀγαθός is standard inscriptional fare.
²⁴⁵ *AJ* 15.18 (cf. 19).
²⁴⁶ *AJ* 15.310-316. The benefaction terminology includes ἐπιμέλεια (15.310, 315, 316), χάρις (15.311, 315), φιλοτιμία (15.312, 316), σπουδή (15.312), μεγαλόψυχος (15.316), and δόξα (15.316).

difficult times 'was regarded as full compensation (ἀντικατάλλαγμα)'. In the view of some, this somewhat mitigated his insensitivity towards Jewish customs. Further, upon Herod's return to Jerusalem from Rome in 17 BC, he gave thanks (εὐχαρίστει) to God and Caesar Augustus for the emperor's appointment of himself as the arbiter of his sons' succession to the throne. According to Herod, this action of Caesar Augustus bolstered his own advantage and ensured concord (ὁμόνοιαν) within the royal household. The ensuing stability in the kingdom, therefore, would repay (ἀμείβειν) Herod's personal debt to the emperor.[247]

The importance of reciprocity in thanksgiving is also explored by Josephus. For example, the Old Testament law against usury on loans (Deut 23:19) is discussed by Josephus in light of this motif. According to Josephus, one should care for the unfortunate because their gratitude (εὐχαριστία) is God's recompense (ἀμοιβή) for acts of generosity.[248] Like Philo (§4.4.3), Josephus interprets the Mosaic law of honouring parents as a case of the reciprocation of parental favour (ἀμειβόμενος τὰς χάριτας).[249] Two other cases of reciprocity, flowing from the gratitude of the beneficiaries, are found in Josephus. The Israelite spies, who had been hidden from danger by the Canaanite prostitute Rahab, swore in gratitude (χάριν) to her that she would be repaid by some recompense (τὴν ἀμοιβὴν ἀποδώσειν) in the future.[250] Outside the Old Testament period, Archelaus evinced his gratitude (χάριν) for the people's praise, adding that he would repay their devotion (ἀμειβόμενος τὸ πρόθυμον αὐτῶν) to himself.[251]

Undoubtedly, more could be said about the return of εὐχαριστία in Josephus: the focus of its praise[252] and the danger of ingratitude.[253] Instead,

---

[247] BJ 1.457-458. The word ὁμόνοια is often employed in the honorific inscriptions to describe the harmonious relationships that benefactors sponsor. Queen Apollonis Eusebes of Pergamon is said to have dealt with her children 'with all concord' (ὁμονοίας Michel 541 [Hierapolis: II cent. BC]). The judge Herokrates is praised for establishing concord between the various parties involved in legal suits (I. Priene 53: II cent. BC: cf. IG VII[1] 121). Finally, an inscription from Phalanna praises Glaukos for bringing about concord (ὁμόνοια[ν] between divided groups (IG IX[2] 1230: II cent. BC). For discussion of ὁμόνοια, see E. Skard, Zwei Religiös-Politische Begriffe Euergetes-Concordia (Oslo 1932), 67-105.
[248] AJ 4.266.
[249] Ap. 2.206.
[250] AJ 5.12-13. See Josephus' comments in AJ 5.30 on the way that Rahab's recompense (ἀμοιβή) came about due to the spies' gratitude (χάρις) for her protection.
[251] AJ 17.201-204. For another example, see BJ 5.530 (τὴν χάριν ἀνθ᾽ ὧν).
[252] Eg: God's salvation, AJ 2.339; Moses, 3.65; Gods glory, 7.95.
[253] Eg: AJ 2.56; 3.312; 4.41; 7.299, 305; 10.139; 13.388; 14.182-183; 15.233; 16.209; 19.272, 362. BJ 1.237, 401.

we turn to Josephus' critique of contemporary views of divine and human beneficence.

4.5.4. Josephus' critique of charis in its benefaction context

To what extent does Josephus theologically critique the beneficence of the hellenistic deities? In *Against Apion* 2.248-250 Josephus responds as a Jew to the religious challenge that the gods posed. After lampooning the multiplicity of the pagan deities, their crude anthropomorphism, and their lecherous appetites, Josephus presses home his attack against the inventers of such fables:

> They have even deified Terror and Fear, nay Frenzy and Deceit (which of the worst passions have they not transfigured into the nature and form of a god?), and have induced cities to offer sacrifices to the more respectable members of this pantheon. Thus they have been absolutely compelled to regard some of the gods as givers of blessings and to call others "(gods) to be averted". They then rid themselves of the latter, as they would of the worst scoundrels of humanity, by means of favours and presents (χάρισι καὶ δώροις), expecting to be visited by some serious mischief if they fail to pay their price.[254]

Significantly, Josephus argues that these 'erroneous conceptions of the deity' have a theological origin:

> For my part, I trace it to the ignorance of the true nature of God with which their legislators entered their task, and to their failure to formulate even such correct knowledge of it as they were able to attain and to make the rest of their constitution conform to it.

However, the precise nature of God — and the way that His beneficence differs to that of the pagan deities — is more to be inferred from Josephus' arguments elsewhere than from any explicit statement in the text.[255] But, at the very least, the unpredictable nature of the pagan gods and their demand to be appeased with χάριτες and δωρεαί is underscored by Josephus. In Josephus' estimation of Graeco-Roman piety, the beneficence of the gods was manipulated by the cult.

Does Josephus portray God's relationship with the Jewish nation as a reciprocal contract? In his portrayal of Solomon's prayer of dedication for the Jerusalem temple, Josephus decisively rejects any notion of reciprocity as regards Israel's gratitude to God:

> Not by deeds is it possible for men to return thanks to God (ἀποδοῦναι θεῷ χάριν) for the benefits they have received, for the Deity stands in need of nothing, and is above any such recompense (ἀμοιβῆς).[256]

---

[254] Elsewhere Josephus speaks of the gods bestowing gifts (ἐχαρίσαντο): *AJ* 19.167.

[255] For theological clues why Josephus may have regarded the beneficence of the pagan gods as inferior, see *Ap.* 2.190-192.

[256] *AJ* 8.111.

Thus Josephus jettisons any idea of divine obligation, distancing himself from those honorific inscriptions which depict the gods as grateful to the ritually pious.[257] But, in this case, Josephus' theology is not based on a close exegesis of the LXX. Typically, Josephus abandons the LXX emphasis on God's covenant faithfulness found in Solomon's prayer (1 Kgs 8:23; 2 Chr 6:14). Instead, as was the case with Philo (§4.4.4), Josephus' understanding of the divine nature is more Stoic than Jewish.

We have seen that Josephus pays considerable attention to the ethos of reciprocity. But what reservations does he voice regarding the role of reciprocity in the benefaction system? In his discussion of the witch of Endor episode (LXX 1 Sam 28), Josephus moralises on how the witch extended beneficence to King Saul through her divinatory arts:

> And this she did, not in return for any benefit received (ὑπὲρ εὐεργεσίας ἀμειβομένη), nor in quest of any favour to come (χάριν μέλλουσαν θηρωμένη) — for she knew that he was about to die —, whereas men are by nature wont either to emulate those who have bestowed some kindness (φιλοτιμουμένων) upon them or to be beforehand in flattering those from whom they may possibly receive some benefit. It is well, then, to take this woman for an example and show kindness to all who are in need, and to regard nothing as nobler than this or more befitting the human race or more likely to make God gracious and ready to bestow upon us His blessings.[258]

For Josephus, then, self-centredness is the real dynamic of the benefaction system. Ultimately, the emulation of beneficent peers and the flattery of powerful benefactors are at the hub of all benefaction relationships. Moreover, Josephus considers that the only legitimate criterion of generosity is the need of the other person. Nonetheless, traces of a merit theology surface in his observation that our philanthropy may well dispose God to be more gracious in His beneficence.

4.5.5. Conclusion

At the outset, we commented on the failure of modern scholarship to investigate the Josephan understanding of χάρις in its first-century benefaction context. Furthermore, the contribution of benefaction motifs to Josephus' apologetic aims has not been sufficiently appreciated by historians. Our discussion of divine and human χάρις in Josephus has demonstrated the important role that the theme of beneficence plays within Josephus' writings.

---

[257] On the beneficence of the gods in the inscriptions, see §2.7.

[258] *AJ* 6.341-342. The LXX account of the episode treats the entire transaction — in marked contrast to Josephus — as a prophetic witness to the demise of Saul's dynasty over against the rise of the Davidic kingdom (I Sam 28:16-19).

How does Josephus view divine beneficence in comparison to Philo and the LXX? Josephus does not provide the sustained cosmological, metaphysical, and philosophical analysis of divine χάρις that we find in Philo. Nor does Josephus adhere to the traditional Old Testament understanding of God's grace. In this regard, he excises the LXX references to covenantal χάρις and interpets them as God's providential care for his people. Three examples adequately demonstrate the limitations of the Josephan view of divine grace. First, in contrast to the inscriptions, Josephus rejects the idea that God could be placed under counter-favour. But, in this case, his theology is more conditioned by Stoic theology than the LXX. Second, the pagan gods are sharply criticised by Josephus for their unpredictable nature and for their demands to be appeased. Josephus, however, is frustratingly vague about the beneficent character of the Jewish God. Third, in similar vein to Philo, the presence of a merit theology in Josephus blurs the sharp LXX outlines of divine grace.

As regards the operation of human beneficence, the motif of reciprocity is common in Josephus. However, Josephus is not averse to moralising about the self-interested nature of the Graeco-Roman benefaction system. Like Philo, Josephus depicts various Old Testament characters and events against a benefaction backdrop. Last, and most importantly, Josephus confirms at a literary level the inscriptional portrait of the Caesars' beneficence. Again, we are reminded of the fact that by the first century AD χάρις had become the central leitmotiv for an unparalleled display of imperial munificence that eclipsed all rivals. This point would not have been lost on the early Christians as they cast around for terminology that would sum up God's infinite beneficence in Jesus.

4.6. Grace in the Jewish Synagogal and Funerary Inscriptions

4.6.1. Grace in the Jewish synagogal inscriptions

There has been no general investigation of benefaction terminology in the Jewish synagogal inscriptions,[259] let alone χάρις and its cognates. There are several reasons for such an investigation being profitable. First, many rabbis and civic leaders are honoured in the synagogal inscriptions as benefactors.[260]

---

[259] However, see the general study of T. Rajak, 'Benefactors in the Greco-Jewish Diaspora', in H. Cancik (*et al.*, Hrsg.), *Geschichte — Tradition — Reflexion: Festschrift für Martin Hengel zum 70. Geburtstag Band I: Judentum* (Tübingen 1996), 305-319.

[260] See S.J.D. Cohen, 'Epigraphical Rabbis', *JQR* 72 (1981), 1-17. For discussions of synagogal benefactors, see L.M. White, *Building God's House in the Roman World:*

Also, the Jewish synagogues themselves acted as benefactors in extending hospitality to travelling Jews. The Greek inscription of Theodotos, found on Mount Ophel in Jerusalem and (arguably) pre-dating the temple's destruction, well illustrates the commitment of the synagogal community to beneficence:

Theodotos, son of Vettenos, priest and head of the synagogue, son of a head of the synagogue, grandson of a head of the synagogue, built the synagogue for the reading of the Law and the teaching of the commandments, and the hostel and the side rooms and water facilities, as lodging for those from abroad who need (it). His fathers and the elders and Simonides founded (the synagogue).[261]

Second, the existence of Jewish trade guilds ensured the spread of benefaction terminology throughout the Diaspora communities.[262] These Jewish guilds, which existed from the Old Testament era (1 Chron 4:14, 21), would have been exposed to the benefaction culture of the hellenistic trade guilds.[263] To be sure, the ties of pagan cult would normally have ruled out guild membership for more devout Jews. But the Jewish artisans of Roman Egypt still joined the trade corporations, while absenting themselves from participation in their religious ceremonies.[264]

Moreover, the familiarity of the Jewish trades with benefaction ideology was reinforced in the synagogues. The large synagogue in Alexandria (the Basilica) provided new-comers with the opportunity to be linked to crafts and guilds. *Tosefta Peah* 4.5 informs us that the synagogue members were

---

Architectural Adaptation among Pagans, Jews, and Christians (Baltimore and London 1990), 77-85; M.P. Bonz, 'Differing Approaches to Religious Benefaction: The Late Third-Century Acquisition of the Sardis Synagogue', *HTR* 86/2 (1993), 139-154.

[261] For the Greek text with French translation, B. Lifshitz, *Donateurs et fondateurs dans les synagogues juives* (Paris 1967), §79. For discussion and an English translation, see B.J. Brooten, *Women Leaders in the Ancient Synagogue* (Atlanta 1982), 24-26. E. Frisch (*op. cit.*, 36) points to *Pesachim* 101a which mentions 'strangers who ate, drank and slept in the synagogue'.

[262] See M. Wischniter, 'Notes to a History of the Jewish Guilds', *HUCA* 33/2 (1950), 245-263.

[263] The Jewish inscriptions from Beth She'arim (III cent. AD) reveal trades likely to have had guilds in the period following the New Testament. See M. Schwabe and B. Lifshitz, (*op. cit.*): clothdyer (§188); perfume merchants (§79, §168: cf. the merchant corporation, *Michel* 998); goldsmiths (§61). In the latter case, Schwabe and Lifshitz (*op. cit.*, 39) point to an inscription from the same period (Palmyra: 258 BC) which mentions a goldsmith's guild: συντέ[λεια τῶν χρυσοχ]όων καὶ ἀργ[υροκόπων] (*IGRR* III 1031). There is an inscription in honour of the artisans, Marinos and Aninos, who executed the mosaic in the synagogue at Beth-Alpha (B. Lifshitz, *op. cit.* [1967], §77 [IV cent. AD]). Other examples: 'a presidency of the purple dyers' and 'synedrion of carpet weavers' (Phrygian Hierapolis: *CIJ* II 793), and a guildmaster of goldsmiths (Corycus: *CIJ* II 793). Note, too, Philo's comment (*Flacc.* 57) that amongst Alexandrian Jewry was the 'ship owner, merchant, and artisan'.

[264] M. Wischniter, *art. cit.*, 253. See also the discussion of A. Kasher, *The Jews in Hellenistic and Roman Egypt: The Struggle for Equal Rights* (Tübingen 1985), s. v. Index 'Craftsmen'.

organised according to craft and occupation 'in order that, in case a stranger came, he might join his craft and thence came his livelihood'.[265] Thus the likely presence of Jewish artisans at the Corinthian synagogue would have provided Paul the tentmaker with profitable evangelistic contacts and exposed him to the synagogal benefaction ideology of the Diaspora (Acts 18:3-4, 8).[266]

Third, the New Testament attests to the role which synagogues and their benefactors played in the spread of benefaction ideology throughout Jewish society. In Luke 7:3-5 the Jewish elders approach Jesus and earnestly (σπουδαίως) beseech him concerning the sick slave of their centurion benefactor: 'This man deserves (ἄξιος) to have you do this, because he loves our nation and has built our synagogue (τὴν συναγωγὴν αὐτὸς ᾠκοδόμησεν ἡμῖν)'.[267] As L.M. White correctly notes, the text's authenticity is secured by its 'conventionalized honorific language commonly found in building inscriptions among both Jews and pagans'.[268]

When we examine the Jewish inscriptions erected in honour of the benefactors and founders of Diaspora synagogues, we find cognates of χάρις appearing alongside a range of conventional benefaction terminology. For example, in a third-century AD decree from Phocaea, Tation is accorded conventional honours in the standard eulogistic vocabulary:

Tation, daughter (or wife) of Straton, son of E(m)pedon, having erected the assembly hall and the enclosure of the open courtyard with her own funds (ἐκ τῶ[ν ἰδ]ίων), gave them as a gift (ἐχαρίσατο) to the Jews. The synagogue of the Jews honoured (ἐ[τείμη]σεν) Tation, daughter (or wife) of Straton, son of E(m)pedon, with a golden crown (χρυσῷ στεφάνῳ) and the privilege of sitting in the seat of honour (προεδρίᾳ).[269]

---

[265] Cited by E. Frisch, *op. cit.*, 35-36.

[266] Note Paul's contacts with the 'seller of purple' at Philippi (Acts 16:14) and a coppersmith in Ephesus (2 Tim 2:14). According to J. Murphy-O'Connor (*St Paul's Corinth: Texts and Archaeology* [Wilmington 1983], 79), evidence on Greek Jewry at Corinth is 'virtually non-existent'. On the trades at Corinth, *Strab.* 8.6.23. On the archaeological evidence for workshops, *id., op. cit.*, 168-169.

[267] F.W. Danker (*Jesus and the New Age: A Commentary on St. Luke's Gospel* [Philadelphia 1988], 158-159) cites *CIG* III 5361 as background. The inscriptions draw attention to the care that benefactors, of different citizenship and racial extraction, lavish on the local communities in which they presently reside. Iunia Theodora, who held multiple citizenship (Roman, Corinthian, Lycian), cared for any Lycian citizens arriving at Corinth, her abode (*SEG* XVIII 143). Doctors (*SEG* XXIV 1100), judges (*Michel* 235, 477, 542; *I. Priene* 53; *I. Assos* 8) and veterinary surgeons (*Michel* 297) are honoured for their work in other cities. Ephesus grants citizenship to Agathocles of Rhodes for his lowering of corn prices (*Ephesos BMI* 455).

[268] L.M. White, *op. cit.*, 86, 181 n.84.

[269] B. Lifshitz, *op. cit.* (1967), §13. Tr., B.J. Brooten, *op. cit.*, Appendix No.3. For discussion, *ibid.*, 143-144.

Furthermore, the routine vocabulary of thanksgiving to benefactors (human and divine) is employed.[270] A conventional inscriptional pairing is utilised in an inscription honouring several benefactors for their 'solicitude and zeal (εὐνοίαν τε καὶ σπουδήν)' for the synagogue.[271] Last, the phrase ἐκ τῶν ἰδίων — much-vaunted in the inscriptional catalogues of ἀρετή ('merit') — regularly appears in the Jewish and Greek inscriptions because it pithily sums up the reliance of beneficiaries upon the funds of the benefactor.[272]

4.6.2. Grace in the Jewish funerary inscriptions

Three Jewish funerary inscriptions of the Diaspora throw considerable light on the hellenisation of first-century Judaism and its impact upon the Jewish understanding of grace.[273] However, a word of caution is apposite. It would be premature to assume that the sentiments on the epitaph reflect the views of the deceased or family: the views may well originate in the world-view of the poet hired to compose the verses.[274] Given the brevity of the epitaphs and their occasion, it would also be unwise to infer that they are articulating a far-ranging theology or philosophy of grace. Notwithstanding, an epitaph from Apollonia in Phrygia (I—II cent. AD), cited below, is typical of the hellenistic reciprocity system, seen its use of χάρις with an ἀντί-compound. There the female honorand, praised for her chastity and children, is graced with a public monument in recompense of her unsullied virtue in marriage:

Antiochene (by race), a descendant of ancestors who filled well the public positions in the country, of the name of Debbora, given (in marriage) to an illustrious man, Pamphylos ... who loved his children ... [I am buried here] receiving (from him this monument) as a token of his recognition (χάριν) in return for ([ἀν]τιλαβοῦσα) a chaste marriage-bed.[275]

A first-century AD funerary stele from Tell el-Yehoudieh in Egypt links χάρις and πίστις to a father's faithfulness towards his deceased daughter:

---

[270] εὐχαριστεῖν (and cognates): B. Lifshitz, *op. cit.* (1967), §70, §73a. εὐχαριστεῖν τῷ θεῷ: *ibid.*, §70, §72, §88.

[271] B. Lifshitz, *op. cit.* (1967), §33 (probably I cent. AD). For the inscriptional coupling of εὔνοια and σπουδή, see *SIG*³ 799; *SEG* II 663; XVIII 143; *IG* IV 2. Additional benefaction vocabulary in the Jewish synagogal inscriptions: δωρέα (and cognates): B. Lifshitz, *op. cit.* (1967), §1, §9, §10, §20, §22; σπουδάζοντος, *ibid.*, §15.

[272] B. Lifshitz, *op. cit.* (1967), §13, §16, §33. For inscriptional examples of ἐκ τῶν ἰδίων and the benefits spawned: *Michel* 163 (Dionysiac processions), 475 (votive offerings), 1007 (sacrifices); *I. Priene* 114 (maintenance of the city's livelihood); *I. Stratonikeia* 15 (an atrium for a bathing room); *I. Mylasa* 106 (public works), 107 (a stoa).

[273] For general discussion, see P.W. van der Horst, *Ancient Jewish Epitaphs* (Kampen 1991). See also, L.H. Kant, 'Jewish Inscriptions in Greek and Latin', *ANRW* II 20/2 (1987), 672-713.

[274] V.A. Tcherikover (*et. al.*, eds), *CPJ* III (Cambridge, Mass. 1964), 162.

[275] *CIJ* II 772.

... and now stop, O traveller. For the one who has fathered me mourns and grieves himself with family and friends. And if you wish, you will be able to know what faith (πισ[τ]ίς) and what recognition (χάρις) (he keeps me in) and what is the lamentation of all. Come here, and ask Samuel, son of Dora, who and what quality it is ...[276]

Our final inscription — dated to 28 January AD 5 and of the same provenance — represents a remarkable fusion of hellenistic and Jewish hopes. The 'pagan' formula of Fate (*Moira*) is used to explain the vicissitudes of Arsinoe's life and is paralleled in other Greek inscriptional epitaphs.[277] While the use of *Moira* in this inscription is undoubtedly 'une personnification poétique',[278] the fickle twists of Fortune (Τύχη) are nicely captured by the adjectives ἀτυχής and αἰνόμορος. Here χάρις sums up the single, crowning benefaction which Fortune allotted the tragic Arsinoe — a radiant soul which finds rest with the saints (ἀγνοτραφές):

Here is the tomb of Arsinoe, O traveller. Weep in considering how she was unlucky (ἀτυχῆν), unfortunate, overcome by destiny (αἰνόμορον). For, though little, I was left bereft of my mother. And when the flower of youth ripened for marriage, my father gave me to Phabeis as husband. But Fate (Μοῖρα), in the pains of the birth of my first-born child, led me to the end of life. In truth, it was a short space of time which I received, but I had a better favour (χάρις): a beautiful radiance of soul. The tomb which here receives in its bosom my body, kept in purity; but the soul has gone from there towards the saints (ἀγνοτραφές). Epitaph of Arsinoe. The year 25, the 2nd day of the month Mechir.[279]

In conclusion, the honorific inscriptions of the Jewish synagogues have clearly imbibed hellenistic benefaction ideology. Jewish craftsmen, who held synagogue membership, would also have been exposed to benefaction terminology via their guilds. And, if the Jewish funerary inscriptions are in any way representative, the first-century Judaism of the Diaspora had hellenised its concept of grace to a surprising extent.

However, these observations need to be tempered by the strong understanding of unilateral grace exhibited in the synagogal preaching of Pseudo-Philo. We now turn to an investigation of his two sermons on justifying grace.

---

[276] *CIJ* II 1451. Note, too, the I cent. AD inscription from Leontopolis in honour of Abramos: 'For you were honoured with the headship of two places, graciously (χάρισιν) performing the double duty' (*CPJ* III 1530).

[277] For Μοῖρα and χάρις, see *SEG* XV 670 (discussed in §2.5).

[278] J.B. Frey, *op. cit.*, 42.

[279] *CIJ* II 1510. In view of the Greek body-soul dualism espoused by the inscription, it is difficult to determine whether the Jewish resurrection state is envisaged.

4.7. Grace in the Jewish Synagogal Sermon

There are no extant examples of early Jewish preaching on grace from the Greek-speaking synagogues apart from the Armenian translation of Pseudo-Philo's *De Jona* and *De Sampsone*.[280] Unfortunately, the Greek original is missing in each case. F. Siegert has proposed that the Armenian original of Pseudo-Philo's text originated with an Alexandrian Jew who was probably a member of a hellenophile school.[281] Owing to the fact that the Armenian intelligentsia maintained a close familiarity with Greek thought and language, the devotional literature of Pseudo-Philo has been preserved in translation. Although the Armenian translator has tried to mimic the Greek syntax, he did not always sucessfully reproduce it. Also mistakes were made in copying the manuscripts.[282] Siegert notes that while both texts have a sermon-like character, they are much longer than what is traditionally designated a 'sermon'. Nonetheless, the genre of sermon is appropriate because each text pastorally addresses its audience and is closely connected to the biblical text. A free theological discussion of each Old Testament book is undertaken rather than a verse-by-verse exegesis.[283]

It is worth remembering that Paul as a diaspora Jew would have been very familiar with the preaching of the Greek-speaking synagogues, including the apologetics against the early Christians (Acts 6:9; 8:1a). Before and after the Damascus road experience, Paul regularly attended synagogue meetings (Acts 9:2, 20; 13:5, 14, 42; 14:1; 15:21; 17:1, 2, 10, 17; 18:4, 7, 19, 26; 19:8; 22:19; 24:12; 26:11; cf. 2 Cor 11:24). In all likelihood, Paul would have had debates with his fellow Jews as much about the nature of grace in the old and the new covenants as about the Messiahship of Jesus (Rom 9:1-18; 9:30-10:4; 11:1-6;

---

[280] For German translations of both sermons, see F. Siegert, *Drei-jüdische Predigten: Ps.-Philon, „Über Jonah", „Über Simson" und „ Über die Gotesbezeichnung, wohltätig verzehrendes Feuer". I. Übersetzung aus dem Armenischen und sprachliche Erläuterungen* (Tübingen 1980). M. Hengel and A.M. Schwemer (*Paul Between Damascus and Antioch: The Unknown Years* [Louisville 1997], 73-74) briefly discuss *De Jona*. On Jewish Synagogue sermons, see W.R. Stegner, 'The Ancient Jewish Synagogue Homily', in D.E. Aune (ed.), *Greco-Roman Literature and the New Testament* (Atlanta 1988), 51-69. More generally, P. Borgen, 'The Early Church and the Hellenistic Synagogue', *ST* 37/1 (1983), 55-78.

[281] F. Siegert, *op. cit.*, 2.

[282] *Ibid.*, 6.

[283] In the words of Siegert (*ibid.*, 6-7), the sermons are 'free omissions by a theologically trained orator ... on a biblical story ... using all the means of the genus epidictum ... Playful practises are interspersed with the genus judiciale and the genus deliberativum ... (as) clear recollections of the orator to his school'.

Acts 13:16ff, esp. 38-41 [cf. v.43: ἔπειθον αὐτοὺς προσμένειν τῇ χάριτι τοῦ θεοῦ]).

Paul's skills in oratory and hermeneutics would have been sharpened by his exposure to and interaction with the rhetoric and exegesis of the synagogue homily.[284] A.D. Nock isolates this as an important area of influence upon Paul:

> The style of Paul is the key to the understanding of his attitude to the world. He saw life in terms of the Septuagint and of Jewish apologetics, of the sermons which he heard at Tarsus as a boy.[285]

The fact that Paul uses homiletic material in Romans 1-4 and 9-11, 'with its heavy use of Scripture as proof',[286] is a strong testimony to the rhetorical impact of synagogal preaching upon the apostle.

Another point worth observing is that the commendation of Jewish law and customs,[287] including the widespread exaltation of Abraham as a model of Torah obedience,[288] would have been a regular part of the Sabbath instruction in Diaspora synagogues.[289] So, in addressing the scriptural arguments of the Galatian judaizing agitators (e.g. Gal 3:10ff; 4:21ff),[290] Paul may well have been responding elements of synagogal exegesis and apologetics that his opponents had marshalled for their own purposes. Thus the importance of Pseudo-Philo's sermons as evidence for one side of the synagogal debate about grace in first-century Judaism should not be underestimated.

The theme of *De Jona* is the graciousness of God. According to Jonah, his divinely appointed confinement in the great fish resulted in his distress becoming proverbial. But, more importantly, the fact that God had punished

---

[284] On Paul and synagogal rhetoric, see M. Hengel, *The Pre-Christian Paul* (London 1991), 58-59.

[285] A.D. Nock, 'The Vocabulary of the New Testament', in *id.*, *Essays on Religion and the Ancient World* Vol.1 (Oxford 1972), 347.

[286] R. Scroggs, 'Paul as Rhetorician: Two Homilies in Romans 1-11', in R. Hamerton-Kelly and R. Scroggs (eds), *Jews, Greeks and Christians. Religious Cultures in Late Antiquity: Essays in Honor of William David Davies* (Leiden 1976), 290.

[287] J.G.M. Barclay, *Obeying the Truth: Paul's Ethics in Galatians* (Minneapolis 1988), 67-68.

[288] G.W. Hansen, *Abraham in Galatians: Epistolary and Rhetorical Contexts* (Sheffield 1989); B.W. Longenecker, *The Triumph of Abraham's God: The Transformation of Identity in Galatians* (Edinburgh 1998).

[289] J.G.M. Barclay, *Jews in the Mediterranean Diaspora from Alexander to Trajan (323 BCE-117 CE)* (Edinburgh 1996), 416-417.

[290] C.K. Barrett, 'The Allegory of Abraham, Sarah, and Hagar in the Argument of Galatians', in *id.*, *Essays on Paul* (London 1982), 154-170; J.G.M. Barclay, *op. cit.*, (1988), 65-67.

him for his disobedience as as a prophet was a striking example of His grace and deliverance:

> Is that not an example which one can see in me? I get stuck in a stomach which encloses me like a tube. I am surrounded by a copper ceiling and steel walls, and explore the world without touching anything. The life of a sea animal has become mine. Prepared for my nourishment, the beast lets me live off its own mass. Look: through its mouth I allow prayers to rise, I see with its eyes, and with its fins I travel. It doesn't really hurt me to be enclosed in the animal, in fact it makes me happy, and even merry. I see the world as in a mirror. And the grace which has been given to me I see more clearly than in a mirror.[291]

The town elders of Ninevah also made a public speech of thanksgiving to God for graciously sparing the Ninevites from judgement when they repented:

> As much as it lay with us, dear Friends, we were already dead. We had already spoken the judgement which damned us together with the town to fall, and now we live through the goodness of the Lord! Under these circumstances it is only fitting and right, that we give Him, from whom we have received life as a part of His grace, thanks through this our life.[292]

The repentance of the Ninevites was a paradigm of the response that both Jews and Gentiles needed to exercise towards God:

> The Ninevites, too, were once without fruits of piety. They did not know the fruits of divine righteousness, and they showed to this world the honour which is due to its Creator. But now they no longer give thanks to nature for its fruits and no longer hold worship for the warming power of the elements; but they confess and honour the Giver of fruits for the fruits, and have committed themselves to worshipping the Architect of this world rather than this world itself.[293]

It is obvious from the texts above that Pseudo-Philo is sympathetic to benefaction ideology and to the theology of the philosophers. The importance of reciprocity for divine beneficence is heavily underscored. God is to be returned 'fitting' thanks for His goodness in graciously sparing the Ninevites from judgement. He is also accorded honour as the Creator and Giver of nature's fruits. Significantly for our purposes, the failure of the pre-conversion Ninevites to thank and worship God finds points of contact with Paul's portrait of human ingratitude and idolatry in Rom 1:19-23 (cf. Wis 13-15). Finally, the description of God as 'Architect of this world' belongs more to the world of philosophical discourse than to the Septuagint.[294] M. Hengel and A.M. Schwemer succinctly capture the tenor of *De Jona*:

---

[291] F. Siegert, *op. cit.*, *De Jona* §21(79-81).

[292] F. Siegert, *op. cit.*, *De Jona* §39(153).

[293] F. Siegert, *op. cit.*, *De Jona* §52(216-217).

[294] Plato (*Ti.* 28c) asks: 'However, let us return and inquire concerning the Cosmos, after which of the Models did its Architect construct it?' Vitr., *De Arch.* 9.1.2 comments regarding the zodiac and the planets: 'The Architect at these points was the power of Nature, and she put the pivots there, to be, as it were, centres, one of them above the earth and sea at

This sermon expresses the liberal attitude of a Jewish synagogue preacher who is open to his environment and to Stoic ideas, but nevertheless, while not 'watering down' the biblical story of Jonah, woos his pagan fellow-citizens so that they attain the knowledge of God's love for humankind.[295]

In the case of *De Sampsone*, the main theme is the justified Jew. This is highlighted in a lengthy digression upon grace at the beginning of the sermon. Pseudo-Philo's understanding of justification comes to the fore in the way that he reflects upon and handles the Old Testament narrative of Samson's birth (Judg 13:1-25). In his digression, Pseudo-Philo excises all mention of the angelic visitation to Manoah and his barren wife: God is the sole actor on the stage. The stipulation that Sampson be a Nazarite from the womb is also bypassed, as is the angel's miraculous ascension to heaven. Moreover, the focus upon Samson as the deliverer of Israel from the hands of the Philistines is universalised. Samson's birth becomes a demonstration of God's power and love for humanity. The text opens with a strong affirmation of God's miraculous deeds as Redeemer, Lord and eschatological Judge:

Now God in other miraculous deeds sets about to bring to fruition one of the other (ones): either He shows His might, or He proclaims His love for people, or He reveals His lordship, or He teaches His patience, or He shows the good things which have been kept for the enjoyment of the righteous, or He announces the judgement which has been kept ready for the sinner. That, however, through Simson God would show His whole power together with His love for humanity, is something He let be recognised in the gifts He gave even to the unborn Simson. Since He found the favour of the living God after his birth, this is obviously payment for the fact that he received his strength for the purpose of righteous actions. Since he was first only begotten and hidden in his mother's womb, and the gift from above had already come to the world as she who conceived him gave birth, the grace and gift of the gracious love of humanity are not the rewards for righteous dealing.[296]

Intriguing here is Pseudo-Philo's strong focus upon God's electing grace and predestination. Samson's gifts were given to him before his birth in order that he might be the channel of God's power and love to humanity. That God's favour was also poured out upon Samson after his birth should not be misinterpreted as a reward for human righteousness. Rather, in light of God's electing and predestinating grace, the divine favour was given solely for the strenghening of God's righteous purposes through Samson. Pseudo-Philo draws from this a fundamental theological lesson. God's grace and love of humanity is not merited by any righeous act of a human being, but is entirely determined by God's anterior decision to bless the world with His gifts. The

---

the very top of the firmament and even beyond the stars composing the Great Bear, the other on the opposite side under the earth in the regions of the south.'

[295] M. Hengel and A.M. Schwemer, *op. cit.*, 74.

[296] F. Siegert, *op. cit.*, *De Sampsone* §3. The Armenian translation renders Samson's name 'Simson'.

intersection of 'gift', 'grace' and 'gracious love of humanity' underscores the unilateral and unconditioned nature of divine beneficence.

Nor is God's grace withdrawn from any of His servants who later become disobedient to their divine vocation:

> God showed His power anew in that He gave him strength, with which he was placed above all others; and He convincingly showed the power of His work wherein He gave him power over those who belonged to foreign peoples. Because it is clear that those who overcome those who honour foreign gods, overcome them as well as their 'higher' helpers. Whoever God has accepted, once and for all, will be recognised by the gifts given to him. He also made His criteria known: As long as the chosen one keeps his commission uninjured, God keeps him in His grace uninjured. But if he rejects his task, He does not take His grace away from him, but carries out His judgement because of his mistake. After that He comes back to His love for humanity, although He doesn't give him all His gifts anymore, since it would not be just if the defeat were to be crowned as well, but He gives, so to speak, still a drop of grace in order to — out of the greatest love for humanity — divert the judgement sentence of the future which will bring death and not let His grace be quenched right to the very last.[297]

Pseudo-Philo asserts here that God continually renews His grace for His dependents. God had appointed His chosen vessel, Samson, to be the leader of the Israelites and had empowered Him not only to subjugate the surrounding foreign peoples but also to conquer their attendant deities as well. Certainly God's grace remains undiminished for those who are faithful to the divine commission. But what of those who, like Samson, become disobedient to the task entrusted to them? Pseudo-Philo's answer is that God maintains His grace even to the last, notwithstanding His imposition of corrective judgement upon the disobedient and His withdrawal of some of His gifts from them. A 'drop of grace', motivated by God's love for humanity, ensures that the individual is spared the sentence of death at the eschaton. Above all, in this extraodinary response of God, we see that divine love and grace can never be exhausted or extinguished by the provocation of human sinfulness.

But a critical question remains for Pseudo-Philo regarding the operation of grace in the career of Samson. If Samson had truly received God's gift of the Spirit of strength, how does one explain its temporary disappearance from the Israelite judge? To say that it occurred because of Samson's overwhelming desire for Delilah is superficial. God subsequently replenished Samson's strength (Judg 16:15ff), notwithstanding his unrighteous behaviour. Alternatively, should one conclude that Samson's experience of great strength did not originate with God at all? Pseudo-Philo grapples with these issues in an extended discussion of the grace-gifts later in the sermon:

> Had Simson received the Spirit of righteousness and level-headedness, you would criticise

---

[297] F. Siegert, *op. cit.*, *De Sampsone* §4.

with justice; if however he only received the Spirit of strength, what then? (cf. Isa 11:2). If Simson did not with other things receive this Spirit straight away, why then would you overlook the man in him and reprimand the Spirit of strength, in so far as you expect the deeds of righteousness from him? Not incorrectly the reproached Spirit could answer, that the gifts are different, according to the will of the Almighty and Great One, and that every gift in His way is only partial and every benevolent gift of grace is limited. To one would be sent the Spirit of truth, to another the Spirit of knowledge and understanding, to another the Spirit of strength and power, and to another the Spirit of the fear of God. Had Simson therefore received the gifts of each Spirit, he must have proved himself to be a sinful man.[298]

Anticipating (to some degree) Paul's teaching on the χαρίσματα, Psuedo-Philo says that the gifting of human beings is diverse. Differing gifts of the Spirit are dispensed as God sees fit. The extent of their influence is partial and limited. Nor should one assume that righteousness or level-headedness must somehow characterise Samson as an Israelite judge. Both characteristics were gifts given to other Israelite judges by the Spirit, in the same way that strength was given to Samson by the Spirit. However, if Samson had been given the Spirit of righteousness and had lived unrighteously as a judge, then he would indeed be culpable for his highhanded sin.

In light of this, the question poses itself whether Samson should have sought more gifts of the Spirit from the wealth of divine gifting available:

But of course if from the source he received only a drop of grace from the great oceon, how is it right and proper that he had only a share from much, over against the whole he is able to have at his disposal?[299]

Once again Pseudo-Philo points to the diverse equipping of the Spirit who gives particular gifts to select individuals. On this occasion, however, Pseudo-Philo appeals to a cavalcade of patriarchal heroes as proof that divine grace was a reality in Samson's life.[300] The Spirit of righteousness was allocated to Abraham in order that he might have life-giving faith (Gen 15:6). Joseph received the Spirit of self-control so that he might conquer the fleshly desire that the seductive advances of Potiphr's wife aroused (Gen 39:7-20). The murder of Shechem the Hivite was a manifestation of the Spirit of zeal poured out upon Simeon and Levi (Gen 34). Last, that Judah was apportioned the Spirit of a righteous judge was confirmed by his just judgement of his daughter-in-law (Gen 38). So, in the same way, the Spirit of strength characterised Samson's life. In other words, the impact of the 'gift of grace' upon each patriarch points to the continuing reality of the divine grace behind the gift.

---

[298] F. Siegert, *op. cit.*, *De Sampsone* §24-25.
[299] F. Siegert, *op. cit.*, *De Sampsone* §25.
[300] *Ibid.*

Pseudo-Philo concludes his discussion with a stinging denunciation of those who deny that Samson experienced the gift of grace throughout His entire life:

> If the Spirit had disappeared with his strength as a result of Simson's covetousness, then we would have known nothing of the whole promise. Obviously those who incorrectly hold, in contradiction to the Scripture, that Simson has not received the Spirit of strength at all, and that it is called 'Gift of grace' without any foundation, are sharpening their tongues against God himself; if he had received it, we would definitely have seen it in his deeds.[301]

The fact that God continued to endow Samson with the Spirit of strength even at the very end of his life — notwithstanding the fact that he had previously been covetous — demonstrates the triumph of God's gracious promises over all human failure.

It seems reasonable to conclude that some first-century Greek-speaking synagogues — at least those whom Pseudo-Philo represents — displayed a strong understanding of the unilateral nature of divine grace in the homiletic tradition. But what of the rabbinic literature postdating the New Testament, to which we now turn? Has the rabbinic corpus managed to include any accurate proto-rabbinic traditions about divine grace from the first century AD?

4.8. Grace in the Rabbinic Literature

4.8.1. Methodological issues

Several scholars have recently highlighted the methodological problems of using the rabbinic corpus, which post-dates AD 200, as background to the New Testament.[302] There is the constant danger of anachronism. Difficulty exists in determining the *ipsissima verba* of the early rabbinic teachers. The resulting mixture of anonymous and attributed material is selective and a product of skilled literary redactors.[303] There is disagreement over the extent

---

[301] F. Siegert, *op. cit.*, *De Sampsone* §26.

[302] G.W. Buchanan, 'The Use of Rabbinic Literature for New Testament Research', *BTB* 7 (1977), 111-122; P.S. Alexander, 'Rabbinic Judaism and the New Testament', *ZNW* 74 (1983), 237-246; S.T. Lachs, 'Rabbinic Sources for New Testament Studies — Use and Misuse', *JQR* 74/2 (1983), 159-173.

[303] On anachronism, see M. Smith, 'A Comparison of Early Christian and Early Rabbinic Tradition', *JBL* 82 (1963), 169-171; J. Neusner, 'The Teaching of the Rabbis: Approaches Old and New', *JJS* 27/1 (1976), 34-35; *id.*, 'The Formation of Rabbinic Judaism: Yavneh (Jamniah) from AD 70-100', *ANRW* II 19/2 (1979), 8. On the *ipsissima verba* of rabbis, see J. Neusner, 'The History of Earlier Rabbinic Judaism: Some New Approaches', *HR* 16 (1977), 229-233; G.W. Buchanan, *op. cit.*, 112-113. On rabbinic redaction, W.S. Green, 'Context and Meaning in Rabbinic "Biography"', in *id.* (ed.),

to which we can reconstruct anything like a rabbinic theology.[304] Therefore, we must devise a method which will unravel the rabbinic traditions regarding grace without imposing foreign categories upon the literature. Also, given the size of the rabbinic corpus and its different concerns, any discussion of the 'rabbinic' view of grace can hardly be representative.[305]

Perhaps one way forward is to examine the rabbinic exegesis of the Hebrew Old Testament texts employing *ḥen* ('grace', 'favour') and its cognates (*ḥannun*: 'gracious'; *ḥanan*: 'to be gracious', 'to be merciful').[306] To be sure, as noted above (§4.2), the Hebrew understanding of grace in the Old Testament was not confined to a single word or expression, but embraced a spread of terminology. But, importantly for our purposes, *ḥen* was the Hebrew word which the translators of the LXX rendered as χάρις (§4.2). The *ḥen* texts may help us to silhouette Paul's understanding of χάρις against the *later* exegetical traditions of rabbinic Judaism.[307]

We will treat the rabbinic discussions of the Old Testament *ḥen* texts chronologically. This should help us to see how the *editors* of the various written collections (spanning the period of AD 200—600) understood the traditions of grace that they had inherited and selected for publication.[308] But we cannot assign any of these traditions with certainty to the proto-rabbinism of the first century AD. Nor can we date with precision when these traditions — if they belong to the later period — came into existence.

Approaches to Ancient Judaism Vol.2 (Ann Arbor 1980), 97-111. See also A.J. Saldarini, '"Form Criticism" of Rabbinic Literature', *JBL* 96/2 (1977), 275-314.

[304] J. Neusner ('Mr Sanders' Pharisees and Mine: A Response to E.P. Sanders, Jewish Law from Jesus to the Mishnah', *SJT* 44 [1991], 76) argues that 'the theological side to Pharisaic Judaism before 70 AD ... is not easily accessible'. Contra, E.P. Sanders, 'Puzzling out Rabbinic Judaism', in W.S. Green (ed.), *op. cit.*, 69; A.F. Segal, 'Covenant in Rabbinic Writings', in *id.*, *The Other Judaisms of Late Antiquity* (Atlanta 1987), 147-165.

[305] See especially the cautionary comments of P.S. Alexander ('Torah and Salvation in Tannaitic Literature', in D.A. Carson [*et al.* ed.], *op. cit.*, 298) regarding the radical difference in authorial context, intention and community between Paul and the *Mishnah*.

[306] I have followed Neusner's dating of the rabbinic literature: *Mishnah* (AD 200); *Sifre* (Leviticus, Deuteronomy: c. AD 200—300); *Tosefta*, *Talmud of the Land of Israel* (AD 400); *Rabbah* (Genesis, Leviticus), *Pesiqta deRab Kahana* (c. AD 400—500); *Rabbah* (Lamentations, Ruth, Esther, Song of Songs: c. AD 500—600); *Talmud of Babylonia* (AD 600).

[307] See the useful coverage of H. Dittmann, *art. cit.*, 347-351.

[308] Note, for instance, the comments of J. Neusner ('The Use of the Later Rabbinic Evidence for the Study of Paul', in W.S. Green [ed.], *op. cit.*, 52) on how the *Sifre* provides an exegetical foundation for the earlier *Mishnah* because the latter work 'notoriously avoids scriptural proof texts'. P.S. Alexander (*art. cit.*, in D.A. Carson [*et al.*, ed.], *op. cit.*, 299) observes that the later generation of Amoraim interpreters of the Tannaitic texts 'were involved in a close reading of the earlier sources and their insights are often highly suggestive as to the theological implications of the Tannaitic texts'.

It is possible that elements of the later rabbinic exegesis arose in response to the Pauline theology of grace and perhaps echo some of the earlier proto-rabbinic formulations of Paul's day.[309] One imagines that the pre-Christian Paul, an educated tri-lingual Pharisee of Palestine, would have been as conversant with proto-rabbinic discussions of ḥen as the hellenistic benefaction context of χάρις.[310] Presumably, in its Jewish context, Paul's theology of grace operated on several fronts. Paul may have been confronting (what he perceived to be) an incipient merit theology within elements of first-century proto-rabbinic thought,[311] as well as the hellenisation of divine and human χάρις among sectors of Greek-speaking Judaism.

---

[309] For an example of the rabbinic rebuttal of the Christian theology of God's electing grace, see E. Mihaly, 'A Rabbinic Defense of the Election of Israel: An Analysis of Sifre Deuteronomy 32:9, Pisqa 312', *HUCA* 35 (1964), 103-135. See also P.S. Alexander's discussion of *Pisqa* 312 in D.A. Carson (*et al.*, ed.), *op. cit.*, 288-291.

[310] On Paul's tri-lingualism, see M. Hengel, *op. cit.* (1991), 38.

[311] Traditionally, two pieces of Pauline polemic (Rom 10:2-3; Phil 3:5-6) have been appealed to as confirmatory evidence for the rise of a Jewish merit theology in the first century AD. Recently, several scholars have challenged this understanding of the Pauline texts. They claim that the traditional position of a so-called 'merit theology' misrepresents the texts themselves, as well as first-century Judaism. F. Watson (*Paul, Judaism and the Gentiles* [Cambridge 1986], 78) has argued that Phil 3:5ff involves a sociological contrast between Jewish law-based communities and Paul's Christ-oriented congregations. The contentious issue which Paul agonises over is Jewish covenant-status, not merit theology. E.P. Sanders (*Paul, the Law, and the Jewish People* [Philadelphia 1983], 140) rejects the merit-grace distinction, proposing instead two dispensations of righteousness: one by law, the other through Christ. See also J.D.G. Dunn, *op. cit.* (1990), 68-69; *id.*, *op. cit.*, (1991), 120-122; N.T. Wright, *The Messiah and the People of God: A Study in Pauline Theology with Particular Reference to the Argument of the Epistle of Romans* (unpub. Ph.D. diss. Oxford University 1980), 98. In my opinion, these suggestions overlook clear textual indications of merit. While Paul boasts in the boundary markers of Jewish covenant-status (3:5), he also spotlights personal achievements credited to his profit and righteousness (3:6). Paul's use of pronouns underlines that a personal pursuit of righteousness was involved here, not just a zealous defence of Israel's distinctiveness (μοι κέρδη, 3:7; ἐμὴν δικαιοσύνην, 3:9a: contra Dunn [1991]). Paul's contrast is neither sociological nor dispensational. Rather he distinguishes between a personal law-based righteousness (ἐμὴν δικαιοσύνην τὴν ἐκ νόμου: 3:9a) and a faith-based righteousness given by God (τὴν ἐκ θεοῦ δικαιοσύνην ἐπὶ τῇ πίστει: 3:9b). See R.H. Gundry, *op. cit.*, 13-14; T. Deidun, *art. cit.*, 50-51; S. Kim, *op. cit.*, 75-81; S. Westerholm, *op. cit.*, 114-115. N.T. Wight has proposed that Israel's pursuit of τὴν ἰδίαν [δικαιοσύνην] in Rom 10:3 involved an exclusivist 'national righteousness' unwilling to submit to Jesus as Messiah (10:4). See *id.*, *art. cit.*, 65; *id.*, *op. cit.*, 97-98; *id.*, *The Climax of the Covenant: Christ and the Law in Pauline Theology* (Edinburgh 1991), 241. Also E.P. Sanders, *op. cit.* (1983), 44-45, 156; J.G. Gager, *The Origins of Anti-Semitism: Attitudes Toward Judaism in Pagan and Christian Antiquity* (Oxford 1985), 224; F. Watson, *op. cit.*, 165; L. Gaston, *op. cit.*, 33; J.D.G. Dunn, *op. cit.* (1990), 69. Paul would have agreed that national righteousness did blind the Jews to the shift of the covenant brought about by the work of Christ (e.g. 2 Cor 3:4-18; Phil 3:8). But here his contrast is between a works-based righteousness and faith. Whereas the elect were chosen by God's mercy (τοῦ ἐλεῶντος θεοῦ: Rom 9:16) and not by works (οὐκ ἐξ ἔργων: 9:11-12), the historical Israel pursued a law of righteousness by works (ὡς ἐξ ἔργων) and not

In suggesting such a possibility, we are not implying that the theology of the first-century proto-rabbis and Greek-speaking Jews was fundamentally synergistic, legalistic, or merit-based. That would fly in the face of much countervailing evidence of the later rabbinic literature and both Philo's and Pseudo-Philo's strong emphasis on the unilateral nature of divine grace. Nonetheless, in my opinion, Paul challenged any theological viewpoint — whether Graeco-Roman or Jewish — that relativised the *priority* of divine grace and the need to rely on it *exclusively*.

The later rabbinic traditions may be valuably compared with Paul's view of grace in another area. Both the New Testament and other first-century Jewish authors confirm an important leitmotiv that appears in the later rabbinic literature. As noted, the pronounced rabbinic concentration on the Merits of the Fathers finds first-century parallel in the various merit theologies present in Philo (§4.4.2), Josephus (§4.5.1), and the intertestamental literature (§4.3).[312] It has also been proposed that Paul himself shares elements of the 'Merits of the Fathers' theology (Rom 9:5; 11:28).[313] If such a construction is correct, how does Paul relate patriarchal merit to his overall view of χάρις? We now turn to the rabbinic evidence.

4.8.2. The rabbinic exegesis of Old Testament grace texts

Owing to its avoidance of scriptural proof texts, there are only two sparse references to Old Testament *ḥen* texts in the Mishnah (c. AD 200). *Sheqalim*

---

righteousness by faith (οὐκ ἐκ πίστεως: 9:32). Israel pursued righteousness with the wrong motive (ὡς: 9:32), divorcing obedience from faith (10:6ff) and erecting instead its own righteousness (τὴν ἰδίαν: 10:3). See R.H. Gundry, *op. cit.*, 18; T. Deidun, *art. cit.*, 51; S. Westerholm, *op. cit.*, 114-115; G.N. Davies, *Faith and Obedience in Romans: A Study in Romans 1-4* (Sheffield 1990), 124. Instead, Israel should have submitted to God's gift of righteousness, summed up in Christ and appropriated by faith (παντὶ τῷ πιστεύοντι: 10:4). Tragically, just as historical Israel was disobedient to the law (10:21; cf. 2:17ff), so too was the Israel of Paul's day to the gospel (10:16). In sum, while Paul believed that a shift of the covenant had occurred with the coming of Christ, he also asserted that the merit-based and exclusivist theologies of certain sectors of Judaism were expressions of sinful human nature. See B.L. Martin, *Christ and the Law in Paul* (Leiden 1989), 135-138; F. Thielman, *op. cit.*, 111-115.

[312] A.F. Segal (*Paul the Convert: The Apostolate and Apostasy of Saul the Pharisee* [New Haven and London 1990], xv) argues that the New Testament evidence is methodologically superior for validating 'mishnaic recollections of first-century Jewish life' than vice versa. For discussions of merit theology generally, see D.A. Carson, *op. cit.*, 1981, *passim*. For merit theology in Philo and the rabbinic literature, see *id.*, *art. cit.*, 162-163; A. Marmorstein, *The Doctrine of Merits in Old Rabbinical Literature* (New York 1968: rpt. 1920), *passim*; E.P. Sanders, *op. cit.* (1977), s.v. Index, 'Merit'; E.E. Urbach, *The Sages: Their Concepts and Beliefs* (Jerusalem 1987), 496-508.

[313] G.F. Moore (*Judaism in the First Centuries of the Christian Era* Vol.1 [New York 1927], 542) and W.D. Davies (*Paul and Rabbinic Judaism* [London 1948], 272) argue that the doctrine of the 'Merits of the Fathers' appears in Rom 9:5 and 11:28.

3.2 specifies the correct attire for the person collecting and taking the heave offering to the *sheqel* chamber in the Temple. The reason for this is that no cause for suspicion should be given to the Omnipresent if His favour is to be maintained (Prov 3:4: *ḥen*). *Abot* 6.7 cites the frequently used 'chaplet of grace' text (Prov 1:9; 4:9: *ḥen*) in reference to the Law: 'Great is the Law, for it gives life to them that practise it in this world and the world to come'.

Other Tannaitic works from the period AD 200—300 widen the Mishnaic perspective on grace. *Mekhilta* interprets the outpouring of 'favour' upon the Davidic house (Zech 12:10: *ḥen*) as a reference to the Holy Spirit.[314] *Sifre Deuteronomy* applies *ḥen* in Prov 4:9 to the study of the Torah.[315] *Sifre Numbers*, in a commentary on the Aaronic blessing, relates several *ḥen* texts to conventional items such as answered prayer (Exod 33:19), favour in the view of others (Esth 2:15; Prov 3:4), and the study of the Torah (Prov 1:9; 4:9).[316]

As far as the Midrashim, *Rabbah Numbers* (AD 400—500) uses a series of *ḥen* and *ḥanan* texts to expound the meaning of the Aaronic blessing.[317] God's grace (*ḥen*) is variously interpreted as His appointment of the prophets (Zech. 12:10), His impartation of grace to individuals (Gen 39:21; Esth 2:15; Dan 1:9; Prov 3:4), and the study of the Torah (Prov 1:9; 4:9). Similarly, God demonstrates His mercy (*ḥanan*) through His undeserved gifts (Ps 123:2-3) and acts of redemption from foreign bondage (Ps 123:3; Isa 33:2). Elsewhere, *Rabbah Numbers* interprets Prov 3:4 (*ḥen*) and Isa 30:18 (*ḥanan*) as a reference to the sufferings of Diaspora Judaism and its hope of recompense through God's grace:

> *But unto the humble (anawim) He giveth grace* (Prov 3:4). '*Anawim* applies to Israel who are poor ('*aniyim*) among the nations and go about in humility ('*anawah*) in their midst and suffer the burden imposed upon them, in order to sanctify the name of the Holy One, blessed be He, and to whom the Holy One, blessed be He, will show future grace, executing justice upon their traducers.[318]

The other Midrashim focus on the relationship of divine grace to prayer and philanthropy. For example, *Rabbah Deuteronomy* cites Exod 33:19 (*ḥanan*) as a proof text to demonstrate that God answered Moses' prayers 'as an act of grace'.[319] Likewise, *Pesiqta deRab Kahuna* (AD 400—500) affirms that God

---

[314] *Mek. Pisha* 13.III.(8G).
[315] *Sifre Deut.* 48.
[316] *Sifre Num.* 41.2. Other Old Testament texts (Ps 132:2-3; Isa 33:2) are cited to amplify the idea of God's unmerited favour.
[317] *Num. Rab.* 11.6.
[318] *Num. Rab.* 11.1.
[319] *Deut. Rab.* 2.1.

answers the prayers of the righteous and generous with His grace (Ps 37:21-22: *hanan*).[320] Last, an important rabbinic perspective on beneficence is found in *Rabbah Genesis*. There it is argued that God's cancellation of the debt of sin should motivate His people to be compassionate towards the poor (Exod 22:27: *hannun*).[321]

Finally, in the *Babylonian Talmud* (AD 600), R. Simeon b. Laqish understood God's gift of grace to the humble (Prov 3:34: *hen*) as a reference to their ritual purity: 'If someone comes wanting to be purified, he is helped to do so; if he comes wanting to be made unclean, they open the way for him'.[322]

Since we have exhausted the rabbinic discussion of the Old Testament *hen* texts, a brief examination of more general references to grace in the rabbinic corpus is apposite. The controversial Mishnaic reference of R. Akiba may well be seen as endorsing a synergistic mixture of works and grace at the Judgement: 'All is foreseen, but freedom of choice is given; and the world is judged by grace, yet all is according to the excess of works [that be good or evil]'.[323] But since there is a textual variant in some of the best manuscripts — which (if adopted) emphasises reliance on God's grace as the grounds of acquittal — one should not be dogmatic about the relationship of grace to works in this instance.[324]

The *Mishnah* also gives detailed directions concerning the recitation of prayers such as the *Shema* and the *Shemoneh 'Esreh* (the Eighteen Benedictions).[325] The latter exhibits a pronounced covenantal understanding of grace. God bestows 'abundant grace' on His creation and, over against the ancestral merit theologies, remembers His 'promises of grace' to the

---

[320] *Pesiq. R.* 2.28.II(4).

[321] *Gen. Rab.* 33.1.

[322] *b. Menah.* Vol.XXIX.A. Ch.3(II.7).

[323] *m. Abot.* 3.15. For discussions of the text, see C.G. Montefiore, 'Impressions of Christianity from the Points of View of the Non-Christian Religions', *HibJ* 3 (1904), 663; S. Schechter, *Aspects of Rabbinic Theology* (New York 1961), 15-16; W. Foerster, *Palestinian Judaism in the New Testament* (London 1964), 221-222; E.P. Sanders, 'On the Question of Fulfilling the Law in Paul and Rabbinic Judaism', in C.K. Barrett (*et. al.*, eds), *Donum Gentilicium: New Testament Studies in Honour of David Daube* (Oxford 1978), 112. See, however, the new translation and interpetation of *m. Abot.* 3.15 offered by C.L. Quarles ('The Soteriology of R. Akiba and E.P. Sanders' Paul and Palestinian Judaism', *NTS* 42/2 [1996], 185-195).

[324] Even if the variant, 'And not according to the amount of work', does not reflect the viewpoint of the historical Akiba, certainly some of Akiba's redactors possessed a unilateral view of grace. Contra, D.A. Hagner, *art. cit.*, 118 n.37.

[325] *m. Ber.* 1.1—5.2. The Shema (Deut 6:4-9, 11:13-21; Num 15:37-41) existed pre-AD 70 whereas the Eighteen Benedictions flourished c. AD 70—100. The Babylonian recension, which consists of nineteen benedictions, is the version used here (*b. Bavli. Ned.* Vol.XV.B. Appendix 2[1-19]). On rabbinic prayers as expressions of covenantal grace see A.F. Segal, *op. cit.* (1987), 154-156.

Fathers.[326] Reigning over His people 'in grace and mercy', God freely justifies them at the final Judgement because He is 'gracious, rich in forgiveness'.[327]

In the case of the *Babylonian Talmud*, R. Hiyya interprets the Song of Solomon 7:2 as a reference to 'acts of philanthropy and of grace'.[328] R. Simeon b. Laqish, on the basis of Ps 42:9, observes that anyone who studies the Torah 'draws out the thread of grace' in this world and in the world to come. When the Sadducees criticise R. Zira for entering Israel with undue haste, he speaks effusively of the 'grace of entering' the very Land that Moses and Aaron had missed 'the heavenly favour of seeing'.[329] Last, in the Babylonian Talmud's commentary on M. Meg. 4.8(9), the Amoraim explain why the *Mishnah* brands as heretical certain teachings regarding God's mercy. As the Amoraim elaborate, the heretic 'makes the commands of the Holy One, blessed be He, acts of grace, whereas they are only decrees'.[330] R.T. Herford has justifiably speculated that this may represent a veiled rabbinic protest against the Pauline antithesis of law and grace.[331]

In conclusion, the rabbinic exegesis of the Old Testament *ḥen* texts, spanning the period of AD 200—600, manifests continuity and development. The element of continuity resides in the emphasis on the study of Torah and the maintenance of God's favour. However, as the Tannaim and Amoraim increasingly provide an exegetical base for the Mishnaic rulings, the rabbinic perspective on grace widens. Traditional motifs appear: the bestowal of grace in response to prayer and the redemption from foreign oppression. But divine grace also embraces pneumatology, the sufferings of Diaspora Judaism, the concerns of ritual purity, and the motivation for philanthropy. Further, as evidenced in *Shemoneh 'Esreh*, the proto-rabbinism of the late first century AD had a strong liturgical understanding of God's covenantal grace. Admittedly, elements of synergism (in the case of, possibly, R. Akiba) may have obscured this emphasis and there are glimmerings of a late rejection of the Pauline priority of grace over law. Notwithstanding, a blanket dismissal of

---

[326] *b. Ned.* Vol.XV.B. Appendix 2 (benedictions 1, 2). Like the first-century proto-rabbinic prayers, the earlier pseudepigraphic work, the *Prayer of Manasseh* (II cent. BC—I cent. AD), strongly emphasises God's forgiveness and mercy (*PrMan* 12-14).

[327] *b. Ned.* Vol.XV.B. Appendix 2 (benedictions 6, 11). Cf. *ibid.*, benedictions 18 ('Merciful One whose grace increases') and 19 ('grace and favour and mercy').

[328] *b. Moed Qat.* Vol.XI. Ch.3(II.25). *b. B. Bat.* Vol.XXII.B. Appendix 1(I:33) refers to devotion to the Torah and 'doing deeds of grace'. Thus the grazing of sheep on the Sabbath 'may be done as an act of grace' (*b. Moed Qat.* Vol.XI Ch.2[I.9]).

[329] *b. Ketub.* Vol.XIV.C. Ch.13(III.46).

[330] *b. Meg.* Ch.4(25a).

[331] R.T. Herford, *Christianity in Talmud and Midrash* (London 1903), 202-203.

rabbinic Judaism as legalistic is entirely premature.[332] Significantly, on one occasion, God's gracious cancellation of the debt of sin is linked to beneficence.[333]

A cautionary comment on the doctrine of the Merits of the Fathers is apposite at this stage. To some degree, an emerging rabbinic merit theology compromised the freedom of divine grace to exercise unconditioned beneficence towards it recipients.[334] However, two important qualifications need to be made. First, the rabbinic stress on the Merits of the Fathers means (at times) little else than God's remembrance of His covenantal promises, as is demonstrated by the accompanying Old Testament covenantal texts.[335] Second, on certain occasions when merit theology is aired, God's grace is still emphatically stated. This is apparent in the *Mekhilta* where God is praised for His grace: 'It was an act of steadfast love that you did with us, for we did not have to our credit deeds [to gain for us the merit that would make us worthy of being redeemed]'.[336] Similarly, *Sifre* denies that the Merits of the Fathers can save their children: 'Isaac cannot save Ishmael, nor can Jacob save Esau. Even if one were to offer all the money in the world, he cannot be granted atonement'.[337]

Finally, we earlier referred to the view that the rabbinic doctrine of ancestral merit finds first-century endorsement in Paul (§4.8.1: Rom 9:5; 11:28). This view, however, misrepresents what Paul is saying. First, Paul rejects any suggestion of ancestral merit in the case of Abraham (Rom. 4:1ff; Gal 3:1-9) and — apart from one occasion (ἀρετή: cf. Phil 4:8) — studiously avoids merit terminology. Second, in its context, Rom 11:28 explains why

---

[332] See R. Brooks, *The Spirit of the Ten Commandments: Shattering the Myth of Rabbinic Legalism* (San Francisco 1990), *passim*; R.N. Longenecker, *Paul: Apostle of Liberty* (Grand Rapids 1976), 84.

[333] The relation between the imitation of God and beneficence is present in the rabbinic literature. See A Marmorstein, 'The Imitation of God (Imitatio Dei) in the Haggadah', in *id.*, *Studies in Jewish Theology* (Oxford 1950), 114-115. For further references, *Gen. Rab.* 33.3; *Exod. Rab.* 31.1.

[334] S. Westerholm (*op. cit.*, 148) notes that Paul's position — over against strands of rabbinic Judaism — is that God's covenantal grace is divorced from Israel's ancestral merit. In my opinion, the Old Testament emphasis on the priority of divine grace in covenantal election (§4.3 n.80) can be vitiated by the ancestral merit theology of Judaism. For examples of ancestral merit theology which obscure covenantal grace in the rabbinic literature, see *Pesiq. R.* 1.8.II(8); *Sifre Deut.* 304, 311; *Mek.* 16.III.(4C); 22.I.(17A); 40.II.(8D, F).

[335] E.g. *Deut. Rab.* 2.23; *Mek.* 16.III.(4B).

[336] *Mek.* 34.I.(5B). See also H.J. Schoeps, *op. cit.*, 206.

[337] *Sifre Deut.* 329. For additional examples, C.G. Montefiore and H. Loewe, *op. cit.*, §590, §597. Contra, *Deut. Rab.* 4.10. Note, too, the rejection of a 'works'-based theology in Antigonos of Sokho (*m. Abot* 1.3 III A, B): 'Do not be like servants who serve the master on condition of receiving a reward, but [be] like servants who serve the master not on condition of receiving a reward'.

God still chooses to love the hardened Israel. God's irrevocable promises to the patriarchs, not ancestral merit, account for the continuation of divine grace towards Israel.

4.9. Conclusion

What was the understanding of grace and its relation to beneficence in first-century Judaism? At the outset, it must be admitted that χάρις in the LXX does not capture in nascent form the theological emphases that Paul was later to develop in his letters. The genesis of Paul's use of χάρις as the standard theological description of beneficence (human and divine) has to be sought elsewhere.

By contrast, the Apocrypha and the Pseudepigrapha have a more theologically pronounced understanding of grace, with χάρις being occasionally linked to almsgiving (ἐλεημοσύνη). This latter trend may be attributed to the inroads that hellenistic benefaction ideology were making into Judaism by the early second century BC, as seen in the *Letter of Aristeas*.

Electing and predestinating grace occupies a dominant position in the synagogal sermons of Pseudo-Philo. Our author is keen to highlight God's general love of humanity. Nor is grace dependent upon continuing human obedience, as the career of Samson amply demonstrates. God's anterior decision to bless His people is what really matters. To some extent, Pseudo-Philo's emphasis on the Spirit's diverse gifting of individuals anticipates Paul's teaching on the χαρίσματα. But in contrast to Paul he never speaks of a corporate gifting of God's covenant people. Pseudo-Philo, too, highlights the importance of reciprocity in a manner reminiscent of traditional benefaction ideology: God is to be returned 'fitting' thanks for His beneficence. Last, grace is never explicitly related in Pseudo-Philo to human beneficence.

Philo and Josephus are invaluable sources for charting the progress that benefaction terminology had made in conquering large tracts of Jewish theological terrain by the first century AD. Both authors use an extensive range of inscriptional benefaction terminology and motifs (including χάρις) in contexts of human and divine beneficence. Philo leans towards a Graeco-Roman conception of merit in describing covenantal χάρις, whereas Josephus excises any LXX reference to covenantal χάρις and dresses the Old Testament narrative in benefaction garb.

Each author critiques the Graeco-Roman understanding of beneficence. Philo caricatures the χάριτες of the benefaction system and contrasts this in Stoic manner with the unconditioned generosity of God. Josephus compares the character of the true God with the χάριτες of the pagan gods and moralises about the self-interest of Graeco-Roman beneficence. Such a critique of the Graeco-Roman benefaction system by Jewish writers had not been undertaken since Ben Sira's exposé of the hostility underlying benefaction rituals earlier in the second century BC. Josephus confirms the inscriptional portrait of the beneficence of the Caesars within Judaea and the wider empire. Again we see the centrality of χάρις as a leitmotiv for imperial generosity.

An important task for later discussion will be to locate Paul within this Jewish debate on the Graeco-Roman benefaction system. We will then be able to determine how far Paul interacts with contemporary assumptions about χάρις. Are Paul's methods of critique as explicit as Philo's, or are they carried out implicitly? What aspects of benefaction rituals does Paul tacitly endorse? Does he expose (like Ben Sira and the Graeco-Roman moralists) the darker side of the social conventions underpinning the benefaction system?

The rabbinic evidence points to a variegated understanding of grace. Although there are synergistic elements and a late reaction to the Pauline teaching on grace, the *Shemoneh 'Esreh*, a late first-century prayer, carries a strong understanding of God's covenantal grace. While the linkage of grace with philanthropy is rare in the rabbinic literature, other theological motifs are used to encourage beneficence. Remarkably, the Jewish funerary inscriptions point to a pronounced hellenisation of χάρις. Further, the Jewish synagogal inscriptions in honour of local benefactors draw on traditional benefaction terminology and motifs, including cognates of χάρις. The presence of Jewish artisans in the synagogues would have promoted familiarity with Graeco-Roman benefaction ideology through their trade-guild contacts. As an apostle and artisan, Paul would probably have used such personal contacts and terminological opportunities for his missionary outreach and teaching.

Chapter 5

The Role of *Charis* in the Philosophers

5.1. Charis, *the Philosophers, and Benefaction Studies*

5.1.1. Paul's exposure to the philosophers' discussions of charis

We know from Diogenes Laertius' *Lives of Eminent Philosophers* that χάρις was a popular topic of intellectual discussion in the philosophical handbooks of antiquity. Theophrastus (c. 370—288/285 BC), Epicurus (341—270 BC), Cleanthes (331—232 BC), Dionysius (c. 328—248 BC) and Demetrius (fl. 50 BC) wrote contributions on the subject, but unfortunately none of their works have survived intact.[1] It is difficult to estimate the extent to which Paul may have been exposed — if at all — to the arguments of the philosophers concerning beneficence. Notwithstanding, several tentative proposals concerning the openness of Paul to these traditions are apposite.

First, we possess the hotly disputed Lucan tradition of Paul's interaction with Stoic and Epicurean philosophers at the Areopagus in Athens.[2] There

---

[1] Respectively, Περὶ χάριτος (Diog. Laert., 5.48: 'On Gratitude'); Περὶ δώρων καὶ χάριτος (10.28: 'Of Benefits and Gratitude'); Περὶ χάριτος (7.175: 'Of Gratitude'); Περὶ πλούτου καὶ χάριτος καὶ τιμωρίας (7.167: 'Of Wealth, Popularity and Revenge'); Περὶ χάριτος (5.81: 'Of Favour'). Further, N.W. DeWitt ('The Epicurean Doctrine of Gratitude', *AJP* 58 [1937], 325) claims that Horace, *Epistle* 7, is 'a Latin sermon based on Epicurus' essay *On Gifts and Gratitude*'. F.-R. Chaumartin ('Les désillusions de Sénèque devant l'évolution de la politique néronienne et l'aspiration à la retraite: le *De vita beata* et le *De beneficiis*', *ANRW* II 36/3 [1987], 1698-1702) has argued that Seneca's *De Beneficiis* is indebted to the lost work of Hecaton (Περὶ χάριτος or Περὶ χαρίτων), alluded to in Cicero, *Off.* 3.63. Finally, the only ancient philosophical handbook on grace that has come down to us is Philodemus' Π[ερὶ χ]άριτος (*P. Herc.* 1414: Col. XIX). Unfortunately this large text, comprising some 19 columns, is highly fragmentary, especially in the contexts where χάρις and its cognates appear. Χάρις occurs 8 times (Cols. IV, V, VI, XII, XIV, XIX); ἀχάριστος 3 times (Cols. I, III, IV); εὐχάριστος 2 times (Cols. IX, X); εὐχαριστία 4 times (Cols. VIII, XI, XV, XVI). For the Greek text and discussion, see A.T. Guerra, 'Philodemo sulla Gratitudine', *Cronache Ercolanesi* 7 (1977), 96-113. In regard to Cols. X and XVI, C.E. Glad (*Paul and Philodemus: Adaptability in Epicurean and Early Christian Psychagogy* [Leiden-New York-Köln 1995], 130 n.112) observes that 'good-will, and gratitude for benevolent help, is basic to the Philodemean ideal of mutual psychagogy and friendship'.

[2] M. Dibelius ('Paul on the Areopagus', in *id.*, *Studies in the Acts of the Apostles* [London 1956], 25-77) regards the entire speech as a invention of the author of Acts.

exists (at least) the possibility that Paul may have reflected theologically on divine and human beneficence in similar apologetic contexts.³

Second, the frequency of the philosophers' discussion of beneficence would have ensured that their ideas spread from the narrow confines of the philosophical schools to more popular settings.⁴ In this respect, one should not underestimate the contribution that Paul's informal discussions with his Gentile converts may have had in prompting him to grapple with the social and theological dimensions of χάρις. As the apostle to the Gentiles, Paul was well aware of the idolatry of his converts' past (1 Thess 1:9; Gal 4:8; 1 Cor 12:2) and the danger which popular philosophies posed to them (Col 2:8: φιλοσοφία).⁵ Moreover, Paul's teaching, by virtue of its concentration upon ethics, would (initially) have been assessed by hellenistic audiences against the psychagogy of the various philosophical schools.⁶ From their viewpoint, the

---

Contrast B. Gärtner (*The Areopagus Speech and Natural Revelation* [Lund 1955]), N.B. Stonehouse (*Paul before the Areopagus and Other New Testament Studies* [London 1957], 1-40) and F.F. Bruce (*Paul: Apostle of the Free Spirit* [Exeter 1977], 238-247) who all point to its Pauline contacts as an argument for its authenticity. Similarly, C.K. Barrett, 'Paul's Speech in the Areopagus', in M.E. Glasswell and E.W. Fasholé-Luke (eds), *New Testament Christianity for Africa and the World* (London 1974), 69-77.

³ E.g. in Acts 14:17 Paul and Barnabas, after rejecting divine honours (vv.11-14, 18), remind the inhabitants of Lystra of God's beneficence towards them by using the participles ἀγαθουργῶν, διδούς, and ἐμπιπλῶν.

⁴ On the popularisation of philosophical ethics (Vulgärethik), see E.A. Judge, 'St. Paul and Classical Society', *JAC* 15 (1972), 32f and the literature cited (especially, A. Dihle, 'Ethik', *RAC* 6 [1966], 666ff). On the range of settings for the teaching of popular philosophical ethics, see A.J. Malherbe, *Moral Exhortation: A Greco-Roman Sourcebook* (Philadelphia 1986), 13. In this regard, R.P.C. Hanson (*The Acts* [Oxford 1967], 191) and H. Conzelmann (*Acts of the Apostles* [Philadelphia 1987: Gmn. orig. 1972], 163) have argued that Luke depicts Paul 'as a Christian philosopher' when the apostle lectures in the hall of Tyrannus (Acts 19:9). Contrariwise, A.J. Malherbe (*Social Aspects of Early Christianity* [Philadelphia 1983: 2nd ed.], 89-91) opts for the setting of a guild hall, not a philosophical σχολή. It is possible (but not provable) that some of Paul's wealthy patrons may have hosted lectures given by wandering philosophers in their salons prior to their conversion. Was it precisely such patrons who drew invidious comparisons between Paul and other more rhetorically and philosophically gifted luminaries at Corinth (2 Cor 10:3-11)? Cf. A. Malherbe, 'Antisthenes and Odysseus, and Paul at War', in *id.*, *Paul and the Popular Philosophers* (Minneaplis 1989), 91-119. On Paul's independence of the philosophical schools, see E.A. Judge, 'St. Paul and Socrates', *Interchange* 14 (1973), 109-110; on Paul as sophist, *id.*, 'The Early Christians as a Scholastic Community, Part II', *JRH* 1/3 (1961), 125-137. Contra, B.W. Winter, 'Is Paul among the Sophists?', *The Reformed Theological Review* 53/1 (1994), 28-38. On the philosophic school as a model for early Christianity, see W.A. Meeks, *The First Urban Christians: The Social World of the Apostle Paul* (New Haven and London 1983), 81-84.

⁵ See A.J. Malherbe, 'Paul: Hellenistic Philosopher or Christian Pastor?', in *id., op. cit.* (1989), 67-77; *id.*, 'NT, Traditions and the Theology of Care In', in R.J. Hunter (*et al.*, ed.), *Dictionary of Pastoral Care and Counselling* (Nashville 1990), 789-792.

⁶ Note the comment of E.A. Judge, 'The Early Christians as a Scholastic Community, Part II', *JRH* 1/3 (1961), 135: 'Another feature that marks Paul's teaching as philosophical

ethical implications of divine and human χάρις — as aired by the popular philosophers at the imperial court, in the salons of the rich, or on the street corners — provided points of contact and collision with the κήρυγμα of Paul.

Third, first-century Judaism was not immune to the influence of the popular philosophers. We have already demonstrated how Philo, a synthesiser of Greek philosophy and Judaism, reworked the LXX from a benefaction perspective and critiqued contemporary benefaction ideology. The same Josephus who dressed the LXX narrative in benefaction garb also drew parallels between the Jewish sects and the famous Greek philosophical schools.[7] Many other intertestamental Jewish writers — e.g. Aristobulus, Ben Sira, the *Letter of Aristeas*, the authors of *4 Maccabees* and the *Wisdom of Solomon* — exhibited considerable familiarity with popular Greek philosophical concepts.[8] It is likely that Paul, in pastoring and evangelising hellenistic Jews of the Diaspora, encountered Jewish audiences familiar with the philosophical discussions of χάρις.[9]

---

rather than religious is its concentration upon ethics'. For pioneering discussions of the impact of philosophical traditions upon Paul, see the collection of A.J. Malherbe, *op. cit.* (1989). Additionally, *id.*, *Paul and the Thessalonians: The Philosophic Tradition of Pastoral Care* (Philadelphia 1987). More generally, *id.*, *op. cit.* (1986); *id.*, 'Greco-Roman Religion and Philosophy and the New Testament' in E.J. Epp and G.W. MacRae (eds), *The New Testament and Its Modern Interpreters* (Philadelphia 1989), 3-26; *id.*, 'Hellenistic Moralists and the New Testament', *ANRW* II 26/1 (1992), 267-333. Useful, too, is D.L. Balch (*et al.*, ed.), *Greeks, Romans, and Christians: Essays in Honor of Abraham J. Malherbe* (Philadelphia 1990); D.L. Balch, 'Neopythagorean Moralists and the New Testament Codes', *ANRW* II 26/1 (1992), 380-410.

[7] For our discussion of Philo and Josephus, see §4.4—4.5. For Josephus' philosophical rendering of the Jewish sects, *Vita* 10-12; *AJ* 13.171-173; 18.11-25; *BJ* 2.119-166.

[8] On philosophical concepts in Aristobulus (II cent. BC), see J.D. Newsome, *Greeks, Romans, Jews: Currents of Culture in the World of the New Testament* (Philadelphia 1992), 234-237. On Ben Sirach (II cent. BC): M. Hengel, *Judaism and Hellenism*. Vol.1 (London 1974), 147-150. On the *Letter of Aristeas* (II cent. BC): G. Boccaccini, *Middle Judaism: Jewish Thought 300 BCE to 200 CE* (Minneapolis 1991), 161-185. On *4 Maccabees* (I cent. AD): G.W.E. Nickelsburg, *Jewish Literature Between the Bible and the Mishnah: An Historical and Literary Introduction* (London 1981), 223-227. On *Wisdom of Solomon* (I cent. BC—I cent. AD): M.E. Stone (ed.), *Jewish Writings of the Second Temple Period: Apocrypha, Pseudepigrapha, Qumran Sectarian Writings, Philo, Josephus* (Assen 1984), 301-313.

[9] The tendency of modern Pauline scholarship to labour under the weight of unhistorical preconceptions is rightly questioned by A. Malherbe (*art. cit.* [1989], 7): 'there is still a tendency on dogmatic grounds to deny any real Hellenistic influence on Paul and to speak of analogies and verbal borrowings. Paul's indebtedness to Jewish traditions, however, is accepted as somehow preserving his theological integrity'. Prior to the dominance of II cent. AD rabbinic Judaism, substantial inroads had been made into the Jewish traditions by Hellenism. The *real* issue is whether Paul draws from sectors of Judaism which adopt *exclusive* or *inclusive* reactions to the impact of Hellenism upon their traditions. For the latter

5.1.2. The contribution of the philosophers to benefaction studies

We lack a thoroughgoing investigation of the role of χάρις in the popular philosophers. There are several compelling reasons for embarking on such an enterprise.

1. C.P. Jones has noted the important corrective provided by the literary evidence (especially the popular philosophers) to the excessively positive tone of the honorific inscriptions. In his view, the unrestrained enthusiasm of various city-states for their benefactors in the honorific inscriptions stands in contrast to the increasingly disillusioned account of Dio Chrysostom concerning his own benefactions in the later Bithynian speeches. The inscriptions, as Jones observes, 'tend to display only the bright side of benefaction, its honours and privileges: it is mainly the literary record that supplies the shadows'.[10]

   We have already seen how Philo etches in some of these shadows by reducing the benefaction system to a financial transaction and then contrasting its vested self-interest with the unconditioned generosity of God.[11] An important task, therefore, is to find out whether this Jewish critique of χάρις is duplicated in the works of the Greek and Roman philosophers. Do the philosophers leave the inscriptional portrait of benefaction largely untouched or, with deft brush strokes, expose the flaws behind its public image?

2. Another important issue is to determine how far Greek ethical theory diverged from the exclusively civic-minded focus of the inscriptions. Were the ethics of beneficence the preserve of the wealthy patrons alone, and thus solely directed towards the citizens of various *poleis*? Were there alternative forms of community (e.g. the household, or the communities of Pythagoreans and Epicureans) which self-consciously began to shape their own understanding of beneficence and its recipients? The import of such questions becomes readily apparent when one remembers the role of hospitality in the early Christian households, and the wide range of communities that contributed to the Jerusalem collection.[12]

---

distinction, see J.D. Crossan, *The Historical Jesus: The Life of a Mediterranean Jewish Peasant* (San Francisco 1991), 418.

[10] C.P. Jones, *The Roman World of Dio Chrysostom* (London 1978), 104. Similarly, R.M. Kidd (*Wealth and Beneficence in the Pastoral Epistles* [Atlanta 1990], 88-90) touches on the evidence of both Dio Chrysostom and Plutarch to illustrate the darker social reality behind the inscriptions.

[11] See our discussion in §4.4.4.

[12] On house church patrons and hospitality, see L.M. White, 'Social Authority in the House Church Setting and Ephesians 4:1-16', *ResQ* 29/4 (1987), 216-218. For the churches contributing to the Jerusalem collection, see K.F. Nickle, *The Collection: A Study in Paul's*

A striking judgement from Plutarch's *The Parallel Lives* concerning charity will illustrate the point.[13] Plutarch, in a discussion of Cato's inhumanity towards his household slaves,[14] states that the good man (ὁ χρηστός) exercises care towards his animals and slaves, even when they have grown old and useless. Thus the evidence for a gentle nature, according to Plutarch, is that we 'extend our goodness (εὐεργεσίαι) and charity (χάριτες) even to irrational creatures'. On this basis, V.L. Johnson has suggested that Plutarch

> ... encountered some new religious ideas — Christian or otherwise — about faith in God and love of God and charity, and attached these concepts of πίστις and ἀγαπή and χάρις to a more or less Platonic system of metaphysics, with a conviction that these non-intellectual elements must be accepted and accounted for.

Now, if Johnson is correct,[15] we see here in miniature how new religious sentiments could challenge and subvert the ethics of beneficence operative in the society of Paul (here, its household relationships). Furthermore, we have already observed how the markedly individual view of φιλία found in *P. Mert.* 1.12 undermined the conventional dynamics of reciprocity in gratitude.[16] Again, the ethical imperatives of the traditional benefaction system are relativised in their social expression.

Subsidiary issues arise from this. If the philosophers do provide an alternative model of beneficent community, is this attributable to some new idea of χάρις on their part, or does it stem from other dynamics such as φιλία? Overall, do the philosophers still endorse traditional notions of χάρις, along with the benefaction system and its honours?

3. The attitude of the popular philosophers towards reciprocity should be investigated if we are to locate Paul properly in his benefaction context. The few scholars who have touched on the topic come to differing conclusions.

Earlier this century R.C. Trench argued that the philosophical schools approved the concept a favour freely done with no expectation of return.[17] More recently, F.G. Downing has drawn attention to the Cynic 'unconcern

---

Strategy (Chatham 1966), 68-70.

[13] V.L. Johnson, 'The Humanism of Plutarch', *CJ* 66/1 (1970), 35.

[14] Plutarch, *Cat. Mai.*, 5.

[15] Over against the view of V.L. Johnson, the silence of Plutarch concerning Christianity tells against any Christian influence. In this respect, P. Decharme (*La critique des traditions religieuses chez les grecs des origines au temps de Plutarch* [Paris 1904], 484) has observed that Christianity remained obscure and hidden for Plutarch precisely because there were many oriental religions competing for recognition throughout the Graeco-Roman world.

[16] See our discussion in §3.3.

[17] R.C. Trench, *Synonyms of the New Testament* (Grand Rapids 1948), 168.

for reciprocation' as background to the Q strand of the gospel traditions.[18] Yet Downing equally insists that Paul adopts a socially conformist stance as opposed to the counter-cultural life-style of the Q Christians and the Cynics.[19] Alternatively, A. Malherbe points out that Paul occasionally abandons the convention of reciprocating gratitude for benefits received (e.g. 1 Thess 1:3) — contrary to the teaching given in Stoic, Platonist and Epicurean psychagogy.[20]

This spectrum of conflicting opinion demonstrates the difficulty of discerning how radical a social critic Paul may have been while the role of reciprocity in the philosophers remains largely unexplored.

4. Although the statements of the philosophers about the gods are more cosmological than theological, there nonetheless exists a substantial body of philosophical reflection on divine beneficence.[21] Scholars have occasionally drawn attention to the collision between the Christian understanding of χάρις and the world-views of popular philosophies. N.W. DeWitt, referring to Paul's opening salutation in 1 Thessalonians, draws the following contrast:

> One item that Paul deliberately chose to write into the new salutation was the doctrine of grace, which Epicurus, by persistently denying the interest of the gods in human affairs, had rendered indispensable for a living religion.[22]

In similar vein, A.H. Armstrong asserts that fundamental differences between the Christian faith and popular philosophy are best appreciated

> (a) by considering the Christian doctrines of the love of God for man and the free gift of grace; and (b) by comparing the benevolence of the philosophers with that 'folly of the Cross', or inversion of the world's values, which leads the Christians to see Christ more clearly in the beggar, the leper, or the fool than in the Philosopher-King himself; and

---

[18] F.G. Downing, *Cynics and Christian Origins* (Edinburgh 1992), 128-129. In his stimulating book (*Cynics, Paul and the Pauline Churches: Cynics and Christian Origins II* [London and New York 1998]), Downing discusses the Cynic understanding of grace in relation to Paul's (*ibid.*, Index s.v. 'Grace', esp. 227-231). However, he focuses on soteriological terminology rather than on the language of grace in Paul and the Cynic sources. Also disappointing in this regard is the recent book of T. Engberg-Pedersen (*Paul and the Stoics* [Edinburgh 2000]). While he touches upon Paul's understanding of grace in Galatians (*ibid.*, 141-146), we gain no understanding of how the Stoics themselves understood grace.

[19] *Ibid.*, 11, 16-17, 115, 142, 169. For a similar exposition of Q to that of Downing, see L.E. Vaage, *Galilean Upstarts: Jesus' First Followers According to Q* (Valley Forge 1994). Contra, C.M. Tuckett, 'A Cynic Q?', *Bib* 70/2 (1989), 349-376.

[20] A. Malherbe, *op. cit.*, 1987, 90. See also N.W. DeWitt, *art. cit.*, 320-328.

[21] For an excellent discussion of the gods and the philosophers, see H.W. Attridge, 'The Philosophical Critique of Religion under the Early Empire', *ANRW* II 16/1 (1978), 45-78; P. Decharme, *op. cit.*, *passim*.

[22] N.W. DeWitt, *St. Paul and Epicurus* (Minneapolis 1954), 43.

makes him leave the company of the righteous and intelligent to pursue with passionate love the salvation of some highly undesirable sinner.[23]

While such observations are helpful, they by-pass the central concerns of the philosophers in their discussion of the gods and χάρις. Instead, we need to focus on the nature of divine beneficence as perceived by the philosophers, and how it was dispensed. For instance: what were the attitudes of the philosophers towards the sacrificial cults as the means of acquiring the divine favour? Were there any specific attitudinal traits required of the worshippers for the sacrifice to be effective? What were the bonds of reciprocity established between human beings and the gods? How were these mutual obligations discharged? With such questions answered, we will be well placed to test A. Deissmann's assertion, already mentioned, that Paul's apologetic for grace was directed as much at the Gentile cults as Judaism.[24]

At the outset, a survey of χάρις and its cognates in the Greek philosophers and moralists will open up the wider ideological terrain (§5.2). In subsequent sections, we will more narrowly focus our attention on the ethos of reciprocity (§5.3) and the beneficence of the gods (§5.4). A brief examination of the philosophical critique of χάρις will conclude our discussion of the Greek evidence (§5.5).[25] Last, in an attempt to compare beneficence cross-

---

[23] A.H. Armstrong, 'The Gods in Plato, Plotinus, Epicurus', *CQ* 32 (1938), 196.

[24] See §3.1.1 and §3.4. Note, too, the interesting comment of S.C. Mott, *The Greek Benefactor and Deliverance from Moral Distress* (unpub. Ph.D. diss. Harvard University 1971), 302: 'grace is not lacking among the Greek and Roman moralists. An increased dependence upon God is seen in the late Stoics such as Seneca, Epictetus, and Marcus Aurelius'.

[25] The Greek philosophers and moralists I have examined are: Plato (429—347 BC); Aristotle (384—322 BC); Theophrastus (370—288/285 BC); Epicurus (342—270 BC) and the later Epicurean writers (Philodemus [110 BC—40/35 BC], *P. Oxy.* II. 215 [I cent. BC], and *The Vatican Collection of Epicurean Sayings* [undated]); Cercidas (c. 250 BC); the Pythagorean writers (Theano [IV—II cent. BC] and Iamblichus [AD 250—325]); Teles (III cent. BC); Posidonius (135 BC—50/50 BC); Cornutus (b. c. AD 20); Musonius Rufus (AD 30—102); Dio Chrysostom (AD 40—112); Plutarch (AD 50—120); Epictetus (AD 55—135); *The Cynic Epistles* (I cent. AD); *The Epistles of Pseudo-Heraclitus* (I cent. AD); Hierocles (AD 117—138); Lucian (AD 120—180); Diogenes Laertius (III cent. AD). Our selection represents a range of the views on beneficence found in the established philosophical schools, as well as in the popular ethics propagated by the itinerant philosophers and moralists. There are also references to the fables of Aesop (VI cent. BC) scattered throughout the footnotes below. I am not thereby implying that Aesop is the author of all the fables traditionally attributed to him. The material is cited to illustrate the longevity of benefaction ethics in Greek moral discourse. The French edition (Société d'Édition *Les Belles Lettres*) of Aesop has been used: É. Chambry, *Ésope: Fables* (Paris 1960).

culturally, the role of *gratia* (the Latin equivalent of χάρις) will be examined in the works of three Roman moralists (§5.6): Cicero (106—43 BC), Valerius Maximus (fl. early I cent. AD), and Seneca (4 BC/1—AD 65).

5.2. *A Survey of* Charis *and its Cognates in the Philosophers*

In this section we will survey the use of χάρις with reference to giving and receiving in the philosophical literature. The stance of the philosophers towards the Graeco-Roman benefaction system is largely the same as that found in the honorific inscriptions and in the papyri. We will also examine any occurrences of χάρις outside its traditional benefaction context. Hopefully, these may further illustrate the New Testament understanding of grace.

5.2.1. *The bestowal of a favour or a gift*

The earlier philosophers concentrate on what constitutes true benevolence. In Aristotle's view, a favour (χάρις) loses its prized status as an act deserving of gratitude when the benefactor has the wrong motives (e.g. self-interest or compulsion). Favours are devalued when they are a chance 'one-off' or a requital of previous obligation. In either case, the recipients are rendered ungrateful (ἀχαρίστους).[26] Plato delicately balances the altruism of the benefactor against his self-interest. He is to confer benefits (χαρίζεσθαι) on the most needy, not on the best, because the former would be the most grateful (πλείστην χάριν). But care must be exercised here: favours should only be granted to the most deserving, and to those most able to repay.[27]

The later philosophers largely endorse the ethos of beneficence. This is readily apparent in Dio Chrysostom's fulsome praise for the advantages of the traditional benefaction system:

For those who take seriously their obligations toward their benefactors (εὐεργέτας) and mete out just treatment to those who have loved them, all men regard as worthy of their favour (χάριτος ἀξίους), and without exception each would wish to benefit them to the best of his ability; and as a result of having many who are well-disposed and who give assistance whenever there is occasion, not only the state as a whole, but also the citizen in private station lives in greater security.[28]

---

[26] Aristotle, *Rh.*, 2.7.4-6.
[27] Plato, *Phd.*, 233D-E. In regard to friends (φίλοι), Plato (*Leg.*, 5.729C-D) argues that one should set more value on the services received than on benefits (χάριτας) conferred. On friendship and benefaction, see also Plutarch, *Mor.*, 63C-D.
[28] Dio Chrysostom, *Or.*, 31.7 (cf. 31.50, 75.6). On the beneficence of the Caesars in

Plutarch waxes lyrical on the indestructibility of the public honours accorded the benefactor. As the decisive measure of moral greatness, beneficence acquires a quasi-eternal dimension, is popularly regarded by all, and evokes a divine aura in the public perception:

> ... rather the love of honour (τὸ φιλότιμον) and beneficence (φιλάνθρωπον) reaches out to eternity as it strives for the crown by deeds and benefactions (χάρισιν) that bring the doer a pleasure impossible to describe. Even when he tries a good man cannot escape thanks, which come to meet him from all sides and flock around him, as multitudes rejoice in benefits conferred
> And as he goes about the town,
> Gaze upon him as a god.[29]

Diogenes Laertius, by contrast, preserves some of the more radical views of the earlier philosophers and their schools concerning beneficence. For example, the school of Hegesias denied that was any such thing as gratitude (χάρις), friendship (φιλία), or beneficence (εὐεργεσία) because benefactors always operated from motives of self-interest.[30] Presumably, such views may well have prompted the modest Arcesilaus to conceal his favours.[31]

Finally, the most extended discussion of the ambiguity of the benefaction system is found in Plutarch. In terms of the beneficiary, benefactions may evoke his reproach and ill-will.[32] No position of neutrality exists: the acceptance of a favour is either shameful or honourable.[33] As for the benefactor, he either fears being outdone in favour,[34] or dreads seeing his well-directed favour disgraced through its rejection.[35]

5.2.2. The return of gratitude

The philosophers regard gratitude as a noble expression of the human spirit. Several examples will secure the point. Aristotle argues that virtue in human beings is manifested through acts of liberality, whereas the base are entirely acquisitive. As a result, gratitude (χάρις) is solely conferred on the

---

Tarsus (Paul's native city: Acts 9:11; 21:39; 22:3), see *id.*, *Or.*, 34.7, 25 (cf. 46.4).

[29] Plutarch, *Mor.*, 1098E.

[30] Diog. Laert. 2.93. Contrast Bion (*ibid.*, 4.49) who said that 'to grant favours to another was preferable to enjoying the favours of others (χαρίζεσθαι)'. Cf. Acts 20:35.

[31] Diog. Laert., 4.37. Also, Theophrastus (Maximus Confessor, *Commonplaces* 46): 'one ought not to get honours as a result of one's manner and charm (χάριτος) [alternatively: 'as a result of association and favour'], but as a result of deeds'.

[32] Plutarch, *Mor.*, 64A (χάρις ἄχαρις); 808B (χάριτες). Dio Chrysostom (*id.*, *Or.*, 45.7) avows that he has neither paraded nor cast favours (χάριτας) in the teeth of his beneficiaries.

[33] Plutarch, *Mor.*, 584C.

[34] *Ibid.*, 178C; *id.*, *Alex.*, 59.4; *id.*, *Flam.*, 1.1-2.

[35] Plutarch, *Mor.*, 582F.

benefactor, not upon those who habitually receive benefits.³⁶ Theophrastus observes that decency of character is better expressed by thankfulness (τὸ εὐχαριστεῖν) than by retribution.³⁷ In the viewpoint of Epicurus, grateful recollection heals the embittering effects of personal misfortune and provides safe harbourage for those who are old.³⁸ Teles comments in this regard that even the misfortune of a thankless (ἀχάριστος) native land ought to be construed as an occasion for gratitude (χάρις).³⁹ Dio Chrysostom believes that the ideal king, in contrast to the despot, repays kindness with gratitude.⁴⁰ And, finally, the *Cynic Epistles* reinforce the propriety of rendering gratitude.⁴¹

Above all, it is Plutarch who provides the most extensive discussion of the return of gratitude. At the most basic level, even the animals display gratitude for benefits (χάριτες εὖ παθόντων).⁴² But gratitude is elevated from the mundane to the extraordinary whenever the καλοκἀγαθοί receive praise for their services to the state. The state, in publicly praising such men, strives to give a tangible and commensurate expression of gratitude for their benefactions. On each occasion, the honorific rituals of the state enhance the brilliance which perpetually shines out from the virtue of the καλοκἀγαθός:

> Yes, and moreover kindly gratitude (χάρις), bearing witness to the acts, and praise (ἔπαινος), competing with gratitude and ushering in deserved goodwill (εὐνοίας δικαίας), add, as it were, a light and brilliance to the joy that comes from virtue (ἀρετῆᾳ).⁴³

What attitude do the philosophers adopt towards the ungrateful? A few select examples will suffice. Epicurus trenchantly attacks the ungrateful greed of the soul (τὸ τῆς ψυχῆς ἀχάριστον) which desires the delicacies of life alone,⁴⁴ or forgets its past blessings.⁴⁵ According to Dio Chrysostom, the Rhodian practice of switching the honorific inscriptions of previous benefactors for those of contemporary καλακἀγαθοί — thereby avoiding the cost of a new

---

³⁶ Aristotle, *Eth. Nic.*, 4.1.8.

³⁷ Theophrastus, *Gnomologium Vaticanum*, No.328.

³⁸ Epicurus, *Sententiae Vaticanae*, 17, 55.

³⁹ Teles, *On Exile*, 3.26H.

⁴⁰ Dio Chrysostom, *Or.*, 1.20 (ἀποδοῦναι χάριν). Cf. *ibid.*, 6.49: 'despots are the only persons who receive no thanks (χάριν) for the favours they bestow'. See *ibid.*, 44.4 and 47.22 for further examples of gratitude.

⁴¹ Pseudo-Diogenes, *Ep.*, 38.3; Pseudo-Socrates, *Ep.*, 1.23; Socratics, *Ep.*, 30.3.

⁴² Plutarch, *Mor.*, 966B. Also, the world of humans: *id.*, *Phil* 21.6: 'benefactors ought always receive reward and gratitude (χάριν) from their beneficiaries'.

⁴³ Plutarch, *Mor.*, 786F. In his *Letter on Friendliness* (*Fragment* 160), Plutarch encourages the return of gratitude so that future benefactors would not be discouraged and their beneficiaries injured.

⁴⁴ Epicurus, *Sententiae Vaticanae*, 69.

⁴⁵ *Ibid.*, 75 (ἀχάριστος).

statue — is an act of monstrous ingratitude.⁴⁶ Last, Lucian pictures Frankness (παρρησία) railing at Plato for ignoring his helpful advice: 'Take care, then, that you yourselves are not acting like most of our present-day philosophers by showing yourselves ungrateful (ἀχάριστοι) and hasty and inconsiderate toward a benefactor'.⁴⁷

Finally, Plutarch warns that Fortune chastises those who are ungrateful for either its benefits or blows.⁴⁸ Indeed, Fortune may even work to obscure the virtue of those who, like Phocion, deserved much more from her hands. As Plutarch sees it, 'instead of the honour and gratitude (τῆς ἀξίας τιμῆς καὶ χάριτος) which are their due, she brings base censure upon some, and so weakens the world's confidence in their virtue'.⁴⁹ More positively, the divinely inspired choice of Timoleon as *strategos* by the Corinthians illustrates how Fortune would encircle his future career with grace.⁵⁰

Overall, the disposal of grace by τύχη is entirely capricious: it cannot be counted on. One was never really sure whether any offence had been given, or whether the withdrawal of favour was entirely arbitrary.⁵¹ Recently D. Georgi has argued for a more positive view of the dependabilty of τύχη.⁵² He observed that the Roman goddess Fortuna and the various hellenistic city-goddesses who resembled the Greek goddess τύχη were regularly invoked for the welfare of the state. But to suggest, as Georgi does, that this somehow parallels Paul's invocation of grace and peace at the beginning of his letters is

---

⁴⁶ Dio Chrysostom, *Or.*, 31.125 (ἀχαριστία). For a fuller discussion of this oration, see §5.3.

⁴⁷ Lucian, *The Dead Come to Life*, 5. Cf., *id.*, *The Dance* 41 (περὶ τὴν εὐεργέτιν ἀχαριστία); *Disowned*, 13 (ἀχαριστότερος), 19 (ἀχαριστία). Further examples: Posidonius, *Diod. Sic.*, 33.17.3; Pseudo-Heraclitus, *Ep.*, 3.

⁴⁸ Plutarch, *Mor.*, 470C-D (ἀχαριστία), 610E (ἀχαριστεῖν). Cf. Dio Chrysostom, *Or.*, 3.101 (ἄχαρις); Posidonius, *Diod. Sic.* 7.1 (ἀχαριστία). Note, too, the comment of Aesop ('The Stag and the Vine': É. Chambry, *op. cit.*, §103): 'This fable shows that those who do evil to their benefactors are punished by God'. Some type of providential over-ruling is perhaps implied in 'The Swan and the Master' (É. Chambry, *op. cit.*, §174): 'When people will not do a thing as a favour (χαρίσασθαι), they are sometimes made to do it against their will'.

⁴⁹ Plutarch, *Phoc.*, 1.3.

⁵⁰ *Id.*, *Tim.*, 3.3 (χάρις).

⁵¹ In the midst of Lucius Aemilius Paullus' victory triumph over the Macedonian king Perseus at Pydna (168 BC), Paullus heard of the death of his two younger sons. *De Viris Illustribus* 56 sums up the capriciousness of Fortune in this manner: 'In the midst of this rejoicing, he lost two sons. He went before the people and gave thanks to Fortune (*gratias fortunae egit*) because whatever adversity had threatened the state had been ended by his own calamity'.

⁵² D. Georgi, 'Reflections of a New Testament Scholar on Plutarch's Tractates *De Alexandri Magni Fortuna aut Virtute*', in B.A. Pearson (*et al.*, ed.), *The Future of Christianity: Essays in Honor of Helmut Koester* (Minneapolis 1991), 22.

surely stretching the point. For Paul, the entire reliability of God's grace is visibly expressed in Christ, without any equivocation on God's part (2 Cor 1:19-20).

5.2.3. Charis *outside its benefaction context*

The philosophers also used χάρις in contexts other than benefaction. χάρις operated as a potent word for describing various human relationships (such as love, reconciliation and marriage). It embraced with equal versatility a range of other topics (including grace of speech, ethics and forensic settlements).

First, in the area of human relationships, Plato reflects upon the favours extended by lovers.[53] Plutarch employs χάρις to describe the restoration of family relationships. In this instance, he confirms the papyrological use of χάρις, discussed previously, which speaks of the reconciliation of a son to his father.[54] Our final example is a striking use of χάρις for the marital relationship. Theano, in a letter to Nikostrate regarding her husband's adultery, encourages the offended party not to respond in kind:

> ... you will manifestly err: You are not convinced that love of one's husband resides in conduct that is noble and good (ἐν τῇ καλοκαγαθίᾳ). For this is the grace of marital association (ἡ χάρις τῆς κοινωνίας). Recognise the fact that he goes to the courtesan in order to be frivolous but that he abides with you in order to live a common life; that he loves you on the basis of good judgement, but her on the basis of passion. The moment for this is brief... My dear, this is how you must live: not defending yourself against courtesans but distinguishing yourself from them by your orderly conduct towards your husband, by your careful attention to the house, by the calm way in which you deal with the servants, and by your tender love for your children.[55]

Second, χάρις functions as the standard description for grace of speech. Plutarch, for instance, states that the Cynic virtue of παρρησία ('frankness') has room for tact and urbanity, provided that such graciousness (ἡ χάρις) does not undermine the exalted position of frankness.[56]

---

[53] Plato, *Phdr.*, 231B-C (χάρις, χαριεῖσθαι), 234B-C (χαρίζεσθαι, χάρις), 241A-C (χάρις χαρίζεσθαι), 256A (χαρίσασθαι).

[54] Plutarch, *Mor.*, 482E (χάρις). See *P. Mich.* VIII 485 and our discussion in §3.2.1.

[55] Theano, *Ep.* (Hercher, 604 No.5). See the translation and discussion in M.E. Waithe (ed.), *A History of Woman Philosophers. Volume 1: Ancient Woman Philosophers 600 BC—500 AD* (Dordrecht 1987), 43-47. Contrast 2 Cor 8:4: τὴν χάριν καὶ τὴν κοινωνίαν τῆς διακονίας. For discussion, see §7.2.1.1.

[56] Plutarch, *Mor.*, 67F (cf. 72F). Cf. Epictetus (Arr., *Epict. Diss.*, 3.22.90): '...the Cynic ought to possess great natural charm (χάριν) and wit'. On παρρησία, see A.J. Malherbe, *op. cit.*, 1987 and 1989, *passim*. Philodemus (Περὶ παρρησίας, Xb 11 [χάρις], XIVb 2-3 [χάρις]) says that one ought to display 'gratitude' towards those who beneficially employ frankness of speech. For the Pauline linkage of salt and grace (in speech: Col 4:6), see Plutarch, *Mor.*, 697D (χάρις, κεχαρισμένα).

Third, χάρις is integrated into Greek ethical theory. Plutarch claims that virtue (ἀρετή) and justice (δικαιοσύνη) engender leadership qualities such as goodwill (εὔνοια), ardour (προθυμία), and favour (χάρις).[57] Human baseness is overcome by frequent benefactions and, more fundamentally, altered by a sense of gratitude.[58] Here Plutarch seems to refer to giving and receiving as an example of a much wider programme of ethical change.

Finally, Plutarch employs a forensic sense of χάρις which is important for the New Testament lexical background. Demosthenes, in the trial of his three guardians for maladministration, sued each man for a penalty of ten talents and gained their conviction. However, as Plutarch continues, 'he exacted no part of the penalty, for he let them off, some for money, and some as an act of grace (χάριτος)'.[59] Similarly, in an aside concerning the unjust fine imposed on Demosthenes, Plutarch comments that it was unlawful to remit an assessment by an act of grace (χάριτι).[60] Such texts may well throw light on the forensic aspects of Paul's doctrine of justification by grace.

From our survey we have seen that the philosophers make no dramatic departures from standard benefaction ideology, and occasionally add to the inscriptional portrait of the benefactor. Can the same be said of their presentation of the ethos of reciprocity?

5.3. Charis *and the Ethos of Reciprocity in the Philosophers*

Aristotle was the first philosopher to open up a wide-ranging discussion on the ideology of reciprocity. All subsequent exploration of the issue in the philosophical literature isolates facets of its operation in society and then addresses its ramifications.

In the view of Aristotle, the doctrine of reciprocity operates with a measure of ambivalence in social relationships. On the one hand, where people seek the right to exact retaliation, justice is totally absent from reciprocity.[61] But, in the interchange of services, justice is upheld when reciprocity bonds together the association of the participants.

---

[57] Plutarch, *Dion*, 10.4. Cf. *id.*, *Mor.*, 786F.
[58] Plutarch, *Dion*, 47.9 (χάρις); cf. *id.*, *Mor.*, 1068D-E. On the importance of a gracious character, see Plato, *Resp.*, 7.2.486D—487A; Plutarch, *Mor.*, 485A; Dio Chrysostom, *Or.*, 43.3.
[59] Plutarch, *Mor.*, 844D. Dio Chrysostom (*Or.*, 34.43) advises the citizens of Tarsus to put aside their anger towards the people of Mallus, by graciously forgiving (χαρισάμενοι) them and not seeking due revenge over the boundary dispute.
[60] Plutarch, *Dem.*, 27.8.
[61] Aristotle, *Eth. Nic.*, 5.5.4. Cf. Seneca, *Clem.*, 1.7.3.

How, then, does Aristotle envisage the social expression of this doctrine? Reciprocity operates proportionately, not on the basis of equality (μὴ κὰι ἰσότητος).⁶² The state will exhibit justice when it requites evil with evil, and repays good with good.⁶³ Indeed, the very presence of a shrine to the Χάριτες should remind us of the cardinal principle of the proportional recompense of favour (ἵν' ἀνταπόδοσις ᾖ).⁶⁴ Aristotle then concludes by developing for his readers a step-by-step guideline on how to effect proportionate requital.⁶⁵

Elsewhere, Aristotle addresses himself to a hypothetical dilemma posed by the obligation of reciprocity. Should we repay our obligation to a benefactor or make a gift to a comrade when the exigencies of life make both options impossible? He gives qualified assent to the first alternative.⁶⁶

Overall, Aristotle helps us see how the ancients struggled with the social complexities of reciprocity. The evidence of Aristotle throws sympathetic light on the struggles Paul had in encouraging reciprocal beneficence among the various Christian communities — different in their ethnicity, social status and wealth — and stands in marked contrast to the solution that the apostle adopted.⁶⁷

Philosophers such as the Pseudo-Aristotelian author of Letter 4 endorse the reciprocation of honours implicit in the benefaction system. In his view, the benefaction system, with its strong emphasis on reciprocity, holds together the social fabric:

> For to speak generally, returning favour and giving (it) (χάριτος ἀμοιβὴ καὶ δόσις) holds together the lives of men, some giving and others receiving and others in turn again giving back (ἀνταποδιδόντων).⁶⁸

As support, the author cites the opinion of Theophrastus that beneficence (τὴν χάριν) earns for the benefactor the 'noble fruit' (καλὸν καρπόν) of

---

⁶² Aristotle, *Eth. Nic.*, 5.5.6. Elsewhere, Aristotle (*ibid.*, 9.1.7) recognises that since the valuation of a service is often difficult to determine, so too is the measurement of the projected return on the part of the beneficiary. In such cases, 'the return (ἡ ἀμοιβή) made should be in proportion to the intention of the benefactor, since intention is a measure of a friend, and of virtue'.

⁶³ *Ibid.*, 5.5.6-7.

⁶⁴ *Ibid.*, 5.5.7. For further discussion of this important passage, see §5.4.1.

⁶⁵ *Ibid.*, 5.5.8ff. In contrast, Paul lets his emphasis fall on disproportionate requital which results in communal equality (2 Cor 8:13-15: ἰσότης).

⁶⁶ Aristotle, *Eth. Nic.*, 9.2.1-5.

⁶⁷ See our discussion in §7.3.2.2.

⁶⁸ Pseudo-Aristotle, *Letters*, 4.1-5. Aesop underscores the necessity of reciprocity to benefactors for harmonious social relations: 'This fable shows that it is necessary to return favour (χάριν ἀποδιδόναι) to benefactors' ('The Ant and the Dove', É. Chambry, *op. cit.*, §242: also §6 [ἀμοιβὰς τοῖς εὐεργέταις παρέχειν], §84 [χάριτας ἀποδιδόναι]).

praise (ἔπαινου). From this he draws the conclusion that widespread favour earns the benefactor both good repute and the reciprocation of favour from grateful beneficiaries (τῶν εὐεργετηθέντων ἀποδώσειν χάριν).[69]

The philosophers also urge the reciprocation of parental benefaction by their progeny. Pythagoras, as rendered by Iamblichus, reminds the young men at the gymnasium of Kroton that they owed their parents gratitude (ὀφείλειν χάριν) as benefactors:

> Our parents alone are our first benefactors (εὐεργεσίας), even before our birth, and ancestors are responsible for all the achievements of their descendants. We cannot go wrong if we show the gods that we do good to our parents (ἑαυτοὺς εὐεργετεῖν) before all others. The gods, we may suppose, will pardon those who honour their parents above all, for our parents taught us to honour the gods.[70]

However, it is Hierocles who gives the doctrine of reciprocation of parental favour its fullest and finest exposition in the philosophical literature:

> But we must begin with the assumption that the only measure of our gratitude (εὐχαριστίας) to them is perpetual and unyielding eagerness (προθυμία) to repay their beneficence (τὸ ἀμείβεσθαι τὰς εὐεργεσίας αὐτῶν), since, even if we were to do a great deal for them, that would be far too inadequate ... So, in order to choose our duties to them easily, we should have this summary statement at hand, namely, that our parents are the images of the gods (θεῶν εἰκόνες), and, by Zeus, domestic gods, benefactors (εὐεργέται), kinsmen, creditors, lords, and the warmest of friends ...They are lenders of the most valuable things, and take back only things which will benefit us (ἡμῶν εὐεργεσία) when we repay (ἡ ἀπόδοσις) them. For what gain is so great to a child as piety and gratitude (εὐχάριστον) to his parents?[71]

Of particular interest here is the perpetuity of obligation towards parents imposed upon the children.[72] Whilst the children are totally incapable of ever properly reciprocating parental benefactions, nonetheless it is a mark of their piety that they do. This emphasis on perpetuity probably stems from the status that parents have as earthly images of the heavenly gods. Caution, however, must be exercised here: the rhetoric of benefaction ideology

---

[69] Pseudo-Aristotle, *op. cit.*

[70] Iamblichus, *Vit. Pyth.*, 38. Cf. Dio Chrysostom, *Or.*, 12.42-43; Aristotle, [*Mag. Mor.*], 2.12.1; *id.*, *Pol.*, 7.14.2; Plutarch, *Mor.*, 497B; *id.*, *Cor.*, 4.4, 36.3.

[71] Hierocles, *On Duties*, 'How to Conduct Oneself Toward One's Parents' (Stob. 3.52).

[72] In a speech to the Council of Apameia, Dio Chrysostom (*Or.*, 41.5; cf. 41.6) uses a familial metaphor to compare his native citizenship of Prusa with his adoptive citizenship of Apameia. He expresses his lasting sense of personal obligation to them in this manner: 'he who cherishes those to whom he owes his being would never neglect those who have become parents as an act of grace (τῶν χάριτι γονέων)'. This type of imagery may have appealed to Paul. According to him, Abraham had become the father of both native born Jews and adopted Gentiles because of God's promise of grace through faith (κατὰ χάριν: Rom 4:16; cf. Eph 1:5-6).

traditionally placed emphasis on the never-ending obligation of the beneficiary.[73]

The obligation of posterity to maintain the reciprocation of honour for past favours features prominently in the thought of other philosophers. In his Rhodian Oration, Dio Chrysostom displays the disbelief aroused when the traditional reciprocation of honours for benefactions is treated with contempt. As noted before, the Rhodians were simply switching the inscriptions, which belonged to the public statues erected in honour of former benefactors, and thereby not incurring the expense of new statues for contemporary civic luminaries. Dio Chrysostom registers the shock he felt over the practice of the Rhodians with characteristic directness:

> And besides, there are the official records of those transactions of which I have spoken; for the decrees by which honours are given are recorded, I take it, and remain on public record for all time. For though repaying a favour (ἀποδοῦναι χάριν) is closely guarded by you, yet taking it back from the recipients is practised with no formality at all.[74]

What ultimately was the mistake of the Rhodians? The obligation of cities to return favour for benefactions extended to all posterity: that was why the honours remained on the public record for all time. To remove the honorific inscriptions of past benefactors from their public statues was at heart an act of ingratitude.[75]

Plutarch, too, endorses the responsibility of posterity to requite its former benefactors. For example, the posterity of Heracles should continue to receive the customary honours (τὰς τιμάς) and rewards (τὰς χάριτας) because Heracles 'had received no adequate thanks or compensation himself (οὐκ ἔτυχεν αὐτὸς ἀξίας χάριτος οὐδὲ ἀμοιβῆς)'.[76] The overall principle to be followed is plain:

> For if we preserve in the descendants our gratitude (τὴν χάριν) for virtue (τῆς ἀρετῆς), we must in reason expect that neither should the punishment of crime flag or falter in its course, but that it should keep pace with gratitude, matching it in requiting men as they deserve.[77]

---

[73] E.g. *I. Priene* 112 speaks of the 'eternal report of (Zosimos') beneficence bestowed towards the people'.

[74] Dio Chrysostom, *Or.*, 31.53.

[75] *Ibid.*, 31.60: 'Would you, then, be willing to give back the favours (ἀποδοῦναι τὰς χάριτας) in return for which you voted those honoured men their statues?'. Cf. *ibid.*, 31.68-69, 125.

[76] Plutarch, *Mor.*, 558B.

[77] *Ibid.*, 558C. Notwithstanding, Plutarch (*Pyrrh.* 8.4) argues that debts to creditors can be repaid to their heirs, whereas the favours of friends must be reciprocated (χαρίτων ἀμοιβαί) within opportune time.

However, sometimes the burden of obligation works in reverse.[78] Dio Chrysostom highlights the unseen moral pressure placed upon benefactors by the community expectation aroused after they had promised benefactions to their city. To be tardy in fulfilling his promise places the benefactor in a position of indebtedness to his community. Therefore the debt must be repaid with interest added:

> For there is nothing more weighty, no debt bearing higher interest, than a favour (χάριτος) promised. Moreover, this is the shameful and bitter kind of loan, when, as one might say, because of tardy payment the favour (χάρις) turns into an obligation, an obligation the settlement of which those who keep silent demand altogether more sternly than those who cry aloud.[79]

Finally, the *Cynic Epistles* apply the ethos of reciprocity to friendships. In a letter attributed to Socrates, the lasting rewards which committed friendship bring to its bearer are praised:

> ... it is clear that for a favour (τῆς χάριτος) of short duration the remuneration (τὰς ἀμοιβάς) is of short duration, but that long lasting good deeds (τῶν εὐεργεσιῶν) bring forth a remuneration equal to the benefit (ἴσην τῇ ὠφελείᾳ τίκτουσι τὴν ἀμοιβήν).[80]

To conclude, the ethos of reciprocity as expressed in the documentary evidence finds its counterpart in the discussions of the philosophers. There were, as we will see, dissenting voices, but these rather aired concern over the abuses of the system than advocated its demise.[81] However, we must first examine the substantial corpus of evidence in the philosophers concerning χάρις and divine benefaction.

5.4. Charis *and the Gods of the Philosophers*

The philosophers invested considerable effort in probing the operation of divine beneficence and our response to it. The boundaries of their interest

---

[78] Normally the benefactor is in the privileged position of being able to cast his favours (χάριτας) in the teeth of his beneficiaries (Dio Chrysostom, *Or.*, 45.7; 45.10 [ἐμοὶ χάριν ὀφείλοντα]). In this respect, Posidonius underscores the obligation of requiting the benefactor's favours (Diod. Sic. 34/35.2.8-9, 40-41; 34/35.38.2). Similarly Plutarch, *Mor.*, 583C, 842B-C; *id.*, *Cor.*, 4.4; *id.*, *Crass.*, 12.1; *id.*, *Dem.*, 5.4, 6.3; *id.*, *Luc.*, 23.1-2; *id.*, *Marc.*, 10.3; *id.*, *Pel. and Marc.*, 3.6; *id.*, *Phoc.* 7.2; *id.*, *Pomp.* 21.5. Lucian (*My Native Land* 7; *Disowned* 13) argues that gratitude (χάριν) to benefactors should also lead one to requite (ἀμείβεσθαι) one's country with its due.

[79] Dio Chrysostom., *Or.*, 40.3. See our discussion in §7.2.2.3. Similarly, Seneca, *Ben.*, 2.1.2; 2.5.2.

[80] Pseudo-Socrates *Ep.*, 6.9; Pseudo-Anacharsis *Ep.*, 5.

[81] See §5.6.2.

ranged far beyond what we meet in the inscriptions and the papyri. Topics of discussion roamed from the impact of grace upon the human character, its role in the cult, to the nature of divine beneficence and its relation to human generosity. At times it was possible to verge upon the contradictory. For example, Epictetus so deepened the gulf of our gratitude to gods that we could only stand before divine grace with total humility; but other philosophers felt that it was obligatory for the gods to recompense the ritually pious.

In this section we will undertake a general survey of philosophical views of divine χάρις, the role of χάρις in the cults, and the understanding which the ancients had of χάρις in relation to divine recompense.

5.4.1. Charis and the gods: a general survey

What picture of divine beneficence is unveiled by the philosophers? In answering this question the philosophers take two tracks. They either concentrate on the gifts of the gods, or plumb the reaction of human beings to divine grace.

First, the deity instils in his devotees gifts of grace that shape their characters. According to Plutarch, truth (ἀληθεία) and the virtues (including kindness, χάρις) are the principal agents of transformation.[82] In similar fashion, Epictetus argues that God gives to each person control over the moral purpose. This enables us to make sound judgements that preserve the social fabric. Consequently, love in the household, concord in the state, peace among the nations, and gratitude to God (πρὸς θεὸν εὐχάριστον) are enhanced by morally wise decisions.[83]

Second, the gods display such extravagant munificence that human beings should be profoundly thankful. At the outset, however, it is crucial that we approach the gods as our benefactors with the correct ritual and motivation. For example, Aphrodite may grant (χαρίσασθαι) a wife to the worshipper who ingratiates himself with the goddess by offering her some boon (δωρεάν) or favour (χάριν).[84] Iamblichus portrays Pythagoras exhorting the Thousand, the councillors of Kroton, to administer their city justly. According to

---

[82] Plutarch, *Mor.*, 351C-D (χαρίσασθαι) and 764E. Cf. See Epictetus (Arr., *Epict. Diss.*, 1.4.31-32) on truth as a matter of thanksgiving to God (εὐχαριστήσωμεν τῷ θεῷ). Interestingly, John 1:14 lays strong emphasis on grace and truth (χάριτος καὶ ἀληθείας) being revealed in the incarnation of Jesus (σὰρξ ἐγένετο). By contrast, Plutarch (*Num.*, 3) finds it hard to believe that 'an immortal god should take carnal pleasure in a mortal body and its beauty (χάρις)'.

[83] Arr., *Epict. Diss.*, 4.5.35. Cf. *ibid.*, 2.23.5-15 (ἀχάριστος εὐχαρίστει τῷ θεῷ). Furthermore, we should be thankful to the gods (εὐχαριστεῖς τοῖς θεοῖς) since we are only held accountable by them for the proper use of our impressions (*ibid.*, 1.12.32-35).

[84] Dio Chrysostom, *Or.*, 20. 21. Cf. Plutarch, *Mor.*, 759F (ἡ τῆς Ἀφροδίτης χάρις).

Pythagoras, the motivation of the Kroton councillors should spring from their gratitude for the kindness which Heracles, the hero-founder of the city, had returned.[85] For Plutarch, what is pleasing to the gods should take precedence over everything else.[86] Plutarch also castigates the self-interest of the ἀχάριστοι, and then elaborates on the beneficence of the gods:

> ...(the ἀχάριστοι) continue to profit by divinity's love for man, which is everywhere dispensed and at no point fails him in his needs...Deity does not abandon man even when he is sick: there is a special God whose mission it is to bring help and strength at such a time. Not even when a man dies is he forsaken: there is a God who cares for him and leads him to the other world, who is for the dead a lord of repose, an escort of souls to Pluto's realm...[87]

But, above all, it is Epictetus who brings to sharp focus our need to show gratitude for God's beneficence.[88] In the passage cited below, Epictetus makes clear our total dependence upon God our Creator, and the privilege, however short-lived, of participating intellectually and socially in the pageant of his rule. The rhetorical force of Epictetus' diatribe deflates our petty pretensions and meanness of spirit:

> And so, when you have received everything, and your very self, from Another, do you yet complain and blame the Giver, if He take something away from you? Who are you, and for what purpose have you come? Did not He show you the light? Did not He give you fellow-workers? Did not He give you the senses and reason? And as what did He bring you into the world? Was it not as a mortal being? Was it not as one destined to live upon earth with a little portion of paltry flesh, and for a little while to be a spectator of His governance, and to join with Him in His pageant and holiday? Are you not willing, then, for so long as has been given you, to be a spectator of His pageant and His festival, and then when He leads you forth, to go, after you have made obeisance and returned thanks (εὐχαριστήσας) for what you have heard and seen?[89]

Last, Epictetus prefaces an imaginary presentation of his own death by acknowledging the superiority of a life of beneficence (εὐεργετικόν). However, for the philosopher, the task is to maintain ἀπάθεια without abandoning natural human relationships, and to avoid error and rashness of judgement.[90] Epictetus' rendering of his last words represents a summary of

---

[85] Iamblichus, *Vit. Pyth.*, 50 (τὴν χάριν τῆς ἀποδοθείσης εὐεργεσίας).

[86] Plutarch, *Fragment* 85 (κεχαρισμένος).

[87] *Id., Mor.*, 758A-B. On gratitude towards the gods in Plutarch, *ibid.*, 480C and 485D (τοῖς θεοῖς χάρις). On the requital of the ungrateful by Fortune (*ibid.*, 470 C-D [ἀχαριστίας]) and, correspondingly, the requital of the pious (*ibid.*, 610E [ἀχαριστεῖν, ἀποδίδωσι καρπόν]).

[88] On thanksgiving in Epictetus, see P. Schubert, *Form and Function of the Pauline Thanksgivings* (Berlin 1939), 132-142; H.-J. Klauck, 'Dankbar leben, dankbar sterben. εὐχαριστεῖν bei Epiktet', in *id., Gemeinde, Amt, Sakrament: Neutestamentliche Perspektiven* (Würzburg 1989), 373-390.

[89] Arr., *Epict. Diss.*, 4.1.103-105.

[90] *Ibid.*, 4.10.13 (cf. 3.2.2; 3.5.7-11).

the philosophic ideal. Accordingly, his faculties enable him to live contentedly under God's rule, and have provided him insight into his preconceptions and the divine order.[91] Epictetus concludes by affirming God's grace:

For that Thou didst beget me I am grateful (χάριν ἔχω); for what Thou hast given I am grateful (χάριν) also. The length of time for which I have had the use of Thy gifts is enough for me. Take them back again and assign them to what place Thou wilt, for they were all Thine, and Thou gavest them me.[92]

In sum, Epictetus' attitude towards the deity is perhaps best encapsulated in this aside: 'we should be giving thanks to God (ηὐχαριστοῦμεν τῷ θεῷ) for those things for which we ought to give Him thanks (εὐχαριστεῖν)'.[93]

Another fundamental question involves the nature of the gods. Does beneficence originate from the generous character of the deity — or is it induced by a correct cultic approach on the part of the worshipper?

The philosophers rarely link χάρις or χαρίζεσθαι with any extended discussion of the character of the gods. Plutarch speculates that the gods confer their benefits (εὐεργετεῖν) secretly 'since it is their nature to take pleasure in the mere act of being gracious (χαρίζεσθαι) and doing good'.[94] Elsewhere, he adds that God is consummately good and lacks none of the virtues (such as δικαιοσύνη and φιλία). These social virtues, therefore, ensure that the divine focus is other-centred:

For not in relation with Himself nor with any part of Himself is there any exercise of justice (δικαιοσύνης) or benevolence (χάριτος) or kindness (χρηστότητος), but only in relation with others.[95]

---

[91] *Ibid.*, 4.10.14-15.

[92] *Ibid.*, 4.10.16. For additional examples of the necessity of gratitude towards God, see *ibid.*, 1.16.15-16 ('hymning and praising the Deity and rehearsing his benefits [χάριτας]'). Also, Dio Chrysostom, *Or.*, 38.20 (χάρις) and 74.21 (τοῖς θεοῖς χάρις). Aesop, like Epictetus, emphasises the importance of humility in front of God's beneficence: 'This fable shows that God (Κύριος) resists the proud but gives grace (δίδωσι χάριν) to the humble' ('The Two Cocks and the Eagle', É. Chambry, *op. cit.*, §20).

[93] Arr., *Epict. Diss.*, 4.4.18. A gulf nonetheless exists between Epictetus and the Christian idea of God and His grace. Note the astute comment of J. Hershbell ('The Stoicism of Epictetus: Twentieth Century Perspectives', *ANRW* II 36/1 [1987], 2161): 'Epictetus' God is all but identical with the world, and there is no concept of divine salvation: for Epictetus salvation is not God's work, but that of human beings striving for moral perfection'. More generally, see P. Oakes, 'Epictetus (and the New Testament)', *Vox Evangelica* 23 (1993), 39-56.

[94] Plutarch, *Mor.*, 63F. On Plutarch's view of God, see L. Valentin, 'De l'idée de Dieu dans Plutarche', *RevThom* 14 (1914), 313-327; F.E. Brenk, 'From Mysticism to Mysticism: The Religious Development of Plutarch of Chaironeia', in G. MacRae (ed.), *Society of Biblical Literature 1975 Seminar Papers* (Cambridge, Mass. 1975), 193-198; *id.*, 'An Imperial Heritage: The Religious Spirit of Plutarch of Chaironeia', *ANRW* II 36/1 (1987), 248-349.

[95] *Id.*, *Mor.*, 423D.

Charis *and the Gods of the Philosophers* 187

The brevity of the foregoing references demonstrates that the Greek philosophers seldom reflected on how χάρις related to the divine character. Overall, they assumed its bestowal through the cult.

Related questions emerge at this stage. Does the beneficence of the gods ever translate to a human setting, in which generosity is experienced in communities alternative to the city-state? What type of self-understanding undergirds these groups? Is it based on divine grace or something else?

The nearest we come to this type of phenomenon in antiquity is in the Epicurean and Pythagorean groups. There φιλία (human and divine) is the dynamic which animates all community relations. Plutarch, in arguing (contrary to Epicurus) that God's nature is to bestow favour (χαρίζεσθαι),[96] comes close to linking divine beneficence with the philosophical ideal of friendship. The friendship which the gods experience causes them to be generous to a select community of the good:

All things belong to the gods, as Diogenes said; among friends all property is in common (καὶ κοινὰ τὰ τῶν φίλων); good men are friends of the gods (καὶ φίλοι τοῖς θεοῖς οἱ ἀγαθοί); and it cannot be that one dear to the gods should fail to prosper or that the temperate and upright man should fail to be dear to the gods.[97]

This should lead — although Plutarch doesn't say as much — to the philosophical community of the wise sharing all things in common.[98] In Plutarch, however, the link between divine χάρις, φιλία and some alternative form of beneficent community is never as explicitly forged as the nexus found in the New Testament.[99]

A final question remains. Is the raison d'être for human beneficence at any stage related to the gods by the Greek philosophers? In a revealing aside, Aristotle links both the return of beneficence and its unsolicited expression to the Charites:

That is why we set up a shrine of the Graces (Χαρίτων) in a public place, to remind men to

---

[96] *Id., Mor.,* 1102E.

[97] *Id., Mor.,* 1102F. See also Dio Chrysostom, *Or.,* 3.110, 115 (110: χαριζόμενος, κοίνα τὰ φιλῶν). On the happiness of the gods due to their friendships, see Philodemus, *De Dis* III, frag. 84, col. 1, 2-4.

[98] The Greek proverb κοίνα τὰ φιλῶν ('the belongings of friends are held in common') is widely found in the philosophical literature: Plato, *Resp.,* 5.46.2c; Aristotle, *Eth. Nic.,* 9.8.1168b; Cicero, *Off.,* 1.16.51; Philo, *Prob.* 75-86; Diog. Laert. 6.72. Pythagorean groups took the communal ideal behind the proverb quite literally (Iamblichus, *Vit. Pyth.,* 30.167-168).

[99] See Acts 2:43-47 (εἶχον ἅπαντα κοινά, v.44; χάριν, v.47), 4:32-35 (ἅπαντα κοινά, v.32; χάρις, v.33); John 15:12-17 (ἠγάπησα ὑμᾶς, ἀγαπᾶτε ἀλλήλους vv.12, 17; φίλοι, vv.13, 14, 15). Cf. M. Hengel, *Property and Riches in the Early Church* (Philadelphia 1974), 31: 'Luke has stylised his picture of the early community along the lines of popular philosophical terminology'.

return a kindness (ἡ ἀνταπόδοσις ᾖ); for that is a special characteristic of grace (χάριτος), since it is a duty not only to repay a service done one (τῷ χαρισαμένῳ), but another time to take the initiative in doing a service (χαριζομένον) oneself.[100]

However, the public prominence of the shrines set up to the Χαρίτες indicates that χάρις (at least for Aristotle) is a primarily civic virtue. As far as the relation of human χάρις to the Χαρίτες, it is cultic in nature. Further, it functions more by mnemonic association than any notion of divine grace impelling human beneficence, as is the case with the early Christians.

5.4.2. Grace and the cults

The role that cultic sacrifice plays in securing divine beneficence features prominently in the discussions of philosophers over several centuries. Apart from the Epicureans and the savage attack of Lucian on sacrifice — both discussed in §5.5 — the philosophers largely endorse conservative cultic practice, using χάρις and its cognates to convey the gods' pleasure at correct ritual. The conservatism of the philosophers in such issues spans the centuries. For example, Plato's *Euthyphro* states that holiness, embodied in prayer and sacrifice, was gratifying to the gods (κεχαρισμένα τοῖς θεοῖς) and brought salvation to individual families and states.[101] Dio Chrysostom points out that sacrifice is only acceptable (κεχαρισμένη) to the gods when the participants in cultic feasts share in friendship.[102] Even the cynical Lucian can acknowledge that sacrifices are pleasing (κεχαρισμένα) to the gods when the participants perform the ceremony in their own native lands.[103]

The most extensive discussion of cultic sacrifice is found in Theophrastus, whose work *On Piety* is epitomised for us by Porphyry. Theophrastus argues that the sacrifice of animals is not as agreeable (εὐχάριστον) to the gods as the sacrifice of fruits.[104] Several arguments are adduced by Theophrastus to bolster his position.

---

[100] Aristotle, *Eth. Nic.*, 5.5.8. For other linkages of χάρις and its cognates with the Χαρίτες, see Dio Chrysostom, *Or.*, 31.37; Plutarch, *Mor.*, 141F and 778C-D; Cornutus, *Summary of Greek Theology* 8 (10.2-3 Lang), 15 (18.14-20.14 Lang).

[101] Plato, *Euthphr.* 14B. Cf. *id.*, *Resp.*, 3.6.A (κεχαρισμένος).

[102] Dio Chrysostom, *Or.*, 3.97.

[103] Lucian, *My Native Land*, 5.

[104] Theophrastus, Περὶ εὐσέβειας, 9.1 (tr. W.W. Fortenbaugh [*et. al.*, ed.], *Theophrastus: Sources for His Life, Writings, Thought and Influence* Vol.2 [Leiden-New York-Köln 1992], §584A). For discussions of this work, see F. Solmsen, 'Theophrastus and Political Aspects of the Belief in Providence', *GBRS* 19/1 (1978), 91-98; P.A. Meijer, 'Philosophers, Intellectuals and Religion in Hellas', in H.S. Versnal (ed.), *Faith, Hope and Worship: Aspects of Religious Mentality in the Ancient World* (Leiden 1981), 250-259; D. Obbink, 'The Origin of Greek Sacrifice: Theophrastus on Religion and Cultural History', in W.W. Fortenbaugh and R.W. Sharples (eds), *Theophrastean Studies* Vol.3 (New Brunswick

First, in his view, the return of beneficence evidenced in the sacrificial cult necessitates the most honourable offerings.[105] Thus, the gift of fruits is precious because it preserves life, whereas animal sacrifice is more expensive and deprives the unwilling creature of its soul.[106] Second, the divinity looks more to the character of those sacrificing than the costliness or quantity of their sacrifices.[107] More important for our purpose, however, are the side-comments which Theophrastus makes concerning the place of grace in cultic sacrifice. He states that

> ... there are three reasons one ought to sacrifice to the gods: either on account of honour (τιμήν) or on account of gratitude (χάριν) or on account of a want of good things ... We honour the gods either because we seek to deflect evils or to acquire goods for ourselves, or because we have first been treated well or simply to do great honour to their good character ... And at any rate we agree that we will do injustice if in the course of sacrificing we destroy those animals that do no injustice. It follows that none of the other animals is to be sacrificed for the sake of honour. Nor indeed (should we sacrifice animals) when we return a favour (χάριν ἀποδιδόντας) to them (the gods) for their kindnesses (εὐεργεσιῶν). For when one makes a just return for kindness (τὴν δικαίαν ἀμοιβὴν τῆς εὐεργεσίας ἀποδιδούς) and an equivalent one (τὸ ἀντάξιον) for a good deed, one ought not to provide these as a result of treating others in an evil manner. For one will no more seem to make a return (ἀμείβεσθαι) than if one, after stealing the property of his neighbour, should reward others as if returning favour and honour (χάριν ἀποδιδοὺς καὶ τιμήν). But neither (should we sacrifice animals) for some want of good things. For when one seeks to be treated well by means of an unjust deed, there is suspicion that even after being well-treated one will feel no gratitude (χάριν). It follows that when a kindness (εὐεργεσίας) is expected, one ought not to sacrifice animals to the gods.[108]

This passage affords us considerable insight into the dynamic underlying the ancient cults. In sacrificing to the gods the ancients either adopt a posture of coercion (designed to avert evil or induce favour) or one of veneration

---

and Oxford 1988), 272-295. For the sake of argument, I have assumed that Theophrastus' work has come down to us substantially intact. The important question whether genuine fragments of Theophrastus' *On Piety* can be retrieved from the epitome of Porphyry, a representative of the later neo-Pythagorean vegetarianism, still remains.

[105] Theophrastus, Περὶ εὐσέβειας, 12.2: Τῶν εὐεργεσιῶν τὰς ἀμοιβὰς καὶ τὰς χάριτας.

[106] *Ibid.*, 12.3-4. Theophrastus (*ibid.*, 12.4) speaks against depriving unwilling animals of their souls through sacrifice: 'No one is holy who returns favours (ἀποδίδωσι χάριτας) by taking from the property of another, even if one takes fruits, even if plants, when the other is unwilling'.

[107] *Ibid.*, 15.3. Cf. Plutarch, *Mor.*, 1102A: '...it is not the abundance of wine or the roast meats that cheer the heart at festivals, but good hope and the belief in the benign presence of the god and his gracious acceptance (κεχαρισμένως) of what is done'. However, as Plutarch observes (*Mor.*, 818C-D), cultic worship could be used by politicians and the demos as a cynical pretext for philanthropic beneficence (χάριν τινὰ φιλάνθρωπον) or private ambition (φολοτιμίαν).

[108] Theophrastus, Περὶ εὐσέβειας, 24.1-5.

(rendering honour or gratitude). Grace is subsumed under the rubric of reciprocity: the favour and honour of the gods are to be returned in a manner commensurate with their kindnesses. The terminology of exchange — ἀποδιδόναι χάριν, ἀμοιβή, ἀμείβεσθαι — makes this contractual element explicit, as does the emphasis on commensurate return by means of δικαία and τὸ ἀντάξιον. Some of Theophrastus' disquiet over the cult may have originated in his perception that animal sacrifice did not reciprocate the gods' beneficence in a manner sufficiently pleasing to them.

In sum, the cultic understanding of grace differs from the Pauline conviction that divine grace was unable to be requited: conversely, the ancients were confident that it could.

The philosophers also devote their attention to the role of grace in other areas of cultic ritual. The statues of the deities, when skilfully rendered by craftsmen, honour the god and win his favour (χάρις).[109] According to Plato, young Athenian boys and girls should be taught dances for the religious processions, and thereby cultivate the favour of the goddess (τὴν τῆς θεοῦ χάριν).[110] Last, Plutarch advises the wife that she is more likely to find divine favour (κεχαρισμένως) if she worships her husband's gods.[111]

In conclusion, the idea that the grace of God was exclusively mediated by the correct performance of cultic ritual was a pervasive one in antiquity. It contributed to groups such as the Epicureans and Christians being labelled atheists, precisely because of their criticism of the traditional cults as mediators of divine beneficence.[112]

5.4.3. Grace and recompense

In the theological world-view of the ancients, the outworking of recompense has a tidal quality: it flows from the gods over the human shoreline, and then slowly ebbs back towards them. χάρις and its cognates are the central terms used to chart this process.

Plutarch, in *The Parallel Lives*, highlights the way in which the gods recompense the καλοκἀγαθοί for their display of ἀρετή in conducting the

---

[109] *Ibid.*, 12.46. Cf. *ibid.*, 12.51 (τῷ θεῷ χάριν) and 12.77 (χαριζομένῳ). Similarly, Plato, *Leg.* 11.931A: 'the living gods beyond feel great good-will towards us and gratitude (εὔνοιαν καὶ χάριν)'.

[110] Plato, *Leg.* 7.796C.

[111] Plutarch, *Mor.*, 140D. Cf. *id., ibid.*, 141F: Χάριτες, χαρίτες.

[112] For the II cent. AD categorisation of Epicureans and Christians as atheists, see A.D. Simpson, 'Epicureans, Christians, Atheists in the Second Century', *TAPhA* 72 (1941), 372-381.

affairs of state. In each case, the presumption is that the gods reward with grace those who have demonstrated the requisite merit.

For example, Dion exhorted his mercenaries with the promise of commensurate reward from the gods (χάριν ἀξίαν κομίζοισθε παρὰ τῶν θεῶν) because they had demonstrated bravery and zeal.[113] Darius prayed to the Persian gods to requite (ἀμείψασθαι) Alexander for the magnificent funeral which he had given the captive Persian queen.[114] The banishment of Camillus from Rome resulted in retribution for the city, since the god did not leave his virtue unrequited (ἀρετῆς ἀχαριστουμένης).[115] Before his assassination Gaius Gracchus prayed that the goddess Diana would requite the ingratitude (ἀντὶ τῆς ἀχαριστίας) and treachery of the Roman people towards himself with servitude.[116]

However, the tide turns and grace returns to the gods, with the result that they are then placed under constraint. The deities on occasion are obligated to return gratitude to their worshippers; the operation of reciprocity in the household causes them intense pleasure; and, as the beneficiaries of the cult, they too can have benefits conferred upon them. This studied reciprocation of grace to the gods can be seen in the following examples.

Plato states that when statues are set up as images of worship, 'the living gods beyond feel great good-will (εὔνοιαν) towards us and gratitude (χάριν)'.[117] According to Plutarch, the gods are gratified (κεχαρισμένον θεοῖς) when children repay their parental favours (χάριτας) — as an act of goodwill and zeal (εὐμενῶς καὶ προθύμως) on their part — by maintaining harmonious sibling friendships.[118] Last, Croesus conferred a benefit upon the god (τῷ θεῷ τὴν χάριν ἀμείψασθαι) in the form of a golden statue of the royal baker. This honorific image simultaneously celebrated the poisoning of the king's dynastic rivals, and requited the baker who had revealed to Croesus the plot against his life.[119]

To sum up, the gods honour the ethos of reciprocity, and subject themselves to the legitimate counter-claims of the ritually pious. We now turn to the criticisms which the philosophers brought against the benefaction system.

---

[113] Plutarch, *Dion*, 43.5.
[114] *Id.*, *Alex.*, 43.4 (ἀποδιδόναι τὴν χάριν).
[115] *Id.*, *Cam.*, 13.2.
[116] *Id.*, *C. Gracch.*, 16.5.
[117] Plato, *Leg.*, 11.931A.
[118] Plutarch, *Mor.*, 479F.
[119] *Ibid.*, 401E-F.

5.5. The Philosophical Critique of Charis

We have seen that the philosophers conservatively endorse the traditional benefaction system at a divine and human level. Nonetheless, they subject the Graeco-Roman benefaction system and its honours to moral censure from a variety of viewpoints. Further, in their view, the ethos of reciprocity was undermined by the self-interest of the participants. Additionally, the mediation of divine grace through the sacrificial cult is held up to ridicule by Lucian in particular. Finally, Plutarch attacks the theology of Epicurus as demeaning in its attitude to divine beneficence, whilst the Cynic Cercidas struggles to reconcile the competing claims of divine grace and divine justice.

5.5.1. The moral critique of benefaction ideology

Epictetus' critique of the benefaction system and its honours is incidental to his overriding concern of training the moral will of his students. In a discussion of the overweening superiority of tyrants and those who flatter them, Epictetus argues that we deceive ourselves when we make judgements outside the moral purpose (τὰ προαιρετικά).[120] By contrast, the individual who has set a high value on his moral purpose (τὴν προαίρεσιν τὴν ἑαυτοῦ) is freed by Zeus.[121] Such a person will not be beguiled by the inflated importance assigned to tyrants — or by the wider Graeco-Roman honour system.

To reinforce this point, Epictetus cites three examples from imperial Rome of the absurd opinions that arise when the moral purpose is ignored.[122] First, there is the fawning respect accorded a cobbler by his former owner, Epaphroditus, when the same cobbler later became a member of Caesar's household.[123] Second, there is the ephemeral fame of the καλοκἀγαθοί who buy a priesthood of Augustus in order to have their names inscribed on the deeds of sale and to be personally honoured with crowns of gold.[124] Last, and importantly for us, there is the folly of the tribune who, having been honoured by all, climbs up the Capitol and offers sacrifice. Epictetus' assessment of the tribune's piety is caustic:

Now who ever sacrificed as a thank-offering for having had right desire, or for having

---

[120] Arr., *Epict. Diss.*, 1.19.23.

[121] *Ibid.*, 1.19.8-9; cf. 2.17.23-25. On the importance of προαίρεσις in Epictetus, see J. Hershbell, *art. cit.*, 2157, 2159-2160 and the literature there cited.

[122] Arr., *Epict. Diss.*, 1.19.16.

[123] *Ibid.*, 1.19.19-23.

[124] *Ibid.*, 1.19.26-29.

exercised choice in accordance with nature (κατὰ φύσιν)? For we give thanks to the gods (θεοῖς εὐχαριστοῦμεν) for that wherein we set the good (τὸ ἀγαθὸν τιθέμεθα).[125]

Tragically, according to Epictetus, people fail to render gratitude to the gods for the central principles of Stoic morality (κατὰ φύσιν) that shape correct ethical decisions.[126] Instead, they foolishly sacrifice thank-offerings to the gods for the fleeting honours accorded to them by their contemporaries. For Epictetus, the social trappings of first-century honorific culture — embodied in the offices, favours and privileges which the Caesars as εὐεργέται dispensed (1.19.19-29) — hold no attraction to the philosopher whose moral purpose is strong and disciplined.

Elsewhere, Epictetus returns to this familiar refrain. If we live outside the moral purpose, our desires (such as zeal for the honours of the benefaction system) will come to grief:

Give (your desires) to health; you will come to grief; so, also if you give them to offices (ἀρχαῖς), honours (τιμαῖς), country, friends (φιλοῖς), children, in short to anything that lies outside the domain of the moral purpose (τῶν ἀπροαιρέτων).[127]

The theological solution which Epictetus posits for regaining the moral ground is straightforward:

But give (χάρισαι) them to Zeus and the other gods; entrust them to their keeping, let them exercise the control; let your desire and your aversion be ranged on their side — and how can you be troubled any longer?[128]

A limited moral critique of the benefaction system is also found in Musonius Rufus. Musonius draws a telling contrast between two approaches to benefaction. Whereas the wealthy élite build luxurious houses to establish *clientes*, the civic-minded benefactor displays unstinting sacrifice. The alternatives are sharply posed:

How much nobler (καλοκἀγαθικώτερον) than spending money for sticks and stones to spend it on men. How much more profitable than surrounding oneself with a great house to make many friends (φίλους πολλούς), the natural result of cheerfully doing good (τῷ προθύμως εὐεργετοῦντι). What would one gain from a large and beautiful house comparable to what he would gain by conferring (χαρίζεσθαι) the benefits of his wealth upon the city and his fellow citizens?[129]

---

[125] *Ibid.*, 1.19.25.

[126] On the role of nature in Stoic thought, see F.H. Sandbach, *The Stoics* (London 1975), 53-59.

[127] Arr., *Epict. Diss.*, 2.17.24.

[128] *Ibid.*, 2.17.25.

[129] Musonius Rufus, Περὶ σκέπης. See C.E. Lutz, 'Musonius Rufus "The Roman Socrates"', in A.R. Bellinger (ed.), *YClS* 10 (1947), §XIX.

5.5.2. Critical responses to the ethos of reciprocity

The philosophers, as we have seen, promote the ethos of reciprocity.[130] On one occasion, however, Plutarch responds to Epicurus' observation that reciprocity in the household originates from a fundamentally self-interested relationship. As Plutarch renders Epicurus' position, 'it is for pay that a father loves his son, a mother her child, children their parents'.[131] Plutarch contrasts the altruistic care of the animal world for its progeny with the position of Epicurus:

For it is shameful — great Heaven! — that the begetting and the pains of travail and the nurture of beasts should be 'Nature' and 'a free gift' (χάριν), but that those of men should be loans and wages and caution-money, all given on condition of a return.

Plutarch has here rejected one of the cardinal tenets of ancient reciprocity: that children *must* reciprocate their parents' favours.[132] Epicurus had exposed the raw nerve of the benefaction system in alluding to its base of self-interest at the household level. By contrast, Plutarch does not prohibit children from reciprocating the past generosity of their parents. But parents should not expect any reciprocation of beneficence in nurturing their children: this would disqualify the very freedom of grace to serve without any expectation of return.

In similar vein, the philosophers also highlight the exploitation of the reciprocity ethos that may occur between φίλοι. In the opinion of Epicurus, the friend who continually requests help makes gratitude (χάρις) a matter of commercial transaction (ἀμοιβή).[133] The wise man will avoid parasitic requests of his friends, and thereby ensure the hope of good in the future.[134] Thus Epicurus believes — along with *P. Mert.* 1.12 — that reciprocity between friends demands a more sensitive approach than that found in orthodox benefaction ideology.[135]

Finally Dio Chrysostom, in a comment on the Homeric account of Telemachus' refusal to benefit a swineherd,[136] exposes the self-interest of the reciprocity system. The reason why Telemachus rejected needy strangers such as the swineherd is that the poor are unable to render a commensurate

---

[130] See our discussion in §5.3.

[131] Plutarch, *Mor.*, 495B.

[132] For the inscriptional evidence, see §2.5 n.82. Papyrological evidence, §3.2.2 and §3.3. Jewish evidence, §4.5.3 and §4.6.3. For the philosophers (especially Hierocles), §5.3.

[133] Epicurus, *Sententiae Vaticanae*, 39.

[134] *Ibid.* See J.M. Rist, 'Epicurus on Friendship', *CPh* 75 (1980), 121-129.

[135] On *P. Mert.* 1.12, see §3.3.

[136] Homer, *Od.*, 17.10ff.

return, unlike the rich.[137] The reciprocity system, in the view of Dio Chrysostom, calculates in advance the projected economic return, including the social status earned as a dividend:

> ... for what seem to be acts of kindliness (θιλοφρονήσεις) and favours (χάριτες) turn out, when examined rightly, to be nothing more or less than accommodations and loans, and that too at a high rate of interest as a usual thing ...[138]

In conclusion, Plutarch, Epicurus and Dio Chrysostom approach the type of sustained critique of the benefaction system that we saw earlier in Philo.[139] Each throws light on differing ethical dilemmas of reciprocity: the need for parents to abandon any expectation of return from their progeny; the possible exploitation of the reciprocity ethos by φίλοι; and, last, the underlying social bias of the benefaction system.

5.5.3. The critique of the cult

Previously, we have examined the dominant belief in antiquity that the grace of the god(s) was mediated through the cult.[140] While many philosophers endorsed this position as axiomatic, Plutarch qualified the belief, whereas Lucian ferociously attacked it.

Plutarch, in *Moralia* 355D, does not reject the established rites of worship per se. Nevertheless, he labels as superstition and atheism any approach to the deity which fails to recognise his true nature. Therefore, the mediation of grace through the cult is relativised by Plutarch: 'no sacrifice that you can offer, no deed that you may do will be more likely to find favour (κεχαρισμένον) with the gods than your belief in their true nature'.[141] The cult certainly continues: but its effectiveness is dependent on correct theological belief, not our performance.

Lucian, in *On Sacrifices*, subjects the sacrificial system — including its feasts and processions in honour of the gods — to sustained criticism from a largely Epicurean theological viewpoint. At the outset, he dismisses as dolts those who adhere to traditional religion. Their piety is irreligious and pestilent because it involves a fundamental misunderstanding of the nature of the gods: namely, that the deities are 'so low and mean as to stand in need of men and to enjoy being flattered and to get angry when they are slighted'.[142] The gods, in Lucian's view, simply cannot be manipulated by the cult.

---

[137] Dio Chrysostom, *Or.*, 7.88.
[138] *Ibid.*, 7.89.
[139] For Philo, see §4.4.4.
[140] See our discussion in §5.4.2.
[141] See also Plutarch, *Mor.*, 1102A (κεχαρισμένως).
[142] Lucian, *On Sacrifices*, 1.

He then cites several satirical examples to lampoon the traditional cult. The disasters which befell the Aetolians are not attributable to the grudge of Artemis over not being invited to Oeneus' sacrifice.[143] Nor could the Ethiopians legitimately claim divine recompense — as if

> Zeus is really paying them back for the kindness (ἀπομνημονεύει τὴν χάριν) that they showed him in dining him for twelve days running, and that too when he brought along the other gods![144]

Overall, in the opinion of Lucian, the traditional sacrificial system is at heart a commercial transaction. The gods are seen as selling human beings their blessings (health, wealth, a royal throne, safety from war and misadventure) at inflationary prices (a calf, up to a hundred oxen, nine bulls, a king's daughter).[145] This 'prosperity theology' so inflates the pride of human beings that they believe that the gods should reciprocate their favours. We see this when the priest Chryses, after failing to secure the return of his daughter from Agamemnon, demanded his due (τὴν ἀμοιβήν) from Apollo because, as Lucian observes, he had loaned his good works (τὴν χάριν) to the god. Chryses parades his piety before Apollo in this revealing prayer:

> My good Apollo, I have often dressed your temple with wreaths when it lacked them before, and have burned in your honour all those thighs of bulls and goats upon your altars, but you neglect me when I am in such straits and take no account of your benefactor (εὐεργέτην).[146]

It is perhaps such Gentile cultic attitudes — mocked with satirical exaggeration by Lucian — which spurred Paul into magnifying justification by grace in his role as the apostle to the Gentiles. It is interesting to speculate whether diaspora Jews in similar fashion had come to view God's covenantal grace as being attracted to the ritually pious. Perhaps circumcision and the Law had come to represent not only a purity boundary marker, but also a badge of ancestral merit that became a ground for Jewish claims of divine recompense.

5.5.4. Epicureans, cynics, and the debate on divine beneficence in antiquity

The theological views of Epicurus and his disciples provoked heated philosophical debate in antiquity.[147] Some of the ancients took offence at the famous statement of Epicurus concerning the divine nature:

---

[143] *Ibid.*

[144] *Ibid.*, 2.

[145] *Ibid.*

[146] *Ibid.*, 3. Lucian adds that Apollo requited Chryses by shooting down the Achaeans with the plague.

[147] For discussions of Epicurus' view of the gods, see D.P. Hadzsits, 'Significance of Worship and Prayer among the Epicureans', *TAPhA* 39 (1908), 73-88; R. Philippson, 'Zur

The blessed and immortal nature knows no trouble itself nor causes trouble to any other, so that it is never constrained by anger or favour (οὔτε ὀργαῖς οὔτε χάρισι). For all such things exist only in the weak.[148]

Elsewhere, in an Oxyrhynchus papyrus identified as coming from Epicurus, other elements of doctrine surface which would have distressed his contemporaries. In the papyrus Epicurus suggests that the gods are to be approached by contemplation (founded upon a proper conception of the gods) and not by the traditional cult.[149] In the view of Epicurus, then, it is totally unnecessary for wise men 'to beg for signs of favour (τῆς χάριτ[ος]) from the gods in their fear of being neglected by them'.[150]

What was so provocative about the position which Epicurus espoused? According to Plutarch, the irreligion of Epicurus' letters resides precisely in their denial of the wrath and favour of God.[151] Any hope of continuing divine beneficence is dashed by Epicurus' approach. As Plutarch puts it, we 'leave ourselves no hope of divine favour (χάριν), no confidence in prosperity, and in adversity no refuge in God'.[152] The position adopted by Epicurus demeans the character of God, whose nature is 'to bestow favour (χαρίζεσθαι) and lend aid', and not 'to be angry and do harm'.[153]

To sum up, the Epicureans entirely removed the possibility of God demonstrating any kindness (χάριν), anger or concern towards humanity. Instead, they consigned the Deity to the clear spaces between the galaxies, remote from all terrestrial care, in order that He could indulge Himself in a life

---

epikureischen Götterlehre', *Hermes* 51 (1916), 568-608; A.H. Armstrong, *art. cit.*, 190-196; W. Schmid, 'Götter und Menschen in der Theologie Epikurs', *RhM* 94 (1951), 97-156; H.W. Attridge, *art. cit.*, 51-56.

[148] Epicurus, *Principal Doctrines*, 1. Cf. Diog. Laert., 10.139. N.W. DeWitt (*art. cit.*, 320 n.1), argues — contrary to Bailey's translation above — that χάρισι should be rendered 'feelings of gratitude'. The issue is complex. Epicurus either means that the gods cannot be induced to dispense benefactions, or be placed under any obligation of gratitude. He may well have agreed with both positions, and chose χάρις precisely because of its ambiguity. Whatever the viewpoint of Epicurus, Plutarch definitely understood him to be referring to divine benefaction. Philodemus (Περὶ εὐσέβειας, Fr.38 [ed. Usener], *ll*.10-11) says that the pious man deems the god separate from anger or 'favour' (or 'gratitude': χάριτος).

[149] *P. Oxy.* II 215. For discussions of the papyrus, see W. Schmid, *art. cit.*, 133ff; A.J. Festugière, *Epicurus and His Gods* (New York 1955), 63-56; H.W. Attridge, *art. cit.*, 53.

[150] *P. Oxy.* II. 215 Col. iii. 5-9.

[151] Plutarch, *Mor.*, 1101B (τὴν χάριν ἐκ τοῦ θείου, μετὰ τῆς ὀργῆς).

[152] *Ibid.*, 1101B-C. Similarly, *ibid.* 1107C: 'the surgery of Epicurus cuts out of our lives ... all hope of help from Heaven and all bestowal of grace (χάρισιν)'.

[153] *Ibid.*, 1102E. On this occasion Plutarch partly agrees with Epicurus in playing down the wrath of God. However, a closer examination of Plutarch's tractate 'On the Delays of the Divine Vengeance' (*Mor.*, 548-568) is required for a fuller appreciation of his views regarding divine wrath. On this issue, see P.G. Bolt, *Plutarch's 'Delay of the Divine Vengeance' and Pauline Eschatology* (unpub. MAHons diss. Macquarie University 1994).

of ease and comfort.[154] Given the visible manifestation of God's grace in the incarnation of Jesus, Paul would probably have sided with Plutarch against the Epicureans on the issue of divine benefaction and divine anger.[155]

The Cynics, in spite of their overall agnosticism,[156] contribute incisively to the ancient debate on divine beneficence. Cercidas, a Cynic from the second century BC, typically airs the thorny issue of the impotence of divine providence, and then proposes a novel theological solution to his dilemma. In a searing critique of traditional mythology, Cercidas rails against the inconsistency and indifference of Zeus in meting out justice:

> For it is easy for a god to accomplish everything whenever it comes into his mind, and to empty of his swinish wealth the dirty usurer and hoarder or this outpourer and ruin of his substance, and to give the squandered means to the man who takes his bite in season and shares his cup with a neighbour. Is then the eye of Right blinded like a mole's? Does Phaethon see crookedly with a single orb, and is the vision of fair Justice dimmed? How can they who have neither hearing or inlet of sight be yet taken for deities? Nay, the august lightning-compeller sits on mid Olympus holding even the balance and in no wise signifies his will ... For why does not he who controls the weights, if he is upright, incline them to me, or to Phrygia at the ends of the earth?[157]

Moreover, Zeus as the universal Father arbitrarily discriminates between his children in the disposal of his providential favour. For Cercidas, even the astrologers would be unable to divine the selection criteria that Zeus uses to determine which of his children receive beneficence:

> To what sort of lords, then, or to what children of Heaven can one go to find how he may get his deserts, when the son of Cronos, the begetter and parent of us all, is found to be a father to some and a stepfather to others? Better to leave these questions to the astrologers, for they, I expect, will have no manner of trouble.[158]

The solution for Cercidas lay in a wholesale rejection of the traditional pantheon of deities, and its replacement by a more just and beneficent alternative: 'For us let Paean (Παιάν) and Giving (Μετάδως) be our care, for

---

[154] Plutarch, *Pyrrh.*, 3-4

[155] On the issue of divine anger in the theology of Paul, see K.N.E. Newell, 'St. Paul and the Anger of God', *Irish Biblical Studies* 1 (1979), 99-114; P.G. Bolt, *op. cit.*

[156] Contrast the attitude of Aesop who highlights the surety of divine justice: 'Even when you are dead you can get even with an enemy. For nothing escapes the eye of divine Justice: it weighs crimes in the balance and allots the appropriate punishment' ('The Rat and the Frog', É. Chambry, *op. cit.*, §244). For a fine discussion of Cynic attitudes to traditional religion, see M.-O. Goulet-Cazé, 'Le cynisme à l'époque impériale', *ANRW* II 36/4 (1992), 2781-2788. Also, F.G. Downing, *op. cit.*, 39-44. If one considers Epictetus to be a Cynic — as opposed to a Stoic — philosopher, the judgement of Goulet-Cazé regarding the overall agnosticism of the Cynics would have to be modified.

[157] *P. Oxy.* VIII 1082. Col. ii. *l.*5 — Col. iii. *ll.*1, 4-5.

[158] *Ibid.*, Col. iii. *ll.*8-14.

she is a goddess, with Retribution (Νέμεσις), on earth'.[159] This earthly triad of Παιάν (the god Apollo as Healer), Μετάδως (the hypostasis of Beneficence), and Νέμεσις (the goddess of Retribution) combines a concern for body and soul, and dispenses both grace and justice. As a result, we are to honour the deity for any 'favouring breeze', and cultivate a Cynic distaste for acquisitiveness and the gifts of Fortune.[160]

Unfortunately, we possess no contemporary reaction to the Cynic theology of Cercidas. Its antagonism to traditional polytheism flows from the very real dilemma of reconciling divine justice and divine grace. The novel solution that it adopts illustrates how some ancients grappled with the problem, and exposes for us some of the intellectual ground into which Paul's gospel of grace would fall.

5.6. Beneficence in the Roman Moralists: A Study of the Role of Gratia

So far we have looked at the role of χάρις in the Greek documentary and literary evidence. At no stage in our coverage has the Latin evidence been combed for the perspective of the Roman West on grace and beneficence. To find out whether there was a uniformity of viewpoint between Greeks and Romans in these matters, we will now investigate the evidence of the three Roman moralists Cicero (106—43 BC), Valerius Maximus (early I cent. AD) and Seneca (4 BC/AD 1—AD 65). We will confine ourselves to occurrences of *gratia* (the Latin equivalent of χάρις) and sift the evidence through the same thematic sieves.

Such a cross-cultural comparison of beneficence is not foreign to antiquity. Valerius Maximus undertook precisely this task in his parallelism of Roman and foreign moral examples in *De liberalitate, De gratis,* and *De ingratis.*[161] It still remains for New Testament scholars to plumb the riches of his work.[162]

5.6.1. A survey of gratia *and its cognates in the Roman moralists*

Cicero regards gratitude as one of the fundamental laws of nature.[163] Nature, upon which all justice is founded, holds together all the social virtues:

---

[159] *Ibid.*, Col. iii. *ll*.15-16.

[160] *Ibid.*, Col. iii. *l.*16 — Col. iv. *l.*4.

[161] All are found in Valerius Maximus, *Noteworthy Doings and Sayings*.

[162] See, however, R. Hodgson, 'Valerius Maximus and the Social World of the New Testament', *CBQ* 51/4 (1989), 683-693. Seneca has been served well by J.N. Sevenster, *Paul and Seneca* (Leiden 1961).

[163] Cicero, *Inv. Rhet.*, 2.22.65-67; 2.53.161. For modern discussions of *gratia*, see §2.1

generosity (*liberalitas*), love of country (*patriae caritas*), loyalty (*pietas*), and the demonstration of gratitude for favours received (*referendae gratiae*).[164] On one occasion, Cicero even accords gratitude the honour of heading all the virtues.[165]

The role of gratitude as a pre-eminent social virtue is regularly aired by Cicero. For example, in his viewpoint, only the shameless man would prefer payment to gratitude for his service to the state.[166] Not surprisingly, Cicero was distressed when the Roman people, due to the exigencies of the times, were unable to accord Racilius gratitude commensurate with his own.[167] In his own case, Cicero acknowledges the continual thankfulness accorded him by the *publicani*, and also the overflowing measure of Vatinius' gratitude.[168]

Last, in his letter of 19 March 49 BC, Cicero invites Caesar to end the Civil War by reconciling himself to Pompey and the Senate. In a cleverly calculated appeal, Cicero wields to full effect the rhetoric of reciprocal obligations imposed by gratitude and friendship in order to manipulate Caesar into abandoning his chosen course:

> ... you may devote some time to considering how I may be enabled by your kindness to be what decency and gratitude (*ut tuo beneficio bonus vir, gratus*), nay good-feeling, require, in remembering my great debt to Pompey ... I, a friend (*amicum*) of peace and of both of you, should be so supported by you that I may be able to work for peace between you and peace amongst our fellow-citizens. I thanked you (*tibi gratias egissem*) formerly in the matter of Lentulus, for having saved him, as he had saved me. Yet on reading the letter he has sent me full of thankfulness (*gratissimo*) for your generous kindness (*liberalitate beneficioque*), I feel that his safety is my debt as much as his. If you understand my gratitude (*esse gratum*) to him, pray give me the opportunity of showing my gratitude to Pompey too.[169]

Seneca pays considerable attention to the attitudes which benefactors and their beneficiaries ought to display towards each other in the benefaction ritual. On the one hand, the benefactor should not manifest any reluctance or delay in fulfilling his promises.[170] He must make absolutely clear the value of his gift to the beneficiary — gauged by the resources of each party — so that no reproach is given.[171] Those who are backward in acknowledging their debt

---

n.20.

[164] *Id., Leg.*, 1.15.43. Cf. *id., Mur.*, 41. It is not surprising to see Cicero correcting (what he perceives to be) the unsatisfactory ethical teaching of the philosophical schools regarding beneficence (*ibid.*, 65).

[165] *Id., Planc.*, 33.80.

[166] *Id., Inv. Rhet.*, 2.34.115.

[167] *Id., Planc.*, 32.77.

[168] Respectively, *id., QFr.*, 1.1.36; *id., Fam.*, 5.11.1.

[169] *Id., Att.*, 9.11a.

[170] Seneca, *Ben.*, 2.1.2; 2.5.2.

[171] *Ibid.*, 2.15.1-3.

of gratitude may need to have their memories refreshed by the benefactor.[172] In this respect, a wiser approach is to avoid the dilemma entirely by not benefiting those with an ungrateful character.[173]

Conversely, the person who decides to accept a benefaction must do so cheerfully and publicly.[174] Accordingly, the greater the favour the greater is the range of compliments to be returned the benefactor.[175] Neither is it inappropriate for the beneficiary 'not merely to equal, but to surpass in deed and spirit those who have placed us under obligation'.[176]

However, should a benefactor subsequently cause his beneficiary harm, this does not entitle the latter to repudiate his debt of gratitude.[177] Only the wise demonstrate genuine gratitude,[178] with virtue its reward.[179] Indeed, to return gratitude is part of love and friendship.[180] So, instead of undertaking retribution in return for the injury,[181] the wise person lets the benefactor's prior generosity outweigh the injury,[182] choosing voluntarily to forget the harm he perpetrated.[183]

Thus, whether benefactor or beneficiary, Seneca believes that we must 'be taught to give willingly, to receive willingly, to return willingly'.[184] Ingratitude, by contrast, is regarded as the cardinal social sin.[185] The ingrate justifiably feels the weight of social disapproval.[186] Nonetheless, social shame has its limits too. True, the shame over the desecration of a benefit may well incur the unremitting hatred of the benefactor,[187] but, in the view of Seneca, it

---

[172] *Ibid.*, 5.22.2; 5.25.6. In this respect, Seneca agrees with Epicurus that we should remember past favours (*ibid.*, 3.4.1-2).

[173] *Ibid.*, 4.27.5; 4.34.2. Aesop echoes a similar sentiment: 'This fable shows that when one does a bad man a service, the only recompense one can hope for is that he will not add injury to ingratitude' ('The Wolf and the Heron', É. Chambry, *op. cit.*, §224).

[174] Seneca, *Ben.*, 2.23.1-2; 4.21.1-3.

[175] *Ibid.*, 2.24.4.

[176] *Ibid.*, 1.4.3.

[177] Seneca, *Ep.*, 81. Also, *id.*, *Ben.*, 6.4.1; 6.5.1; 6.6.2-3. According to Aesop, the character of the benefactor has to be carefully studied by his prospective recipients: 'This fable shows that favours (χάριτες) are frightening when they come from evildoers' ('Zeus and the Serpent', É. Chambry, *op. cit.*, §122).

[178] Seneca, *Ep.*, 81.10ff, 13ff, 17ff, 24ff.

[179] *Ibid.*, 81.19ff.

[180] *Ibid.*, 81.12.

[181] *Ibid.*, 81.7.

[182] *Ibid.*, 81.8ff, 15ff.

[183] *Ibid.*, 81.24ff.

[184] *Id.*, *Ben.*, 1.4.3.

[185] *Ibid.*, 4.16.1-3; 4.20.3; 4.24.2; 4.26.1-3.

[186] *Ibid.*, 1.3.1.

[187] *Id.*, *Ep.*, 80.32.

is no worse than the social humiliation induced by the benefactor who continually reminds his dependants of his services.[188]

5.6.2. Gratia *and the ethos of reciprocity in the Roman moralists*

Cicero assumes the axiomatic nature of the reciprocation of favour.[189] The poor man who cannot return a favour in kind should at the very least express thankfulness of heart to his benefactor.[190] Kindness must therefore be requited as proof of gratitude.[191] In this respect, Cicero appeals authoritatively to Hesiod for the principle of reciprocation with interest, and illustrates it by referring to the fecund return of the fields.[192] Generosity undertakes and requites kindness: the failure to do so is only excusable when the rights of others are violated.[193] Under normal circumstances, however, the greater the favour the greater is the obligation. Nevertheless, this ought not become an incentive for self-interest where benefactors calculate in advance the projected return rather than meet the individual needs of people.[194]

Also, helpfully for us, Cicero brings to his exposition the acute sensitivity of a *novus homo* who, unlike established Roman nobles, did not inherit large numbers of *clientes*. He would have been dependent on networks of patronage and *amicitia*, and was therefore imbued with a heightened sense of the shame and obligation that such a system engendered. We see this in Cicero's profuse outpouring of gratitude for his recall by the Roman people in 4 August 57 BC from self-imposed exile:

I should show gratitude (*gratiam*) for services received, I should cherish the friendships (*amicitias*) that have proved sterling in the fire ... Were I for the rest of my life permitted to discharge no other duty save that of giving proof of adequate gratitude (*satis gratus*) towards merely the chief promoters and foremost champions of my restoration, I should nevertheless count the years that yet remain to me all too scanty a span even for the mere verbal expression of my gratitude (*gratiam*), far more for its translation into deeds.[195]

---

[188] *Ibid.*, 2.11.1-6. Valerius Maximus was well aware of the social humiliation involved in accepting gifts. Hiero, king of Syracuse, sent the Romans wheat, barley, and gold after their heavy loss at Lake Trasimenus (217 BC). As Valerius (*Noteworthy Doings and Sayings*, 4.8. Ext.1) continues, 'And not being ignorant of the modesty of the Romans in receiving such gifts, he made as if he presented them a congratulation of victory, that he might compel them, moved by religion, to accept his munificence'.

[189] Cicero, *Inv. Rhet.*, 2.22.65: 'Gratitude has regard for remembering and returning services, honour, and acts of friendship'. Cf. *ibid.*, 2.53.161; *id.*, *Phil.*, 3.6.14.

[190] *Id., Off.*, 2.20.69.

[191] *Ibid.*, 1.15.47.

[192] *Ibid.*, 1.15.48.

[193] *Ibid.*

[194] *Ibid.*, 1.15.49. Cf. *id., Amic.*, 9.31: 'we do not put out our favours at interest'.

[195] *Id., Red. Sen.*, 9.23-24.

Above all, it is in Cicero's letters that we feel the cutting edge of reciprocal obligation. He consistently acknowledges the obligation of gratitude.[196] As with Seneca, he concedes that even in discharging a debt he still remains a moral debtor.[197] Moreover, he can react with considerable anger when his own favours are not properly reciprocated.[198]

Two letters, each from 43 BC, accentuate the deeply personal sense of obligation on the part of the beneficiary, Plancus, to his benefactor, Cicero. Whatever the force of the rhetorical protestation which Plancus adopts as he affirms to Cicero his (in reality, flagging) loyalty to the Republic, his approach differs markedly to the dismissive attitude that *P. Mert.* 1.12 has towards the reciprocation of gratitude amongst φίλοι.[199] On one occasion, Plancus speaks of his 'undying gratitude' (*immortales gratias*) to Cicero because of his inabilility to requite the support that Cicero accorded him in the Senate:

So great have been your services that I do not think that I can rise to the requital of them, unless indeed, in your own impressive and eloquent words, you intend to regard me as paying the debt of gratitude (*referre gratiam*) so long as I bear that debt in remembrance.[200]

On another occasion, Plancus confesses 'with a sense of shame' that he cannot do justice to Cicero's generosity:

For neither does the intimate connection you have encouraged between us appear any expression of thanks (*gratiarum*), nor is it any pleasure to me to repay your wonderful kindnesses (*beneficiis*) by employing the cheap currency of words; and I had rather prove to you that I am not forgetful by my respectful consideration for you, and unfailing attention to you when we meet.[201]

Moreover, Cicero's total indifference towards any obligatory requital from his intimate friends stirs Plancus to even greater efforts 'to outdo all the gratitude (*gratas*)' of his friends and kinsfolk.[202]

In what way does the approach of Valerius Maximus, a collector of moral *exempla*, differ to that of Cicero? Valerius parades a host of Roman and foreign luminaries to illustrate the importance of reciprocation of gratitude to benefactors. A brief selection from *De Gratis* and *De Ingratis* will suffice.

---

[196] *Id., Fam.*, 3.5.1; 13.18.2.
[197] *Id., Planc.*, 28.68.
[198] *Id., Fam.*, 5.5.2-3.
[199] For our discussion of *P. Mert.* 1.12, see §3.3. Cicero comes close to the spirit of *P. Mert.* 1.12 in *Fam.* 12.28.2: 'I am gratified (*gratum*) too that you should not think it necessary to thank me (*quod mihi gratias agendas non putat*) on your account; you and I should not do that sort of thing'.
[200] *Id., Fam.*, 10.11.1.
[201] *Ibid.*, 10.24.1.
[202] *Ibid.*

There is the case of L. Petronius, a man of humble birth, who had advanced to the Equestrian Order through the patronage (*beneficio*) of Caelius. Although Petronius was unable to render Caelius adequate thanks (*gratum*) in prosperous times, he reciprocated his gratitude in adversity. Caelius, who faced execution as governor upon the fall of Placentia to Cinna, was spared an ignoble death when Petronius, in an act of piety to his patron's magnanimity, took both his own life and that of Caelius.[203]

Another case involved two women from the pro-Carthaginian town, Capua. Vedia Opidia and Cluvia Facula had exercised good will towards Rome by supplying the needs of the Roman captives and by daily sacrificing for the success of the Romans. On the capture of Capua in 211 BC by Rome, the Senate requited their faithfulness by freeing them and restoring their possessions. As Valerius concludes, 'it is remarkable that the Conscript Fathers should have found leisure at a time of such rejoicing, to return thanks (*referre gratiam*) to two very humble women, let alone to do so with so hearty a will'.[204]

Again, Terentius Culleo, a Praetorian and Senator, demonstrated gratitude for his release from Carthaginian captivity in 201 BC by walking bareheaded, freedman's cap in hand, behind the chariot of the triumphant Scipio Africanus Major. Valerius portrays the motivation behind Terentius' action in traditional terms: 'he very properly made acknowledgment before the Roman people of the benefaction he had received (*accepti beneficii confessionem*) to the author of his freedom, as though to a former master'.[205]

However, Valerius also employs Scipio Africanus Major as an example of the bitter revenge unleashed when favours were not requited. Notwithstanding his adulation for delivering Rome from disaster, the conqueror of Hannibal subsequently suffered the ignominy of being confined to a small village near a stinking lake. The inscription placed upon Scipio's tomb in c. 184—183 BC simmers with the rage of a *nobilis* whose *dignitas* has been spurned: *ingrata patria, ne ossa quidem mea habes*. With sympathetic insight Valerius editorialises on the ungratefulness of Rome:

What could be more unfitting than the necessity, more just than the complaint, more moderate than the reprisal? He denied his ashes to a city, which he had not let collapse into ash.[206]

---

[203] Valerius Maximus, *Noteworthy Doings and Sayings*, 4.7.5.
[204] *Ibid.*, 5.2.1.
[205] *Ibid.*, 5.2.5.
[206] *Ibid.*, 5.3.2b. The tomb inscription, translated, is: 'Ungrateful country, you do not even have my bones'. As Aesop comments: 'Those who have shown ingratitude to benefactors will not find others to help them when they are in a fix' ('The Crow and

Last, the return of gratitude for past favours overrides even the accepted norms of international diplomacy. For example, King Mithridates exchanged all his Rhodian prisoners for one Leonicus, who had in the past rescued the King from danger. Although the act of the King violated conventional military wisdom, it upheld the sacred conventions of reciprocity. In the view of Valerius, Mithridates 'judged it better to be overreached by his bitter foes than not to repay one who had served him well (*quam bene merito gratiam non referre*)'.[207]

Finally, the exhaustive coverage that Seneca devotes to the etiquette of reciprocity may deceive the reader into thinking that he is an undisciplined thinker who arrives at contradictory conclusions. The opposite is true. Rather, Seneca is very sensitive to the complexity of benefaction relationships. He therefore seeks to endorse the traditional reciprocation ethos, while alerting his readers to the abuses of the system and the potential for personal insult if inexpertly handled.[208]

Seneca consistently exhorts communities and individuals to recompense all acts of generosity from their benefactor.[209] The person who is grateful must either accept and owe benefits in good spirit, or make an appropriate return for favours received.[210] Indeed, philosophy demands that gratitude 'honourably avow the debt of benefits received, and honourably pay them; sometimes, however, the acknowledgment itself constitutes payment'.[211] At the very least, repayment should be made with gratitude,[212] or with a range of compliments commensurate to the benefaction.[213] If the original benefaction has indeed been repaid, the beneficiary ought to regard himself as still indebted to his benefactor in the reciprocation of gratitude.[214]

Hermes', É. Chambry, *op. cit.*, §166).

[207] *Ibid.*, 5.2. *Ext.* 1.2. The Romans also gave away kingdoms as benefactions to various client-kings in order to create bonds of gratitude in international relations. For an example, see Valerius Maximus' discussion of the gift of Asia to King Attalus (*ibid.*, 4.8.4). *De Viris Illustribus* 54 speaks of the diplomatic favour owed the Syrian king Antiochus III by the Roman Scipio Africanus thus: 'Antiochus had captured the son of Scipio Africanus during the sailing, and he returned him to his father, who, as if to return the favour (*reddenda gratia*), tried to persuade him to seek the friendship of Rome'.

[208] For Seneca's critique of reciprocity, see §5.6.4.

[209] Seneca, *Ben.*, 3.1.1: 'not to return gratitude for benefits (*non referre beneficiis gratiam*) is a disgrace'. Also, *id.*, *Hercules Furens*, 1337-1338; *Ep.*, 74.13.

[210] *Id.*, *Ben.*, 4.21.1-3.

[211] *Id.*, *Ep.*, 73.9.

[212] *Id.*, *Ben.*, 2.17.6.

[213] *Ibid.*, 2.24.4.

[214] *Ibid.*, 2.35.1-5; 2.18.5-6.

Alternatively, the ungrateful man feels no obligation for what he receives,[215] and repays his favour without interest.[216] Moreover, the ingrate clings to any subsequent injury perpetrated by the benefactor as justification for not returning the original favour,[217] and thereby undermines the social desirability of a voluntary return.[218] Last, it is also ungrateful for the beneficiary to try and ease out of his obligation by praying to the gods for the opportunity to counter-benefit the benefactor.[219]

5.6.3. Gratia and the gods in the Roman moralists

Both Cicero and Seneca assert the fundamental importance of gratitude to the gods. However, the range of reasons adduced for thankfulness to the various deities is more diverse than that found in the Greek philosophers.

Cicero, like Seneca, regards Natural Philosophy as the basis for our gratitude to the gods.[220] Indeed, *Gratia* is one of the hypostasised deities mentioned by Cicero.[221] Only on one occasion, in a letter (29 April 58 BC) addressed to his wife, does Cicero make a significant departure from orthodox benefaction ideology in relation to the gods. There he says that the pious worship of the gods undertaken by Terentia had (to his surprise) not induced their gratitude.[222] The exception, however, proves the rule. Elsewhere, even death becomes an occasion for joy and thanksgiving to God: it is precisely then that we abandon the prison of our body and pass on to our eternal home.[223] Finally, Cicero views wealth, honour, and security as evidence of divine benefaction, whereas the virtues flow entirely from our own moral achievement.[224]

According to Seneca, gratitude to the gods originates in the beneficence of the gods as lords of creation,[225] and in their generous appointment of human beings as their under-lords on earth.[226] Humanity, therefore, is not 'a hasty

---

[215] *Id., Ep.* 98.11.
[216] *Id., Ep.* 81.18-19.
[217] *Ibid.*, 81.23-26. Seneca (*ibid.*, 81.31-32) believed that 'paying back injuries instead of benefits' was characteristic of his age.
[218] *Ibid.*, 81.9-10.
[219] *Id., Ben.*, 6.27.1-2; 6.35.1-5.
[220] Cicero, *Fin.*, 3.22.73.
[221] *Id., Nat. D.*, 3.17.44.
[222] *Id., Fam.*, 14.4.1-2. Notwithstanding, Cicero (*Cat.*, 4.3) still speaks of the gods' requital.
[223] *Id., Tusc.*, 1.49.118.
[224] *Id., Nat. D.*, 3.36.87-88.
[225] Seneca, *Ben.*, 2.30.2.
[226] *Ibid.*, 2.29.3.

and purposeless creation'.[227] An orderly universe, with a fixed purpose, has been set in motion for our sake. We are endowed with an audacious mind to explore the entire domain of Nature and, in so doing, seek the gods and commune with the powers divine.[228] Further, in His providential ordering of history God appoints as rulers only those with the requisite personal or ancestral merit, so that the debt of gratitude owed them (or their family) is requited.[229] Overall, in the view of Seneca, it is total foolishness to ignore the unconditioned generosity of the gods:

> What madness it is to quarrel with the gods over their gift! How shall a man show gratitude (*gratus*) to those to whom he cannot return gratitude (*gratia referri non potest*) without expenditure, if he denies that he has received anything from beings from whom he has received most of all, from those who are always ready to give and will never expect return?[230]

In addressing the gods as benefactors, however, there are prayers which are illegitimate for the pious person. For instance, to pray for the injury of earthly benefactors in order to gain advantage over them by becoming their counter-benefactor is reprehensible.[231] Rather, it is evidence of an ungrateful spirit that is unwilling to remain under obligation. A more righteous prayer would be that

> ... (the benefactor) never have lack of benefits (*beneficiorum*) to bestow nor regret for those bestowed; may his nature that of itself is inclined to pity, kindness, and mercy find stimulus and encouragement from a host of grateful persons (*gratorum*), and may he be fortunate enough to find them without the necessity of testing them ... may Fortune continue to bestow on him such unbroken favour that it will be impossible for anyone to show gratitude (*ut nemo possit esse gratus*) to him except by feeling it.[232]

Last, Seneca links human beneficence more tightly to its divine counterpart than the Greek philosophers.[233] We are to imitate the unconditional generosity of the gods who, in dispensing their blessings among the nations and peoples, neither discriminate as to the worth of the recipients, nor expect

---

[227] *Ibid.*, 6.23.6-7.
[228] *Ibid.*, 6.23.3-7.
[229] *Ibid.*, 4.32.1-4.
[230] Seneca, *Ben.*, 6.23.7. See also *id.*, *Ep.*, 74.11; 93.8.
[231] *Seneca, Ben.*, 6.25.1 — 6.27.7.
[232] *Ibid.*, 6.29.1; cf. 3.17.3. Conversely, Valerius Maximus (*Noteworthy Doings and Sayings*, 5.3.2ff) refers to P. Lentulus 'who prayed to the Immortal Gods that his ungrateful country (*ingratum populum*) might never have occasion to use him again'.
[233] For the Greek philosophers on divine beneficence, see §5.4.1.

any reward.²³⁴ Notwithstanding, Seneca believes that we should astutely discriminate whether it is in our interest to benefit the ungrateful.²³⁵

5.6.4. The philosophical critique of gratia in the Roman moralists

Do the Roman moralists and philosophers undertake a critique of the benefaction system comparable to that found in the Greek philosophers? While our sample of the Latin evidence is truncated by comparison, similar features nonetheless emerge.

First, like the Greek philosophers, our Latin authors closely scrutinise the motivation of the benefactor. According to Seneca, the benefactor should aim at being of service to his beneficiary, without any thought of inducing a return in exchange. To do otherwise constitutes bargaining, not benefaction.²³⁶ In similar vein, Cicero denies the reputation for generosity and the associated kudos of gratitude to any person who lends money for gain.²³⁷

Second, in a novel addition to the Greek philosophers, Seneca does not regard obligation as a dynamic worthy of reciprocity. In his view, it stifles gratitude which, by its very nature, thrives on spontaneity. As Seneca elaborates,

> ... although to repay gratitude (*referre gratiam*) is a most praiseworthy act, it ceases to be praiseworthy if it is made obligatory; for in that case no one will any more praise one who has returned a deposit of money, or paid a debt without being summoned before a judge.²³⁸

Third, in line with the Greek philosophers, Cicero rejects popular Epicurean theology. The famous maxim of Epicurus concerning God's indifference to anger and favour is aired and draws a stinging response.²³⁹ According to Cicero, Epicurus suffers from theological short-sightedness. He exalts God's goodness and excellence, whilst overlooking the supreme expression of those attributes in divine benevolence. Religion is thereby extinguished from the human heart — a god devoid of beneficence simply does not care for the other gods, let alone mankind!²⁴⁰ Furthermore, cultic holiness is totally compromised if, as Epicurus asserts, the gods pay no attention to terrestrial affairs.²⁴¹

---

²³⁴ Seneca, *Ben.*, 3.15.4; 4.25.1-3; 4.28.1-6; 7.31.3-4. Seneca's teaching is reminiscent of the synoptic teaching of Jesus (e.g., Matt 5:43ff; 6:25ff).
²³⁵ Seneca, *Ben.*, 4.26.1-3; 4.28.6.
²³⁶ Seneca, *Ben.*, 2.31.2-3. Similarly, *ibid.*, 4.13.1 — 4.14.4.
²³⁷ Cicero, *Fin.*, 2.35.117. Similarly, *id.*, *Leg.*, 1.18.48.
²³⁸ Seneca., *Ben.*, 3.7.2-3.
²³⁹ Cicero, *Nat. D.*, 1.17.45. For Epicurus, see §5.5.4 above.
²⁴⁰ *Ibid.*, 1.43.121.
²⁴¹ *Ibid.*, 1.44.122-123.

Cicero also appeals to Posidonius' *On the Nature of the Gods* for theological support. In that work, Posidonius argues that Epicurus' theology — in which God is reduced to a feeble human being — is at heart practical atheism. For if God cares for no-one, and does nothing at all, His existence becomes an absolute impossibility.[242] In a final riposte to Epicurus, Cicero states that he too would become an atheist if the gods were as Epicurus suggests:

> ... even if God exists, yet is of such a nature that He feels no benevolence (*gratia*) or affection (*caritate*) towards men, good-bye to Him, I say — not 'God be gracious (*propitius*) to me', why should I say that? for He cannot be gracious (*propitius*) to anybody, since as you tell us, all benevolence (*gratia*) and affection (*caritas*) is a mark of weakness.[243]

5.7. Conclusion

The philosophers enthusiastically endorse the civic-minded focus of the honorific inscriptions. Benefactors should exercise beneficence unstintingly and with the correct motivation. Significantly, only on two occasions in the philosophers have we encountered that extremely rare reversal of status where a benefactor is benefited by a social inferior. The propriety of returning gratitude by means of the honour system is also strongly emphasised. Indeed, one risks the chastisement of Fortune by displaying ingratitude for benefits.

Moreover, whatever ambiguities and misunderstandings may be implicit in benefaction rituals, there is no dispensation from the moral obligation of reciprocity. In this respect, the philosophers also heavily underscore the perpetual reciprocation of parental favour by their progeny. In all of the foregoing, χάρις and its cognates function in a way entirely typical of the inscriptional parlance. Usefully, the philosophers provided some interesting cases of χάρις in non-benefaction contexts, including one example which throws light on the forensic background of Pauline justification by grace.

Only on rare occasions do we get any glimpse of an alternative philosophical community such as the Pythagoreans — separate from the *polis* — in which benefaction is practised. φιλία, not χάρις, is its dynamic. If our Pythagorean traditions are reliable, it is at very best a pale imitation of the friendship shared amongst the self-sufficient gods.

---

[242] *Ibid.*, 1.44.123.
[243] *Ibid.*, 1.44.124.

We had occasion to observe that the philosophers verged on contradiction in thinking about divine grace. On the one hand, human beings should exhibit total humility in the face of the gods' unsolicited beneficence. Correct ritual, belief and motivation is essential in order to secure the divine favour. On the other hand, a counter-claim on our part is entirely legitimate. We can demand the obligatory divine recompense for our ritual piety, and even as inferiors we may confer a benefit upon God.

Although the gods bestow gifts of grace that shape the human character, this is never related to human beneficence with the same theological rigour as the Christians. Apart from Seneca, who encourages us to imitate the divine munificence, only Aristotle grapples with the problem. His solution was to link human beneficence and reciprocity to the Χάριτες by virtue of the obvious mnemonic association. And even in this instance, the understanding of grace is cultic.

As an apostle, Paul faced Gentile converts whose minds would have been moulded by such belief systems. Surely Deissmann is correct in supposing that Paul's doctrine of justification by grace was aimed as much at the Gentile cults and popular philosophy as certain theological strands within first-century Judaism (including judaising Christianity). The issues were varied and complex. As the paramount theologian of grace, Paul probably agreed with those philosophers who objected to the devaluation of divine grace found in the theology of Epicurus. Like Lucian in a later century, he had no sympathy for that ancient 'prosperity theology' which dispensed the divine favour exclusively through the cult. Ultimately, Paul's solution to the conundrum of Cercidas — how to reconcile the impotence of divine justice with divine grace — was found in the cross of Christ (Rom 8:31-39).

Like Philo, other Greek philosophers launched a critique of the benefaction system, subjecting it to their moral censure at various junctures. In their view, the ethos of reciprocity was riddled with self-interest and social bias. Notwithstanding, their faith in the overall system remains intact. Finally, in our cross-cultural comparison, we confirmed that the philosophers and moralists of the Latin West approached the issue of beneficence in generally the same way as the Greek East.

Chapter 6

Paul and Divine Beneficence

That the gods were beneficent was an axiom of the first-century Graeco-Roman world. The so-called 'atheism' of the Epicureans concerning divine beneficence was viewed as a dangerous aberration by most of the philosophical schools. The god(s) and demi-god(s), the spirit-world, and the Caesars were thanked for their χάριτες and placed under counter-obligation through cultic piety.[1] The language of grace figured prominently in this exchange and informed its conventions of honour. At a social level, divine grace was a reciprocal arrangement. The Caesars were munificent towards client-states that hosted the imperial cult; the local aristocrats who presided over the prestigious civic cults defrayed the daily running costs and benefited their city; the patrons of private associations were honoured with public inscriptions for their piety towards the deities. How did Paul relate χάρις to the religious assumptions and yearnings of the Graeco-Roman world when instructing his converts or engaging in evangelism?

We have earlier noted how Philo and Josephus engaged in an explicit theological critique of the gods and the Graeco-Roman reciprocity system (§4.4.4 [*Cher.* 122-123]; §4.5.4 [*Ap.* 2.248-250; *AJ* 6.341-342]). This chapter will argue that Paul engages in a similar enterprise, though — in contrast to his Jewish contemporaries — implicitly and more positively. In responding to Graeco-Roman views of divine beneficence, Paul tailors his presentation of χάρις to the social contexts of the Roman and Eastern Mediterranean churches (§6.1.1—§6.1.3.2). Paul clarifies the relationship between divine and human beneficence by the impoverished benefactor motif (§6.2). Paul's

---

[1] An important inscription of the late Augustan era (*I. Kyme* 19) says that divine honours were reserved for the gods and those who, like the emperor, were 'godlike' (ἰσόθεοι). See the discussion of S.R.F. Price, *Rituals and Power: The Roman Imperial Cult in Asia Minor* (Cambridge 1984), 50-51. Similarly, in AD 19, the Alexandrians acclaimed Germanicus, 'hailing him as equal to the gods' (A.S. Hunt and C.C. Edgar, *Select Papyri Vol.II* [Cambridge, Mass. 1934] §211). We should not conclude, however, that the Caesars and their family members were universally seen as divine. This was conspicuously not the case in Thessalonica. See the discussion of H. Hendrix, 'Beyond "Imperial Cult" and "Cults of Magistrates"', in H.R. Kent (ed.), *Society of Biblical Literature 1986 Seminar Papers* (Chico 1986), 300-308.

portrait of the impoverished Christ also interacted with contemporary philosophical debates about the character of patronal leadership (§6.3). We have also noted how important the social expression of divine grace was for the ancients. What differentiated Paul's understanding of grace in the body of Christ from its Graeco-Roman religious and social context (§6.4.1—§6.4.3)? The final issue to be explored is the beneficence of the gods (§6.5). How did Paul's understanding of divine χάρις differentiate him from the attitudes of Graeco-Roman cults, the popular philosophers, and the monotheism of his first-century Jewish contemporaries?

6.1. Paul, Charis, *and the Salvation of God*

The epistle to the Romans provides the most systematic exposition of divine χάρις within the Pauline corpus. It has recently been claimed that the language of grace in Romans (χάρις, χάρισμα, χαριτᾶν and χάριζεσθαι) sums up Paul's gospel under a single rubric.[2] Although the centre of Paul's thought remains a matter of controversy among New Testament scholars,[3] χάρις is undoubtedly Paul's preferred leitmotiv for any full-orbed description of divine beneficence.

We cannot penetrate Paul's deepest intentions in Romans unless we keep in view its contingent nature,[4] the first-century cultural codes that it

---

[2] C.E.B. Cranfield, *The Epistle to the Romans* Vol.1 (Edinburgh 1975), 71. M. Hengel (*The Pre-Christian Paul* [London 1991], 145) argues that *sola gratia* is central for Romans: 'Romans is no chance product, but a fundamental theological account by the apostle. Paul, the persecutor and enemy of Christ, had experienced in himself the significance of radical grace'. More generally, C.J.A. Hickling ('Centre and Periphery in the Thought of Paul', *Studia Biblica* III [1978], 214 n.327) states that 'The doctrine of grace ... is in Paul the root of nearly everything else'.

[3] E.E. Ellis (*Paul and His Recent Interpreters* [Grand Rapids 1961], 24-34) summarises older debates concerning the centre of Pauline thought. For recent debate, H. Ridderbos, *Paul: An Outline of His Theology* (Grand Rapids 1975), 13-90; C.J.A. Hickling, *art. cit.*, 215-223; E.P. Sanders, *Paul and Palestinian Judaism: A Comparison of Patterns of Religion* (London 1977), 434-447; J.C. Beker, *Paul the Apostle: The Triumph of God in Life and Thought* (Edinburgh 1980), 11-19, 135-212; R.Y.K. Fung, 'The Status of Justification by Faith in Paul's Thought: A Brief Survey of a Modern Debate', *Themelios* 6/3 (1981), 4-11; C.A. Wanamaker, 'A Case against Justification by Faith', *Journal of Theology for Southern Africa* 42 (1983), 37-49; L. Cope, 'Analogy, the Pauline Centre, and Doing Theology Today', *Bangal. Theol. For.* 15/2 (1983), 128-133; J. Becker, *Paul: Apostle to the Gentiles* (Louisville 1993; Gmn. orig. 1989), 373-379; J.D.G. Dunn, 'Prolegomena to a Theology of Paul', *NTS* 40/3 (1994), 407-432, esp. 423-431; D.N. Howell, 'The Centre of Pauline Theology', *BSac* 151 (1994), 50-70.

[4] J.C. Beker, *op. cit.*, 59-93.

preserves,⁵ and the polemics that the apostle was engaged in. It is worth noting that the famous theologians of grace (Augustine, Martin Luther, and Karl Barth) interpreted Paul for their contemporaries against the cultural backdrop of their own times.⁶ In this hermeneutical process, Paul's understanding of χάρις was reduced to timeless theology without any historical connection.⁷ But the wealth of first-century social metaphor throughout Romans should caution us against proceeding down this path. Paul wrote his letter to Gentile Roman Christians (Rom 1:5-6; 11:13) who had experienced an eschatological 'age of grace' well before their conversion to Christ.⁸ In antiquity, the reign of Augustus represented a turning point in

---

⁵ S.K. Stowers, *A Rereading of Romans: Justice, Jews, and Gentiles* (New Haven and London 1994), 6ff.

⁶ Augustine, Luther, and Barth wrote their commentaries on Romans and works of theology in polemical contexts. Augustine faced the threat of the Manichees and Pelagius; Luther confronted the merit theology of medieval Catholicism; Barth struggled with the post-war crisis of 1918 and struggled against the anthropocentric theologies of A. Harnack and F. Schleiermacher. The first-century context of grace was ignored in each case.

⁷ Typically, K. Barth (*The Epistle to the Romans* [London 1933], 8) regarded Romans as 'a dogmatics in outline' and called for theological (as opposed to historical) exegesis.

⁸ It is beyond our scope to identify in detail the occasion and recipients of Romans. For recent scholarship, see K.P. Donfried (ed.), *The Romans Debate* (Rev. ed. Edinburgh 1991 [orig. 1977]); A.J.M. Wedderburn, *The Reasons for Romans* (Edinburgh 1988); L.A. Jervis, *The Purpose of Romans: A Comparative Letter Structure Investigation* (Sheffield 1991); S.K. Stowers, *op. cit*; J.C. Miller, *The Obedience of Faith: The Eschatological People of God, and the Purpose of Romans* (Atlanta 2000). However, two observations are apposite. First, in reconstructing the audience of Romans, far too much weight is placed by scholars on the (so-called) expulsion of Jews and Jewish Christians under Claudius in AD 49 (Suet., *Claudius* 25:4; cf. Acts 18:2). Contra, see E.A. Judge and G.S.R. Thomas, 'The Origin of the Church at Rome: A New Solution', *Reformed Theological Review* 25/3 (1966), 81-94; S. Benko, 'The Edict of Claudius of AD 49 and the Instigator Chrestus', *TZ* 25/6 (1969), 406-418; E.A. Judge, 'Judaism and the Rise of Christianity: A Roman Perspective', *TynBul* 45/2 (1994), 354-368; M.D. Nanos, *The Mystery of Romans: The Jewish Context of Paul's Letter* (Minneapolis 1994), 41-84, 372-387. Second, the evidence of Rom 14:1-23 does not require that the controversy over dietary laws was *specifically* Jewish (or Jewish Christian), emerging (it is alleged) because of the social and theological differences of a mixed Jewish-Gentile congregation. The dispute could have arisen over the influence of Neo-Pythagorean vegetarianism, with the *Gentile* Roman congregation arriving at polarised viewpoints and practices on the issue. For this suggestion, see P. Schubert, *Form and Function of the Pauline Thanksgivings* (Berlin 1939), 85, 139. However, this proposal is somewhat strained and ignores the division over the observance of holy days. Alternatively, Paul may be adapting the psychagogy of the popular philosophers to correct general divisions and abuses that had emerged within the Gentile Roman congregation, rather than dealing with specific theologically polarised groups in the house churches (C.E., Glad, *Paul and Philodemus: Adaptability in Epicurean and Early Christian Psychagogy* [Leiden-New York-Köln 1995]; S.K. Stowers, *op. cit.*, 317ff). Yet, while this approach illuminates Paul's rhetorical strategy, it underplays the fact that Paul nominates aversion from foods (Rom 14:1-2, 6b, 20-23) and observance of holy days (14:5-6a) as signs of 'weak faith' (R.A. Gagnon, 'Why the "Weak" at Rome Cannot Be Non-Christian Jews', *CBQ* 62/1 [2000], 76 n.8). Paul's approach is not hypothetical. More likely is R.A. Gagnon's idea (*ibid.*) that the 'weak in faith' are 'Noahide'

beneficence.[9] The χάριτες of Augustus had acquired soteriological, eschatological, and cosmological status within his own lifetime throughout the Graeco-Roman world. The grace of the Caesars would remain a continuing refrain (§2.5—§2.6, §2.8.4; §3.2.4, §3.5; §4.5.2). It was precisely in this context that Paul announced God's reign of grace through Christ.

Paul's presentation of divine χάρις in Romans splits, prism-like, into a rich spectrum of theological *and* social colour. First, the apostle delineates his understanding of divine grace within Graeco-Roman conventions of honour and dishonour (§6.1.1—§6.1.2.3). Second, Paul interprets the eschatological work of Christ for his Roman auditors against the backdrop of Augustan patronage (§6.1.2.4—§6.1.2.5).

Our first major section on Romans (§6.1.1—§6.1.2.3) will concentrate on how Paul pictures the relationship between the divine Benefactor and his human dependants. How does he resolve the dilemma caused by the human dishonouring of God's beneficence?

6.1.1. *Graeco-Roman benefaction and the honour-and-shame dynamic of Paul's letter to the Romans*

Until recently, New Testament scholarship has not viewed the honour-and-shame dynamic of Romans in its Graeco-Roman context.[10] Paul silhouettes

---

Christian Gentiles — remembering that the implied audience of Romans is Gentile (Rom 1:5-6, 13-15; 11:13-14; 15:15-18) — who wish to observe Jewish standards. Whatever the truth of the matter, a vocal Jewish Christian minority in the Roman church is not necessary to explain the evidence. By contrast, S. Mason ('Paul, Classical Anti-Jewish Polemic, and the Letter to the Romans', in D.J. Hawkin and T. Robinson [eds], *Self-Definition and Self-Discovery in Early Christianity: A Study in Changing Horizons* [Lewiston-Queenston-Lampeter 1990], 181-223) argues that Romans is a letter addressed to Christian Jews. R. Oster ('"Congregations of the Gentiles" (Rom 16:4): A Culture-Based Ecclesiology in the Letters of Paul', *ResQ* 40/1 [1998], 47) asserts that Romans 14:1-15:13 addresses 'judgments and practices that stem from Jewish and Gentile congregational cultures'. Similarly, J.C. Walters, *Ethnic Issues in Paul's Letter to the Romans: Changing Self-Definitions in Earliest Roman Christianity* (Valley Forge 1993). But there is always a danger of misreading the *Jewishness* of Romans to indicate an exclusively Jewish-Christian audience or a mixed Jewish-Gentile Christian audience. A simpler explanation of the Jewishness of Romans is that Paul is teaching his Gentile-Christian auditors about how they came to be incorporated by grace into remnant Israel and why they should overcome their prejudiced and judgemental attitudes towards the Jews and 'Noahide' Gentiles at Rome. On anti-semitism at Rome, see W. Wiefel, 'The Jewish Community in Rome and the Origins of Roman Christianity', in K.P. Donfried (ed.), *The Romans Debate: Revised and Expanded Edition* (Peabody, Mass. 1991), 85-101; R. Penna, 'The Jews in Rome at the Time of the Apostle Paul', in *id.*, *Paul the Apostle: Jew and Greek Alike* (Philadelphia 1996), 19-47.

[9] The Jews, too, were indebted to Augustus. L.M. White ('Finding the Ties that Bind: Issues from Social Description', *Semeia* 56 [1992], 19) surmises that the 'Synagogue of the Augustasians' at Rome developed from 'webs of clientellage'.

[10] The following discussion is indebted to G.M. Corrigan, 'Paul's Shame for the

God's grace against the backdrop of humankind dishonouring His glory and beneficence. This portrait of God as the dishonoured Benefactor may well have surprised Paul's Gentile contemporaries.[11] In the Graeco-Roman world it was axiomatic that honour (τιμή) and repute (δόξα) were owed to the gods for their beneficence (e.g. Seneca, *Ben.*, 2.29-30). In this respect, the honorific inscriptions never question the appropriateness of benefactors reciprocating divine honour. A decree of the Delian guild of the Dionysiac craftsmen (c. 172-167 BC) praises its benefactor, Kraton, for his untiring efforts in maintaining the τιμή and δόξα of the gods.[12] Kraton's beneficence not only recompensed the guild deities for the honour and protection that they had given to the Dionysiac craftsmen but also ensured perpetuation of honour for the guild. As the decree elaborates, Kraton had acted

in order that (the) immortal glory (ἀθάνατος δόξα) proceeding from the craftsmen may remain for ever, whom both the gods and the kings and all the Greeks honour (τιμῶσι), having given to all the craftsmen security and safety (both) in war and peace ...[13]

Whereas the honorific inscriptions endorse the cultic honouring of the god(s) with gifts, Paul's emphasis is upon human beings *morally* honouring God.[14]

Gospel', *BTB* 16 (1986), 23-27; H. Moxnes, 'Honour and Righteousness in Romans', *JSNT* 32 (1988), 61-77; *id.*, 'Honor, Shame and the Outside World in Paul's Letter to the Romans', in J. Neusner (*et al.*, ed.), *The Social World of Formative Christianity and Judaism: Essays in Tribute to Howard Clark Kee* (Philadelphia 1988), 207-218; *id.*, 'The Quest for Honour and the Unity of the Community in Romans 12 and in the Orations of Dio Chrysostom', in T. Engberg-Pedersen (ed.), *Paul in His Hellenistic Context* (Edinburgh 1994), 203-230; R.W. Pickett, 'The Death of Christ as Divine Patronage in Romans 5:1-11', in E.H. Lovering (ed.), *SBL 1993 Seminar Papers* (Atlanta 1993), 726-739.

[11] Pseudo-Crates (*Ep.*, 10.2: ἀτιμᾶν) warns against dishonouring God's gift of wine (τὸ δῶρον τοῦ θεοῦ) by being drunk.

[12] *IG* XI(4) 1061 *ll.*6-8. On account of Megakles' piety towards the gods of Chios, 'δόξα shines forth' for him (*SEG* XXVI 1021: I cent. BC). τιμή and δόξα occur together in regard to human benefaction. The Ephesian gymnasiarch Diodoros is described as being 'in nothing neglectful of what relates to honour and fame (*I. Ephesos* Ia. 6: II cent. BC [πρὸς τιμὴν καὶ δόξαν])'.

[13] *IG* XI(4) 1061 *ll.*11-14. Paul speaks of the 'eternal weight of glory' at the eschaton (2 Cor 4:17: αἰώνιον βάρος δόξης [cf. 2 Tim 2:10]), deliberately avoiding the inscriptional use of ἀθάνατος δόξα. As noted in §4.5.2 n.128, ἀθάνατος is standard inscriptional fare. Since Paul regards the world as under the dominion of death (e.g. Rom 5:14, 17: θάνατος), he reserves αἰώνιος for God (Rom 16:26; Christ: 1 Tim 6:16), the eschatological existence of the Christian (Rom 2:7, 5:21, 6:22-23; 2 Cor 4:18—5:1; Gal 6:8; 1 Tim 6:12; 2 Thess 2:16) and the destruction of the disobedient (2 Thess 1:9). In Paul's view, the honours accorded the civic, military, and sporting elite — if the inscriptional crowning rituals are representative — are perishable (1 Cor 9:25: φθαρτὸν στέφανον).

[14] In antiquity, the unpredictable nature of divine anger ensured that the gods were placated with cultic gifts. Note R. Lane Fox (*Pagans and Christians in the Mediterranean World From the Second Century AD to the Conversion of Constantine* [New York 1986], 38) who writes: the gods 'were not just superior patrons, but powers of immense superiority: they were particularly touchy, then, about honor and were not committed to giving regular

Paul argues that the Gentiles have dishonoured God's glorious character by participating in idolatrous cults (Rom 1:23b, 25b), with the result that they have either degraded themselves with impure lusts (1:24a: ἐν ταῖς ἐπιθυμίαις τῶν καρδιῶν) or exhibit an attitude of self-sufficiency (1:22a: φάσκοντες εἶναι σοφοί [cf. 1:32; 3:18]).[15] God is not rendered appropriate honour because fallen human beings suppress the truth concerning Him (Rom 1:18-19). Nonetheless, God's invisible nature — His eternal power and deity (Rom 1:20: ἥ τε ἀίδιος αὐτοῦ δύναμις καὶ θειότης) — has been indelibly stamped in creation. The glory of the immortal God (Rom 1:23a: ἡ δόξα τοῦ ἀφθάρτου θεοῦ) belongs to Him for ever (Rom 11:36, 16:27: εἰς τοὺς αἰῶνας [cf. 1 Tim 1:17; 6:16]) and cannot be shared with idolatrous rivals (Rom 1:23b, 25).[16]

Moreover, the falsehood and unfaithfulness of some Jews only serves to underline the truthfulness of God's revelation and enhance His glory (Rom 3:3, 7: ἐπερίσσευσεν εἰς τὴν δόξαν αὐτοῦ). In this gospel age, God has more narrowly defined the content and locus of His honour. The correct response for Jew and Gentile — prefigured in the uncircumcised Abraham — is to glorify God by believing His covenantal promises (Rom 4:20: δοὺς δόξαν τῷ θεῷ), and by regarding Christ as the visible fulfilment of the divine

---

gifts in return'. Similarly, S.J. Case, *The Social Triumph of the Ancient Church* (rpt. New York 1971: orig. 1933), 4-5. The inscriptions honour benefactors for their part in maintaining the *pax deorum*. For example, in *I. Priene* 117 (I cent. BC), Herakleitos is praised for his piety (εὐσέβεια) towards the god and for his justice (δικαιοσύνη) and goodwill towards the people. The inscriptions also spell out in detail the dire consequences of dishonouring the gods' cults. For examples, see *SIG*[3] 997 (A.L. Connolly, 'Standing on Sacred Ground', *New Docs* 4 [1987], §25, 105); *id.*, 'χολάω', *New Docs* 4 [1987], §91. In particular, Antiochus I of Kommagene invokes elaborate divine curses on those who would violate the sanctity of his own mausoleum and that of his father, Mithridates Kallinikos. See F.W. Danker, *Benefactor: Epigraphic Study of a Graeco-Roman and New Testament Semantic Field* (St. Louis 1982), §41 *ll.*228-237, §42 *ll.*210-237. Paul, by contrast, dismisses Graeco-Roman ideas of cultic propitiation as idolatry. Ironically, in Paul's view, God's anger is provoked precisely by the ἀσέβεια and ἀδικία of the cults (Rom 1:18: cf. vv.23, 25). For discussion of a cultic inscription which (like Paul) requires the worshippers to adhere to a basic morality, see S.C. Barton and G.H.R. Horsley, 'A Hellenistic Cult Group and the New Testament Churches', *JAC* 24 (1981), 7-41.

[15] Paul countenances legitimate cultic approaches to God. Because of the Passover sacrifice of Christ (1 Cor 5:7), Christians should offer themselves as living sacrifices to God out of gratitude for His mercies (θυσία ζῶσα ἁγία εὐάρεστος τῷ θεῷ: Rom 12:1). This surpasses contemporary Jewish and Hellenistic aspirations for a more spiritual worship. On this, see D. Peterson, *Engaging with God: A Biblical Theology of Worship* (Leicester 1992), 174-176. Other Christian sacrifices (θυσίαι) which are acceptable to God include the life of faith (θυσία καὶ λειτουργία τῆς πίστεως: Phil 2:17), Paul's apostolic ministry to the Gentiles (ἡ προσφορὰ τῶν ἐθνῶν: Rom 15:16), and acts of Christian beneficence (θυσία δεκτή, εὐάρεστος τῷ θεῷ: Phil 4:18).

[16] H. Moxnes, *art. cit.* ('*Honor, Shame*', 1988), 212: 'Honor here is not a civic virtue but is reserved exclusively for God'.

glory in patriarchal history (Rom 9:4-5: ἡ δόξα καὶ αἱ διαθῆκαι; 2 Cor 3:18: ἡ δόξα κυρίου; 2 Cor 4:4 [cf. v.6]: τῆς δόξης τοῦ Χριστοῦ). Thus, for Paul, it is inconceivable that God could ever be recompensed (Rom 11:35), precisely because of the wealth of kindness and glory that He has displayed as cosmic Benefactor and Redeemer (11:33: βάθος πλούτου; 2:4: ὁ πλοῦτος τῆς χρηστότητος; 9:23: ὁ πλοῦτος τῆς δόξης [cf. Eph 1:18, 3:16; Phil 4:19; Col 1:27]).

Further, in contrast to the honorific inscriptions, Paul depicts unregenerate humanity as incapable of rendering appropriate τιμή and δόξα to God. The bleakness of Paul's portrait is better appreciated when one remembers the antagonism provoked in antiquity when the generosity of benefactors was met with ingratitude.[17] The idolatrous Gentiles had neither honoured God as Creator or even thanked Him (Rom 1:21: οὐχ ὡς Θεὸν ἐδόξασαν ἢ ηὐχαρίστησαν).[18] Therefore God abandoned them to their dishonourable physical passions (Rom 1:24: τοῦ ἀτιμάζεσθαι τὰ σώματα αὐτῶν; 1:26: εἰς πάθη ἀτιμίας).

Conversely, *some* Jews boasted in their covenantal status (Rom 2:17-20; cf. 3:3 τινες) but had dishonoured their Benefactor by living a life unworthy of His beneficence and Law (2:23: τὸν θεὸν ἀτιμάζεις).[19] The boasting of such Jews was misplaced. God extends grace towards people on the basis of faith as opposed to 'works of law' (Rom 3:27-28), choosing in His mercy to make some vessels for honour (9:21b: εἰς τιμήν; 9:23b: προητοίμασεν εἰς δόξαν) and others for dishonour (9:21b: εἰς ἀτιμίαν; 9.22b: κατηρτισμένα εἰς ἀπώλειαν). In this respect, the Jewish remnant of the present age is as much chosen by grace as was the faithful remnant of Elijah's time (Rom 11:5: κατ' ἐκλογὴν χάριτος; 6a: χάριτι, οὐκέτι ἐξ ἔργων; cf. 11.2-4).[20] To

---

[17] For the ancients on ingratitude, see §3.1.3; §4.3 (Ben-Sirach) and §4.5.3; §5.2.2. B. Byrne (*Romans* [Collegeville], 1996) makes the following observation in regards to Romans 1:21: 'In 2 Cor 4:15 Paul portrays the "overflow" of thanksgiving to God on the part of human beings as the goal of the entire Christian mission'.

[18] See D.W. Pao, *Thanksgiving: An Investigation of a Pauline Theme* (Downers Grove 2000), 159-162.

[19] According to E. Krentz ('The Name of God in Disrepute: Romans 2:17-29 [22-23]', *CurTM* 17/6 [1990], 429-439), Paul's arguments concerning the dishonouring of God are best located within the exegetical traditions of Hellenistic Judaism. Although Krentz makes a compelling case, one must ask how far first-century Palestinian and Diaspora Judaism had been exposed to Graeco-Roman benefaction ideology through the public inscriptions and popular philosophers. Was Paul reacting to the danger (real or perceived) that divine grace might be seen by some as a reciprocal contract where God only honours the ritually pious (e.g. Rom 2:17, 23a; 3:27a)?

[20] See especially R.E. Clements, '"A Remnant Chosen by Grace" (Romans 11:5): The Old Testament Background and Origin of the Remnant Concept', in D.A. Hagner and M.J. Harris (eds), *Pauline Studies: Essays Presented to F.F. Bruce* (Exeter 1980), 106-121.

suggest otherwise is to nullify the grace underlying both the Abrahamic covenant and its fulfilment in Christ (Rom 11:6b: ἡ χάρις οὐκέτι γίνεται χάρις). Thus, in refusing to acknowledge their status as beneficiaries, Jew and Gentile have fallen short of the glory of God (Rom 3:23: ἡ δόξα τοῦ θεοῦ) and rendered themselves subject to His wrath (1:18, 32a; 2:2-3, 5, 8; 3:5b, 8b). Significantly, Paul's emphasis falls more on God's wrath over His *own* dishonouring than — as was the case with Seneca — the gods' anger towards city-states that had failed to requite their human benefactors.[21]

For Paul, the theme of divine impartiality provides a proper perspective on honour and dishonour. In antiquity, impartiality was one of the qualities encouraged in benefactors. For example, Seneca highlights the impartiality of the gods in conferring cosmic benefits,[22] a disposition which he attributes to their decision at creation to look after the interests of humankind.[23] A decree from Busiris (AD 22—23) praises Gnaeus Pompeius for his impartiality (ἀδεκάστως) in considering the construction of dykes for the production of crops.[24] But Paul's understanding of divine impartiality is eschatological. God, as an impartial Benefactor (Rom 2:11; cf. 2:6), will reward those who, in a life of well-doing, seek to attain glory, honour and immortality (2:7: δόξα, τιμή, ἀφθαρσία).[25] All believers — Jew and Gentile — will be recompensed

---

[21] Seneca, *Ben.*, 3.17.3; 6.30.1; 6.40.2. In Seneca's view, the gods dispense benefactions without any expectation that the divine honour should be acknowledged, because they only possess the power of doing good (*Ben.*, 4.9.1; 4.25.1—4.26.1; 4.28.1-3; 7.31.4). Paul's stance on the cosmic beneficence of God is different. While God always dispenses the cosmic benefit of His revelation (Rom 1:19-20), He responds to His own dishonouring with wrath (1:18), in the present (1:24, 26, 28) and at the eschatological judgement (2:5-6, 12a, 15-16). Paul's emphasis also differs from that later found in a III cent. AD tomb inscription from Akmonia (B. Laum, *Stiftungen in der griechischen und der römischen Antike* Vol.II [Berlin 1914], §174). There Aurelius Aristeas threatens that the 'justice of God' (πρὸ[ς τὴ]ν δικαιοσύ[νην] τοῦ θεοῦ) would fall upon the neighbourhood of Protopuletai if its residents did not annually decorate the tomb of his life-long companion Aurelia with roses. This act of piety towards Aurelia was intended to recompense Aristeas' gift of fallow land and tools to the community. The inscription reminds us that in antiquity — at least in benefaction contexts — the gods were often more concerned about the dishonouring of civic benefactors than about their own honour. However, for examples of inscriptions where there is concern about the dishonouring of the gods' cults, see n.14 above.

[22] Seneca, *Ben.*, 4.28.1-3; 7.31.4; cf. Matt 5:45.

[23] Seneca, *Ben.*, 6.23.1-3.

[24] *SEG* VIII 527. A decree from Mylasa describes Limnaios as unbribed (ἀνερίθευτος) and incorruptible (ἀδωροδόκητος) in his office as choregus (*I. Mylasa* 110: II cent. BC).

[25] J.M. Bassler (*Divine Impartiality: Paul and a Theological Axiom* [Chico 1982], 136) observes that Paul underscores God's impartiality in Rom 1:16—2:10 by using πᾶς (1:16, 18, 29; 2:1, 9, 10) and by emphasising God's justice (1:18, 24, 26, 28, 32; 2:2-3, 5) and cosmic benefaction (1:20). The Old Testament regards impartiality as an integral aspect of God's character (Deut 10:17; 2 Chron 19:7; Job 34:19) that must inform human ethics (Lev 19:15; Deut 1:17; 16:19).

with eternal life (2:7: ζωὴ αἰώνιος) when their quest for divine honour concludes at the eschaton (Rom 2:10: δόξα, τιμή, εἰρήνη; cf. 5:2b; 8:18b; 8:30b). In the present, however, God mercifully delays His judgement in the hope that some may repent (Rom 2:4: see §6.1.2.1 n.37).

How would first-century auditors have responded to the honour-and-shame dynamic of Romans? The postponement of honour until the eschaton would have cut against the cultural grain.[26] The honorific inscriptions regularly voiced their concern that city-states should not be remiss in the return of honour to benefactors.[27] The six-year delay in the crowning of Demosthenes for his benefactions — outlined in *De Corona* — caused him considerable rancour and testified to the importance of promptly reciprocating favour in antiquity. But Paul's up-ending of the honour system excludes all human boasting (Rom 3:27): God is the One who allocates and receives praise (2.29b; 15:11).

Other facets of Paul's argument would have puzzled contemporaries familiar with benefaction ideology. Surely beneficiaries have to respond worthily to their benefactor — or admit their inability to do so — if munificence was to be extended and maintained?[28] Yet God had responded in an unprecedented way to His dishonouring as the cosmic and covenantal Benefactor. Instead of avenging His honour, He had demonstrated forbearance and extended χάρις to the ungrateful in his crucified Son. The prized status of possessing merit (ἀρετή) — until now the preserve of benefactors — was transferred to the entire church, with the result that ordinary Christians actualised in their communities the merit traditionally assigned to the καλοκἀγαθοί.[29] For Paul, the gift of righteousness (δικαιοσύνη) is the linchpin of this new approach to divine beneficence. We turn to a fuller consideration of these issues in our next section.

---

[26] G.M. Corrigan (*art. cit.*, 25) sums up Paul's stance: 'For Paul, God grants honor in the future. The promise of "eternal life" must have surely sounded queer to a culture which, much like our own, sought "instant gratification"'.

[27] See our discussion of χάρις in the manifesto clause of the honorific inscriptions (§2.4).

[28] See especially the Roman moralists in §5.6.1.

[29] See our arguments in §6.2.

6.1.2. Graeco-Roman benefaction and the age of grace: Paul and the Roman Christians

6.1.2.1. Paul's solution to the honour-and-shame dynamic in Romans does not diminish the demands of divine righteousness

First, in contrast to contemporary benefaction ideology, Paul more sharply focuses the dilemma caused by the human dishonouring of God's beneficence. According to Paul, the challenge issued to God's honour (δόξα) by the sin of Jew and Gentile (Rom 3:9, 23) demands a just response from the divine Benefactor.[30] God, as Benefactor of the Jews (Rom 3:2: ἐπιστεύθησαν τὰ λόγια τοῦ θεοῦ [cf. 9:4-5]), must exercise covenant loyalty (3:3: ἡ πίστις τοῦ θεοῦ), precisely because the covenantal privileges of Israel cannot be arbitrarily revoked (11:29: τὰ χαρίσματα). Thus God must maintain His truthfulness (3:7: ἡ ἀλήθεια τοῦ θεοῦ [cf. 9:6a; 15:8-9]) and justice (3:5-6: ἡ δικαιοσύνη τοῦ θεοῦ [cf. 9:14]).[31] In the case of the Gentiles, as we have seen, God had responded to the dishonouring of His beneficence with wrath and ongoing mercy, and would settle the issue at the eschaton with impartiality (Rom 2:6, 9, 11-12, 14-16; 3:9).

What solution does Paul propose to this dilemma? God has manifested His righteousness — independent of the Jewish Law (Rom 3:21a, 28) and human success at law-keeping (3:19-20) — without either diminishing the demands of His justice or abandoning His loyalty to His dependants.[32] As covenantal

---

[30] G.M. Corrigan (*art. cit.*, 26) has argued that God as the superior did not necessarily have to respond to the challenge of human sinfulness. This underestimates the universal expectation of benefactors in antiquity that beneficiaries should *worthily* acknowledge their benefits. It also ignores the covenantal and forensic dimensions of Paul's theological argument in Romans 1-3. It is inconceivable to Paul that the covenantal God would act untruthfully or unjustly when confronted by human falsehood (Rom 3:4-7). A response of some kind on His part is demanded.

[31] Paul draws several telling contrasts between the character of God as Benefactor (Rom 3:3: ἡ πίστις τοῦ θεοῦ; 3:4, 7: ὁ θεὸς ἀληθής, ἡ ἀλήθεια τοῦ θεοῦ; 3:5: ἡ δικαιοσύνη τοῦ θεοῦ) and the unresponsiveness of His covenant people (3:3: ἡ ἀπιστία αὐτῶν; 3:4, 7: ψεύστης, ψεῦσμα; 3:5: ἡ ἀδικία ἡνῶν), with a view to establishing God's justice in punishing any Jews who dishonoured His name (2:23-24; 3:8, 19-20). For discussions of the antitheses, see R.B. Hays, 'Psalm 143 and the Logic of Romans 3', *JBL* 99/1 (1980), 110-111; S.K. Williams, 'The "Righteousness of God" in Romans', *JBL* 99/2 (1980), 268. This scrupulous attention to the divine attributes and their relation to rendering God appropriate honour is largely missing from Graeco-Roman discussions of divine beneficence. Overall, the ancients either believed that correct cultic ritual satisfies the demands of divine honour or that the gods are unconcerned about their honour (either because they only act beneficently — see §5.4.1 — or are indifferent to human beings).

[32] I agree with commentators who differentiate between δικαιοσύνη as an attribute of God (Rom 3:5, 25b, 26a) and δικαιοσύνη as a status conferred by God (3:21, 22; cf. 1:17). These include W. Sanday and A.C. Headlam (Edinburgh 1895); A.M. Hunter (London 1955); C.K. Barrett (London 1957); F.-J. Leenhardt (London 1961); F.F. Bruce (Leicester

Benefactor (Rom 3:5 [cf. v.3], 21b), God vindicated His own righteousness by offering His Son as a ransom-payment (3:24: διὰ τῆς ἀπολυτρώσεως) and propitiatory sacrifice (3:25: ἱλαστήριον ἐν τῷ αὐτοῦ αἵματι) for Jew and Gentile (3:29-30).[33] The centrality of divine honour in Paul's argument is gauged by the repetition of the purpose clause in Romans 3:25-26 (εἰς [v.26: πρὸς τὴν] ἔνδειξιν τῆς δικαιοσύνης αὐτοῦ).[34] God's forbearance under the Old Covenant, Paul argues, should not be viewed as indifference to the countervailing claims of His justice (Rom 3:25b) — then or now (3:26a). The costliness of God's redemptive act (Rom 3:25b: ἐν τῷ αὐτοῦ αἵματι) precludes such a conclusion. Rather, God has equally maintained His justice (Rom 3:26b: δίκαιον) and covenant loyalty (3:26b: δικαιοῦντα). Finally, God had vindicated His own honour and that of His crucified Son by raising Him from the dead and installing Him as the Lord of glory (Rom 6:4: διὰ τῆς δόξης τοῦ πατρός; Phil 2:11: εἰς δόξαν θεοῦ πατρός; 2 Cor 2:8: τὸν κύριον τῆς δόξης).

1963); J. Murray (London 1967); M. Black (Grand Rapids 1973); C.E.B. Cranfield (Edinburgh 1975); J.A.T. Robinson (London 1979); L. Morris (Leicester 1992). Commentators who argue that δικαιοσύνη in Rom 3:21, 22, 25b, 26a is uniform in its reference (either God's salvific power or the status conferred by Him) include: C.H. Dodd (London 1932); R.C.H. Lenski (Minneapolis 1936); A. Nygren (Philadelphia 1949); P.M.-J. Lagrange (Paris 1956); E. Käsemann (Grand Rapids 1980: Gmn. orig. 1973); P.J. Achtemeier (Atlanta 1985); J. Ziesler (London 1989). J.D.G. Dunn (Dallas 1988), D. Moo (Grand Rapids 1996), J.A. Fitzmyer (New York 1992), B. Byrne (Collegeville 1996), and T.R. Schreiner (Grand Rapids 1998) adopt a mediating position.

[33] On Paul's ransom and propitiation motifs in Rom 3:24-25, see C.E.B. Cranfield, *The Epistle to the Romans* Vol.1 (Edinburgh 1975), 206-208, 214-218; L. Morris, *The Apostolic Preaching of the Cross* (London 1955), 184-202. For a strong defence of ἱλαστήριον as 'mercy seat', see D. Moo, *Romans* (Grand Rapids 1996), 231ff.

[34] The weakness of E. Käsemann's interpretation (*op. cit.*; *id.*, '"The Righteousness of God" in Paul', in *id., New Testament Questions of Today* [London 1969], 168-193) of δικαιοσύνη θεοῦ becomes apparent precisely at Rom 3:25-26. Käsemann, on the basis of the Qumran and intertestamental literature (*IQS* 10:25; *IQM* 4:6; 11:12; *CD* 20:20; *T. Dan.* 6:10), posits an apocalyptic background for δικαιοσύνη θεοῦ (cf. Rom 1:17: ἀποκαλύπτα; 3:21: πεφανέρωται). Käsemann takes δικαιοσύνη θεοῦ (Rom 1:17) to be a subjective genitive that describes God's acts of salvific power and extends this understanding to all of Paul's subsequent references (3:5, 21, 25, 26; 10:3). In my view, Käsemann fails to appreciate the extent to which Paul heightens — in contrast to his Graeco-Roman contemporaries (see nn.14, 16, 21, 30, 31) — the honour-and-shame dynamic of Romans 1-3. As a result, Käsemann dilutes Paul's insistence in Rom 3:25-26 that God has satisfied all the demands of His righteousness (*id., op. cit.* [1980], 99: 'God has nothing to prove'). For decisive arguments against Käsemann's interpretation of the Jewish evidence, see E.P. Sanders, *Paul and Palestinian Judaism: A Comparison of Patterns of Religion* (London 1977), 308-309; M.L. Soards, 'Käsemann's "Righteousness" Re-examined', *CBQ* 49/2 (1987), 264-267; D. Moo, *op. cit.*, 85-86. G.N. Davies (*Faith and Obedience in Romans: A Study in Romans 1-4* [Sheffield 1990], 105) observes that the meaning of δικαιοσύνη θεοῦ throughout Romans should be determined by context rather than driven by one's understanding of Rom 1:17.

How would Graeco-Roman auditors have perceived Paul's relentless insistence upon the demands of divine justice and honour? The Graeco-Roman philosophers and moralists had struggled to reconcile the beneficence of the gods with the perceived injustice of their rule. Seneca argued that divine Providence placed tyrants on the throne only as an act of reciprocation to their more virtuous ancestors.[35] Cercidas was so frustrated by the indifference and arbitrariness of Zeus in disposing His providential favour that he devised an alternative pantheon which would rule with justice and grace.[36] Epicurus resolved the entire issue by asserting that the divine nature was motivated neither by beneficence nor judgement.[37]

It is difficult to gauge the reaction that Gentiles, exposed to such popular philosophy,[38] might have had to Paul's preaching (cf. Acts 17:18, 32). Paul's auditors may have been impressed by his refusal to dodge the whole issue of divine justice.[39] However, Paul's insistence that God avenges the dishonouring of His δόξα would have been unpalatable to the Epicureans. Moreover, in a world full of the ambiguities so eloquently articulated by Cercidas (cf. Rom 8:20, 35b-36), it would have been strange to learn that God had exposed His own Son to the arbitrariness and blindness of human justice

---

[35] Seneca, *Ben.*, 4.31.1—4.32.4.

[36] See our discussion in §5.5.4.

[37] On Plutarch's response to Epicurus, *ibid.* Seneca criticises Epicurus' theological views on divine beneficence from a Stoic viewpoint (*Ben.*, 4.4.1-3; 4.19.1-4). See also P.G. Bolt (*Plutarch's "Delay of the Divine Vengeance" and Pauline Eschatology* [unpub. MAHons diss. Macquarie University 1994], *passim*), especially in regard to texts such as Rom 2:4. For Bolt's discussion of χαρίζεσθαι and χάρις, see *ibid.*, 193-197.

[38] On the familiarity of Paul's audiences with popular philosophy, see §5.1.1.

[39] A.J. Guerra (*Romans and the Apologetic Tradition: The Purpose, Genre and Audience of Paul's Letter* [Cambridge 1995]) has argued that in view of Paul's strong apologetic aims Romans is an example of hellenistic protreptic discourse. Paul's overall strategy, according to Guerra, is directed at 'persuading Jewish Christians as well as Gentile Christians in Rome that his planned efforts in the West are worthy of support' (*ibid.*, 42). More specifically, Guerra identifies the intent of Paul's apology for divine justice in Rom 3:5-6 as follows: 'Paul is aware of the potential objections which may occur to his contemporary audience and which the members of the Roman Christian community may themselves raise and/or be confronted with in their interaction with outsiders' (*ibid.*, 68). Our suggestion that Paul may have been responding to popular philosophical discussions on the issue of divine justice and beneficence strengthens Guerra's proposal, especially when one remembers that Seneca was a celebrated resident of Rome in the 50's and early 60's. For further discussion of the protreptic genre and Romans, see D. Aune, 'Romans as a Logos Protreptikos in the Context of Ancient Religious and Philosophical Propaganda', in M. Hengel and U. Heckel (Hrsg.), *Paulus und das antike Judentum* (Tübingen 1992), 91-121. On the Jewish side, the evidence is delicately poised. G. Schrenk ('δικαιοσύνη', *TDNT* 2 [1964], 197) has argued that intertestamental Judaism tried in vain to relate God's goodness to His justice. Alternatively, the Rabbinic literature continued to endorse the Old Testament nexus between human sin and God's retributive justice. See D. Kraemer, *Responses to Suffering in Classical Rabbinic Literature* (Oxford 1995), *passim*.

(1 Cor 2:6-8). But Paul argues that in abandoning His Son to the cross God had demonstrated His unswerving commitment to beneficence (Rom 8:32: χαρίσεται). God had intervened to requite His unrequited Benefactor and thereby relocated and re-defined honour and its rewards.[40] Audiences familiar with popular philosophers and the honorific inscriptions must have found the novelty of Paul's solution not easily assignable to any contemporary understanding of divine beneficence.

6.1.2.2. Paul's solution to the honour-and-shame dynamic in Romans involves a novel understanding of righteousness

As we have seen, God has responded to His dishonouring as cosmic and covenantal Benefactor with an unprecedented act of favour. Paul's approach to divine beneficence involves a radical departure from the Graeco-Roman understanding of the cardinal virtue, δικαιοσύνη.[41] In the honorific inscriptions δικαιοσύνη ('justice', 'uprightness') was the 'quality exhibited by a superior (such as a benefactor) to an inferior, not the reverse'.[42] But, in sharp contrast, Paul denies that a superior moral status is the preserve of any human being (Rom 3:10: οὐκ ἔστιν δίκαιος), let alone the benefactor (5:7: ὁ

---

[40] According to Paul, every believer participates in God's δόξα: progressively in the present age (2 Cor 3:18: ἀπὸ δόξης εἰς δόξαν) and permanently at the eschaton (Rom 5:2: καυχώμεθα ἐπ᾿ ἐλπίδι τῆς δόξης τοῦ θεοῦ [cf. 8:18, 21; Col 1:27]) when God will reverse all dishonour (1 Cor 15:43: ἐν ἀτιμίᾳ, ἐν δόξῃ [cf. Phil 3:21]). However, since the allocation of honour is God's preserve, all entitlement to honour is waived (Rom 2:10). At the social level, Christians experience either honour or dishonour (2 Cor 6:8a: διὰ δόξης καὶ ἀτιμίας; 1 Cor 4:10: ὑμεῖς ἔνδοξοι, ἡμεῖς δὲ ἄτιμοι) according to the response of people to the gospel. Within the body of Christ, mutual honouring is the norm (Rom 12:10). It should be directed towards the weak (1 Cor 12:23-26), parents (Eph 6:2), widows (1 Tim 5:3), pastor-teachers (1 Tim 5:17), masters (1 Tim 6:1) and outside dignitaries (Rom 13:7). On the honouring of widows in early Christianity, see my article, 'Benefaction Ideology and Christian Responsibility for Widows', in S.R. Llewelyn (ed.), *New Docs* 8 (Grand Rapids 1998), 106-116.

[41] On the cardinal virtues, see H.F. North, 'Canons and Hierarchies of the Cardinal Virtues in Greek and Latin Literature', in L. Wallach (ed.), *The Classical Tradition: Literary and Historical Studies in Honor of Harry Caplan* (New York 1966), 165-183. For general discussions of δικαιοσύνη, see G. Schrenk, *art. cit.*, 192-210; E. Käsemann, *art. cit., op. cit.*; J.A. Ziesler, *The Meaning of Righteousness in Paul: A Linguistic and Theological Enquiry* (Cambridge 1972); C. Brown, 'Righteousness', in *id., The New International Dictionary of New Testament Theology* Vol.3 (Exeter 1978: Gmn. orig. 1971), 352-377; R.B. Hays, *art. cit.*, 107-115; S.K. Williams, *art. cit.*, 241-290; F.W. Danker, *op. cit.*, 345-348; J. Reumann, *Righteousness in the New Testament* (Philadelphia 1982); P. Stuhlmacher, 'The Apostle Paul's View of Righteousness', in *id., Reconciliation, Law and Righteousness* (Philadelphia 1986), 68-93; R.K. Moore, 'Issues Involved in the Interpretation of ΔΙΚΑΙΟΣΎΝΗ ΘΕΟΥ in the Pauline Corpus', *Colloquium* 23/2 (1991), 59-70; J.D.G. Dunn, 'The Justice of God: A Renewed Perspective on Justification by Faith', *JTS* 43/1 (1992), 1-22.

[42] G.H.R. Horsley, 'δικαιοσύνη', *New Docs* 4 (1987), 145.

ἀγαθός) or the ritually pious (3:20: ἐξ ἔργων νόμου οὐ δικαιωθήσεται; 3:21: χωρὶς νόμου; 4:1-7).[43]

For Paul, the entire process of moral transformation is now 'democratised'. Members of God's covenant family — whether Jew or Gentile (Rom 4:16: κατὰ χάριν [cf. Gal 3:18: κεχάρισται]; 11:5-6: χάριτι, οὐκέτι ἐξ ἔργων) — are freely declared righteous in an act of divine benefaction (Rom 3:24: δικαιούμενοι δωρεὰν τῇ αὐτοῦ χάριτι).[44] As noted, God as supreme Benefactor demands that the claims of His own righteousness be satisfied: but ultimately He abandons the exalted status of Benefactor by bridging the distance between Himself and His beneficiaries and accounting them righteous through faith (πίστις).[45] Rather than facing God's wrath over His dishonouring (Rom 5:1: εἰρήνην ἔχομεν), the Christian has continual access through Christ to the favour of the divine Benefactor (5:2: εἰς τὴν χάριν ταύτην ἐν ᾗ ἑστήκαμεν; cf. 2 Thess 2:16; Titus 3:7).[46]

6.1.2.3. The gift of divine righteousness is extended to unworthy beneficiaries through a dishonoured benefactor

The paradox is that God accords the status of righteousness to believers through a dishonoured Benefactor. Whereas contemporary benefactors generally restricted their munificence to their own citizens,[47] Christ died for

---

[43] On ὁ ἀγαθός (Rom 5:7) as a reference to the benefactor, see A.D. Clarke, 'The Good and the Just in Romans 5:7', *TynBul* 41/1 (1990), 128-142. More generally, *id.*, *Secular and Christian Leadership in Corinth: A Socio-Historical and Exegetical Study of 1 Corinthians 1-6* (Leiden-New York-Köln 1993). In regard to Rom 4:4 (κατὰ χάριν), see our discussion (§3.2.1) of *P. Mich.* II 123-124.

[44] The adverb δωρεάν ('freely', 'as a free gift') was standard benefaction parlance. Zosimos of Priene (*I. Priene* 112, 113: 84 BC) provided 'as a free gift' (δωρεάν) a bath for the young men and their instructors at the gymnasium, and for citizens and foreigners at festivals. Cf. *IG* IX(2) 1230 (II cent. BC: δωρεάν). J.D.G. Dunn (*The Theology of Paul the Apostle* [Grand Rapids 1998], 322) notes the striking way in which Paul links χάρις to δωρεά ('gift': Rom 5:15, 17; 2 Cor 9:15; Eph 3:7; 4:7) and δωρεάν ('as a gift', 'undeservedly': Rom 3:24; Gal 2:21). See also our discussion of Dio Chrysostom, *Or.*, 41.5 as background to Rom 4:16 (§5.3 n.72).

[45] Rom 1:17; 3:22-31; 4:1-22; 5:1-2; 9:30-32; 10:6-17;11:20. Paul uses πίστις 27 times in these passages. Note the comment of R.M. Pickett (*art. cit.*, 793): 'God is a patron who doesn't act like a patron'.

[46] On προσαγωγή, see *BAGD* (Chicago 1979²) for reference to ambassadors gaining admission to an audience with the Great King (Xen., *Cyr.* 7.5.45: προσάγειν).

[47] It is a matter of comment that Zosimos of Priene (*I. Priene* 112, 113: 84 BC) provided a bath even for the Romans and their women and children. Similarly, Kleanax 'entertained sumptuously in the Town Hall for several days many of the citizens and Romans' (*SEG* XXXII 1243: late I cent. BC—early I cent. AD). R.A. Kearsley ('A Civic Benefactor of the First Century in Asia Minor', *New Docs* 7 [1994], §10, 237) points out that the scope of Kleanax' beneficence included 'all definable social categories in Graeco-Roman cities'. See also R.K. Sherk, *The Roman Empire: Augustus to Hadrian* (Cambridge

the ungodly and ungrateful enemies of God who had spurned divine beneficence (Rom 5:6, 10). The social dishonour involved in Christ's death stirs Paul to underscore the divine love which prompted it (Rom 5:8: τὴν ἑαυτοῦ ἀγάπην εἰς ἡμᾶς). He airs the possibility that one might, as a remarkable act of honour and gratitude, reciprocate the generosity of one's benefactor by dying for him (ὁ ἀγαθός: Rom 5:7b).[48] We have already drawn attention to Pseudo-Demetrius who envisages the precise situation of Rom 5:7b in describing the indebtedness of a beneficiary to his benefactor:

I hasten to show in my actions how grateful I am to you for the kindness you showed me in your words. For I know that what I am doing for you is less than I should, for *even if I gave my life for you*, I should still not be giving adequate thanks (ἀξίαν ἀποδώσειν χάριν) for the benefits I have received.[49]

Moreover, Valerius Maximus refers to L. Petronius who reciprocated the munificence of his benefactor, Caelius, in costly manner.[50] Petronius took his own life and that of Caelius, thereby sparing his benefactor an ignominious death at the hands of his enemies. But, in the view of Paul, the death of Christ surpasses in scope all contemporary Graeco-Roman beneficence precisely because it was conditioned by ἀγάπη rather than by reciprocity. The unworthiness of those who receive the benefits of Christ's death also poses a problem for traditional benefaction ideology. The philosophers stress that the benefactor should carefully study the disposition of his projected beneficiaries in order to circumvent the humiliation of an unworthy response.[51] Christ, however, took no such precaution.

1988), §7II.E. Typical of a more discriminatory approach to ancient beneficence is the prefect of Nero who repudiates the notion that veterans somehow possessed unqualified access to imperial χάρις. See our discussion of *P. Fouad.* 21 in §3.5. As a general rule, beneficence was only extended to 'hometown, neighbours, relations, and friends' (Pliny, *Ep.*, 9.30.1).

[48] See A.D. Clarke, *art. cit.*, 128-141; T.R. Schreiner, *Romans* (Grand Rapids 1998), 262. F.W. Danker (*op. cit.*, 417) cites Rom 5:6-8 as another example of the endangered benefactor motif.

[49] Pseudo-Demetrius, Τύποι Ἐπιστολικοί, 21 (II cent. BC—III cent. AD), discussed in §3.1.3. G.W. Peterman (*Paul's Gift from Philippi: Conventions of Gift Exchange and Christian Giving* [Cambridge 1997], 82, 194) has noted the same text in discussing Rom 5:7, though he has incorrectly referred to the author as 'Ps-Dionysius' in *ibid.*, 194.

[50] Valerius Maximus, *Noteworthy Doings and Sayings*, 4.7.5, discussed in §5.6.2. Other paradigms for Christ's vicarious death may be relevant. On Maccabean martyrology, see J.S. Pobee, *Persecution and Martyrdom in the Theology of Paul* (Sheffield 1985), 13-92; D. Seeley, *The Noble Death: Graeco-Roman Martyrology and Paul's Concept of Salvation* (Sheffield 1990), 83-112. On vicariousness in its Graeco-Roman context, see M. Hengel, *The Atonement: The Origins of the Doctrine in the New Testament* (London 1981), 1-32; D. Seeley, *op. cit.*, 113-141; G.W. Bowersock, *Martyrdom and Rome* (Cambridge 1995).

[51] See §5.6.1 for a general discussion of the appropriate attitudes between benefactor and beneficiary in benefaction rituals. Seneca (*Ben.*, 4.27.5; 4.34.2) argues that benefactors should avoid benefiting those with an ungrateful disposition. On the Jewish side, see Sir

In our second major section on Romans (§6.1.2.4—§6.1.2.5), we turn to the Augustan context of divine χάρις. How would Gentile Christians at Rome have understood Paul's exposition of God's eschatological reign of grace?

6.1.2.4. The reign of grace in Romans 5:12-21 must be situated as much within the Roman eschatology of Augustus as within the Jewish apocalyptic literature

The gift of Christ's righteousness (Rom 5:18-19) heralds the eschatological reign of grace, in the present age and at the eschaton.[52] Paul's focus is simultaneously theocentric and christocentric. Christ's death is an act of God's patronage that inaugurates the reign of grace (Rom 5:15:b: ἡ χάρις τοῦ θεοῦ); it is also a deliberate act of Christ as Benefactor that leads to righteousness (15a, 16b: τὸ χάρισμα [cf. 6:23]; 15b: ἡ δωρεὰ ἐν χάριτι; 16a: τὸ δώρημα).[53] The Jewish eschatology underlying the Adam-Christ typology in Romans 5:12ff is well known.[54] For example, in regard to Romans 5:15b, M. Theobald has argued that Paul employs apocalyptic and rabbinic traditions (2 Esdr 4.29ff; 8.31ff; *Sifre* Lev 5:17 [120a]) — in conjunction with περισσεύειν — to underscore the eschatological fullness of God's grace.[55] Further, as D. Moo has observed, Paul's language of 'reigning'

12.1-2.

[52] Contrast Rom 5:15b (ἡ χάρις τοῦ θεοῦ καὶ ἡ δωρεὰ ἐν χάριτι ... ἐπερίσσευσεν) with 5:17b (οἱ τὴν περισσείαν τῆς χάριτος καὶ τῆς δωρεᾶς ... λαμβάνοντες ... βασιλεύσουσιν). In this regard, M. Theobald (*Die überströmende Gnade: Studien zu einem paulinischen Motivfeld* [Würzburg 1982], 107) comments: '"Leben" und "Tod" haben in Christus einen präsentisch- und futurisch-eschatologischen Sinn'.

[53] See D. Moo, *op. cit.*, 334ff; D.J. Doughty, 'The Priority of ΧΑΡΙΣ: An Investigation of the Theological Language of Paul', *NTS* 19 (1973), 172-175. Similarly, W. Grundmann ('Die Übermacht der Gnade: Eine Studie zur Theologie des Paulus', *NovT* 2/1 [1957], 54) writes: 'Die Äonenwende ist durch die gerechte Tat Jesu Christi eingetreten'. In regard to Paul's use of χάρισμα in Rom 5:15b, O. Michel (*Der Brief an die Römer* [Göttingen 1978], 189 n.11) observes: 'Χάρισμα (Sir. 38,30; 7,33 vl.) ist zunächst ein hellenistischer Begriff und bezeichnet hier den konkreten Erweis der Gnade und Güte Gottes'.

[54] See J.R. Harrison, 'Paul, Eschatology and the Augustan Age of Grace', *TynBul* 50/1 (1999), 79-91, esp. 80-83 for the Jewish background.

[55] M. Theobald, *op. cit.*, 94-96. See also W. Sanday and A.C. Headlam, *A Critical and Exegetical Commentary on the Epistle to the Romans* (Edinburgh 1902), 136-138; J. Moffatt, *Grace in the New Testament* (London 1931), 221-224; R. Scroggs, *The Last Adam: A Study in Pauline Anthropology* (Philadelphia 1966), *passim*; H. Schlier, *Der Römerbrief* (Freiburg 1977), 183-189; O. Michel, *op. cit.*, 193-197. On Paul's apocalyptic theology, J.C. Beker, *op. cit.*, 135-181. Note the comment of K. Berger ('χάρις', H. Balz and G. Schneider [eds], *Exegetical Dictionary of the New Testament* Vol.3 [Grand Rapids 1993], 459): 'Romans 5 relates the messianic category of superabundance to the apocalyptic vision of the increase of evil: the overabundance of evil is reversed and simultaneously eclipsed by increased fullness'.

alludes to the familiar idea of 'dominions' (or *aeons* in Jewish apocalyptic thought).[56] Thus the new age of grace and its gift of righteousness (Rom 5:17b; 21b: βασιλεύειν) has supplanted the current age of sin and death (5:14a; 17a; 21a: βασιλεύειν). The eschatological newness of χάρις is underscored by the accompanying language of abundance (Rom 5:15: ἐπερίσσευσεν; 5:17: τὴν περισσείαν; 5:20: πλεονάσῃ, ἐπλεονάσεν, ὑπερεπερίσσευσεν; cf. 6.20: πλεονάσῃ; cf. 2 Cor 4:15; 8:7; 9:8; Eph 1:7b-8; 1Tim 1:14) and by the death-and-life contrasts (5:12, 14, 17, 21: θάνατος; 5:17, 18, 21: ζωή).[57]

New Testament exegetes have been reluctant to situate the reign of grace described in Romans 5:12-21 as much in the Roman eschatology of the Augustan era as in the traditions of Jewish apocalyptic literature.[58] However, D. Georgi has noted that 'the gospel according to Augustus had the world spellbound',[59] including (presumably) some of the Roman Christians to whom Paul later wrote. From the late first century BC, as the Julian house eclipsed its rivals, beneficence was monopolised by the Caesars. As noted,[60] the one-sidedness of this contest struck contemporary observers as a turning-point in Roman history and this was reflected in the Augustan propaganda.

It is worth speculating whether Paul's Roman auditors may have interpreted the reign of Christ's beneficence (Rom 5:21: ἡ χάρις βασιλεύσῃ; cf. 5:17b: βασιλεύσουσιν) against its Augustan counterpart.[61]

---

[56] D. Moo, *op. cit.*, 349. Regarding ὑπερεπερίσσευσεν ἡ χάρις (Rom 5:20), B. Eastman (*The Significance of Grace in the Letters of Paul* [New York 1999], 132) says: 'ὑπερεπερισσεύω, in a manner typical of Jewish apocalyptic, signifies eschatological abundance and makes a fitting climax to the sequence of contrasts begun in vs. 15'. He cites 4 *Ezra* 4:50 as corroboration (*ibid.*, 173 n.123).

[57] D. Zeller (*Charis bei Philon und Paulus* [Stuttgart 1990], 135 n.19) cites two cases of Philo employing χάρις with περισσεύειν (*Leg. All.* 1.34; 3.163), correctly observing that Paul's use was not unique. As we will see, περισσεύειν (and cognates) was part of benefaction parlance. J. Wobbe (*Der Charis-Gedanke bei Paulus: Ein Beitrag zur neutestamentlichen Theologie* [Münster 1932], 41) notes how Paul employs a range of abundance terminology (περισσεύειν, πλοῦτος, ὑπερβάλλειν) to express the fullness of grace instead of resorting to the plural χάριτες. For a fine discussion of abounding grace in 2 Cor 4:15, see B. Eastman, *op. cit.*, 47-49. On Paul's eschewal of the plural χάριτες see §6.5 below. Generally, see also J. Guillet, 'Grâce', *Catholicisme* 5 (1951), col.137; C. Spicq, *Théologie morale du nouveau testament* Tome 1 (Paris 1965), 115 nn.4-5.

[58] See, however, F.W. Danker, *op. cit.*, 347. Note the eschatological motifs used by Statius (*Silv.*, 4.1-3) of Domitian and (more controversially) by the Einsiedeln *Eclogues of Nero*.

[59] D. Georgi, 'Who is the True Prophet?', *HTR* 79/1-3 (1986), 104. D. Georgi (*ibid.*, 100-26) and B. Witherington III (*Conflict and Community in Corinth: A Socio-Rhetorical Commentary on 1 and 2 Corinthians* [Grand Rapids 1995], 295-298) have discussed Roman eschatology in regard to select New Testament texts.

[60] See our survey of the χάρις of the Caesars in §2.5, §2.8.4.

[61] See the insightful comparison of Christ and Augustus in E. Stauffer, *Christ and the*

It would be injudicious to press for an exclusively Caesarian reference when trying to explain the origin of Paul's regnal imagery in Romans 5:21.[62] Nonetheless, the enormity of Augustus' beneficence was apparent to his contemporaries and successors. A letter of the Roman Proconsul to the Asian League (9 BC) admits that 'it is difficult to return for (Augustus') many great benefactions thanks in equal measure (κατ' ἴσον ε[ὐχαρισ]τεῖν)'.[63] In his letter to the city of Gytheion (AD 15), Tiberius referred to 'the great size of the benefits of my father to all the world'.[64] In similar vein, Germanicus would later describe Augustus as 'the true saviour and the benefactor of the entire race of men'.[65]

An overpowering sense of eschatological destiny had gripped the minds of the contemporaries of Augustus when they honoured the *princeps*. For example, the first decree of the Asian League concerning the new provincial calendar (Priene: 9 BC) explodes with praise as it recounts Augustus' merits:

[S]ince Providence, which has divinely disposed our lives, having employed zeal and ardour, has arranged the most perfect (culmination) for life (τὸ τελητότατον τῶι βίωι) by producing Augustus, whom for the benefit of mankind (εἰς εὐεργεσίαν ἀνθρώ[πων]) she has filled with excellence (ἐπλήρωσεν ἀρετῆς), as [if she had granted him as a saviour] ([σωτῆρα χαρισαμένη]) for us and our descendants, (a saviour) who brought war to an end and set [all

---

Caesars: Historical Sketches (London 1955), 90-111.

[62] An overt allusion to Caesarian beneficence in Rom 5:21 is (probably) ruled out when it is remembered that Augustus and his beneficiaries avoided regnal imagery in describing the principate. In view of the fact that the Romans had ousted the monarchy and the Caesars emphasised their superiority to both client-kings and the monarchs of enemy nations (e.g. Augustus: *Res Gestae* 4, 27, 31-33; Caligula: R.K. Sherk, *op. cit.*, §42B), this is perfectly understandable. Further, Paul's imagery could equally be alluding to the beneficence of eastern potentates or the Herods of Palestine. Significantly, in this regard, Antiochus I of Kommagene refers to his 'royal grace' (βα[σι]λικαῖς χάρισιν: §2.8.2). We must not also discount the possibility that Paul chose βασιλεύειν because it evoked the Old Testament portrayal of God as King (e.g. 1 Sam 8:7; Isa 6:5; Ps 24:7ff; Jer 51:57 etc). In this respect, it is worth remembering J.L. White's contention (*The Apostle of God: Paul and the Promise of Abraham* [Peabody 1991], 204-205) that Paul's portrait of Christ's lordship equally drew upon idealised images of the Roman emperor and the Jewish-Christian idea of the Davidic Messiah.

[63] V. Ehrenberg and A.H.M. Jones, *Documents Illustrating the Reigns of Augustus and Tiberius* (London 1954: 2nd ed.), §98a (*ll*.15-17). The first decree of the Asian League concerning the new provincial calendar (Priene: 9 BC) asserts that the officials of Augustus had 'bestowed benefits on the province, the size of which benefits no speech would be adequate to relate' (*ibid.*, 98b *ll*.46-47). B.W. Winter (*Seek the Welfare of the City: Christians as Benefactors and Citizens* [Grand Rapids 1994], 125) cites a fragment from Nicolaus of Damascus (*F.Gr.H.* 90 F 125.1), the court historian of Herod the Great and a contemporary observer of Augustus. He spoke of the eagerness of cities to revere Augustus with temples and cultic worship due to 'the greatness of his virtue and the scale of his benefactions to them'. See also Philo, *Leg.* 147.

[64] R.K. Sherk, *op. cit.*, §31.

[65] *Ibid.*, §42B (AD 18—19).

things] in peaceful order (κοσμήσοντα δὲ [εἰρήνην]); [and (since) with his appearance] Caesar exceeded the hopes (τὰς ἐλπίδας [ὑπερ]έθηκεν) of all those who had received [glad tidings] ([εὐανγέλια]) before us, not only surpassing ([ὑπερβα]λόμενος) those who had been [benefactors] before him, but not even [leaving any] hope [of surpassing him] (ἐλπίδ[α] ὑπερβολῆς) for those who are to come in the future; and (since) the beginning of glad tidings (εὐαγγελί[ων]) on his account for the world was [the birthday] of the god ...[66]

The beneficent reign of Augustus is given quasi-cosmological significance by the Roman proconsul in his letter to the Asian League (Priene: 9 BC):

It is subject to question whether the birthday of our most divine Caesar spells more of joy or blessing, this being a date that we could probably without fear of contradiction equate with the beginning of all things (τῆι τῶν πάντων ἀρχῆι), if not in terms of nature, certainly in terms of utility, seeing that he restored stability, when everything was collapsing and falling into disarray, and gave a new look to the entire world that would have been most happy to accept its own ruin had not the good and common fortune of all been born: Caesar. Therefore people might justly assume that his birthday spells the beginning of life and real living (ἀρχὴν τοῦ βίου καὶ τῆς ζωῆς) and marks the end and boundary of any regret that they had themselves been born.[67]

As seen above, the imperial propaganda laid heavy emphasis on the pre-eminent merit of Augustus as benefactor.[68] He had established peace, inaugurated an era of unparalleled beneficence, and secured hope for the

---

[66] V. Ehrenberg and A.H.M. Jones, *op. cit.*, §98b (*ll*.32-41). For its relevance to Rom 5:12-13 and 8:18-19, note the comment of J. Rouffiac (*Caractères du Grec,* 72ff cited by C. Spicq, *Theological Lexicon of the New Testament* Vol. 3 [Peabody 1994: Fr. orig. 1978], n.44 353-354) regarding the Priene inscription of Augustus:

It probably would not have required much touching up of this text for a Christian to be able to apply it to Christ fifty years later. A saviour who realised ancestral hopes; who has a unique importance for humanity; who is so great that he will be never surpassed; whose birth marks the beginning of a new era: so many descriptions that one might think were created by Christian piety, but which nevertheless are found in a pagan inscription from not long before the birth of Jesus.

BMI 894 (Halicarnassus: 2 BC [*ll*.8-12]) combines realised and future eschatological elements in addressing Augustus as σωτήρ: 'there is peace (εἰρηνεύο[υσ]ι) on land and at sea; cities are in bloom with good order, harmony, and prosperity; every good thing is at its zenith and point of maturity; there is a culmination of auspicious hopes (ἐλπίδων χρηστῶν) for the future, and there is the present cheerfulness of men who have been filled'. The same inscription states that Nature freely gave (ἐχαρίσατο) to humankind the greatest good in the form of Augustus' immeasurable beneficence (τὸ [μέγ]ιστον πρὸς ὑπερβαλλούσας εὐεργεσίας). In short, 'Providence not only made full (ἐπλήρωσε) the prayers of all but also transcended (them)'. Suetonius (*Aug.* 98) reports the Alexandrian sailors' praise of Augustus: 'it was through him they lived, through him that they sailed the seas, and through him that they enjoyed their liberty and fortunes'. For the invocation of Fortune to protect Augustus, see Horace, *Carm. Saec.*, 29-32. On εὐαγγέλιον and the Caesar cult, P. Stuhlmacher, *Das paulinische Evangelium I: Vorgeschichte* (Göttingen 1968), 197-203.

[67] V. Ehrenberg and A.H.M. Jones, *op. cit.*, §98a (*ll*.4-11).

[68] The inscription on the golden shield placed in the Curia Julia recognised Augustus' valour (ἀρετή), clemency (ἐπείκεια), justice ([δ]ικαιοσύνη), and piety (εὐσέβεια). *Res Gestae* 34.

future.⁶⁹ Elsewhere, we also hear of Augustus' clemency towards his enemies.⁷⁰ These motifs may well have resonated within the minds of Paul's auditors as they heard about Christ's reign of grace. The merit of Christ — seen in His righteous act of obedience to the Father (Rom 5:18b, 19b) — has secured peace with God (5:2: εἰρήνην πρὸς τὸν θεόν) and the eschatological hope of glory for His beneficiaries (5:2: ἐπ' ἐλπίδι τῆς δόξης).⁷¹ However, whereas Augustus had responded with clemency to those who were politically astute enough to sue for peace after the battle of Actium (31 BC), Christ took the initiative and reconciled those who were at the time God's enemies through an act of acquittal (Rom 5:6a, 8b, 10a, 19b).

The imperial propaganda also portrays Augustus as an eschatological figure.⁷² His principate represents the culmination (τὸ τεληότατον) of

---

⁶⁹ For the imperial ideology of peace, see Augustus, *Res Gestae* 12 (Ε[ἰρ]ήνης Σεβαστῆς), 13 (εἰρηνευομένης), 26 (εἰρηνεύεσθαι). Cf. *ibid.*, 34: 'I had extinguished the flames of civil war'. Similarly, Horace (*Carm.*, 3.14.14-16; cf. 1:2; 1.12.49-60; 4.2.41-52; 4.15.17-20): 'Neither civil strife nor death by violence will I fear, while Caesar holds the earth'. Additionally, Virgil (*G.*, 1.498-514; 2.170-172), Seneca (*Apocol.* 10), and Velleius Paterculus (2.89.1-6; 2.126.3-4). Note the more critical stance of Epictetus (Arr., *Epict. Diss.*, 3.13.9-11) who contrasts the peace offered by the Caesars with that of the philosophers.

On the role of benefactors in restoring peace, see F.W. Danker, *op. cit.*, 398-399. On hope in imperial propaganda, see M.E. Clark, 'Images and Concepts of Hope in the Imperial Cult', in H.R. Kent (ed.), *Society of Biblical Literature 1982 Seminar Papers* (Chico 1982), 39-43. For the benefactions of Augustus, see *Res Gestae* 15-24. Augustus, in imitation of the honorific inscriptions of Republican *nobiles* (e.g. *CIL* I. 2), promotes an eschatological aura around his acts of beneficence and deliverance: 'I was the first and only one (*primus et [s]olus omnium*) to do this' (*Res Gestae*, 16). On this feature of Augustus' *Res Gestae*, see P. Veyne, *Bread and Circuses: Historical Sociology and Political Pluralism* (London 1990; Fr. orig. 1976), 258. Again, as commissioner of the grain supply, Augustus speaks of his generosity in pressing times: 'I freed the entire people, at my own expense, from the fear and danger in which they were' (*Res Gestae* 5).

⁷⁰ Augustus, *Res Gestae* 3 (cf. *ibid.*, 34: ἐπιείκεια): 'when victorious I spared all citizens who sued for pardon'.

⁷¹ Note the widespread peace and hope terminology in Romans. εἰρήνη: Rom 1:7; 2:10; 8:6; 10:15; 14:17, 19; 15:13, 33; 16:20. ἐλπίς 5:4-5; 8:20; 12:12; 15:4, 13. ἐλπίζειν: 8:24-25. In relation to Paul's glory terminology (Rom 5:2), Horace (*Carm.*, 3.25.4-5) speaks of 'peerless Caesar's immortal glory (*aeternum decus*)'. On Paul's linkage of εἰρήνη with χάρις (Rom 1:7; 1 Cor 1:3; 2 Cor 1:2; Gal 1:3; Eph 1:2; Col 1:2; 1 Thess 1:1; 2 Thess 1:2; Phlm 3; 1 Tim 1:2; 2 Tim 1:2; Titus 1:4), see J.M. Lieu, '"Grace to You and Peace": The Apostolic Greeting', *BJRL* 68/1 (1985), 161-178.

⁷² In Augustan propaganda the battle of Actium (31 BC) acquired a special eschatological significance (Virgil, *Aen.*, 2.675ff; Horace, *Epod.*, 9; cf. *Res Gestae* 25). According to Virgil (*Ecl.*, 4), a golden age had been ushered in by Augustus. On the latter, see I.S. Ryberg, 'Virgil's Golden Age', *TAPhA* 89 (1958), 112-131. The portent of Caesar's comet (Horace, *Carm.*, 1.12.46-48; Virgil, *Ecl.*, 9.46-50; cf. Suetonius, *Iul.*, 88) heralded the eschatological fruitfulness of the Augustan era and its enduring brightness. On the battle of Actium and its centrality to Augustan numismatic propaganda, see R.A. Gurval, *Actium and Augustus: The Politics and Emotions of Civil War* (Ann Arbor 1995), 47-65.

Providence in the universal history of mankind. The superiority of Augustus as world-benefactor for all time is reinforced by the language of excess (ὑπερβάλλειν, ὑπερβολή).[73] Paul's language of abundance, cited above, also features in the Priene inscription: the cities of Asia are encouraged to celebrate the birthday of Augustus 'in an even more extraordinary manner (περισσότερον)'.[74] In similar vein to the documents above, Paul highlights the fact that Christ died for the ungodly 'at the right time' (Rom 5:6: κατὰ καιρόν; cf. Gal 4:4: τὸ πλήρωμα τοῦ χρόνου). In the context, D. Moo is correct in interpreting *kairos* as 'the culminating, eschatological time of God's intervention in Christ'.[75] Later, Paul would identify Jesus as the culmination of the Jewish quest for righteousness by law (Rom 10:4: τέλος νόμου).

Additionally, the Pauline language of abundance — περισσεύειν and cognates (including a ὑπερ- compound) — points to the supplanting of the Adamic reign of sin and death by Christ's reign of grace and eternal life.[76] Thus, by the time of Paul, Roman auditors were confronted with two competing eschatological hopes. The imperial version — if Suetonius (*Aug.*, 28.2) has accurately rendered an edict of Augustus — looked beyond the grave to the continuing stability of the *res publica*: 'I ... bear with me the hope (*spem*) when I die that the foundations which I have laid for the State will remain unshaken'.[77] Alternatively, Paul proclaimed the defeat of death itself (Rom 5:21; 8:38-39; cf. 1 Cor 15: 20-28, 51-57).

---

[73] The language of excess (ὑπερβάλλειν) typified benefactors in honorific inscriptions. Benefactors 'excelled' in a range of virtues: e.g. good will (εὔνοια: *SEG* XXII 128), benevolence (φιλανθρωπία: *IG* XIII[7] 395), courage (ἀνδρεία: *I. Prusa Olymp.* 2), love of glory (φιλοδοξία: *Caria. Aphro.* 270) and honour (φιλοτιμία: *I. AnkyraBosch.* 131, 108), greatness of mind (μεγαλοφροσύνη: *TAM* II[1-3] 579), moderation (σωφροσύνη: *TAM* V 62), merit (ἀρετή: *FD* III[1] 546a) and ancestral honour (φιλοτειμία προγονική: *SEG* XXXVII 1210). In contrast to the honorific inscriptions, Paul usually reserves the language of excess (ὑπερβάλλειν, ὑπερβολή) for the overflow of divine grace (2 Cor 9:14; Eph 2:7), glory (2 Cor 3:10, 17), power (2 Cor 4:7; Eph 1:19), revelation (2 Cor 12:7) and love (Eph 3:19). Where Paul employs ὑπερβολή in ethical contexts, it refers to the excess of sin (Rom 7:13; Gal 1:13) or, more positively, the excellence of love (1 Cor 12:31).

[74] V. Ehrenberg and A.H.M. Jones, *op. cit.*, §98a (*l.*23). Examples of the inscriptional language of abundance are easily multiplied. In honour of Tiberius Caesar, the Ephesians dedicate through their agonothetēs two stoa 'from the superfluous money (ἐκ τῶν περισσῶν χρημάτων) of the games of Augustus Caesar' (*I. Ephesos* VII 3420). See also *I. Ephesos* Ia 17 (*l.*43: περισσῇ δαπάνῃ), 18 (*l.*15: περισσῇ δαπάνῃ). Flavius Diadumenos is honoured 'on account of the extraordinary good-will and love of honour (τὴν περ[ισσὴν] εὔνοιαν καὶ] φιλοτιμίαν) in (his) offices and liturgies' (*I. Tralleis* 81: AD 217).

[75] D. Moo, *op. cit.*, 307.

[76] In addition to M. Theobald (*op. cit., passim*), note the comment of W. Sanday and A.C. Headlam (*op. cit.*, 133) concerning Rom 5:12-21: 'ὑπερεπερίσσευσεν ἡ χάρις is the keynote of the passage'. Similarly, H. Schlier (*op. cit.*, 172): 'Wir werden auf die Überfülle, den Überfluß, man könnte sagen: dem Exzeß der Gnade aufmerksam gemacht'.

[77] See E. Stauffer, *op. cit.*, 109-110.

Finally, the imperial propaganda ascribed a cosmic status to Augustus. The reason was obvious to all. He had brought about a decisive reversal of the social disintegration unleashed by the *triumvirs* (and, indeed, Marius and Sulla before them), as they and their factions struggled for political ascendancy (59—31 BC). When Roman civilisation had tottered on the precipice, Augustus offered a new beginning (ἀρχή) that would bring real life (βίος; ζωή) and an end to all regret. The poet Horace (65—8 BC) affords us insight into the profound sense of relief that Augustus brought to a generation wearied by war-guilt and the snubbing of traditional Roman values.[78] Horace's idyllic description of the fertility of the Augustan age is replete with the motifs of redemption and the restoration of the *mos maiorum*:

...(the) country yearns for Caesar. For when he is here, the ox in safety roams the pastures; Ceres and benign Prosperity make rich the crops; safe are the seas over which our sailors course; Faith shrinks from blame; polluted by no stain, the home is pure; custom and law have stamped out the taint of sin; mothers win praise because of children like unto their sires; while Vengeance follows close on guilt.[79]

Furthermore, in the *Carmen Saeculare*, Horace depicts Augustus as a new Aeneas, who according to later legend was Rome's founder (*Carm. Saec.* 37-48). An eschatological figure, Augustus establishes a worldwide reign of fruitfulness (*Carm. Saec.* 29-32) and peace (49-56) that embodies the quintessential Roman values (57-60).[80]

The inscriptions replicate this blend of eschatological and cosmological expectation regarding Augustus. The island of Phylae, located at the first waterfall of the Nile, honoured Augustus' conquest of Egypt some twenty-three years after the event and accorded him a quasi mythological status:

The emperor, ruler of oceans and continents, the divine father among men, who bears the same name as his heavenly father—Liberator, the marvellous star of the Greek world, shining with the brilliance of the great heavenly Saviour.[81]

---

[78] According to Horace, atonement for Roman guilt — rendered necessary because 'citizen whetted against citizen the sword' (*Carm.*, 1.2) — was more than satisfied by the deliverance that Augustus had brought.

[79] Horace, *Carm.*, 4.5.16-24; cf. 4.15. See also Virgil, *G.*, 1.24-42. Generally, see W. Deonna, 'La légende d'Octave-Auguste: dieu, sauveur et maître du monde', *RHR* 83 (1921), 32-58, 163-195; 84 (1921), 77-107; A. Wallace-Hadrill, 'The Golden Age and Sin in Augustan Ideology', *P&P* 95 (1982), 19-36. For Augustus' stated faithfulness to the *mos maiorum*, see *Res Gestae* 5, 8.

[80] See the excellent discussion of D. Georgi, *art. cit.*, 115-117; H. Koester, 'Memory of Jesus' Death and the Worship of the Risen Lord', *HTR* 91/4 (1998), 335-50. The *Ara Pacis* (Altar of Peace), erected in the Campus Martius between 13 and 9 BC to celebrate Augustus' return from Gaul, includes a representation of Aeneas arriving in Italy.

[81] Cited in E. Stauffer, *op. cit.*, 99. The astronomical appellation — 'the marvellous star of the Greek world, shining with the brilliance of the great heavenly Saviour' — alludes to

Even Philo, the Jewish philosopher of Alexandria, ascribes to Augustus the role of social and cosmic healer:

> The whole human race exhausted by mutual slaughter was on the verge of utter destruction had it not been for one man and leader, Augustus, whom men fitly call the averter of evil. This is the Caesar who calmed the torrential storms on every side, who healed pestilences common to Greeks and barbarians, pestilences which descending from the south and the east coursed to the west and north sowing seeds of calamity over the places and waters which lay between them.[82]

Paul's portrayal of Christ as the eschatological figure of world and cosmic history would have registered with Romans imbued with the Augustan eschatology (and who may well have been alienated by imperial successors such as Caligula and Nero). According to Paul, humanity is held hostage to sin and death through the disobedience of Adam its founder (Rom 5: 12-14). The entire creation, which was subjected by God to futility at Eden (Rom 8:22; cf. 15:30; Gen 3:17-19), groans (Rom 8:23) and awaits the culmination of the redemption hope, equally for itself and for Christians at the eschaton (8:20b-21, 23b). But, as the first-born from the dead (Rom 8:29; cf. Col 1:18), Christ is the beginning of a new humanity (Col 1:18: ἀρχή; cf. Rom 5:14b; 1 Cor 15:21-22, 45-48). Set free to live without the crippling legacy of its founder

---

the *sidus Iulium*. This was the comet observed shortly after Caesar's death in 44 BC when Augustus was celebrating the *Victoria Caesaris*. A coin issue of 18 BC displays the oak-wreathed head of Augustus on the obverse and an eight-rayed comet with a fiery tail on the reverse. Across the field of the coin and between the rays is the legend DIVVS IVLIVS. See H. Mattingly, *Coins of the Roman Empire* Vol.1 (London 1965), 59 §323-328. In a cameo of Augustus' victory at Actium, Virgil (*Aen.* 2.680-684) links two supra-cephalic flames issuing from Augustus' helmet with his father's star, the *sidus Iulium*, which dawns over its crest. For discussion of the coins, see R. Oster, 'Numismatic Windows into the Social World of Early Christianity', *JBL* 101/2 (1982), 195-223, esp. 208-212; idem, '"Show me a denarius": Symbolism of Roman Coinage and Christian Beliefs', *ResQ* 28/2 (1985-1986), 107-115, esp. 108-111. For an excellent general discussion of Augustus' coins, see E. Stauffer, *op. cit.*, 86-88. More generally, L.J. Kreitzer, *Striking New Images: Roman Imperial Coinage and the New Testament World* (Sheffield 1996). Note, too, the cosmological dimension of *I. Perge* 381: '(This monument is dedicated to) Imperator Caesar Augustus, Son of a God, Guardian of all the earth and sea'. Cf. Rev 10:6; 14:7. For a late first-century BC prophecy in honour of Augustus' victory at Actium — or is it possibly a reference to Caesar's triumph at Pharsalus? — see *I. Hadrianoi* 24:

> I, Gauros, have received the trustworthy words of prophets and have inscribed the victory of Caesar and the contests of (the) gods, through whom by prayers I grasped all things from beginning to end and, repaying ungrudgingly the gifts, I exult. Gauros, son of Asklepiades, from Torea, (has erected) the statue from his own (money).

According to Paul, the gospel of the risen Son of God in power was 'promised beforehand through (God's) prophets in the Holy Scriptures' (Rom 1:2; 16:25-26). D. Georgi (*Theocracy in Paul's Praxis and Theology* [Minneapolis 1991: Gmn. orig. 1987], 87) argues that Rom 1:3-4 is 'an alternative to the social utopia of Caesarism'.

[82] Philo, *Leg.* 144-145. For a sensitive discussion of Philo's eulogy of Augustus, see D.L. Tiede, *Jesus and the Future* (Cambridge 1990), 25-26.

(ζωή: Rom 5:17b, 18b, 21b; εἰς πνεῦμα ζῳοποιοῦν: 1 Cor 15:45b) the new humanity experiences through Christ a restoration of the original righteousness of Eden (5:16b, 17b, 19b, 21b).[83] In contrast to the Priene inscription of Augustus, an eschatological reserve characterises Paul's εὐαγγέλιον.[84] With the advent of Augustus all regret is banished: the believer, however, waits in hope for the eschatological glory (Rom 5:2: 8:20, 24-25). But, given the inevitability of suffering (Rom 5:3-5; 8:18, 35-36), worldly and cosmic powers cannot separate the believer from the love of Christ (8:35-39), precisely because His death is the guarantee of God's beneficence towards His people (8:32: χαρίσεται).

In conclusion, although Paul formulates his understanding of the eschatological fullness of grace within a Jewish matrix, his presentation of Christ's work in Romans 5 and 8 might remind listeners of the eschatological motifs of Augustan beneficence, along with the implicit hint for contemporary auditors that Christ's generosity surpassed even that of the Caesars.[85]

6.1.2.5. Paul's metaphor of Christians as obligated beneficiaries in Romans 6:12-23 is drawn from the familia Caesaris

The obligations and rewards of Christians as slaves of God and Christ are subsumed under the motif of divine beneficence. Only recently have New Testament scholars considered the possibility that Paul is employing the slavery metaphor of Romans 6:12-23 within the wider context of Caesarian patronage. W.A. Meeks has made the valuable suggestion that the Pauline images of being 'a slave of God' or 'a slave of Christ' should be viewed against the backdrop of the *familia Caesaris* (that is, the slaves and freedmen of the emperor's household). In the view of Meeks, the slavery metaphor loses its stigma when it is remembered that many slaves of the emperor were 'exercising enormous power and even enjoying extraordinary, though reflected, honour'.[86] In the first century AD, many talented members of Caesar's household — regardless of their freedman or servile status[87] — acquired

---

[83] Righteousness was the characteristic of Eden and its inhabitants (1 *Enoch* 32.3; 60.8, 23; 70.3; 77.3).

[84] Note the comment of B. Eastman (*op. cit.*, 131): 'But grace is not only responsible for the gift of righteousness: there is an eschatological element, a "not-yet" aspect, to the fullness of grace'.

[85] F.W. Danker (*op. cit.*, 347): 'Such grace was beyond a Caesar Augustus'.

[86] W.A. Meeks, *The Origins of Christian Morality: The First Two Centuries* (New Haven and London 1993), 169. For full discussion, see P.R.C. Weaver, *Familia Caesaris: A Social Study of the Emperor's Freedmen and Slaves* (Cambridge 1972).

[87] Typically, Paul up-ends all distinctions in social status between the *Caesaris servus* (the slave of Caesar) and the *Augusti libertus* (the freedman of Augustus) as far as social

significant career opportunities in the emperor's personal staff, the Roman civil service, and the imperial estates.

Additionally, F. Lyall has argued that behind Romans 6:16-22 lies the metaphor of the yielding (6:13a, 16: παριστάνειν; 6:13b, 19: παριστάναι) or self-sale of individuals into slavery.[88] Although Lyall has correctly identified the method of enslavement behind the metaphor, he views Paul's imagery in too negative a light and thus distorts its function.[89] Lyall overlooks the fact that Paul thanks God (χάρις τῷ θεῷ) for the transfer of believers *as slaves* from sin to righteousness (Rom 6:17-19). If Paul's metaphor of two types of slavery (one positive, the other negative) is to be successful, it must resonate in its Roman social context.[90]

Romans 6:12-23 functions best as a social metaphor when we regard entry into the *familia Caesaris* as the background to vv.16b, 18b, 19b, 20b, 22b-23. It is entirely possible that there were Christians at Rome belonging the imperial household (Phil 4:22; Rom 16:11) — presuming, of course, a Roman origin for Philippians and that τοὺς ἐκ τῶν Ναρκίσσου refers to members

---

relationships between Christians (1 Cor 7:22).

[88] F. Lyall, *Slaves, Citizens, Sons: Legal Metaphors in the Epistles* (Philadelphia 1984), 33-35. Similarly, F.S. Malan, 'Bound to Do Right', *Neot* 15 (1981), 118-138. Note the reference of Tacitus (*Germ.*, 24) to the reckless gambling of the Germans: 'they stake personal liberty on a last and final throw: the loser faces voluntary slavery'.

[89] S.R. Llewelyn ('"Slaves obey your masters": The Legal Liability of Slaves', *New Docs* 7 [1994], 194) has correctly noted that slavery is spoken of as 'an evil force' in Rom 6:6b, 16a, 17a, 20a. But, contra Lyall and Malan (n.88 above), Paul portrays slavery positively in Rom 6:16b, 18b, 19b, 20b, 22b-23. In these verses, Paul focuses on the status and privilege of Christians as much as their obedience to righteousness. For discussion of positive portraits of slavery in Paul, see I.A. Combes, *The Metaphor of Slavery in the Writings of the Early Church From the New Testament to the Beginning of the Fifth Century* (Sheffield 1998), 83; M.J. Harris, *Slave of Christ: A New Testament Metaphor for Total Devotion to Christ* (Leicester 1999), 142-156. For Harris' discussion of Romans 6, see *ibid.*, 81-85. Note the comment of D.B. Martin (*Slavery as Salvation: The Metaphor of Slavery in Pauline Christianity* [New Haven 1990], 50): 'Paul's positive application of slavery to one's relationship to God (Romans 6) is not generally found in the moral philosophers'. Further, *ibid.*, 60-62. For a general discussion of slavery and freedom metaphors in Paul, see D.J. Williams, *Paul's Metaphors: Their Context and Character* (Peabody 1999), 111-140.

[90] J.L. White (*op. cit.*, 41-42 n.49) argues that Paul's description of slavery is inaccurate because the radically different results (death, eternal life) rob the image of verisimilitude. That Paul depicts slaves as being free to choose their master does not, in White's view, correspond to social reality. Admittedly, Paul does stretch the image well beyond its normal limits. But for the image to register both negatively and positively with his Roman auditors, Paul had to invest the image with (at the very least) a modicum of social authenticity. Furthermore, irrespective of Paul's intentions, his converts would have normally interpreted the positive slavery image within the imperial context they were familiar with at Rome. For example, Seneca's story about the compassionate treatment of Vedius Pollio's slave by Augustus, in contrast to his master's cruelty, would have been well known (T.W. Wiedemann, *Greek and Roman Slavery* (London and Canberra 1981), §190.

from the household of the wealthy freedman of Claudius, Narcissus.[91] Imperial slaves in the Roman house churches would surely have drawn a contrast between their slavery to God through their heavenly Lord (Rom 6:22-23; cf. 1:3-4) and their experience of slavery under Caesar the earthly Lord (cf. 1 Cor 2:6, 8; 8:5).[92]

Contemporaries knew well the lucrative rewards and status that accrued to those belonging to the *familia Caesaris*. For example, *P. Oxy.* 3312 mentions Hermaios — possibly a private citizen — who journeyed to Rome 'and became a freedman of Caesar in order to take appointments'.[93] We have already referred to the fawning respect accorded a cobbler by his former owner, Epaphroditus, when the same cobbler was subsequently admitted into Caesar's household.[94] However, for slaves outside the *familia Caesaris* there was much less scope for social advancement.[95] Epictetus portrays the abject situation of a manumitted slave who, although legally free, was now deprived of the patronage of his master.[96] Thus the greater the social status of the

---

[91] See M.J. Brown, 'Paul's Use of ΔΟΥΛΟΣ ΧΡΙΣΤΟΥ ΙΗΣΟΥ in Romans 1:1', *JBL* 120/4 (2001), 723-737. R.A. Horsley ('The Slave Systems of Classical Antiquity and Their Reluctant Recognition by Modern Scholars', *Semeia* 83/84 [1998], 59) is correct in saying that 'we have no idea whether such "saints" were menial or "managerial" slaves'. Whatever the status of believers in the *familia Caesaris*, the superior benefits of slavery to God and His righteousness — as enunciated by Paul in Romans 6 — must have stood in contrast to the benefits offered to those believers who were slaves of Caesar in Rome. Otherwise why did they risk attachment to a group that would soon be categorised a 'superstitio' by its Roman critics in AD 64 (Tacitus, *Ann.*, 15.44; Suetonius, *Ner.* 16.2)? S. Briggs ('Paul on Bondage and Freedom in Imperial Society', in R.A. Horsley [ed.], *Paul and Politics: Ekklesia, Israel, Imperium, Interpretation. Essays in Honor of Krister Stendahl* [Harrisburg 2000], 122-123) suggests that the early believers diluted the social stratification underpinning slavery and thereby unwittingly contributed to the Roman persecution of Christians in AD 64.

[92] Note the comment of M.J. Brown (*ibid.*, 735): 'Paul's strategy in this regard is rather clever. He appeals to them based on their own status as slaves of the emperor'.

[93] See the discussions of G.H.R. Horsley, 'Joining the Household of Caesar', *New Docs* 3 (1983), §1; E.A. Judge, *Rank and Status in the World of the Caesars and St. Paul* (University of Canterbury 1982), 18-20.

[94] Arr., *Epict. Diss.*, 1.19.32. See our discussion of Epictetus in §5.5.1.

[95] Philo (*Quod Omn. Prob.* 35) speaks generally of the promotion of slaves by their masters into positions of status and power. On first-century social mobility and voluntary slavery, see the discussion of B.W. Winter (*op. cit.*, 154-159), especially in relation to Petronius (*Sat.*, 57). Also, S.S. Bartchy, *First-Century Slavery and 1 Corinthians 7:21* (Atlanta 1971), 47-48; G. Theissen, *Social Reality and the Early Christians: Theology, Ethics, and the World of the New Testament* (Edinburgh 1992), 190-196. Lucian impugns the motives of educated Greeks who attached themselves to the households of the Roman elite (*On Salaried Posts in Great Houses*, 7-9). Although such Greeks acquired the status of belonging to the inner circle of the first household in the Roman Empire (*ibid.*, 20-21), Lucian quips that they are really slaves instead of freedmen (*ibid.*, 9, 23).

[96] Arr., *Epict. Diss.*, 4.1.33-38. For further discussion of the abject position of slaves generally, see R.A. Horsley, *art. cit.*, 19-66; O. Patterson, *Slavery and Social Death: A*

master, the greater were the career prospects for his slaves. Lucian affords us an insider's view of the substantial privileges that the members of Caesar's household and the Roman civil service possessed:

> ... there is a very great difference between entering a rich man's house as a hireling, where one is a slave and endures what my essay describes, and entering public service, where one administers affairs as well as possible and is paid by the Emperor (παρὰ βασιλέως) for doing it ... You are paid in both cases and are under a master's orders, but there is a world of difference ... In one case the slavery is obvious, and those who enter on these conditions are not much different from slaves, whether bought or bred at home, while those who handle public business and make themselves of service to states and whole provinces cannot rightly be criticised merely because they are paid, or be brought down to the same level of general denunciation.[97]

According to Paul, the munificence and status that God as Master confers upon His slaves renders obsolete the advantages of belonging to the *familia Caesaris*.[98] Christians, as the favoured slaves of God's household (Rom 6:16-18, 20-23), are no longer enslaved to the old Mosaic dominion of sin and death (6:12: μὴ βασιλευέτω; 6:14a: οὐ κυριεύσει; 6:14b, 15: οὐκ ὑπὸ νόμον). Instead, they experience a new dominion of grace (6:14, 15: ἀλλὰ ὑπὸ χάριν) because their divine Master has incorporated them into Christ's death and resurrection (6:3-11). Christ as Son has maintained loyalty to the dependants of His Father's household. He has delivered them from the enslaving powers of Adamic existence: Sin, Death, the Law, the Cosmic and Spirit forces (Rom 6:6, 10; 7:4; 8:38-39).[99] Furthermore, He has freed His

---

Comparative Study (Cambridge, Mass. 1982).

[97] Lucian's comments (*Apology*, 11) are partially skewed by his own defence against the charge of hypocrisy. He had accepted a salaried post in the Roman civil service of Egypt, although he was critical of such ambitions in *On Salaried Posts in Great Houses*.

[98] Note W. Meeks' comment (*The Moral World of the First Christians* [Philadelphia 1986], 128) that the metaphor of slavery to God was 'rare in Greek or Roman religious sentiment'. See, however, the famous discussion of A. Deissmann (*Light from the Ancient East* [2nd ed., 1927]; rpt. [Grand Rapids 1978], 319-331) on sacral manumission. Cf. Epictetus (Arr., *Epict. Diss.*, 1.19.9; cf. 4.7.20): 'Zeus has set me free. Or do you really think that he was likely to let his own son be made a slave?'. For criticism of Deissmann's proposal, see S.R. Llewelyn, 'The Slave of God (Rom 6:22) and Sacral Manumission', *New Docs* 6 (1992), 70-76.

[99] R.A. Horsley ('Paul and Slavery: A Critical Alternative to Recent Readings', *Semeia* 84/84 [1998], 173-176) argues that Paul's slavery metaphors in Romans 6 are not linked to the positive image of upward mobility found in the *familia Caesaris*. Rather Paul's portrait of humanity's slavery to superhuman forces (Sin, Death, Law) originates in the Israelite traditions of bondage to human rulers (Egypt, Rome). Conversely, the believer's freedom in Christ and slavery to God recalls the Exodus traditions that demanded a continuing covenantal obedience to God. Such LXX overtones may well be present. But the reality was that at Rome and throughout the Mediterranean basin Augustus was venerated as an eschatological liberator and dispenser of grace (§6.1.2.4), while his successors provided the possibility of lucrative career paths for their slaves. This imperial gospel demanded a decisive

beneficiaries for the service of righteousness (6:18: ἐδουλώθητε τῇ δικαιοσύνῃ; cf. 6:13b, 16b, 19b). As a result, the slaves of God's household exhibit gratitude (Rom 6:17; 7:24-25a: χάρις τῷ θεῷ; 14:6-7: εὐχαριστεῖ τῷ θεῷ) and obedience to their Master (6:12, 16, 17: ὑπακούειν; 6:16: ἡ ὑπακοή). As their Patron, God sponsors the new life of Christians (Rom 6:13: ἐκ νεκρῶν ζῶντας) and has graciously made provision for its transformation after death (6:23: τὸ χάρισμα τοῦ θεοῦ ζωὴ αἰώνιος ἐν Χριστῷ Ἰησοῦ).[100] Thus the eternal rewards that accrued to the obedient slaves of God's household are set by Paul over against the ephemeral rewards of the *familia Caesaris*.[101] The transfer of believers to a new Patron relativises the rulers of this age whose doom is sealed (cf. 1 Cor 2:6, 8; Rom 13:1-6, 11b-14).

The oaths of personal loyalty towards the Caesarian house, modelled on Hellenistic precedent,[102] may also be relevant here.[103] The loyalty oath of the Paphlagonians to Augustus and his descendants (6 March 3 BC), sworn by the inhabitants and Roman businessmen of the province, affirmed their goodwill towards the *imperator*. This involved a costly personal identification with the interests of Augustus and a radical reorientation of one's relationships and responsibilities:

I swear by Zeus, Earth, Sun, all the gods [and] goddesses, and Augus[t]us himself that I will

---

response from the apostle for the sake of his Roman auditors. Therefore it is difficult to believe that Paul's language of grace and slavery metaphors, as formulated in Romans 5-6, is not in part aimed at pricking the inflated soteriological claims of the Caesars.

[100] German and French commentators on Romans have compared χάρισμα in Rom 6:23 with the *donativum* or bounty dispensed by a victorious general or new emperor. See T. Zahn (Leipzig 1910, 326); F.J. Leenhardt (London 1961, 175), U. Wilckens (Zürich 1980, 40 n.154). G.P. Wetter (*Charis: Ein Beitrag zur Geschichte des ältesten Christentums* [Leipzig 1913], 23) points out that in Rom 6:23 'Tertullian übersetzt χάρισμα mit *donativum*'. See also J. Wobbe, *op. cit.*, 61; C. Spicq, *op. cit.*, 460 n.6; U. Brockhaus, *Charisma und Amt: Die paulinische Charismenlehre auf dem Hintergrund der frühchristlichen Gemeindefunktionen* (Wuppertal 1972), 132-133 n.23. O. Michel (*op. cit.*, 216 n.18) cites a variety of sources as background: Tacitus, *Ann.* 1.8; 12.41; 14.11; Suetonius, *Aug.*, 10; *Claud.*, 10; *Ner.*, 7; Dio Cassius 56.32.2; 59.2.1ff; Josephus, *AJ* 19.247.

[101] Note the astute observation of A. Deissmann (*op. cit.*, 376): '(δοῦλος Χριστοῦ) certainly aroused sensations of contrast when heard beside the frequent title of "slave of the Emperor"'.

[102] See M. Hammond, 'Hellenistic Influences on the Structure of the Augustan Principate', *Memoirs of the American Academy in Rome* 17 (1949), 7-10. For examples of Hellenistic oaths towards Antiochus I/II and Seleucus II, see respectively S.M. Burstein (*The Hellenistic Age from the Battle of Ipsos to the Death of Kleopatra VII* [Cambridge 1985], §22) and R.S. Bagnall and P. Derow ([eds], *Greek Historical Documents: The Hellenistic Period* [Chico 1981], §29B).

[103] For discussion of the Caesarian oaths, see E.A. Judge, *The Social Pattern of Christian Groups in the First Century* (London 1960), 34-35; *id.*, 'The Decrees of Caesar at Thessalonica', *Reformed Theological Review* 30/1 (1971), 5-7.

be favourably disposed toward [Caes]ar Augustus (εὐνοή[σειν Καί]σαρι Σεβαστῶι) and his children and descendants all the time of my [life] in word and deed and thought, considering as friends those whom they may consider (friends) and holding as enemies those whom they may judge to be (enemies), and for things that are of interest to them I will spare neither my body [nor] my soul nor my life nor my children, but in every way for the things that affect them I undergo every danger; and whatever I might perceive or hear against them being said or plotted or done, I will report it and I will be an enemy to the person saying or plotting or doing [any of] these things; and whomever they may judge to be their enemies, these, on land and sea, with arms and steel I will pursue and ward off.[104]

This oath concludes with an invocation of total destruction upon those who break its terms, including their descendants: 'may neither the [bodies] of my family and of my descendants by earth or [sea] be received, nor may (earth or sea) bear fruit (μηδὲ καρποὺς) [for them]'.[105] Even more interesting are the additions made to the stereotyped format in the Cypriot loyalty oath to Tiberius. As E.A. Judge observes, the Cypriot pledge of goodwill includes vows of obedience and reverence towards the new emperor:

We, ourselves and our Children, [swear] to harken unto (ὑπακούσεσθαι) and to obey (πειθαρχήσειν) alike by land and sea, with regard to loyalty (εὐνοήσειν) and to worship (σεβάσεσθαι) Tiberius Caesar Augustus, son of Augustus, with all his house, to have the same friends and the same foes as they ...[106]

The foregoing loyalty oaths are not specifically related to the *familia Caesaris* or to the institution of slavery. However, Epictetus cites the oath of Nicopolis to the Caesars as an ironic confession of slavery. In a discourse on freedom, Epictetus pictures an imaginary interlocutor of consular rank expostulating: 'But who can put me under compulsion, except Caesar, the lord of all?'. Epictetus replies:

There, you have yourself admitted that you have one master. And let it not comfort you that he is, as you say, the common master of all men, but realise that you are a slave in a great house. So also the men of Nicopolis are wont to shout: "Yea, by the fortune of Caesar, we are free men!"[107]

---

[104] See V. Ehrenberg and A.H.M. Jones, *op. cit.*, §315. Augustus (*Res Gestae* 25) speaks of all Italy voluntarily taking an oath of allegiance to himself as ἡγεμῶν after Actium. For the arrangements of Samos concerning a loyalty oath towards Augustus, see P. Herrmann, *Der römische Kaisereid* (Göttingen 1968), 125-126 §6. For Latin and Greek loyalty oaths towards Caligula, see *ibid.*, 122-123 §1, §3.

[105] V. Ehrenberg and A.H.M. Jones, *op. cit.*, §315 *ll*.33-35.

[106] E.A. Judge, *art. cit.*, 7. For a discussion of the decree, T.B. Mitford, 'A Cypriot Oath of Allegiance to Tiberius', *JRS* 50 (1960), 75-79. H.L. Hendrix ('On the Form and Ethos of Ephesians', *USQR* 42/4 [1988], 8) has argued that the 'obligated beneficiary' motif, found in the Cypriot oath and *Res Gestae* 25, explains the moral demands of Ephesians 4-6.

[107] Arr., *Epict. Diss.*, 4.1.12-14. In regard to the Nicopolis oath W.A. Oldfather, the Loeb translator of Epictetus (Vol.1 Cambridge [Mass.] and London 1925, 249 n.1), pithily comments: 'The very form of the oath contradicts the statement made'.

Therefore it is important to ask what contrast Paul's Roman audience may have drawn between the loyalty demanded by the Caesars and that of God or Christ as Master.[108] As already noted, Paul heavily underscores in Romans 6 the importance for God's δοῦλοι to obey Him as Master. In the loyalty oath of the Paphlagonians the inhabitants of the province swear loyalty to Augustus in thought, word and deed; in similar fashion, Paul praises God that the Romans have become obedient from the heart to the apostolic teaching (Rom 6:17: ὑπηκούσατε ἐκ καρδίας; cf. 10:16; 15:18; 2 Cor 2:9; Phil 2:12; 2 Thess 1:8, 3:14).

But, whereas the Paphlagonian loyalty oath exclusively focuses upon the unfruitfulness (μηδὲ καρπούς) that disobedience to Caesar brings, Paul contrasts the unfruitfulness of sin (Rom 6:21: τίνα καρπόν εἴχετε;) with the fruitfulness of a sanctified life (6:22 [cf. 6:19b]: τὸν καρπὸν ὑμῶν εἰς ἁγιασμόν).[109] Over against the Cypriot loyalty oath, Paul does not use σεβάσεσθαι for obedience to God, presumably on account of its lexical connection with the Caesar cult (Σεβαστός). Significantly, its sole New Testament occurrence refers to false worship (Rom 1:25: ἐσεβάσθησαν).

Moreover, Paul would have agreed with Epictetus that the much-vaunted freedom under the lordship of the Caesars was illusory.[110] The freedom of the virtuous man was a frequent *topos* in the popular philosophers, with the slavery metaphor the common parlance for *impediments* to moral virtue. But Paul turns the metaphor of slavery to God and His righteousness (6:18b: ἐδουλώθητε τῇ δικαιοσύνῃ; 6:22a: δουλωθέντες τῷ θεῷ) into a *positive* image of freedom from sin and death (Rom 6:18a, 22a: ἐλευθερωθέντες).[111] In sharp contrast, Philo totally avoids the language of slavery to God in his discussion of the free man. He opts for the term 'friend of God' (an echo of *amicus Caesaris*?).[112] The reason for Philo's choice is plain: 'no one is

---

[108] Note the comment of R.W. Pickett (*art. cit.*, 735-736): 'For Paul God is the ultimate patron who as creator expects exclusive loyalty (πίστις) from humanity'.

[109] See the excellent discussion of D.B. Martin, *op. cit.*, 60-62. Note how Paul links χάρις τοῦ θεοῦ with the imagery of fruitfulness in Col 1:6 (1:6a: καρποφορούμενος; 1:10b: καρποφοροῦντες).

[110] In addition to the oath of Nicopolis, note the boast of Augustus (*Res Gestae* 1): 'I restored liberty ([ἠλευ]θέ[ρωσα]; *libertatem*) to the republic, which had been oppressed by the tyranny (δουλήας) of a faction'.

[111] In the popular philosophers there are many examples of slavery metaphors that are used of *impediments* to virtue. E.g. the treatises of Dio Chrysostom (*Or.* 14-15); Epictetus (Arr., *Epict. Diss.*, 4.1); Philo (*Quod Omn. Prob.*, passim). Additionally, Cicero, *Paradoxa Stoicorum* 33-41; Pseudo-Crates, *Ep.*, 34.3; Pseudo-Heraclitus, *Ep.*, 9.5-8); Pseudo-Cebes, *Tabula* 9, 22 (cf. Lucian, *On Salaried Posts in Great Houses*, 42).

[112] Philo, *Quod Omn. Prob.*, 42.

willingly a slave'.¹¹³ Paul's stance is different: the Spirit of Jesus liberates believers from servile fear by testifying to their sonship and to their eschatological inheritance as co-heirs of Christ (Rom 8:14-17). For Paul — and undoubtedly for his readers — the paradox is that they remain slaves to righteousness (Rom 6:16-18).

Overall, Paul eschews the stylised conventions of loyalty oaths when exhorting his converts to submit to the moral demands of grace.¹¹⁴ One simple reason may have been that the ethical motivation behind the Caesarian oaths is driven by εὔνοια.¹¹⁵ It is a far cry from the soteriological and pneumatological basis of Paul's ethics. Further, many of the Caesarian oaths are cultic, sworn as they were 'in the temple of Augustus by the [altar of] Augustus'.¹¹⁶ I suspect, too, that the punitive stipulations invoked as part of the oath-making ritual may have caused a certain theological unease for Paul. God's faithfulness to His household is not conditioned by human loyalty or disloyalty. According to Paul, the acceptance (Eph 2:8-9) *and* the maintenance of salvation (1 Cor 1:4, 8-9; cf. Phil 1:6) originates solely in the grace of God: it is effected by the faith-union of believers with their Lord and by the continuous work of His Spirit in their lives.¹¹⁷ It is as a reminder of

---

¹¹³ *Ibid.*, 36. Note the ambivalence of Seneca (*De Prov.*, 5.6): 'nor am I God's slave, but I give my assent to Him'.

¹¹⁴ In sharp contrast to Paul, Epictetus (*Epict. Diss.*, 1.14.15-17) draws an extended comparison between loyalty to a beneficent God and the loyalty oath that soldiers swore to Caesar: 'to this God you also ought to swear allegiance, as the soldiers do to Caesar ... and shall you, indeed, who have been counted worthy of blessings so numerous and so great be unwilling to swear, or, when you have sworn, to abide by your oath? And what shall you swear? Never to disobey under any circumstances, never to prefer charges, never to find fault with anything that God has given, never to let your will rebel when you have either to do or to suffer something that is inevitable' (*ibid.*, 16).

¹¹⁵ On the sparsity of εὐ-compounds — widespread in the eulogistic inscriptions — in the New Testament, see E.A. Judge, 'Moral Terms in the Eulogistic Tradition', *New Docs* 2 (1982), 105-106.

¹¹⁶ V. Ehrenberg and A.H.M. Jones, *op. cit.*, §315.

¹¹⁷ C.F.D. Moule, 'Jesus, Judaism, and Paul' in G.F. Hawthorne and O. Betz (eds), *Tradition and Interpretation in the New Testament: Essays in Honor of E. Earle Ellis for His 60th Birthday* (Grand Rapids 1987), 48. On Phil 1:6, see J.M. Gundry Volf, *Paul and Perseverance: Staying In and Falling Away* (Tübingen 1990), 33-47. Elsewhere C.F.D. Moule writes ('Obligation in the Ethic of Paul', in *id.*, *Essays in New Testament Interpretation* [Cambridge 1982], 265-266): 'It is not that grace abolishes law, but that dependence on grace, instead of the attitude of legalism, is the only way to fulfil God's law. There is obligation, but it is to grace, not law'. Further, G.M. Styler, 'The Basis of Obligation in Paul's Christology and Ethics', in B. Lindars and S.S. Smalley (eds), *Christ and Spirit in the New Testament: Studies in Honour of C.F.D. Moule* (Cambridge 1973), 175-187. Similarly, P. Enns, 'Expansions of Scripture', in D.A. Carson (*et al.*, ed.), *Justification and Variegated Nomism. Volume 1 — The Complexities of Second Temple Judaism* (Tübingen 2001), 97-98. In endorsing the position of C.F.D. Moule, I signal my disagreement with E.P. Sanders regarding Paul's assurance of salvation. In the view of

this central truth that Paul concludes all his letters with the χάρις benediction.[118]

We will now consider Paul's presentation of divine χάρις in an Eastern Mediterranean context. How does Paul adapt his theology of grace to the cultural situation of the Ephesian Christians living in the Roman East?

6.1.3. Graeco-Roman benefaction and the age of grace: Paul and the eastern Mediterranean Christians

6.1.3.1. Paul's doctrine of grace in Ephesians is directed against local manifestations of counterfeit spirituality at Ephesus

In our discussion of the magical papyri, we observed that a spread of benefaction ideology (including χάρις) was employed by practitioners of the occult to secure χάριτες and δύναμις outside of the mainstream benefaction system. χάρις also possessed independent pneumatic status as one of the

---

Sanders (*Paul and Palestinian Judaism: A Comparison of Patterns of Religion* [London 1977], 517-518), Paul's position is — in line with Palestinian Judaism — that one is *saved by* God's elective grace *and stays in* by works of the law. However, the Pauline texts that Sanders cites do not substantiate his emphasis on law as the means of sanctification for the believer. First, the continuance of the believer envisaged by Paul in Rom 11:22 is not motivated by works of the law but rather by God's kindness (χρηστότης θεοῦ). Second, the righteousness that distinguishes the lifestyle of believers from their Graeco-Roman contemporaries (1 Cor 6:9-11) flows from their new identity in Christ and in the Spirit (6:11; cf. 19-20) as opposed to works of the law. Third, the obedience envisaged in Gal 5:21 is clearly driven by the Spirit (Gal 5:5, 16-18, 22, 25; 6:8; cf. 3:2-5; Rom 8:4-5), by love as the fulfilment of the law (Gal 5:6b, 13b-14, 22; 6:2; cf. Rom 13:8-10), and by the continuing impact of Christ's redemptive death (Gal 5:1-5a, 11, 24; 6:14; cf. 3:1; Rom 8:3-4a). In each of the above cases, the continuing obedience of believers has a distinctive edge that surpasses anything found in Palestinian Judaism. Ultimately, in my opinion, Sanders' proposal diminishes the role of Spirit as the guarantee and dynamic of the obedience of believers (J.M. Gundry Volf, *op. cit.*, 27-33; F.F. Bruce, *Paul: Apostle of the Free Spirit* [Exeter 1977], 188-211). Given the enslaving role of the law, as enlisted by sin (Rom 5:20; 6:14; 7:8-13; 1 Cor 15:56; Gal 4:3, 9-10, 21-31), only the law of the Spirit of life can bring to completion the just requirements of the law in the life of the believer (Rom 7:6; 8:2, 4, 5b, 6b, 13b). See especially R.B. Sloan, 'Paul and the Law: Why the Law Cannot Save', *NovT* 33/1 (1991), 35-60. Further, Sanders insufficiently emphasises the fact that Paul, in locating believers in the eschatological reign of grace (Rom 5:21; 6:14), extends this not only to their *entry* into God's covenantal community but also to their *continued walk* in righteousness (§6.1.2.4—§6.1.2.5). Thus, along with R.Y.K. Fung and several others ('The Status of Justification by Faith in Paul's Thought: A Brief Survey of a Modern Debate', *Themelios* 6/3 [1981], 4-11), I would propose that justification by grace — along with the eschatological dimension of *Heilsgeschichte* as an important addition to the traditional Reformation perspective — still remains the centre of Paul's theological message. Contra Sanders, see also T. Deidun, 'E.P. Sanders: An Assessment of Two Recent Works. 1. "Having His Cake and Eating It"', *HeyJ* 17 (1986), 43-52; R.H. Gundry, 'Grace, Works, and Staying Saved in Paul', *Biblica* 66/1 (1985), 1-38.

[118] Rom 16:20, 24; 1 Cor 16:23; 2 Cor 13:13; Gal 6:18; Eph 6:24; Phil 4:23; Col 4:18; 1 Thess 5:28; 2 Thess 3:18; 1 Tim 6:21; 2 Tim 4:22; Titus 3:15; Phlm 25.

voces magicae.[119] It is therefore possible that Paul's theology of grace, as formulated in Ephesians, is directed against the influence that magic and the Artemis cult wielded in Ephesus and throughout the province of Asia. Admittedly, the converted magicians who belonged to the Ephesian house churches had made a decisive break with the past by burning their magical books (Acts 19:19). But the threat posed by occult competition was real. There were periodic visits of itinerant Jewish and Greek exorcists,[120] the fame of the *ephesia grammata* ('Ephesian Letters'),[121] the celebrated power of Ephesian Artemis over magic,[122] and (relatedly) the presence of the Lydian-Phrygian and Artemis mysteries.[123] This would have ensured a continuing struggle for Paul against several forms of counterfeit spirituality.

It is worth remembering that Paul links χάρις with the language of glory (Eph 1:6a; cf. 6b: χαριτοῦν), wealth (1:7; 2:7), mystery (3:2-3) and power (3:7) — themes that appear throughout Ephesians.[124] This can hardly be coincidental when it is remembered that the same motifs are found in the

---

[119] See §3.6.1—§3.6.3.

[120] Acts 19:13-17; Philostratus, *Vita Apol.*, 4:10-11.

[121] For discussion of the six Ephesian magical terms, see C.C. McCown, 'The Ephesia Grammata in Popular Belief', *TAPhA* 54 (1923), 128-140; C.E. Arnold, *Ephesians: Power and Magic. The Concept of Power in Ephesians in Light of its Historical Setting* (Cambridge 1989), 15-16.

[122] The superiority of Artemis over magical power is seen in an inscription from Koloe (F. Graf, 'An Oracle against Pestilence from a Western Anatolian Town', *ZPE* 92 [1992], 267-279). The oracle of Apollo suggests, as a remedy for a local outbreak of pestilence, that the community place an image of Artemis from Ephesus in a temple. As the oracle elaborates, Artemis 'will provide deliverance from your affliction and will dissolve the poison (or: 'magic') of pestilence, which destroys men, and will melt down with her flame-bearing torches in nightly fire the kneaded works of wax, the signs of the evil art of a sorcerer'.

[123] G.H.R. Horsley, 'Petition Concerning Ephesian Mysteries', *New Docs* 4 (1987), §22; R.A. Kearsley, 'The Mysteries of Artemis at Ephesus', *New Docs* 6 (1992), §29. On the Artemis mysteries, see R.A. Kearsley, *ibid.*, 201-202. Note also Vedia, a priestess of Artemis and a descendant of asiarchs (*I. Ephesos* VII[1] 3072; cf. Acts 19:31), who 'completed the mysteries on account of her father Gaius and of her family worthily'. In regard to Acts 19:31, L.W. Countryman ('Welfare in the Churches of Asia Minor under the Early Roman Empire', in P.J. Achtemeier [ed.], *Society of Biblical Literature 1979 Seminar Papers* [Missoula 1979], 143) views the episode as a case of the intervention of powerful patrons on behalf of Paul.

[124] Glory terminology: δόξα (Eph 1:6, 12, 14, 17, 18; 3:13, 16, 21); ἔνδοξος (5:21). Wealth terminology: πλούσιος (2:4); πλοῦτος (1:7, 18; 2:7; 3:8, 16). Mystery terminology: μυστήριον (1:9; 3:3, 4, 9; 5:32; 6:19). Power terminology: δύναμις (1:19; 3:7, 20); ἐξουσία (1:21; 2:2; 3:10; 6:12); ἀρχή (1:21; 3:10; 6:12). C. Spicq (*op. cit.*, 112 n.4) observes that χαριτοῦν is ignored by Philo, the inscriptions, and the papyri. Also Spicq (*op. cit.*, 119 n.6) notes that in Paul's epistles χάρις and δύναμις are frequently synonymous, adding later on that Philo identifies χάριτες and δυνάμεις (*op. cit.*, 129 n.6; cf. Philo, *Abr.* 54).

magical papyri and in the Ephesian inscriptions of Artemis and the mysteries. Ephesian auditors of Paul would have been alert to their prominence. First, we have previously drawn attention to several magical papyri that request glory in conjunction with χάρις, either as a triad (σωτηρία, εὐδοξία, χάρις) or as a pairing (δόξα, χάρις).[125] Glory terminology is also a feature of the Artemis inscriptions. Artemis, the designated leader of the Ephesians, had made Ephesus 'the most illustrious (ἐνδοξοτέραν) of all cities through her divine nature'. On account of the piety displayed towards Artemis during the sacred month Artemision, the goddess reciprocates by ensuring that Ephesus will be 'more illustrious ([ἐ]δοξοτέρα) and more blessed for all time'.[126]

Second, we have noted how *PGM* VIII 16-20 summons Hermes to make benefactors unreservedly generous in their beneficence. Similarly, the wealth deposited in the Temple of Artemis was proverbial (Dio Chrysostom, *Or.* 31.54).[127] An Ephesian proconsular decree (*I. Eph.* 1a.18b: AD 44), which forbids the embezzlement of the temple funds, boasts of 'the abundance of revenues restored by Augustus to the goddess'. The industries that the Temple of Artemis spawned also provided lucrative incomes for the Ephesian citizens (Acts 19:23-25).

Third, G.P. Wetter has pointed out long ago that χάρις often occurs in conjunction with δύναμις in the magical papyri,[128] whereas more recently C.E. Arnold has comprehensively covered the power ideology underlying the Artemis cult.[129] Especially significant is the power of Artemis over the onslaughts of astrological Fate, celebrated in the iconography of the cult statue of the goddess.[130] How does this relate to Paul's doctrine of grace in Ephesians?

---

[125] See our discussion in §3.6.

[126] R.E. Oster, 'Holy Days in Honour of Artemis', *New Docs* 4 (1987), §19. Also, R.A. Kearsley, 'Ephesus: *Neokoros* of Artemis', *New Docs* 6 (1992), §30. See the two important articles of R.E. Oster, 'The Ephesian Artemis as an Opponent of Early Christianity', *JAC* 19 (1976), 27-44; *id.*, 'Ephesus as a Religious Centre under the Principate, I. Paganism before Constantine', *ANRW* II 18/3 (1990), 1661-1728. C. Spicq (*op. cit.*, 133 n.1) draws attention to the formula νικήσας ἐνδόξως, found in the *agonistic* inscriptions, as 'une «mention» attribueé à la carrière «brillante» des athlètes victorieux'.

[127] On the economics of Artemis, see P. Trebilco, 'Asia', in D.W.J. Gill and C. Gempf (eds), *The Book of Acts: Volume 2. Graeco-Roman Setting* (Carlisle 1994), 324-326. Note the hymn of Isis (*SEG* VIII 550 [*ll.*21-22]: I cent. AD) which refers to the 'men to whom you have granted wealth (πλοῦτόν) and great blessings (χάριτας μεγάλας)'.

[128] See our references to G.P. Wetter, *op. cit.*, in §3.1.1; §3.6. Also, J. Nolland, 'Grace as Power', *NovT* 28/1 (1986), 26-31.

[129] C.E. Arnold, *op. cit.*, 21ff.

[130] See R.E. Oster, *art. cit.* (1987), 81; P. Trebilco, *art. cit.*, 318 n.129.

H. Hendrix has convincingly argued that the opening blessing of Ephesians (Eph 1:3-14) fits the genre of the honorific decree in its 'expansive recital of divine benefactions'.[131] More fundamentally, Paul tailors his presentation of divine beneficence (χάρις) to counter the rival claims of magic and Artemis as benefactors of the Ephesians. The glory of God's freely-given grace (Eph 1:6a: εἰς ἔπαινον δόξης τῆς χάριτος; 1:6b: ἐχαρίτωσεν; cf. 2 Thess 1:12) is displayed in His predestinating love (Eph 1:4-5; Rom 8:29). This would provide security for Ephesian believers who, in their pre-conversion state, had feared the ravages of astrological Fate (Eph 6:10-20). Further, whereas *only* the city of Ephesus is made ἐδοξοτέρα through the benefaction of Artemis,[132] an international community of citizens (Eph 2:11-16, 19) is now made ἔνδοξος through the benefaction of Christ (5:27).[133]

Since the Ephesians have been included in God's vindication of Christ (Eph 1:20-21) — made alive, raised, and seated in the heavenly realms (1:3; 2:5-6) — they experience the riches of divine grace, in the present and in the coming age (1:7: τὸ [2:7: ὑπερβάλλον] πλοῦτος τῆς χάριτος; cf. 1 Cor 1:4-5a). In contrast to the 'prosperity theology' of the magical papyri and the Artemis cult, God lavishes soteriological wealth on His beneficiaries by redeeming and forgiving them in Christ (Eph 1:7; 4:32 [cf. Col 2:13: χαρισάμενος; 3:13b: ἐχαρίσατο]). For Paul, God's beneficence cannot be manipulated by either ritualistic magic or sacrificial cult (Eph 2:8b: οὐκ ἐξ ὑμῶν; 2:9a: οὐκ ἐξ ἔργων; cf. 2 Tim 1:9). God, as a loving and merciful Benefactor (Eph 2:4), acts in grace to deliver His dependants from their sin and passions (2:5, 8: χάριτί ἐστε σεσῳσμένοι; cf. Titus 2:11).[134] Ultimately, even the faith of God's dependants (Eph 2:8: διὰ πίστεως) is a divine gift and not an occasion for boasting (2:8b-9: θεοῦ τὸ δῶρον).

Paul's own ministry at Ephesus was an expression of God's beneficence (Eph 3:2a, 7a: τὴν οἰκονομίαν [v.7a: τὴν δωρεὰν] τῆς χάριτος τοῦ θεοῦ; 3:8a: ἡ χάρις) and power (3:7b: τὴν ἐνέργειαν τῆς δυνάμεως αὐτοῦ; cf. 2 Tim 2:1). As an apostle, Paul had made known the mystery of God's eschatological plan of salvation (Eph 1:9-10; 3:2-4, 8-9; 5:32; 6:19: τὸ

---

[131] H.L. Hendrix, *art. cit.*, 8. Similarly, F.W. Danker, *op. cit.*, 451.

[132] On the beneficence of Artemis, see G.H.R. Horsley, 'Giving Thanks to Artemis', *New Docs* 4 (1987), §28; P. Trebilco, *art. cit.*, 317.

[133] R.E. Oster, *art. cit.* (1987), 78.

[134] S.C. Mott (*The Greek Benefactor and Deliverance from Moral Distress* [unpub. Ph.D. diss. Harvard University 1971], 37) claims that nowhere in the ruler cult 'is a ruler addressed as σωτήρ with reference to providing immortality or providing refuge from sin or the passions'. However, Horace, *Carm.*, 4.5.16-24 (above) comes close in regard to refuge from sin. See too S.K. Stowers, *op. cit.*, 55ff on self-mastery and the virtues in the Augustan revolution.

μυστήριον). R.A. Kearsley has claimed that Paul may be contrasting the 'plan of the mystery' (Eph 3:9: οἰκονομία τοῦ μυστηρίου) — revealed in the universal gospel of Christ (1:10; 3:6; 6:19) — with the Lydian-Phrygian mysteries, in order to counter their influence on the Asian churches.[135] Even if Paul is primarily drawing from the LXX (Dan 2:28-29: ὁ ἀνακαλύπτων μυστήρια), his Ephesian audience would in all probability have transferred the theological inference anyway. Paul, as the steward of God's grace (Eph 3:2), heralds for the Gentiles the total superiority of God's revelation over the mysteries at Ephesus (3:8: τὸ ἀνεξιχνίαστον πλοῦτος τοῦ Χριστοῦ).[136]

Simultaneously, the grace which animates Paul's ministry is an expression of God's δύναμις (Eph 3:7). Paul has already referred to the 'immeasurable greatness' (τὸ ὑπερβάλλον μέγεθος) of God's resurrection δύναμις at work in the Ephesians' lives (Eph 1:19). It is entirely possible that Paul has chosen this μέγα-cognate to contrast the life-giving power of the risen Christ with the so-called 'greatness' of Artemis (Acts 19:27-28, 34-35: μεγάλη).[137] Certainly the Ephesian converts who had dabbled in the magical arts would have been left in no doubt about the power of God's grace in their lives: it was the same resurrection power that had installed Christ as Lord over the underworld powers (Eph 1:19-21; Phil 2:9-10: ἐχαρίσατο).

Finally, as a brief sidelight to Ephesians, Paul does not view the power of grace as either triumphalism or the preserve of a secret society. This is clear from Paul's response to the factions within the Corinthian church who had misunderstood and misrepresented him as their benefactor (2 Cor 11:7-11; 12:11-19). Paul inverts traditional benefaction ideology and hellenistic rhetorical *topoi* in portraying himself as the endangered servant-benefactor of the Corinthian church (11:16-33).[138] Although a figure of weakness in the view of some (2 Cor 10:9-10), the apostle had discovered the sufficiency of divine grace in the midst of suffering and social dishonour (2 Cor 12:8-10).[139]

---

[135] R.A. Kearsley, *art. cit.* ('Mysteries', 1992), 202.

[136] While J. Wobbe (*op. cit.*, 96) maintains that χάρις was not a technical term of the mystery cults, he observes that the full content of divine grace was clear only to Christians. Christians, as Wobbe continues, proclaimed 'das große Geheimnis des Christentums' that had been unveiled in Christ.

[137] BAGD (Chicago 1979²) tentatively suggests a link between the Ephesian inscriptions (e.g. *I. Ephesos* Ia. 27 [*ll.*224-225, 324: μεγίστη]) and μέγεθος in Eph 1:19. For additional references, see P. Trebilco, *art. cit.*, 318 n.129.

[138] See our discussion in §7.4.2.

[139] J. Wobbe (*op. cit.*, 72) contends that ἡ χάρις μου (2 Cor 12:9a) and ἡ δύναμις τοῦ Χριστοῦ (12:9b) are synonymous. In Wobbe's view, this spotlights the power of divine grace available to Paul for the accomplishment of his apostolic work. Granted the parallelism that exists between vv.9a and 9b, Wobbe's proposal partially misrepresents Paul's power-weakness dynamic: for Paul (a) divine grace is simultaneously experienced as power *and*

The paradox is that Christ's grace (χάρις) is experienced as weakness (ἀσθένεια) and power (δύναμις) in the present aeon, in conformity with the paradigm of Christ's crucifixion and resurrection (2 Cor 13:4a).

The apostle knows the weakness of the crucified Christ (2 Cor 13:4a: ἡμεῖς ἀσθενοῦμεν ἐν αὐτῷ; 4:10a, 11a, 12a; Phil 3:10b; 1 Cor 15:31) when he suffers for the gospel or undergoes reversal in social status (I Cor 4:9-13; 2 Cor 6:4-10). The grace of Christ, experienced in weakness, divests Paul of boastful self-reliance (2 Cor 1:8-9; 12:7a) and provides him the right perspective on his apostolic accomplishments and spirituality (10:13-18; 11:9-11, 16-33; 12:1-10). Elsewhere, Paul refers to the Philippians as partakers of grace with him (Phil 1:7: συγκοινωνούς μου τῆς χάριτος) because they too had been granted the privilege of suffering for Christ (1:29: ὑμῖν ἐχαρίσθη τὸ ὑπὲρ Χριστοῦ ... πάσχειν).

Simultaneously, Paul knows the power of the risen Christ (2 Cor 13:4b: ζήσομεν σὺν αὐτῷ ἐκ δυνάμεως θεοῦ: cf. 4:10b, 11b, 12b; Phil 3:10a) even when Satan mimics aspects of the apostle's ministry at Corinth (2 Cor 11:3, 13-15) or tries to deflect him from his appointed course by means of the (unspecified) 'thorn in the flesh' (12:7). The grace of Christ, experienced as divine power, conquers the sophistry of Paul's opponents (2 Cor 10:3-6: δυνατὰ τῷ θεῷ; 11:6), provides the confirmatory signs of true apostleship (12:12: δυνάμεσιν), and strengthens Paul in his resolve to discipline any unrepentant Corinthians (12:20-13:10; cf. 13:3: δυνατεῖ ἐν ὑμῖν).[140]

6.1.3.2. Paul and the honorific inscriptions stress the obligation of beneficiaries to respond worthily of their benefactor

We have seen how Paul sketches for Roman Christians their responsibilities as slaves of righteousness against the backdrop of the *familia Caesaris*. The same theological principle is formulated for eastern Mediterranean Christians within the conventions of the honorific inscriptions. According to Paul, the acceptance of divine beneficence imposes an obligation to live worthily of the Benefactor.[141] In ancient benefaction ideology there was emphasis upon the

---

weakness (12:10b) and (b) divine power is perfected *in* weakness (12:9b; 13:4a; cf. 1 Cor 1:25b).

[140] See especially the discussions of C.K. Barrett, *The Signs of an Apostle* (Philadelphia 1972); J.H. Schütz, *Paul and the Anatomy of Apostolic Authority* (Cambridge 1975), 238-248; D.A. Black, *Paul, Apostle of Weakness: Astheneia and Its Cognates in the Pauline Literature* (New York 1984), 129-172; J. Jervell, 'The Signs of an Apostle: Paul's Miracles', in *id.*, *The Unknown Paul* (Minneapolis 1984), 77-95. For an insightful discussion of the relationship of power to grace in 2 Cor 12:9, see B. Eastman, *op. cit.*, 45-46.

[141] In this respect, note the telling comment of E. Käsemann (*art. cit.*, 170): 'Paul knows no gift of God which does not convey both the obligation and the capacity to serve'.

necessity of appropriate behaviour towards the benefactor. In 197 BC Queen Laodike III, wife of Antiochus III, reminded the people of Iasos of the responsibility that her benefactions entailed: 'as for you, you should act toward my brother and our house in general as is proper and be mindful of all our benefactions'.[142] Benefactors such as Phainios of Gytheion (AD 41—42) advised the Spartans against the folly of neglecting his grace.[143] An anonymous first-century benefactor warned his community that should the citizens hinder the erection of his monument — and the allocation of associated honours — they would incur the wrath of the gods because they had been forgetful of his favour.[144]

In the wider Pauline corpus there emerges a strong sense of one's moral indebtedness to God as Benefactor. As an apostle, Paul had been placed under obligation by his Benefactor both to Greeks and barbarians (Rom 1:14: ὀφειλέτης εἰμί; cf. 15:15-21: τὴν χάριν τὴν δοθεῖσάν μοι ὑπὸ τοῦ θεοῦ; Gal 1:15-16: καλέσας διὰ τῆς χάριτος αὐτοῦ). In speaking to the Corinthian believers, Paul magnifies the fact that God's grace (χάρις) had not been displayed in vain (1 Cor 15:10a: οὐ κενή). What he was as a person (15:10a) and the very industry of his apostleship amply testified to the grace at work in his life (15:10b).[145] Later, Paul pleads with the Corinthians not to accept God's grace in vain (2 Cor 6:1: εἰς κενὸν τὴν χάριν τοῦ θεοῦ; cf. Gal 3:4-5). As R.P. Martin assesses the situation, the frustration of grace on the part of the Corinthian converts 'is an example of (their) ingratitude for God's love'.[146] Tragically, the Corinthians demonstrated that they were still living for themselves (2 Cor 5:15) in failing to support Paul as their founding apostle over against interloping rivals (2 Cor 2:17; 3:1-18; 4:2-6; 6:11-13; 7:2-3; 10.1-13.14).

Finally, Paul airs his astonishment that the Galatian converts are in danger of deserting the electing grace of Christ (Gal 1:6: ἐν χάριτι [Χριστοῦ]). In reverting to Jewish circumcision as a requirement for converts, the Galatians nullify the grace of God (Gal 2:21: τὴν χάριν τοῦ θεοῦ; 5:4: τῆς χάριτος). The results are far-reaching. The gospel is perverted (Gal 1:6-9); the death of Christ is robbed of its redemptive power (3:1; 5:1, 4a, 11); the Spirit as the dynamic of the new creation is ignored (3:2, 5; 4:6; 5:16-24; 6:6, 15); and love

---

[142] S.M. Burstein,, *op. cit.*, §36 (ll.26-28).

[143] See our discussion in §2.8.3.

[144] B. Laum, *op. cit.*, §78a.

[145] For discussion of 1 Cor 15:10a, see O. Glombitza, 'Gnade — Das entscheidende Wort: Erwägungen zu 1 Kor XV 1-11, eine exegetische Studie', *NovT* 2/3-4 (1959), 281-290.

[146] R.P. Martin, *2 Corinthians* (Waco 1986), 166. See also J.M. Gundry Volf, *op. cit.*, 277-280.

as the fulfilment of the Law is obscured (5:13-15; 6:2-4).[147] Above all, Christ would have died 'for nothing' (Gal 2:21: δωρεάν). As F.W. Danker notes,[148] the tragic irony is that the honorific inscriptions used δωρεάν of the free bounties of civic benefactors (cf. Rom 3:24: δικαιούμενοι δωρεάν τῇ αὐτοῦ χάριτι). Ultimately, the Galatians were in danger of rejecting the free bounty of their Benefactor: His death on their behalf (Gal 3:1; 6:14-15).

Finally, Paul's heavy emphasis on responding worthily to a divine benefactor who had expended everything on his dependents was particularly apposite for the Galatians. A remarkable inscription from North Galatia highlights the plight of parents faced with the demand of reciprocity towards the gods: how do parents return thanks to the gods who indifferently preside over the death of their three children? The answer is simple: as per the demands of the reciprocity system, one returns 'thanks' to the gods — but, in this case, a 'thankless thanks' (ἄχαρις χάρις). Although the inscription postdates the New Testament period, belonging to the mid third century AD, it eloquently captures the dilemma of the ancients as they struggled to reconcile the reciprocity system with the fickle justice of the gods:

> The fates have seen the place which is always just, and fixed the end of life as our portion. For they have snatched away the finest bloom of beloved youth and we shall no more arrive at the prime (?) of life. This tomb conceals first of all our virgin sister, called Olympias, and then to us, prematurely dead. Theseus was the eldest brother, and my name was Amemptos, a child, younger in age. His cheeks bloomed with a thin down and he was in the flower of youth, like the gods. Theseus died in the winter, then Amemptos in the fourth month, at the beginning of summer. Here may be seen the thankless thank offering (ἄχαρις χάρις) of their wretched parents, a libation on the tomb for their children who died before their wedding day. First virgin Olympias, then Theseus with the unflawed bloom on his cheeks, then a third end took away Amemptos. They lie here as a common family and the tomb has joined their remains together.[149]

In our next section we will examine how Paul links human beneficence to divine grace. How would Graeco-Roman auditors have understood Paul's portrayal of Christ as the impoverished benefactor who enriches His dependants?

---

[147] See J. Lambrecht, 'Transgressor by Nullifying God's Grace: A Study of Gal 2:18-21', *Bib* 72/2 (1991), 217-236. On Gal 5:4, see J.M. Gundry Volf, *op. cit.*, 203-216.

[148] F.W. Danker, *op. cit.*, 451. For evidence, see our discussion in n.44 above. On Gal 2:21, see B. Eastman, *op. cit.*, 82-83.

[149] S. Mitchell, *Regional Epigraphic Catalogues of Asia Minor. The Ankara District: The Inscriptions of North Galatia II* (Oxford 1982), §392.

6.2. Paul, Charis, and the Impoverished Benefactor Motif

The *locus classicus* for divine beneficence in the Pauline epistles is (arguably) 2 Corinthians 8:9. In encouraging the Corinthian house-churches to contribute their part of the collection for needy Jewish Christians at Jerusalem, Paul sets forth the grace of Christ as the reason for all Christian generosity. He reminds them in 2 Corinthians 8:9 that they

know the grace (τὴν χάριν) of our Lord Jesus Christ, that though He was rich (πλούσιος ὤν), yet for your sakes He became poor (ἐπτώχευσεν), so that you through His poverty (τῇ ἐκείνου πτωχείᾳ) might become rich (πλουτήσητε).

Paul's portrait of Christ as an impoverished benefactor may be his counterpart to the inscriptional vignettes of civic beneficence.[150] More importantly, the text functions at several levels: the combination of christology, ethics and benefaction perspectives adds to its overall moral force.

Traditionally interpreted, 2 Corinthians 8:9 focuses on the divine Christ who abandoned His heavenly pre-existence (πλούσιος) for his earthly incarnation (ἐπτώχευσεν).[151] His self-abandonment has provided for the salvation enrichment (πλουτήσητε) of spiritually impoverished humanity (πτωχείᾳ). Seemingly, in reminding the Corinthians of their new status in front of God, Paul is encouraging the Corinthians — in view of Christ's beneficence (χάρις) and as an expression of their new identity in Him — to act with commensurate generosity towards the poor. However, since the christological dimension of 2 Corinthians 8:9 has been aired elsewhere, we will concentrate upon its ethical and benefaction implications.[152]

---

[150] Occasionally the inscriptions provide miniature portraits of beneficence in similar vein to that found in 2 Cor 8:9. One is here reminded of the quick sketch of Epigone's generosity (§7.3.1.1: A.R. Hands, *Charities and Social Aid in Greece and Rome* [London and Southampton, 1968], §D13), framed by the much larger inscription in honour of her husband-benefactor, Euphrosynus.

[151] For Paul's affirmation of the deity of Christ as θεός (Rom 9:5; Titus 2:13 [if Pauline]), see M.J. Harris, *Jesus as God: The New Testament Use of Theos in Reference to Jesus* (Grand Rapids 1992). For the application of LXX texts and categories, originally referring to Yahweh, to Jesus, see R.T. France, 'The Worship of Jesus: A Neglected Factor in Christological Debate?', in H.H. Rowdon (ed.), *Christ the Lord: Studies in Christology Presented to Donald Guthrie* (Leicester 1982), 17-36; D.R. de Lacey, '"One Lord" in Pauline Christology', in *ibid.*, 191-203; L.W. Hurtado, *One God One Lord: Early Christian Devotion and Ancient Jewish Monotheism* (Philadelphia 1988); D.B. Capes, *Old Testament Yahweh Texts in Paul's Theology* (Tübingen 1992).

[152] For discussion of the christology of 2 Cor 8:9, see A. Ross, 'The Grace of our Lord Jesus Christ', *EvQ* 13/3 (1941), 219-225; F.B. Craddock, 'The Poverty of Christ', *Int* 22/2 (1968), 158-170; G. Panikulam, *Koinōnia in the New Testament: A Dynamic Expression of Christian Life* (Rome 1979), 51-53; J.D.G. Dunn, *Christology in the Making: An Inquiry*

In its ethical context, the impoverishment of Christ acquires paradigmatic force. Paul has already pointed to the grace of God operative in the impoverished Macedonian churches, which wells up in rich generosity towards their Jewish brethren at Jerusalem (2 Cor 8:1-2: ἡ κατὰ βάθους πτωχεία; τὸ πλοῦτος τῆς ἁπλότητος). He reminds the Corinthians that they will be made rich in God's righteousness, in order that they can be generous on every occasion (2 Cor 9:11: πλουτιζόμενοι εἰς πᾶσαν ἁπλότητα). Elsewhere, in answer to critics of his ministry, Paul highlights the impoverishment of his own apostleship which, contrary to its discreditable appearance, makes many spiritually rich (2 Cor 6:10: ὡς πτωχοὶ πολλοὺς δὲ πλουτίζοντες). Thus the poverty-riches paradigm, grounded in Christ's self-abandonment, is echoed in various ethical contexts. Although the paradigm is qualified in the force of its application — equality of resources among believers is Paul's preferred option (2 Cor 8: 13-15) — the implicit analogy drawn between the results of Christ's generosity and that of the Christian churches is made clear.

However, the question — posed by J.D.G. Dunn[153] — whether Christ's freely embraced poverty is *literal* in its reference requires attention. What difference is brought to our understanding of the Pauline text if it is interpreted in its benefaction context? At the most basic level, Paul presents an image of an impoverished benefactor.[154] While it is true that Paul's audience were Gentile converts from the synagogue — and who as proselytes or God-fearers were exposed to the LXX — this does not prevent Paul from choosing images which communicate theologically and culturally at an ecclesiastical and social level.[155]

---

into the *Origins of the Doctrine of the Incarnation* (London 1980), 121-123; R. Brändle, 'Geld und Gnade (zu II Kor 8, 9)', *TZ* 41/3 (1985), 264-271; C.E.B. Cranfield, 'The Grace of Our Lord Jesus Christ', *Comm. Viat.* 32/3 (1989), 105-109; R.R. Melick, 'The Collection for the Saints: 2 Corinthians 8-9', *Criswell Theological Review* 4/1 (1989), 101-102; S.J. Joubert, 'Behind the Mask of Rhetoric: 2 Corinthians 8 and the Intra-Textual Relation Between Paul and the Corinthians', *Neot* 26/1 (1992), 108.

[153] J.D.G. Dunn, *op. cit.*, 121-122.

[154] See the attempt of J.P. Brown ('Inversion of Social Roles in Paul's Letters', *NovT* 33/4 [1991], 325) to interpret 2 Cor 8:9 against the background of the rehabilitated bankrupt. Of the impoverished benefactor, P. Veyne (*op. cit.*, 6) writes: 'The great notables who presided over these associations ruined themselves in order to make a festival more splendid, or endow the province with a temple for the Imperial cult, or an amphitheatre'.

[155] On Paul's audience, see J.G. Dunn, *art. cit.*, 417-418. A survey of twentieth-century commentators on 2 Corinthians reveals that F.W. Danker (*2 Corinthians* [Minneapolis 1989], 126) is unique in relating 2 Cor 8:9 to its benefaction context. Most commentators concentrate exclusively on the christological dimensions of the text: see A. Menzies (London 1912), A. Plummer (Edinburgh 1915), H.L. Goudge (London 1927), R.H. Strachan (London 1935), R.C.H. Lenski (Minneapolis 1937), R.P.C. Hanson (London 1954), R.V.G. Tasker

The motif of the impoverished benefactor — absent from the corpus of eulogistic inscriptions — makes its appearance in the philosophical literature.[156] Poverty was a well-known feature of the Cynic lifestyle, as L.E. Vaage has documented.[157] Here we are more interested in a highly unusual feature of ancient benefaction: excessive divestiture of wealth by a benefactor which imperils his status and resources. Our evidence is sparse, but tantalising. Dio Chrysostom provides us with this striking vignette of Heracles:

...he went unclothed and unarmed except for a lion's skin and a club, and they add that he did not set great store by gold or silver or fine raiment, but considered all such things nothing save to be given away and bestowed upon others (χαρίσασθαι). At any rate he made presents to many men, not only of money without limit and lands and herds of horses and cattle, but also of whole kingdoms and cities. For he fully believed that everything belonged to him exclusively and that gifts bestowed would call out the good-will of the recipients.[158]

(London 1958), P.E. Hughes (Grand Rapids 1962), M.E. Thrall (Cambridge 1965; Edinburgh 2000), J. Héring (London 1967), C.K. Barrett (London 1973), W.P. Furnish (New York 1984), H.D. Betz (Philadelphia 1985), M. Carrez (Geneva, 1986), R.P. Martin (Grand Rapids 1986), C.G. Kruse (Grand Rapids 1987), E. Best (Atlanta 1987); D.E. Garland (Nashville 1999). Incredibly, R. Bultmann (Minneapolis 1985) does not discuss the text at all! Only Héring, Betz and Kruse (above) raise the issue of Christ's identification with the economically poor. Several commentators (Hughes, Furnish, Martin, Danker) recognise a link with 2 Cor 6:10, as does J. Koenig (*New Testament Hospitality: Partnership with Strangers as Promise and Mission* [Philadelphia 1985], 75).

[156] See, too, the related inscriptional motif of the endangered benefactor. F.W. Danker, 'The Endangered Benefactor in Luke-Acts', in H.R. Kent (ed.), *Society of Biblical Literature 1981 Seminar Papers* (Chico 1981), 39-48; *id.*, *op. cit.*, 417-427; *id.*, 'Graeco-Roman Cultural Accommodation in the Christology of Luke-Acts', in H.R. Kent (ed.), *Society of Biblical Literature 1983 Seminar Papers* (Chico 1983), 404-406. The attempt of J.D.G. Dunn (*op. cit.*) to excise any reference to the pre-existence of Christ remains exegetically flawed. Contra, R.P. Martin, *op. cit.*, 263-264.

[157] L.E. Vaage, *Q: The Ethos and Ethics of an Itinerant Intelligence* (unpub. Ph.D. diss. Claremont Graduate School 1987), 316-318. This section has been omitted from Vaage's subsequent book (*Galilean Upstarts: Jesus' First Followers According to Q* [Valley Forge 1994]). See also Plutarch, *Mor.*, 581C on the voluntary poverty of Socrates and his refusal to be benefited.

[158] Dio Chrysostom, *Or.*, 1.61-62; cf. Arr., *Epict. Diss.*, 3.26.31-32. Note the interesting parallel between Heracles, who believed that 'everything belonged to him', and the Pauline 'all things are yours' (1 Cor 3:21). J. Wettstein (*Novum Testamentum Graecum* Vol.2 [Amsterdam 1752; rpt. Graz 1962]) cites the example of Odysseus as background to 2 Cor 8:9: 'Odysseus, for all his being a beggar (πτωχός) and begging of the suitors, was nonetheless a king and the owner of the house' (Dio Chrysostom, *Or.*, 14.22; cf. *ibid.* 1.21). See also E. Skard, *Zwei religiös-politische Begriff Euergetes-Concordia* (Oslo 1932), 42-43, 56-57; R. Höistad, 'Cynicism', in P. Wiener (ed.), *Dictionary of the History of Ideas* Vol.1 (New York 1968), 627-634, esp. 632-633; S.C. Mott, *op. cit.*, 286-300; D.E. Aune, 'Heracles and Christ: Heracles Imagery in the Christology of Early Christianity', in D.L. Balch (*et al.*, ed.), *Greeks, Romans, and Christians: Essays in Honor of Abraham J. Malherbe* (Philadelphia 1990), 3-19.

Dio Chrysostom himself lets fall a revealing snippet concerning his pet project of embellishing Prusa, his native city. He comments that 'I have grown much thinner than I was when I came in'.[159] The thrust of his comment is fully appreciated when one remembers his continuing financial hardship after his return from exile (AD 96), and what had been for him the genuine risk of poverty prior to that.[160] Notwithstanding, Dio Chrysostom gives himself unstintingly to his efforts on behalf of his citizens.

The Roman collector of moral *exempla*, Valerius Maximus, nominates Fabius Maximus as a case of such liberality. The Senate had refused to honour the agreement he had secured with Hannibal for the release of Roman captives. Instead he sent his son to Rome, sold the only farm he possessed, and paid Hannibal. Valerius provides us this homily on his actions:

> If we consider the sum, (it is) but small, as being the price but of seven acres of land, and those lying in Pupinia; but considering the soul of the giver, (it is) a most large sum, and far exceeding the money. For he would rather himself to be destitute in patrimony, than that his country should be poor in credit. So (his act is) much more to be commended, as it is a more certain sign of favourable study, to stretch beyond ability, rather than to do the same act out of superfluity. For the one can do what he performs, the other more than he is able.[161]

Another example of the impoverished benefactor motif is found in Lucian's portrait of Timon, the semi-legendary misanthrope of Periclean Athens. There Timon rails against the social misfortune that befalls benefactors like himself who sacrifice everything for their beneficiaries. Now reduced to farm labouring and wearing animal skins, Timon sums up his fate in terminology reminiscent of 2 Corinthians 8:9:

> After raising so many Athenians to high station and making them rich when they were wretchedly poor before (πλουσίους ἐκ πενεστάτων ἀποφήνας) and helping all who were in want, nay more, pouring out my wealth (τὸν πλοῦτον) in floods to benefit my friends (εἰς εὐεργεσίαν τῶν φίλων), now that I have become poor thereby (πένης διὰ ταῦτα ἐγενόμην) I am no longer recognised or even looked at by the men who formerly cringed and kowtowed and hung on my nod.[162]

Last, the liberator of Syracuse, Dion, was led beyond his resources by his generosity (τῇ μεγαλοψυχίᾳ) when distributing thanks to his friends (φίλοις χάριτας) and rewards to his allies (συμμάχοις δωρεάς).[163] In light of the above examples, flashes of cultural recognition may well have been occasioned by Paul's presentation of the impoverishment of Jesus, the

---

[159] Dio Chrysostom, *Or.*, 47.20.
[160] *Id.*, 47.21; 40.2.
[161] Valerius Maximus, *Noteworthy Doings and Sayings*, 4.8.1. Cf. Mk 12:41-44.
[162] Lucian, *Timon*, 5.
[163] Plutarch, *Dion*, 52.1.

infinitely rich benefactor, who in his self-emptying became the model for all Christian beneficence (2 Cor 8:9).

The impoverished benefactor imagery of 2 Corinthians 8:9 gains force when viewed against the background of the honorific inscriptions. F.W. Danker has correctly observed that 'Graeco-Roman benefactors could generally rely on reserves'.[164] Indeed, to prevent benefactors exhausting their funds, communities often designated their civic luminaries ἀλειτούργητος ('free from public services').[165] No such exemptions were demanded by Christ: he literally impoverished himself in a life of unremitting benefaction.

Further, the humiliation brought about by Christ's impoverishment is intriguing in its benefaction context. Valerius Maximus was well aware of the social humiliation involved in benefaction rituals. The reversal of status which the consul, Metellus Pius, accepted as a patron is a case in point. Although he was the sponsor of Q. Calidius' praetorship, Metellus assumed a position of social inferiority towards his client. This sprang from his gratitude for Calidius' part in the recall of his father, Metellus Numidicus, from exile. Valerius Maximus (*Noteworthy Doings and Sayings*, 5.2.7) sums up the affair in this way:

Indeed (Metellus) always referred to Calidius as the patron of his house and family. Nor did he thereby detract in any way from the position of leadership which was his beyond question, because he lowered his outstanding dignity (*eximiam dignitatem*) before the signal desert of one much his inferior not in a spirit of humility but of gratitude (*quia non humili, sed grato animo*).[166]

Correspondingly, the social humiliation of Jesus originates in his *own* decision to become both δοῦλος (Phil 2:6-8: ἑαυτὸν ἐκένωσεν, v.7; ἐταπείνωσεν ἑαυτόν, v.8) and πτωχός (2 Cor. 8:9: ἐπτώχευσεν) than from an obligation to return gratitude — as was the case with Metellus.[167] The selfless example

---

[164] F.W. Danker, *op. cit.* (1989), 126.

[165] Michel 475, 998; R.K. Sherk, *Roman Documents from the Greek East: Senatus Consulta and Epistulae to the Age of Augustus* (Baltimore 1969), §49; *I. Délos* IV 1520, 1521.

[166] See also Plutarch (*Mor.*, 172B) for King Artaxerxes' willingness to be benefited by social inferiors. Lucian's portrait of Timon (*Timon* 5) emphasises the social disdain felt towards the impoverished benefactor by his former beneficiaries: ' ... if I chance to meet any them in the road, they treat me as they would the gravestone of a man long dead which time has overturned, passing by without even a curious glance. Indeed, some of them, on catching sight of me in the distance, turn off in another direction, thinking that the man who not long ago showed himself their saviour and benefactor (σωτῆρα καὶ εὐεργέτην) will be an unpleasant and repulsive spectacle'.

[167] Another telling example of the impoverished benefactor motif is found in Plutarch's *Sol.*, 2.1. There Plutarch links the impoverishment of Pericles' family estate, which had been precipitated by his father's excessive beneficence, with Pericles' subsequent social humiliation as a young man: 'he was ashamed to take from others, since he had belonged to

of Christ afforded Paul the opportunity, in the face of Corinthian recalcitrance, to observe that genuine Christian beneficence is not rendered under compulsion (2 Cor 9:7: μὴ ἐξ ἀνάγκης). Furthermore, Christ's experience of dishonour through His impoverishment became the paradigm for the apostles (2 Cor 6:8: διὰ δόξης καὶ ἀτιμίας; 6:9: ὡς πτωχοὶ πολλοὺς δὲ πλουτίζοντες), and for prominent Christians struggling with their loss of social status.[168] Presumably, one purpose of this alternative model of beneficence sponsored within the Christian communities was to eliminate inevitable tensions and misunderstandings.

Concomitant with the social humiliation of Christ is the reversal in status for his beneficiaries. By means of the impoverishment of Christ (2 Cor 8:9a), Christians are endowed with the status which — in the ideology of the inscriptions — typified the benefactor: the possession of wealth (8:9b) and the requisite merit for its disposal (ἵνα ἡμεῖς γενώμεθα δικαιοσύνη θεοῦ ἐν αὐτῷ: 5:21). Further, as a series of ethnically and socially diverse communities, Christians are encouraged to adopt the role of benefactors themselves. This stripped the Christian communities of the suppliant position that — if the inscriptions are representative — traditionally characterised eastern Mediterranean city-states in front of their benefactors.[169] The return of honour is redirected: the praise accorded benefactors within early Christian house churches now redounds to God as the Supreme Benefactor (2 Cor 9:11-15).

What would Graeco-Roman auditors, familiar with the honorific inscriptions, have made of this? It would have been puzzling. Benefactors, as

---

a family which had always helped others'. See also F.W. Danker's reference to Menander's *Dyskolos*, 767-769 in *id.*, 'Menander and the New Testament', *NTS* 10 (1963—1964), 368. G. Hamel (*Poverty and Charity in Roman Palestine, First Three Centuries CE* [Berkeley and Los Angeles 1990], 189-190) notes that proselytes were commanded to impoverish themselves for the sake of the Torah (*b. Yev.* 47a). On the shame of financial humiliation, G.W. Peterman, *op. cit.*, 140-141. Note, too, the comment of R. Corriveau (*The Liturgy of Life: A Study of the Ethical Thought of St. Paul in His Letters to the Early Christian Communities* [Bruxelles-Paris 1970], 104 n.38) regarding 2 Cor 8:9: 'in speaking simply of the "beggaring" of Christ without any limitation or further development, it seems difficult to exclude the ignominious death of the cross as part of the concrete human condition of Christ's impoverishment'.

[168] See especially L.W. Countryman, *The Rich Christian in the Church of the Early Empire: Contradictions and Accommodations* (New York and Toronto 1980), 162-166. On status discrepancy, see R.L. Rohrbaugh, 'Methodological Considerations in the Debate over the Social Class Status of Early Christians', *JAAR* 52/3 (1984), 519-546.

[169] From *SEG* XI 948 we observe the suppliant role which the *polis*, Cardamylae, adopts towards its benefactor, Poseidippos. There, Cardamylae deferentially states that it gives Poseidippos a share of 'the *lesser* favour (ἐλάττονος χάριτος)' in returning honours to its benefactor.

we have seen, were cushioned against exhausting their reserves. In contrast, Christ as Benefactor was exposed to ridicule (1 Cor 1:18a, 21b, 23, 25a; Gal 5:11b), weakness (1 Cor 1:25b; 2 Cor 13:4a), the desolation of God's judgement (Gal 3:13), and an ignominious death (1 Cor 2:8; Phil 2:8).[170] In regard to beneficence, the *entire* Christian community was called to ethical action, not just a select circle of wealthy citizens enticed by the promise of civic honours. Conversely, the only ethical responsibility demanded of hellenistic *poleis* was to return honours commensurate with the original benefactions, and thereby maintain a reputation of gratitude in front of its contemporaries and posterity.[171] Other aspirants, it was hoped, would step in and fill the breach in civic munificence. Finally, the idea of an impoverished deity was a matter of ridicule in antiquity.[172]

However, our discussion of the impact of 2 Corinthians 8:9 in its benefaction context upon Paul's auditors has not yet been fully exhausted. We turn now to the rhetorical topos of the enslaved and impoverished leader as found in Antisthenes.

6.3. Paul and Antisthenes on the Charis *of the Enslaved Leader*

In our previous section, we noted how members of the patronal class occasionally impoverished themselves on behalf of their dependents. It is likely that Paul's auditors would have recognised the social implications implicit in Paul's image of the 'impoverished benefactor'. But 2 Corinthians 8:9 is also profitably silhouetted against the rhetorical topos of the enslaved leader. Some of Paul's auditors may have evaluated his portrait of the impoverished Christ against contemporary philosophical debates about the character of patronal leadership.

The issue for the Corinthians had more than theoretical relevance. Paul was calling his auditors to divest themselves of wealth in order to complete, as

---

[170] In Lucian's *Timon* 8, the god Hermes is critical of Timon because the Athenian benefactor did not show sufficient discrimination regarding the character of his recipients: '... (Timon) was ruined by kind-heartedness and philanthropy and compassion on all those who were in want; but in reality it was senselessness and folly and lack of discrimination in regard to his friends. He did not perceive that he was showing kindness to ravens and wolves'. As we have seen (§6.1.2.3), the grace of Christ — in contrast to the traditional benefaction ideology outlined above — did *not* discriminate regarding the worthiness of the recipients.

[171] See §6.4.1 below.

[172] Plutarch (*Mor.*, 235E) preserves this revealing jest: 'A Spartan, seeing a man taking up a collection for the gods, said that he did not think much of gods who were poorer than himself (θεῶν πτωχοτέρων ἑαυτοῦ)'. The reference is cited by J. Wettstein (*op. cit.*) in relation to 2 Cor 8:9.

trustworthy religious benefactors, the Jerusalem collection.¹⁷³ But in accomplishing this, they were to be regulated by a principle of mutual assistance (2 Cor 9:13: ἐξ ἰσότητος) that would ensure the divine goal of equality (9:14: ὅπως γένηται ἰσότης), rather than the continued dominance of the patronal elite. ¹⁷⁴ What, then, was the debate regarding the ancient ideal of servant leadership and to what extent did χάρις inform its rationale? How did Paul differentiate his understanding of the servant benefactor from the contemporary Cynic alternatives?

The debate over the true nature of the servant benefactor brought aristocratic and populist models of leadership into collision. From the fifth-century BC onwards, the patronal view of social relations — according to which the upper class ruled as a benevolent patriarch over its social inferiors — was increasingly challenged by the Cynic model of the populist leader. ¹⁷⁵ The Cynics argued that the true leader should be a slave of the people, lowering himself to the inferior status of those he served, and accommodating himself to their lifestyle and speech. For the Cynics, Odysseus and Heracles represented the ideal slave king who endured suffering and privation for the sake of others.¹⁷⁶ The reaction of the upper class to the Cynic populist model was predictably negative. In its view, the Cynics had reduced the leader of the polis to a chameleon-like flatterer whose adaptability was nothing but a disguise for self-interest. The versatile Odysseus was nominated as such an opportunist.¹⁷⁷

The so-called 'father' of the Cynics, Antisthenes (c.445—c.360 BC),¹⁷⁸ makes an incisive contribution to the Athenian debate regarding political

---

¹⁷³ On the use of ἐπιτελέω ('to complete': 2 Cor 8:6, 11) in association decrees, see R.S. Ascough, 'The Completion of a Religious Duty: The Background of 2 Cor 8:1-15', *NTS* 42/4 (1996), 584-599.

¹⁷⁴ G. Stählin, Ἴσος, ἰσότης, ἰσότιμος, *TDNT* 3 (1965), 348.

¹⁷⁵For discussion, see R. Höistad, *Cynic Hero and Cynic King: Studies in the Cynic Conceptions of Man* (Lund 1948), esp. 92-102; D.B. Martin, *op. cit.*, 86-116; D. Seeley, 'Rulership and Service in Mark 10:41-45', *NovT* 35/3 (1993), 234-250, esp. 234-245.

¹⁷⁶ On Heracles and Christianity, see M. Simon, *Hercule et le Christianisme* (Paris 1955); D.E. Aune, *art. cit.*, in D.L. Balch (*et al.*, ed.), *op. cit.*

¹⁷⁷ In an imaginary conversation between Odysseus and Gryllus, Plutarch (*Mor.* 987C) contrasts the guileless nature of wild beasts with the deceitfulness of Odysseus. Undoubtedly, Gryllus' tirade against Odysseus represents the typical upper class reaction to the populist Cynic hero: 'Take, first, if you please, courage, in which you take great pride, not even pretending to blush when you are called "valiant" and "sacker of cities". Yet you, you villain, are the man who by tricks and frauds have led astray men who knew only a straightforward, noble style of war and were unversed in deceit and lies'.

¹⁷⁸ For the ancient controversy as to whether Antisthenes was the true father of the Cynics, see Diog. Laert. 1.15; 6:13; Pseudo-Crates, *Ep.*, 19.

leadership.[179] Among the surviving fragments of Antisthenes are the speeches of Ajax and Odysseus. Each man claims for himself the (now vacant) military command of the Greeks at Troy. Consequently, before the assembled Greek soldiers, each man mounts a spirited rhetorical defence of his right to the weapons of the fallen Achilles.[180] Antisthenes captures the difference between the speakers with a striking vignette of each man's valour.

In the case of Ajax, Antisthenes confronts his auditors with the traditional portrait of a noble warrior, a figure who is more the man of deeds than words. Ajax insists that the Greeks were quite capable of forming a definite opinion regarding the differing leadership styles of Odysseus and himself. Whereas Odysseus came to Troy 'not willingly but unwillingly' (οὐχ ἑκὼν ἀλλ' ἄκων), Ajax was the first in battle formation, always standing alone, far away from the security of the walls.[181] Consequently Ajax bristles at the idea that the ἀρετή of the great man should be open to the judgement of his contemporaries. As Ajax reminds his troops, he is the king of Salamis and therefore is not subject to the scrutiny of inferiors.[182]

The populist manner of Odysseus, who is disguised in a pauper's rags and fights with rude weapons, stands in sharp antithesis to the elitism of Ajax, the royal warrior.[183] According to Odysseus, Ajax fights on the city walls only

---

[179] For discussion of Antisthenes in relation to Paul, see H. Funke, 'Antisthenes bei Paulus', *Hermes* 98 (1970), 459-471; A.J. Malherbe, in 'Antisthenes and Odysseus, and Paul at War', in *id.*, *Paul and the Popular Philosophers* (Minneapolis 1989), 91-119; D.B. Martin, *op. cit.*, 105-107; F.G. Downing, *Cynics, Paul and the Pauline Churches* (London and New York 1998), 138-141.

[180] For Antisthenes' speech of Odysseus (ΟΔΥΣΣΕΥΣ Η ΠΕΡΙ ΟΔΥΣΣΕΩΣ), see G. Giannantoni, *Socraticorum Reliquiae* Vol.2 (Naples 1983), §54. For Antisthenes' speech of Ajax (ΑΙΑΣ Η ΑΙΑΝΤΟΣ ΛΟΓΟΣ), see *ibid.*, §53. I am grateful to Professor Albrecht Dihle for first bringing this text to my attention.

[181] *Socraticorum Reliquiae* Vol.2 §53 (9).

[182] *Ibid.*, §53 (4, 7).

[183] Epictetus (Arr. *Epict. Diss.* Fragment 11) also cites Odysseus' impoverishment as a moral paradigm: 'shall the man of noble nature make a poorer showing than Polus, and not play well any role to which the Deity assigns him? And will he not follow the example of Odysseus, who was no less pre-eminent in his rags than in his rich and purple cloak?'. Similarly, Pseudo-Diogenes (*Epistle* 34.2; cf. 7.2): 'And that Odysseus, son of Laertes, returned home from Ilium in a torn cloak, caked with kitchen dirt and smoke. Now do my clothing and begging still seem disgraceful to you or are they noble and admirable to kings and to be taken up by every sensible person for frugality's sake?'. Dio Chrysostom (*Or.* 14.22; cf. 33.15) illustrates the paradox that the free man is a king, notwithstanding adverse circumstances, by referring to Odysseus: 'Odysseus, for all his being a beggar (πτωχὸς ὤν) and begging of the suitors, was none the less a king and the owner of the house'. Note, however, the tradition that Odysseus, 'alone and naked and shipwrecked', enriched himself 'abundantly' in exile (Musonius Rufus, *Fragment* 10: C.E. Lutz, 'Musonius Rufus "The Roman Socrates"', in A.R. Bellinger [ed.], *Yale Classical Studies* Vol.10 [1947], 3-147). Lucian (*The Parasite* 10) also asserts that Odysseus, 'after flogging himself and putting on

during daylight, protected by an impregnable bull's-hide shield and accompanied by his troops. Odysseus scorns the way that Ajax insulates himself against harm or danger by means of his superior military equipment:

> Don't you know that the well-born man must not suffer the least mite of harm either by himself or by a comrade or by the enemy? But just like children you are delighted that these men say that you are courageous; but I (say that) you (are) the most cowardly of all and the most fearful of death — you being the one who has in the first place unbroken and invulnerable weapons, on account of which they say you are invulnerable! However, what would you do if someone of the enemy approached you with such weapons? Surely there might be something both honourable and admirable, if neither of the two of you were able to do anything? Again, do you think there is any difference between having such weapons and sitting inside a wall? But don't you also have a 'wall', as you say? Accordingly, you go around alone holding a seven bulls' hide 'wall' in front of yourself.[184]

By contrast, Odysseus approaches the walls unarmed, neither fleeing the danger of battle nor its humiliation.[185] He fights as much in the night as in the day in order to save his dependents. Acting as an endangered benefactor, Odysseus' motivation is the delivery of his dependents not his own safety:

> But I come unarmed not (only) towards the walls of the enemy but (up) to the (very) walls themselves, and I overpower the wakeful advance guards of the enemy with their weapons and all. I am a general and a guard both of you and all the other men, and I know both what is in this place and what is the condition of the enemy. (This is) not because I send another man to spy the situation out, but just as the helmsman looks out day and night in order to save the sailors (ὅπως σώσουσι τοὺς ναύτας), (so) in this way I myself also save both you and all the other men. For there is not any danger (ὅντινα κίνδυνον) I fled thinking it shameful, (especially) during the time that I was about to harm the enemy. Not even if some men were going to see me, would I have dared to cling to appearances. But even if as a slave (δοῦλος) or a pauper (πτωχός) and whipping-boy (μαστιγίας) I was about to harm the enemy I would attempt it, even if no one saw (me).[186]

As a result, the safety of Ajax and his fellow Greeks is secured by Odysseus' self-sacrifice and by his acceptance of a reversal of social status:

> ...but whenever you are snoring, I am saving you (ἐγὼ σώζω σέ) at that precise time, and always I am going to harm the enemy, having (only) these slavish weapons and rags and scourges, on account of which you sleep securely.[187]

---

wretched Stoic rags', went on to live the Epicurean life of a parasite in Calypso's isle. For the varying estimates of Odysseus in antiquity, see A.J. Malherbe, *art. cit.* in *id., op. cit.*, 105-109.

[184] *Socraticorum Reliquiae* Vol.2, §54 (6-7). Since ἐγώ does not agree with δειλότατόν, Reiske suggests the emendation of σέ as a replacement for τε in τε καί (ἐγὼ δὲ δειλότατόν γε ἁπάντων σέ καί: §54:7: *ibid.*, n.36 342). I have followed Reiske's emendation.

[185] In a manner reminiscent of the endangered benefactor motif, Antisthenes emphasises the many dangers Odysseus faces in order to save the city (κίνδυνος, κινδυνεύω: *ibid.*, §54 (1, 2, 3, 9); σώζω: ibid., §54 (5, 8, 10).

[186] *Ibid.*, §54 (8-9).

[187] *Ibid.*, §54 (10).

Not unexpectedly, Ajax misrepresents Odysseus' behaviour as secretive, ignominious and self-serving. In his view, the contrast between his own lifestyle and that of Odysseus is stark. Ajax underscores the dissimilarity in a series of powerful antitheses:

> For while there is nothing which he might do openly (φανερῶς), I would not dare to do anything covertly (λάθρᾳ). And while I would not endure being in bad repute (κακῶς ἀκούων) or, moreover, (endure) being in an evil plight (κακῶς πάσχων), he would endure being strung up, if he was going to gain something (εἰ κερδαίνειν τι μέλλοι). (For) being the one who used to give himself up to his slaves to flog (him) and to beat his back with sticks and his face with fists, and then putting on rags, he entered into the walled city of the enemy during the night, robbed a temple and departed.[188]

Finally, Antisthenes highlights the fact that the χάρις of Odysseus had not been properly requited by the Greeks, as he deserved. In this regard, Odysseus complains that he had been wrongly accused of temple robbery by Ajax. The accusation, Odysseus claims, was entirely malicious. The truth of the matter was that Odysseus re-captured an image of the god which had been stolen from the Greeks. Up till then, the Greek forces — stripped of their divine benefactor — were unwilling to attack the impregnable fortress of Troy. But, because of Odysseus' daring strategy, they could now expect a resurgence in their military fortune. Although the Greeks had experienced considerable grace at Odysseus' hands, his favour remained unappreciated by his comrades. As Odysseus laments, his assumption of the role of endangered benefactor had not been properly appreciated by his fellow Greeks:

> For we have not come here in order that we might fight with the Trojans, but in order that we might both take back Helen and conquer Troy. But all this together was among my dangers (ἐν τοῖς ἐμοῖς κινδύνοις). For at the time when it was a declared (fact) that Troy was impregnable, if we did not seize beforehand the image of the god stolen from us, who is the one who fetched back the image here — some other person or I, the one whom you judge for sacrilege? For you know nothing, you call 'sacrilegious' the man who recovered the image of the god, but not Alexandros who filched it away from us. And while you all boast that Troy was taken, do you call me sacrilegious who contrived the means whereby that this would be (accomplished)? Although, if at all events, it was fine to conquer Troy, it is also fine to procure the cause of this. While the others experience favour (χάριν), you cast reproaches upon me; for by reason of ignorance you know nothing of the benefits which you received (at my expense).[189]

It is interesting to speculate whether Graeco-Roman auditors would have made any connection between the Cynic topos of the enslaved leader and Paul's servant-benefactor christology. Few New Testament scholars have asked whether there is a relationship between Antisthenes' portrait of

---

[188] *Ibid.*, §53 (5-6). See Lucian, *The Dialogues of the Dead* 23 (29); *The Parasite* 49.
[189] *Socraticorum Reliquiae* Vol.2 §54 (2-4).

Odysseus — or even Cynic thought more generally — and Paul's portrait of Christ's self-impoverishment in 2 Corinthians 8:9. A singular exception is F.G. Downing who claims that

> Paul's Christ is himself an Odysseus-like figure, accepting tribulation (1 Thess 1:6) and poverty (2 Cor 8:9), adopting the role of a slave, serving others (Phil 2:7; Rom 15:8) as Paul in turn strove to do. The Paul who urged his hearers to emulate a human model *of just this character* would be remarkably reminiscent of those Cynics who took Odysseus for their ideal.[190]

In other words, the Cynic apostle imitates his Cynic Lord.[191] But, as we will see, Downing overlooks distinctive features of Paul's christology which do not fit the Cynic mould.

By contrast, D.B. Martin has convincingly demonstrated the relevance of the Cynic enslaved leader topos to Paul's apostolic practice in 1 Corinthians 9:19-22.[192] Paul does not seek personal gain (κερδαίνειν) in his self-lowering, as Achilles alleges of Odysseus. Rather Paul enslaves himself (1 Cor 9:19a: ἐμαυτὸν ἐδούλωσα) and surrenders his freedom (9:19a: ἐλεύθερος) so that he might win as many as possible to the gospel of Christ (κερδαίνειν: 9:19b, 20a, 20b, 21b, 22a; σῴζειν: 9:22b). Martin also suggests that the status reversal of Christ's cross involves a social lowering similar to the humiliation experienced by the enslaved leader in antiquity.[193] Although Martin refers to 2 Corinthians 8:9 in this regard, he does not expand on the christological implications of the verse.

It should also be observed here that Paul's focus on his 'gain' (κερδαίνειν) is equally Christ and people-centered in the epistle to the Philippians. In Phil 3:5ff Paul dismisses his status and achievements — whether they be Jewish (Phil 3:5-7: ἅτινα ἦν μοι κέρδη [v.7a]) or apostolic (3:8) — as 'loss' in order to gain Christ (3:8b: ἵνα Χριστοῦ κερδήσω).[194] He experiences Christ's resurrection power and the fellowship of His sufferings as he dies in service of the risen Lord and His church (Phil 3:10; cf.

---

[190] F.G. Downing, *op. cit.*, 211. Emphasis added by Downing.

[191] The adoptionist christology of F.G. Downing (*Jesus and the Threat of Freedom* [London 1987], 159) views Jesus as a Jewish Cynic teacher whose earthly life God made His own.

[192] D.B. Martin, *op. cit.*, 117-146. See, too, A.J. Malherbe, *art. cit.*, in *id.*, *op. cit.* for the relevance of the Antisthenes' paradigm to 2 Cor 10:3-6.

[193] D.B. Martin, *op. cit.*, 136-142.

[194] The change in tense from the perfect ἥγημαι in Phil 3:7 ('I have come to consider') to the present ἡγοῦμαι in 3:8 ('I consider') indicates that everything is considered as loss for the sake of Christ up to the time of writing. See P.T. O'Brien, *The Epistle to the Philippians* (Grand Rapids 1991), 386. R.P. Martin (*Philippians* [Leicester 1959], 145) sums up the force of Paul's change in verb tense thus: 'all the privileges he could claim as a Jew (verses 5-7) and as a Christian (verse 8) were offset by inestimable gain'.

1:29-30; 1 Cor 15:31; 2 Cor 4:10-12; 6:9; 12:8-10; 13:4-5; Col 1:24). Although Paul looks forward to death as 'gain' (Phil 1:21b: τὸ ἀποθανεῖν κέρδος), he must remain imprisoned for Christ in the present (1:12-14, 29-30). He rejoices in the advance of the gospel, notwithstanding the efforts of his rivals to belittle him (Phil 1:15-18). While the apostle would prefer to be with the heavenly Christ (Phil 1:32; cf. 3:20-21), he accepts God's extension of his earthly ministry for the sake his converts (Phil 1:19, 24-26).

To be sure, Paul's focus in 1 Corinthians and Philippians is more on his apostolic self-understanding than on his christology. But, again, it is surprising that scholars — F.G. Downing excepted — have not canvassed whether there are any thematic links between Antisthenes' topos of the enslaved leader and Paul's portrait of the obedient servant who emptied himself and died on a cross (Phil 2:5-8: μορφὴν δούλου λαβών [v.7]).[195] Two examples will suffice. Although He was in the form of God (Phil 2:6: ὅς ἐν μορφῇ θεοῦ ὑπάρχων), Christ had assumed — like Odysseus — the form of a slave for the sake of his dependents (2:7 [cf. Rom 15:8]: μορφὴν δούλου λαβών). Furthermore, as Odysseus had endured scourgings in order to save his fellow countrymen, so Christ underwent the ignominy of the cross for the benefit of humankind (Phil 2:8; cf. 1 Cor 1:23; 1 Thess 1:6).

In drawing such comparisons, I am not proposing that Paul's servant christology was directly informed by Antisthenes' topos of the enslaved leader. In Philippians 2:6-11 Paul's christology clearly originates in the Jesus tradition (John 13:3-17; cf. Mark 10:35-45 / Matt 20:25-28 / Luke 22:24-27; Mk 9:35; Matt 11:29; 23:11) and — less assuredly — in the servant theology of Isaiah (Isa 53:5-6, 10-12), as well as in the Jewish tradition of the vindicated righteous sufferer (e.g. Wis 2; 2 Macc 6-7).[196] But, as we have indicated, several of the christological motifs in verses 6-8 may have resonated

---

[195] K. Wengst (*Humility: Solidarity of the Humiliated* [Philadelphia 1988: Gmn. orig. 1987], 49-50) argues that the career of Christ, as portrayed in Phil 2:6-8, runs in an opposite direction to Roman upward social mobility.

[196] For discussion, see L.W. Hurtado, 'Jesus as Lordly Example in Philippians 2:5-11', in P. Richardson and J.C. Hurd (eds), *From Jesus to Paul: Studies in Honour of Francis Wright Beare* (Waterloo 1984), 113-126; G. Wagner, 'Le Scandale de la croix expliqué par le chant du Serviteur d'Isaïe 53. Réflexion sur Philippiens 2/6-11', *ETR* 61 (1986), 177-187; R.P. Martin, *A Hymn of Christ: Phil 2:5-11 in Recent Interpretation and in the Setting of the Early Christian Worship* (Downers Grove 1997); M. Bockmuehl, *The Epistle to the Philippians* (London 1998), 135-137. For criticism of the view that Isaianic servant theology lies behind the Synoptic and Pauline servant traditions, see M.D. Hooker, *Jesus and the Servant: The Influence of the Servant Concept of Deutero-Isaiah in the New Testament* (London 1959); D. Seeley, *art. cit*. In a more circumscribed manner, P.T. O'Brien (*op. cit.*, 220, 268-271) discounts an Isaianic background to Phil 2:7. For a recent coverage of both sides of the debate, see W.H. Bellinger and W.R. Farmer (eds), *Jesus and the Suffering Servant: Isaiah 53 and Christian Origins* (Harrisburg 1998).

with Gentile auditors who were attuned to Cynic popular philosophy. Undoubtedly, Paul was well aware that he was articulating a cruciform theology of servant leadership which not only challenged the upward social mobility of Graeco-Roman culture but also which interacted with the Cynic critique of aristocratic leadership.[197]

But, to return to the focus of our discussion, what of the self-impoverishment of Christ in 2 Corinthians 8:9?[198] Like the slave-beggar Odysseus, Christ is portrayed as having experienced a dramatic reversal of social status. The infinitely rich benefactor had became poor (2 Cor 8:9a: ἐπτώχευσεν πλούσιος ὤν). It is important to realise that the self-lowering of Christ and Odysseus, as rendered by Paul and Antisthenes, involved each man becoming a pauper (ἐπτώχευσεν [2 Cor 8:9a]; πτωχός [*Socraticorum Reliquiae* Vol.2 §54.9]). How would contemporary auditors have responded to such a portrait? Those with an aristocratic bias may well have concluded that Christ had dishonoured himself by his injudicious generosity and by his assumption of pauper status. Two different strands of evidence will establish the point.

First, in the Septuagint, the πτωχός stood powerless against the exploitation of oppressors.[199] As a result, he was socially despised by his peers and even by his relatives.[200] His only hope was prayer to God for deliverance because God had commanded His covenant people to give alms to the poor.[201] Above all, it is perhaps Sirach's description of the πτωχός as an

---

[197] For discussion of how Graeco-Roman competition for honour was inimical to a servant mentality, see T.B. Savage, *Power through Weakness: Paul's Understanding of the Christian Ministry in 2 Corinthians* (Cambridge 1996), 23-24. For the benefaction background to the text, see N.H. Young ('An Aristophanic Contrast to Philippians 2:6-7', *NTS* 45/1 [1999], 153-155). Young points out that Aristophanes (*Women in Government* 777-783) depicts the gods as holding out their hands palms up because they expected gifts from their suppliants rather than act beneficently in reply to their petitions. As Young comments (*art. cit.*, 154), 'The contrast with Phil 2:6-7 could not be more stark'.

[198] The precise reference underlying the ingressive aorist ἐπτώχευσεν (2 Cor 8:9: 'he became poor') has long puzzled scholars. C. Brown (Brown, C., 'Poor', in *id.*, [ed.], *The New International Dictionary of New Testament Theology* Vol.2 [Exeter 1976: Gmn. orig. 1971], 828) incisively sums up the issue: 'The passage implies the pre-existence of Christ, though it does not define the manner of Christ's becoming poor in the way that Phil 2:6ff speaks of the self-emptying of Christ'.

[199] On the πτωχός being unjustly oppressed by the powerful and wealthy, see (LXX) Pss 9:2(10:2); 9:30 (10:9); 11(12):5; 13(14):5; 36(37):14; Pr 22:7; 28:3; Amos 2:7; 4:1; 5:11; 8:4; Ezek 18:12; 22:29; Isa 3:15; 10:2; Sir 4:2. As a result, the πτωχός makes a meagre living and is close to death (LXX: Ps 87[88]:15; Sir 31:4).

[200] Pss 14:20; 19:7; Sir 13:21. On the πτωχός being mocked, hounded and despised, see (LXX) Ps 108(109):16; Pr 17:5; Sir 10.23. The πτωχός faces troubles and disdain (LXX: Pss 21[22]:24; 33[34]:6).

[201] On God as deliverer of the πτωχός, see (LXX) Pss 39(40):17; 40(41):1; 69(70):5;

'abomination to the rich' which most graphically captures the social dishonour of the pauper in a Jewish context.[202]

Second, in the classical world the social consequences of impoverishment for the benefactor are spelt out in the texts of the Anonymus Iamblichi. The authors of these texts, anonymous fifth-century philosophers, had reflected on the nature of the social obligation which impelled private acts of beneficence in the Greek city-states. Especially pertinent for our purposes is the text cited below. It underscores the fact that the ancients regarded ambivalently any unrestrained display of munificence that resulted in self-impoverishment:

> If, by giving financial support (to others), a man becomes a benefactor of his region, he will necessarily become 'bad' (κακός) when he gathers wealth again. What is more, he could not accumulate the money, the capital, in such a great amount that his resources would not fail while he makes his gifts and presentations. This second evil (δευτέρα κακία) will also appear if the benefactor, after he has collected the money having been a rich man, becomes a poor man (πένης γένηται) and from having been a member of the propertied class (ἐκ πλουσίου), sinks down into the non-propertied class.[203]

In the world-view of the Anonymus Iamblichi, benefactors had to be prepared to lose their property if they were to relieve the poverty of their fellow citizens. But there were very strict limits to their financial support. There was the real danger that, by excessive liberality, benefactors might sink to the status of the non-propertied classes and not have sufficient money to fulfil their gifts. This, the Anonymus Iamblichi assert, would spell social ruin (κακία) for the benefactor and result in him becoming a κακός. As W. Den Boer notes, the word κακός here implies 'poverty, a low social status, and moral inferiority'.[204] Furthermore, as the first sentence makes clear, should the benefactor attempt to reverse his inferior position by accumulating wealth again, he would only reinforce his position as κακός. The hierarchy of wealth, as allocated by the gods, had to be maintained if the polis was to function hamoniously. What ultimately mattered in antiquity was the preservation of the status quo.

71(72):4, 12, 13; 85 (86):1; 112(113):15; 139(140):12. For a prayer of the πτωχός to God, see (LXX) Ps 101(102) *tit*; Job 29:12; 34:28. On almsgiving and the πτωχός, see (LXX) Tob 4.7; 9.20. On the dependence of the πτωχός on the gleanings of the field, see (LXX) Lev 19:10; 23:22; Deut 24:19.

[202] Sir 13.20.

[203] Diels, *Vorsokr.* §89[82]: Anonymus Iamblichi 3.4. For discussion, see W. Den Boer, *Private Morality in Greece and Rome: Some Historical Aspects* (Leiden 1979), 173-176. It was precisely because the munificence of the emperor Augustus was never exhausted that he became the benchmark for generosity in antiquity.

[204] W. Den Boer, *op. cit.*, 175.

According to the Anonymus Iamblichi, it was inconceivable that a wealthy benefactor should become a πένης ('day-labourer', 'poor man'), let alone sink to the pathetic state of being a πτωχός ('beggar', 'pauper'). It was bad enough that the benefactor, having become a πένης, would now be unable to live on his income without working.[205] But, in a daring move, Paul asserts that Christ had abandoned His status of being a πλούσιος ('a wealthy man') and became a πτωχός instead. Paul's choice of the ingressive aorist ἐπτώχευσεν (2 Cor 8:9a: 'he became poor', 'he became a beggar') instead of πένης γενέσθαι ('to become poor') is surely deliberate. The social background underlying the imagery is clear enough. Whereas the πένης earned a frugal living because he had no property, the πτωχός had suffered an extreme reversal of fortune.[206] Reduced to total destitution, the πτωχός was forced to beg for financial support and was treated with contempt by the social elite and his relatives alike.[207] What, then, was Paul trying to convey in designating Christ a πτωχός?

Paul's image of the destitute beggar in 2 Corinthians 8:9 — as interpreted against the backdrop of Antisthenes' portrait of Odysseus — plumbs the depths of the social humiliation and self-sacrifice which Christ experienced in His incarnation and upon the cross.[208] Furthermore, it pricks the arrogance

---

[205] F. Hauck, πένης, πενιχρός, *TDNT* 6 (1968), 37-40. C. Brown (*art. cit.*, 820) states that 'the term includes the handworker and small peasant, who, subsequent to Solon's legislation, were the main supporters of the Athenian democracy.

[206] F. Hauck and E. Bammel, πτωχός, πτωχεία, πτωχεύω, *TDNT* 6 (1968), 885-915. It might be countered that Paul's use of πτωχός is synonymous for πένης and simply functions as a general reference to the economically oppressed. Paul, it could be argued, is reflecting the LXX usage which obscured the difference in meaning between each word in the classical world — that is, between 'pauper' (πτωχός) and 'day-labourer' (πένης). See C. Brown (*art. cit.*, 820) for the LXX references. But Paul mostly uses πτωχός (Rom 15:26; 2 Cor 6:10; Gal 2:10; cf. 4:9) and πτωχεύω (2 Cor 8:9) in benefaction contexts. The sole occurrence of πένης in Paul (2 Cor 9:9) is found in his LXX citation of Ps 111(112):9. Given Paul's clear preference for πτωχός over against πένης, it is reasonable to assume that he opts for the classical meaning of pauperism.

[207] Note that the emperor Tiberius was only willing to make subventions to poor senators. Tiberius, Tacitus informs us (*Ann*. 2.48), distinguished between 'the honorable poverty of the innocent' (*honesta paupertas innocentium*) — e.g. aristocrats who inherited a reduced patrimony — and the 'spendthrift poor' (*prodigi egentes*). The latter group, who had either squandered their wealth on the unworthy or on luxuries, or who always had belonged to the destitute in a daily search for food, were dismissed as dishonourable. As Sallust observed (*Cat*. 12.1), poverty was considered 'a disgrace' (*probrum*). I am indebted to R. Saller ('Poverty, Honor and Obligation in Imperial Rome', *Criterion* 37/2 [1998], 12-20) for these references.

[208] B. Witherington III ('Christology', in G.F. Hawthorne [*et al*., ed.], *Dictionary of Paul and His Letters* [Downers Grove-Leicester 1993], 109) observes that 'the significant events of Jesus' earthly career between his Incarnation and death is (*sic*.) scarcely mentioned (cf. 2 Cor 8:9, though this may also refer to the circumstances into which Jesus was born).'

and self-sufficiency of the wealthy. For, paradoxically, it is precisely through Christ's poverty (2 Cor 8:9b: τῇ ἐκείνου πτωχείᾳ) that others are made rich (2 Cor 8:9b: ἵνα ὑμεῖς πλουτήσητε). Thus the social hierarchy founded on wealth has been overturned by an unprecedented act of benefaction.

Paul also realised that the Corinthians were competing for power and status in a manner similar to the agonistic culture of the times. Unexpectedly, he inverts the contest. The Corinthians were to compete against the Macedonians by divesting themselves of the trappings of their wealth so that they might enrich others (2 Cor 8:8b-15; 9:1-5). In this regard, nothing would have quite as dramatically exposed the self-centeredness of the Corinthians as Paul's appeal to the self-impoverishment of Christ (2 Cor 8:9 [ἐπτώχευσεν]; cf. 2 Cor 6:10b [ὡς πτωχοὶ πολλοὺς δὲ πλουτίζοντες]; cf. 1 Cor 4:7 [ἤδη ἐπλουτήσατε]) and to the liberality of the Macedonian churches notwithstanding their deep poverty (2 Cor 8:2: ἡ κατὰ βάθους πτωχεία αὐτῶν). Paul measures the sincerity of Corinthian love for the poor at Jerusalem (2 Cor 8:8b: τὸ τῆς ὑμετέρας ἀγάπης γνήσιον) against the divine yardstick of grace given to the Macedonian believers (2 Cor 8:1a [τὴν χάριν τοῦ θεοῦ]; cf. 8:8b [διὰ τῆς ἑτέρων σπουδῆς]) and supremely revealed in the incarnation of Christ (2 Cor 8:9a [τὴν χάριν τοῦ κυρίου ἡμῶν Ἰησοῦ]).

Significantly, it is precisely in relation to grace that Paul diverges from Antisthenes. For although Antisthenes underlines the costliness and selflessness of Odysseus' humiliating service, he depicts Odysseus as demanding requital for his benefits and venting annoyance that others had unjustifiably received his favour (χάριν). The only reciprocation of his beneficence he had so far received, Odysseus complains, was to be reproached as 'sacriligious'. In contrast, Paul spotlights the fact that the grace of Christ expected no requital. The humiliation and self-sacrifice of the incarnation is totally other-centered (2 Cor 8:9: δι' ὑμας, ἵνα πλουτήσητε).[209] In light of this, Paul insists that generosity of the Corinthians should not originate in the demands of the reciprocity system (2 Cor 9:7a: μὴ ἐκ λύπης ἢ ἐξ ἀνάγκης) but be motivated by the joy flowing from their experience of divine grace (2 Cor 9:7b-9; cf. 8:1-2).

Elsewhere in his epistles, Paul makes a similar point regarding Christ's beneficence with several different images. Christ had died for His rebellious enemies who would not reciprocate His beneficence with gratitude (Rom 5:6-8). He had died in weakness for those who are still weak in Him (2 Cor 13:4;

---

[209] ὑπὲρ ἡμῶν: Rom 5:8; 8:32; 1 Cor 15:3; 2 Cor 5:21; Gal 3:13. ὑπὲρ ἐμοῦ: Gal 2:20. Eph 5:2: ὑπὲρ αὐτῆς: Eph 5:25.

cf. 11:21, 29-30; 12:5, 9-10). The sinless One had became sin on their behalf so that they might become the righteousness of God in Him (2 Cor 5:21). He had redeemed them from the curse of the law by becoming a curse for them on the cross (Gal 3:13; 4:4b-5). In sum, Christ identified with His dependents and vicariously represented them on the cross, transferring to unworthy recipients all His soteriological benefits in an extraordinary display of grace.

Finally, for Paul the real dynamic behind Christ's grace is God's love. The distinctiveness of Paul's approach can be better appreciated if one examines Epictetus' description of Diogenes the Cynic, the famous pupil of Antisthenes.

> Come, was there anybody that Diogenes did not love (ἐφίλει), a man who was so gentle and kind-hearted that he gladly took upon himself all those troubles and physical hardships for the sake of the common weal? But what was the manner of his loving (ἐφίλει)? As became a servant (διάκονον) of Zeus, caring for (κηδόμενος) men indeed, but at the same time subject unto God. That is why for him alone the whole world, and no special place, was his fatherland; and when he had been taken prisoner he did not hanker for Athens nor his acquaintances and friends (φίλους) there, but he got on good terms with the pirates and tried to reform them. And later when he was sold into slavery at Corinth he kept on living there just as he had formerly lived at Athens ...[210]

In considering this passage there emerge two significant differences between the Cynic world-view and Paul's undertsanding of divine love. First, the verb used for Diogenes' love is φιλεῖν. The word belongs to the language of friendship (φιλία) and forms part of the Graeco-Roman reciprocity system.[211] Very rarely does Paul use φιλ- compounds of human love and avoids them entirely in regards to divine love.[212] Paul's overwhelming preference for ἀγάπη ('love'), ἀγαπητός ('beloved') and ἀγαπᾶν ('to love') is probably explained by the fact that the apostle wishes to differentiate God's love and its outworking from the operations of the Graeco-Roman reciprocity system (Rom 4:4-5; 11:5-6; 35; 13:6-10; 1 Cor 4:7). Moreover, as C. Spicq observes, 'friendship is properly used only of a relationship between equals'.[213] As a description of God's love for humankind, then, ἀγάπη was much better suited to relationships involving parties of different status (inferiors / superiors).

Second, as Epictetus elaborates, the secret of Diogenes' equanimity lay in his close adherence to Antisthenes' teaching. Antisthenes had taught his pupil Diogenes that a philosopher only had the power to deal with his external

---

[210] Arr., *Epict. Diss.*, 3.24.64-66.
[211] See E.A. Judge, *art. cit.* (1982), 105-186; C. Spicq, ἀγάπη, in *id.*, *Theological Lexicon of the New Testament Vol.1* (Peabody 1994), 10-11.
[212] φιλεῖν: 1 Cor 16:22; cf. Titus 3:15. φιλόστοργος: Rom 12:10.
[213] C. Spicq, *art. cit.*, 13.

impressions. It was by cultivating a radical detachment from one's circumstances and attachments that one was progressively freed from the disturbances of life.[214] It was for this reason that Diogenes was able to be affectionate to everyone, no matter what the circumstance. What, then, distinguishes Diogenes' love from its early Christian counterpart?

For Paul, God's love is not found in the philosopher's detachment from the world. Rather grace, motivated and empowered by God's love and mercy (Eph 2:4; 2 Thess 2:16; cf. 1 Tim 1:14), assumes a cruciform shape in a broken and suffering world. God's love had been demonstrated once and for all by Christ's death on behalf of His enemies (Rom 5:8), with the result that nothing in creation can now separate believers from God's predestinating love (Eph 1:4-5; Rom 8:28, 35, 37, 39). Nor did the Son go to the cross unwillingly but rather gave Himself up voluntarily to the Father in an astonishing act of personal love for His dependents (Gal 2:20; Eph 5:2, 25). The Father's love for the Son also ensures that believers experience His glorious grace (Eph 1:6) and that they have been transferred to the Kingdom of His Son (Col 1:13).

Grace, as the invading power of God's love, risks everything in its personal involvement with its terrestrial dependants.[215] It chooses to enter the world of pain rather than retreat from it; it unveils the glory of God in the disgrace of the Son; it simultaneously reveals the weakness and the power of a merciful God in the crucified Christ. Loveless acts towards one's fellow-believers, therefore, overlook the fact that Christ has died for them too (Rom 14:15). As God's dearly loved (Col 3:12a; 1 Thess 1:4; 2 Thess 2:13), believers are to clothe themselves with love (Col 3:12b-14). Such is the mark of the grace of the Father (Rom 5:5a), the Son (2 Cor 5:14; Phil 2:1; Eph 3:17b-19) and the Holy Spirit (Rom 5:5b; Eph 5:22) in the life of the believer.

For Paul, then, God's grace ushered His dependants into a servant community that continued to experience the loving kindness of its Benefactor. In this respect, Paul's language of grace accumulates around three themes: thanksgiving, apostleship, and the χαρίσματα. Each of these will be explored in the next section.

---

[214] Arr., *Epict. Diss.*, 3.24.67-70.
[215] J.D.G. Dunn (*op. cit.* [1998], 320) writes regarding Paul's thought: 'More than any other, these two words, "grace" and "love", together sum up and most clearly characterise his whole theology'.

6.4. Paul, Charis, and the Body of Christ

6.4.1. Charis *and gratitude*

The importance of rendering honour and gratitude to the gods for their beneficence was a commonplace of the Graeco-Roman world.[216] What has not been sufficiently appreciated is the extent to which the Pauline thanksgivings (χάρις; χάριν ἔχω; εὐχαριστία; εὐχάριστος; εὐχαριστεῖν) both draw upon and diverge from well-established hellenistic inscriptional convention. In this respect, P. Schubert has noted that 'the Pauline thanksgivings certainly serve — along with other purposes — to honour the churches to which the letters are addressed'.[217] Thus Paul regularly gives thanks to God for the divine grace animating the fledgling house churches (1 Cor 1:4: εὐχαριστῶ τῷ θεῷ μου περὶ ὑμῶν ἐπὶ χάριτι τοῦ θεοῦ). The most frequent honour that Paul accords Christian communities is a generalised reference to their faith — viewed singly (Rom 1:8: πίστις; cf. 1 Tim 1:12; 2 Tim 1:3-5) or in tandem with other graces (Eph 1:15-16, Col 1:3-4, 1 Thess 3:6-9, 2 Thess 1:3, Phlm 3-4: πίστις, ἀγάπη; 1 Thess 1:2-3: πίστις, ἀγάπη, ἐλπίς).

Further, Paul frames his portraits of Christian faithfulness within Graeco-Roman thanksgiving conventions. Although Paul's honouring of individuals and communities reflects gratitude to God, a strong tone of public praise for his converts and co-workers remains: the partnership (κοινωνία) of the Philippians in defending the gospel (Phil 1:3, 5); the earnestness (σπουδή) of Titus in finalising the Jerusalem collection (2 Cor 8:16); the suffering that the Thessalonians experienced in receiving God's Word worthily (1 Thess 2:13-15); and, last, the personal cost for Prisca and Aquila in serving Paul and the Gentile churches (Rom 16:4). Only on one occasion does Paul use thanksgiving to humiliating effect. There the apostle thanks God for

---

[216] See our discussion of the inscriptions (§2.7), papyri (§3.2.2; §3.6.2), and the philosophers (§5.2.2; §5.4.1—§5.4.2). On thanksgiving to Artemis and Asklepios, see respectively G.H.R. Horsley, *art. cit.* ('Giving Thanks' [1987]) and F.W. Danker, *op. cit.* (1982), §28. On thanksgiving to the gods in the inscriptions and papyri, see especially P. Schubert, *op. cit.*, 142-179. More generally, T. Schermann, 'Εὐχαριστία und εὐχαριστεῖν in ihrem Bedeutungswandel bis 200 n. Chr.', *Philologus* 69 (1910), 375-410. For additional discussion of the Pauline thanksgivings, see J. Wobbe, *op. cit.*, 81-95; G.P. Wiles, *Paul's Intercessory Prayers: The Significance of the Intercessory Prayer Passages in the Letters of Paul* (Cambridge 1974); P.T. O'Brien, 'Thanksgiving and the Gospel in Paul', *NTS* 21 (1974—1975), 144-155; *id., Introductory Thanksgivings in the Letters of Paul* (Leiden 1977); *id.*, 'Thanksgiving in Pauline Theology', in D.A. Hagner and M.J. Harris (eds), *op. cit.*, 50-66; D. Zeller, *op. cit.*, 192-196; D.W. Pao, *op. cit.*

[217] P. Schubert, *op. cit.*, 148. Schubert (*ibid.*) adds that the 'personal dat. obj. τῷ θεῷ to εὐχαριστῶ must not deceive us about the fact that the Pauline thanksgivings are an indirect yet definite compliment to the addressee'.

providentially curtailing his baptism of new converts at Corinth (1 Cor 1:11-16: εὐχαριστῶ [τῷ θεῷ] ὅτι οὐδένα ὑμῶν ἐβάπτισα). This rhetorical tactic is aimed at shaming the factions ripping apart the Corinthian church. But, overall, the Pauline thanksgivings fall within the ambit of the honorific inscriptions. Ultimately, Paul's Godward focus (τῷ θεῷ) and his avoidance of the inscriptional warnings against ingratitude (cf. 2 Tim 3:2: ἀχάριστος) are what differentiate the Christian approach from its Graeco-Roman civic counterpart.

In similar vein to the inscriptions, Paul also insists that the Christian churches return gratitude to their Benefactor and articulates several reasons for honouring God (Rom 6:17; 7:24-25a; 2 Cor 2:14; Col 1:12).[218] Any differences in theological conviction among believers concerning Christian lifestyle must be respected and not become points of contention so that thanksgiving in the body of Christ is maintained (Rom 14:5-6; 1 Cor 10:30 [cf. 11:24]; 1 Tim 4:3-4). Paul does not sponsor a cult of individualism. Individuals should gratefully acknowledge the divine origin of their giftedness, irrespective of their status in the body of Christ (1 Cor 14:18).[219] Above all, the χαρίσματα will only produce genuine corporate thanksgiving to God (Eph 5:4, 20; Phil 4:6; Col 2:7; 3:15, 17; 4:2; 1 Thess 5:18; 1 Tim 2:1) when love and mutual edification are the rule (1 Cor 14:16-17; cf. 13:1-3).

But differences do emerge between Paul and the honorific inscriptions as regards the motivation for thanksgiving. Greek city-states regarded the return of thanks as a matter of public honour. It was the traditional method by which the hellenistic *poleis* cultivated their contemporaries and ensured that their reputation would withstand the scrutiny of posterity. Three typical formulations from the inscriptions will establish the point.

First, the people of Delphi honoured Nicomedes III 'in order that the city might be manifest (in) distributing fitting thanks (καταξίας [χ]άριτας) to those who intend to benefit it'.[220] As previously noted, the epithets ἀξία and καταξία, which often accompanied χάρις in the honorific inscriptions, plunge us into the Homeric world of gifts and counter-gifts. The use of these epithets within the Graeco-Roman reciprocity system reinforced the fact that the honours ascribed were commensurate with the original benefaction.[221] How comfortably do the Pauline thanksgivings fit into this grid?

---

[218] D. Zeller (*op. cit.*, 193) cites Epictetus (Arr., *Epict. Diss.*, 4.4.7) and Philo (*Som.* 2.213) as background to Rom 6:17ff and Rom 7:25a respectively.

[219] D. Zeller (*ibid.*, 119, 193) cites Philo, *Leg. All.* 1.82 and *Quod Deus* 5ff as background to 1 Cor 14:16ff.

[220] *FD* III(4) 77 (94 BC).

[221] See our discussion in §2.4.

Paul consistently associates the return of gratitude with the motif of abundance: τὴν εὐχαριστίαν περισσεύσῃ (2 Cor 4:15b); περισσεύουσα διὰ πολλῶν εὐχαριστιῶν τῷ θεῷ (9:12b); περισσεύοντες ἐν εὐχαριστίᾳ (Col 2:7b). The return of thanks, however, cannot be measured against the infinite generosity of the divine Benefactor: 'For what thanksgiving can we return to God ... ?' (1 Thess 3:9: τίνα γὰρ εὐχαριστίαν δυνάμεθα τῷ θεῷ ἀνταποδοῦναι). Instead, for Paul, εὐχαριστία simply abounds! Christian gratitude spontaneously responds to the divine blessing (τὸ χάρισμα) that comes from the answered prayers of fellow Christians (2 Cor 1:11); it rejoices in the extension of divine grace (ἡ χάρις πλεονάσασα) through the suffering apostles to others (4:15 [cf. vv.7-11]); it celebrates the spiritual maturity and generosity of the Gentile Christians as they meet the needs of their impoverished Jewish brethren (9:11b-12). Thus, since Paul applies the same abundance terminology to χάρις (§6.1.2.4), the conclusion of D. Zeller is inescapable: in the Christian gospel 'Gnade ist der Grunde der εὐχαριστία'.[222]

Second, a first-century BC decree of an Ionian religious guild accords honours to a priestess of Dionysos 'in order that the benevolence of Hediste and the thankfulness (εὐχαριστία) of the religious guild may become manifest to posterity'.[223] The Pauline thanksgivings, however, are not framed with the judgement of posterity in mind. As D. Georgi has astutely observed,

> Paul was eager to show that his mission had resulted, not in the establishment of some disintegrated clubs, but in genuine communities willing to remember *in gratitude* their origin and, hence, were bound to the church as an ecumenical body. As such these congregations did not shrink away from giving material proof of their individual responsibility.[224]

Paul's focus is simultaneously theocentric and ecclesiastical. In 2 Corinthians 9:11-15, Paul promotes 'a cycle of grace' that embraces Jew and Gentile in an international community of dependence and interdependence.[225] God, in an

---

[222] D. Zeller, *op. cit.*, 196. See also our discussion of *P. Warren* 13 in §3.4. Similarly, C. Spicq (*op. cit.*, 141): 'La vie chrétienne est la gratitude en acte'. Note, however, Paul's use of the language of commensurability in 2 Thess 1:3: εὐχαριστεῖν ὀφείλομεν τῷ θεῷ ... καθὼς ἄξιόν ἐστιν. C. Spicq (*op. cit.*, 134 n.2) correctly observes that this corresponds to hellenistic usage (Aristotle, Philo, and the honorific inscriptions).

[223] *SEG* IV 598.

[224] D. Georgi, *Remembering the Poor: The History of Paul's Collection for Jerusalem* (Nashville 1992: Gmn. orig. 1965), 55 (my emphasis).

[225] On the 'cycle of grace', see D. Georgi, *op. cit.*, 151-152; R. Corriveau, *op. cit.*, 106; J. Koenig, 'Occasions of Grace in Paul, Luke and First-Century Judaism', *ATR* 64/4 (1982), 566-567; D. Zeller, *op. cit.*, 192. For an interesting contrast to Paul in this instance, see our discussion of the cycle of divine reciprocity in the hymn of Isidoros to Isis-Hermouthis (§2.7).

act of grace towards His dependants, provides both the finances (2 Cor 9:10a, 11a [ἐν παντί], 12a, 13a) and the spiritual maturity (9:10b, 11b [ἐν παντί]) for the Gentile Christians to finalise the Jerusalem collection for the poor. The Jerusalem Christians, in returning the grace of thanksgiving (2 Cor 9:11c, 12b), express their dependence upon God as Benefactor and their interdependence as part of the universal body of Christ (9:14: cf. Rom 1:11-12: χάρισμα πνευματικόν).[226]

In the view of Paul, this cycle of grace promotes a work of solidarity in his missionary work.[227] What ought to motivate the Corinthian Christians is the thanksgiving and glory that their Jerusalem brethren render to God for the διακονία of the Gentile churches (2 Cor 9:12b-13).[228] Moreover, as M. Theobald argues,[229] Paul deepens theologically the ancient letter *topos* of longing when he describes the projected response of the Jerusalem church (2 Cor 9:14a). The longing of the Jerusalem Christians will be expressed in prayer for their Gentile brothers as they observe the 'surpassing grace of God' at work in them (2 Cor 9:14b: τὴν ὑπερβάλλουσαν χάριν τοῦ θεοῦ). Thus Paul anticipates and initiates the thankfulness of the Jerusalem churches when he praises God for the 'inexpressible gift' of God's grace in the Gentile Christians (2 Cor 9:15: χάρις τῷ θεῷ).[230] In short, the unity of Christ's church — not the judgement of posterity — is what really matters for Paul in thanksgiving.

Third, a Mylasan benefactor is honoured with a gold crown and an inscribed image 'in order that (the tribe of) the Otorkondeis may manifestly distribute appropriate gratitude (τὴν καταξίαν χάριτα) and honour (τιμήν) to those who choose to seek honour (φιλοδοξεῖν)'.[231] The contrast with the Pauline thanksgivings is pointed: there God is the ultimate focus of all honour (2 Cor 4:15: τὴν δόξῆν τοῦ θεοῦ; 9:12b-13: δοξάζοντες τὸν θεόν).[232]

---

[226] M. Theobald (*op. cit.*, 300) draws attention to the 'wish motif' common to Rom 1:11 (ἐπιποθῶ) and 2 Cor 9:14 (ἐπιποθούντων).

[227] D. Zeller, *op. cit.*, 192: 'Die Judenchristen preisen Gott ... für das Werk der Solidarität'. Similarly, M. Theobald (*op. cit.*, 301) argues that 'ein geistlicher Austausch' between the Jewish and Gentile communities was Paul's objective.

[228] In regard to 2 Cor 9:12b, H.D. Betz (*2 Corinthians 8 and 9* [Philadelphia 1985], 118) observes that 'the collection had a spiritual purpose, and for Paul this constituted an overriding concern'.

[229] M. Theobald, *op. cit.*, 300.

[230] G.P. Wiles, *op. cit.*, 240; M. Theobald, *op. cit.*, 301; H.D. Betz, *op. cit.*, 128.

[231] *I. Mylasa* 110 (II cent. BC).

[232] On δόξα and χάρις in 2 Cor 8-9, see D. Georgi, *op. cit.*, 102, 107-109, 151. In regard to 2 Cor 4:15, M. Theobald (*op. cit.*, 224) writes that grace is not transformed into 'die Gabe der Herrlichkeit Gottes' through the apostle. Rather it reveals itself in its fullness and so magnifies the greater glory of God. Note, too, the comment of G.P. Wiles (*op. cit.*,

6.4.2. Charis *and apostleship*

A consciousness of mission appears in the first-century Cynic-Stoic philosophers, Epictetus and Dio Chrysostom. New Testament scholars have been alert to the potential parallels that such evidence affords.[233] Nonetheless, there needs to be further exploration of the relationship between this material and Paul's self-understanding as an apostle chosen by divine grace. How did the terminology of the Cynic-Stoic mission contrast to that of Paul? What portrait of the divine and its intersection with the human world was promoted in each case? What perception of authority impelled their missionary endeavours? In other words, what legitimation was appealed to and why? How would Paul's Graeco-Roman contemporaries have perceived his apostolic persona?

In the view of Epictetus, the true Cynic has a twofold commission from the deity. First, as the scout of Zeus, he must identify and accurately diagnose the external circumstances that divert people from correct moral behaviour. Second, as the messenger of Zeus, he must so apply the truth to his audience that they are called back to the true moral path within themselves from which they have strayed. The following extract best encapsulates Epictetus' understanding of the mission of the Cynic:

> ...he has been sent by Zeus (ἀπὸ τοῦ Διὸς ἀπέσταλται) to men, partly as a messenger (ἄγγελος), in order to show them that in questions of good and evil they have gone astray, and are seeking the true nature of the good and evil where it is not, but where it is they never think; and partly, in the words of Diogenes, when he has taken off to Philip, after the battle, as a scout (κατάσκοπος). For the Cynic is truly a scout (κατάσκοπος), to find out what things are friendly to men and what hostile; and he must first do his scouting accurately (ἀκριβῶς κατασκεψάμενον), and on returning must tell the truth (ἀπαγγεῖλαι τἀληθῆ), not driven by fear to designate as enemies those who are not such, nor in any other fashion be distraught or confused by his external impressions.[234]

In his missionary task, it is preferable that the Cynic is free from the distraction of private duties to a family. The Cynic, as an itinerant preacher, must be 'devoted to the service of God (ὅλον πρὸς τῇ διακονίᾳ τοῦ θεοῦ)', in order that he might fulfil his role as 'the messenger (ἄγγελος), the

---

240) on 2 Cor 4:15 and 9:11-15: 'that thanksgivings may be multiplied from many believers and due honour may be given to God ... was a theme of importance for Paul'. On the interrelation of thanksgiving and δόξα in 2 Cor 4:15 and 9:12-13, see G.H. Boobyer, *"Thanksgiving" and the "Glory of God" in Paul* (Leipzig 1929), 79ff.

[233] D. Georgi, *The Opponents of Paul in Second Corinthians* (Edinburgh 1986; Gmn. orig. 1964), 151-164; K.H. Rengstorf, 'ἀποστέλλω, ἀπόστολος', *TDNT* 1 (1964), 398-447; V.C. Pfitzner, *Paul and the Agon Motif: Traditional Athletic Imagery in the Pauline Literature* (Leiden 1967), 191-192; F.G. Downing, *op. cit.* (1987), 73-75; *id.*, *Christ and the Cynics* (Sheffield 1988), 46.

[234] Arr., *Epict. Diss.*, 3.22.23-25.

scout (κατάσκοπος), the herald of the gods (κῆρυξ τῶν θεῶν)'.[235] Since the Cynic's true family is humanity, he performs a servant role on behalf of Zeus (ὑπηρέτης τοῦ Διός) by upbraiding his complacent kinsfolk in a fatherly and brotherly manner (ὡς πατήρ, ὡς ἀδελφός).[236] Moreover, the Cynic is presented by Epictetus 'as a witness summoned by God (ὡς μάρτυς ὑπο τοῦ θεοῦ κεκλημένος)'.[237] The Cynic points to the real nature of the moral purpose (προαίρεσις).[238] In other words, the true Cynic demonstrates by his behaviour and teaching that external circumstances — whether good or evil — should not divert people from making responsible ethical choices and acting morally.[239]

What is remarkable about Epictetus' portrayal of the Cynic mission is its overlap in terminology with Paul's view of his apostleship. As an apostle, Paul had been summoned (καλεῖν: Gal 1:15; καλεῖσθαι: 1 Cor 15:9; κλητός: Rom 1:1; 1 Cor 1:1) and sent out by God (ἀποστέλλειν: 1 Cor 1:17; ἀποστολή: Rom 1:5; ἀπόστολος: Rom 1:1; 1 Cor 1:1 etc). An important feature of Paul's apostolic service (διακονία: Rom 11:13; 2 Cor 3:7, 8, 9; 4:1; 5:18; 6:3; cf. 1 Tim 1:12; διάκονος: Eph 3:7; ὑπηρέτης: 1 Cor 4:1) was his proclamation of the gospel (κῆρυξ: cf. 2 Tim 1:11; κηρύσσειν: 1 Cor 1:23; 9:27; 15:11-12; 2 Cor 1:19; 4:5; Gal 2:2; 5:11; Col 1:23; 1 Thess 2:9). Above all, this involved testimony to God (μαρτυρεῖν: 1 Cor 1:6; 2:1; 15:15; cf. 2 Tim 1:8; μάρτυς: cf. Acts 22:15; 26:16) as well as a commitment to His revealed truth (ἀλήθεια: 2 Cor 4:2; 6:7; 11:10; 13:8; Gal 2:5, 14; Phil 1:18; Col 1:5-6). Last, Paul regarded himself as the apostolic father of his congregations and co-workers (ὡς πατρὶ τέκνον: Phil 2:22; ὡς πατὴρ τέκνα: 1 Thess 2:11).

Significantly, two of the pivotal words that Epictetus chooses to describe the Cynic mission — κατάσκοπος and ἄγγελος — are used disparagingly by Paul of impediments to the gospel. Thus Paul's thorn in the flesh is styled a 'messenger of Satan' (2 Cor 12:7: ἄγγελος Σατανᾶ) because it might deflect him from his apostolic mission. The Judaizers at Galatia are identified as scouts who spy on the liberty of the Christian church (Gal 2:4: κατασκοπῆσαι). In each case, the tone is negative. But whether Paul felt equally uneasy about the Cynic overtones of κατάσκοπος and ἄγγελος as descriptions of his *own* apostolic mission is impossible to tell.

---

[235] *Ibid.*, 3.22.69-70.
[236] *Ibid.*, 3.22.82 (95: ὡς φίλοις τοῖς θεοῖς, ὡς ὑπηρέτης).
[237] *Ibid.*, 1.29.47; 3.24.112.
[238] *Ibid.*
[239] *Ibid.*, 1.29.47-49; 3.24.113-114.

Dio Chrysostom provides us the closest Graeco-Roman parallel to a divinely impelled mission which dispenses the grace of the deity to its human recipients. From AD 82 Dio became increasingly conscious of a mission after his expulsion from Rome, Italy, and native Bithynia during the reign of Domitian. Dio visited the temple of Delphi to consult the oracle and was commanded to persevere in his mission as an itinerant philosopher until he came 'to the uttermost parts of the earth' (*Or.*, 13.9; cf. Acts 1:8; 22:21).[240] He would later tell the citizens of Tarsus that he 'came by divine guidance (κατὰ τὸ δαιμόνιον) to address and counsel (them)' (*Or.*, 34.4). As a result, his missionary message had none of the ambiguities associated with traditional divination (*Or.*, 34.5).

At Alexandria, Dio distinguished himself from the disreputable type of philosopher who either avoided the exposure of public proclamation or (like the Cynics) resorted to mendicancy for remuneration (*Or.*, 32.8-11).[241]

---

[240] For examples of missionary guidance in the inscriptions and papyri, see the Delian aretalogy of Sarapis (F.W. Danker, *op. cit.* [1982], §27) and the letter of Zoilos (*PSI* IV. 435: A. Deissmann, *op. cit.*, 152-161). Plutarch (*Mor.*, 329C) tells us that Alexander the Great 'believed that he came as a heaven-sent governor (θεόθεν ἁρμοστής) to all, and as a mediator for the whole world'. Alexander of Abonuteichus (Lucian, *Alexander the False Prophet*, 36) sent out oracle-mongers into the Roman empire with warnings of impending disaster. For discussion of Paul and other Hellenistic cult founder figures, see H.D. Betz, 'Transferring a Ritual: Paul's Interpretation of Baptism in Romans 6', in T. Engberg-Pedersen (ed.), *Paul in His Hellenistic Context* (Edinburgh 1994), 86ff.

[241] In each instance, Paul would not have met with Dio Chrysostom's approval. First, as E.A. Judge, S.K. Stowers, and C. Forbes point out, Paul rarely preached in the open air like the Cynics. Usually he taught in the hellenistic synagogues and (after his arrival at Philippi in Macedonia) in the salons of wealthy patrons, as was the practice of itinerant sophists. In the estimation of Dio, Paul would have discredited himself by lecturing in the hall of Tyrannus (Acts 19:9). This was the tactic of pseudo-philosophers who wanted to avoid healthy public scrutiny: 'others exercise their voices in what we call lecture-halls, having secured as hearers men who are in league with them and tractable' (Dio Chrysostom, *Or.*, 32.8). See too Pseudo-Socrates, *Ep.*, 1.2: 'I neither practise philosophy shut up inside'. Second, much of the rancour that Paul occasioned revolved around his refusal to accept remuneration (2 Cor 11:7-11; 12:14-16), preferring either to work himself (Acts 18:1-3; 20:34; 2 Thess 3:8; cf. 1 Cor 9:14-15) or to accept benefactions from congregations *other than* the church at which he was currently ministering (Phil 4:10-19; 2 Cor 11:8-9). Undoubtedly, Paul was well aware of the fraudulent reputation of mendicants (e.g. Aristotle, *Rh.*, 3.2; cf. Pseudo-Socrates, *Ep.*, 1.2). Therefore, Paul reserved for himself the right of a benefactor to preach the gospel 'free of charge' to the Corinthians (1 Cor 9:18: ἀδάπανον). In so doing, Paul called upon a commonplace of the honorific inscriptions to express his generosity. Two examples will be adequate. A decree from Sestos in honour of Menas says that he 'spares himself no expense (οὔτε δαπάνης) or public service' (*Michel* 327: 133-120 BC). Zosimos of Priene, as secretary of the Council, bore the expense (δαπάνη) of producing double copies of the public records on skins and papyrus rolls, knowing that he was assured of the good faith of the People towards himself (*I. Priene* 112: 84 BC). Generally, see E.A. Judge, 'The Early Christians as a Scholastic Community, Part II', *JRH* 1/3 (1961), 125-137; *id.*, 'First Impressions of St. Paul', *Prudentia* 2/2 (1970), 52-58.

Instead, he promoted himself as the philosopher chosen by Providence to dispense the benefactions of Sarapis at Alexandria. On this occasion, the miraculous cures of Sarapis would not be divinatory in origin. Instead, the beneficence of the deity would be found in the wisdom of Dio, the philosopher-physician, who cares for souls:

> I have chosen that role, not of my own volition, but by the will of some deity (ὑπὸ δαιμονίου τινὸς γνώμης). For when divine providence is at work (οἱ θεοὶ προνοοῦσιν) for men, the gods provide, not only good counsellors who need no urging, but also the words that are appropriate and profitable to the listener. And ... here in Alexandria the deity is most in honour, and to you especially does he display his power (τὴν αὐτοῦ δύναμιν) through almost daily oracles and dreams ... But your deity, I think, being more potent (τελειότερος), wishes to confer his benefits upon you through the agency of men ... not by means of a few words, but with strong, full utterance and in clear terms, instructing you regarding most vital matters — if you are patient — with purpose and persuasiveness.[242]

There is no overlap in terminology between Dio's understanding of mission and the apostleship of Paul. Dio's appeal to divine πρόνοια is simply not found in the New Testament. But the issue of legitimation is more complex. Paul uses several expressions for his claim that God's will was the sole origin of his apostleship.[243] By contrast, Dio alludes only to the *daimonion* of Socrates.[244] This is consistent with the parallels which Dio draws, in the hope of legitimating his mission, between himself as a wandering preacher and the

---

Contra, see B.W. Winter, 'Is Paul among the Sophists?', *Reformed Theological Review* 53/1 (1994), 28-38. A more qualified response is found in S.K. Stowers, 'Social Status, Public Speaking and Private Teaching: The Circumstances of Paul's Preaching Activity', *NovT* 26/1 (1984), 59-82; C. Forbes, 'Finding a Place for St Paul', *Society for Early Christianity Newsletter* (Macquarie University, No.8, 1990), 5-7. Also, R.F. Hock, *The Social Context of Paul's Ministry: Tentmaking and Apostleship* (Philadelphia 1980); P. Marshall, *Enmity in Corinth: Social Conventions in Paul's Relations with the Corinthians* (Tübingen 1987), 218-258.

[242] Dio Chrysostom, *Or.*, 32.12-13. Dio's inflated claim that the divine power (δύναμις) was reaching eschatological consummation (τελειότερος) in the wisdom of noble philosophers like himself would have provoked a sharp reaction from Paul. Christ is the embodiment of wisdom and power (Rom 10:4: τέλος νόμου; 1 Cor 1:24: θεοῦ δύναμιν καὶ θεοῦ σοφίαν [cf. 1:30]) because God has eschatologically overturned the age of the sophist through the death of His Son (1 Cor 1:18-23; 1 Cor 4:20). For Paul, earthly wisdom (σοφία σαρκική) and the grace of God (χάρις τοῦ θεοῦ) are diametrically opposed (2 Cor 1:12). The grace of God also empowers Paul's apostleship (δύναμις: Rom 15:15-19 [v.15: χάρις]; 1 Cor 4:20-21; 2 Cor 12:9 [v.9a: χάρις]; 13:4b) and brings believers to completion in Christ (τέλειος: Rom 12:2; Phil 3:15; Col 1:28; 4:12; τελειοῦν: 2 Cor 12:9).

[243] διὰ θελήματος θεοῦ: 1 Cor 1:1; 2 Cor 1:1; Eph 1:1; Col 1:1. διὰ Ἰησοῦ Χριστοῦ: Gal 1:1. κατ' ἐπιταγὴν θεοῦ: 1 Tim 1:1; Titus 1:3. κλητὸς ἀπόστολος: Rom 1:1; 1 Cor 1:1. Paul also styles his calling 'a necessity' (1 Cor 9:16: ἀνάγκη).

[244] See especially Plato, *Ap.*, 23b, 29d, 30e-31a. Pseudo-Socrates (*Ep.*, 1.2) says that Socrates applied himself 'to the philosophic life at the command of God' (τοῦ θεοῦ κελεύσαντος φιλοσοφεῖν) and was commanded to stay in the city of Athens (*ibid.*, 1.7). For further examples of Socrates' divine guidance, *ibid.*, 1.9-10.

unimpeachable figure of Socrates (*Or.*, 13.14ff).[245] As previously noted, Epictetus resorted to this type of legitimation in referring to Diogenes' role as scout. Similarly, Dio appeals to Diogenes as a missionary figure through the familiar theme of the 'care of souls' (*Or.*, 8:5; 9:2; 27:7; 32:10), and leaves his readers to draw the appropriate inference concerning himself.[246] From the foregoing evidence we can observe a clear similarity between Dio Chrysostom and the way that Paul legitimates his apostleship. This is especially obvious in Galatians 1:15-16. There Paul links his vocation as the apostle to the Gentiles (Gal 1:15) with the commissioning of the Old Testament prophet Jeremiah (1:16: cf. Jer 1:5) and the Servant of Yahweh of Deutero-Isaiah (1:16: cf. Isa 49:1, 5-6).[247]

However, although Paul presents his commission partially in Old Testament prophetic categories, the ἀποκαλύψις Ἰησοῦ Χριστοῦ (Gal 1:12, 16) remains for him the fundamental legitimation of his apostleship, along with — appropriately for a Cynic or an Old Testament prophetic context — his ongoing sufferings (2 Cor 11:20-12:11). It is important to realise that Paul's commission (Gal 1:16b) is inseparable from his election and conversion (1:15-16a).[248] Paul's experience of divine grace through His risen Son on the Damascus road (Gal 1:16a: ἀποκαλύψαι τὸν υἱὸν αὐτοῦ ἐν ἐμοί; cf. 1 Cor 9:1; 1 Cor 15:8; 2 Cor 4:6; Phil 3:12b) was the outcome of God's beneficent intention (Gal 1:15a: εὐδόκησεν). As A. Denis notes, God's election of Paul was distinct from and anterior to his apostolic commission.[249] Having been set apart by God before his birth (Gal 1:15a) and

---

[245] For discussion, W.L. Liefeld, *The Wandering Preacher as a Social Figure in the Roman Empire* (unpub. Ph.D. diss. Columbia University 1967), 47-48.

[246] *Ibid.*, 48-49. On Peregrinus as 'the new Socrates', see Lucian, *The Passing of Peregrinus*, 12.

[247] For discussion, see J. Munck, *Paul and the Salvation of Mankind* (London 1959: Gmn. orig 1954), 24ff; A.-M. Denis, 'L'élection et la vocation de Paul, faveurs célestes: Étude thématique de Gal 1,15', *RevThom* 35 (1957), 408, 413; A. Satake, 'Apostolat und Gnade bei Paulus', *NTS* 15 (1968), 97. Both Satake (*op. cit.*, 97 n.2) and Denis (*art. cit.*, 422-426) set Paul's use of καλεῖν in Gal 1:15 against the backdrop of Deutero-Isaiah. For criticism of Satake's overall approach, see S. Kim, *The Origin of Paul's Gospel* (Tübingen 1981), 288-296; H. von Lips, 'Der Apostolat des Paulus — ein Charisma? Semantische Aspekte zu χάρις-χάρισμα und anderen Wortpaaren im Sprachgebrauch des Paulus', *Bib* 66/3 (1985), 305-343. Recently, S. Kim (*Paul and the New Perspective: Second Thoughts on the Origin of Paul's Gospel* [Grand Rapids-Cambridge 2002], 101-127) has argued that Isa 42:6-7 also lies behind Gal 1:15.

[248] See J. Guillet, *art. cit.*, col.138; F.F. Bruce, *The Epistle of Paul to the Galatians* (Exeter 1982), 93.

[249] A.-M. Denis, *art. cit.*, 427. Contra, see G. Bornkamm ('The Revelation of Christ to Paul on the Damascus Road and Paul's Doctrine of Justification and Reconciliation: A Study in Galatians 1', in R.J. Banks [ed.], *Reconciliation and Hope: New Testament Essays on Atonement and Eschatology Presented to L.L. Morris on His 60th Birthday* [Exeter 1974],

called by divine grace to belong to Christ (1:15b: καλέσας διὰ τῆς χάριτος; cf. 1:6: καλέσαντος ὑμᾶς ἐν χάριτι), he was also graciously called to preach Him to the Gentiles (1:16: ἵνα εὐαγγελίζωμαι αὐτον; 2:9: τὴν χάριν τὴν δοθεῖσάν μοι [cf. Rom 12:3; 15:15; 1 Cor 3:10; Eph 3:2, 7, 8]; Rom 1:5: χάριν καὶ ἀποστολήν).[250] God's beneficence, therefore, is entirely unsolicited: it is primordial in origin, transforming in its power, and missionary in its agenda. It afforded Paul the confidence that in spite of his previous persecution of God's church he was by God's grace what he was (1 Cor 15:9-10: χάριτι θεοῦ) — an apostle of Christ.

Moreover, the idea that the deity called out individuals well before their performance of the requisite cult at a sanctuary was highly unusual in a Graeco-Roman context. When one wanted to approach the deity for revelation or beneficence, the initiative lay — as we saw with Dio — entirely with the suppliant. The case of M. Julias Apellas is an instructive exception to the rule. After having suffered severe digestive upsets, Apellas 'was sent [for] by the god', and only then did he embark on the trip to the sanctuary of Asclepius at Epidaurus (*SIG*³ 117: II cent. AD). On the journey, at Aegina, he was commanded by the god not to lose his temper so much and on his arrival at Epidaurus was given the prescription that led to his cure.[251] In contrast to Paul, however, there is no sense in Apellas' testimony of a primordial grace leading to the consciousness of mission.

How would Paul's Graeco-Roman contemporaries have perceived Paul's divine mission? It is precisely the language of grace, among other things, that differentiated the apostle of the Gentiles from itinerant hellenistic preachers Dio Chrysostom and the Cynic 'scouts' of Epictetus. Whereas Dio preached a message of ideal kingship over against the tyranny of the emperor (Domitian's reign: *Or.*, 7.12; 14.1ff; 45.5ff; Trajan's reign: *Or.*, 1-4; 62), Paul heralded Christ's reign of grace over sin and death (Rom 5:17, 21; 6:14). Whereas Epictetus exalted the impoverished Cynic as king and master over his audience (Arr., *Epict. Diss.*, 3.22.49: βασιλεὺς καὶ δεσπότης),[252] Paul regarded the Philippians as 'my fellow-sharers of grace' (Phil 1:7:

90-103). Bornkamm argues that Paul more emphasises his call rather than his conversion in Gal 1:15-16. In my view, this is a false dilemma: conversion and call are inseparable, with grace undergirding each. See J. Becker, *op. cit.*, 69-81.

[250] J. Wobbe (*op. cit.*, 73-74) argues that Rom 1:5 (χάριν καὶ ἀποστολήν) is a case of hendiadys and is therefore to be translated 'the grace of apostleship'.

[251] See also C. Forbes (*Prophecy and Inspired Speech in Early Christianity and its Hellenistic Environment* [Tübingen 1995], 304-308) on the rare phenomenon of spontaneous or unsolicited oracles in antiquity.

[252] On the Cynic use of regnal imagery, see R. Höistad, *op. cit.*; *id.*, 'Cynicism', in P. Wiener (ed.) *Dictionary of the History of Ideas* Vol.1 (New York 1968), 627-634, esp. 632ff.

συγκοινωνούς μου τῆς χάριτος) in his imprisonment and defence of the gospel. Admittedly, Paul's insistence upon the ethical obedience of his Gentile converts (Rom 1:5: εἰς ὑπακοὴν πίστεως ἐν πᾶσιν τοῖς ἔθνεσιν [cf. 15:18; 16:26]; 6:1, 15; 1 Thess 1:9: δουλεύειν θεῷ) may initially have sounded similar to aspects of the Cynic-Stoic mission.[253] However, such moral change was motivated and empowered by divine grace rather than a Cynic cultivation of self-mastery for the masses.

6.4.3. Charis *and spiritual gifts*

In grappling with Paul's understanding of χάρισμα in its Graeco-Roman context, we are immediately confronted with the problem that the earliest assured occurrence of the word in Greek literature is from the second century AD (Alciphron *Ep.* 3.17.4).[254] On the Jewish side, the evidence is equally unpromising. The evidence of the Jewish apocrypha is textually suspect (cf. the variant readings of *Sir.* 7:33 [cod.B] and 38:30 [cod.S]). The Jewish pseudepigraphic work, the *Sibylline Oracles*, describes the soul as a 'gracious gift of God' (*Sib. Or.* 2:54): but this appears in a passage which is clearly a Christian interpolation. The twofold occurrence of χάρισμα in Philo, referring to the 'free grace of God' dispensed in creation (*Leg. All.* 3.78), probably represents the first time in antiquity that the word was used with theological reference.[255] It is likely, therefore, that Paul borrowed χάρισμα

---

[253] However, as regards 1 Thess 1:9, note the perceptive comment of W.H. Rengstorf (*art. cit.*, 412 n.37) that δοῦλος τοῦ θεοῦ was 'never used by Cynics or Stoics as a self-designation and would be quite impossible from their standpoint'.

[254] On χάρισμα in Paul, see G.P. Wetter, *op. cit.*, 168-187; J. Wobbe, *op. cit.*, 63-75; A.C. Piepkorn, 'Charisma in the New Testament and the Apostolic Fathers', *CTM* 42/6 (1971), 369-389; U. Brockhaus, *op. cit., passim*; H. Conzelmann, 'χάρισμα', *TDNT* 9 (1974), 402-406; J.D.G. Dunn, *Jesus and the Spirit: A Study of the Religious and Charismatic Experience of Jesus and the First Christians as Reflected in the New Testament* (London 1975), 205-207, 259-300; H.A. Lombard, 'Charisma and Church Office', *Neot* 10 (1976), 31-52; F.S. Malan, 'The Relationship Between Apostleship and Office in the Theology of Paul', *Neot* 10 (1976), 53-68; R. Banks, *Paul's Idea of Community: The Early House Churches in Their Historical Setting* (2nd edit. Peabody, Mass. 1994: orig. edit. 1978), 88-108; R.Y.K. Fung, 'Ministry, Community and Spiritual Gifts', *EvQ* 66/1 (1984), 3-20; N. Baumert, 'Charisma und Amt bei Paulus', in A. Vanhoye (ed.), *L'apôtre Paul: personnalité, style et conception du ministère* (Leuven 1986), 203-228; D.S. Lim, *The Servant Nature of the Church in the Pauline Corpus* (unpub. Ph.D. diss. Fuller Theological Seminary 1987), 138-158; D. Zeller, *op. cit.*, 185-189; E. Nardoni, 'The Concept of Charism in Paul', *CBQ* 55/1 (1993), 68-80; M. Turner, *The Holy Spirit and Spiritual Gifts Then and Now* (Carlise 1996), 261-285; T.R. Schreiner, *Paul: Apostle of God's Glory in Christ. A Pauline Theology* (Downers Grove 2001), 351-370.

[255] The position of D. Zeller, *op. cit.*, 36 n.21. By contrast, R. Banks (*op. cit.*, 91) unnecessarily plays down the theological content of Philo's reference. Contrary to Zeller, U. Brockhaus (*op. cit.*, 128) claims that the earliest and clearest reference to χάρισμα in the extant Greek literature is that of Paul. This is because there remains text-critical argument

from contemporary colloquial language (with the sense of 'gift' or 'present') and was the first to use it as a technical term.[256] Unfortunately, in the case of χάρισμα, we do not have any access to the familiar first-century cultural codes that may have been embedded in its colloquial use. Further, in view of Paul's innovative understanding of the word, meaningful cultural comparison becomes increasingly difficult.

In his treatment of χάρισμα, R. Banks makes a breach in our impasse by contrasting the community of the early Christians with the hellenistic religious associations.[257] But his contribution is brief, impressionistic, and confined to the literary evidence. For our purposes, three inscriptions of the popular voluntary associations invite comparison with the Pauline assemblies: the *Rule of the Iobacchoi* (*SIG*³ 1109: 178 BC); the *Rule of the Andanian mysteries* (*SIG*³ 736: 92—91 BC); and, finally, the *Philadelphian Association* (*SIG*³ 985: I cent BC). At the outset, the connection between divine χάρις and the giftedness of Christ's body must be clarified.

Several of Paul's uses of χάρισμα have a general non-technical sense. As argued above (§6.1.2.4; §6.1.2.5), χάρισμα refers three times to the beneficent act of God in Christ which secures righteousness (Rom 5:15a, 16b) and eternal life for His dependants (6:23). Acts of divine beneficence towards individuals are also embraced by χάρισμα: Paul's delivery from deadly peril in Asia through the prayer of his fellow Christians (2 Cor 1:11); or, again, the gift of celibacy which enables Christians (single and married) to exercise self control over their sexual desires (1 Cor 7:7).[258] χάρις and χάρισμα acquire a specific technical connotation when they designate the manifestation and operation of divine grace either within the nation of Israel (Rom 11:29: τὰ χαρίσματα [cf. 9:4]) or the body of Christ (χάρις: Eph 4:7; χάρισμα: Rom 1:11; 12:6; 1 Cor 1:7; 12:4, 9, 28, 30-31; cf. 1 Tim 4:14; 2 Tim 1:6).

Four important conclusions can be drawn from Paul's technical use of χάρισμα.

1. Paul does not regard χάρις and χάρισμα as simply interchangeable. As E. Nardoni points out, χάρισμα is the direct result of God's χάρις.[259] The rich variety of gifting within Christ's church is always the product of

---

among scholars concerning the presence of χάρισμα in *Leg. All.* 3.78. See also J. Wobbe (*op. cit.*, 64) and H. Conzelmann (*art. cit.*, 403 n.4). Either way, Paul embarks on the most extended and original use of χάρισμα in antiquity.

[256] These are the positions respectively of E. Nardoni (*art. cit.*, 69) and R. Banks (*op. cit.*, 91).

[257] R. Banks, *op. cit.*, 107-108.

[258] On 1 Cor 7:7, see especially J.D.G. Dunn, *op. cit.*, 206-207.

[259] E. Nardoni, *art. cit.*, 71.

God's grace (Rom 12:6: χαρίσματα κατὰ τὴν χάριν; 1 Cor 1:7 [cf. v.4]).

2. The eschatological fullness of the Spirit is grounds for the diversity of gifting.[260] The Spirit helps Christians to understand the gifts bestowed on them by God (2 Cor 2:12: τὰ ὑπὸ τοῦ θεοῦ χαρισθέντα) and animates the gifts themselves (Rom 1:11: χάρισμα πνευματικόν; 1 Cor 12:1: περὶ τῶν πνευματικῶν; 1 Cor 12:7: ἡ φανέρωσις τοῦ πνεύματος). At the sovereign discretion of the Spirit (1 Cor 12:11: καθὼς βούλεται), each member of Christ's body is apportioned a gift (or gifts). Nonetheless, as central as the Spirit is in this process (1 Cor 12:4, 8, 9, 11: τὸ αὐτὸ πνεῦμα), the Trinitarian Godhead (12:4-6) is ultimately the source of the unity and diversity within the body of Christ.[261]

3. God equips His church with gifted people (χάρις: Eph 4:7, 11; cf. 1 Cor 12:28), along with their specific ministries (χαρίσματα: Rom 1:11; 1 Cor 1:7; 12:4, 9, 28, 30-31; cf. 1 Tim 4:14; 2 Tim 1:6).

4. The χαρίσματα promote a variety of social relationships that ultimately invert the hierarchical structure of Graeco-Roman society.[262] There occurs a reciprocal exchange that mutually strengthens and encourages Christians (Rom 1:11-12). Unity in the Spirit among believers (1 Cor 12:12-13) enables them to work together in love (12:31-14:1) for the 'common good' (12:7). This is variously understood as the edification of Christ's body (14:3-5, 12, 17, 26), its equipment for service through the grace-gifts (Eph 4:11-12), and its growth towards fullness in Christ (1:22-23; 4:12-13; Col 1:18-19; 2:19). Each Christian, as an interdependent and complementary member of Christ's body (Rom 12:4-8; 1 Cor 12:12-27), is uniquely gifted and therefore indispensable for its overall health. In this regard, Paul's body metaphor summons Christians to abandon the Cynic-Stoic ideal of αὐτάρκεια (1 Cor 12:14-21, 25b-26); it asserts the unity of Christ's church (12:4-6, 12-13) over against the fragile concord of the body politic (Republican and Caesarian); it undermines the pecking order of the *cursus honorum* at Rome and in the colonies (12:22-25a); it overturns the

---

[260] D. Zeller, *op. cit.*, 186. Note L. Cerfaux's observation ('La théologie de la grâce selon Saint Paul', *VSpir* 83 [1950], 11): 'Les charismes sont l'explosion extérieure d'un don l'intérieur ou de la présence de l'Esprit'.

[261] L. Cerfaux (*art. cit.*, 11) says that in 1 Cor 12:4-6 we are presented 'un panorama trinitaire'.

[262] Note the astute comment of E.A. Judge on Paul's body imagery ('Demythologizing the Church: What is the Meaning of "The Body of Christ"?', *Interchange* 11 [1972], 164): 'this leads to the conclusion that what Paul is regularly concerned with is the question of status and the social obligations consequent upon faith in Christ, and that his use of body language is designed to raise these to the highest place in the estimation of his readers'.

entrenched social power of the καλοκάγαθός in honouring the socially disenfranchised (12:22-25a).[263]

How does Paul's understanding of the charismatic body of Christ differ from our three voluntary religious associations? Each is cultic, little emphasis on divine beneficence (apart from the *Philadelphian Association*: *SIG*³ 985, *ll*.60-64). But Paul's communities can hardly be described as cultic. All the traditional practices of cultic ritual were absent. The apostle underscores this by transferring Jewish cultic terminology to the believers themselves and to their ministries. Also each association survives on the generosity of human benefactors, the payment of compulsory fees, and the imposition of various fines for the misdemeanours of their members. By contrast, Paul envisages local communities of believers, inaugurated by God's salvific patronage, which proclaim His beneficence and act as benefactors on His behalf.[264]

There is no notion of the *giftedness* of each member in the cultic associations, as there is in Paul's house churches. The closest approximation occurs in the *Rule of the Iobacchoi*: there 'every member is expected to participate in word or deed or confer some special benefit' (*SIG*³ 1109 *ll*.45-46). But this largely refers to members taking part in the dramatic presentation associated with the society's celebrations (*SIG*³ 1109 *ll*.64-66, 111ff).

Further, there is little understanding of ethical conduct being grounded in and transformed by divine grace. To be sure, the *Philadelphian Association* (*SIG*³ 985 *ll*.15-51) and the *Rule of the Andanian mysteries* (*SIG*³ 736 Sect.1) make various ethical vows to the deities. While there is a strong interest in sexual self-control, this is hardly regarded as a χάρισμα from God (cf. 1 Cor 7:7). Instead the gods demand obedience, dispensing grace to those who obey and punishments to those who transgress (*SIG*³ 985 *ll*.45-51). According to Paul, grace is the real dynamic behind Christian ethics (§6.1.2.5): it touches believers as much in their language (χάρις: Eph 4:29; Col 4:6) as in the weightier matters of personal reconciliation (χαρίζεσθαι: 2 Cor 2:7, 10; 12:13; Eph 4:32; Col 3:13; Phlm 22).

---

[263] On 'αὐτάρκεια' ('self-sufficiency'), see G. Kittel, *TDNT* 1 (1964), 466-467. Also, A.N.M. Rich, 'The Cynic Conception of *Autarkeia*', *Mnemosyne* 9 (1956), 23-29. In regard to Paul's use of αὐτάρκεια (2 Cor 9:8: cf. 1 Tim 6:6) and αὐτάρκης (Phil 4:11), note the comment of D. Georgi (*op. cit.* [1992], 160): 'Autarky means, for Paul, the simplicity of an open, trusting, and faithful heart'. On the Republican and Caesarian body metaphors, see E.A. Judge, 'Contemporary Political Models for the Inter-Relations of the New Testament Churches', *Reformed Theological Review* 22/3 (1963), 65-76; G. Theissen, *op. cit.*, 196-201. On the *cursus honorum* at Corinth and Paul's discussion of gifts, see A.D. Clarke, *op. cit.*, 13-18; B. Witherington III, *op. cit.*, 259-261.

[264] F.W. Danker, *op. cit.* (1982), 156.

Finally, the *Rule of the Iobacchoi* strove to enhance the social status of its members by recognising their attainment of new civic honours and by highlighting recent personal achievements of note (*SIG*^{3} 1109 *ll*.127-136). While Paul rejoiced in the appropriateness of honouring fellow Christians (Rom 12:10b; 1 Cor 12:26b), there was simply no room for inflated self-importance (Rom 12:3) or the dishonouring of the weak in the body of Christ (1 Cor 12:22-25). Furthermore, the *Rule of the Iobacchoi* vaunted its superiority over the other Bacchic societies (*SIG*^{3} 1109 *l.*27). But, for Paul, the wild olive was not entitled to boast over the branches (Rom 11:17-18). Divine grace had become the great social leveller in the body of Christ.[265]

6.5. Paul, Charis, and the Gods of the Gentiles

As an Israelite from birth (Rom 9:3b-4; Phil 3:5; 2 Cor 11:22) and as a committed Pharisee before his conversion (Phil 3:5b, 6b; Gal 1:14), Paul was a strict Jewish monotheist who rejected the idolatry and syncretism of Graeco-Roman religion (Rom 3:30; 1 Cor 8:4, 6; 15:28; Gal 3:20; Eph 4:6; cf. 1 Tim 2:5; cf. Ex 20:1-4). God as the Creator and Judge of humanity, Paul says, commands everyone to turn from their idolatry (Rom 1:18ff; 1 Thess 1:9-10; Gal 4:8-9). While the gods are irrelevant powers (1 Cor 8:4-5: 'no real existence', 'so-called gods'; 12:2: 'dumb idols'; Gal 4:8: 'by nature are no gods'), they still belong to the demonic world which awaits God's judgement and arouses His divine jealousy in the present (1 Cor 10:7-8, 14-22). No compromise, therefore, is envisaged for Christians (2 Cor 6:14-16):

... what fellowship can light have with darkness? What harmony is there between Christ and Belial? ... What agreement is there between the temple of God and idols?[266]

We must not conclude, however, that Paul was disinterested in popular ideas concerning the nature of the Graeco-Roman deities. Such a blinkered

---

[265] S.J. Case (*The Social Origins of Christianity* [rpt. New York 1975: orig. 1923], 134) writes: 'No herald in the Christian assemblies announced, after the model of the Eleusinian mysteries, that admission to the cult was open only to those who could meet specified tests of a ritual or moral sort'. In focusing on the differences between the cultic associations and Paul's house churches regarding divine grace, I am not suggesting there were no similarities in group behaviour between the associations and the house churches. For discussion of the similarities and the various problems it posed for the Corinthian church, see J.R. Harrison, 'Paul's House Churches and the Cultic Associations', *Reformed Theological Review* 58/1 (1999), 31-47, esp. 40-45.

[266] On Paul and idolatry, see J. Becker, *op. cit.*, 107-108; P.J. Tomson, *Paul and the Jewish Law: Halakha in the Letters of the Apostle to the Gentiles* (Assen 1990), 151-220.

attitude would place him at a considerable pastoral and evangelistic disadvantage. Surely A. Deissmann is correct in noting that Paul's understanding of grace was as much directed against the Graeco-Roman cults as at sections of first-century Judaism (§3.1.1; §3.4). Perhaps D. Georgi sums up the issue best:

> Paul argues emphatically for a God engaged in the human demise and impoverishment; Paul fights against a distant and unengaged deity. The deficiency of the pagan deities in his eyes would not be that they were too human, but that they were too little involved in the human dilemma. Justification is not merely important between God and the individual, but it comes about and manifests itself in the interrelatedness of God, the world, and all humanity.[267]

Furthermore, as previously argued, Paul interacts with the traditions of the popular philosophers (§6.1.2.1) and the magical papyri (§6.1.3.1) in formulating his understanding of divine χάρις. But there are several other facets of Graeco-Roman religious belief which equally provoked Paul's heavy emphasis on the unilateral nature of God's grace.[268]

1. The *do ut des* ('I give that you may give') mentality of Graeco-Roman religion reduced human piety to a mere business transaction. We have already referred to Deissmann's discussion of *PSI* IV 435 in this regard (§3.4).[269] Similarly, in an inscription of the cult of Apollo in Attica (*SEG* XXI 469C: II cent. BC), the people and council assert that they will

> watch closely not only the institutions of the ancestors, but also further increase both the sacrifices and the honours well and piously, in order that they also may gain the appropriate favours (χάριτας) proceeding from the gods.

For Paul, all such attempts at manipulating the divine favour (likewise §3.4: *P. Warren* 13) amounted to a fatal reliance on works rather than upon God's grace (§6.1.2—§6.1.3).

2. Relations between the Graeco-Roman gods and human beings were subsumed under the motif of reciprocity. As noted, the gods were placed under obligation by cultic piety and thus were constrained to reciprocate with gratitude (§2.7: *Hands* D.9; §3.4: *UPZ* 1.41; §5.4.3: Plato, *Leg.* 2.931A). Moreover, Theophrastus well articulates the dominant belief in antiquity that cultic sacrifices adequately requite divine grace (§5.4.2). Only the 'atheist' Epicurus (§5.5.4; §5.6.4), satirists such as Lucian

---

[267] D. Georgi, *op. cit.* (1992), 159.

[268] On grace as a unilateral act of God, J.D.G. Dunn, *op. cit.*, 202; J.C. Beker, *op. cit.*, 264. See also the discussion of S.C. Mott (*op. cit.*, 300-307) which highlights the theme of dependence upon God's grace in both Philo and the popular philosophers. Further, see §4.3 n.80.

[269] For additional modern literature and ancient sources, see H.D. Betz, *op. cit.*, 109 nn.150-151.

(§5.5.3), or Delphic priests like Plutarch (§5.5.3) ever question this orthodoxy. In contrast, Paul magnifies grace precisely because human beings are morally incapable of reciprocating God's infinite generosity (Rom 11:35; 1 Cor 4:7).
3. Paul's idea that God's grace animates and impels human beneficence is highly unusual in Graeco-Roman religion. Certainly the philosophers can speak of human beings imitating the munificence of the gods (§5.6.3; also Arr., *Epict. Diss.*, 2.14.11-13). Aristotle highlights the mnemonic association of χάρις with the Χάριτες in regard to beneficence (§5.4.1). The link between the φιλία of the gods and the communal generosity of the Pythagorean groups is never really made explicit (§5.4.1).[270] In my opinion, nothing cited above approximates to Paul's *tour de force* in 2 Corinthians 8:9 (§6.2).

Two questions remain. First, why did Paul avoid the plural χάριτες — in contrast to Philo — as a description of divine beneficence? Undoubtedly, Paul's monotheism is the fundamental explanation: God's grace would have been all too easily confused with the Greek goddesses, the *Charites*, if the plural was used.[271] As J. Wobbe adds, Paul captures the fullness of grace implied by χάριτες by employing a range of alternative terminology with χάρις (πλοῦτος; περισσεία; περισσεύειν; ὑπερβάλλειν; τὸ ὑπερβάλλον).[272] It is also likely that Paul restricts himself to the singular χάρις to underline the fact that the reign of grace is founded on the decisive eschatological act of God in Christ.[273] Finally, we must not overlook the fact that two Hebrew words lie behind Paul's use of χάρις. In the LXX *ḥen* ('grace', 'favour') is invariably rendered χάρις, apart from two instances where *ḥesed* ('mercy', 'kindness') is translated by χάρις (§4.2). Importantly, *ḥen* is always used in the singular in the Hebrew scriptures, while *ḥesed* is almost always so.[274] Given the fact that *ḥen* always appeared in the singular,

---

[270] See also G.H.R. Horsley, '"Charity Motivated by Piety" in an Epitaph', *New Docs* 2 (1982), §16. Unfortunately, the referent of εὐσέβεια is not explicit: does it mean piety towards the gods or towards human beings?

[271] J. Wobbe, *op. cit.*, 41. On the *Charites*, see especially K. Deichgräber, *Charis und Chariten: Grazie und Grazien* (München 1971). I cannot agree with G.P. Wetter's argument (*op. cit.*, 26) that χάρις in Gal 1:15 is used as a hypostasis of God in regard to the 'means of vocation'. Rather the expression διὰ τῆς χάριτος αὐτοῦ is typical of Paul (e.g. Rom 1:5; 12:3; 15:15; 2 Cor 9:14; Gal 1:6; 2:9) and simply conveys the idea of divine mediation.

[272] J. Wobbe, *op. cit.*, 41.

[273] D. Georgi (*op. cit.* [1992], 97) comments: 'for Paul there is only one divine grace, no matter how varied it may appear in its results'. J.D.G. Dunn (*op. cit.* [1998], 322) states that 'it also presumably reflects the fact that for Paul grace had a single source (God) and a single focal expression (the redemptive act of Christ)'.

[274] In the MT there are 226 verses containing the singular *ḥesed* and only another 17

it would have been almost inconceivable for Paul to use χάριτες instead of χάρις.

Second, why does Paul opt for χάρις over against ἔλεος ('mercy') as the central description of divine benevolence? In a previous chapter (§4.2) we noted the suggestion that there was an increasing tendency for first-century Jewish authors (e.g. Philo) to supplant ἔλεος in the LXX with χάρις. However, in my opinion, Paul was not just reflecting Philo's type of Judaism or absorbing late hellenistic philological trends. More likely, Paul deliberately chose χάρις as the most positive and widespread word for beneficence (human and divine) in his culture. As observed above, there was the added advantage that the word had acquired an eschatological, cosmological, and soteriological dimension in its Augustan context. Moreover, ἔλεος may well have carried a negative connotation in early first-century benefaction parlance. Although the reference postdates Paul, Nero said of his liberation of Greece (AD 67) that 'it is not out of pity (οὐ δι' ἔλεον) for you but out of goodwill (δι' εὔνοιαν) that I bestow this benefaction' (*SIG*³ 814).[275]

In §4.2 we also suggested that Paul's preference for χάρις over the LXX ἔλεος, might be partially explained by the overtone of reciprocity attached to *ḥesed* in the Hebrew Old Testament. Furthermore, *ḥen* ('grace', 'favour') — invariably rendered χάρις in the LXX — carried the idea of the bestowal of favour by a superior (human or divine). Perhaps this emphasis better

---

verses that use the plural (with 18 instances of the plural form itself). See the discussion of J.D.G. Dunn, *ibid.*, 322.

[275] J. Moffatt, *op. cit.*, 118. Note, too, Epictetus (Arr., *Epict. Diss.*, 4.1.4): 'who wishes to live in grief, fear, envy, pity (ἐλεῶν), desiring things and failing to get them, avoiding things and falling into them?'. A revealing case of divine ἔλεος is found in an aretalogy of Isis (G.H.R. Horsley, 'A Personalised Aretalogy of Isis', *New Docs* 1 [1981], §1 *ll.*18-20). Isis has only regard for those whose righteousness merits her mercy (*ll.*37-38): 'I legislated for mercy (ἐλεᾶν) to be shown to suppliants. I have regard for those who defend themselves with justification (τοὺς δικαίως ἀμυνομένους)'. See the discussion of M. Strom, *Reframing Paul: Conversations in Grace and Community* (Downers Grove 2000), 118-119. On the Stoic rejection of pity, see A.R. Hands, *op. cit.*, 77-88. G.W. Peterman (*op. cit.*, 150) notes that, in contrast to the Jewish and Christian ethos, money given out of mercy for another's condition was 'never considered meritorious' in the Graeco-Roman world. Instead 'one gives benefits to those who are worthy to receive', both in terms of their character and their ability to reciprocate (*ibid.*). See J.C. Beker (*op. cit.*, 266) for extra suggestions why Paul preferred χάρις to ἔλεος in the Jewish context. K.R. Snodgrass ('Justification by Grace — to the Doers: An Analysis of the Place of Romans 2 in the Theology of Paul', *NTS* 32/1 [1986], 91 n.51) suggests that Paul avoided ἔλεος because some Jews may have presumed on God's mercy in regard to the final Judgement. This argument is at odds with Paul's use of ἔλεος and ἐλεεῖν in Romans 9-11. Paul does not shy away from the Old Testament emphasis on God's unconditional mercy (Rom 9:15-16, 18, 23); nor does he baulk at its extension to *both* Jew and Gentile (11:30-32; 15:9).

preserved for Paul the nuance of a unilateral transaction in describing divine beneficence. As J.D.G. Dunn incisively notes,

> It would appear, then, that Paul preferred *charis*, presumably because in its usage he could combine the most positive features of the two Hebrew words: *charis* denotes, as it were, the unilateralness of *chen* and the lasting commitment of *chesed*.[276]

But, as we noted, the irony was that in choosing the word χάρις Paul opted for the central *leitmotiv* of the Graeco-Roman reciprocity system.

Ultimately, in contrast to ἔλεος, there was a greater semantic versatility to χάρις. It embraced both sides of the benefaction ritual, referring to the gratitude of the beneficiary as well as the favour of the benefactor. As such, χάρις provided Paul the opportunity to interact with the prevalent ethos of reciprocity and to formulate his radical theological and social alternative to the Graeco-Roman benefaction system.

6.6. Conclusion

What portrait of divine grace does Paul sketch for first-century Christians living in the Western and Eastern Mediterranean basin? Against the backdrop of the universal dishonouring of God as the cosmic and covenantal Benefactor, God extends His χάρις to ungrateful enemies, while still maintaining the righteous demands of His honour. The prized status of δικαιοσύνη — reserved for the καλοκἀγαθοί in antiquity — is 'democratised' and extended to the entire Christian community through Christ as the dishonoured and impoverished Benefactor.

This dramatic reversal in status frees Christians from dependence on the generosity of civic luminaries: instead the house churches should adopt the role of benefactor for themselves. Significantly for the Roman Christians, Christ's act of divine patronage supersedes the eschatological beneficence of Augustus both at Rome and throughout the Empire. While God demands loyalty of the dependants in His household, God's reign of grace provides a security and status that totally surpasses the lucrative career prospects within the *familia Caesaris*. God's grace is also superior to any of its spiritual counterfeits at Ephesus — whether it be the mysteries, the cults, or magic. More generally, Paul endorses conventions from the honorific inscriptions that stress the obligation of the beneficiary to respond worthily of the Benefactor.

---

[276] J.D.G. Dunn, *op. cit.* (1998), 321.

Social relationships within the body of Christ are radically transformed by divine grace. The Pauline thanksgivings imbibe a different spirit to the stylised conventions of recompense found in the honorific inscriptions. There is no hint of the Homeric world of gift and counter-gift; the unity of Christ's church matters more than the estimate of posterity; God is the ultimate focus of all honour. Paul's language of grace differentiates his apostolic mission from the itinerant Cynic-Stoic preachers like Epictetus and Dio Chrysostom. Nothing in the popular voluntary associations really approximates the dynamic of grace in Paul's assemblies. Further, in the following chapter, it will be argued that Paul's understanding of divine grace up-ends the hellenistic ethics of beneficence.

Finally, Paul's description of divine beneficence may well have intrigued, puzzled, or alienated the popular philosophers — depending on the viewpoint of their school and the overall context of the discussion. In this regard, it is noteworthy that the closest approximation of a 'servant theology' in antiquity, Antisthenes' portrait of the enslaved and impoverished Odysseus, is still driven by the demand for reciprocation. Only the grace of Christ — in sharp contrast to the beneficence of the gods and human beings — is unilateral, not reciprocal.

Chapter 7

Paul and Human Beneficence

7.1. Introduction

The popularity of Christian beneficence among the general populace attracted the attention of the opponents of Christianity in antiquity. The Emperor Julian (AD 332—363) was forced to provide imperial subsidies so that the high priests of the traditional cults could counter the charitable distributions of the Christian churches. As Julian believed, the influence of Graeco-Roman religion was waning precisely because the so-called love feasts (ἀγάπη), service of tables (διακονία), and hospitality (ὑποδοχή) of the Galileans had led many into atheism (ἀθεότης).[1]

Likewise, many modern scholars have been struck by (what they perceive to be) the novelty of Christian philanthropy in its social context. A.D. Nock argues that Christianity democratised the mystery cults. As he elaborates,

(Christianity) expected liberality of the wealthy but gave its rites to the poor and needy, just as it gave to them the advantages of burial societies and more: even a poor man's guild required subscriptions and was in danger of liquidation.[2]

---

[1] Julian, *Fragment of a Letter to a Priest* 305B-C; cf. *id.*, *Letter to Arsacius, High-priest of Galatia* 429C—431B. E.A. Judge (*The Conversion of Rome: Ancient Sources of Modern Social Tensions* [Macquarie University 1980], 14) has argued that Julian understood with greater clarity than his contemporaries 'the social and intellectual dynamics of the movement he was determined to stop'.

[2] A.D. Nock, *Conversion: The Old and the New in Religion from Alexander the Great to Augustine of Hippo* (Oxford 1933), 57. S.J. Case, citing the Latin inscription of the funerary society at Lanuvium as a test case (J.-P. Waltzing, *Étude historique sur les corporations professionnelles chez les Romains III* [Hildesheim/New York 1970], 642-666), observes that 'the tenor of the numerous inscriptions can hardly be said to reflect a beneficent temper' (*The Social Triumph of the Ancient Church* [1933; rpt. New York 1971], 26). For a translation of the inscription, see A.R. Hands, *Charities and Social Aid in Greece and Rome* (London and Southampton 1968), §D.28. G. Theissen (*Social Reality and the Early Christians: Theology, Ethics, and the World of the New Testament* [Edinburgh 1992], 280) states that *liberalitas* was as much the preserve of the poor (Mk 12:41-44) as the rich and powerful in early Christianity.

L.M. White asserts that while the early church adopted the conventions of existing social structures (e.g. household, hospitality, and patronage), the redemptive act of Christ provided the ethical framework for the ἀγάπη and κοινωνία underlying Christian service.³ A.R. Hands and P. Veyne, following H. Bolkestein, claim that traditional Graeco-Roman euergetism had little connection with religion because its focus was entirely civic. Conversely, Christian and Jewish almsgiving to the poor was motivated by divine mercy and directed towards the genuinely destitute as opposed to the citizens of the *poleis* alone. But, overall, such views tend to overstate the contrast between Graeco-Roman and Christian beneficence.⁴

---

³ L.M. White, 'Social Authority in the House Church Setting and Ephesians 4:1-16', *ResQ* 29/4 (1987), 209-228. Also, W.A. Meeks, *The Origins of Christian Morality: The First Two Centuries* (New Haven and London 1993), 212. C.F. Whelan (*'Amica Pauli*: The Role of Phoebe in the Early Church', *JSNT* 49 [1993], 83) writes that 'Paul certainly thinks of his churches as clients and is quick to invoke the principles of reciprocity'. Nonetheless, as we will see, Paul overturns traditional reciprocity conventions, while endorsing their validity (§7.3.2).

⁴ A.R. Hands, *op. cit.*, 47-48; P. Veyne, *Bread and Circuses: Historical Sociology and Political Pluralism* (London 1990: Fr. orig. 1976), 19-34. Similarly, S.C. Mott ('The Power of Giving and Receiving: Reciprocity in Hellenistic Benevolence', in G.F. Hawthorne, *Current Issues in Biblical and Patristic Interpretation* [Grand Rapids 1975], 72): 'Hellenistic beneficence ... made little penetration into the lower classes'. Note, too, the comment of H. Bolkestein (*Wohltätigkeit und Armenpflege im vorchristlichen Altertum* [rpt. New York 1979: Gmn. orig. Utrecht 1939], 107): 'Beistehen soll man — nicht den Armen — sondern den „Guten", nicht so sehr deshalb weil die „Schlechten" es nicht verdienen, sondern weil man nur von guten Menschen Vergeltung der χάρις (freundlichen Hilfe) mit χάρις (Dank, Gegengabe) erwarten kann'. Moreover, H. Bolkestein and W. Schwer ('Almosen', *RAC* I [1950], 301) argue that the extension of the meaning of 'mercy' (ἔλεος) to 'compassion towards the poor' and 'almsgiving' (ἐλεημοσύνη) occurred in the Greek-speaking Orient (LXX Prov 21:26; Dan 4:24; Ps-Phoc. 23). S. Joubert (*Paul as Benefactor: Reciprocity, Strategy, and Theological Reflection in Paul's Collection* [Tübingen 2000], 130) also argues that in Graeco-Roman society 'benefactors used their benefactions to increase their own honour and not to alleviate the material needs of others'. However, L.W. Countryman (*The Rich Christian in the Church of the Early Empire: Contradictions and Accommodations* [New York and Toronto 1980], 105-106) rightly cautions against misrepresenting Graeco-Roman beneficence in this regard. Public benefactions such as the grain dole and feasts ensured that the needs of the poor were catered for as much as the general citizen populace. A few examples will establish the point. In a discussion of *SEG* XXXII 1243 (late I cent. BC to early I cent. AD), R. Kearsley ('A Civic Benefactor of the First Century in Asia Minor', *New Docs* 7 [1994], §10) comments on the wide range of people provided for by Kleanax' banquets. A benefactor of Akraiphia (*IG* VII[2] 2712: AD 37) gave breakfast to his town, including in his invitation not only the citizens, but also all the foreigners living there, as well as the freedmen and the slaves of the citizens. In his bequest to his city, Phainios of Gytheion (*SEG* XIII 258: AD 41/42) states that 'I wish also the slaves to share in the gift of oil for six days each year'. Countryman (*op. cit.*, 106) sums up the difference between Oriental and Graeco-Roman beneficence in this fashion: 'the

L.W. Countryman provides a more nuanced view regarding the novelty of Christian beneficence. He argues that a similarity in role existed between the hosts of the house churches and the rich patrons of Graeco-Roman clubs. Countryman also asserts that the Christian patron, unlike his civic peers, was not able to manipulate the distribution of gifts to his own advantage; nor could he be recompensed with commensurate public honours.[5] In my opinion, Countryman's position is overly optimistic. At Corinth, for example, several of the house church patrons had manipulated the Lord's Supper in favour of the wealthier Christians belonging to the urban elite (1 Cor 11:17-34). The same abuse of patronal power is further reflected in the litigation occurring among the Corinthian believers (1 Cor 6:1-11).[6] Perhaps the very desire for commensurate honours on the part of the social elite within the Christian community had led several of the Corinthian house church patrons to act arrogantly and with intimidation towards the weak (1 Cor 12:14-26).

However, irrespective of the validity of these observations, Paul's most extended discussion of beneficence — the Jerusalem collection — still awaits in-depth coverage against the backdrop of the honorific inscriptions.[7] This is a curious oversight given the substantial overlap in benefaction language and motifs between Paul's treatment of the Jerusalem collection and the honorific inscriptions. Recent scholarship on the Jerusalem collection has gravitated either towards the theological meaning of the collection (§7.2.2) or towards the use of ἰσότης in 2 Cor 8:13-14.[8] Recently, W.A. Meeks has drawn attention

---

difference was that the Hellenic world was reluctant to single the poor out for special treatment'. Moreover, even P. Veyne (*op. cit.*, 20-21) admits that the poor were increasingly singled out for philanthropy in the Imperial epoch. For further criticism of Bolkestein, see M.R.P. McGuire, 'Epigraphical Evidence for Social Charity in the Roman West', *AJP* 67 (1946), 129-150; W. Den Boer, *Private Morality in Greece and Rome: Some Historical Aspects* (Leiden 1979), 165-169; G. Theissen, *op. cit.*, 277 n.26.

[5] L.W. Countryman, 'Welfare in the Churches of Asia Minor under the Early Roman Empire: Part I — The Christian Practice of Almsgiving', in P.J. Achtemeier (ed.), *Society of Biblical Literature 1979 Seminar Papers* (Missoula 1979), 142-143. Also *id.*, 'Patrons and Officers in Club and Church', in P.J. Achtemeier (ed.), *Society of Biblical Literature 1977 Seminar Papers* (Missoula 1977), 135-143.

6 See G. Theissen, *The Social Setting of Pauline Christianity: Essays on Corinth* (Philadelphia 1982), 145-174; J.K. Chow, *Patronage and Power: A Study of Social Networks in Corinth* (Sheffield 1992), 113-166. For other constructions of 1 Cor 11:17-34, see B. Winter, 'The Lord's Supper at Corinth: An Alternative Reconstruction', *Reformed Theological Review* 37/3 (1978), 73-82; G.C. Nicholson, 'Houses for Hospitality', *Colloquium* 19/1 (1986), 1-6.

7 See the brief discussion of F.W. Danker, *Benefactor: Epigraphic Study of a Graeco-Roman and New Testament Semantic Field* (St. Louis 1982), 437-438. More elaborately, *id.*, *2 Corinthians* (Minneapolis 1989), 116-147.

8 On ἰσότης, see D. Georgi, *Remembering the Poor: The History of Paul's Collection*

to the novelty of a collection put together by disparate Gentile Christian groups without patronal status, and directed towards unknown Jews who were separated from their benefactors by geography, culture and (to some extent) theology.[9] But terms such as 'novel' and 'unique' are notoriously slippery in such contexts.[10] Primarily, we need to ask how the Jerusalem collection — which, for Paul, was a tangible expression of divine and human χάρις (2 Cor 8:1, 4, 7, 8, 9, 16, 19; 9:8, 14, 15) — would have been perceived in its Graeco-Roman benefaction context. Further, what significance should be attributed to the overlaps, omissions, and inversions of traditional benefaction terminology and motifs found in Paul? Only then will we be in a position to gauge whether Paul is up to something new. In sum, a more nuanced approach is required.

The writings of E.A. Judge are suggestive for the way ahead. Judge argues that Paul

> ...takes up existing social institutions and subjects them on the one hand to a radical critique from his new point of view, and on the other hand to careful cultivation because of the advantages they have to bring to what he has to do.[11]

In Judge's view, Paul abandons the terminology of patronage and friendship because of the trappings of status and obligation inherent in its social world-

---

for Jerusalem (Nashville 1992: Gmn. orig. 1965), 84-91, 138-140; P. Vassiliadis, 'Equality and Justice in Classical Antiquity and in Paul: The Social Implications of the Pauline Collection', *St. Vladimir's Theological Quarterly* 36/1-2 (1992), 51-59. Unfortunately, Vassiliadis' book on the Jerusalem collection (Χάρις—Κοινωνία—Διακονία: *The Social Character of the Pauline Collection* [Thessaloniki 1985]), written in Greek, was unavailable to me. Similarly, B. Beckheuer, *Paulus und Jerusalem: Kollekte und Mission im theologischen Denken des Heidenapostels* (Frankfurt a.M. 1997).

[9] W.A. Meeks, *op. cit.*, 107.

[10] See the discussion of J.Z. Smith, *Drudgery Divine: On the Comparison of Early Christianities and the Religions of Antiquity* (Chicago 1990), 36-53. Furthermore, there are (admittedly loose) Graeco-Roman parallels to Paul's collection. For example, one could cite Iamblichus' story of Abaris (*Vit. Pyth.* 91-92), a priest of Apollo, who had collected gold for his god. After meeting Pythagoras, Abaris was persuaded "to share the gold he had collected with those companions who had been led by reason to confirm in action the precept "friends have all in common"'(*ibid.*, 92). To be sure, the differences between Abaris' collection and Paul's are easily spotted. But my point is that some Christian scholars (W. Meeks excepted) have a propensity to invoke too readily a judgement of 'uniqueness' when comparing early Christianity with Graeco-Roman institutions and thought. Conversely, to dismiss arbitrarily all such judgements as merely *apologetische* is historical dogmatism of the worst kind. Note too the claim of VD. Verbrugge (*Paul's Style of Church Leadership Illustrated by His Instructions to the Corinthians on the Collection: To Command or not to Command* [San Francisco 1992], 145-243, esp. 244) that Paul's fund-raising practices were 'virtually unknown in antiquity'.

[11] E.A. Judge, 'St. Paul and Socrates', *Interchange* 14 (1973), 109.

Introduction

view. By reaction, Paul adopts the language of servitude and subordination to redefine the obligation of all believers, irrespective of their social status, to each other.[12] This abandonment of status prepares the way for a new order of human relationships that affirms the divine giftedness of the individual and, in conjunction with other diversely gifted believers, embraces service of the weak and strong.[13] Is Paul embarking on a similar enterprise in his arrangements for the Jerusalem collection? Ultimately, to what extent did Paul's preaching of grace give theological expression to a new set of social values in regard to beneficence?[14]

At the outset, this chapter will examine the range of terminology — including χάρις — that Paul applies to the Jerusalem collection (§7.2.1). We will then be better placed to assess recent scholarly interpretations of the collection (§7.2.2). Can we easily discern Paul's intentions regarding the collection (especially in view of the apostle's complex intermingling of social and theological argument)? Moreover, Paul's apprehension about his fate in Jerusalem (Rom 15:30-32; cf. Acts 24:17-19) may well have resulted in a measure of allusiveness and restraint in argument on his part. So, in assessing Paul's motivations, how much credence should be accorded modern arguments that heavily rely on historical inference? Further, was Paul's understanding of the entire enterprise congruent with that of the participating Gentile churches and the mother church at Jerusalem? Certainly, as we will see, there were heated disagreements between Paul and the Corinthians on the issue (§7.4.1—§7.4.2). The majority of the chapter, however, will concentrate on situating the Jerusalem collection in its Graeco-Roman context and assessing Paul's attitude to the ethos of reciprocity (§7.3.1—§7.3.3; §7.4.3). In this section, we will focus on the evidence of the honorific inscriptions to elucidate Paul's use of rivalry and imitation motifs and his appeal to the ethos of reciprocity.

---

[12] *Id.*, 'Paul as a Radical Critic of Society', *Interchange* 16 (1974), 196-197; *id.*, 'The Social Identity of the First Christians: A Question of Method in Religious History', *JRH* 11 (1980), 214-215; *id.*, 'The Reaction against Classical Education in the New Testament', *Journal of Christian Education* 77 (1983), 12.

[13] E.A. Judge, *op. cit.* (1980), 5; *id.*, *art. cit.* (1983), 14; *id.*, 'Cultural Conformity and Innovation in Paul: Some Clues from Contemporary Documents', *TynBul* 35 (1984), 6.

[14] See especially G. Theissen, *op. cit.* (Edinburgh 1992), 204. Note, too, L.M. White (*art. cit.*, 225): 'ethics are the reciprocal response for a divine act of human benefaction'.

7.2. Paul, Charis, and the Jerusalem Collection

7.2.1. Paul's description of the Jerusalem collection

7.2.1.1. The Jerusalem collection as χάρις

T.N. Schulz, commenting on the semantic versatility of χάρις, notes the difficulty of determining the precise connotation of the word in each of its ten occurrences in 2 Cor 8 and 9.[15] Four broad uses of χάρις can be detected in those chapters: (1) the objective manifestation of God's favour towards humankind in the incarnation (8:9: cf. §6.2-§6.3); (2) the effects of God's grace in the life of the believer (8:1; 9:8, 14: cf. §6.1.2.5; §6.1.3.2; §6.4.3); (3) the collection for the poor saints in Jerusalem (8:6, 7, 19; cf. 1 Cor 16:3); (4) human thanksgiving and gratitude to God (8:16; 9:15; cf. §6.4.1).[16] If, as G. Fee argues,[17] χάρις in 2 Cor 1:15 also refers to the 'kindness' of the Jerusalem collection, there exist (at most) five Pauline references to grace as a description of human beneficence (1 Cor 16:3; 2 Cor 1:15; 8:6, 7, 19).[18]

---

[15] T.N. Schulz, *The Meaning of Charis in the New Testament* (Genova 1971), 63.

[16] See especially R. Corriveau, *The Liturgy of Life: A Study of the Ethical Thought of St. Paul in His Letters to the Early Christian Communities* (Bruxelles-Paris 1970), 105-106; T.N. Schulz, *op. cit.*, 63. Corriveau and Schulz disagree on whether 2 Cor 8:6 refers to the Jerusalem collection or to the effects of grace in the believer's life. Whereas Corriveau regards v.6 as a clear reference to the collection, Schulz (*loc. cit.*) believes that the verse deals with 'the disposition of the givers'. But, in my opinion, since Titus — and not God — is bringing τὴν χάριν ταύτην to completion, v.6 must refer to the administration of collection and not to the disposition of the Corinthians. To be sure, a positive response on their part will ensure a successful outcome for Titus: but Paul is unequivocal about God being the agent of dispositional change (2 Cor 8:1-2, 5, 7a, 8-9, 16; 9:6-15). As regards 2 Cor 8:4, Corriveau (*op. cit.*, 106 n.46) only gives qualified assent to v.4 as a reference to the collection, whereas Schulz has no doubts on the issue. As will be argued below, Paul's use of χάρις in 2 Cor 8:4 is not a strict reference to the collection.

[17] G.D. Fee, 'ΧΑΡΙΣ in 2 Corinthians 1:15: Apostolic Parousia and Paul-Corinth Chronology', *NTS* 24 (1977), 533-538. Contra, K. Berger ('χάρις', in H. Balz and G. Schneider [eds], *Exegetical Dictionary of the New Testament* Vol.3 [Grand Rapids 1993], 457) argues that 2 Cor 1:15 is a reference to the 'apostolic parousia': 'Paul's presence in a church means the presence of grace'. Notwithstanding the general truth of Berger's comment, the twofold mention of Macedonia (2 Cor 1:16a, 16b; cf. 8:1; 9:2, 4) probably seals the case for the referent being the Jerusalem collection.

[18] Moreover, four of Paul's grace-gifts (Rom 12:6: χαρίσματα κατὰ τὴν χάριν) involve acts of beneficence and almsgiving to the needy. This is clear from the use of the terms elsewhere in the New Testament. (1) εἴτε διακονίαν, ἐν τῇ διακονίᾳ (Rom 12:7: cf. 15:25; 2 Cor 8:4; 9:12, 13; Acts 6:1-2). (2) ὁ μεταδιδοὺς ἐν ἁπλότητι (Rom 12:8). L.W. Brandt (*Diest und Dienen im Neuen Testament* [Gütersloh 1931], 156) notes that the meaning of μεταδιδόναι is clearly established as almsgiving in Lk 3:11 and Eph 4:28. (3) ὁ προϊστάμενος ἐν σπουδῇ (Rom 12:8; cf. 16:2). See the discussions of προστάτης and προστάτις by E.A. Judge, *art. cit.* (1984), esp. 21-22 and G.H.R. Horsley ('Sophia, "The

The final use of χάρις in 2 Cor 8:4 eludes easy categorisation. Modern translations, as A.J. Malherbe observes,[19] fail to capture the richness of Paul's statement. There, three of Paul's central theological motifs — χάρις, κοινωνία, διακονία — are brought into close relation with each other. However, not only is the translation of 2 Cor 8:4 difficult, its overall import is unclear. Is Paul merely referring to the administration of the Jerusalem collection — or is he embarking on a more theological description of the collection?

It is possible that the two accusatives in τὴν χάριν καὶ τὴν κοινωνίαν τῆς διακονίας (v.4b) are accusatives of respect. The Macedonians, therefore, were begging (δεόμενοι) Paul and his co-workers *'in regard of* this grace and the fellowship in the ministering to the saints' (RV).[20] But, more likely, τὴν χάριν is the direct object of δεόμενοι. If this is the case, and if the ensuing καί is epexegetic, then the Macedonians were pleading for *'this privilege* (χάρις: NIV), *namely, sharing* (κοινωνία: NIV, JB) *in this service* (διακονία: NIV, JB) *to the saints'*.[21] Alternatively, should τὴν χάριν καὶ

Second Phoibe'", *New Docs* 4 [1987] §122, esp. 242ff). M. Zappella ('A proposito di Febe ΠΡΟΣΤΑΤΙΣ [Rm 16,2]', *RivB* 37/2 [1989], 167-171) refers to the inscription of Iunia Theodora of Solomos (*SEG* XVIII 143 *ll.76-77*: c. AD 43) who 'welcomes in her own house Lycian travellers and our citizens ... supplying them with everything, displaying her patronage (προστασίαν) of those who are present'. According to Zappella, προστάτις in Rom 16:2 — and, presumably, ὁ προϊστάμενος in 12:8 (cf. Titus 3:14: προΐστασθαι) — 'indicante una persona che offre ospitalità ad itineranti' (*ibid.*, 171). Further, see R.A. Kearsley, 'Women in Public Life in the Roman East: Iunia Theodora, Claudia Metrodora and Phoibe, Benefactress of Paul', *Ancient Society: Resources for Teachers* 15/3 (1985), 124-137. L.W. Countryman (*art. cit.*, 133) says of ὁ προϊστάμενος in Rom 12:8 that 'the Greek expression suggests a patron-client relationship'. Additionally, on hospitality in Paul (Rom 12:13; 16:23; Phlm 22; cf. 1 Tim 3:2; 5:10; Titus 1:8), see D.W. Riddle, 'Early Christian Hospitality: A Factor in the Gospel Transmission', *JBL* 57 (1938), 141-154; J.B. Mathews, *Hospitality and the New Testament Church: An Historical and Exegetical Study* (unpub. Ph.D. diss. Princeton University 1965); J. Koenig, *New Testament Hospitality: Partnership with Strangers as Promise and Salvation* (Philadelphia 1985). (4) ὁ ἐλεῶν ἐν ἱλαρότητι (Rom 12:8; cf. 2 Cor 9:7). For more general Pauline references to benefaction, see 1 Cor 13:3; Phil 4:10-19; cf. 1 Tim 6:17-19. J.G. Strelan ('Burden-Bearing and the Law of Christ: A Re-examination of Galatians 6:2', *JBL* 94/2 [1975], 266-276) suggests that Gal 6:2 refers to the bearing of financial burdens. Furthermore, L.W. Hurtado ('The Jerusalem Collection and the Book of Galatians', *JSNT* 5 [1979], 53ff) proposes that Gal 6:6-10 exhorts the Galatians to be involved in the Jerusalem collection.

[19] A.J. Malherbe, 'The Corinthian Contribution', *ResQ* 3 (1959), 229 n.44.

[20] For the following, I am indebted to P.E. Hughes, *The Second Epistle to the Corinthians* (Grand Rapids 1962), 291-292 n.11.

[21] The translation of 2 Cor 8:4 which we have adopted here is that of the NIV. Other translations differ over the precise meanings of χάρις κοινωνία, and διακονία. χάρις 'favour' (RSV, NASB, JB). κοινωνία: 'taking part' (RSV); 'participation' (NASB).

κοινωνίαν be taken as a case of hendiadys, then the Macedonians were requesting '*the privilege of sharing in this service of the saints* (NIV)'.[22]

It is obvious, then, that διακονία functions as a circumlocution for the Jerusalem collection and would probably carry for its auditors associations of beneficence, administration, and delegation.[23] What is unclear to modern scholars is whether χάρις and κοινωνία carry any theological and social weight in 2 Cor 8:4.[24]

First, as regards χάρις in 2 Cor 8:4, the wider context is theological.[25] The grace of God, at work in the impoverished Macedonian churches (2 Cor 8:1a: ἡ χάρις τοῦ θεοῦ), had manifested itself in a social paradox: those who were poor had become benefactors. Paul employs the language of abundance (περισσεύειν and cognates) to underscore the point and draws an implicit parallel between Christ and the Macedonians by means of the poverty/riches antithesis.[26] In 2 Cor 8:2 Paul writes that the joy and poverty of the suffering Macedonians (8:2a: ἡ περισσεία τῆς χαρᾶς; ἡ κατὰ βάθους πτωχεία) had unexpectedly overflowed in rich liberality to the Jewish brethren at

---

διακονία: 'the relief' (RSV); 'the support' (NASB).

[22] Commentators on 2 Corinthians who regard καί as epexegetic include A. Plummer (Edinburgh 1915) and R.C.H. Lenski (Minneapolis 1937). Commentators who understand the Greek construction to be hendiadys include F.F. Bruce (London 1971), V.P. Furnish (New York 1984), H.D. Betz (Philadelphia 1985), M.E. Thrall (Vol II: Edinburgh 2000). P. Barnett (Grand Rapids 1997 [395 n.31]) vacillates between the two. See also S. Joubert (*op. cit.*, 137). H.J. Seesemann (*Der Begriff Koinônia im Neuen Testament* [Göttingen 1933], 67-68 n.2) notes the conjunction of χάρις and κοινωνία in Plutarch, *Num.* 4. Similarly, see also our discussion of the letter of Theano (ἡ χάρις τῆς κοινωνίας) in §5.2.3. On the conjunction of χάρις with κοινωνία in the declaration of Antiochus I of Kommagene, see §2.8.2.

[23] On beneficence, see the parallel (*T. Job* 11.1-3) cited by V.P. Furnish, *2 Corinthians* (New York 1984), 401. On administration and delegation, see respectively H.D. Betz (*2 Corinthians 8 and 9* [Philadelphia 1985], 46) and J.N. Collins (*DIAKONIA: Re-Interpreting the Ancient Sources* [Oxford 1990], 218, 230). Nevertheless, the force of the genitive in τὴν κοινωνίαν τῆς διακονίας (2 Cor 8:4) should not be ignored. As K.F. Nickle (*The Collection: A Study in Paul's Strategy* [Chatham 1966], 109) writes, 'By designating his collection διακονία, Paul was regarding it as an essential act of Christian fellowship fulfilled in the service of the Lord'.

[24] F.W. Danker (*op. cit.* [1989]) writes that 'the terms χάρις and κοινωνία are characteristic of administrative and business documents'. Similarly, H.D. Betz, *op. cit.*, 46. Other commentators on 2 Corinthians — including R.C.H. Lenski (Minneapolis 1937), F.F. Bruce (London 1971), C.K. Barrett (London 1973), and R.P. Martin (Waco 1986) — allow for varying degrees of theological significance.

[25] H.J. Seesemann (*op. cit.*, 67-68) states that χάρις simply cannot mean 'favour' in 2 Cor 8:4 due to its theological use in 8:1. Similarly, D. Georgi, *op. cit.*, 81.

[26] On the abundance terminology, see M. Theobald, *Die überströmende Gnade: Studien zu einem paulinischen Motivfeld* (Würzburg 1982), 279-282.

Jerusalem (8:2b: ἐπερίσσευσεν εἰς τὸ πλοῦτος τῆς ἁπλότητος).²⁷ The unexpected generosity of the Macedonian believers embodied the sacrifice of Christ's incarnational poverty (2 Cor 8:9a: ἐπτώχευσεν) and, at least in this instance, expressed *at a social level* Christ's salvation-enrichment of His dependants (8:9b: ἵνα πλουτήσητε).²⁸ Moreover, the grace of God that animated the lives of the Macedonians was also the grace of His Son (2 Cor 8:1a, 9a: ἡ χάρις τοῦ θεοῦ, ἡ χάρις τοῦ κυρίου ἡμῶν ᾿Ιησοῦ). This overflow of divine grace was displayed for all in the way that Macedonians had committed themselves both to God and Paul by voluntarily contributing beyond their means to the Jerusalem collection (2 Cor 8:3, 5). The effects of grace in the lives of the Macedonians became the paradigm for the recalcitrant Corinthians (8:7: ἐν ταύτῃ τῇ χάριτι περισσεύητε). In conclusion, the Macedonian request to participate in the Jerusalem collection in 2 Cor 8:4 should be viewed as a free act of grace, prompted by the effects of divine grace in their lives (8:1, 7a, 9b),²⁹ and modelled on the grace of God's impoverished benefactor (8:9; cf. 6:10).³⁰

Second, what is the relation of χάρις to κοινωνία in 2 Cor 8:4? H.J. Seesemann is confident that 'κοινωνία muß für [Paulus] einen tieferen, innerlicheren, religiösen Klang gehabt haben'.³¹ In my opinion, Seesemann is

---

[27] G. Panikulam (*Koinōnia in the New Testament: A Dynamic Expression of Christian Life* [Rome 1979], 48) observes that '*chara* is closely bound to the *charis* in v.1, and is rightly seen as the effect of the latter'.

[28] As we have seen (§6.2), Paul employs the same poverty-riches paradigm to describe the spiritual effects of his apostolic ministry (2 Cor 6:10). Conversely, we must not forget that Paul's theological argument in 2 Cor 8:9 pivots on a social metaphor.

[29] D. Georgi (*op. cit.*, 82) comments that in 2 Cor 8:7 Paul is trying 'to make the Corinthians see that participation in the collection was the consequence of all the gifts of grace (*charismata*) they had previously been granted'.

[30] I agree with the assessment made by K.F. Nickle (*op. cit.*, 125 n.205) regarding 2 Cor 8:4: 'If grace retains its primary theological significance of "the free gift of God" ... then Paul was saying that (the Macedonians) considered the opportunity to help the Jerusalem Christians to be a gift of God's grace to them, and κοινωνία has the sense of "fellowship" with the accent on "sharing in"'. Finally, S. Joubert (*op. cit.*, 174, 179) claims that Paul neither explicitly appeals to the self-impoverishment of the Macedonians (2 Cor 8:1-5) nor to the poverty of Christ (8:9) as an exemplum for the Corinthians. In my opinion, Joubert plays down the theological links that Paul makes between Christ's ministry and his own, as well as the divine grace equally animating the ministry of Christ and the Macedonians. Paul highlights both theological motifs as a challenge to the 'ungracious' Corinthians. For discussion, see P. Barnett, *op. cit.*, 333-334, 408. Furthermore, Joubert overlooks how the 'impoverished benefactor' and 'enslaved leader' motifs (2 Cor 6:10; 8:9; cf. Mk 10:42-45; 12:41-44) — each of which is present in the Jesus tradition — were rhetorically employed as exempla in various contexts in antiquity. See my discussion in §6.2—§6.3.

[31] H.J. Seesemann, *op. cit.*, 68. He translates κοινωνία in 2 Cor 8:4 as 'participation', referring to 1 Cor 10:16. Note, too, the comment of W.M. Franklin (*Die Kollekte des Paulus*

correct. Later, in reference to the Corinthian involvement in the Jerusalem collection, Paul mentions (what he hopes would be) the 'generosity of (your) contribution' to the Jewish believers (2 Cor 9:13b: ἁπλότητι τῆς κοινωνίας; cf. Rom 15:26; Gal 2:9; κοινωνεῖν: Rom 15:27 [cf. 12:13]; cf. Phil 4:15). The response of the saints in Jerusalem to the surpassing grace of the Corinthians (2 Cor 9:14b: τὴν ὑπερβάλλουσαν χάριν τοῦ θεοῦ), Paul projects, would be their longing and prayers of thanksgiving for their Gentile brethren (9:14a), prompted by the selfless διακονία of the Gentile churches on their behalf (διακονία: Rom 15:31; 2 Cor 8:4; 9:12, 13; διακονεῖν: Rom 15:25; 2 Cor 8:19, 20).[32] Thus, the solidarity of ecumenical fellowship — initiated by God through the gracious act of the Macedonians (2 Cor 8:1, 4) and followed up with the overflowing grace of the Corinthians (8:6, 7, 19) — finds reciprocation in the fellowship of the Jerusalem saints (9:14).[33]

[Scottdale 1938], 60): 'Paulus schrieb τὴν κοινωνίαν τῆς διακονίας weil der Dienst an den Heiligen ein Ausdruck einer tiefen religiösen Gedankens war, und der Dienst war der Beweis dafür, dass eine brüderliche Liebe existierte'. See also J. Hainz, *Koinônia: »Kirche« als Gemeinschaft bei Paulus* (Regensburg 1982), 141-161. The attempt of J.P. Sampley (*Pauline Partnership in Christ: Christian Community and Commitment in Light of Roman Law* [Philadelphia 1980], 21-50) to link the partnership involved in the Jerusalem collection with the Roman conception of *societas* is highly speculative. Cf. *id.*, 'Roman Law and Paul's Conception of the Christian Community', in J. Jervell and W.A. Meeks (eds), *God's Christ and His People* (Oslo 1977), 158-174. See especially the critique of Sampley's arguments regarding Phil 4:10-12 and Rom 15:26 in G.W. Peterman, *Paul's Gift from Philippi: Conventions of Gift Exchange and Christian Giving* (Cambridge 1997), 124-127, 177-178.

[32] On 'yearning' for the absent friend as an epistolary *topos*, see H. Koskenniemi, *Studien zur Idee und Phraseologie des griechischen Briefes bis 400 n. Chr.* (Helsinki 1956), 169-172; K. Thraede, *Grundzüge griechisch-römischer Brieftopik* (München 1970), 165-173.

[33] As A.J. Malherbe recognises (*art. cit.*, 225 n.18), Paul was not only interested in forging an ecumenical bond between the Gentile and Jewish churches, but also in preventing the real danger of fragmentation within the Corinthian house churches (e.g. 1 Cor 1:10-17; 3:1-9, 16-23; 6:1-7; 11:17-34; 2 Cor 12:20-21). Thus, as Malherbe sums it up (*loc. cit.*), 'a common concern, such as the contribution, would unite them'. Furthermore, although there is no direct evidence, there may also have been unresolved tensions between Macedonian and Corinthian believers over the contrasting policy that Paul adopted towards each group on the issue of patronage (Phil 4:10-19; 1 Cor 9:1-18; 2 Cor 11:7-12; 12:13-18). As a result, the Corinthians may well have felt 'less loved' than the other Pauline churches (2 Cor 11:11; 12:15). Further, the fact that Paul had made his promised second visit to Corinth after his Macedonian journey (2 Cor 2:13; 7:5) may have made the Corinthians increasingly suspicious that Paul was not impartial in his church relations (2 Cor 1:15-22), especially given the fiasco of his initial visit to Corinth (1:22—2:11). Again, the Jerusalem collection would have promoted unity among the contributing Gentile churches. In this regard, Paul was careful to boast *publicly* of the readiness of *both* the Corinthian and Macedonian churches to contribute to the collection (2 Cor 8:1-5; 9:1-4).

Paul, as G.W. Peterman reminds us,[34] displays an acute sensitivity towards Graeco-Roman social conventions of giving and receiving in his discussion of the Jerusalem collection. 2 Cor 8:4 may well represent Paul's attempt at theologically and socially redefining Graeco-Roman conventions of beneficence for Corinthian house churches that were in danger of operating on the basis of reciprocity rather than grace (2 Cor 9:5-11).[35] For Paul, human beneficence is motivated by divine grace and seeks to establish fellowship with its recipients — as opposed to the reciprocal obligation of his Graeco-Roman contemporaries — through serving their needs (Rom 13:8). If the Corinthians had heeded Paul's implicit critique of the Graeco-Roman reciprocity system (§7.3.2), they would not have so misunderstood and misrepresented Paul's own beneficence towards themselves (§7.4).

Finally, what would readers of the honorific inscriptions have made of Paul's use of χάρις (and cognates) in 2 Cor 8-9? I suspect that initially they would have been surprised by the profuse occurrence of χάρις in Paul's epistles and by the apostle's consistent use of the singular case (§6.5). In the inscriptions χάρις and its cognates normally appear in the manifesto clause (§2.4), but much less frequently elsewhere. Moreover, Paul employs the language of abundance in conjunction with χάρις (§6.1.2.4; §6.5) over and against the inscriptional language of commensurability (§2.4: ἄξιος, κατάξιος). From Paul, one derives the impression of the absolute centrality and availability of divine and human grace for the believer — a grace which neither demands nor expects commensurate return.

Also surprising is the 'three dimensional' understanding of grace sponsored by Paul.[36] Whereas the honorific inscriptions, like Paul, register the disposal and return of χάριτες by benefactors and their beneficiaries, the transaction is an entirely civic affair and is very seldom related to the divine realm. Furthermore, on these rare occasions, the gods are invariably placed under counter-obligation by the cultic piety of the benefactor or community. The Pauline understanding of a unilateral display of divine grace that motivates and empowers human beneficence — along with its corresponding return of gratitude — is conspicuously absent from the inscriptions and constitutes something novel in the Graeco-Roman context (§6.5: *pace*, J.Z. Smith, cited in §7.1 n.10).[37]

---

[34] G.W. Peterman, 'Romans 15:26: Make a Contribution or Establish Fellowship?', *NTS* 40/3 (1994), 457-463.

[35] For the latter point, see B. Witherington III, *Conflict and Community in Corinth: A Socio-Rhetorical Commentary on 1 and 2 Corinthians* (Grand Rapids 1994), 427.

[36] G. Panikulam, *op. cit.*, 39-40.

[37] Note the comment of R.R. Melick ('The Collection for the Saints: 2 Corinthians 8-9',

7.2.1.2. The honorific inscriptions and Paul's descriptions of the collection

The range of terminology which Paul applies to the Jerusalem collection has intrigued modern scholars. According to W.C. Linss, Paul hardly ever describes his appeal for the Jerusalem saints as 'a collection' (1 Cor 16:1, 2: λογεία) and studiously avoids all mention of the word 'money'.[38] N.A. Dahl notes Paul's predilection for 'circumlocution' when referring to the collection,[39] while H.A. Seesemann also speaks of Paul 'umschreibenden Worten für die äußerliche Sache der Geldsammlung'.[40] Although these observations are valid, it is simply assumed that Paul's tactics, like his terminology, are somehow determined by his theology.[41] To be sure, Paul's terminology for the collection does reflect fundamental theological concerns. Unfortunately, the presence of an impressive range of benefaction terminology and motifs is often overlooked in discussions of the collection (§7.2.1.2; §7.2.2.3; §7.3.1.1—§7.3.1.2).

Moreover, Paul's strategy of using a variety of circumlocutions for the collection draws upon a well known convention of the honorific inscriptions. It will be interesting to determine how far Paul's emphasis either aligns with or diverges from the stereotyped portraits of beneficence in the honorific inscriptions.

Criswell Theological Review 4/1 [1989], 101): 'Ultimately Paul considers all human responses to God outworkings of grace'. The attempt of S. Joubert (*op. cit.*, 138) to play down Paul's unilateral understanding of divine grace for a more reciprocal relationship between the deity and human beings is unconvincing. The evidence cited by Joubert (Philo, *Spec. Leg.* I. 283) well illustrates the very type of counterclaim made upon the deity by human beings that Paul so vigorously resists (Rom 11:35; 1 Cor 4:7; 15:10b). Whereas Paul highlighted the total impossibility of repaying God, the ancients never doubted their capacity to do so: 'as far as it is humanly possible to repay the benefactions from the gods, we continue repaying eagerly' (*I. Ephesos* Ia. 21: AD 138). J. Chacko ('Collection in the Early Church', *ERT* 24/2 [2000], 181) sums up Paul's understanding of reciprocity thus: 'Our response in gratitude to (Christ's) self-impoverishment must be self-giving, for giving to others is giving to Christ who gave himself for us. Thus reciprocity between God and his people issues in reciprocity between people themselves — vertical and horizontal are bound together'.

[38] W.C. Linss, 'The First World Hunger Appeal', *CurTM* 12/4 (1985), 212.

[39] N.A. Dahl, 'Paul and Possessions', in *id.*, *Studies in Paul* (Minneapolis 1977), 37.

[40] H.A. Seesemann, *op. cit.*, 68.

[41] Thus E. Best (*Second Corinthians* [Atlanta 1987], 88) writes that Paul's choice of theological terms for the collection 'gives the whole discussion a theological orientation'. According to L.E. Keck ('The Poor among the Saints in the New Testament', *ZNW* 56 [1965], 129), Paul's terminology reveals that he 'saw the fund as an occasion of the grace of God to do its work in particular acts'. For extended discussion of several of these theological terms, see K.F. Nickle, *op. cit.*, 102-111; G. Panikulam, *op. cit.*, 38-45; A.J. Malherbe, *art. cit.*, 227-231.

Turning to Paul's terminology, we have already touched on three of the central theological terms denoting the collection: 'grace' (χάρις: 1 Cor 16:3; 2 Cor 1:15; 8:6, 7, 19), 'fellowship' (κοινωνία: Rom 15:26; 2 Cor 8:4; 9:13; κοινωνεῖν: Rom 15:27 [cf. 12:13]), and 'service' (διακονία: Rom 15:31; 2 Cor 8:4; 9:12, 13; cf. διακονεῖν: Rom 15:25; 2 Cor 8:19, 20). Additional theological terms for the collection include 'public service' or '(priestly) ministry' (λειτουργία: 2 Cor 9:12; cf. λειτουργεῖν: Rom 15:27), 'blessing' (εὐλογία: 2 Cor 9:5; cf. ἐπ' εὐλογίαις: 9:6), 'proof of your love' (τὴν ἔνδειξιν τῆς ἀγάπης: 2 Cor 8:24), and 'harvest of your righteousness' (τὰ γενήματα τῆς δικαιοσύνης: 2 Cor 9:10). Of these terms, only χάρις (§2.1—§2.9), δικαιοσύνη and λειτουργία regularly appear in the honorific inscriptions. εὐλογία features prominently in the Jewish inscriptions.[42] A range of secular and metaphorical terms also appear: 'liberality' or 'generosity' (ἁπλότης: 2 Cor 8:2; 9:11, 13), 'liberal gift' or 'abundance' (ἁδρότης: 2 Cor 8:20), 'earnestness' (σπουδή: 2 Cor 8:8), 'willingness' (προθυμία: 2 Cor 8:11, 12, 19; 9:2), 'abundance' (περίσσευμα: 2 Cor 8:14), 'good work' (ἔργον ἀγαθόν: 2 Cor 9:8), and 'fruit' (καρπός: Rom 15:28).

In contrast to Paul, the honorific inscriptions employ the stereotyped language of moral virtue as a circumlocution for the benefactor's financial contributions to his community.[43] This is especially apparent in the resolution proper of the honorific inscriptions, in which the grounds for the city's conferral of civic honours upon its benefactor was outlined (§2.3).[44] The inscriptional eulogies elevate the whole transaction to a moral plane, and thereby establish an aristocracy of merit — normally confined to the καλοκἀγαθοί — among the citizenry. One example of this phenomenon will suffice. An honorific decree from Delos, erected by a corporation of merchants, directs that its benefactor, Patron, be crowned

with a gold crown in the sacrifices celebrated for Poseidon, on account of (his) merit and goodness (ἀρετῆς ἕνεκεν καὶ καλοκἀγαθίας), which he continues holding towards the corporation of the merchants and the owners of ships of Turoi Herakleistoi ...[45]

---

[42] The formula, ευλογία (and its variations: ευλογία πᾶσι, ευλογία δοίοις), is especially common (e.g. *CIJ* I 25, 173, 652; II 732, 798, 799a, 803).

[43] E.A. Judge ('The Teacher as Moral Exemplar in Paul and in the Inscriptions of Ephesus', in D. Peterson and J. Pryor [eds], *In the Fullness of Time: Biblical Studies in Honour of Archbishop Donald Robinson* [Homebush West 1992], 187) pithily sums up the situation: 'The money has purchased merit'. At times the inscriptions emphasise the fact that benefactions, not just moral excellence, are being rewarded with the honour of a crown: ἀρετῆς ἕνεκεν καὶ εὐεργεσίας (*Michel* 1011).

[44] See, too, the discussion of E. Nachmanson, 'Zu den Motivformeln der griechischen Ehreninschriften', *Eranos* 11 (1911), 180-196.

[45] *I. Délos* IV 1519.

Sometimes the grounds for the benefactor's crown are encapsulated in a single abstraction (ἀρετή; εὔνοια).⁴⁶ More regularly, traditional pairings are employed, the first of which was normally ἀρετή. A sample of the accompanying virtues includes ἀνδραγαθία, δικαιοσύνη, εὔνοια, εὐσέβεια, καλοκἀγαθία, φιλοδοξία, and φρόνησις.⁴⁷ However other pairings occur, often identifying the audience that witnesses or benefits from the virtue (εὐσεβείας ἕνεκεν τῆς εἰς τὰς θεὰς καὶ φιλοτιμίας τῆς εἰς ἑαυτούς).⁴⁸ Finally, triads appear (ἀρετή, εὔνοια, καλοκἀγαθία; ἀρετή, δικαιοσύνη, εὔνοια),⁴⁹ again with their respective audiences specified (ἀρετῆς ἕνεκεν καὶ εὐνοίας [τῆς πρὸ]ς τὸν δῆμον καὶ εὐσεβείας τῆς πρὸς τοὺς θεούς).⁵⁰ In sum, the resolution proper of the honorific inscriptions affords us a stylised portrait of the καλοκἀγαθός and the civic virtues esteemed by late hellenistic society.

How does Paul's use of circumlocution in 2 Cor 8-9 compare to that found in the honorific inscriptions? There are several interesting points of contact. First, Paul's use of circumlocution in describing his financial arrangements was not only a clever theological tactic on his part: it was also a well known convention of eastern Mediterranean honorific culture. Second, Paul's blend of secular and theological terminology for the collection is paralleled in the inscriptions, which were as much interested in the εὐσέβεια of the benefactor as in his εὔνοια.

Third, the inscriptional pairings and triads of virtue also find a counterpart in Paul. The Corinthians had been enriched by God's grace (1 Cor 1:4: ἐπὶ τῇ χάριτι τοῦ θεοῦ τῇ δοθείσῃ) with all speech and all knowledge (1:5: ἐπλουτίσθητε ἐν παντὶ λόγῳ καὶ πάσῃ γνώσει). Subsequently, in 2 Cor 8:7, Paul expands his coupling of 'speech' and 'knowledge' into the first of two triads of virtue.⁵¹ The first triad of v.7a underscores the continuing

---

⁴⁶ ἀρετή: *SIG*³ 800; *IGRR* I 864. εὔνοια: *I. Kalchedon* 1.

⁴⁷ ἀνδραγαθία *Michel* 515. δικαιοσύνη: *Michel* 235, 983; *IG* VII(1) 21, VII(2) 4130. εὔνοια: *SEG* XII 306; *I. Priene* 53, 112, 113, 117; J. Benedum, 'Griechische Arztinschriften aus Kos', *ZPE* 25 (1977), 265-276, No.4. εὐσέβεια: *Michel* 985. καλοκἀγαθία *Michel* 998; *I. Délos* IV 1519. φιλοδοξία: *I. Mylasa* 106, 110; *I. Délos* IV 1504. φρόνησις: *Michel* 515.

⁴⁸ *Michel* 982; cf. *SEG* XVIII 20, XXI 419.

⁴⁹ Respectively, *Michel* 550; *ibid.*, 477 and *I. Assos* 8. In *I. Délos* IV 1507 an adverbial triad occurs (ἴσως, δικαίως, ἀδωροδοκήτω[ς]).

⁵⁰ *I. Priene* 117.

⁵¹ For discussions of the two triads of virtue in 2 Cor 8:7, see H.D. Betz, 'The Problem of Rhetoric and Theology According to the Apostle Paul', in A. Vanhoye (ed.), *L' apôtre Paul: personnalité, style et conception du ministère* (Leuven 1986), 45-47; R.R. Melick, *art. cit.*, 108-109. On virtue lists more generally, see J.T. Fitzgerald, 'Virtue/Vice Lists', in D.N. Freedman (ed.), *The Anchor Bible Dictionary* Vol.6 (New York 1992), 857-859. For

overflow of grace in the Corinthians' lives (1 Cor 1:5: ἐπλουτίσθητε; 2 Cor 8:7a: ἐν παντὶ περισσεύητε) by referring to the addition of faith to their original wealth: 'Now as you excel in everything — in faith (πίστει), in utterance (λόγῳ), in knowledge (γνώσει)'. Whereas the first triad concentrates on the God-centred virtues (2 Cor 8:7a), Paul's second triad of virtue (8:7b) commends an overflow of Corinthian benevolence towards their Jewish brethren in the collection: 'in all earnestness (πάσῃ σπουδῇ), and in your love for us (ἐν ὑμῖν ἀγάπῃ) — see that you also excel in this gracious work (ἐν ταύτῃ τῇ χάριτι περισσεύητε)'.[52]

Nonetheless, a significant difference emerges as regards the dynamics of beneficence. What is remarkable about Paul's pairings and triads of virtue is their communal nature. Divine grace causes an increase of virtue in the personal *and* corporate life of believers.[53] In the case of the eulogistic inscriptions, the virtues of the καλοκἀγαθοί are merely the accolades accorded the benefactor by his appreciative fellow-citizens as part of the honour system. Precisely because these virtues are confined to the civic elite, the only task of the citizen-body is to summon its prospective benefactors to munificence and to maintain a reputation for gratitude. By contrast, Paul's circumlocutions for the collection engage his auditors in theological thought about the true nature of beneficence and their *own* responsibility towards God and their fellow-believers. In sum, Paul calls his churches to active beneficence, not just to the return of honour.

7.2.2. Theological and social dimensions of the Jerusalem collection

In the history of interpretation of the Jerusalem collection, three basic positions have been espoused by scholars regarding Paul's motivations. Since these have been so influential — and to some extent have blurred appreciation of the Jerusalem collection in its wider Graeco-Roman context — a brief appraisal of each position is in order.

---

additional pairings and triads in Paul, see respectively Gal 5:6 (πίστις, ἀγάπη) and 1 Cor 13:13 (πίστις, ἐλπίς, ἀγάπη). Gal 5:22 may well be considered three triads.

[52] As H.D. Betz (*art. cit.*, 47) writes, 'What is to be added now concerns practical ecumenical stewardship and assistance going beyond the local concerns of Corinth'.

[53] J.M. Bassler (*God and Mammon: Asking for Money in the New Testament* [Nashville 1991], 109): 'Grace is not static'.

7.2.2.1. The eschatological interpretation

The representatives of this viewpoint argue that the Jerusalem collection was an eschatological event for Paul. Not only is the collection intended to fulfil the Old Testament prophecies of the end-time pilgrimage of the nations to Jerusalem (Rom 15:25-31; cf. Isa 60:1-7; 61:6; 66:18-20; Zeph 3:10) but, as an integral part of the apostle's priestly work for 'the fullness of the nations' (Rom 11:25; 15:16, 28), Paul expected that it would also provoke the conversion of Israel (Rom 11:11ff, 26) and precipitate the return of Christ as the Messiah (Rom 15: 28-29; Isa 66:20 [cf. *Pss. Sol.* 17.34; 4 Ezra 13.13]).[54]

Additional evidence is invoked to buttress this interpretative edifice. The eschatological force of ἐν τῷ νῦν καιρῷ (2 Cor 8:14a; cf. Rom 11:5), it is argued, points to Paul's growing awareness of the momentous significance of the collection.[55] Similarly, Paul's exegesis of the two LXX texts — Isa 55:10 and Hos 10:12 — in 2 Cor 9:10 are (supposedly) fraught with eschatological significance.[56] Paul's mention of Spain (Rom 15:24, 28; cf. LXX 'Tarshish' Is 66:19) evokes the end-time pilgrimage of the nations, as does the presence of so many Gentile delegates accompanying the collection (Acts 20:4).[57] Finally, the collision between Paul and his opponents in 2 Corinthians may be partially explained by the latter alleging the superiority of Jerusalem over Paul's Gentile pilgrims in the dawning eschatological age.[58] What can be said about the viability of this interpretation of the Jerusalem collection?

J. Bassler has astutely observed that such arguments are 'intriguing but highly inferential'.[59] I would further add that the struts of the 'eschatological' thesis can be explained in more viable ways, especially when they are connected sympathetically with Paul's explicit statements concerning the collection in its Graeco-Roman context. A series of 'negative' observations will expose the highly inferential nature of the overall thesis. In discussing the

---

[54] Representatives of this viewpoint include J. Munck (*Paul and the Salvation of Mankind* [London 1959: Gmn. orig. 1954], 42-55, 285-308); D. Georgi (*op. cit.*); K.F. Nickle (*op. cit.*); F.F. Bruce ('Paul and Jerusalem', *TynBul* 19 [1968], 22-25); R.D. Aus ('Paul's Travel Plans and the "Full Number of the Gentiles" of Rom 11:25', *NovT* 21/3 [1975], 232-262); J. Koenig (*op. cit.*, 73-74); C.H. Talbert, 'Money Management in Early Mediterranean Christianity: 2 Corinthians 8-9', *RevExp* 86/3 (1989), 360-361.

[55] R.R. Melick, *art. cit.*, 105.

[56] D. Georgi, *op. cit.*, 99-102; K.F. Nickle, *op. cit.*, 137.

[57] R.D. Aus, *art. cit.*, 242-246.

[58] W.D. Oostendorp, *Another Jesus: A Gospel of Jewish-Christian Superiority in 2 Corinthians* (Kampen 1967), 75-79.

[59] J.M. Bassler, *op. cit.*, 113. Similarly, P. Barnett, *op. cit.*, n.33 397: 'Paul makes no explicit connection between the collection for the saints and the bringing of the Gentiles to Jerusalem as an offering to the Lord, whether in 2 Corinthians 8-9 or in Rom 15:15-33'.

collection, Paul does not cite any of the key LXX texts regarding the pilgrimage of the nations.[60] (Consequently, we should not mirror-read a 'pilgrimage' theology out of 2 Cor 10-13 and then attribute that to Paul's opponents).[61] Further, he makes no explicit reference to the conversion of Israel in such contexts.[62] Nor does he betray any awareness of the intertestamental messianic expectations associated with Isa 66:20 — let alone the actual text itself! Thus, while it is likely that the rabbinically trained Paul knew such eschatological theology, he fails to draw the inference as regards the collection, although the Jerusalem church and his opponents at Corinth may well have understood or portrayed the collection differently.[63] More

---

[60] R.D. Aus (*art. cit.*, 260) argues that the πλήρωμα τῶν ἐθνῶν (Rom 11:25) will be completed when Paul returns from Spain (15:24, 28; cf. Is 66:20) to Jerusalem with new converts bearing gifts. This is vitiated by Paul's total silence concerning his intentions after his projected mission to Spain.

[61] On the dangers of 'mirror reading', see L.T. Johnson, 'On Finding the Lukan Community: A Cautious Cautionary Essay', in P.J. Achtemeier (ed.), *Society of Biblical Literature 1979 Seminar Papers* (Missoula 1979), 87-100; J.M.G. Barclay, 'Mirror Reading a Polemical Letter: Galatians as a Test Case', *JSNT* 31 (1987), 73-93. E.E. Ellis ('Paul and His Opponents: Trends in the Research', in *id.*, *Prophecy and Hermeneutic in Early Christianity* [Grand Rapids 1978], 97) warns against 'reading an adversary theology out of Paul's statements'.

[62] Note the special pleading of K.F. Nickle (*op. cit.*, 140-142) on the issue. Similarly, R. Aus (*art. cit.*, 261-262). I suspect that such scholars read Rom 15:25-31 and 2 Cor 8-9 through the lens of Rom 11:25-26 to the exclusion of other equally valid interpretations. L.E. Keck (*art. cit.*, 127) provides a damning assessment of such approaches: 'not only is there no hint of Paul's trip or of the fund in Rom 9-11, but the entire construction stems from a steadfast refusal to believe what Paul himself says in Rom 15:30ff'. B. Holmberg (*Paul and Power: The Structure of Authority in the Primitive Church as Reflected in the Pauline Epistles* [Philadelphia 1980], 38 n.134) correctly observes that 'Munck and Nickle have a too rigidly and literally "apocalyptic" understanding of Paul's eschatology'.

[63] On different understandings of the collection by Paul's contemporaries, see W.D. Oostendorp, *op. cit.*; K. Berger, 'Almosen für Israel: Zum historischen Kontext der Paulinischen Kollekte', *NTS* 23 (1976), 180-204; B. Holmberg, *op. cit.*, 39-41; W.A. Meeks, *The First Urban Christians: The Social World of the Apostle Paul* (New Haven and London 1983), 110. Strangely, the wider context of gift-giving in antiquity is often ignored in such discussions. Were certain groups within the Jerusalem church secretly resentful that they were being placed under obligation through the collection to return commensurate favour? Note the strained tone of Ammonius to his bureaucratic superior, Apollonius, in *P. Oxy.* XLII 3057: 'I don't want you, brother, to load me with these continual kindnesses, since I can't repay them (ἀμείψασθαι)'. In this regard, Paul is very careful to depict the Gentile churches as *debtors* to Jerusalem (Rom 15:27). Was Paul's emphasis on equality in 2 Cor 8:13-15 designed to allay as much Jewish as Corinthian fears over the collection? For discussion of the ethos of reciprocity in first-century Judaism, see §4.4.4 and §4.5.2. For additional suggestions as to why some of the Jerusalem Christians may have considered refusing the collection, see G. Hamel, *Poverty and Charity in Roman Palestine: First Three Centuries CE* (Berkeley and Los Angeles 1990), 189. Indeed, A.J.M. Wedderburn ('Paul's

probably, Paul is simply reflecting the Graeco-Roman ethos of reciprocity at this point (Rom 15:27; cf. 1 Cor 9:11), but locates its rationale in gratitude for divine grace and in the unique position that the Jew — and the Jerusalem church — had in salvation-history (Rom 1:16b; 2:17-20; 3:1-2; 10:4-5; 11:29).[64]

Furthermore, where specific exegetical warrant for the 'eschatological' thesis is claimed, the texts cited are over-interpreted. For example, in its context, the phrase ἐν τῷ νῦν καιρῷ (2 Cor 8:14a) simply refers to those occasions when the Corinthians have a surplus of goods and the Jerusalem believers are in need — not to a climactic moment of eschatological significance.[65]

Collection: Chronology and History', *NTS* 48/1 [2002], 110) argues that 'the evidence suggests that the collection may have failed in its basic purpose and that the Jerusalem church refused to accept any of it for itself'. For further discussion, see J. Eckhert, 'Die Kollekte des Paulus für Jerusalem', in P.-G. Müller and W. Stenger (Hrsg.), *Kontinuität und Einheit: Für Franz Mussner* (Freiburg 1981), 65-80, esp. 77-79; S. Joubert, *op. cit.*, 204-215; M.E. Thrall, *op. cit.*, 518. Was the Corinthian recalcitrance in finalising the collection (2 Cor 9:1-4) explained by Paul's refusal to accept their offer of remuneration over against that of the Macedonians (11:7-9)? As a parallel, one might cite the case of Julius Graecinus who earned the censure of contemporaries by refusing the monetary gift of Fabius for the public games, while simultaneously accepting contributions from others (Seneca, *Ben.*, 2.21.5-6). On the refusal of friendship, see P. Marshall (*Enmity in Corinth: Social Conventions in Paul's Relations with the Corinthians* [Tübingen 1987], 13-18, 243ff). If certain factions in the Corinthian house churches, therefore, regarded themselves as 'insulted' benefactors (§3.1.3: Pseudo-Libanius, 53, 64, 80; Pseudo-Demetrius, 3), Paul's collection would have been viewed as an unwarranted imposition (2 Cor 12:16-18). Again, was Paul's emphasis on equality (2 Cor 8:13-15) and voluntariness in generosity (8:3, 12; 9:5, 7) designed to counter lingering Corinthian resentments? Further, any additional requests from Paul for money would have been viewed by some Corinthians as deception (2 Cor 7:2-3; 6:8b-9a; 12:13-18). Presumably, this explains why Paul devotes so much space to the integrity of the Gentile delegates accompanying the collection (2 Cor 8:16-23). See P. Marshall, *op. cit.*, 321-323. On the Graeco-Roman background to the delegates in 2 Cor 8, see M.M. Mitchell, 'New Testament Envoys in the Context of Greco-Roman Diplomatic and Epistolary Conventions: The Example of Timothy and Titus', *JBL* 111/4 (1992), 641-662.

[64] A.J. Malherbe (*art. cit.*, 229) writes concerning Rom 15:26ff: 'Instead of openly asking the Corinthians to reciprocate materially, Paul appeals to their spirituality. Since they have received the grace of God, they should in turn be gracious'. Here Paul stands in marked contrast to the Epicureans who denied the beneficence of the gods, while emphasising the obligation to return gratitude toward Nature and friends. See N.W. DeWitt, 'The Epicurean Doctrine of Gratitude', *AJP* 58 (1937), 320-328.

[65] V.P. Furnish, *op. cit.*, 408. Similarly, R.P. Martin (*2 Corinthians* [Waco 1986], 267-270) over-interprets the ἵνα clause of 2 Cor 8:14b in suggesting that it looks forward to Israel's eschatological reconciliation. Paul's emphasis, however, is clearly on equality of resources for all believers *in the present*.

Again, Paul's citation of Isa 55:10 and Hos 10:12 in 2 Cor 9:10 will not bear the eschatological weight that D. Georgi attributes to them.[66] First, in the case of Isa 55:10, the prophet illustrates the dependability of Yahweh's salvific word by referring to His reliability as cosmic Benefactor.[67] Likewise, in 2 Cor 9:10, Paul highlights for the recalcitrant Corinthians the total reliability of God as Benefactor (χορηγήσει καὶ πληθυνεῖ τὸν σπόρον) and Saviour (αὐξήσει τὰ γενήματα τῆς δικαιοσύνης).

Second, in the case of Hos 10:12, the prophet reminds faithless Israel that the security of her agricultural life resides in loyalty to covenantal righteousness. So, in encouraging the Corinthians to abandon the mores of the Graeco-Roman reciprocity system (2 Cor 9:5b, 7), Paul unveils for his converts a new model of beneficence: the righteous man of the Psalms (2 Cor 9:9: cf. Ps 112:9). In antiquity, benefactors feared the shame of having their gifts ignored by their recipients. Thus Seneca (*Ben.*, 4.27.5; 4.34.2) advises benefactors to assess carefully the disposition of their dependants so that gifts would be received with gratitude. But, according to Paul, the righteous man of the LXX is totally secure about his generosity to others (2 Cor 9:6b, 7b-8, 10a, 11a). God has promised that he will reap the fruit of his covenantal loyalty (2 Cor 9:10b: cf. Hos 10:12; 1 Cor 9:10-11). In sum, it is more likely that Paul is correcting Graeco-Roman understandings of beneficence that the Corinthians have unwisely appropriated rather than saying anything specifically eschatological (§7.2.2.3 below).[68]

7.2.2.2. The ecumenical interpretation

According to this interpretation, the collection is a powerful manifestation of the unity of Christ's church (Rom 12:5; 1 Cor 12:13; Gal 3:28; Eph 2:18; 4:4-6).[69] God's grace (τὴν χάριν τὴν δοθεῖσάν μοι), Paul says, had so forged

---

[66] S. McKnight ('Collection for the Saints', in G.F. Hawthorne [*et al.*, ed.], *Dictionary of Paul and His Letters* [Downers Grove-Illinois 1993], 143) posits that Paul could be contending in 2 Cor 9:10 'that the gifts of the Corinthians will actually turn out to enlarge the harvest (the conversion of Israel?)'. Note the comment of D. Zeller (*Charis bei Philon und Paulus* [Stuttgart 1990], 191) on 2 Cor 9:6-14: 'Paulus schreibt eine traditionelle Gnadentheologie aus, die in agrarischen Metaphern einhergeht'. For a full coverage of Paul's agrarian theology, H.D. Betz, *op. cit.*, 98-100; R.R. Melick, *art. cit.*, 110-113. See also in this regard our discussion (§2.7) of the Isis-Hermouthis hymns of Isidoros in *SEG* VIII 549-550.

[67] Whereas D. Georgi (*op. cit.*, 100) draws attention to the pilgrimage theme present in the wider context (Isa 55:5), Paul conspicuously does not.

[68] On the eschatological interpretation, see the astute comments of M.E. Thrall, *op. cit.*, 512-513.

[69] See A. Harnack, *The Mission and Expansion of Christianity in the First Three Centuries* (rpt. Gloucester, Mass. 1972: 2nd Gmn. edit. 1905), 183; F. Rendall, 'The

a bond of fellowship (κοινωνίας) between the Jewish and Gentile apostolic missions that a collection for the Jerusalem poor was agreed upon and implemented (Gal 2:9-10; cf. 1 Cor 16:1-4).[70] For Paul, the collection expressed the indebtedness not only of Jew and Gentile to each other (Rom 15:26-27; 2 Cor 8:13-15; 9:12-14) but also of the Body of Christ to God (2 Cor 8:9, 16; 9:11b, 12b, 15).

It was further hoped that the voluntariness of the collection (1 Cor 16:2: 'as he may prosper'; 2 Cor 8:3, 12; 9:5, 7) would accelerate the unity of purpose and love (2 Cor 8:8, 24). The Gentile delegates accompanying the collection (2 Cor 8:16-24; Acts 20:4) would also be a provocative demonstration to any Judaizers present at Jerusalem that God's grace had justified the ungodly without any recourse to the national emblems of legal righteousness.[71] As O. Cullmann eloquently writes,

> It is much more than a collection for help in winter-time or any other kind of work: a sacrifice for the unity of the Body of Christ. Truly because they are separated not only geographically but also through differently oriented theologies and through different missionary organisations to form two separate Churches, the collection is a sacrifice, and truly the blessing is sealed which keeps together the separated members of the early Church in spite of an already existing gulf.[72]

Thus, while Paul was realistic about the potential pitfalls of the entire exercise (Rom 15:30-31a; cf. Acts 21:27-30), he was nonetheless confident of its acceptability to the Jerusalem saints (Rom 15:31b).

Overall, I only have one minor quibble concerning the 'ecumenical' interpretation of the collection. As noted above,[73] the Jerusalem collection promoted unity as much between the contributing Gentile churches as the Jewish and Gentile missions. Paul's vista is often wider than we imagine.

Pauline Collection for the Saints', *The Expositor* 8 (4th series: 1893), 332; E.B. Allo, 'La portée de la collecte pour Jérusalem dans les plans de Saint Paul', *RB* 45 (1936), 536; O. Cullmann, 'The Early Church and the Ecumenical Problem', *ATR* 40 (1958), 181-189, 294-301; K.F. Nickle (*op. cit.*, 111-129); C.H. Talbert, *art. cit.*, 360; M.E. Thrall, *op. cit.*, 514-515.

70 Conceptually, Gal 2:9-10 best approximates the inter-relationship of χάρις, κοινωνία, and διακονία found in 2 Cor 8:4 (§7.2.1.1).

71 B. Holmberg, op. cit., 37; D. Georgi, op. cit., 117-120. J. Becker (*Paul: Apostle to the Gentiles* [Louisville 1993: Gmn. orig. 1988], 260) writes that 'Paul plainly challenges the Judaizing forces ... to see the collection as a test of whether Jewish Christianity still recognises the equality of Gentile Christianity or really wants to terminate fellowship despite the council decision'.

72 O. Cullmann, *art. cit.*, 299.

73 See n.33 above.

7.2.2.3. The obligation interpretation

A variety of interpretative positions have been grouped under this general heading.[74] The famous 1928 essay of K. Holl, which argues that the collection was a tax imposed upon Paul and his Gentile churches by the leaders of the Jerusalem church, has rightly been rejected as too extreme.[75] A more nuanced approach to the relationship of the Gentile churches with the mother church in Jerusalem is found in K. Berger. The collection, Berger asserts, is an expression of the unity of the church as opposed to the supremacy of Jerusalem and the dependency of the Pauline congregations.[76] Berger's overall view is that the collection best approximates the institution of 'alms for Israel' in which uncircumcised Gentile God-fearers gave alms to the poor of Israel in order that they might belong to and participate in God's covenant community.[77] According to B. Holmberg, the idea of obligation was implicit in the collection from the beginning, irrespective of whether the viewpoint is that of Jerusalem or Paul. In contrast to the supremacist views of the Jerusalem church, Paul gave the collection 'a more theological interpretation as an acknowledgment of Jerusalem's actual importance in God's election- and salvation-history', without thereby compromising the independence and achievement of the Gentile mission.[78] G.W. Peterman, after a useful coverage of Graeco-Roman reciprocity conventions, speaks of the collection as a social debt: it is a material reciprocation of the gratitude of the Gentile churches for sharing in the spiritual heritage of Israel and the Jerusalem church.[79] But if the idea of obligation is implicit from the beginning, as Holmberg and Peterman argue, why is the language of grace so profuse in 2 Corinthians 8-9, especially in its emphasis on *voluntary* giving?

---

[74] For a general coverage of the obligation interpretation, see M.E. Thrall, *op. cit.*, 511-512.

[75] K. Holl, 'Der Kirchenbegriff des Paulus in seinem Verhältnis zu dem der Urgemeinde', in K.H. Rengstorf (ed.), *Das Paulusbild in der neueren deutschen Forschung* (Darmstadt 1969), 144-178. Contra, K.F. Nickle, *op. cit.*, 90-93; B. Holmberg, *op. cit.*, 35-37.

[76] K. Berger, *art. cit.*, 199. Gal 2:10, Berger elaborates, sums up the legitimacy of the Jewish and Gentile missions and understands the connection of the Gentiles with Jerusalem in 'traditioneller jüdisch-theologischer Kategorien' (*loc. cit.*).

[77] Berger's proposal is ultimately flawed because the collection is more an expression of reciprocity than traditional almsgiving (Rom 15:26-27; 2 Cor 8:13-15). See J.M. Bassler, *op. cit.*, 94.

[78] B. Holmberg, *op. cit.*, 41.

[79] G.W. Peterman, (*op. cit.*), 177-178. P. Vassiliadis ('The Collection Revisited', *Delt. Bib. Mel.* 21/1 [1992], 42-48) argues that the purpose of the collection was the equal distribution and continuous sharing of wealth.

Finally, S. Joubert has recently proposed that the Jerusalem collection agreement of Gal 2:9-10 — when viewed from the perspective of agonistic gift exchange — was a reciprocal agreement.[80] The benefit conferred by the Jerusalem church was official recognition of Paul's apostleship. The extension of the right hand of fellowship, initiated by the 'pillar-apostles', visibly confirmed the benefit they had bestowed: affirmation of his apostleship to the Gentiles.[81] In the viewpoint of the 'pillar-apostles', then, the collection was a caritative project designed to place Paul and Barnabas in debt to Jerusalem for a long time.[82]

---

[80] S. Joubert, *op. cit.*, *passim*. Notwithstanding the ubiquity of the reciprocity system in antiquity, I remain unconvinced that Paul felt somehow obligated to the Jerusalem 'pillar-apostles' for recognition of his apostleship. Paul strongly emphasises his independence from the Jerusalem apostles (Gal 1:1, 10, 12, 15-17, 18-19, 22; 2:6b) and adopts a somewhat 'ironic or dismissive tone' in referring to them (2:2b, 6a, 9: R.N. Longenecker, *Galatians* [Dallas 1990], 57). This does not accord with the suppliant position usually adopted by beneficiaries before their benefactors, if the honorific inscriptions and papyri are sufficiently representative in this regard. If we view the reciprocity system primarily through the lens of the literary evidence (e.g. Seneca), as Joubert does, we will inevitably subsume everything under the rubric of 'payback' and gloss over important distinctives that point in a different direction.

[81] *Ibid.*, 100-101. Once again, Paul's acceptance of the right hand of fellowship (Gal 2:9) does not necessarily indicate his submission to the Jerusalem apostles as part of ancient reciprocity rituals. Most commentators on Galatians (e.g. E. De Witt Burton [Edinburgh 1921], 95-96; R.N. Longenecker, *op. cit.*, 58; F.J. Matera [Collegeville 1992], 77; J.D.G. Dunn [Peabody 1993], 110-111; J. Louis Martyn [New York 1997], 205; B. Witherington III [Grand Rapids 1998], 143-144) see the ritual as signifying not the submission of the Gentile mission to the mother-church at Jerusalem but rather as representing what the Jerusalem apostles had in common with Paul (cf. Phil 1:5: κοινωνία). It is entirely possible, as Witherington suggests (*op. cit.*, 144), that Paul interpreted the handshake as a gesture of mutual friendship, while the 'pillar-apostles' regarded it as Paul's tacit admission of their superiority. Notwithstanding, Paul distances himself from this implication in regard to his apostleship and the collection. In sum, much of Joubert's thesis for interpreting the Jerusalem collection as 'benefit exchange' depends upon the limited evidence of an ambiguous ritual (Gal 2:9) which, incidentally, can be understood in a different way. In this regard, it is more likely that the *ancient* context of the handshake in Galatians 2:9 is the bond of ritualised friendship that concluded alliances in antiquity. Significantly, the bond of ξενία ('friendship') was maintained even when those participating in the ritual were not strictly social equals. For a fine discussion of ritualised handshakes in the literary, documentary, and archaeological evidence, see G. Herman, *Ritualised Friendship and the Greek City* (Cambridge 1987), 37, 46, 5-53, 63, 64, 134. It is interesting that Polybius designates the extension of the right hand (δεξιά) as a 'sign of friendship' (Polybius 29.27: τῆς φιλίας σύνθημα). In Galatians 2:9, therefore, does Paul appropriate in a well-known cultural ritual and reinterpret the *missionary alliance* forged between himself and the 'pillar-apostles' in light of the gospel (δεξιὰς κοινωνίας)? If this is the case, an important strut of Joubert's 'reciprocity' thesis falls.

[82] S. Joubert, *op. cit.*, 106.

For Paul, however, it was clear that he was now obligated to Jerusalem along with his Gentile churches (Rom 15:25-27). Thus, the collection represented a reciprocation of tangible material benefits that would secure his apostolic honour upon its completion, thereby creating a solidarity (Gal 2:9: κοινωνία) and balanced reciprocity within the early Christian movement (2 Cor 8:13-15).[83] Moreover, with Paul successfully discharging the collection, the original benefactors at Jerusalem were placed under counter-obligation to return thanks to God and bestow honour (2 Cor 9:11-15).[84] According to Joubert, Paul moves from a *foundational* understanding of the collection as 'benefit exchange' to a more theological formulation of the venture as χάρις.[85]

As insightful as many of these observations are, modern scholars still underestimate the complexity of Graeco-Roman reciprocity conventions in regard to the collection. As a result, they fail to see how Paul engages in an implicit critique of the Graeco-Roman benefaction system and shapes an alternative vision of social relations by means of his theology of grace. Joubert, in particular, pays insufficient attention to the christological foundations of Paul's unilateral view of grace: its incarnational and cruciform focus (e.g. Rom 5:6-8; 2 Cor 8:9; Gal 2:20-21; Eph 2:4-8) subverts the very 'benefit exchange' perspective that (as Joubert alleges) underpins Paul's approach to the collection. How then do we account for Paul's profuse language of grace in 2 Corinthians 8-9?[86]

First, we have already drawn attention to the potential social misunderstandings that the Jerusalem collection may have provoked.[87] Some of the Jewish Christians at Jerusalem may have felt duty-bound to reciprocate commensurately in the future. As we argued in Chapter 4, reciprocity ideology had certainly made an impact on first-century Judaism, if Philo and Josephus are sufficiently representative. Furthermore, some Corinthians felt

---

[83] *Ibid.*, 102-103, 114-115, 121-124, 128-134, 140-144.

[84] *Ibid.*, 144-152.

[85] *Ibid.*, 152-153, 202-203.

[86] I register in advance my disagreement with V.D. Verbrugge (*op. cit., passim*) regarding the role of grace in the collection. Verbrugge argues that Paul's apostolic imperatives in 1 Cor 16:1-2 regarding the collection are progressively abandoned for a less authoritarian and more conciliatory emphasis on χάρις in 2 Corinthians 8-9. Similarly, S. Joubert (*op. cit.*, 168). This change in leadership style and rhetoric on Paul's part, Verbrugge argues, is occasioned by the fallout over his 'painful' letter (2 Cor 2:4; 7:8). χάρις, according to Verbrugge (*op. cit.*, 329), is merely employed by Paul 'to motivate the Macedonians and Achaians'. It does not function as a central theological description of the collection: rather Paul's main emphasis is on 'duty' (*op. cit.*, 330). As I will seek to demonstrate, Paul's frequent use of χάρις in 2 Corinthians 8-9 underscores his theological understanding of beneficence over against the obligations of the Graeco-Roman reciprocity system.

[87] See nn.33 and 63 above.

that they had been unfairly imposed on — in their perception at least — by a second-rate sophist who had refused their patronage (2 Cor 10:9-10; 11:6). Moreover, this was taking place in an internally divided church that was (in the view of some) competing with the Macedonians for Paul's affection.

The real sticking point for the Corinthians, however, was that they had promised to contribute to the collection but, as benefactors, had been remiss in their promise (2 Cor 9:2, 5). We see the social consequences of such unfulfilled obligations well illustrated in the experience of Dio Chrysostom. He had failed to honour his promise of embellishing his native city and shamefacedly admits his oversight to his fellow citizens:

> But since the question before us concerns my not proving false toward my native land and not defrauding you of the promise I made under no compulsion (μηδενὸς ἀναγκάζοντος), a promise by no means easy to make good and involving no small outlay of money, this I conceive to be a difficult matter and one calling for much serious cogitation. For there is nothing more weighty, no debt (ὀφειλόμενον) bearing higher interest, than a favour (χάριτος) promised. Moreover, this is the shameful and bitter kind of loan (τὸ ἀναίσχυντον δάνειον καὶ πικρόν), when, as one might say, because of tardy payment the favour (χάρις) turns into an obligation, an obligation the settlement of which those who keep silent demand altogether more sternly than those who cry aloud. For nothing has such power to remind those who owe you (τοὺς ὀφείλοντας ὑμῖν) such obligations as your having utterly forgotten them.[88]

Increasingly, an invisible moral pressure was imposed upon Dio Chrysostom the longer he delayed his munificence. His initial promise to Prusa, free of any compulsion, was transformed into an obligation that ultimately could not be postponed. We are seeing here the reverse side of the Graeco-Roman reciprocity system. Normally, the obligation to reciprocate χάριτες with public honours entrenched the moral and social status of the benefactor. But, in this case, the shift of the burden of indebtedness onto the benefactor not only stifled the gratitude of the recipient (Seneca, *Ben.*, 2.1.2; 2.5.2) but also exposed the benefactor to social shame. Not that many in antiquity were actually impolite enough to broach the issue with the benefactor — only Paul and the opponents of Demosthenes' crowning did that! But the silent demand and feigned forgetfulness of a beneficiary could become a powerful weapon for provoking recalcitrant benefactors into action. This was especially so in a culture where reciprocity conventions were everything.

The parallel with the Corinthian church is particularly revealing. Some of the Corinthians, resentful that they had been rebuffed as patrons by Paul, were now under the increasing obligation, because of their procrastination over the collection, to reciprocate with the promised χάρις. Indeed, Paul had said

---

[88] Dio Chrysostom., *Or.*, 40.3-4.

as much in regard to the collection (Rom 15:27: ὀφειλέται, ὀφείλουσιν).⁸⁹ The Corinthians were probably aware that if they chose not to reciprocate, they ran the risk of being regarded as false brothers or (worse) open enemies. Moreover, even when (to borrow Dio Chrysostom's words) that 'shameful and bitter kind of loan' was repaid, the Corinthians would still be permanently in debt to their Christian brethren: that is, through the debt of love (Rom 13:8-10: ὀφείλετε). Paul, as the apostle of God's grace (§6.4.2), was also under obligation to Jew and Gentile (Rom 1:14: ὀφειλέτης εἰμί) and, like Dio Chrysostom, would be exposed to shame along with the Corinthians if the promised contribution to the collection was not ready when the delegates came (Rom 9:4: καταισχυνθῶμεν).⁹⁰

The situation, then, that Paul faced at Corinth required considerable cultural and pastoral sensitivity if the collection was to be completed. Perhaps Paul's secret fear was that the Corinthians might ultimately comply with his request and fulfil their promised contribution, not because of any sense of gratitude for the divine grace revealed in the impoverished Christ (2 Cor 8:9), but more due to the silent demands of Graeco-Roman reciprocity system. Little wonder that Paul pleaded with the Corinthians, in terminology reminiscent of Dio Chrysostom and Philo (§4.4.4 n.180), that the contribution be 'ready not as an exaction but as a willing gift' (2 Cor 9:7: μὴ ἐκ λύπης ἢ ἐξ ἀνάγκης).

Second, grace is the central dynamic that animates the new set of social obligations that the collection embodies. As an act of benevolence (1 Cor 16:3; 2 Cor 8:6, 7, 19: χάρις), the collection is 'a visible sign of invisible grace' that meets people's needs (2 Cor 8:14; 9:12: τὸ ὑστέρημα).⁹¹ That same collection helps the participating groups involved — Jew and Gentile, Macedonian and Corinthian, the apostle and his (at times) factionalised and disloyal house-churches — to view themselves as 'recipients of divine grace', united by the reciprocal obligation of love and by a recognition of the salvation-history priority of the Jews.⁹² The focus of Paul's theology of grace, as we have seen (§6.1.2.4), can be eschatological: but, as far as the Jerusalem collection goes, it is strictly ecclesiological and christological. Last, as argued above, the collection allows Paul to interact with the first-century eastern Mediterranean understandings of human χάρις and propose a

---

⁸⁹ On Paul's debt terminology, see K.F. Nickle, *op. cit.*, 120 n.174.
⁹⁰ See also B. Witherington III, *op. cit.*, 426.
⁹¹ J.M. Bassler, *op. cit.*, 105.
⁹² *Ibid.*, 94.

radically different model of beneficence. We now turn to the Jerusalem collection in its wider Graeco-Roman context.

7.3. The Jerusalem Collection in its Graeco-Roman Context

7.3.1. Paul and the inscriptional motifs of rivalry and imitation

Several authors have drawn attention to the rivalry motifs that Paul employs regarding the Jerusalem collection.[93] A.R. Hands, S.C. Mott, P. Veyne, and W.A. Meeks also refer to the competitive element present in the Graeco-Roman benefaction system.[94] However, most writers assume that the rivalry alluded to in 2 Cor 9:2 is either 'friendly'[95] or 'mild'.[96] I have tentatively suggested that this may not necessarily have been the case. There could have been (unspoken) tensions between the Corinthians and the Macedonians over the issue of Paul's remuneration. Paul's sole acceptance of Macedonian patronage may have led the Corinthians to conclude that the Macedonians had simply outclassed them as rival patrons of Paul, that Paul had not only operated deceptively but also had displayed open inconsistency and partiality, and that they themselves were 'second class citizens' in the apostle's affections. Furthermore, because patronage conferred status and power over others, the Corinthians may have been perceived by their Christian contemporaries as having suffered social dishonour over against the ascendant Macedonians. Support for the collection may not have been entirely unanimous in Macedonia either. As H.D. Betz points out,[97] the expression οἱ πλείονες (2 Cor 9:2: 'most', 'the majority') could imply that there remained 'a sceptical minority' who did not willingly support the collection. Whether the reluctance of this minority regarding the collection is explained by the poverty of the Macedonian churches (2 Cor 8:1-4) or is due to other factors is impossible to say.

---

[93] E.g. R.R. Melick, *art. cit.*, 107-108 n.39; J. Koenig, *op. cit.*, 81.

[94] A.R. Hands, *op. cit.*, 31; S.C. Mott, *art. cit.*, 61; P. Veyne, *op. cit.*, 78, 108; W.A. Meeks, *op. cit.* (1993), 41. Note the helpful comment of C.H. Talbert (*art. cit.*, 362): 'Paul is here using the ancient rhetorical technique of comparison to motivate the Corinthians. He in effect is proposing a contest between the two regional churches to see who would be first in generosity'.

[95] See J. Koenig, *loc. cit.*; W.A. Meeks, 'The Circle of Reference in Pauline Morality', in D.L. Balch (*et al.*, ed.), *Greeks, Romans, and Christians: Essays in Honor of Abraham J. Malherbe* (Minneapolis 1990), 312. It must be noted that the competitive element inherent in the Graeco-Roman benefaction system was largely friendly.

[96] R.R. Melick, *art. cit.*, 107 n.108.

[97] H.D. Betz, *op. cit.*, 93.

In what follows I will argue that Paul employs traditional inscriptional rivalry and imitation motifs to encourage the Corinthians not to become benefactors of himself but rather of others through the Jerusalem collection.[98] The unhealthy rivalry between the Corinthians and Macedonians may well have forced his hand on the issue, as well as the shame of unfulfilled obligation in regard to the promised Corinthian contribution (§7.2.2.3). Nonetheless, there remain several significant departures from inscriptional convention that highlight what is central for Paul: χάρις and ἀγάπη.

7.3.1.1. The ἵνα and ὅπως clause in the resolution proper of the honorific inscriptions

The ἵνα or ὅπως clause in the resolution proper of honorific decrees unlocks for New Testament scholars a wealth of evidence concerning ethical exhortation and modelling in a hellenistic civic context.[99] A series of formulaic ethical motifs recur: the maintenance of honour in front of peers and posterity, the competition for honour among peers, and the ethical imitation of models of beneficence.

First, in hellenistic decrees the *polis* acknowledges its moral accountability in civic affairs: the city must preserve its reputation for honour before contemporaries and future generations. A decree of the Amphictyonic Council stipulates honours for a Thessalian benefactor 'so that (ὅπως) all the Greeks may know that the [Amphictyonic] Council knows how to return adequate favours (χάριτας ἀξίας ἀποδιδόναι) to those who confer benefactions on them and all the Greeks'.[100] Occasionally the honour of both the honorand

---

[98] Note the comment of B. Witherington III (*op. cit.*, 420 n.30) in this regard: 'Paul is trying hard to convince the Corinthians to complete the collection by showing them that they can thus fulfil their desire to be benefactors, only of other Christians'. S. Joubert (*op. cit.*, 173-176) correctly labels 2 Cor 8:1-6 an 'agonistic exemplum'.

[99] The publication of E.A. Castelli on Pauline imitation (*Imitating Paul: A Discourse of Power* [Louisville 1991]) typically ignores the epigraphic evidence. In viewing Pauline imitation from a Foucaultian perspective — and not from its hellenistic civic context — Castelli distorts the apostle's social and ethical stance. According to Castelli, Paul's paradigm of imitation imposes an ideological sameness and social exclusivity (difference) upon his converts. In my view, Paul sponsors several models of beneficence which up-end Graeco-Roman conventions of patronal power, without diminishing the social importance of traditional benefaction ethics and its rewards. S.C. Mott (*The Greek Benefactor and Deliverance from Moral Distress* [unpub. Ph.D. diss. Harvard University 1971], 150-151) draws attention to the motives behind the expressions of gratitude contained in the inscriptional ὅπως clauses.

[100] *SIG*³ 613A. For similar formulations, *SIG*³ 800; *Michel* 983; *SEG* XVI 255; *I. Magnesia* 92a; *I. Délos* IV 1520 (*ll.*17-20); *IG* V(1) 931 (*ll.*21-24), VII(2) 4130 (*ll.*55-57), IX(2) 11 (*ll.*33-36).

and the *polis* is brought into sharp focus. The stele of a first-century AD benefactor, Poseidippos of Cardamylae, is set up in the gymnasium

> ...in order that (ἵνα) those who confer benefits may receive favour (χάριν) in return for (ἀντί) love of honour (φολοτειμίας), and that those who have been benefited, returning honours (ἀποδιδόντες τειμάς), may have a reputation for thankfulness (εὐχαριστίας) before all people, never coming too late for the sake of recompense (ἀμοιβήν) of those who wish to do kindly (acts).[101]

Moreover, the perspective of posterity is never far removed from the mind of those who frame the decrees.[102] The effusive language of eternity is used to enhance the status of the honours conferred. Thus, in a decree honouring Eumenes II and his brother Attalos, the Athenian *demos* must keep on their horizon the gratitude of future generations for benefactions to their city:

> In order, therefore, that (ὅπως ἄν) the People may appear foremost in the return of a favour (ἐγ χάριτος ἀποδόσει) and be conspicuous in honouring those voluntarily benefiting the People and its friends and in committing the goodness of their deeds to eternal memory (εἰς ἀΐδιομ μνήμην) ...[103]

Or, again, the second-century BC decree honouring the grammarian Dioskourides:

> Further, in order that (ὅπαι) the earnest policy of the city may also be everlasting (ἀείμναστος) for posterity and that goodwill may be manifest (both) to those who have been set nobly and gloriously over the most honourable customs and to those who intend to increase goodwill towards (the city), inscribe this decree on a stone monument and erect (it) in the temple of Apollo Delphidios.[104]

In the above cases, the inscriptional language of eternity underscores the determination of the *polis* not to be dubbed ἀχάριστος either in the judgement of its contemporaries or later generations.[105]

Second, another important result of public recompense of benefactors is the competition for honour that was engendered among their peers. The inscriptions speak positively of this phenomenon, since the outcome of the

---

[101] *SEG* XI 948. See our discussion of this decree in §2.6.

[102] See P. Veyne (*op. cit.*, 258-259) on posterity as the audience of the eulogistic inscriptions.

[103] *OGIS* 248 (175—174 BC). ὅπως clauses employ the language of eternity to describe either the honours accorded benefactors or the glory of particular institutions (such as guilds). ἀείμνηστος τιμή: *I. Délos* IV 1521 (*ll*.27-28). ἀΐδιοι τιμαί: *I. Délos* IV 1520 (*l*.58). ἀθάνατος δόξα: *IG* XI(4) 1061 (*ll*.11-12).

[104] *SIG*³ 721. See also J. Benedum, *art. cit.*, No.2.

[105] A *polis* could compete with its own past record in rendering honour. For example, in returning thanks to Antiochus III and his Queen, the city Teos boasts in 'surpassing ourselves in the honours given to them for their benefactions'. See S.M. Burstein, *The Hellenistic Age from the Battle of Ipsos to the Death of Kleopatra VII* (Cambridge 1985), §33.

competitors' quest for glory is the advancement of the public good. Two examples will suffice. The city of Akraiphiae praises the people of Larissa for sending them three exemplary judges and stipulates that the decree itself be set up as a votive gift

> ...in order that (ὅπως) it may be manifest to all that the Akraiphiae are able to return appropriate honours and favours (τὰς καταξίας τιμὰς καὶ χάριτας ἀποδιδόναι) to the benefactors of themselves, and that the judges who are present thereafter for us, observing the gratitude of the Akraiphaia, may compete (ἀμιλλῶνται) for (a reputation of) nobleness.[106]

Similarly, a second-century BC Attic inscription decrees a crown of myrtle for its honorand

> ...in order, therefore, that ([ὅ]πως) it may be rivalling (ἐφάμ[ιλλον]) for those who strive eagerly to offer themselves in the common interest, seeing that they receive favours worthy of whatever kindnesses they have performed.[107]

Third, and significantly for the New Testament context, the *polis* or guild often calls upon its more zealous members — in view of the honours accorded their benefactors — to imitate in the civic arena the acts of beneficence eulogised in the decree. The language of zeal (ζηλωταί) is often employed in the honorific inscriptions to encourage the imitation of civic benefactors. The ethical dimension of this modelling is well captured in a Boeotian decree which honours its benefactor Epaminondas

> ...in order that (ἵνα), when these (foregoing honours) are completed in this manner, our city may appear (to be) grateful towards the benefactors, and that many may become zealous imitators (ζηλ[ωταί]) of the virtuous (acts) ([τῶν ἀγαθῶν]) of the foremost (τῶν πρώτων), which are given good report to the city.[108]

From this decree we see that imitation of meritorious action (τὰ ἀγαθά) is confined to aristocratic models (οἱ πρῶτοι) whose reputation for civic

---

[106] *Michel* 235 (146 BC). Indeed, the very act of publicly honouring magistrates places pressure upon them to act with probity. For example, the people of Demetrias honour three magistrates 'in order that the rest, contemplating (those) who were honoured, may stimulate such men to govern fairly and rightly' (*SEG* XII 306).

[107] *SEG* XXI 419. Also, *Michel* 985 (*ll*.20-22: ἵνα οὖν ἐφάμιλλον ᾖ τοῖς ἀεὶ φιλοτιμουμένοις). Plutarch (*Mor.*, 817D) exhorts the statesman in these terms: 'One should, however, always vie (διαμιλλητέον) with every official in zeal, forethought (προνοίᾳ) for the common good, and wisdom ... allowing them ... to be held in high esteem because they are benefactors of the community'. For further examples of πρόνοια in rivalry contexts, see Josephus, *AJ*, 18.289; Plutarch, *Mor.*, 92 C-D.

[108] *IG* VII(2) 2712 (AD 37). In a II cent. BC decree, the Ephesian people agree that a statue in honour of the gymnasiarch Diodoros be set up in the gymnasium, thereby 'guiding everyone to become emulators (ζηλωτάς) of excellent deeds' (*I. Ephesos* Ia. 6). For further examples employing ζηλωτής, see *Michel* 1011; *SEG* XVI 94, XXI 452; *I. Délos* IV 1520, 1521; *IG* XII(9) 239, 899.

honour was well known. Occasionally, an inscription more sharply focuses the mind of its audience by providing its own portrait of a civic luminary who imitated the moral qualities of another benefactor:

> Epigone, indeed, a woman of saintly dignity and devoted to her husband, imitated his example herself by taking up the priesthood ordained for every goddess, worshipping the gods reverently at sacrificial expense, in providing all men alike with a festive banquet.[109]

Finally, the idea of zealous imitation is sometimes coupled with the motif of competition to reinforce the moral pressure brought to bear upon the audience. We see this in an honorific decree from Delos, erected in the second century BC by a corporation of merchants. The resolution proper exhorts guild members to compete with each other by performing acts of beneficence on behalf of the guild. The incentive for this competition stems from the positive ethical model provided by Patron as the guild's benefactor and, moreover, by the guild itself in its desire for recompense commensurate with Patron's original generosity. As the decree explains:

> ...in order, therefore, that (ἵνα) for the remaining time (Patron) may also render himself (to be one who does not need to be) summoned (in regard to beneficence) and that the guild may manifestly take thought of the men who are benevolently disposed to itself and that it may return worthy favours (ἀξίας χάριτας ἀποδιδοῦσα) to the benefactors and that more of the other (members) from the guild may be zealous imitators (ζηλωταί) on account of the (guild's) thankfulness (εὐχαριστίαν) for this (generosity of Patron) and that those who love honour (φιλοτιμούμενοι) may outdo (παραμιλλῶνται) (each other) to achieve something for the guild ...[110]

It is worth pondering the reaction of the early Christians to these civic motifs. The early Christians must have confronted such benefaction ideology since it had thoroughly permeated the hellenistic and imperial city-states of the eastern Mediterranean basin. Several questions emerge at this stage. How could Paul encourage the Corinthians to fulfil their promise of beneficence without entirely alienating them? Was it Paul's intention that the beneficence of believers be impelled by traditional motifs such as imitation and competition, or by some other dynamic, or both? What aspects of Paul's presentation would have sounded odd to Graeco-Roman auditors?

7.3.1.2. Paul's redefinition of the inscriptional motifs of rivalry and imitation

Although Paul inverts the elitist values of Graeco-Roman society (§6.2-§6.3; §6.4.3), he employs familiar inscriptional motifs such as imitation and rivalry to buttress his ethical exhortation. However, he does this without

---

[109] A.R. Hands, *op. cit.*, §D.13. In *SEG* XVIII 27 honours are accorded a priest of Asklepios so that the other priests might be zealous imitators (ζηλωταί) of their peers.

[110] *I. Délos* IV 1519.

compromising what is distinctive for him (χάρις and ἀγάπη). As we have already shown, the ἵνα and ὅπως clauses of the honorific inscriptions exhort the social elite to imitate the munificence of the civic benefactors, with the incentive that they will be recompensed by the *polis* with honours and gratitude. The imitation motif in the honorific inscriptions, however, functions quite differently to its Pauline counterpart. In terminology, the honorific inscriptions invariably choose ζηλωτής, whereas Paul opts for μιμητής or μιμεῖσθαι. Possibly the reason that Paul avoided ζηλωτής in imitation contexts was its association with Jewish zeal for the Law from the Maccabean era onwards.[111] The inscriptional terminology of imitation would have sat uneasily with the Christ-centred ethic of Paul.[112]

Further, the point of ethical imitation — apart from the general replication of beneficence — was rarely defined in the inscriptions. The merit of the καλοκἀγαθοί was simply assumed: since their benefactions amply testified to their moral rectitude, there was no need to elaborate on the precise characteristics to be imitated by their successors. In this respect, an early third-century BC decree from Gazoros is unusually explicit in its parallelism: the care that the benefactor of Gazoros had lavished upon the city should be duplicated in his aspirants (πρ[ο]ενοήσατο τοῦ διασωθῆ[να]ι [*ll*.10-12]; πρόνοιαν τοῦ διασώιζειν [*ll*.24-25]).[113]

---

[111] For a discussion of ζηλωτής (and its cognates) in Paul and in Judaism more generally, see R.A. Horsley, *Jesus and the Spiral of Violence: Popular Jewish Resistance in Roman Palestine* (San Francisco 1987), 121-129; J.D.G. Dunn, *The Partings of the Ways: Between Christianity and Judaism and Their Significance for the Character of Christianity* (London 1991), 120-122. Paul does retain one use of ζηλωτής which could have overtones of Maccabean zeal (Gal 1:14: cf. v.13). Yet, at best, it is only presented as a model of mistaken zeal (cf. Rom 10:3; Phil 3:6-7). On μιμεῖσθαι in the Jewish world, W.P. De Boer, *The Imitation of Paul* (Kampen 1962), 8-13.

[112] D. Stanley has observed that the συν-compounds of Paul's later epistles, which apply the death-and-life paradigm of Christ to moral contexts, supplant the ethical imitation of Christ found in the earlier letters. *Id.*, 'Imitation in Paul's Letters: Its Significance for His Relationship to Jesus and to His Own Christian Foundations', in P. Richardson and J.C. Hurd (eds), *From Jesus to Paul: Studies in Honour of Francis Wright Beare* (Waterloo 1984), 132 n.15.

[113] C. Veligianni, 'Ehrendekret aus Gazoros (Ostmakedonien)', *ZPE* 51 (1983), 105-114. For a discussion of this decree, see my article, 'Benefaction Ideology and Christian Responsibility for Widows', in S.R. Llewelyn (ed.), *New Docs* 8 (1997), 106-116. Similarly, Epigone (A.R. Hands, *op. cit.*, §D.13), discussed in §7.3.1.1. Josephus depicts the companions of Judas Maccabaeus, after his death, begging Jonathon 'to imitate (μιμεῖσθαι) his brother who in his concern (πρόνοιαν) for his countrymen had died on behalf of the liberty of them all' (*AJ*, 13.5).

Paul, like the Gazoros decree, aims for precision: the models to be imitated are clearly defined,[114] and the theological content argued with rigour.[115] Nevertheless, the differences outweigh the similarities. Whereas the citizens of Gazoros envisage continued dependence upon benefactors with aspirants filling the breach, Paul presents himself as a model of financial independence to the Thessalonian church (2 Thess 3:7-10). The Thessalonian Christians, he argues, must reject the temptation to remain dependent as clients (2 Thess 3:11-12) and instead learn to exercise the role of benefactor (3:13).[116]

But what of the inscriptional rivalry motifs? Paul promotes a rivalry in beneficence between the Macedonian and Corinthian congregations by employing the zeal terminology of the honorific inscriptions (σπουδή, προθυμία). He pressures the recalcitrant Corinthians to fulfil their part of the Jerusalem collection by drawing invidious comparisons between their lack of preparation and the generosity of their Macedonian brethren. The earnestness of the Macedonian Christians (διὰ τῆς ἑτέρων σπουδῆς: 2 Cor 8:8; cf. 8:1-4) should provoke the Corinthians to match their initial readiness (τὴν προθυμίαν τοῦ θέλειν: 8:11; cf. v.10) with their contribution to the Jerusalem collection. Nonetheless, Paul avoids the inscriptional terminology of competition (ἐφάμιλλος; ἁμιλλᾶσθαι; παραμιλλᾶσθαι). The omission is surely deliberate.[117] The real issue for the Corinthians, in Paul's view, is simply the genuineness of their love (ἀγάπη: 2 Cor 8:8, 24). Only this new understanding of beneficence as an expression of love (cf. 1 Cor 13:3) would ensure that the rivalry between the Corinthian and Macedonian Christians did

---

[114] In contexts employing μιμητής or μιμεῖσθαι, the models appealed to are: 1 Thess 1:6a (ἡμῶν: Paul, Silvanus, and Timothy [cf. 1:1]; τοῦ κυρίου: Christ); 1 Thess 2:14 (the churches in Judaea); 2 Thess 3:7, 9 (ἡμᾶς: Paul, Silvanus, and Timothy [cf. 1:1]). 1 Cor 4:16 (μου: Paul); 1 Cor 11:1 (μου: Paul; Χριστοῦ: Christ). Other examples: Phil 3:17 (μου and ἡμᾶς: Paul and Timothy [1:1]). Gal 4:12 (ἐγώ: Paul). Eph 5:1 (God).

[115] On the theological content, see D.M. Stanley, 'Become Imitators of Me: The Pauline Conception of Apostolic Tradition', *Bib.* 40 (1959), 859-877; id., *art. cit.*; B. Sanders, 'Imitating Paul: 1 Cor 4:16', *HTR* 74/4 (1981), 353-363; B. Fiore, *The Function of Personal Example in the Socratic and Pastoral Epistles* (Rome 1986), 164-190; N. Onwu, '*Mimetês* Hypothesis: A Key to the Understanding of Pauline Paraenesis', *African Journal of Biblical Studies* 1/2 (1986), 95-112; E. Best, *Paul and His Converts* (Edinburgh 1988), 58-72; E.A. Judge, *art. cit.* (1992), 195-199; J.A. Brant, 'The Place of *Mimêsis* in Paul's Thought', *SR* 22/3 (1993), 285-300.

[116] See B.W. Winter, '"If a man does not wish to work ...". A Cultural and Historical Setting for 2 Thessalonians 3:6-16', *TynBul* 40/2 (1989), 305-315.

[117] E.A. Judge (*art. cit.* [1992], 187) comments on the use of ἁμιλλᾶσθαι in *I. Ephesos* Ia. 27 (AD 104), observing that the term, absent from the New Testament, 'pin-points one of the principal motives of civic generosity, to outshine one's peers in benefactions'.

not degenerate into the heated competitions for honour so typical of the καλοκἀγαθοί.

In similar vein to the inscriptions, Paul reminds the Corinthians of the importance of maintaining a reputation for beneficence in front of their Christian contemporaries. The apostle has already boasted about their readiness to the Macedonian churches and to the other congregational delegates responsible for the collection (2 Cor 8:24; 9:2), whom he had sent to test their preparedness (ἵνα παρεσκευασμένοι ἦτε: 9:3b). He reminds them that any reticence on their part would be carefully noted before the churches (εἰς πρόσωπον τῶν ἐκκλησιῶν: 2 Cor 8:24). Further, Paul resorts to the language of dishonour (καταισχύνειν) in describing the humiliation that the Corinthians and himself, as their founding apostle, would experience should his boasting in their readiness prove unfounded.

It is the reputation of the Corinthians and Paul *as benefactors* that is at risk here: the inscriptions are more concerned about the reputation of the *polis* in returning honours commensurate with their benefactions. Paul's boldness in confronting recalcitrant co-benefactors like the Corinthians differs from the deferential politeness normally accorded benefactors in antiquity. This does not mean that Paul, in line with the inscriptions, is indifferent to highlighting the rewards that accrue to those who are beneficent. Paul's focus remains on God who, in the disposal of His blessings upon the Corinthians (2 Cor 9:7-11), undergirds their beneficence by His grace (χάρις: 9:14b; cf. 8:1, 9) and as a result will reward both the Corinthians (9:10, 11a, 13a) and their beneficiaries (9:12, 14a).

7.3.2. Paul and the ethos of reciprocity

Reciprocity governed the entire gamut of relationships — human and divine — in antiquity (§2.6; §3.3; §4.4.3; §4.5.3; §5.3). We have already seen that the gods could be placed under obligation through cultic piety, reciprocating with gifts and gratitude. Even first-century Jews such as Philo and Josephus interpreted God's Old Testament covenantal Law through the lens of reciprocity (§4.4.3; §4.5.3). As noted, Paul rejects the idea that God could be put under obligation (§6.5). God's infinite generosity simply cannot be requited (Rom 11:35: ἀνταποδοθήσεται αὐτῷ; [LXX: Job 35:7; 41:11]; 1 Cor 4:7; 1 Thess 3:9). When God does choose to act reciprocally, He blesses the beneficent in the present (2 Cor 9:6-11 [v.10: LXX Isa 55:10; Hos 10:12]) and, as the impartial Judge of all at the eschaton (Rom 2:6: ἀποδώσει ἑκάστῳ κατὰ ἔργα αὐτοῦ), rewards the faithful (Col 3:24: τὴν ἀνταπόδοσιν) and judges the wicked (ἀνταποδοῦναι: Rom 11:9; 12:19 [LXX Lev 19:18; Deut 32:35]; 2 Thess 1:6). In such cases, divine recompense is either a matter of God's free grace or His retributive justice.[118] However, in contrast to Philo (§4.4.4: Philo, *Cher* 122-123), Paul does not resort to Stoic theology in order to criticise Graeco-Roman views of divine reciprocity. At this juncture, Paul's thought clearly imbibes the LXX portrait of God, outlined above, not that of the popular philosophers.

Human relationships, too, were governed by the ethos of reciprocity. By the first century AD, reciprocity embraced the international relations between Rome, her client-states (§2.6: *I. Ephesos* II. 233), and the various local associations (§3.5: *Pap. Agon.* 6). At the local level, the conventions for the return of honour between benefactors and their local *poleis* were subsumed under the ethos of reciprocity (§2.6: *SEG* XI 948). Finally, at a personal level, reciprocity undergirded the hierarchical relationships of the family (§2:5: *SEG* XVIII 365; §3.3: *P. Turner* 18; §4.6.2: *CIJ* II 772; §5.3: Hierocles, *On Duties* [Stob. 3.52]), as much as the mutually convenient arrangements made between equals (φίλοι). The dominance of reciprocity in social relations can also be gauged by the rarity of any critique of the institution in antiquity (§3.3: *P. Mert.* I 12; §4.4.4: Philo, *Cher* 122-123). J.D. Crossan sums up the situation well:

In the Roman Mediterranean, therefore, the web of patronage and clientage, with accounts that could never be exactly balanced because they could never be precisely computed, was the dynamic morality that held society together.[119]

7.3.2.1. *Paul's critique of the Graeco-Roman reciprocity system*

At the outset, we should ask to what extent Paul engages in a critique of the Graeco-Roman reciprocity system. E.A. Judge has correctly observed that Paul ultimately subverts the patronal system — based as it was on the obligation of a socially inferior client to a socially superior patron — by subjecting everyone to a common Master who outshines all.[120] The terminology of servitude and subordination that Paul universally applies to social relations within the body of Christ undermines the status conventions

---

[118] On this entire topic, see F.V. Filson, *St. Paul's Conception of Recompense* (Leipzig 1931), *passim*.

[119] J.D. Crossan, *The Historical Jesus: The Life of a Mediterranean Jewish Peasant* (San Francisco), 65. A.R. Hands (*op. cit.*, 29-31) helpfully summarises the critique of the popular philosophers regarding the Homeric reciprocity system. Nonetheless, note Hand's estimate (*ibid.*, 30-31) as to the outcome of debate among the popular philosophers regarding reciprocity: 'a return, even though it may no longer decently be asked for, is confidently expected'.

[120] E.A. Judge, *art. cit.* (1974), 196-197. Elsewhere, Judge (*art. cit.* [1983], 6) states that 'the deliberate abandonment of status...open(s) the way to a new spirit of human cooperation through mutual service'.

associated with the reciprocity system.[121] The honorific titles and privileges accorded the officials and patrons of the Sarapis association (*Michel* 1553), the sacred association of the Great Mother (*Michel* 984), and the Bacchic society (*SIG*³ 1109) are simply absent from Paul's house churches.[122] Significantly, as regards the reciprocation of honour, the weakest was to be accorded the greatest honour in the body of Christ (1 Cor 12:22ff).

But more than honorifics is involved here. Paul's language of grace subtly undermines the social expectations aroused by the Graeco-Roman reciprocity system. A case in point is the Jerusalem collection. D. Georgi has argued that Paul regards acts of patronage as 'the return of divine grace, mediated through *charismata* and accumulated thanksgiving'.[123] Unfortunately, Georgi's view is too abstract for our purposes. How *did* Paul differentiate the Jerusalem collection from the range of social conventions that made up the Graeco-Roman reciprocity system? What precisely were the issues that Paul was addressing?

In this regard, we have previously argued that the procrastination of the Corinthians regarding the Jerusalem collection created a delicate pastoral and social problem for Paul (§7.2.2.3). A sense of unspoken obligation — fuelled by the expectations of the other Gentile churches and the Jerusalem believers themselves — would have increasingly gripped the Corinthians the longer that they delayed on the issue. From a Graeco-Roman perspective, this obligation would not be requited until the Corinthians had fulfilled their promised contribution . Thus the emphasis of Paul on voluntariness and divine grace as the dynamic of human generosity was probably designed to extricate the Corinthians from the burdensome demands of the Graeco-Roman reciprocity system (§7.2.2.1 n.63). At the very least, it challenged the Corinthians to understand the obligation of reciprocity differently to the prevailing ethos of their culture. The language of abundance associated with grace also liberated them from the tyranny of commensurability that characterised the reciprocity system (§2.4; §6.1.2.4; §6.5; §7.2.1.1). It ensured that joy (2 Cor 9:7) — not the resentfulness of obligation — was the by-product of their generosity and that this would then overflow into thankfulness towards God (2 Cor 9:12ff).[124]

---

[121] E.A. Judge, *art. cit.* (1974), 196-197.

[122] F.W. Danker, *op. cit.* (1982), §20, §21, §22. See L.M. White (*art. cit.*, 221 n.49) for additional examples.

[123] D. Georgi, *op. cit.*, 161.

[124] E.F. Bruck ('Ethics vs Law: St. Paul, the Fathers of the Church and the "Cheerful Giver" in Roman Law', *Traditio* 2 [1944], 102) refers to Cornutus in discussing the Graeco-Roman context of 'cheerful giving' (cf. 2 Cor 9:7b: ἱλαρῶς). Cornutus, arguing that the

But what of the recipients of the Jerusalem collection? Does Paul tackle the ticklish issue of the return of favour with the Jerusalem believers as well? The question is difficult to answer since Paul's letters are directed to Gentile churches and not to the church at Jerusalem. Unfortunately, we do not know whether Paul ever informally explained the rationale behind the collection to the Jerusalem church in the same way that he had to the churches at Rome and Corinth (cf. Gal 2:9-10; Acts 24:17). We can only assume that Paul would have wanted to allay any fears of the Jerusalem church that they would be obligated to return favour for the collection. He does this by simply reversing the direction of indebtedness (§7.2.2.1 n.63). The Gentiles, Paul argues, were in debt to the Jerusalem church because God's grace had been initially mediated through the Jews to the Gentile nations (§7.2.2.1). Seemingly, the only obligation of the Jewish believers is — as an expression of their longing for their Gentile brethren — to thank God in prayer for the generosity of the Gentile churches and for the divine grace at work in their lives (2 Cor 9:14-15). However, as we will argue in our next section (§7.3.2.2), the intensity of feeling conveyed here for their benefactors surpasses anything found in the honorific inscriptions.

More generally, as we have seen (§6.4.3), Paul's language of grace also provides a new vision of social relationships within the body of Christ, partially inverting the hierarchical structure of Graeco-Roman society that was promoted by the reciprocity system.

In conclusion, the beneficence of believers is not motivated by the obligation to return favour or, conversely, the expectation of the return of favour. The only legitimate dynamic for Paul is love (Rom 13: 8-10; 1 Cor 13:3).[125]

7.3.2.2. Paul's endorsement of the Graeco-Roman reciprocity system

To what extent did reciprocity conventions inform Paul's ecclesiastical relations and his understanding of human beneficence? L.M. White argues that

---

Χάριτες were etymologically derivative from χαρά ('joy', 'cheerfulness'), explains the derivation thus: 'By doing good cheerfully (ἱλαρῶς), (the *Charites*) render cheerful (ἱλαρῶς) the receivers of their good deeds as well'. *Id., Summary of Greek Theology*, 15 [20.5-8 Lang]. As enlightening as this background material is, Paul studiously avoids the plural χάριτες in discussions of divine and human beneficence (§6.5). For discussion of the relationship between χάρις, χαρά, and the Χάριτες, see O. Loew (ΧΑΡΙΣ Diss. Marburg), 1908.

[125] C.K. Barrett (*The Epistle to the Romans* [London 1957], 249-250) well captures the thrust of Paul's teaching: 'Paul means that the only debt Christians ought to incur is that which they are bound to incur and can never completely discharge — the debt of mutual love'.

Paul adheres to many of the reciprocity conventions of the traditional patronage system.[126] We have also seen that C.F. Whelan argues that Paul treats his churches as clients, invoking their allegiance to himself as father/benefactor and expecting reciprocity in their relationship.[127] Arguably, several items of evidence point to the continuing importance of reciprocity conventions for Paul.

These are: (1) Paul's use of reciprocity terminology for his relationship with the Corinthians (2 Cor 6:13: ἀντιμισθίαν), for the patronage of the Philippians (Phil 4:15: εἰς λόγον δόσεως καὶ λήμψεως), and — if 1 Timothy is Pauline — for beneficence towards widows (1 Tim 5:4: ἀμοιβὰς ἀποδιδόναι); (2) Paul's recommendation of Phoebe (Rom 16:1-2); (3) Paul's use of προπέμπειν in Rom 15:24 as a technical term; (4) a selection of passages that contain reciprocity motifs (Rom 15:27 [cf. 1 Cor 9:11]; 2 Cor 8:13-15; Phil 4:10-20); (5) finally, the complex web of reciprocal relationships in Paul's letter to Philemon. For the sake of brevity, I will register my agreement with (what I consider to be) assured cases of reciprocity and offer caveats where they are warranted.

First, the three cases of reciprocity terminology (2 Cor 6:13; Phil 4:15; 1 Tim 5:4) certainly do point to Paul's endorsement of traditional reciprocity conventions.[128] Nonetheless, in 2 Cor 6:13, Paul, as the apostolic benefactor, displays an intensely personal affection (6:13b: πλατύνθητε καὶ ὑμεῖς: cf. v.11b; 7:2) towards his Corinthian converts. In the case of the honorific inscriptions, however, such displays of personal emotion are rare. Only occasionally do we find in the inscriptions a departure from the formulaic honorifics that reveals genuine affection for the benefactor. One such case was Theokles of Olbia who became 'as a brother in regard to the men of his own age, as a son in regard to the more aged, as a father in regard to the more young' (*CIG* II 2059: §2.3; cf. 1 Tim 5:1; cf. Arr., *Epict. Diss.*, 3.22.81-82).

Second, that Paul was recommending the reciprocation of Phoebe's patronage and hospitality (Rom 16:1-2) is not necessarily assured, especially if Rom 16 is addressed to the Roman house churches as opposed to (conjecturally) Ephesus.[129] As R. Jewett observes,

It is not clear, however, why Paul would have expected that the Roman house churches,

---

[126] L.M. White, *art. cit.*, 216-222.

[127] C.F. Whelan, *loc. cit.*

[128] For a discussion of εἰς λόγον δόσεως καὶ λήμψεως (Phil 4:15) in contexts of social reciprocity, see P. Marshall, *op. cit.*, 157-164; G.W. Peterman, *op. cit.*, 53-65. On 2 Cor 6:13, *ibid.*, 189-192. On 1 Tim 5:4, see J.R. Harrison, *art. cit.*

[129] For a convenient summary of the respective arguments for a Roman or Ephesian provenance of Rom 16, see C.F. Whelan, *art. cit.*, 71ff.

which owed nothing to him for their formation and growth, could have felt obligated to repay Phoebe on his behalf.[130]

Jewett may be correct in asserting that Paul was recommending Phoebe to the Romans so that she could create a logistical base there for his projected mission to Spain.[131] But, in my opinion, Jewett's suggestion is (at best) inferential and (at worst) entirely conjectural. Perhaps a simpler and more likely alternative is that Paul expects the Romans to accept Phoebe worthily of the saints (ἀξίως τῶν ἁγίων): that is, in a manner worthy of the debt of love owed to all believers (Rom 13:8-10). If my suggestion is correct, then love is a distinctive that redefines the Graeco-Roman reciprocity system for believers.

Third, in the case of Rom 15:24, προπέμπειν seems to bear elements of reciprocity. The elements of exchange are clear enough: after a period of the reciprocal sharing of spiritual gifts while at Rome (Rom 1:11-12), Paul anticipates a financial subsidy for his projected mission to Spain (ὑφ' ὑνῶν προπεμφθῆναι: 15:24; cf. εἰς λόγον δόσεως καὶ λήμψεως: Phil 4:15), as had been the custom on other occasions (1 Cor 16:6, 11; 2 Cor 1:16; cf. Titus 3:13).[132] But what holds true for Rome is more ambiguous at Corinth. Paul's rejection of patronage while at Corinth — in order to avoid being placed under obligation as a client[133] — would have sat uneasily (in the minds of some) with his acceptance of Corinthian finances upon his departure from Corinth. Paul probably justified his (apparent) inconsistency by regarding the latter financial arrangement as a case of the Corinthians legitimately sponsoring his missionary work *elsewhere*. While *at* Corinth, however, Paul vigorously resists the claims of reciprocity, insisting on the right of parents to benefit their children. But, in the case of the church at Rome, where Paul was not the founding apostle, he assumes the mantle of reciprocity — redefined as the mutual sharing of χαρίσματα — for ease of relations with believers he has not as yet met.

Fourth, G.W. Peterman is correct asserting that while the reciprocity of Phil 4:10-20 shows familiarity with Graeco-Roman reciprocity conventions, it

---

[130] R. Jewett, 'Paul, Phoebe, and the Spanish Mission', in J. Neusner (*et al.*, ed.), *The Social World of Formative Christianity and Judaism* (Philadelphia 1988), 161 n.83.

[131] R. Jewett, *art. cit.*, 151-155. Contra, C.F. Whelan, *art. cit.*, 84-85.

[132] On προπέμπειν as a technical expression referring to material help, see C.E.B. Cranfield, *The Epistle to the Romans* Vol.II (Edinburgh 1979); L.M. White, *art. cit.*, 217; R. Jewett, *art. cit.*, 143; G.W. Peterman, *op. cit.*, 165.

[133] E.A. Judge, *art. cit.* (1980), 214. For an in-depth coverage, see P. Marshall, *op. cit.*, 165-277.

is primarily animated by the Old Testament and the gospel.[134] We have argued similarly in regard to Rom 15:27 (§7.2.2.1). Again, as far as 1 Cor 9:11 (cf. Gal 6:6; 1 Tim 5:17-18), Paul endorses reciprocity conventions, but redefines their rationale. The patronage of the apostles in the early church reciprocates their spiritual ministry: but the obligation derives from the Old Testament (1 Cor 9:9 [LXX: Deut 25:4]; 9:13 [LXX Num 18:18ff]), the command of Christ (9:14 [Matt 10:10; Luke 10:7-8]; cf. 1 Tim 5:18), the example of the other apostles (9:4-5), and Paul's agricultural theology (9:7b). Finally, in 2 Cor 8:13-15, the same pattern emerges. We have noted Aristotle's comment that the very presence of a shrine to the Χάριτες should remind its observers of the principle of proportional recompense of favour (§5.3: κατ' ἀναλογίαν καὶ μὴ κατ' ἰσότητα [Aristotle, Eth. Nic., 5.5.6-7]; cf. §4.4.3 n.179; §4.5.1 n.205).[135] Paul's emphasis, however, falls on a disproportionate requital (2 Cor 8:14a-b) that will result in communal equality (8:13: ἐξ ἰσότητος; 8:14c: ὅπως γένηται ἰσότης). Moreover, he grounds his argument in the mutual sharing of the Israelite wilderness experience (2 Cor 8:15: LXX Exod 16:18) and perhaps, more generally, in the socio-economic ethics of LXX land theology.[136] Above all, as P. Vassiliadis convincingly argues,[137] New Testament equality is not based on the legal principle of Greek philosophy but rather on the act of divine grace. Christ, who is equal to God

---

[134] J. Koenig, op. cit., 71-73; G.W. Peterman, op. cit., 121-161; S. Fowl, 'Know Your Context: Giving and Receiving Money in Philippians', Int 56/1 (2002), 45-58. For a brief discussion of reciprocity in Philippians, see L. Bormann, Philippi: Stadt und Christengemeinde zur Zeit des Paulus (Leiden-New York-Köln 1995), 179-181.

[135] The language of equality is found elsewhere in reciprocation contexts. For example, Pseudo-Libanius (Ἐπιστολιμαῖοι Χαρακτῆρες 80) reminds his reader that he had 'received many favours when he was not able to repay me measure for measure (τοῖς ἴσοις ἀμείφασθαι)'. Similarly, the author of P. Mert. I. 12 acknowledges that he might not be able 'to render something equivalent (τὰ ἴσα)'.

[136] On the latter, see the suggestions of C.J.H. Wright in regard to New Testament κοινωνία: id., Living as the People of God: The Relevance of Old Testament Ethics (London 1983), 98ff; id., God's People in God's Land: Family, Land, and Property in the Old Testament (Exeter 1990), 112ff.

[137] P. Vassiliadis, art. cit. ('Equality', 1992), 55. W.A. Meeks, art. cit., in D.L. Balch (et al., ed.), op. cit., 312-313: 'Paul is thus making the pattern of Christ's self-giving a model by which to revise the notion of equity within the Christian movement. At the same time, his citation of Exod 16:18 (2 Cor 8:15) undoubtedly indicates that, at least in his own mind, the movement is continuous with Israel and that therefore the same pattern of equity is to be seen in God's dealings with (biblical) Israel'. For extra discussion, see D. Georgi, op. cit., 84-91, 138-140; H.D. Betz, op. cit., 67-70; B. Witherington III, Conflict and Community in Corinth: A Socio-Rhetorical Commentary on 1 and 2 Corinthians (Carlisle 1995) 421 n.37.

(Phil 2:6: τῷ εἶναι ἴσα θεῷ), had disproportionately impoverished Himself in order to enrich the poor (2 Cor 8:9).

Fifth, and finally, Paul's letter to Philemon regarding his slave Onesimus unveils a series of client-patron relationships.[138] Paul is the father/benefactor of Onesimus (Phlm 10) and intercedes as his patron before Philemon, his aggrieved master. Simultaneously, the apostle is the father/benefactor of Philemon (Phlm 19b) and therefore expects (but does not demand) requital from his beneficiary. Equally, Paul endorses Philemon as the patron of a house church (Phlm 1-2, 5, 7, 22) and assumes that Philemon will continue to act as a host to himself and his new client Onesimus, as well as to the other local believers. What is especially puzzling for the modern interpreter — and presumably for the original auditors! — is the way that Paul both endorses and subverts the traditional conventions of reciprocity in each case.

At the outset, I wish to signal my agreement with the recent strand of scholarship that interprets the occasion of the epistle against the evidence of certain first-century jurists (e.g. Proculus: *Digest* 21.1.17.4; cf. *Digest* 21.1.17.5; 21.1.43.1).[139] According to this interpretation, Onesimus was not a

---

[138] For recent discussion of Philemon, see P. Lampe, 'Keine »Sklavenflucht« des Onesimos', *ZNW* 76 1/2 (1985), 135-137; N.R. Petersen, *Rediscovering Paul: Philemon and the Sociology of Paul's Narrative World* (Philadelphia 1985); S.C. Winter, 'Paul's Letter to Philemon', *NTS* 33/1 (1987), 1-15; J.D.M. Derrett, 'The Functions of the Epistle to Philemon', *ZNW* 79 1/2 (1988), 63-91; J.M.G. Barclay, 'Paul, Philemon and the Dilemma of Christian Slave-Ownership', *NTS* 37/2 (1991), 161-186; L.A. Lewis, 'An African American Appraisal of the Philemon-Paul-Onesimus Triangle', in C.H. Felder (ed.), *Stony the Road We Trod: African American Biblical Interpretation* (Minneapolis 1991), 232-246; J.G. Nordling, 'Onesimus *Fugitivus*: A Defence of the Runaway Slave Hypothesis in Philemon', *JSNT* 41 (1991), 97-119; B.M. Rapske, 'The Prisoner Paul in the Eyes of Onesimus', *NTS* 37/2 (1991), 187-203; P. Arzt, 'Brauchbare Sklaven: Ausgewählte Papyrustexte zum Philemonbrief', *Proto Bib* 1/1 (1992), 44-58; S.S. Bartchy, 'Philemon, Letter to', in D.N. Freedman (ed.), *The Anchor Bible Dictionary* Vol.5 (New York 1992), 305-310; A.D. Callahan, 'Paul's Epistle to Philemon: Toward an Alternative *Argumentum*', *HTR* 86/4, (1993) 357-376; *id.*, *Embassy of Onesimus: The Letter of Paul to Philemon* (Valley Forge 1997); P.V. Kea, 'Paul's Letter to Philemon: A Short Analysis of Its Values', *Perspectives in Religious Studies* 23 (1996), 223-232; R.A. Horsley, 'Paul and Slavery: A Critical Alternative to Recent Readings', *Semeia* 83/84 (1998), 153-200, esp. 178-182; M.J. Harris, *Slave of Christ: A New Testament Metaphor for the Total Devotion to Christ* (Leicester 1999), 57ff; M. Barth and H. Blanke, *The Letter to Philemon: A New Translation with Notes and Commentary* (Grand Rapids-Cambridge 2000).

[139] P. Lampe (*art. cit.*), followed by B.M. Rapske (*art. cit.*) and S.S. Bartchy (*art. cit.*). L.A. Lewis (*art. cit.*, 245-246) speaks of Paul being 'the envoy' of Onesimus. M. Barth and H. Blanke (*op. cit.*, 228) argue against Lampe's thesis thus: 'Lampe seems to overlook the fact that only the *acceptance* of a letter of intercession exempted the slave from official or private prosecution, and from subsequent punishment — if he was caught after his escape. Neither the search for a person who might intervene nor an oral or written plea in the slave's

runaway slave, but had *deliberately* sought out Paul as the respected father/benefactor of Philemon. The legal basis for Onesimus' decision to contact Paul was plain: a slave, facing chastisement from his master for wrong-doing, could leave his household and seek a friend of his master to intercede on his behalf. But, unexpectedly to everyone, Onesimus had become a Christian during his stay with Paul. Paul was now *formally* the patron of Onesimus and *spiritually* both his father/benefactor and brother in Christ. As a result, a new web of social relationships and obligations bound together Paul, Onesimus, Philemon and the church that met in his house. But how this new dynamic of reciprocity was to be worked out in the context of first-century slavery remained unclear to Paul.[140] So the apostle moved cautiously, affirming traditional reciprocity conventions, while providing a glimpse for us of their social transformation in Christ.

At first glance, Paul's reply to Philemon could be viewed as reversing the direction of obligation between patrons and clients, as dictated by the expectations of the Graeco-Roman reciprocity system. The ancients well understood that the client was obligated to reciprocate his patron's favours. It would seem that Paul, the father/benefactor of Philemon (Phlm 19b: σεαυτόν μοι προσοφείλας), abandons his traditional right to reciprocity from Philemon, his client, when he offers to reimburse personally any losses that Philemon may have incurred through Onesimus' absence (v.18: εἰ δέ τι ἠδίκησέν σε ἢ ὀφείλει, τοῦτο εμοὶ ἐλλόγα;. v.19a: ἐγὼ ἀποτίσω).[141] Arguably, Paul is upholding — over against the Graeco-Roman reciprocity system (§7.3.2.2) — the right of parents to benefit their children without expectation of return. However, the issue is more complex than this. It must be remembered that Paul is acting as the formal patron of Onesimus. So Paul, as the father/benefactor of Philemon, is simply committing himself to further beneficence on behalf of his new client. But it is also likely that Philemon perceived no real difference between Paul acting as the formal patron of Onesimus and Paul acting as his own patron to ensure a favourable reception

---

interest *automatically* assured impunity and liberty' (original emphasis). Although this is *legally* true, the objection is not decisive. Onesimus may well have been hoping that Philemon's obligation to his greatly revered father/benefactor-in-the-faith, the apostle Paul, would override whatever legal technicalities arose in the event of his capture. Finally, the thesis of A.D. Callahan (*art. cit., op. cit.*) that Onesimus is not a slave at all is unconvincing. Callahan argues that the use of ὡς in v.16 prefacing δοῦλος points to a virtual, not an actual, state of affairs. For sound arguments to the contrary, see M. Barth and H. Blanke, *op. cit.*, 418-420.

[140] See especially J.M.G. Barclay, *art. cit.*

[141] On Paul's debt metaphor in Philemon, see N.R. Petersen, *op. cit.*, 74ff. For a fine discussion of Phlm 17-19, see G.W. Peterman (*op. cit.*, 185-192).

for Onesimus. Philemon would have been left with little choice: either maintain his honour as a benefactor in front of his house church and before Paul — or face social shame.[142]

Again, Paul seems to relativise the dynamic of reciprocity that binds together himself and Philemon in the relationship of father/benefactor and beneficiary. The obedience that Paul expects of Philemon in taking back Onesimus (Phlm 21: ἡ ὑπακοή; cf. v.14: τὸ ἀγαθόν; v.20: ἐγώ σου ὀναίμην) must not be conditioned by the obligation of reciprocity (v.14: μὴ ὡς κατὰ ἀνάγκην: cf. v.8-9) but rather by free will (v.14: ἀλλὰ κατὰ ἑκούσιον) and love (v.9: διὰ τὴν ἀγάπην; cf. v.4, 7). Nonetheless, in this regard, Paul echoes a traditional reciprocity motif (Seneca, Ben., 1.4.3) when he says that Philemon will outdo his own expectations as an apostle (Phlm 21b: ὑπὲρ ἃ λέγω).[143] Furthermore, Paul has no hesitation in reminding Philemon of the personal debt owed to himself as an apostle (Phlm 19b: ὅτι καὶ σεαυτόν μοι προσοφείλεις) and the appropriateness of recompense (20a: ἐγώ σου ὀναίμην ἐν κυρίῳ).[144]

Paul does not display any reservations regarding Philemon's role as benefactor. The reason for this ringing endorsement arose out of Philemon's gracious example as a patron of a house-church, a servant role that he would continue to exercise (Phlm 2, 5, 7, 22). However, notwithstanding the status of Philemon as patron of his house-church and of Paul, a reversal of social obligation occurs in the reception of Onesimus. As J. Koenig writes,

Here the screw turns, but not without laughter. Philemon, the expert in hospitality, is bidden to receive his own slave as a guest, indeed as an emissary from the apostle who must be honoured as the latter's own presence.[145]

Further, as N.R. Petersen notes,[146] Philemon has to reassess in what capacity he would greet his returned slave at his doorstep. Onesimus was now a freedman in Christ: Philemon, his master, had become a slave of Christ (1 Cor 7:22: Gal 3:28-29). In sum, the relationship of obligation between Philemon and Onesimus has been socially redefined: by divine grace (Phlm 3,

---

[142] See S.S. Bartchy, art. cit., 306, 309.

[143] J.M.G. Barclay (art. cit., 174), in discussing the ambiguity of Phlm 21, entirely misses out on Paul's use of a traditional reciprocity motif.

[144] G.W. Peterman (op. cit., 188-191) argues that Paul employs the language of social reciprocity (ὀφείλειν, ἀποτίνειν) in Phlm 18-19. In addition to the examples that Peterman (ibid., 189 nn.116-117) cites from Dio Chrysostom, Plutarch, and Dionysius Halicarnassus, note also the comment of Pseudo-Demetrius, Τύποι Ἐπιστολικοί 21: 'demand a return (χάριν). For I am in your debt (ὀφείλω)'.

[145] J. Koenig, op. cit., 79.

[146] N.R. Petersen, op. cit., 269-270.

25), they are now brothers in Christ and partners in the work of the gospel (Phlm 16-17).[147] In this regard, the public reading of Paul's letter to Philemon would have strengthened the social coercion contained in it.[148] The same, too, can be said of Paul's pointed reminders that Onesimus represented his personal presence (Phlm 12, 17b) and that he would be a useful co-worker for the gospel (Phlm 11, 13).

Why does Paul simultaneously affirm and partially invert the ethos of reciprocity in his letter to Philemon? As noted above, it seems likely that it was an expression of Paul's uncertainty regarding the extent to which the institution of slavery should be tolerated, transformed, or subverted within the Christian community.[149] Presumably, Paul resisted the temptation to impose too precise a solution so that Philemon's decision regarding Onesimus would be motivated by grace rather than by obligation. Theologically, it also reflects Paul's struggle in the first-century benefaction context to achieve the fine balance between the freedom of grace and the obligation that it imposes: that is, between the freedom to serve without the expectation of recompense and the obligation of continuously reciprocating the debt of love. For Paul, as we have observed, love is the dynamic that transforms and subverts the hellenistic ethos of reciprocity (Phlm 1, 5, 7, 9, 16: Rom 13:8-10). Ultimately, this emphasis on divine grace and the debt of love is what differentiates Paul's approach to Philemon from the manipulative techniques that Valerius Gemellus wields in his letter to his brother (*P. Mich.* VIII 502: see §3.4).

In conclusion, Paul treads warily as far as endorsing reciprocity. The intensely personal relationship that the apostle had with his churches involves him in a striking departure from the formulaic patterns of reciprocity found in the honorific inscriptions. Moreover, Paul theologically redefines the nature of the exchange through the LXX and gospel traditions. He displays flexibility in

---

[147] Note the fine insight of E. Lohse (*Colossians and Philemon* [Philadelphia 1971: Gmn. orig. 1968], 205): 'Philemon will understand that within this relationship one can no longer balance debt against debt. Onesimus has experienced the same mercy of God by which Philemon first became a Christian. Therefore he should receive him as a brother in Christ and squelch any stirring of anger, no matter how justifiable it may be'. E.A. Judge (*op. cit.* [1980], 4) makes this general comment concerning the reversal of the social status system: 'a striking new development appears ... The well-established patrons who promoted St Paul and others were expected to draw their domestic servants and clients into a new order of relationships'.

[148] G.W. Peterman, *op. cit.*, 186.

[149] Note the comment of M.J. Harris (*op. cit.*, 59): 'we may say, minimally, that Paul did not object to slave ownership within Christian ranks. Yet he indirectly undermines the institution of slavery by setting the master-slave relation on a new footing when he highlights Onesimus' status as a dearly loved Christian brother'.

his financial arrangements, allowing some churches to recompense his ministry and declining the offer in other cases where the gospel was at risk of being misunderstood as a reciprocal contract. As noted, Paul struggles in *Philemon* to balance the freedom of grace against the obligation that it imposes. The ancient economy, of course, was largely based on slave labour and the generosity of wealthy patrons. Paul affirms the reciprocal obligations inherent in the system. However, he transforms its dynamic through the debt of love and subverts its hierarchy of status through the social levelling brought about by divine grace. Last, Paul's tactic of resisting and promoting reciprocity as occasion demanded left him vulnerable to attack. He could easily be portrayed by his opponents as either inconsistent or deceptive regarding the obligations of the Graeco-Roman benefaction system. We turn to this issue in our next section.

7.4. Paul and Corinthian Disputes Over Beneficence

Paul's opponents at Corinth, as depicted in 2 Cor 10-13, made much of the (so-called) irregularities of the apostle's financial arrangements. Paul had loved the Corinthians less, so the opponents insinuated, by accepting payment from the Macedonians, preferring instead to work as a slavish artisan rather than accept the generous Corinthian offer of remuneration reserved for eloquent sophists (2 Cor 11:7-11; 12:14-15). The apostle to the Gentiles was deceptive, either craftily pocketing the funds of the Jerusalem collection for himself or, alternatively, unfairly imposing his demands on those whom he had recently rebuffed (2 Cor 12:16-18).[150] Recent scholarship has unfolded the richness of the rhetorical conventions that Paul martials to rebut the attack of his opponents.[151] What has been insufficiently observed is the extent to

---

[150] See P. Marshall, *loc. cit.*; R.F. Hock, *The Social Context of Paul's Ministry: Tentmaking and Apostleship* (Philadelphia 1980), *passim*. More generally, C.K. Barrett, 'Paul's Opponents in 2 Corinthians', and *id.*, 'ΨΕΥΔΑΠΟΣΤΟΛΟΙ (2 Cor 11:13)', in *id.*, *Essays on Paul* (London 1982), 60-86, 87-107 respectively.

[151] E.A. Judge, 'The Conflict of Educational Aims in New Testament Thought', *Journal of Christian Education* 9 (1966), 32-45; *id.*, 'Paul's Boasting in Relation to Contemporary Professional Practice', *Australian Biblical Review* 16 (1968), 37-50; H.D. Betz, *Der Apostel Paulus und die sokratische Tradition* (Tübingen 1972); S.H. Travis, 'Paul's Boasting in 2 Corinthians 10-12', *SE* 6 (1973), 527-532; C. Forbes, 'Comparison, Self-Praise and Irony: Paul's Boasting and the Conventions of Hellenistic Rhetoric', *NTS* 32/1 (1986), 1-30; J.P. Sampley, 'Paul, His Opponents in 2 Corinthians 10-13, and the Rhetorical Handbooks', in J. Neusner (*et al.*, ed.), *op. cit.*, 162-177; J.T. Fitzgerald, 'Paul, the Ancient Epistolary Theorists, and 2 Corinthians 10-13: The Purpose and Literary Genre of a Pauline Letter', in

which Paul weaves the colour of benefaction *topoi* into the tapestry of his argument. We will examine Paul's response to his Corinthian opponents against (1) the benefaction terminology and motifs of the honorific inscriptions, the papyri, and the epistolary handbooks; (2) Demosthenes' *De Corona* and (relatedly) Aeschines' *Against Ctesiphon*; (3) and, last, Graeco-Roman reciprocity ideology regarding parents.

7.4.1. Paul's use of benefaction terminology and motifs in 2 Cor 10-13

Paul asserts in 2 Cor 11 that he had dispensed, like his Lord, the gospel 'without cost' (11:7b: δωρεάν; cf. Rom 3:24), waiving his right to any reciprocation of expense. The terminology, as we have seen (§6.1.2.2 n.44), was well known. The first-century BC benefactor, Zosimos of Priene, had provided baths free of charge (δωρεάν) for his fellow citizens and foreigners.[152] Moreover, rather than 'burdening' the Corinthians with the obligations of the reciprocity system (ἐν παντὶ ἀβαρῆ: 2 Cor 11:9: καταναρκᾶν, καταβαρύνειν: 12:13-14, 16; cf. 1 Thess 2:9: πρὸς τὸ μὴ ἐπιβαρῆσαί τινα ὑμῶν) — a 'burden' from which Ammonius begs release in a letter to his bureaucratic superior (§3.3: *P. Oxy.* XLII 3057) — Paul had accepted the support of the Macedonians or worked himself.[153] Paul's

---

D.L. Balch (*et al.*, ed.), *op. cit.*, 190-200; S.B. Andrews, 'Enslaving, Devouring, Exploiting, Self-Exalting, and Striking: 2 Cor 11:19-20 and the Tyranny of Paul's Opponents', in (ed. anon.), *Society of Biblical Literature 1997 Seminar Papers* (Atlanta 1997), 460-490; B.W. Winter, *Philo and Paul among the Sophists* (Cambridge 1997), 203-230; B.K. Peterson, *Eloquence and the Proclamation of the Gospel in Corinth* (Atlanta 1998), *passim*; J.W. McCant, *2 Corinthians* (Sheffield 1999), 101-172; L.L. Welborn, 'The Runaway Paul', *HTR* 92/2 (1999), 115-163. We must not overlook the pioneering articles of A. Fridrichsen, 'Zum Stil des paulinischen Peristasen-Katalogs 2 Cor 11:23ff', *Symbolae Osloenses* 7 (1927), 25-29; *id.*, 'Peristasenkatalog und Res Gestae: Nachtrag zu 2 Cor 11:23ff', *Symbolae Osloenses* 8 (1929), 78-82.

[152] For further examples, F.W. Danker, *op. cit.* (1982), 333-334.

[153] Ammonius writes: 'I don't want you, brother, to load (βαρύνειν) me with these continual kindnesses, since I can't repay them (ἀμείψασθαι)'. See also the fine discussion of G.W. Peterman, *op. cit.*, 168-171. Nero writes to an unidentified city that he does not wish 'to burden you (ἐπιβαρεῖν ὑ]μᾶς) at the beginning of (my reign as) Princeps' (*SB* XII 11012: AD 55). For further examples, see F.W. Danker, *op. cit.* (1982), 334-335. F.W. Danker ('Reciprocity in the Ancient World and in Acts 15:23-29', in R.J. Cassidy and P.J. Sharper (eds), *Political Issues in Luke-Acts* [New York 1983], 57 n.23) draws attention to *OGIS* 669 in which the prefect of Egypt, Tiberius Julius Alexander, assures the Egyptians that the province will not be 'burdened (βαρύνειν) with new and unfair levies'. Similarly, Zosimos of Priene (*I. Priene* 112) is praised for assuming the role of a benefactor at a time when the resources of the citizens and the livelihood of the city were dramatically falling. This had occurred precisely because nobody was willing to face up to 'the burden of public service (διὰ τὸ τῆς λειτουργίας βάρος)'. For further on reciprocity, see *id.*, 'Bridging St. Paul and the Apostolic Fathers: A Study in Reciprocity', *CurTM* 15/1 (1984), 84-94.

rationale is clear: he would 'gladly spend (δαπανήσω) and be spent (ἐκδαπανηθήσομαι) for your souls (2 Cor 12:15)'. Again, as we have seen (§6.4.2 n.241), spending terminology is a commonplace of the inscriptions for the generosity of benefactors like Menas of Sestos and Zosimos of Priene.

As noted (§3.1.2), Paul was probably au fait with the wide range of epistolary conventions of the technical handbooks and found them useful in exposing the downside of the benefaction system. Indeed, the epistolary theorists showed considerable interest in the benefaction *topos* (§3.1.3). At a negative level, then, Paul adopts the epistolary styles of accusation (Κατηγορικός) and reproach ('Ονειδιστική) to expose both the ingratitude of the Corinthians for their benefits (2 Cor 11:7-11; 12:13-15; 12:19-13:9) and their failure to repent of their sin (2 Cor 12:21; 13:5-7).[154] Paul's use of irony (2 Cor 10:1, 12a; 11:19; 12:13b) may well have been prompted by the Εἰρωνικός ('ironic') or Παροξυντική ('provoking') letter types. In this regard, too, Paul's ironic plea for forgiveness in 2 Cor 12:13b (χαρίσασθε) is a rare departure from the universally positive nature of Paul's grace language elsewhere.

More positively, however, Paul portrays himself as the endangered (2 Cor 11:26: κινδύνοις; 1 Cor 15:30: κινδυνεύειν; cf. Rom 15:31) and impoverished benefactor (2 Cor 6:10; 11:27; cf. §6.2), who is consumed with anxiety for his churches (11:28-29: μέριμνα; cf. μεριμνᾶν: 1 Cor 12:25; Phil 2:20).[155]

Thus, by means of his adroit use of benefaction terminology and motifs, Paul portrays himself — among other more jarring and discreditable descriptions ('fool[ish][ness]': 11:1, 16-18, 21; 'madman': 11:23; 'weak[ness]': 11:21, 29, 30; 'servant': 11:23) — as a selfless benefactor who places himself at risk in his missionary work, without any expectation of return from his ungrateful converts. With a series of ripostes from the epistolary theorists,[156] Paul pricks the inflated sense of self-importance that

---

[154] For what follows, I am dependent on J.T. Fitzgerald, *art. cit.*, in D.L. Balch (*et al.*, ed.), *op. cit.*, 197-200, esp. nn.42-43, 46, 48-49. On the 'ironic man', see C. Forbes, *op. cit.*, 10ff.

[155] On the endangered benefactor motif, see F.W. Danker, *op. cit.* (1982), 363, 417-435. Strangely, Danker leaves 2 Cor 11:26 entirely out of his discussion, even though Paul's terminology is that of the inscriptions (*ibid.*, 363: §12, §30; *OGIS* 229). Other benefactors, too, had risked their necks for Paul and the gospel (Rom 16:4; Phil 2:30). On Epaphroditus as endangered benefactor, see F.W. Danker, *op. cit.* (1982), 426. For additional examples of the endangered benefactor motif, see C.B. Welles, *Royal Correspondence in the Hellenistic Period: A Study in Greek Epigraphy* (London 1934), §52 (κίνδυνον), §63 (τῶν συγκεκινδυνευκότων).

[156] J.T. Fitzgerald (*art. cit.*, in D.L. Balch [*et al.*, ed.], *op. cit.*, 200) regards 2 Cor 10-

so marked the spirituality of the Corinthians and calls them back both to repentance towards God and loyalty towards their apostolic benefactor.

7.4.2. Paul as the endangered and cowardly benefactor

The way that Paul contrasts his selfless beneficence with the hubristic behaviour and boasting of his opponents (2 Cor 11:19-29) is reminiscent of the rhetoric of Demosthenes' *De Corona*.[157] The speech is, among other things, the tirade of an unrequited benefactor who had been denied the honour of a golden crown — proposed by Ctesiphon in 336 BC and opposed in court by Aeschines in 330 BC — for his benefits to Athens. After the defeat of Athens at Chaeroneia in 338 BC by Philip II, Demosthenes had been elected as the Commissioner for the Repair of Walls. However, the ten talents entrusted for the task proved to be insufficient and Demosthenes topped up the shortfall with a further three talents from his own funds. Like Paul with the Corinthians (2 Cor 12:14-16), Demosthenes was determined to assert his independence as a benefactor over against any outside interference from the Athenian Board of Auditors:

> So far from claiming, as (Aeschines) invidiously suggested just now, that I am not to be called to account, I fully admit that all my life long I have been accountable for all my official acts and public counsels; but for the donations that I promised and gave at my own expense I do say that I am not accountable at any time — you hear that, Aeschines — nor is there any other man, though he be one of the nine archons. Is there any law so compact of iniquity and illiberality that, when a man out of sheer generosity has given away all his own money, it defrauds him of the gratitude (τῆς χάριτος) he has earned, drags him before a set of prying informers, and gives them authority to hold an audit of his free donations? There is no such law.[158]

Further, in similar vein to Paul, who was highly uncomfortable about his boasting (2 Cor 11:1, 16-19, 21, 23, 30; 12:1, 11), Demosthenes prefers as a matter of principle to remain silent about his munificence (*De. Cor.*, 268). Again, like Paul (2 Cor 12:11:11: ὑμεῖς με ἠναγκάσατε), Demosthenes states that he was compelled (ἀναγκάζομαι) by Aeschines' backbiting and scurrility to outline his generosity with all the modesty he could muster (*De. Cor.*, 256). As Demosthenes later expands,

> My view is that the recipient of a benefit ought to remember it all his life, but that a benefactor ought to put it out of his mind at once, if the one is to behave decently, and the

---

13 as a 'mixed letter type'.

[157] See especially the discussion of F.W. Danker, 'Paul's Debt to the *De Corona* of Demosthenes: A Study of Rhetorical Techniques in Second Corinthians', in D.F. Watson (ed.), *Persuasive Artistry: Studies in New Testament Rhetoric in Honour of George A. Kennedy* (Sheffield 1991), 262-280. Also, *id.*, *op. cit.* (1989), 147-214.

[158] Demosthenes, *De. Cor.*, 112.

other with magnanimity. To remind a man of the good turns you have done to him is very much like a reproach.[159]

F.W. Danker has helpfully drawn attention to a series of rhetorical parallels, supplementary to those above, between *De Corona* and 2 Cor 10-13.[160] What captures my interest, however, is the different ways that Paul and Demosthenes — and Aeschines by reaction — portray their pedigrees and achievements as benefactors over against their opponents.

Demosthenes outlines the advantages that ancestral wealth brought him in his early education and later in serving Athens beneficently (χορηγεῖν, τριηραρχεῖν, εἰσφέρειν) and honourably (μηδεμιᾶς φιλοτιμίας ἀπολείπεσθαι).[161] Conversely, Demosthenes asserts that Aeschines, his prosecutor, lacked merit (ἀρετή) because the abject poverty of his childhood stripped him of the resources to act honourably in public life.[162] Demosthenes concludes with a savage comparison of himself and Aeschines in which he vaunts his superiority over his opponent:

And now, Aeschines, I beg you to examine in contrast, quietly and without acrimony, the incidents of our respective careers... You were an usher, I a pupil; you were an acolyte, I a candidate; you were clerk-at-the-table, I addressed the House; you were cat-called, I hissed; you have ever served our enemies, I have served my country. Much I pass by; but on this very day, I am on proof for the honour of a crown, and acknowledged to be guiltless; you have already the reputation of an informer, and the question at hazard for you is, whether you are still to continue in that trade, or be stopped for ever by getting less than your quota of votes. And that is the good fortune enjoyed by you, who denounce the shabbiness of mine![163]

We also possess Aeschines' invaluable speech *Against Ctesiphon*.[164] The evidence of Aeschines allows us to hear the other side of the debate over Demosthenes' crowning — a luxury that we do not have as far as Paul's Corinthian opponents. Aeschines' tactics largely duplicate those of Demosthenes. After a brief attack on Demosthenes' private life (*In Ctes.*, 49-53), Aeschines launches a major offensive against the orator's public life (*In Ctes.*, 54-168). Then Aeschines counters Demosthenes' charges against himself by denigrating the pedigree and character of Demosthenes (*In Ctes.*,

---

[159] *Ibid.*, 269.
[160] F.W. Danker, *art. cit.*, in D.F. Watson, *op. cit.*
[161] Demosthenes, *De. Cor.*, 256-258.
[162] *Ibid.*, 258-264.
[163] *Ibid.*, 265-266.
[164] There is also the famous speech of Dinarchus (c. 360—c. 290 BC), the fourth-century Carthaginian orator resident at Athens, written against Demosthenes. While we will concentrate on the speech of Aeschines, we will make reference to the evidence of Dinarchus in the footnotes where appropriate. For a translation of Dinarchus' *Against Demosthenes*, see I. Worthington, *Greek Orators II: Dinarchus and Hyperides* (Warminster 1999).

169-214) and also by rebutting point-for-point his slanders (*In Ctes.*, 215-235).

Most revealing for our purposes are the reasons given by Aeschines for not honouring Demosthenes' benefactions with a golden crown. It must be remembered that crowns for civic benefactors, as Aeschines notes (*In Ctes.*, 42, 246), were awarded in recognition of merit (ἀρετή), uprightness (ἀνδραγαθία), and patriotism (εὔνοια). According to Aeschines, however, this was conspicuously not the case with Demosthenes:

> I would like to reckon up in your presence, fellow citizens, with the author of this motion, the benefactions for which he calls on you to crown Demosthenes. For if, Ctesiphon, you propose to cite that which you made the beginning of your motion, that he did good work in excavating the trenches around the walls, I am astonished at you ... But you, Demosthenes, tire us out with your everlasting talk of Thebes and of that most ill-starred alliance, while you are silent as to the seventy talents of the king's gold which you have seized and embezzled. Was it not for lack of money, nay, for lack of five talents, that the mercenaries failed to deliver up the citadel to the Thebans. And when all the Arcadians were mobilised and their leaders were ready to bring aid, did not the negotiations fail for want of nine talents of silver. But you are a rich man, you serve as a choregus — to your own lusts. In a word, the king's gold stays with Demosthenes, the dangers (οἱ κίνδυνοι), fellow citizens, with you ... Now let us compare what is taking place to-day. A politician, the man who is responsible for all our disasters, deserted his post in the field, and then ran away from the city: this man is calling for a crown, and he thinks he must be proclaimed. Away with the fellow, the curse of all Hellas! Nay, rather, seize and punish him, the pirate of politics, who sails on his craft of words over the sea of state.[165]

We have witnessed here the rhetoric martialled by each side as they tried either to defend or denigrate the benefactions of Demosthenes and his right to recompense of honour. What light does it throw on the way that Paul combats the slurs of his opponents in 2 Cor 10-13 regarding his financial arrangements as an apostle?

---

[165] Aeschines, *In Ctes.*, 236, 239-240, 250. Dinarchus (*Against Demosthenes* 71, 80-82) draws a telling conclusion regarding the runaway Demosthenes: 'Is it fitting that ... you are ordering others to take the field when you yourself deserted the battle-line? ... For when (Demosthenes) heard that Philip was intending to invade our land after the battle of Chaeronea he appointed himself envoy in order that he might escape from the city ... In a nutshell he is this sort of man: in the battle line he is a stay-at-home, among those who remain at home he is an envoy, and among envoys he is a runaway'. Demosthenes, of course, claims that he 'did not desert the post of patriotism in the hour of peril' (*De. Cor.*, 173), 'neither shirking nor even counting any personal danger' (*ibid.*, 197: οὐδένα κίνδυνον). See also Plutarch's comparison of Agesilaus' stout defence of his city over against Pompey's cowardly abandonment of Rome ("Comparison of Agesilaus and Pompey' 3.3-5 in *Vit.* Vol.5 [Loeb]). Pliny the Elder's summation of Augustus' reign (*NH* 7.45.147-150), cited in P. Marshall (*op. cit.*, 361-362), is relevant here as another example of the cowardly benefactor *topos*. It represents the reverse image of Augustus' reign as the eschatological age of grace (§6.1.2.4).

At a superficial level, it affords us sympathetic insight into the savage rhetoric that the apostle employs to downgrade the status of his opponents (2 Cor 11:3-5, 12-15, 20). Paul's assertion of the superiority of his pedigree and achievements over against those of his opponents was typical of the exchanges of orators such as Demosthenes and Aeschines (2 Cor 11:12-18; 11:16-23; 12:11-13; cf. Phil 3:2-6).[166] But whereas Demosthenes and Aeschines relentlessly seek to establish the validity of their boasts — despite countervailing claims to modesty on Demosthenes' part — Paul imposes strict limits on the exercise. Paul's use of irony (2 Cor 10:12a), his adoption of the LXX perspective on boasting (2 Cor 10:17: LXX Jer 9:24) and the speech of fools (2 Cor 11:16a, 17b, 21b, 23a: LXX Prov 10:14; 11:1, 16-18, 21; 12:6; 14:3; 15:2, 14; 17:7; 18:6-7; 19:1; Eccl 5:3; 10:14), and his radical eschewal of status (2 Cor 12:11b: οὐδέν εἰμι) and achievement (Phil 3:7b, 8a, 8b: ζημία; 3:8c: σκύβαλα) combine to give the hellenic boasting conventions that he employs an entirely different temper.

More fundamentally, the *topos* of the benefactor who served his city-state 'in the pressing times (ἐν τοῖς ἀναγκαιοτάτοις καιροῖς)' for its advantage, and who unselfishly risked personal danger on its behalf, was a commonplace both of the honorific inscriptions (§4.4.2 n.168; §7.4.1 n.155) and of the speeches of the Athenian orators (Aeschines, *In Ctes.*, 169-170).[167] Paul, as

---

[166] Note also how Dinarchus (*Against Demosthenes* 12-13), in a manner similar to Paul's refutation of his opponents (2 Cor 11:21a-29), rhetorically rebuts point by point the claims of Demosthenes: 'Demosthenes nevertheless goes about both slandering the council and speaking about himself, tales that he will perhaps presently tell you in an effort to deceive you. Thus: "I made the Thebans your allies." No, Demosthenes you harmed the common interests of both our states. "I brought everyone into line at Chaeronea." No again: on the contrary, you yourself and no one else fled from the line there. "I was an ambassador on many embassies on your behalf." I do not know what he would have done or what he would have said if, in connection with these missions, what he had advocated had turned out to be successful! After touring the whole world arranging these misfortunes and disasters he nevertheless claims to be given the greatest privileges: to take bribes against the country and to say and do what he wishes against the people'.

[167] Aeschines (*In Ctes.*, 170) asserts that the friend of the people 'ought to be a man of brave heart, that in danger and peril (τοὺς κινδύνους) he may not desert the people'. In this regard, Aeschines consistently portrayed Demosthenes as a coward who betrayed his endangered city (*ibid.*, 159; 175-176; 226; 253). Similarly, Dinarchus (*Against Demosthenes* 36) portrays Demosthenes 'living well in the midst of the city's hardships, and travelling in a sedan-chair on the road to Piraeus and abusing the needy for their poverty'. Demosthenes' self-serving actions, Dinarchus asserts, stand in stark contrast to the endangered benefactors of the Athenian past: 'Gentlemen, will you not remember the deeds of your ancestors who, when great and numerous dangers (μεγάλων καὶ πολλῶν κινδύνων) were befalling the city, risked peril (ἐκινδύνευσαν) for the well-being of the people, honourably for the city, their own freedom, and just reputation?' (*ibid.*, 37). More generally on beneficence in the Athenian

we have seen, claimed the endangered and impoverished benefactor motif for himself when portraying his selfless commitment to his churches. But this *topos* could also be used to humiliating effect. Aeschines' depiction of the rhetorically-gifted Demosthenes as corrupt and cowardly and, concomitantly, Athens as endangered because of his dereliction of duty, shows how effectively the *topos* could be inverted by one's opponents.

Could it be that in 2 Cor 11:23-33 Paul is playing off against each other two familiar images of the benefactor — one negative, the other positive — in an attempt to clarify the paradox of his apostleship and the Christian life more generally? As an apostle, Paul is both weak and strong, as he daily dies and rises with Christ in the service of the saints (§6.1.3.1) On the one hand, Paul is the endangered benefactor of the inscriptions who risks everything for his churches (2 Cor 11:23-29). On the other hand, he is ironically the 'cowardly' benefactor — as depicted by Aeschines in another context — who abandons his brethren to the dangers of Antioch and disqualifies himself as a man of honour through an ignominious escape (2 Cor 11:30-33).[168] Such a coward, of course, cannot be crowned: either as a soldier who attained the *corona muralis*[169] — or as an endangered benefactor who imperils himself for his citizens. But Paul's point is that, in the present age, the endangered and the 'cowardly' benefactor are exactly the same person. Until his death Paul will continue to experience, like all believers, the tension of living between the 'already' and the 'not yet', as well as the surprise of power in weakness.

Paul's imagery, then, is clearly cross-cultural.[170] It appeals to the Roman Christians at the colony of Corinth; it equally speaks to eastern

---

orators, see the Excursus, 'Private and Public Benefactions in Athenian Litigation', in W.P. Clark, *Benefactions and Endowments in Greek Antiquity* (unpub. Ph.D. diss. Chicago University 1928), 137-146.

[168] D.E. Garland ('Paul's Apostolic Authority: The Power of Christ Sustaining Weakness [2 Corinthians 10-13]', *RevExp* 86/3 [1989], 379) captures Paul's tone well: 'It was not some dramatic, great escape, worthy of TV dramatisation, but rather an undignified stealing away'.

[169] E.A. Judge (*art. cit.* [1966], 44-45) suggests that the metaphor behind 2 Cor 11:30-33 was the award of the *corona muralis*, which was given to the first soldier who scaled the wall in the face of the enemy. As Judge pithily concludes (*ibid.*, 45), 'Paul's point was devastatingly plain: he was first down'. C. Forbes has added flesh to Judge's proposal by drawing attention to passages such as Dionysius of Halicarnassus, *Roman Antiquities*, 10.36.3ff. See *id.*, *"Strength" and "Weakness" as Terminology of Status in St. Paul: The Historical and Literary Roots of a Metaphor, with Specific Reference to 1 and 2 Corinthians* (unpub. BA Hons. thesis Macquarie University 1978), Ch.4 n.63. The problem with Judge's suggestion is that it gives an exclusively Roman provenance to Paul's metaphor in a city that was still as much Greek as it was Roman by the first century AD.

[170] The cross-cultural dimension of Paul's metaphor is further underlined by his

Mediterranean Greek Christians imbued with the inscriptional portrait of the καλοκάγαθός. In each case, Paul upends a popular cultural icon. The reversal of worldly values embodied in the cross (2 Cor 13:4; cf. 1 Cor 1:18-25) allows Paul to re-interpret either image — whether the *corona muralis* or the 'cowardly' benefactor — to his own disadvantage and then to postpone its crowning ritual until the eschaton (1 Cor 9:25; Phil 4:1; 1 Thess 2:19; cf. 2 Tim 2:5; 4:8). Thus Paul pricks the pretensions of the so-called 'superlative apostles' of the Corinthians (2 Cor 11:5) and exposes the superficiality of their care as spiritual benefactors of the Corinthians. As P. Vassiliadis remarks of the apostle:

> ...at any time his opponents (of judaising, enthusiastic, or libertine tendency) challenged his gospel, (Paul) re-interpreted the significance of Jesus' death on the basis of his theology of the cross with all the socio-political consequences this humiliating symbol connoted in contemporary Roman society.[171]

7.4.3. Paul and the reciprocation of parental favour

The ideology of reciprocity embraced household relations as much as the civic arena. The popular philosophers urged the reciprocation of parental benefaction by their progeny.[172] Of all the philosophers, Hierocles gives the doctrine of the pious reciprocation of parental favour its fullest and finest exposition (§5.3). But the Pythagorean philosopher Pempelos (III-II cent. BC) also provides sympathetic insight into the ramifications of ignoring reciprocation of parental favour:

> Neither divinity nor anyone possessing the least wisdom will ever advise anyone to neglect

---

invocation of an oath (2 Cor 11:31; cf. 1:23). As E.A. Judge (*art. cit.* [1966], 45 n.119) notes of the Roman military metaphor, the oath of Paul alludes to the strict verification required for any claim of *corona muralis*. Equally, oaths feature in the Athenian debate over Demosthenes' status as a benefactor. Demosthenes invokes the Attic gods and goddesses as witnesses, along with Pythian Apollo, as to his truthfulness as a patriotic benefactor (*De. Cor.*, 141; cf. 1-2, 8). Correspondingly, Aeschines quips that when Demosthenes 'is cheating you, (he) adds an oath to his lie' (*In Ctes.*, 99). Similarly, Dinarchus (*Against Demosthenes* 64) contrasts the truthfulness of his own oaths over against the deceitfulness of Demosthenes' oaths (47, 86). Ironically, then, Paul invokes an oath to testify to the truthfulness of his claim that he is indeed the cowardly benefactor.

[171] P. Vassiliadis, 'STAUROS: Centre of the Pauline Soteriology and Apostolic Ministry', in A. Vanhoye (ed.), *op. cit.*, 253. Note, too, the helpful comment of Vassiliadis (*ibid.*, 252) on 2 Corinthians generally: 'In 2 Cor with his famous *Peristasenkataloge* (Paul) contrasts the arrogant theology and behaviour of the pseudo-apostles with Christ's voluntary humiliation on the cross and the suffering of the real apostle'.

[172] See Dio Chrysostom, *Or.*, 12.42-43; Aristotle, [*Mag. Mor.*], 2.12.1; *id.*, *Pol.*, 7.14.2; Plutarch, *Mor.*, 479B; *id.*, *Cor.*, 4.4, 36.3; Seneca, *Ben.*, 2.11.5; 5.5.2-4; 6.24.1-2; Iamblichus, *Vit. Pyth.* 38. On the Jewish side, see Sir 7.27-28.

his parents ... For he who honours his parents by gifts will be recompensed by God, for without this the divinities will not pay attention to the prayers of such parents for their children ... For parents, who are divine images that are animated, when they are continually adorned and worthily honoured by us, pray for us, and implore the gods to bestow on us the most excellent gifts, and do the contrary when we despise them ... Every intelligent person, therefore, should honour and venerate his parents, and should dread their execrations and unfavourable prayers, knowing that many of them take effect.[173]

Even the honorific inscriptions occasionally highlighted cases of parental munificence that were worthy of honour. Queen Apollonis Eusebes dealt with her children with such concord that she earned their conspicuous thanks and eternal commendation.[174] In similar vein, the aretalogy of Isis at Kyme says that 'I ruled that parents be loved by their children'.[175]

In 2 Cor 12:14b, Paul's justifies his financial independence as an apostle when ministering at Corinth as follows: 'children ought not to lay up for their parents, but parents for their children'. In view of the examples cited above, Paul's statement would have sounded strange in a culture where the reciprocation of parental favour was the norm. Paul is certainly not unique in his stance. After all, Plutarch had said the same in criticism of Epicurus (§5.5.2). But Paul's comment would certainly have jarred with the Corinthians. Moreover, Paul magnifies his benefactor role in 2 Cor 12:15a when he says 'I will most gladly spend (δαπανήσω) and be spent (ἐκδαπανηθήσομαι) for your souls'. The choice of δαπανᾶν ('to spend') to describe his unstinting service of the Corinthians may well have caught the ear of auditors familiar with the honorific inscriptions. There the word was commonly applied to benefactors who had gone beyond the normal bounds of generosity.[176] Again we are witnessing in 2 Cor 12:14-15 the overturning of Graeco-Roman reciprocity conventions in the hands of Paul. However, we must resist the temptation to overstate our case at this juncture. In the case of

---

[173] Pempelos (Περὶ γονέων, Stob. 4.25.52).

[174] *Michel* 541 (second half II cent. BC).

[175] F.W. Danker, *op. cit.* (1982), §29.

[176] For inscriptional examples, see §6.4.2 n.241. Examples are easily multiplied. Euboulos of Marathon, a priest of Dionysius, spent his own money (ἐκ τῶν ἰδίων δαπανήσας) on the solemn processions of the god (*Michel* 163 [148/147 BC]). Poluxeos of Akraephiae 'performed not a few favours (χάριτας) for the people, foreseeing no harm or expense' (οὐδεμίαν βλ[ά]β[η]ν οὐδὲ δαπάνην π[ρ]οορώ[με]νος: *Michel* 236 [II cent. BC]). Patron, benefactor of a Delian corporation of merchants, undertook an embassy on behalf of the Athenians, going by sea out of his own expense (ἔπλευσεν δαπανῶν ἐκ τῶν ἰδίων: *Michel* 998 [II cent. BC]). Finally, the patrons of the *summoria* of Echinos at Teos brought no expense to the Council (οὐδεμίαν ἀνενέγκαντες τῶι κοινῶι δαπάνην: *Michel* 1007 [II cent. BC]) by lavishly furnishing the sacrifices from their own funds. See also *SIG*³ 748 (71 BC).

2 Cor 6:13, Paul endorses obligation to parents along traditional benefaction lines. There, in addressing the wayward Corinthians as his spiritual children (2 Cor 6:13; 1 Cor 4:14-15; cf. Phil 2:22; 1 Thess 2:11; Phlm 10),[177] Paul employs reciprocity terminology when encouraging his grudging converts to love him 'in return' (2 Cor 6:13a: τὴν αὐτὴν ἀντιμισθίαν).[178] Thus Paul's approach to Graeco-Roman reciprocity conventions can differ markedly according to the outworking of the gospel in its varying pastoral contexts. On the one hand, Paul's gospel affirms the obligation of his converts to reciprocate, materially and spiritually, the debt of love owed to all believers and their leaders (Rom 13:8-10; 15:26-27; 16:1-2; 1 Cor 9:3-11; 2 Cor 6:13a; 8:8-9; Gal 6:6; cf. 1 Tim 5:17-19). On the other hand, Paul's gospel upholds the freedom of believers to serve others without any expectation of return (1 Cor 9:12-23; 2 Cor 11:7-11; 12:14-15). Little wonder that the Corinthians, besotted by the reciprocity and rhetorical conventions of their age, stereotyped their founding apostle as inconsistent and unloving (2 Cor 1:15-23; 10:1b, 10; 12:13).

One final point. Paul does not share the view of Pempelos, cited above, that 'execrations and unfavourable prayers' were somehow the right of parents who had been spurned by their ungrateful children. In the case of the disloyal Corinthians, Paul continues to pray for the improvement of his converts (2 Cor 13:8b).

---

[177] Paul's 'father' image may be viewed against the backdrop of benefaction ideology or imperial propaganda. Respectively, T.R. Stevenson, 'The Ideal Benefactor and the Father Analogy in Greek and Roman Thought', *CQ* 42/2 (1992), 421-436; E.M. Lassen, 'The Use of the Father Image in Imperial Propaganda and 1 Corinthians 4:14-21', *TynBul* 42/1 (1991), 127-136. In this regard, we have already referred to Theokles of Olbia whose concern for his community was 'as a father (πατήρ) to the more young' (*CIG* II 2059: §2.3). Further, τροφεύς ('foster-father') was used in the imperial inscriptions and in Dio Chrysostom (*Or.*, 48.10) as title given to benefactors in recompense of their generosity. See L. Robert, 'Τροφεύς et 'Αριστεύς', *Hellenica* XI-XII (1960), 569-576. G. Herman (*Ritualised Friendship and the Greek City* [Cambridge 1987], 18) points out that familial terminology, including 'father' and 'grandfather', became 'one of the reciprocal appellations used within the entourages of Persian and Hellenistic rulers'. For discussion of Paul's father imagery, see B. Holmberg, *op. cit.*, 77-79; E. Best, *op. cit.* (1988), 29-58; S. Joubert, 'Managing the Household: Paul as *Paterfamilias* of the Christian Household Group in Corinth', in P.F. Esler (ed.), *Modelling Early Christianity: Social-Scientific Studies of the New Testament in Its Context* (London and New York 1995), 213-223; *id.*, *op. cit.*, 167-173; B.K. Peterson, 'Conquest, Control, and the Cross: Paul's Self-Portrayal in 2 Corinthians 10-13', *Int* 52/3 (1998), 258-270, esp. 262ff; T.H. Burke, 'Pauline Paternity in 1 Thessalonians', *TynBul* 51/1 (2000), 59-80.

[178] See the helpful discussion of G.W. Peterman, *op. cit.*, 172-174. Note our comments on 2 Cor 6:13 in §7.3.2.3.

7.5. Conclusion

At the outset, we argued that the interrelationship of χάρις, κοινωνία, and διακονία in 2 Cor 8:4 represents Paul's attempt at socially and theologically redefining Graeco-Roman conventions of beneficence. While the range of circumlocutory terminology that Paul applied to the Jerusalem collection would not have occasioned surprise to readers of the honorific inscriptions, the profusion of χάρις as the leitmotiv of the collection certainly would. Moreover, the dynamic of beneficence operative in the hellenistic city-states was different to that of the early Christian communities. Whereas the *poleis* elicited munificence from local benefactors by means of various moral accolades and honours, it was the common experience of divine grace that impelled the geographically separated and ethnically diverse Christian communities to care for the Jerusalem poor.

In rejecting the prominent eschatological interpretation of the Jerusalem collection, we opted for more exegetically sound approaches that focus on the ecumenical dimension of the collection and on its social obligation. Attention was drawn to possible misunderstandings of the Jerusalem collection on the part of the Jewish Christians who may have felt obligated to reciprocate. Similarly, the Corinthians probably felt that a silent obligation was imposed on them as benefactors due to their failure to meet the deadline for their promised munificence. In tackling these misunderstandings, Paul sets forth grace as the basis for a new set of social obligations that he hoped would animate the collection. We also suggested that Paul's use of the inscriptional rivalry motifs was forced on him by Corinthian recalcitrance concerning the collection and by their resentment over being 'pipped at the post' by the Macedonian believers as benefactors of Paul.

Finally, in regard to the ethos of reciprocity, there is an implicit critique of the Graeco-Roman benefaction system in Paul's letters. Where the apostle does countenance reciprocity rituals, it is usually in a highly qualified way. To be sure, Paul continues to affirm the obligation of believers to each other and to their Graeco-Roman neighbours. But he transforms the dynamic of reciprocity by means of the debt of love. Further, the honour allocated to the wealthy in the reciprocity system is now re-directed to God as the cosmic benefactor and to the socially marginalised in the body of Christ.

Ranging more widely, we looked at how Paul handled disputes over beneficence with the Corinthians in 2 Cor 10-13. We observed how the apostle employed a series of benefaction *topoi* to portray himself as the endangered, impoverished, and cowardly (!) benefactor. These *topoi* were directed against his opponents and designed to recall the disloyal Corinthians back to their apostle and, ultimately, to their Lord.

Chapter 8

Conclusion

This thesis set out to investigate the extent to which Paul interacted with Graeco-Roman benefaction ideology when he instructed his Gentile churches about the manifestation of divine χάρις and its obligations for believers. I have argued that modern scholarship, with the notable exceptions of G.P. Wetter, C. Spicq, and D.A. deSilva has largely ignored the first-century benefaction context of grace. Paul formulated his understanding of the theological and social dimensions of χάρις for Gentile converts who had been exposed to the Augustan 'age of grace' — and the χάριτες of the imperial successors — and who were familiar with the demands of the hellenistic reciprocity system of the Eastern Mediterranean basin.

The public nature of benefaction language would have ensured that χάρις, the leitmotiv of the first-century reciprocity system, was readily recognised by its original auditors and interpreted within that grid. The Herods and the Caesars proclaimed their munificence throughout Palestine and the Eastern provinces. At prominent locations, the honorific inscriptions praised the χάριτες of local benefactors in the Jewish synagogues, in the Greek city-states, and in the meeting places of the trade guilds. In this regard, the evidence of the papyri confirmed that benefaction ideology had penetrated the provincial backwaters of the empire as much as its large urban centres. The ethic of beneficence, a feature of the Delphic canon, was taught to the ἔφηβοι in the gymnasia of the Greek East. Even in death, the epigrams of the funerary inscriptions testified to posterity that the honorand — independent of the traditional civic honours — had possessed or achieved grace.

The Jewishness of Paul would not have shielded him from the impact of benefaction ideology. The Greek documentary and literary evidence of first-century Judaism demonstrates that χάρις was largely understood in the same way as in the eastern Mediterranean as a whole. (The Hebrew literature, by contrast, generally retained the Old Testament emphasis on the unilateral nature of covenantal grace, as did some of the preachers in the first-century Greek-speaking synagogues, if the homilies of Pseudo-Philo are sufficiently representative.) Several of the Jewish funerary inscriptions exhibit a characteristically hellenistic sense of χάρις, while the Jewish papyri point to the spread of the benefaction ideology of the Caesars in diaspora Judaism. Philo appropriates Graeco-Roman conceptions of merit in describing covenantal χάρις, whereas Josephus deletes the LXX references to covenantal χάρις and often stages the Old Testament narrative against a benefaction backdrop. Even aspects of the Mosaic law were subsumed under the rubric of reciprocity.

There also emerges a theological critique of the Graeco-Roman understanding of divine and human beneficence in Philo and Josephus, though its rationale is more Stoic than Hebraic. The self-interest of the benefaction system is caricatured and the χάριτες of the pagan gods are satirised. But the critique of the benefaction system found in Philo and Josephus is largely that of the Graeco-Roman popular philosophers. In sum, while E.P. Sanders has justifiably pointed to the importance of covenantal grace in Tannaitic Judaism, it is possible that Graeco-Roman views of merit and reciprocity were penetrating the theologies of Greek-speaking Judaism by way of the benefaction system. Undoubtedly, in reflecting on his radical experience of grace on the Damascus road (2 Cor 4:1, 6; Gal 1:15-16), Paul felt that all such views stripped the Abrahamic Covenant of grace of its unilateral and unmerited aspect (Rom 4:1-25; Gal 3:6-25; 4:21-31) and obscured its fulfilment in the glorious Covenant of the Spirit (Rom 7:6; 2 Cor 3:4-18; Gal 3:14).

The pervasiveness of benefaction ideology allowed Paul to communicate the gospel of grace attractively at a theological and social level. Nonetheless, unless there was clear definition of Christ's χάρις, the distinctiveness of His self-sacrifice could easily be blurred by reciprocity conventions. Theological questions about the nature of divine beneficence would typically have arisen from Paul's discussions with his Gentile converts who had previously sought the gods' favour through the official cults or by means of magical rites (1 Cor 12:2; Gal 4:8-9; 1 Thess 1:9-10; Acts 19:17-20). This 'prosperity theology' of antiquity was aggressively promoted throughout the eastern Mediterranean region (Acts 8:9ff; 14:8ff; 16:16ff; 19:23ff). Thus the inscriptions lavishly praised the χάριτες of local deities or simply ensured the perpetuity of divine honour with a view to future blessing (Acts 17:23).

Moreover, Paul's portrait of God as a dishonoured Benefactor who benefited the Gentiles on the basis of His grace as opposed to traditional cultic piety would have provoked reaction from outsiders (Rom 1-3; Acts 17:22ff). Gentile enquirers may well have assessed Paul's gospel of justification by grace against the psychagogy of the Epicurean, Stoic, and Cynic philosophers who, in radically different conclusions, either reconciled or dismissed the competing claims of divine beneficence and divine justice

(Acts 17:16-34). Paul's portrait of divine grace was formulated with the Gentiles in mind as much as the judaizing Christians and (possibly) various strands of first-century proto-rabbinism.

Furthermore, the ethos of reciprocity may have raised an expectation of return on the part of the donors and the recipients of the Jerusalem collection. Occasionally the obligation of reciprocation was redirected towards the benefactor. I argued that the procrastination of the Corinthians regarding the Jerusalem collection (2 Cor 8:6-7, 10-12, 24; 9:3-5a) had resulted in the imposition of a silent obligation on them. This, too, was the experience of Dio Chrysostom when he failed to honour his promise of embellishing his native city. For Paul, the freedom of grace to be unreservedly generous towards others was in danger of being subverted at Corinth by the dynamic of a shameful and bitter obligation (2 Cor 8:8a, 11a; 9:5, 7).

We have also seen that the evidence of the epistolary theorists and the papyri stripped away the veneer of politeness that characterised the honorific inscriptions. There the darker social realities underlying the benefaction system, such as the cardinal sin of ingratitude and the enmity that it spawned, were revealed for all to see. This partially explains why Paul's arguments over beneficence in 2 Cor 10-13 were so anguished and vitriolic. Paul, as the father/benefactor of the Corinthians, reflects a variety of epistolary styles from the technical handbooks in exposing the ingratitude of the Corinthians for their benefits (2 Cor 11:7-11; 12:13-15; 12:19-13:9). His portrayal of himself as the impoverished (2 Cor 6:10; 11:27), endangered (11:26), and cowardly benefactor (11:30-32) was designed to prick the pretensions of the Corinthians and redirect them to the sufficiency of divine grace.

Finally, I have suggested that the Corinthians may have been resentful towards the Macedonian believers over being 'pipped at the post' as benefactors of Paul. Paul's discreet choice of οἱ πλείονες in 2 Corinthians 9:2 may also imply, as H.D. Betz suggested, that there was a sceptical minority of the Macedonians who were less than enthusiastic about the Jerusalem collection, even if the majority was supportive (2 Cor 8:1-5). Paul undoubtedly employed the rivalry motifs we see in the inscriptions to overcome the recalcitrance of the Corinthians and to test the reality of their love for their brethren.

What understanding of χάρις has emerged from my study of the eastern Mediterranean reciprocity system? Instead of reiterating the conclusions of Chapters 2—5, I will trace the world-view of Graeco-Roman beneficence under the major themes that have shaped my thesis (§1.4) and outline Paul's response in each case.

8.1. The Ethos of Reciprocity

The semantic versatility of χάρις ('favour', 'thanks') meant that the word could equally refer to the ritual of giving or of receiving. The language of commensurability (ἄξιος, κατάξιος) and reciprocation (ἀμείβειν, ἀμοιβή, ἀντί) that regularly accompanied χάρις evokes the Homeric world of the counter-gift. The conventions of reciprocity applied to a variety of human relationships: inter-state relations, the benefactor and his *polis*, the Caesars and the local associations, the interactions of φίλοι, and the household.

People of inferior social status often felt overwhelmed by the burden to reciprocate. In this respect, Aristotle believed that reciprocity should operate proportionately rather than on the basis of equality. The necessity of returning gratitude was everywhere emphasised. The ἀχάριστοί were universally despised and it was expected that they would be chastised by Fortune or meet with divine justice. Finally, as noted, while several Greek philosophers (Dio Chrysostom, Epicurus, Plutarch) provide a critique of the self-interest underlying the reciprocity system, they were far from advocating its demise. Epictetus alone dismisses the social trappings of first-century honorific culture because it was detrimental to the moral purpose of the philosopher.

At the outset of my thesis, I posed the question whether Paul critiqued the hellenistic reciprocity system. Paul displays reserve regarding the inscriptional language of commensurability. There is no instance of Paul using ἄξιος or ἀξιοῦν with χάρις. Instead, Paul expects believers to live worthily of God (ἀξίως: Eph 4:1; Phil 1:27; Col 1:10; 1 Thess 2:12; ἀξιοῦν: 2 Thess 1:11) and to render honour to their leaders worthily of the debt of love (Rom 16:2 [cf. Rom 13:8-10]; 1 Tim 5:17). Neither does Paul employ ἀμοιβή or ἀντί-compounds with χάρις, with the sole exception of 1 Thess 3:19 (εὐχαριστίαν τῷ θεῷ ἀνταποδοῦναι). As I argued, on the occasions where Paul resorts to reciprocity terminology (2 Cor 6:13; Phil 4:15; 1 Thess 3:9; 1 Tim 5:4) and its motifs (Rom 15:24; 16:1-2; 1 Cor 9:11; 2 Cor 8:13-15), he redefines their rationale in the light of Old Testament and gospel traditions. As an alternative, Paul chooses the language of abundance (πλοῦτος, περισσεύειν, ὑπερβάλλειν and their cognates) to accompany χάρις. The reason for Paul's change of terminology is clear: God operates on the basis of His overflowing grace over against the obligation of reciprocity.

In this regard, it is worth noting that Paul's strong preference for χάρις over the LXX ἔλεος is partially occasioned by the idea of reciprocity attached to *ḥesed* in the Hebrew Old Testament. Thus any implication of reciprocity that might distort the unilateral nature of covenantal grace in

Christ was ruthlessly expunged by the apostle in his choice of terminology, whether its origin was Hebraic or hellenistic.

Further, Paul is not reticent in confronting the Corinthians as reluctant benefactors. Paul's profuse use of χάρις and his emphasis on the voluntariness of grace in 2 Cor 8—9 is best explained by Paul's perception that the Corinthians were in danger of operating on the basis of reciprocity (2 Cor 9:5-11), rather than from divine love, as regards the Jerusalem collection. For Paul, it is love that subverts the dynamics of the Graeco-Roman reciprocity system (Rom 13:8-10; 2 Cor 8:8, 24; 1 Cor 13:3). As I have argued concerning 2 Cor 8:4, this occurs in servant communities where divine grace creates a fellowship among believers that transcends racial, geographical, and religious boundaries (2 Cor 9:6-14). All believers are equipped by divine grace to be benefactors (2 Cor 6:10; 8:2, 9b; 9:11) and are called to abandon the dependency fostered by the benefaction system (2 Thess 3:6-13). Thus Paul models the grace of giving for the Corinthians by abandoning the traditional expectations of reciprocation as their father/benefactor (2 Cor 11:7b; 12:14-16a).

Finally, Paul's implicit critique of the hellenistic reciprocity system is also to be expressed in the social relations of believers. The honorific titles and privileges of the associations are to be absent from the body of Christ. The hierarchical structure of the honour system is radically overturned: all believers are endowed with χαρίσματα; the weak, not the strong, are to be given the first place of honour; all believers are slaves of Christ who must serve each other. However, the social outworking of Paul's radical theological vision was not without difficulty because it demanded considerable sensitivity in the first-century context. As I have argued concerning the epistle to Philemon, Paul moves cautiously, affirming many of the traditional reciprocity conventions of the household, while pointing to their social transformation in Christ.

8.2. The χάριτες of the Gods

Divine beneficence was largely assumed in antiquity, notwithstanding the unpredictable and touchy nature of many deities. Thus the atheism of Epicurus regarding the gods' beneficence and wrath was regarded by most as a dangerous theological aberration. Even the bleak theodicy of Cercidas, the Cynic philosopher, found resolution when he invented his own beneficent pantheon. Overall, the conferral of divine grace was mediated to individuals and communities via a scrupulous performance of the sacrificial cult. The return of gratitude to the gods operated in the same way. Of the philosophers I examined, only the Epicureans and Lucian — who was also much influenced by Epicurean theology — attacked this belief-system.

Moreover, the gods could be placed under counter-obligation by the ritual piety of benefactors or by the faithfulness of individuals to the ancestral traditions. As a matter of honour, the gods would reciprocate with gratitude. Unilateral and unsolicited acts of grace were, therefore, especially rare in the case of the Graeco-Roman deities (§3.4 n.86). Furthermore, divine grace was generally not regarded as the motivation for beneficence to others. To be sure, Aristotle commented on the mnemonic link of χάρις with the public shrine of the Χάριτες in order to highlight the importance of beneficence and its reciprocation. Seneca and Epictetus also spoke briefly of the desirability of imitating the gods' munificence. But divine grace, even in the case of the Pythagoreans, was not explicitly related to specific ongoing beneficent communities. Finally, as regards the underworld deities, χάρις had acquired the status of a *vox magica* and was used to secure far-ranging benefits outside of the traditional benefaction system.

As regards divine beneficence, I have argued that Paul tailors his presentation of χάρις to the social contexts of the Western and the Eastern Mediterranean churches. In the case of the Roman house-churches, Paul's benefaction language and social imagery are reminiscent of the grace of the Caesars (Rom 5:12-21; 6:12-23). However, in addressing the churches of the Greek East, Paul draws on the general conventions of thanksgiving and obligation found in the honorific inscriptions. Sometimes Paul's language of grace has pointed precision for its Eastern audience. The Corinthians, who were besotted with the rhetoric of travelling sophists, would have recognised Paul's allusion to the impoverished and enslaved benefactor motif of the popular philosophers (2 Cor 8:9; cf. Phil 2:7). In Ephesians, Paul associates χάρις with the motifs of power, wealth, mystery, and glory. There Paul asserts the superiority of Christ's grace over against the dominance of magic, the Temple of Artemis, and the mystery-cults at Ephesus.

As much as Paul accommodates his gospel to contemporary benefaction idiom, he retains a distinctiveness of viewpoint regarding divine grace. Divine grace, for Paul, is non-cultic. The χάρις of Christ stands in opposition to the *do ut des* mentality of the Graeco-Roman world. To think otherwise is to return to justification by works (Gal 3:1-5; 4:8-9; 5:4) and to reverse the direction of our indebtedness to God (Rom 11:35; 1 Cor 4:7).

Rather, the divine favour is mediated through the death of God's dishonoured Benefactor on behalf of His ungrateful enemies (Rom 5:2, 6-8). This totally surpasses the expectations of Pseudo-Demetrius and Valerius

Maximus regarding the death of the καλοκἀγαθός for his dependants. It exposes the limitations of servant benefactors such as Odysseus, as rendered by Antisthenes, and Diogenes, as remembered in the Cynic tradition. For Paul, the love and mercy of a reconciling God stands behind the cross (2 Cor 5:18-19) and through the cruciform mediation of Christ the new creation is unveiled in believers' lives by the Father (2 Cor 5:14-15, 17). Christ gives Himself up voluntarily to the Father at Golgotha in an unprecedented act of love on behalf of His unworthy dependants (Gal 2:20b) and thereby secures their eschatological safety (Rom 8:35-38). The gift of the Spirit, a further sign of the grace in which believers stand, transforms believers' lives individually and corporately with their heavenly Benefactor's love (Rom 5:2, 5; Gal 5:13b-14, 22; 6:2). In sum, the very being of God is revealed in the unconditional love that animates and directs His grace.

Significantly, the social and moral power of the καλοκἀγαθός is also relativised. His merit (δικαιοσύνη) is now democratised throughout the body of Christ. The conferral of the Benefactor's salvific wealth on the spiritually impoverished leads to the establishment of ongoing beneficent communities (2 Cor 8:9). Honour, too, is redirected in the body of Christ. Whereas the inscriptions frame their thanksgiving with posterity in view, the gratitude of believers is focused on God and unites Jews and Gentiles in fellowship (2 Cor 9:11-15). Finally, Paul's understanding of the diversity of the χαρίσματα in building up the body of Christ stands in contrast to the limited responsibilities that the members of the Graeco-Roman voluntary religious associations had towards each other. In this regard, it is precisely the language of grace that differentiates Paul's apostleship from the position of intinerant hellenistic preachers like Dio Chrysostom and from the Cynic 'scouts' of Epictetus.

8.3. The Augustan Age of Grace

I have argued that Paul was attracted to χάρις as a leitmotiv for divine beneficence because the Augustan 'age of grace' had, ensured that nobody would be able to compete against the munificence of the Caesars. The grace of the Caesars had eclipsed the munificence of their civic rivals in the first century AD. Caligula's immortal favour was not easily reciprocated. Nero's liberation of the entire province of Achaia more than recompensed the πρόνοια of the Greek deities towards Rome. But, as widespread as the Caesars' beneficence was, the grace of Nero discriminated as regards the worth of its recipients. Last, the grace of the gods towards the Caesars operated within the traditional reciprocity conventions.

The parallel of the Augustan 'age of grace' with the eschatological reign of Christ's grace would have been especially potent for Paul's Roman auditors. I have argued that in Rom 5:12-21 Paul worked on two fronts, employing traditional motifs from the Jewish apocalyptic literature in conjunction with echoes of the Augustan benefaction propaganda. Paul's portrait of believers as obligated beneficiaries in Rom 6:12-23 would probably have been understood by his auditors against the backdrop of the lucrative career prospects offered to slaves in the *familia Caesaris*. But, in contrast to its Augustan counterpart, Paul's gospel of grace maintains an eschatological reserve. The creation still groans for its future liberty (Rom 8:18ff). Nonetheless, the munificence of Christ totally exceeds that of the Caesars and other first-century civic benefactors in its impartiality and scope.

All research climbs up on the shoulders of its forbears and looks afresh at the terrain. I have sought to open up the hellenistic view of grace which seems to be somewhat neglected in modern New Testament scholarship, but which was altogether familiar to the ancient Mediterranean world. There remains much to do. For example, there is need for a major study on the impact of the Roman benefaction system on the cities of the Greek East. This would throw considerable light on many of the major urban centres in which Paul and his co-workers ministered. Jesus' searing critique of the hellenistic reciprocity and honour systems — as rendered in Luke's gospel (6:27-38; 14:12-14; 22:24-27) — requires attention. Jesus, like Philo, may well have sought to undermine the ethos of reciprocity and supplant it with a distinctly theological understanding of beneficence. Finally, Paul's portrayal of Christ as cosmic Benefactor (Rom 8:18ff; 1 Cor 8:4ff; Eph 1:3ff; Col 1:15ff; cf. Heb 1:1ff; John 1:1ff) might profitably be looked at against the background of the eschatological and cosmic claims made about the Caesars. Such studies would surely locate the apostle of grace even more firmly in his Graeco-Roman context.

Bibliography

ABEGG, M., 'Paul, "Works of the Law" and MTT', *BAR* 20/6 (1994), 52–61, 82.
ACHTEMEIER, P.J., *Romans* (Atlanta 1985).
ALEXANDER, P.S., 'Rabbinic Judaism and the New Testament', *ZNW* 74 (1983), 237–246.
–, 'Torah and Salvation in Tannaitic Literature', in D.A. Carson (*et al.*, ed.), *Justification and Variegated Nomism. Volume 1 — The Complexities of Second Temple Judaism* (Tübingen 2001), 261–301.
ALLO, E.B., 'La portée de la collecte pour Jérusalem dans les plans de Saint Paul', *RB* 45 (1936), 529–537.
AMARU, B.H., 'Land Theology in Josephus' *Jewish Antiquities*', *JQR* 71 (1980), 201–209.
–, 'Land Theology in Philo and Josephus', in L.A. Hoffman (ed.), *The Land of Israel: Jewish Perspectives* (Notre Dame 1986), 65–95.
ANDREWS, S.B., 'Enslaving, Devouring, Exploiting, Self-Exalting, and Striking: 2 Cor 11:19–20 and the Tyranny of Paul's Opponents', in (ed. anon.), *Society of Biblical Literature 1997 Seminar Papers* (Atlanta 1997), 460–490.
ARMSTRONG, A.H., 'The Gods in Plato, Plotinus, and Epicurus', *CQ* 32 (1938), 190–196.
ARNOLD, C.E., *Ephesians: Power and Magic. The Concept of Power in Ephesians in Light of Its Historical Setting* (Grand Rapids 1992).
ARZT, P., 'Brauchbare Sklaven: Ausgewählte Papyrustexte zum Philemonbrief', *Proto Bib* 1/1 (1992), 44–58.
–, 'The "Epistolary Introductory Thanksgiving" in the Papyri and in St. Paul', *NovT* 36/1 (1994), 29–46.
ASCOUGH, R.S., 'The Completion of a Religious Duty: The Background of 2 Cor 8:1–15', *NTS* 42/4 (1996), 584–599.
–, 'Translocal Relationships Among Voluntary Associations and Early Christianity', *Journal of Early Christian Studies* 5/2 (1997), 223–241.
–, *What Are They Saying About the Formation of Pauline Churches?* (New York 1998).
–, 'The Thessalonian Christian Community as a Professional Voluntary Association', *JBL* 119/2 (2000), 311–328.
ATTRIDGE, H.W., *The Interpretation of Biblical History in the Antiquitates Judaicae of Flavius Josephus* (Missoula 1976).
–, 'The Philosophical Critique of Religion under the Early Empire', *ANRW* II 16/1 (1978), 45–78.
AUNE, D.E., 'Magic in Early Christianity', *ANRW* II 23/2 (1980), 1507–1557.
–, 'The Apocalypse and Graeco–Roman Revelatory Magic', *NTS* 33/4 (1987), 481–501.
–, 'Heracles and Christ: Heracles Imagery in the Christology of Early Christianity', in D.L. Balch (*et al.*, ed.), *Greeks, Romans, and Christians: Essays in Honor of Abraham J. Malherbe* (Philadelphia 1990), 3–19.
–, 'Romans as a Logos Protreptikos in the Context of Ancient Religious and Philosophical Propaganda', in M. Hengel and U. Heckel (Hrsg.), *Paulus und das antike Judentum* (Tübingen 1992), 91–121.
AUS, R.D., 'Paul's Travel Plans and the "Full Number of the Gentiles" of Rom 11:25', *NovT* 21/3 (1975), 232–262.

AUSTIN, M.M., *The Hellenistic World from Alexander to the Roman Conquest* (Cambridge 1981).
AVEMARIE, R., *Tora und Leben: Untersuchungen zur Heilsbedeutung der Tora in der frühen rabbinischen Literatur* (Tübingen 1996).
–, 'Bund als Gabe und Recht', in *id.* and H. Lichtenberger (Hrsg.), *Bund und Tora: Zur theologischen Begriffsgeschichte in alttestamentlicher, frühjüdischer und urchristlicher Tradition* (Tübingen 1996), 163–216.
–, 'Erwählung und Vergeltung: Zur optionalen Struktur rabbinischer Soteriologie', *NTS* 45/1 (1999), 108–126.
BAGNALL, R.S., and P. Derow, *Greek Historical Documents: The Hellenistic Period* (Chico 1981).
BAIRD, W., 'Letters of Recommendation: A Study of 2 Cor 3:1–3', *JBL* 80/2 (1961), 166–172.
BALCH, D.L., (*et al.*, ed.), *Greeks, Romans, and Christians: Essays in Honor of Abraham J. Malherbe* (Philadelphia 1990).
–, 'Neopythagorean Moralists and the New Testament Codes', *ANRW* II 26/1 (1992), 380–410.
BANKS, R., *Paul's Idea of Community: The Early House Churches in Their Historical Setting* (2nd edit. Peabody 1994: orig. ed. 1978).
BARCLAY, J.M.G., 'Mirror Reading a Cautionary Essay: Galatians as a Test Case', *JSNT* 31 (1987), 73–89.
–, *Obeying the Truth: Paul's Ethics in Galatians* (Minneapolis 1988).
–, 'Paul, Philemon and the Dilemma of Christian Slave–Ownership', *NTS* 7/2 (1991), 161–186.
–, *Jews in the Mediterranean Diaspora from Alexander to Trajan (323 BCE–117 CE* (Edinburgh 1996).
BARNETT, P., *The Second Epistle to the Corinthians* (Grand Rapids 1997).
BARR, J., *The Semantics of Biblical Language* (London 1961).
BARRETT, C.K., *A Commentary on the Epistle to the Romans* (London 1957).
–, *The Signs of an Apostle* (Philadelphia 1972).
–, 'Paul's Speech in the Areopagus', in M.E. Glasswell and E.W. Fasholé–Luke (eds), *New Testament Christianity for Africa and the World* (London 1974), 69–77.
–, 'Paul's Opponents in 2 Corinthians', in *id.*, *Essays on Paul* (London 1982), 60–86.
–, 'ΨΕΥΔΑΠΟΣΤΟΛΟΙ (2 Cor 11:13)', in *ibid.*, 87–107.
–, 'The Allegory of Abraham, Sarah, and Hagar in the Argument of Galatians', in *ibid.*, 154–170.
BARTCHY, S.S., *First–Century Slavery and 1 Corinthians 7:21* (Atlanta 1971).
–, 'Community of Goods in Acts: Idealisation or Social Reality?', in B.A. Pearson (ed.), *The Future of Early Christianity: Essays in Honor of Helmut Koester* (Minneapolis 1991), 309–318.
–, 'Philemon, Letter to', in D.N. Freedman (ed.), *The Anchor Bible Dictionary* Vol.5 (New York 1992), 305–310.
BARTH, K., *The Epistle to the Romans* (London 1933).
BARTH, M. and H. Blanke, *The Letter to Philemon: A New Translation with Notes and Commentary* (Grand Rapids–Cambridge 2000).
BARTON, S.C. and G.H.R. HORSLEY, 'A Hellenistic Cult Group and the New Testament Churches', *JAC* 24 (1981), 7–41.
BASSLER, J.M., *Divine Impartiality: Paul and a Theological Axiom* (Chico 1982).
–, *God and Mammon: Asking for Money in the New Testament* (Nashville 1991).

BAUCKHAM, R., 'Apocalypses', in D.A. Carson (*et al.*, ed.), *Justification and Variegated Nomism. Volume 1 — The Complexities of Second Temple Judaism* (Tübingen 2001), 135–187.
BAUMERT, N., 'Charisma und Amt bei Paulus', in A. Vanhoye (ed.), *L' apôtre Paul: personnalité, style et conception du ministère* (Leuven 1986), 203–228.
BECKER, J., *Paul: Apostle to the Gentiles* (Louisville 1993).
BEKER, J.C., *Paul the Apostle: The Triumph of God in Life and Thought* (Edinburgh 1980).
BELL, H.I., *Jews and Christians in Egypt: The Jewish Troubles in Alexandria and the Athanasian Controversy* (London 1924).
–, *Id.*, and A.D. Nock, *Magical Texts from a Bilingual Papyrus in the British Museum* (London 1932).
BELLINGER, W.H., and W.R. FARMER (eds), *Jesus and the Suffering Servant: Isaiah 53 and Christian Origins* (Harrisburg 1998).
BENEDUM, J., 'Griechische Arztinschriften aus Kos', *ZPE* 25 (1977), 265–276.
BENKO, S., *Pagan Rome and the Early Christians* (London 1985).
–, 'The Edict of Claudius of AD 49 and the Instigator Chrestus', *TZ* 25/6 (1969), 406–418.
BERGER, K., 'Almosen für Israel: Zum historischen Kontext der Paulinischen Kollekte', *NTS* 23 (1977), 180–204.
–, 'Hellenistische Gattungen im Neuen Testament', *ANRW* II 25/2 (1984), 1034–1432.
–, 'χάρις' in H. Balz and G. Schneider (eds), *Exegetical Dictionary of the New Testament* Vol.3 (Grand Rapids 1993), 457–460.
BEST, E., *Second Corinthians* (Atlanta 1987).
–, *Paul and His Converts* (Edinburgh 1988).
BETZ, H.D., *Der Apostel Paulus und die sokratische Tradition* (Tübingen 1972).
–, 'The Formation of Authoritative Tradition in the Greek Magical Papyri', in B.F. Meyer and E.P. Sanders (eds), *Jewish and Christian Self–Definition. Vol.3: Self–Definition in the Graeco–Roman World* (London 1982), 161–170.
–, *2 Corinthians 8 and 9* (Philadelphia 1985).
–, (ed.), *The Greek Magical Papyri in Translation, Including the Demotic Spells.* Vol.1 (Chicago and London 1986).
–, 'The Problem of Rhetoric and Theology According to the Apostle Paul', in A. Vanhoye (ed.), *L' âpotre Paul: personnalité, style et conception du ministère* (Leuven 1986), 16–48.
–, 'Transferring a Ritual: Paul's Interpretation of Baptism in Romans 6', in T. Engberg–Pedersen (ed.), *Paul in His Hellenistic Context* (Edinburgh 1994), 84–118.
BILDE, P., *Flavius Josephus between Jerusalem and Rome: His Life, His Works, and Their Importance* (Sheffield 1988).
BLACK, D.A., *Paul, Apostle of Weakness: Astheneia and Its Cognates in the Pauline Literature* (New York 1984).
BLACK, M., *Romans* (Grand Rapids 1973).
BLAU, P.M., *Exchange and Power in Social Life* (New York 1964).
–, *The Elementary Structures of Kinship* (Boston 1969).
BLOCH, M., 'Feudal Society', in S.W. Schmidt (ed.), *Friends, Followers, and Factions* (Berkeley and Los Angeles 1977), 192–207.
BOAK, A.E.R., 'The Organisation of Gilds in Greco–Roman Egypt', *TAPhA* 68 (1937), 212–220.
BOCCACCINI, G., *Middle Judaism: Jewish Thought 300 BCE to 200 CE* (Minneapolis 1991).
BOCKMUEHL, M., *The Epistle to the Philippians* (London 1998).

BOERS, H., '' Ἀγάπη and Χάρις in Paul's Thought', *CBQ* 59/4 (1997), 693–713.
BOLKESTEIN, H., *Wohltätigkeit und Armenpflege im vorchristlichen Altertum* (rpt. New York 1979: Utrecht 1939).
–, *Id.* and W. Schwer, 'Almosen', *RAC* 1 (1950), cols.301–307.
BOLT, P.G., *Plutarch's 'Delay of the Divine Vengeance' and Pauline Eschatology* (unpub. MAHons thesis Macquarie University 1994).
BONZ, M.P., 'Differing Approaches to Religious Benefaction: The Late Third–Century Acquisition of the Sardis Synagogue', *HTR* 86/2 (1993), 139–154.
BOOBYER, G.H., *"Thanksgiving" and the "Glory of God" in Paul* (Leipzig 1929).
BORGEN, P., 'The Early Church and the Hellenistic Synagogue', *ST* 37/1 (1983), 55–78.
BORMANN, L., *Philippi: Stadt und Christengemeinde zur Zeit des Paulus* (Leiden–New York–Köln 1995).
BORNKAMM, G., 'The Revelation of Christ to Paul on the Damascus Road and Paul's Doctrine of Justification and Reconciliation: A Study in Galatians 1', in R.J. Banks (ed.), *Reconciliation and Hope: New Testament Essays on Atonement and Eschatology Presented to L.L. Morris on His 60th Birthday* (Exeter 1974), 90–103.
BOTHA, P.J.J., 'Greco–Roman Literacy as Setting for the New Testament Writings', *Neot* 26/1 (1992), 195–215.
BOWERSOCK, G.W., *Martyrdom and Rome* (Cambridge 1995).
BRADY, T.A., *Sarapis and Isis: Collected Essays* (Chicago 1978).
BRANDLE, R., 'Geld und Gnade (zu II Kor 8, 9)', *TZ* 41/3 (1985), 264–271.
BRANDT, L.W., *Dienst und Dienen im Neuen Testament* (Gütersloh 1931).
BRANICK, V.P., *The House Church in the Writings of Paul* (Wilmington 1989).
BRANT, J.A., 'The Place of *Mimêsis* in Paul's Thought', *SR* 22/3 (1993), 285–300.
BRAY, G., 'Justification: The Reformers and Recent New Testament Scholarship', *Churchman* 109/2 (1995), 102–126.
BRÉHIER, É., *Les idées philosophiques et religieuses de Philon d' Alexandrie* (Paris 1925: 2nd edit.).
BRENK, F.E., 'From Mysticism to Mysticism: The Religious Development of Plutarch of Chaironeia', in G. MacRae (ed.), *Society of Biblical Literature 1975 Seminar Papers* (Cambridge, Mass. 1975), 193–198.
–, 'An Imperial Heritage: The Religious Spirit of Plutarch of Chaironeia', *ANRW* II 36/1 (1987), 248–349.
BRIGGS, S., 'Paul on Bondage and Freedom in Imperial Society', in R.A. Horsley (ed.), *Paul and Politics: Ekklesia, Israel, Imperium, Interpretation. Essays in Honor of Krister Stendahl* (Harrisburg 2000), 110–123.
BROCKHAUS, U., *Charisma und Amt: Die paulinische Charismenlehre auf dem Hintergrund der frühchristlichen Gemeindefunktionen* (Wuppertal 1972).
BROOKS, R., *The Spirit of the Ten Commandments: Shattering the Myth of Rabbinic Legalism* (San Francisco 1990).
BROOTEN, B., *Women Leaders in the Ancient Synagogue* (Atlanta 1982).
–, 'Iael προστάτης in the Jewish Donative Inscription from Aphrodisias', in B.A. Pearson (ed.), *The Future of Early Christianity: Essays in Honor of Helmut Koester* (Minneapolis 1991), 149–162.
BROWN, C., 'Poor', in *id.*, (ed.), *The New International Dictionary of New Testament Theology* Vol.2 (Exeter 1976: Gmn. orig. 1971), 820–829.
–, 'Righteousness', in *id.*, (ed.), *The New International Dictionary of New Testament Theology* Vol.3 (Exeter 1978: Gmn. orig 1971), 352–377.
BROWN, J.P., 'Inversion of Social Roles in Paul's Letters', *NovT* 33/4 (1991), 303–325.

BROWN, M.J., 'Paul's Use of ΔΟΥΛΟΣ ΧΡΙΣΤΟΥ ΙΗΣΟΥ in Romans 1:1', *JBL* 120/4 (2001), 723–737.
BRUCE, F.F., *The Epistle of Paul to the Romans: An Introduction and Commentary* (Leicester 1963).
–, 'Paul and Jerusalem', *TynBul* 19 (1968), 3–25.
–, 'The New Testament and Classical Studies', *NTS* 22 (1976), 229–242.
–, *Paul: Apostle of the Free Spirit* (Exeter 1977).
–, *The Epistle of Paul to the Galatians* (Exeter 1982).
BRUCK, E.F., 'Ethics vs Law: St. Paul, the Fathers of the Church and the "Cheerful Giver" in Roman Law', *Traditio* 2 (1944), 97–121.
BUCHANAN, G.W., 'The Use of Rabbinic Literature for New Testament Research', *BTB* 7 (1977), 111–122.
BULTMANN, R., *The Second Letter to the Corinthians* (Minneapolis 1987).
BURKE, T.H., 'Pauline Paternity in 1 Thessalonians', *TynBul* 51/1 (2000), 59–80.
BURKERT, W., *Greek Religion: Archaic and Classical* (Cambridge 1985).
BURNISH, R.F.G., *The Doctrine of Grace from Paul to Irenaeus* (unpub. Ph.D. diss. Glascow University 1971).
BURSTEIN, S.M., *The Hellenistic Age from the Battle of Ipsos to the Death of Kleopatra VII* (Cambridge 1985).
BYRNE, B., *'Sons of God' — 'Seed of Abraham'* (Rome 1979).
–, *Romans* (Collegeville 1996).
CADBURY, H.J., 'Erastus of Corinth', *JBL* 50 (1931), 42–58.
CALLAHAN, A.D., 'Paul's Epistle to Philemon: Toward an Alternative Argumentum', *HTR* 86/4, (1993), 357–376.
–, *Embassy of Onesimus: The Letter of Paul to Philemon* (Valley Forge 1997).
CAPES, D.B., *Old Testament Yahweh Texts in Paul's Theology* (Tübingen 1992).
CARREZ, M., *La deuxième épître de Saint Paul aux Corinthiens* (Geneva 1986).
CARSON, D.A., *Divine Sovereignty and Human Responsibility: Biblical Perspectives in Tension* (Atlanta 1981).
–, 'Divine Sovereignty and Human Responsibility in Philo', *NovT* 23/2 (1991), 148–164.
CARSON, D.A. (et al., ed.), *Justification and Variegated Nomism. Volume 1 — The Complexities of Second Temple Judaism* (Tübingen 2001).
CASE, S.C., *The Social Triumph of the Ancient Church* (rpt. New York 1971: New York 1933).
–, *The Social Origins of Christianity* (rpt. New York 1975: Chicago 1923).
CASTELLI, E.A., *Imitating Paul: A Discourse of Power* (Louisville 1991).
CERFAUX, L., 'La théologie de la grâce selon Saint Paul', *VSpir* 83 (1950), 5–19.
CHACKO, J., 'Collection in the Early Church', *ERT* 24/2 (2000), 177–183.
CHARLESWORTH, J.H., *The Old Testament and the New Testament: Prolegomena for the Study of Christian Origins* (Cambridge 1985).
CHAUMARTIN, F.-R., 'Les désillusions de Sénèque devant l'évolution de la politique néronienne et l'aspiration à la retraite: le *De vita beata* et le *De beneficiis*', *ANRW* II 36/3 (1987), 1688–1723.
CHOW, J.K., *Patronage and Power: A Study of Social Networks* (Sheffield 1992).
CLARK, G.R., *The Word Hesed in the Hebrew Bible* (Sheffield 1993).
CLARK, M.E., 'Images and Concepts of Hope in the Imperial Cult', in H.K. Richards (ed.), *Society of Biblical Literature 1982 Seminar Papers* (Atlanta 1982), 39–43.
CLARK, W.P., *Benefactions and Endowments in Greek Antiquity* (unpub. Ph.D. diss. Chicago University 1928).
CLARKE, A.D., 'The Good and the Just in Romans 5:7', *TynBul* 41/1 (1990), 128–142.

–, *Secular and Christian Leadership in Corinth: A Socio–Historical and Exegetical Study of 1 Corinthians 1–6* (Leiden–New York–Köln 1993).
CLEMENTS, R.E., '"A Remnant Chosen by Grace" (Romans 11:5): The Old Testament Background and Origin of the Remnant Concept', in D.A. Hagner and M.J. Harris (eds), *Pauline Studies: Essays Presented to F.F. Bruce* (Exeter 1980), 106–121.
COHEN, S.J.D., 'Epigraphical Rabbis', *JQR* 72 (1981), 1–17.
COMBES, I.A., *The Metaphor of Slavery in the Writings of the Early Church From the New Testament to the Beginning of the Fifth Century* (Sheffield 1998).
CONNOLLY, A.L., 'Standing on Sacred Ground', in G.H.R. Horsley (ed.), *New Documents Illustrating Early Christianity* Vol.4 (1987 Macquarie University), 105–117.
–, 'χολάω', in G.H.R. Horsley (ed.), *New Documents Illustrating Early Christianity* Vol.4 (1987 Macquarie University), 175–176.
CONZELMANN, H., *The Acts of the Apostles* (Philadelphia 1987).
–, *Id.*, and W. Zimmerli, 'χάρις, χαρίζομαι, χαριτόω, ἀχάριστος, χάρισμα, εὐχαριστέω', *TDNT* Vol.9 (1974), 372–415.
COOPER, K.T., 'Paul and Rabbinic Soteriology: A Review Article', *WTJ* 44/1 (1982), 123–139.
COPE, L., 'Analogy, the Pauline Centre, and Doing Theology Today', *Bangal. Theol. For.* 15/3 (1983), 128–133.
CORRIGAN, G.M., 'Paul's Shame for the Gospel', *BTB* 16 (1986), 23–27.
CORRIVEAU, R., *The Liturgy of Life: A Study of the Ethical Thought of St. Paul in His Letters to the Early Christian Communities* (Bruxelles and Paris 1970).
COUNTRYMAN, L.Wm., 'Patrons and Officers in Club and Church', in P.J. Achtemeier (ed.), *Society of Biblical Literature 1977 Seminar Papers* (Missoula 1977), 135–141.
–, 'Welfare in the Churches of Asia Minor under the Early Roman Empire: Part I — The Christian Practice of Almsgiving', in P.J. Achtemeier (ed.), *Society of Biblical Literature 1979 Seminar Papers* (Missoula 1979), 131–146.
–, *The Rich Christian in the Church of the Early Empire: Contradictions and Accommodations* (New York and Toronto 1980).
CRADDOCK, F.B., 'The Poverty of Christ', *Int* 22/2 (1968), 158–170.
CRAFFERT, P.F., 'More on Models and Muddles in the Social–Scientific Interpretation of the New Testament: The Sociological Fallacy Reconsidered', *Neot* 26/1 (1992), 217–239.
CRANFIELD, C.E.B., *A Critical and Exegetical Commentary on the Epistle to the Romans* (Edinburgh 1975–1979). 2 Vols.
'The Grace of our Lord Jesus Christ', *Comm. Viat.* 32/3 (1989), 105–109.
–, '"The Works of the Law" in the Epistle of the Romans', *JSNT* 43 (1991), 89–101.
CROSSAN, J.D., *The Historical Jesus: The Life of a Mediterranean Jewish Peasant* (San Francisco 1991).
CULLMANN, O., 'The Early Church and the Ecumenical Problem', *ATR* 40 (1958), 181–189, 294–301.
DAHL, N.A., 'Paul and Possessions', in *id.*, *Studies in Paul* (Minneapolis 1977), 22–39.
DANIEL, R.W. and Franco MALTOMINI (eds), *Supplementum Magicu. Vols I and II* (Opladen 1989, 1991).
DANIÉLOU, J., *Philon D'Alexandrie* (Paris 1958).
DANKER, F.W., 'Menander and the New Testament', *NTS* 10 (1963–1964), 365–368.
–, 'The Endangered Benefactor in Luke–Acts', in H.R. Kent (ed.), *Society of Biblical Literature 1981 Seminar Papers* (Chico 1981), 39–48.
–, *Benefactor: Epigraphic Study of a Graeco–Roman and New Testament Semantic Field* (St. Louis 1982).

–, 'Graeco–Roman Cultural Accommodation in the Christology of Luke–Acts', in H.R. Kent (ed.), *Society of Biblical Literature 1983 Seminar Papers* (Chico 1983), 391–414.
–, 'Reciprocity in the Ancient World and in Acts 15:23–29', in R.J. Cassidy and P.J. Sharper (eds), *Political Issues in Luke–Acts* (New York 1983), 49–58.
–, 'Bridging St. Paul and the Apostolic Fathers: A Study in Reciprocity', *CurTM* 15/1 (1984), 84–94.
–, *Jesus and the New Age: A Commentary on St. Luke's Gospel* (Philadelphia 1988).
–, *2 Corinthians* (Minneapolis 1989).
–, 'Paul's Debt to the *De Corona* of Demosthenes: A Study of Rhetorical Techniques in Second Corinthians', in D.A. Watson (ed.), *Persuasive Artistry: Studies in New Testament Rhetoric in Honour of George A. Kennedy* (Sheffield 1991).
–, 'Associations, Clubs, Thiasoi', in D.N. Freedman (ed.), *Anchor Bible Dictionary* Vol.1 (New York 1992), 501–503.
DAVIES, G.N., *Faith and Obedience in Romans: A Study in Romans 1–4* (Sheffield 1990).
DAVIES, W.D., *Paul and Rabbinic Judaism* (London 1948).
–, 'Reflections on the Nature of Judaism', *RHPR* 75/1 (1995), 85–111.
DAVIS, S. 'Philanthropy as a Virtue in Late Antiquity and the Middle Ages', in J.B. Schneewind (ed.), *Giving: Western Ideas of Philanthropy* (Bloomington and Indianapolis 1996), 1–23.
DE BOER, W.P., *The Imitation of Paul* (Kampen 1962).
DE LACEY, D.R., '"One Lord" in Pauline Christology', in H.H. Rowdon (ed.), *Christ the Lord: Studies in Christology Presented to Donald Guthrie* (Leicester 1982), 191–203.
DE ROO, J.C. 'The Concept of "Works of the Law" in Jewish and Christian Literature', in S.E Porter and B.W.R. Pearson (eds), *Christian–Jewish Relations through the Centurie.* (Sheffield 2000), 116–147.
DESILVA, D.A., *Honor, Patronage, Kinship and Purity: Unlocking New Testament Culture* (Downers Grove 2000).
DE STE. CROIX, G.E.M., '*Suffragium*: From Vote to Patronage', *British Journal of Sociology* 5 (1954), 33–48.
DEWITT, N.W., 'The Epicurean Doctrine of Gratitude', *AJP* 58 (1937), 320–328.
–, *St. Paul and Epicurus* (Minneapolis 1954).
DE WITT BURTON, E., *A Critical and Exegetical Commentary on the Epistle to the Galatians* (Edinburgh 1921).
DECHARME, P., *La critique des traditions religieuses chez les grecs des origines au temps de Plutarch* (Paris 1904).
DEICHGRÄBER, K., *Charis und Chariten: Grazie und Grazien* (München 1971).
DEIDUN, T., 'E.P. Sanders: An Assessment of Two Recent Works', *WTJ* 44/1 (1986), 43–52.
DEINES, R., 'The Pharisees Between "Judaisms" and "Common Judaism"', in D.A. Carson (*et al.*, ed.), *Justification and Variegated Nomism. Volume 1 — The Complexities of Second Temple Judaism* (Tübingen 2001), 443–504.
DEISSMANN, A., 'Epistolary Literature', *Encyclopaedia Biblica* Vol.2 (1901), 1322–1329.
–, 'Primitive Christianity and the Lower Classes', *Expositor* 7 (1909), 208–224.
–, 'Prolegomena to the Biblical Letters and Epistles', in *id.*, *Bible Studies* (Edinburgh 1923), 1–59.
–, *Light from the Ancient East* (2nd ed. 1927: rpt. Grand Rapids 1978).
DELLING, G., 'παρθένος', *TDNT* Vol. 5 (1967), 826–837.
DEN BOER, W., *Private Morality in Greece and Rome: Some Historical Aspects* (Leiden 1979).

DENIS, A.-M., 'L'élection et la vocation de Paul, faveurs célestes: Étude thématique de Gal 1, 15', *RevThom* 35 (1957), 405–428.
DEONNA, W., 'La légende d'Octave–Auguste: dieu, sauveur et maître du monde', *RHR* 83 (1921), 32–58, 163–195; *RHR* 84 (1921), 77–107.
DERRETT, J.D.M., 'The Functions of the Epistle to Philemon', *ZNW* 79 1/2 (1988), 63–91.
DI BELLA, M.P., 'Name, Blood and Miracles: The Claims to Renown in Traditional Sicily', in J.G. Peristiany and J. Pitt-Rivers (eds), *Honour and Grace in Anthropology* (Cambridge 1992), 151–165.
DIBELIUS, M., 'Paul on the Areopagus', in *id.*, *Studies in the Acts of the Apostles* (London 1956), 25–77.
DICKIE, M.W., 'An Epitaph from Stratonikeia in Caria', *ZPE* 100 (1994), 109–118.
DIHLE, A., *Die goldene Regel: Eine Einführung in die Geschichte der antiken und frühchristlichen Vulgärethik* (Göttingen 1962).
–, 'Ethik', *RAC* 6 (1966), 646–796.
DODD, C.H., *The Epistle of Paul to the Romans* (London 1932).
–, *The Bible and the Greeks* (London 1935).
DONFRIED, K.P., *The Romans Debate* (Edinburgh 1991).
DONLAN, W., 'Reciprocities in Homer', *CW* 75 (1982), 26–48.
DÖRRIE, H., and H. DITTMANN (*et. al.*), 'Gnade', *RAC* Vol.11 (1981), 313–346.
DOTY, W.G., 'The Classification of Epistolary Literature', *CBQ* 31/2 (1969), 183–199.
–, *Letters in Primitive Christianity* (Philadelphia 1973).
DOUGHTY, D.J., 'The Priority of ΧΑΡΙΣ: An Investigation of the Theological Language of Paul', *NTS* 19 (1972–1973), 163–180.
DOWNING, F.G., 'Philo on Wealth and the Rights of the Poor', *JSOT* 24 (1985), 116–118.
–, *Jesus and the Threat of Freedom* (London 1987).
–, 'A Bas Les Aristos: The Relevance of Higher Literature for the Understanding of the Earliest Christian Writings', *NovT* 30/3 (1988), 212–230.
–, *Christ and the Cynics* (Sheffield 1988).
–, *Cynics and Christian Origins* (Edinburgh 1992).
–, *Cynics, Paul and the Pauline Churches: Cynics and Christian Origins II* (London and New York 1998).
DREXLER, H., *Politische Grundbegriffe der Römer* (Darmstadt 1988).
DUNN, J.D.G, *Jesus and the Spirit: A Study of the Religious and Charismatic Experience of Jesus and the First Christians as Reflected in the New Testament* (London 1975).
–, *Christology in the Making: An Inquiry into the Origins of the Doctrine of the Incarnation* (London, 1980).
–, *Romans 1–8, Romans 9–16* (Dallas 1988).
–, *Jesus, Paul, and the Law: Studies in Mark and Galatians* (Louisville 1990).
–, *The Partings of the Ways: Between Christianity and Judaism and Their Significance for the Character of Christianity* (London 1991).
–, 'The Justice of God: A Renewed Perspective on Justification by Faith', *JTS* 43/1 (1992), 1–22.
–, 'Yet Once More — "The Works of the Law": A Response', *JSNT* 46 (1992), 99–117.
–, 'Prolegomena to a Theology of Paul', *NTS* 40/3 (1994), 407–432.
–, *The Epistle to the Galatians* (Peabody 1995).
–, *The Theology of Paul the Apostle* (Grand Rapids 1998).
DU TOIT, A.B., 'Encountering Grace: Towards Understanding the Essence of Paul's Damascus Experience', *Neot* 30/1 (1996), 71–87.
EASTMAN, B., *The Significance of Grace in the Letters of Paul* (New York 1999).

ECKHERT, J., 'Die Kollekte des Paulus für Jerusalem', in P.-G. Müller and W. Stenger (Hrsg.), *Kontinuität und Einheit: Für Franz Mussner* (Freiburg 1981), 65–80.
EHRENBERG, V., and A.H.M. JONES, *Documents Illustrating the Reigns of Augustus and Tiberius* (London 1955).
ELLIOT, J.H., 'Patronage and Clientism in Early Christian Society: A Short Reading Guide', *Forum* 3/4 (1987), 39–48.
–, 'The Fear of the Leer: The Evil Eye from the Bible to Li'l Abner', *Forum* 4/4 (1988), 42–71.
–, *Social–Scientific Criticism of the New Testament* (London 1995).
ELLIS, E.E., *Paul and His Recent Interpreters* (Grand Rapids 1961).
–, 'Paul and His Opponents: Trends in the Research', in *id.*, *Prophecy and Hermeneutic in Early Christianity* (Grand Rapids 1978), 80–115.
–, *Pauline Theology: Ministry and Society* (Grand Rapids 1989).
ENGBERG–PEDERSEN, T., *Paul and the Stoics* (Edinburgh 2000).
ENGELMANN, H., *The Delian Aretalogy of Sarapis* (Leiden 1975).
ENNS, P., 'Expansions of Scripture', in D.A. Carson (*et al.*, ed.), *Justification and Variegated Nomism. Volume 1 — The Complexities of Second Temple Judaism* (Tübingen 2001), 73–98.
ERNST, M., 'Die Funktionen der Phöbe (Röm 16, 1f) in der Gemeinde von Kenchreai', *Prot Bib* 1/2 (1992), 135–147.
ERSKINE, A., 'The Romans as Common Benefactors', *Historia* 43 (1994), 70–84.
ESLER, P.F., *The First Christians in Their Social Worlds: Social–Scientific Approaches to New Testament Interpretation* (London 1994).
–, 'Group Boundaries and Intergroup Conflict in Galatians: A New Reading of Galatians 5:13—6:10', in M.G. Brett (ed.), *Ethnicity and the Bible* (Leiden–New York–Köln 1996), 215–240.
EVANS, C.A., 'Scripture–Based Stories in the Pseudepigrapha' in D.A. Carson (*et al.*, ed.), *Justification and Variegated Nomism. Volume 1 — The Complexities of Second Temple Judaism* (Tübingen 2001), 57–72.
EXLER, F.X., *The Form of the Ancient Greek Letter: A Study in Greek Epistolography* (Ph.D. Catholic University of America 1923).
FALK, D., 'Psalms and Prayers', in D.A. Carson (*et al.*, ed.), *Justification and Variegated Nomism. Volume 1 — The Complexities of Second Temple Judaism* (Tübingen 2001), 7–56.
FEE, G.D., 'ΧΑΡΙΣ in 2 Corinthians 1:15: Apostolic Parousia and Paul–Corinth Chronology', *NTS* 24 (1978), 533–538.
FELDMAN, L.H., 'Abraham the Greek Philosopher in Josephus', *TAPhA* 99 (1968), 143–156.
–, 'Hellenizations in Josephus' Version of Esther (Ant. Jud. 11, 185–295)', *TAPhA* 101 (1970), 143–170.
–, 'Josephus an Apologist to the Greco–Roman World: His Portrait of Solomon', in E.S. Fiorenza (ed.), *Aspects of Religious Propaganda in Judaism and Early Christianity* (Notre Dame 1976), 66–99.
–, 'Josephus' Portrait of Saul', *HUCA* 53 (1982), 45–99.
–, 'Flavius Josephus Revisited: The Man, His Writings, and His Significance', *ANRW* II 21/2 (1983), 763–862.
–, 'Josephus' Portrait of Hezekiah', *JBL* 111/4 (1992), 597–610.
–, 'Josephus' Portrait of Ezra', *VT* 43/2 (1993), 190–214.
–, *Josephus's Interpretation of the Bible* (Berkeley–Los Angeles–London 1998).

FERNAND–COURBY, L'Institut, *Nouveau choix d'inscriptions grecques: textes, traductions, commentaires pour l'Institut Fernand–Courby* (Paris 1971).

FESTUGIÈRE, A.J., *Epicurus and His Gods* (New York 1955).

FILSON, F.V., *St. Paul's Conception of Recompense* (Leipzig 1931).

FINLEY, M.I., 'Marriage, Sale and Gift in the Homeric World', *RIDA* III 2 (1954), 167–194.

–, *The World of Odysseus* (Harmondsworth 1954).

FIORE, B., *The Function of Personal Example in the Socratic and Pastoral Epistles* (Rome 1986).

FITZGERALD, J.T., 'Paul, the Ancient Epistolary Theorists, and 2 Corinthians 10–13: The Purpose and Literary Genre of a Pauline Letter', in D.L. Balch (*et al.*, ed.), *Greeks, Romans, and Christians: Essays in Honor of Abraham J. Malherbe* (Minneapolis 1990), 190–200.

–, 'Virtue/Vice Lists', in D.N. Freedman (ed.), *The Anchor Bible Dictionary* Vol.6 (New York 1992), 857–859.

FITZMYER, J.A., 'Some Notes on Aramaic Epistolography', *JBL* 93/2 (1974), 201–225.

–, 'Paul's Jewish Background and the Deeds of the Law', in *id.*, *According to Paul: Studies in the Theology of the Apostle* (New York 1992), 18–35.

–, *Romans: A New Translation with Introduction and Commentary* (New York 1992).

FLACK, E.E., 'The Concept of Grace in Biblical Thought', in J.M. Myers (ed.), *Biblical Studies in Memory of H.C. Alleman* (Locust Valley 1960), 137–154.

FORBES, C., *"Strength"and "Weakness" as Terminology of Status in St. Paul: The Historical and Literary Roots of a Metaphor, with Specific Reference to 1 and 2 Corinthians* (unpub. BA Hons. thesis Macquarie University 1978).

–, '"Unaccustomed As I Am": St. Paul the Public Speaker in Corinth', *Buried History* 19/1 (1983), 11–16.

–, 'Comparison, Self–Praise and Irony: Paul's Boasting and the Conventions of Hellenistic Rhetoric', *NTS* 32/1 (1986), 1–30.

–, 'Finding a Place for St. Paul', *Society for Early Christianity NewsLetter* 8 (1990), 5–7.

–, *Prophecy and Inspired Speech in Early Christianity and Its Hellenistic Environment* (Tübingen 1995).

FORBES, C.A., *Neoi: A Contribution to the Study of Greek Associations* (Middletown 1933).

–, 'Ancient Athletic Guilds', *CPh* 50 (1955), 238–252.

FORSTER, W., *Palestinian Judaism in the New Testament* (London 1964).

FORTENBAUGH, W.W., *Theophrastus: Sources for His Life, Writings, Thought and Influence* Vol.2 (Leiden–New York–Köln 1992).

FOUCART, P., *Des associations religieuses chez les Grecs: thiases, éranes, orgéons* (Paris 1873).

FOWL, S., 'Know Your Context: Giving and Receiving Money in Philippians', *Int* 56/1 (2002), 45–58.

FRANCE, R.T., 'The Worship of Jesus: A Neglected Factor in Christological Debate?', in H.H. Rowdon (ed.), *Christ the Lord: Studies in Christology Presented to Donald Guthrie* (Leicester 1982), 17–36.

FRANK, R., 'Motivation, Cognition, and Charitable Giving', in J.B. Schneewind (ed.), *Giving: Western Ideas of Philanthropy* (Bloomington and Indianapolis 1996), 130–152.

FRANKLIN, W.M., *Die Kollekte des Paulus* (Scottdale 1938).

FRANZMANN, J.W., *The Early Development of the Greek Concept of Charis* (unpub. Ph.D. diss. Wisconsin University 1972).

FRIDRICHSEN, A., 'Zum Stil des paulinischen Peristasen–Katalogs 2 Cor 11:23ff', *Symbolae Osloenses* 7 (1927), 25–29.
–, 'Peristasenkatalog und *Res Gestae*', *Symbolae Osloenses* 8 (1929), 78–82.
FRIESEN, S.J., *Twice Neokoros: Ephesus, Asia and the Cult of the Flavian Imperial Family* (Leiden–New York–Köln 1993).
FRISCH, E., *An Historical Survey of Jewish Philanthropy from the Earliest Times to the Nineteenth Century* (New York 1924).
FUNG, R.Y.K., 'The Status of Justification by Faith in Paul's Thought: A Brief Survey of a Modern Debate', *Themelois* 6/3 (1981), 4–11.
–, 'Ministry, Community and Spiritual Gifts', *EvQ* 66/1 (1984), 3–20.
FUNK, R.W., *Language, Hermeneutic, and Word of God: The Problem of Language in the New Testament and Contemporary Theology* (New York 1966).
FUNKE, H., 'Antisthenes bei Paulus', *Hermes* 98 (1970), 459–471
FURNISH, V.P., *Theology and Ethics in Paul*. (Nashville 1968).
–, *2 Corinthians: A New Translation with Introduction and Commentary* (New York 1984).
GAGER, J., *Kingdom and Community: The Social World of Early Christianity* (Englewood Cliffs 1975).
–, *The Origins of Anti–Semitism: Attitudes Toward Judaism in Pagan and Christian Antiquity* (Oxford 1985).
GAGNON, R.A., 'Why the "Weak" at Rome Cannot Be Non–Christian Jews', *CBQ* 62/1 (2000), 64–82.
GARDINER, A.W., 'The Norm of Reciprocity: A Preliminary Statement', *American Sociological Review* 25/2 (1960), 161–178.
GARLAND, D.E., 'Paul's Apostolic Authority: The Power of Christ Sustaining Weakness (2 Corinthians 10–13)', *RevExp* 86/3 (1989), 371–389.
–, *2 Corinthians* (Nashville 1999).
GARNET, P., 'Qumran Light on Pauline Soteriology', in D.A. Hagnar and M.J. Harris (eds), *Pauline Studies: Essays Presented to F.F. Bruce* (Exeter 1980), 19–34.
GARRETT, S.R., *The Demise of the Devil: Magic and the Demonic in Luke's Writings* (Minneapolis 1989).
GARTNER, B., *The Areopagus Speech and Natural Revelation* (Lund 1955).
GASTON, L., *Paul and the Torah* (Vancouver 1987).
GELZER, M., *The Roman Nobility* (Oxford 1969).
GEORGI, D., *The Opponents of Paul in Second Corinthians* (Edinburgh 1986).
–, 'Who is the True Prophet?', *HTR* 79/1–3 (1986), 100–126.
–, 'Reflections of a New Testament Scholar on Plutarch's Tractates *De Alexandri Magni Fortuna aut Virtute*', in B.A. Pearson (ed.), *The Future of Christianity: Essays in Honor of Helmut Koester* (Minneapolis 1991), 20–34.
–, *Theocracy in Paul's Praxis and Theology* (Minneapolis 1991: Gmn. orig. 1987).
–, *Remembering the Poor: The History of Paul's Collection for Jerusalem* (Nashville 1992: Hamburg–Bergstedt 1965).
GIANNANTONI, G., *Socraticorum Reliquiae* Vol.2 (Naples 1983).
GILL, C., (*et al.*, ed.), *Reciprocity in Ancient Greece* (New York 1998).
GILL, D.W.J., 'Erastus the Aedile', *TynBul* 40 (1989), 294–301.
GINSBURG, M., 'Roman Military Clubs and Their Social Functions', *TAPhA* 71 (1940), 149–156.
GLAD, C.E., *Paul and Philodemus: Adaptability in Epicurean and Early Christian Psychagogy* (Leiden–New York–Köln 1995).
GLOMBITZA, O., 'Gnade — Das entscheidende Wort: Erwägungen zu 1 Kor XV 1–11, eine exegetische Studie', *NovT* 2/3–4 (1959), 281–290.

GLUECK, N., *ḤESED in the Bible* (New York 1975).
GOODSPEED, E.K., 'Phoebe's Letter of Introduction', *HTR* 44 (1951), 55–57.
GOUDGE, H.L., *The Second Epistle to the Corinthians* (London 1927).
GOULET–CAZÉ, M.–O., 'Le cynisme à l'époque impériale', *ANRW* II 36/4 (1992), 2720–2833.
GOWEN, D.E., 'Wisdom', in D.A. Carson (*et al.*, ed.), *Justification and Variegated Nomism. Volume 1 — The Complexities of Second Temple Judaism* (Tübingen 2001), 215–239.
GRAF, F., 'An Oracle against Pestilence from a Western Anatolian Town', *ZPE* 92 (1992), 267–279.
GRANT, M., *Herod the Great* (New York 1971).
GREEN, W.S., 'Context and Meaning in "Rabbinic Biography"', in W.S. Green (ed.), *Approaches to Ancient Judaism* Vol.2 (Ann Arbor 1980).
GREENBERG, M.S., and S.P. SHAPIRO, 'Indebtedness: An Adverse Aspect of Asking for and Receiving Help', *Sociometry* 34/2 (1971), 290–301.
GREGORY, C.A., *Gifts and Commodities* (London 1982).
GRUNDMANN, W., 'Die Übermacht der Gnade: Eine Studie zur Theologie des Paulus', *NovT* 2/1 (1957), 50–72.
GUERRA, A.J., *Romans and the Apologetic Tradition: The Purpose, Genre and Audience of Paul's Letter* (Cambridge 1995).
GUERRA, A.T., 'Filodemo sulla Gratitudine', *Cronache Ercolanesi* 7 (1977), 96–113.
GUILLET, J., 'Grace', *Catholicisme* 5 (1951), 135–141.
GUNDRY, R.H., 'Grace, Works, and Staying Saved in Paul', *Bib* 66/1 (1985), 1–38.
GUNDRY VOLF, J.M., *Paul and Perseverance: Staying In and Falling Away* (Tübingen 1990).
GURVAL, R.A., *Actium and Augustus: The Politics and Emotions of Civil War* (Ann Arbor 1995).
HADZSITS, D.P., 'Significance of Worship and Prayer among the Epicureans', *TAPhA* 39 (1908), 73–88.
HAGNER, D.A., 'Salvation, Faith, Works', *The Reformed Journal* 29/9 (1979), 25–27.
–, 'Paul and Judaism. The Jewish Matrix of Early Christianity: Issues in the Current Debate', *Bulletin for Biblical Research* 3 (1993), 111–130.
HAINZ, J., *Koinônia: »Kirche« als Gemeinschaft bei Paulus* (Regensburg 1982).
HAMEL, G., *Poverty and Charity in Roman Palestine: First Three Centuries CE* (Berkeley and Los Angeles 1990).
HAMMOND, M., 'Hellenistic Influences on the Structure of the Augustan Principate', *Memoirs of the American Academy in Rome* 17 (1949), 1–25.
HANDS, A.R., *Charities and Social Aid in Greece and Rome* (London and Southampton 1968).
HANSEN, G.W., *Abraham in Galatians: Epistolary and Rhetorical Contexts* (Sheffield 1989).
HANSON, R.P.C., *The Second Epistle to the Corinthians: Christ and Controversy* (London 1954).
–, *The Acts* (Oxford 1967).
HARNACK, A., *The Mission and Expansion of Christianity in the First Three Centuries* (Gloucester, Mass. 1972).
HARRIS, M.J., *Jesus as God: The New Testament Use of Theos in Reference to Jesus* (Grand Rapids 1992).
–, *Slave of Christ: A New Testament Metaphor for Total Devotion to Christ* (Leicester 1999).

HARRIS, W.V., 'Literacy and Epigraphy, I', *ZPE* 52 (1983), 87–111.
HARRISON, J.R., 'Benefaction Ideology and Christian Responsibility for Widows', in S.R. Llewelyn (ed.), *New Documents Illustrating Early Christianity* Vol.8 (Grand Rapids 1998), 106–116.
–, 'Paul's House Churches and the Cultic Associations', *Reformed Theological Review* 58/1 (1999), 31–47.
–, 'Paul, Eschatology and the Augustan Age of Grace', *TynBul* 50/1 (1999), 79–91.
HATCH, E., *The Organisation of the Early Christian Churches* (Oxford and Cambridge 1881).
HAUCK, F., 'πένης, πενιχρός', *TDNT* 6 (1968), 37–40.
HAUCK, F., and E. BAMMEL, 'πτωχός, πτωχεία, πτωχεύω', *TDNT* 6 (1968), 885–915.
HAYS, R.B., 'Psalm 143 and the Logic of Romans 3', *JBL* 99/1 (1980), 107–115.
HELLEGOUARC'H, J., *Le vocabulaire latin des relations et des partis politiques sous la république* (Paris 1963).
HENDRIX, H.L., *Thessalonicans Honor Romans* (unpub. Th.D. diss. Harvard University 1984).
–, 'Beyond "Imperial Cult" and "Cults of Magistrates"', in H.R. Kent (ed.), *Society of Biblical Literature 1986 Seminar Papers* (Chico 1986), 301–308.
'On the Form and Ethos of Ephesians', *USQR* 42/4 (1988), 3–15.
–, 'Benefactor/Patron Networks in the Urban Environment: Evidence from Thessalonica', *Semeia* 56 (1992), 39–58.
HENGEL, M., *Judaism and Hellenism: Studies in their Encounter in Palestine During the Early Hellenistic Period* (London 1974). 2 Vols.
–, *Property and Riches in the Early Church* (Philadelphia 1974).
–, *The Atonement: The Origins of the Doctrine in the New Testament* (London 1981).
–, *The Pre–Christian Paul* (London 1991).
HENGEL, M., and R. DEINES, 'E.P. Sanders' "Common Judaism", Jesus, and the Pharisees', *JTS* 46/1 (1995), 1–70.
HENGEL, M. and A.M. SCHWEMER, *Paul Between Damascus and Antioch: The Unknown Years* (London 1997).
HERFORD, R.T., *Christianity in Talmud and Midrash* (London 1903).
–, *The Pharisees* (London 1924).
HÉRING, J., *The Second Epistle of St. Paul to the Corinthians* (London 1967).
HERMAN, G., *Ritualised Friendship and the Greek City* (Cambridge 1987).
HERRMANN, P., *Der römische Kaisereid* (Göttingen 1968).
HERSHBELL, J., 'The Stoicism of Epictetus: Twentieth Century Perspectives', *ANRW* II 36/1 (1987), 2148–2163.
HEWITT, J, W., 'The Development of Political Gratitude', *TAPhA* 55 (1924), 35–51.
–, 'The Terminology of "Gratitude" in Greek', *CPh* 22 (1927), 142–161.
HICKLING, C.J.A., 'Centre and Periphery in the Thought of Paul', *Studia Biblica* III (1978), 199–214.
HOCK, R., *The Social Context of Paul's Ministry: Tentmaking and Apostleship* (Philadelphia 1980).
HODGSON, R., 'Valerius Maximus and the Social World of the New Testament', *CBQ* 51/4 (1989), 683–693.
HÖISTAD, R., *Cynic Hero and Cynic King: Studies in the Cynic Conception of Man* (Uppsala 1948).
–, 'Cynicism', in P. Wiener (ed.), *Dictionary of the History of Ideas* Vol.1 (New York 1968), 627–634.

HOLL, K., 'Der Kirchenbegriff des Paulus in seinem Verhältnis zu dem der Urgemeinde', in K.H. Rengstorf (ed.), *Das Paulusbild in der neueren deutschen Forschung* (Darmstadt 1969), 144–178.

HOLMBERG, B., *Paul and Power: The Structure of Authority in the Primitive Church as Reflected in the Pauline Epistles* (Philadelphia 1980).

–, *Sociology and the New Testament: An Appraisal* (Minneapolis 1990).

HOOKER, J.T., 'Χάρις and ἀρετή in Thucydides', *Hermes* 102 (1974), 164–169.

HOOKER, M.D, *Jesus and the Servant: The Influence of the Servant Concept of Deutero-Isaiah in the New Testament* (London 1959).

HORN, R.C., 'Life and Letters in the Papyri', *Classical Journal* 17 (1922), 487–502.

HORRELL, D.G., *The Social Ethos of the Corinthian Correspondence: Interests and Ideology from 1 Corinthians to 1 Clement* (Edinburgh 1996).

–, *Social Scientific Approaches to New Testament Interpretation* (Edinburgh 1999).

HORSLEY, G.H.R., 'A Personalised Aretalogy of Isis', in *id.*, *New Documents Illustrating Early Christianity* Vol.1 (Macquarie University 1981), 10–21.

–, '"Charity Motivated by Piety" in an Epitaph', in *id.*, *New Documents Illustrating Early Christianity* Vol.2 (Macquarie University 1982), 55–56.

–, 'Joining the Household of Caesar', in *id.*, *New Documents Illustrating Early Christianity* Vol.3 (Macquarie University 1983), 7–9.

–, 'δικαιοσύνη', in *id.*, *New Documents Illustrating Early Christianity* Vol.4 (Macquarie University 1987), 144–145.

–, 'Giving Thanks to Artemis', in *id.*, *New Documents Illustrating Early Christianity* Vol.4 (Macquarie University 1987), 127–129.

–, 'Petition Concerning Ephesian Mysteries', in *id.*, *New Documents Illustrating Early Christianity* Vol.4 (Macquarie University 1987), 94–95.

–, 'Sophia, "The Second Phoibe"', in *id.*, *New Documents Illustrating Early Christianity* Vol.4 (Macquarie University 1987), 239–244.

–, 'Koine or Atticism — A Misleading Dichotomy', in *id.*, *New Documents Illustrating Early Christianity* Vol.5 (Macquarie University 1989), 41–48.

–, 'The Inscriptions of Ephesos and the New Testament', *NovT* 34/2 (1992), 106–168.

–, *Id.* and S. Mitchell (eds), *The Inscriptions of Central Pisidia* (Bonn 2000).

HORSLEY, R.A., *Jesus and the Spiral of Violence: Popular Jewish Resistance in Roman Palestine* (San Francisco 1987).

–, 'The Slave Systems of Classical Antiquity and Their Reluctant Recognition by Modern Scholars', *Semeia* 83/84 (1998), 19–66.

–, 'Paul and Slavery: A Critical Alternative to Recent Readings', *Semeia* 84/84 (1998), 153–200.

HOWELL, D.N., 'The Centre of Pauline Theology', *BSac* 151 (1994), 50–70.

HUBERT, H., and M. MAUSS, 'Essai sur la nature et la fonction du sacrifice', *Année Sociologique* 2 (1899), 29–138.

HUGHES, P.E., *Paul's Second Epistle to the Corinthians* (Grand Rapids 1962).

HUMMEL, P., 'Le labeur et la grâce: Étude d'une constellation lexicale. δαπάνη, πόνος et χάρις dans Pindare', *Revue de philologie* 70/2 (1996), 247–254.

HUNT, A.S., and C.C. Edgar, *Select Papyri* (Cambridge, Mass. 1934). 2 Vols.

HUNTER, A.M., *The Epistle to the Romans* (London 1955).

HURTADO, L.W., 'The Jerusalem Collection and the Book of Galatians', *JSNT* 5 (1979), 46–62.

–, 'Jesus as Lordly Example in Philippians 2:5–11', in P. Richardson and J.C. Hurd (eds), *From Jesus to Paul: Studies in Honour of Francis Wright Beare* (Waterloo 1984), 113–126.

–, *One God One Lord: Early Christian Devotion and Ancient Jewish Monotheism* (Philadelphia 1988).
HUTT, R.J.H., 'The Concept of God in the Works of Flavius Josephus', *JJS* 31 (1981), 171–189.
JACOB, E., *Theology of the Old Testament* (London 1958).
JAUBERT, A., *La notion d'alliance dans le judaïsme aux abords de l'ère chrétienne* (Paris 1963).
JAUNCEY, E., *The Doctrine of Grace up to the End of the Pelagian Controversy* (London 1925).
JERVELL, J., 'The Signs of an Apostle: Paul's Miracles', in *id.*, *The Unknown Paul* (Minneapolis 1984), 77–95.
JERVIS, L.A., *The Purpose of Romans: A Comparative Letter Structure Investigation* (Sheffield 1991).
JEWETT, R., 'Paul, Phoebe, and the Spanish Mission', in J. Neusner (ed.), *The Social World of Formative Christianity and Judaism: Essays in Tribute to Howard Kee* (Philadelphia 1988), 142–161.
JOHNSON, L.T., 'On Finding the Lukan Community: A Cautious Cautionary Essay', in P.J. Achtemeier (ed.), *Society of Biblical Literature 1979 Seminar Papers* (Missoula 1979), 87–100.
JOHNSON, V.L., 'The Humanism of Plutarch', *CJ* 66/1 (1970), 26–37.
JONES, C.P., *The Roman World of Dio Chrysostom* (London 1978).
JOUBERT, S, 'Behind the Mask of Rhetoric: 2 Corinthians 8 and the Intra–Textual Relation Between Paul and the Corinthians', *Neot* 26/1 (1992), 101–112.
–, 'Managing the Household: Paul as *Paterfamilias* Of the Christian Household Group in Corinth', in P.F. Esler (ed.), *Modelling Early Christianity: Social–Scientific Studies of the New Testament in Its Context* (London and New York 1995), 213–223.
–, *Paul as Benefactor: Reciprocity, Strategy and Theological Reflection in Paul's Collectio* (Tübingen 2000).
–, 'One Form of Social Exchange or Two? "Euergetism," Patronage, and Testament Studies', *BTB* 31/1 (2001), 17–25.
JUDGE, E.A., *The Social Pattern of the Christian Groups in the First Century* (London 1960).
–, 'The Early Christians as a Scholastic Community. Parts I and II', *JRH* 1/1 (1960), 4–15; 1/3 (1961), 125–137.
–, 'Contemporary Political Models for the Inter–Relations of the New Testament Churches', *Reformed Theological Review* 22/3 (1963), 65–76.
–, 'The Conflict of Educational Aims in New Testament Thought', *Journal of Christian Education* 9 (1966), 32–45.
–, *Id.*, and G.S.R. Thomas, 'The Origin of the Church at Rome: A New Solution?', *Reformed Theological Review* 25/3 (1966), 81–96.
–, 'Paul's Boasting in Relation to Contemporary Professional Practice', *AusBR* 16 (1968), 37–50.
–, 'First Impressions of St. Paul', *Prudentia* 2/2 (1970), 52–58.
–, 'The Decrees of Caesar at Thessalonica', *Reformed Theological Review* 30/1 (1971), 1–7.
–, 'Demythologising the Church: What is the Meaning of "The Body of Christ"?', *Interchange* 11 (1972), 155–167.
–, 'St. Paul and Classical Society', *JAC* 15 (1972), 19–36.
–, 'St. Paul and Socrates', *Interchange* 14 (1973), 106–116.
–, 'Paul as a Radical Critic of Society', *Interchange* 16 (1974), 191–203.

–, *The Conversion of Rome: Ancient Sources of Modern Social Tensions* (Macquarie University 1980).
–, 'The Social Identity of the First Christians: A Question of Method in Religious History', *JRH* 11 (1980), 215–246.
–, 'Moral Terms in the Eulogistic Tradition', in G.H.R. Horsley (ed.), *New Documents Illustrating Early Christianity* Vol.2 (Macquarie University 1982), 105–106.
–, *Rank and Status in the World of the Caesars* (University of Canterbury 1982).
–, 'The Reaction against Classical Education in the New Testament', *Journal of Christian Education* 77 (1983), 7–14.
–, 'Cultural Conformity and Innovation in Paul: Some Clues from Contemporary Documents', *TynBul* 35 (1984), 3–24.
–, 'The Teacher as Moral Exemplar in Paul and in the Inscriptions of Ephesus', in D. Peterson and J. Pryor (eds), *In the Fullness of Time: Biblical Studies in Honour of Archbishop Donald Robinson* (Homebush 1992), 85–201.
–, 'Benefactors at Ephesus' (unpublished paper, Macquarie University 1993).
–, 'Judaism and the Rise of Christianity: A Roman Perspective', *TynBul* 45/3 (1994), 354–368.
–, 'The Rhetoric of Inscriptions', in S.E. Porter (ed.), *Handbook of Classical Rhetoric in the Hellenistic Period 330 BC—AD 400* (Leiden–New York–Köln 1997), 807–828.
–, 'Ancient Beginnings of the Modern World', in T.W. Hillard (*et al.*, ed.), *Ancient History in a Modern University. Volume II: Early Christianity, Late Antiquity, and Beyond* (Grand Rapids 1998), 468–482.
KAMSLER, H.M., '*HESED* — Mercy or Loyalty?', *Jewish Bible Quarterly* 27/3 (1999), 183–185.
KANT, L.H., 'Jewish Inscriptions in Latin and Greek', *ANRW* II 20/2 (1987), 672–713.
KÄSEMANN, E., '"The Righteousness of God" in Paul', in (*id.*) *New Testament Questions of Today* (London 1969), 168–193.
–, *Commentary on Romans* (Grand Rapids 1980: Gmn. orig. 1973).
KASHER, A., *The Jews in Hellenistic and Roman Egypt: The Struggle for Equal Rights* (Tübingen 1985).
KEA, P.V., 'Paul's Letter to Philemon: A Short Analysis of Its Values', *Perspectives in Religious Studies* 23 (1996), 223–232.
KEARSLEY, R.A., 'The Mysteries of Artemis at Ephesus', in S.R. Llewelyn (ed.), *New Documents Illustrating Early Christianity* Vol.6 (Macquarie University 1987), 196–202.
–, 'Ephesus: Neokoros of Artemis', in S.R. Llewelyn (ed.), *New Documents Illustrating Early Christianity* Vol.6 (Macquarie University 1992), 203–206.
–, 'A Civic Benefactor of the First Century in Asia Minor', in S.R. Llewelyn (ed.), *New Documents Illustrating Early Christianity* Vol.7 (Macquarie University 1994), 233–241.
–, 'Women in Public Life in the Roman East: Iunia Theodora, Claudia Metrodora and Phoebe, Benefactress of Paul', *TynBul* 50/2 (1999), 189–211.
KECK, L.E., 'The Poor among the Saints in the New Testament', *ZNW* 56 (1965), 100–124.
–, 'The Poor among the Saints in Jewish Christianity and Qumran', *ZNW* 57 (1966), 66–78.
KENNEDY, H.A.A., *Philo's Contribution to Religion* (London 1919).
KEYES, C.W., 'The Greek Letter of Introduction', *AJP* 56 (1935), 28–44.
KIDD, R.M., *Wealth and Beneficence in the Pastoral Epistles: A 'Bourgeois' Form of Early Christianity?* (Atlanta 1990).

KIM, C.-H., *Form and Structure of the Familiar Greek Letter of Recommendation* (Missoula 1972).
–, 'The Papyrus Invitation', *JBL* 94/3 (1975), 391–402.
KIM, S., *The Origin of Paul's Gospel* (Tübingen 1981).
–, *Paul and the New Perspective: Second Thoughts on the Origin of Paul's Gospel* (Grand Rapids–Cambridge 2002).
KITTEL, G., 'αὐτάρκεια', *TDNT* 1 (1964), 466–467.
KLAUCK, H.–J., 'Dankbar leben, dankbar sterben. εὐχαριστεῖν bei Epiktet', in (*id.*), *Gemeinde, Amt, Sakrament: Neutestamentliche Perspektiven* (Würzburg 1989), 373–390.
KLOPPENBORG, J.S., 'Edwin Hatch, Churches, and Collegia', in B.H. McLean (ed.), *Origins and Method: Towards a New Understanding of Judaism and Christianity* (Sheffield 1993), 212–237.
KOENIG, J., 'Occasions of Grace in Paul, Luke and First–Century Judaism', *ATR* 64/4 (1982), 562–576.
–, *New Testament Hospitality: Partnership with Strangers as Promise and Salvation* (Philadelphia 1985).
KOESTER, H., 'Memory of Jesus' Death and the Worship of the Risen Lord', *HTR* 91/4 (1998), 335–350.
KOSKENNIEMI, H., *Studien zur Idee und Phraseologie des griechischen Briefes bis 400 n. Chr.* (Helsinki 1956).
KÖTTING, B., 'Euergetes', *RAC* 6 (1965), 846–860.
KRAEMER, D., *Responses to Suffering in Classical Rabbinic Literature* (Oxford 1995).
KREITZER, L.J., *Striking New Images: Roman Imperial Coinage and the New Testament World* (Sheffield 1996).
KRENTZ, E., 'The Name of God in Disrepute: Romans 2:17–29 (22–23)', *CurTM* 17/6 (1990), 429–439.
KRUSE, C.G., *The Second Epistle of Paul to the Corinthians: An Introduction* (Grand Rapids 1987).
–, *Paul, the Law, and Justification* (Leicester 1996).
LAATO, T., *Paul and Judaism: An Anthropological Approach* (Atlanta 1995).
LACHS, S.T., 'Rabbinic Sources for New Testament Studies — Use and Misuse', *JQR* 74/2 (1983), 159–173.
LAGRANGE, P.M.–J., *Saint Paul: Épître aux Romains* (Paris 1956).
LAMBRECHT, J., 'Transgressor by Nullifying God's Grace: A Study of Gal 2:18–21', *Bib* 72/2 (1991), 217–236.
LAMPE, P., 'Keine »Sklavenflucht« des Onesimos', *ZNW* 76 1/2 (1985), 135–137.
LANE FOX, R., *Pagans and Christians in the Mediterranean World from the Second Century AD to the Conversion of Constantine* (New York 1986).
LANE, W.L., 'Paul's Legacy from Pharisaism: Light from the *Psalms of Solomom*', *Concordia Journal* 8 (1982), 130–138.
LAPORTE, J., *Eucharistia in Philo* (New York and Toronto 1983).
LAPORTE, J.–M., 'The Mystery of God's Abundance', in J. Plevnik (ed.), *Word and Spirit: Essays in Honor of David Michael Stanley on His 60th Birthday* (Willowdale 1975), 371–409.
LASSEN, E.M., 'The Use of the Father Image in Imperial Propaganda and 1 Corinthians 4:14–21', *TynBul* 42/1 (1991), 127–136.
LAUM, B., *Stiftungen in der griechischen und römischen Antike: Ein Beitrag zur antiken Kulturgeschichte* Vol.2 (Berlin 1914).
LEENHARDT, F.–J., *The Epistle to the Romans: A Commentary* (London 1961).

LENSKI, R.C.H., *The Interpretation to St. Paul's Epistle to the Romans* (Minneapolis 1936).
–, *The Interpretation of 1 and 2 Corinthians* (Minneapolis 1937).
LEVICK, B., *Claudius* (London 1990).
LEWIS, L.A., 'An African American Appraisal of the Philemon–Paul–Onesimus Triangle', in C.H. Felder (ed.), *Stony the Road We Trod: African American Biblical Interpretation* (Minneapolis 1991), 232–246.
LEWIS, N., (ed.) *Leitourgia Papyri: Documents on Compulsory Public Service in Egypt under Roman Rule* (Philadelphia 1963: *TAPhA* 53/9).
LIEFELD, W.L., *The Wandering Preacher as a Social Figure in the Roman Empire* (unpub. Ph.D. diss. Columbia University 1967).
LIEU, J.M., '"Grace to You and Peace": The Apostolic Greeting', *BJRL* 68/1 (1985), 161–178.
LIFSHITZ, B., *Donateurs et fondateurs dans les synagogues juives* (Paris 1967).
LIM, D.S., *The Servant Nature of the Church in the Pauline Corpus* (unpub. Ph.D. diss. Fuller Theological Seminary 1987).
LINSS, W.C., 'The First World Hunger Appeal', *CurTM* 12/4 (1985), 211–219.
LLEWELYN, S.R., 'The Slave of God (Rom 6:22) and Sacral Manumission', in *id.* (ed.), *New Documents Illustrating Early Christianity* Vol.6 (Macquarie University 1992), 70–76.
–, 'A Soldier's Letter Home', in *id.* (ed.), *New Documents Illustrating Early Christianity* Vol.6 (Macquarie University 1992), 156–159.
–, '"Slaves Obey Your Masters": The Legal Liability of Slaves', in *id.* (ed.), *New Documents Illustrating Early Christianity* Vol.7 (Macquarie University 1994), 163–196.
LOADER, B., 'Paul and Judaism — Is He Fighting Strawmen?', *Colloquium* 16/2 (1984), 11–20.
LOEW, O., ΧΑΡΙΣ (Diss. Marburg 1908).
LOFTHOUSE, W.F., '*Hen* and *Hesed* in the Old Testament', *ZAW* 51 (1933), 29–35.
LOHSE, E., *Colossians and Philemon* (Philadelphia 1971).
LOMBARD, H.A., 'Charisma and Church Office', *Neot* 10 (1976), 31–52.
LONGENECKER, B.W., *Eschatology and the Covenant: A Comparison of 4 Ezra and Romans 1–11* (Sheffield 1991).
–, *The Triumph of Abraham's God: The Transformation of Identity in Galatians* (Edinburgh 1998).
LONGENECKER, R.N., *Paul: Apostle of Liberty* (Grand Rapids 1976).
–, *Galatians* (Dallas 1990).
LUTZ, C.E., 'Musonius Rufus "The Roman Socrates"', in A.R. Bellinger (ed.), *YClS* 10 (1947), 3–147.
MACLACHLAN, B., *The Age of Grace: Charis in Early Greek Poetry* (Princeton 1993).
MACMULLEN, R., *Roman Social Relations* (New Haven 1974).
MALAN, F.S., 'The Relationship Between Apostleship and Office in the Theology of Paul', *Neot* 10 (1976), 53–68.
–, 'Bound to Do Right', *Neot* 15 (1981), 118–138.
MALHERBE, A.J., 'The Corinthian Contribution', *ResQ* 3 (1959), 221–233.
–, *Social Aspects of Early Christianity* (Philadelphia 1983: 2nd ed.).
–, *Moral Exhortation: A Greco–Roman Sourcebook* (Philadelphia 1986).
–, *Paul and the Thessalonians: The Philosophic Tradition of Pastoral Care* (Philadelphia 1987).
–, *Ancient Epistolary Theorists* (Atlanta 1988).

–, 'Antisthenes and Odysseus, and Paul at War', in *id.*, *Paul and the Popular Philosophers* (Minneapolis 1989), 91–119.
–, 'Greco–Roman Religion and Philosophy and the New Testament', in E.J. Epp and G.W. MacRae (eds), *The New Testament and Its Modern Interpreters* (Philadelphia 1989), 3–26.
–, 'Paul: Hellenistic Philosopher or Christian Pastor?', in *id.*, *Paul and the Popular Philosophers* (Minneapolis 1989), 67–77.
–, 'New Testament, Traditions and the Theology of Care In', in R.J. Hunter (ed.), *Dictionary of Pastoral Care and Counselling* (Nashville 1990), 789–792.
'Hellenistic Moralists and the New Testament', *ANRW* II 26/1 (1992), 267–333.
MALINA, B., *The New Testament World: Insights from Cultural Anthropology* (Atlanta 1981).
–, *Christian Origins and Cultural Anthropology: Practical Models for Biblical Interpretation* (Atlanta 1986).
MALINOWSKI, B., *Argonauts of the Western Pacific* (London 1922).
MANSON, W., 'Grace in the New Testament', in W.T. Whitely (ed.), *The Doctrine of Grace* (London 1932), 33–60.
MARMORSTEIN, A., *The Doctrine of Merits in Old Rabbinical Literature* (New York 1968: orig. 1920).
–, 'The Imitation of God (Imitatio Dei) in the Haggadah', in *id.*, *Studies in Jewish Theology* (Oxford 1950), 106–121.
MARSHALL, I.H., 'Salvation, Grace and Works in the Later Writings in the Pauline Corpus', *NTS* 42/3 (1996), 339–358.
MARSHALL, P., *Enmity in Corinth: Social Conventions in Paul's Relations with the Corinthians* (Tübingen 1987).
MARTIN, B.L., *Christ and the Law in Paul* (Leiden 1989).
MARTIN, D.B., *Slavery as Salvation: The Metaphor of Slavery in Pauline Christianity* (New Haven 1990).
MARTIN, R.P., *Philippians* (Leicester 1959).
–, *2 Corinthians* (Waco 1986).
–, *A Hymn of Christ: Phil 2:5–11 in Recent Interpretation and in the Setting of the Early Christian Worship* (Downers Grove 1997).
LOUIS MARTYN, J., *Galatians: A New Translation with Introduction and Commentary* (1997).
–, *Theological Issues in the Letters of Paul* (Edinburgh 1997).
MASON, S., 'Paul, Classical Anti–Jewish Polemic, and the Letter to the Romans', in D.J. Hawkin and T. Robinson (eds), *Self–Definition and Self–Discovery in Early Christianity: A Study in Changing Horizons* (Lewiston–Queenston–Lampeter 1990), 181–223.
MASSON, O., 'Pape–Benseleriana VII. Le nom *Charis*, feminin et masculin', *ZPE* 37 (1980), 109–113.
MATERA, F.J., *Galatians* (Collegeville 1992).
MATHEWS, J.B., *Hospitality and the New Testament Church: An Historical and Exegetical Study* (unpub. Ph.D. diss. Princeton 1965).
MATTHEWS, V.H., 'The Unwanted Gift: Implications of Obligatory Gift Giving in Ancient Israel', *Semeia* 87 (1999), 91–104.
MATTINGLY, H., 'The Emperor and His Client', in A.J. Dunston (ed.), *Essays on Roman Culture* (Toronto and Sarasoto 1976), 159–186.
MAUSS, M., *The Gift: The Form and Reason for Exchange in Archaic Societies* (London 1990: Glencoe 1954).

–, *A General Theory of Magic* (London and Boston 1972).
MCCANT, J.W., *2 Corinthians* (Sheffield 1999).
MCCOWN, C.C., 'The Ephesia Grammata in Popular Belief', *TAPhA* 54 (1923), 128–140.
MCGUIRE, M.R.P., 'Epigraphical Evidence for Social Charity in the Roman West', *AJP* 67 (1946), 129–150.
MCKNIGHT, S., 'Collection for the Saints', in G.F. Hawthorne (*et al.*, ed.), *Dictionary of Paul and His Letters* (Downers Grove–Illinois 1993), 43–47.
MCLEAN, B.H., 'The Agrippinilla Inscription: Religious Associations and Early Church Formation', in B.H. McLean (ed.), *Origins and Method: Towards a New Understanding of Judaism and Christianity* (Sheffield 1993), 239–270.
MEALAND, D.L., 'Philo of Alexandria's Attitude to Riches', *ZNW* 69/3 (1978), 258–264.
–, 'The Paradox of Philo's Views of Wealth', *JSNT* 24 (1985), 111–115.
MEEKS, W.A., *The First Urban Christians* (New Haven 1983).
–, *The Moral World of the First Centuries* (Philadelphia 1986).
–, 'The Circle of Reference in Pauline Morality', in D.L. Balch (*et al.*, ed.), *Greek, Romans, and Christians: Essays in Honor of Abraham J. Malherbe* (Minneapolis 1990), 305–317.
–, *The Origins of Christian Morality: The First Two Centuries* (New Haven and London 1993).
MEGGITT, J.J., 'The Social Status of Erastus (Rom 16:23)', *NovT* 38/3 (1996), 218–223.
–, *Paul, Poverty and Survival* (Edinburgh 1998).
MEIJER, P.A., 'Philosophers, Intellectuals and Religion in Hellas', in H.S. Versnal (ed.), *Faith, Hope and Worship: Aspects of Religious Mentality in the Ancient World* (Leiden 1981), 216–263.
MELICK, R.R., 'The Collection for the Saints: 2 Corinthians 8–9', *Criswell Theological Review* 4/1 (1989), 91–177.
MENZIES, A., *The Second Epistle of the Apostle Paul to the Corinthians* (London 1912).
MERITT, B.D., *Corinth. Vol.VIII. Pt.1: Greek Inscriptions 1889—1927* (Cambridge, Mass. 1931).
MICHEL, O., *Der Brief an die Römer* (Göttingen 1978).
MIHALY, E., 'A Rabbinic Defence of the Election of Israel: An Analysis of Sifre Deuteronomy 32:9, Pisqa 312', *HUCA* 35 (1964), 103–135.
MILLAR, F., *The Emperor in the Roman World (31 BC—AD 337)* (New York 1977).
MILLER, J.C., *The Obedience of Faith: The Eschatological People of God, and the Purpose of Romans* (Atlanta 2000).
MITCHELL, M.M., 'New Testament Envoys in the Context of Greco–Roman Diplomatic and Epistolary Conventions: The Example of Timothy and Titus', *JBL* 111/4 (1992), 641–662.
MITCHELL, S., *Regional Epigraphic Catalogues of Asia Minor. The Ankara District: The Inscriptions of North Galatia II* (Oxford 1982).
MITFORD, T.B., 'A Cypriot Oath of Allegiance to Tiberius', *JRS* 50 (1960), 75–79.
MOFFATT, J., *Grace in the New Testament* (London 1931).
MONTEFIORE, C.G., 'Impressions of Christianity from the Points of View of the Non–Christian Religions', *HibJ* 3 (1904), 649–667.
–, *Id.*, and H. Loewe, *A Rabbinic Anthology* (New York 1974).
MONTGOMERY, J.A., 'The Religion of Flavius Josephus', *JQR* 1 (1920), 277–305.
–, 'Hebrew *Hesed* and Greek *Charis*', *HTR* 32/2 (1939), 97–102.
MOO, D., '"Law", "Works of the Law", and Legalism in Paul', *WTJ* 45/1 (1983), 73–100.
–, 'Paul and the Law in the Last Ten Years', *SJT* 40 (1987), 287–307.
–, *Romans* (Grand Rapids 1996).

MOON, W.G., 'Nudity and Narrative: Observations on the Frescoes from the Dura Synagogue', *JAAR* 60/4 (1992), 587–658.
MOORE, G.F., *Judaism in the First Centuries of the Christian Era* (New York 1927). 3 Vols.
MOORE, R.K., 'Issues Involved in the Interpretation of ΔΙΚΑΙΟΣΥΝΗ ΘΕΟΥ in the Pauline Corpus', *Colloquium* 23/3 (1991), 59–70.
MORRIS, L., *The Apostolic Preaching of the Cross* (London 1955).
–, *The Epistle to the Romans* (Leicester 1992).
MOTT, S.C., *The Greek Benefactor and Deliverance from Moral Distress* (unpub. Ph.D. diss. Harvard 1971).
–, 'The Power of Giving and Receiving: Reciprocity in Hellenistic Benevolence', in G.F. Hawthorne (ed.), *Current Issues in Biblical and Patristic Interpretation: Studies in Honor of Merril C. Tenney* (Grand Rapids 1975), 60–72.
–, *Biblical Ethics and Social Change* (Oxford 1982).
MOULE, C.F.D., 'A Christian Understanding of Law and Grace', *Christian Jewish Relations* 14 (1981), 52–61.
–, 'Obligation in the Ethic of Paul', in *id.*, *Essays in New Testament Interpretation* (Cambridge 1982), 261–277.
–, 'Jesus, Judaism, and Paul', in G.F. Hawthorne and O. Betz (eds), *Tradition and Interpretation in the New Testament: Essays in Honor of E. Earle Ellis for His 60th Birthday* (Grand Rapids 1987).
MOULTON, J.H., and G. MILLIGAN, *The Vocabulary of the Greek New Testament* (London 1930).
MOUSSY, C., *Gratia et sa famille* (Paris 1966).
MOXNES, H., 'Honor and Righteousness in Romans', *JSNT* 32 (1988), 61–77.
–, 'Honor, Shame and the Outside World in Paul's Letter to the Romans', in J. Neusner (ed.), *The Social World of Formative Christianity and Judaism: Essays in Tribute to Howard Clark Kee* (Philadelphia 1988), 207–218.
–, 'The Quest for Honour and the Unity of the Community in Romans 12 and in the Orations of Dio Chrysostom', in T. Engberg-Pedersen (ed.), *Paul in His Hellenistic Context* (Edinburgh 1994), 203–230.
MULLINS, T.Y., 'Petition as a Literary Form', *NovT* 5 (1962), 44–50.
–, 'Disclosure: A Literary Form in the New Testament', *NovT* 7 (1964–1965), 44–50.
–, 'Greeting as a New Testament Form', *JBL* 87/4 (1968), 418–426.
–, 'Formulas in the New Testament Epistles', *JBL* 91/3 (1972), 380–390.
MUNCK, J., *Paul and the Salvation of Mankind* (London 1959).
MURPHY–O'CONNOR, J., *St. Paul's Corinth: Texts and Archaeology* (Wilmington 1983).
–, 'Prisca and Aquila', *Bible Review* 8/2 (1992), 40–51, 62.
MURRAY, J., *The Epistle to the Romans: The English Text with Introduction, Exposition, and Notes* (London 1967).
NACHMANSON, E., 'Zu den Motivformeln der griechischen Ehreninschriften', *Eranos* 11 (1911), 180–196.
NANOS, M.D., *The Mystery of Romans: The Jewish Context of Paul's Letter* (Minneapolis 1994).
NARDONI, E., 'The Concept of Charism in Paul', *CBQ* 55/1 (1993), 68–80.
NEUSNER, J., *Early Rabbinic Judaism* (Leiden 1975).
–, 'The Teaching of the Rabbis: Approaches Old and New', *JJS* 27/1 (1976), 23–35.
–, 'The History of Earlier Rabbinic Judaism: Some New Approaches', *HR* 16 (1977), 216–236.
–, 'Comparing Judaisms', *HR* 18 (1978), 178–191.

–, 'The Formation of Rabbinic Judaism: Yavneh (Jamniah) from AD 70—100', *ANRW* II 19/2 (1979), 3–42.
–, 'The Use of the Later Rabbinic Evidence for the Study of Paul', in W.S. Green (ed.), *Approaches to Ancient Judaism* Vol.2 (Ann Arbor 1980), 43–63.
–, 'Mr Sanders' Pharisees and Mine: A Response to E.P. Sanders', *Jewish Law from Jesus to the Mishnah*, *SJT* 44 (1991), 73–95.
NEWELL, K.N.E., 'St. Paul and the Anger of God', *Irish Biblical Studies* 1 (1979), 99–114.
NEWSOME, J.D., *Greeks, Romans, Jews: Currents of Culture in the World of the New Testament* (Philadelphia 1992).
NEYREY, J.H., *Paul in Other Words* (Louisville 1990).
NICHOLSON, G.C., 'Houses for Hospitality', *Colloquium* 19/1 (1986), 1–6.
NICKELSBURG, G.W.E., *Jewish Literature Between the Bible and the Mishnah: An Historical and Literary Introduction* (London 1981).
NICKLE, K.F., *The Collection: A Study in Paul's Strategy* (Chatham 1966).
NOCK, A.D., 'The Historical Importance of Cult Associations', *CR* 38 (1924), 105–109.
–, *Conversion: The Old and the New in Religion from Alexander the Great to Augustine of Hippo* (Oxford 1933).
–, 'Greek Magical Papyri', in *id.*, *Essays on Religion and the Ancient World* Vol.1 (Oxford 1972), 176–194.
–, 'The Vocabulary of the New Testament', in *id.*, *Essays on Religion and the Ancient World* Vol.1 (Oxford 1972), 341–347.
–, '*Soter* and *Euergetes*', in *id.*, *Essays on Religion and the Ancient World* Vol.2 (Oxford 1972), 720–735.
NOLLAND, J., 'Grace as Power', *NovT* 28/1 (1986), 26–31.
NORDLING, J.G., 'Onesimus *Fugitivus*: A Defence of the Runaway Slave Hypothesis in Philemon', *JSNT* 41 (1991), 97–119.
NORTH, H.F., 'Canons and Hierarchies of the Cardinal Virtues in Greek and Latin Literature', in L. Wallach (ed.), *The Classical Tradition: Literary and Historical Studies in Honor of Harry Caplan* (New York 1966), 165–183.
NUTTON, V., 'The Beneficial Ideology', in P.D.A. Garnsey and C.R. Whittaker (eds), *Imperialism in the Ancient World* (Cambridge 1978), 209–221.
NYGREN, A., *Commentary on Romans* (Philadelphia 1949).
O'BRIEN, P.T., 'Thanksgiving and the Gospel in Paul', *NTS* 21 (1974–1975), 144–155.
–, *Introductory Thanksgivings in the Letters of Paul* (Leiden 1977).
–, 'Thanksgiving in Pauline Theology', in D.A. Hagner and M.J. Harris (eds), *Pauline Studies: Essays Presented to F.F. Bruce* (Exeter 1980), 50–66.
–, *The Epistle to the Philippians* (Grand Rapids 1991).
OAKES, P., 'Epictetus (and the New Testament)', *Vox Evangelica* 23 (1993), 39–56.
OBBINK, D., 'The Origin of Greek Sacrifice: Theophrastus on Religion and Cultural History', in W.W. Fortenbaugh and R.W. Sharples (eds), *Theophrastean Studies* Vol.3 (New Brunswick and Oxford 1988), 272–295.
OIKONOMIDES, A.N., 'The Lost Delphic Inscription with the Commandments of the Seven and *P. Univ. Athen* 2782', *ZPE* 37 (1980), 179–183.
OLIVER, J.H., *Demokratia, the Gods, and the Free World* (New York 1972).
OLYAN, S.M., 'Honor, Shame, and Covenant Relations in Ancient Israel and Its Environment', *JBL* 115/2 (1996), 201–218.
ONWU, N., '*Mimetês* Hypothesis: A Key to the Understanding of Pauline Paraenesis', *African Journal of Biblical Studies* 1/2 (1986), 95–112.

OOSTENDORP, W.D., *Another Jesus: A Gospel of Jewish–Christian Superiority in 2 Corinthians* (Kampen 1967).
OSTER, R.E., 'The Ephesian Artemis as an Opponent of Early Christianity', *JAC* 19 (1976), 27–44.
–, 'Numismatic Windows into the Social World of Early Christianity', *JBL* 101/2 (1982), 195–223.
–, '"Show me a denarius": Symbolism of Roman Coinage and Christian Beliefs', *ResQ* 28/2 (1985–1986), 107–115.
–, 'Holy Days in Honour of Artemis', in G.H.R. Horsley (ed.), *New Documents Illustrating Early Christianity* Vol.4 (Macquarie University 1987), 74–82.
–, 'Ephesus as a Religious Centre under the Principate, I. Paganism before Constantine', *ANRW* II 18/3 (1990), 1661–1728.
–, '"Congregations of the Gentiles" (Rom 16:4): A Culture–Based Ecclesiology in the Letters of Paul', *ResQ* 40/1 (1998), 39–52.
PANAGOPOULOS, C., 'Vocabulaire et mentalité dans les *Moralia* de Plutarche', *DHA* 3 (1977), 197–235.
PANIKULAM, G., *Koinônia in the New Testament: A Dynamic Expression of Christian Life* (Rome 1979).
PAO, D.W., *Thanksgiving: An Investigation of a Pauline Theme* (Downers Grove 2002).
PARDEE, D., 'An Overview of Ancient Hebrew Epistolography', *JBL* 97/3 (1978), 321–346.
PATTERSON, O., *Slavery and Social Death: A Comparative Study* (Cambridge, Mass. 1982).
PEEK, W., 'Grabepigramm aus Aegypten', *ZPE* 21 (1976), 133–134.
PENNA, R., 'The Jews in Rome at the Time of the Apostle Paul', in *id.*, *Paul the Apostle: Jew and Greek Alike* (Philadelphia 1996), 19–47.
PETERMAN, G.W., *Paul's Gift from Philippi: Conventions of Gift–Exchange and Christian Giving* (Cambridge 1997).
–, 'Romans 15:26: Make a Contribution or Establish Fellowship?', *NTS* 40/3 (1994), 457–463.
PETERSEN, N.R., *Rediscovering Paul: Philemon and the Sociology of Paul's Narrative World* (Philadelphia 1985).
PETERSON, B.K., *Eloquence and the Proclamation of the Gospel in Corinth* (Atlanta 1998).
–, 'Conquest, Control, and the Cross: Paul's Self–Portrayal in 2 Corinthians 10–13', *Int* 52/3 (1998), 258–270.
PETERSON, D., *Engaging with God: A Biblical Theology of Worship* (Leicester 1992).
PFITZNER, V.C., *Paul and the Agon Motif: Traditional Athletic Imagery in the Pauline Literature* (Leiden 1967).
PHILIPP, G.B., 'Kritzeleien eines erleichterten Lehrers auf einem hölzernen Buchdeckel', *Gymnasium* 85 (1978), 151–159.
PHILIPPSON, R., 'Zur epikureischen Götterlehre', *Hermes* 51 (1916), 568–608.
PICKETT, R.W., 'The Death of Christ as Divine Patronage', in E.H. Lovering (ed.), *Society of Biblical Literature 1993 Seminar Papers* (Atlanta 1993), 726–739.
PIEPKORN, A.C., '*Charisma* in the New Testament and the Apostolic Fathers', *CTM* 42/6 (1971), 369–389.
PITT–RIVERS, J., 'Honor and Social Status', in J.G. Peristiany (ed.), *Honour and Shame: The Values of Mediterranean Society* (Chicago 1966), 21–77.
–, 'Postscript: The Place of Grace in Anthropology', in J.G. Peristiany and J. Pitt–Rivers (eds), *Honor and Grace in Anthropology* (Cambridge 1992), 215–246.

PLUMMER, A., *A Critical and Exegetical Commentary on the Second Epistle of St. Paul to the Corinthians* (Edinburgh 1915).
POBEE, J.S., *Persecution and Martyrdom in the Theology of Paul* (Sheffield 1985).
POUILLOUX, J., *Choix d'inscriptions grecques: textes, traductions et notes* (Paris 1960).
PRICE, S.R.F., *Rituals and Power: The Roman Imperial Cult in Asia Minor* (Cambridge 1984).
PROBST, H., *Paulus und der Brief: Die Rhetorik des antiken Briefes als Form der paulinischen Korintherkorrespondenz (1 Cor 8–10)* (Tübingen 1992).
QUARLES, C.L., 'The Soteriology of R. Akiba and E.P. Sanders' *Paul and Palestinian Judaism*', *NTS* 42/2 (1996), 185–195.
QUET, M.-H., 'Rhétorique, culture et politique: le fonctionnement du discours idéologique chez Dion de Pruse et dans les *Moralia* de Plutarque', *DHA* 4 (1978), 51–119.
RAJAK, T., 'Benefactors in the Greco-Jewish Diaspora', in H. Cancik (*et al.*, Hrsg.), *Geschichte — Tradition — Reflexion: Festschrift für Martin Hengel zum 70. Geburtstag Band I: Judentum* (Tübingen 1996), 305–319.
RAPSKE, B.M., 'The Prisoner Paul in the Eyes of Onesimus', *NTS* 37/2 (1991), 187–203.
REED, W.L., 'Some Implications of *Hen* for Old Testament Religion', *JBL* 73/1 (1954), 34–41.
RENDALL, F., 'The Pauline Collection for the Saints', *The Expositor* 8 (1893), 321–336.
RENGSTORF, K.H., 'ἀποστέλλω, ἀπόστολος', *TDNT* 1 (1964), 398–447.
REUMANN, J., *Righteousness in the New Testament* (Philadelphia 1982).
REYNOLDS, J.M., *Aphrodisias and Rome* (London 1982).
RICH, A.N.M., 'The Cynic Conception of *Autarkeia*', *Mnemosyne* 9 (1956), 23–29.
RIDDERBOS, H., *Paul: An Outline of His Theology* (Grand Rapids 1975).
RIDDLE, D.W., 'Early Christian Hospitality: A Factor in the Gospel Transmission', *JBL* 57 (1938), 141–154.
RIGAUX, B., *The Letters of St. Paul: Modern Studies* (Chicago 1968).
RIST, J.M., 'Epicurus on Friendship', *CPh* 75 (1980), 121–129.
ROBERT, L., 'Épigrammes relatives à des gouverneurs', *Hellenica* IV (1948), 78–84.
–, 'Τροφεύς et Ἀριστεύς', *Hellenica* XI–XII (1960), 569–576.
–, 'De Delphes a l'Oxus: inscriptions grecques nouvelles de la Bactriane', *Comptes Rendues de l'Académie des Inscriptions et Belles Lettres*, (1968), 416–457.
ROBERTS, E.S., *An Introduction to Greek Epigraphy. Pt. 1: The Archaic Inscriptions and the Greek Alphabet* (Cambridge 1887).
ROBINSON, J.A.T., *Wrestling with Romans* (London 1979).
ROEHRS, W.R., 'The Grace of God in the Old Testament', *CTM* 23/12 (1952), 895–910.
ROGERS, G.M., *The Sacred Identity of Ephesos: Foundation Myths of a Roman City* (London 1991).
ROHRBAUGH, R.L., 'Methodological Considerations in the Debate Over the Social Class Status of Early Christians', *JAAR* 52/3 (1984), 519–546.
ROLLER, O., *Das Formular der paulinischen Briefe: Ein Beitrag zur Lehre vom antiken Briefe* (Stuttgart 1933).
RONIGER, L., 'Modern Patron–Client Relations and Historical Clientelism: Some Clues from Ancient Republican Rome', *Archives européennes de sociologie* 24/1 (1983), 63–95.
ROSS, A., 'The Grace of our Lord Jesus Christ', *EvQ* 13/3 (1941), 219–225.
ROUSSILLON, J., 'Les termes hébreux en théologie chrétienne: justification de leur choix', *RevThom* 38 (1960), 80–99.
ROUTLEDGE, R., 'ḤESED as Obligation: A Re-examination', *TynBul* 46/1 (1995), 179–196.

RYBERG, I.S., 'Vergil's Golden Age', *TAPhA* 89 (1958), 112–131.
RYDER SMITH, C., *The Bible Doctrine of Grace* (London 1956).
SAKENFIELD, K.D., *The Meaning of HESED in the Hebrew Bible: A New Inquiry* (Missoula 1978).
SALDARINI, A.J., '"Form Criticism" of Rabbinic Literature', *JBL* 96/2 (1977), 275–314.
SALLER, R.P., *Personal Patronage under the Early Empire* (Cambridge 1982).
–, 'Poverty, Honor and Obligation in Imperial Rome', *Criterion* 37/2 (1998), 12–20.
SAMPLEY, J.P., 'Roman Law and Paul's Conception of the Christian Community', in J. Jervell and W.A. Meeks (eds), *God's Christ and His People* (Oslo 1977), 158–174.
–, *Pauline Partnership in Christ: Christian Community in Light of Roman Law* (Philadelphia 1980).
–, 'Paul, His Opponents in 2 Corinthians 10–13 and the Rhetorical Handbooks', in J. Neusner (ed.), *The Social World of Formative Christianity and Judaism* (Philadelphia 1988), 162–177.
SANDAY, W., and A.C. HEADLAM, *A Critical and Exegetical Commentary on the Epistle to the Romans* (Edinburgh 1902).
SANDBACH, F.H., *The Stoics* (London 1975).
SANDERS, B., 'Imitating Paul: 1 Cor 4:16', *HTR* 74/4 (1981), 353–363.
SANDERS, E.P., 'Patterns of Religion in Paul and Rabbinic Judaism: A Holistic Method of Comparison', *HTR* 66/4 (1973), 455–478.
–, 'The Covenant as a Soteriological Category and the Nature of Salvation in Palestinian and Hellenistic Judaism', in R. Hamerton–Kelly and R. Scroggs (eds), *Jews, Greeks and Christians: Cultures in Late Antiquity. Essays in Honour of William David Davies* (Leiden 1976), 11–44.
–, *Paul and Palestinian Judaism: A Comparison of Patterns of Religion* (London 1977).
–, 'On the Question of Fulfilling the Law in Paul and Rabbinic Judaism', in C.K. Barrett (ed.), *Donum Gentilicium: New Testament Studies in Honour of David Daube* (Oxford 1978), 103–126.
–, 'Puzzling out Rabbinic Judaism', in W.S. Green (ed.), *Approaches to Ancient Judaism* Vol.2 (Ann Arbor 1980), 65–79.
–, *Paul, the Law, and the Jewish People* (Philadelphia 1983).
–, 'Judaism and the Grand "Christian" Abstractions: Love, Mercy, and Grace', *Int* 39/4 (1985), 357–372.
–, *Judaism: Practice and Belief 63 BCE—66 CE* (Philadelphia 1992).
SANDMEL, S., 'Virtue and Reward in Philo', in J.L. Crenshaw and J.T. Willis (eds), *Essays in Old Testament Ethics* (New York 1974), 217–223.
–, 'Philo Judaeus: An Introduction to the Man, His Writings, and His Significance', *ANRW* II 21/1 (1983), 3–46.
SATAKE, A., 'Apostolat und Gnade bei Paulus', *NTS* 15/1 (1968), 96–107.
SAVAGE, T.B., *Power through Weakness: Paul's Understanding of the Christian Ministry in 2 Corinthians* (Cambridge 1996).
SCHECHTER, S., *Aspects of Rabbinic Theology* (New York 1961).
SCHERMANN, T., 'Εὐχαριστία und εὐχαριστεῖν in ihrem Bedeutungswandel bis 200 n. Chr.', *Philologus* 69 (1910), 375–410.
SCHLATTER, A., *Wie sprach Josephus von Gott?* (Gütersloh 1910).
SCHLIER, H., *Der Römerbrief* (Freiburg 1977).
SCHMID, W., 'Götter und Menschen in der Theologie Epikurs', *RhM* 94 (1951), 97–156.
SCHNEIDER, J., 'Brief', *RAC* II (1954), 564–587.
SCHOEPS, H.J., *Paul: The Theology of the Apostle in the Light of Jewish Religious History* (Philadelphia 1961).

SCHREINER, T.R., *The Law and Its Fulfilment: A Pauline Theology of Law* (Grand Rapids 1993).
–, *Romans* (Grand Rapids 1998).
Apostle of God's Glory in Christ. A Pauline Theology (Downers Grove 2001).
SCHRENK, G., 'δικαιοσύνη', *TDNT* 2 (1964), 192–210.
SCHUBERT, P., 'Form and Function of the Pauline Letters', *JR* 19 (1939), 365–377.
–, *Form and Function of the Pauline Thanksgivings* (Berlin 1939).
SCHULZ, T.N., *The Meaning of Charis in the New Testament* (Genova 1971).
SCHÜTZ, J.H., *Paul and the Anatomy of Apostolic Authority* (Cambridge 1975).
SCHWABE, M., and B. LIFSHITZ, *Beth She'arim. Volume II: The Greek Inscriptions* (Jerusalem 1974).
SCOTT, M., 'Charis in Homer and the Homeric Hymns', *AClass* 26 (1983), 1–13.
–, 'Charis from Hesiod to Pindar', *AClass* 27 (1984), 1–13.
SCROGGS, R., *The Last Adam: A Study in Pauline Anthropology* (Philadelphia 1966).
–, 'Paul as Rhetorician: Two Homilies in Romans 1–11', in R. Hamerton–Kelly and R. Scroggs (eds), *Jews, Greeks and Christians. Religious Cultures in Late Antiquity: Essays in Honor of William David Davies* (Leiden 1976), 271–298.
–, *Paul for a Day* (Philadelphia 1977).
SEAFORD, R., *Reciprocity and Ritual: Homer and Tragedy in the Developing City–State* (Oxford 1994).
SEELEY, D., *The Noble Death: Graeco–Roman Martyrology and Paul's Concept of Salvation* (Sheffield 1990).
–, 'Rulership and Service in Mark 10:41–45', *NovT* 35/3 (1993), 234–250.
SEESEMANN, H.J., *Der Begriff Koinōnia im Neuen Testament* (Göttingen 1933).
SEGAL, A.F., 'Covenant in Rabbinic Writings', in *id.* (ed.), *The Other Judaisms of Late Antiquity* (Atlanta 1987), 147–165.
–, *Paul the Convert: The Apostolate and Apostasy of Saul the Pharisee* (New Haven and London 1990).
SEIFRID, M.A., *Justification by Faith: The Origin and Development of a Central Pauline Theme* (Leiden–New York–Köln 1992).
–, 'Blind Alleys in the Controversy over the Paul of History', *TynBul* 45/1 (1994), 73–95.
SEVENSTER, J.N., *Paul and Seneca* (Leiden 1961).
SHERK, R.K., *Roman Documents from the Greek East: Senatus Consulta and Epistulae to the Age of Augustus* (Baltimore 1969).
–, *The Roman Empire: Augustus to Hadrian* (Cambridge 1988).
SIEGERT, F., *Drei hellenistisch–jüdische Predigten: Ps.–Philon, „Über Jona", „Über Simson" und „Über die Gottesbezeichnung, wohltätig verzehrendes Feuer". I. Übersetzung aus dem Armenischen und sprachliche Erläuterungen* (Tübingen 1980).
SILVA, M., 'The Law and Christianity: Dunn's New Synthesis', *WTJ* 53/2 (1991), 339–353.
SIMON, M., *Hercule et le Christianisme* (Paris 1955).
SIMPSON, A.D., 'Epicureans, Christians, Atheists in the Second Century', *TAPhA* 72 (1941), 372–381.
SKARD, E., *Zwei religiös–politische Begriffe: Euergetes–Concordia* (Oslo 1932).
SKUTRIS, J., 'Epistolographie', *PWSup* V (1931), 185–220.
SLOAN, R.B., 'Paul and the Law: Why the Law Cannot Save', *NovT* 33/1 (1991), 35–60.
SMITH, C.R., *The Bible Doctrine of Grace* (London 1956).
SMITH, D.E., 'Frederick W. Danker, *Benefactor*', *CBQ* 46/1 (1984), 150–152.
SMITH, J.Z., *Drudgery Divine: On the Comparison of Early Christianities and the Religions of Antiquity* (Chicago 1990).

SMITH, M., 'A Comparison of Early Christian and Early Rabbinic Tradition', *JBL* 82 (1963), 169–176.
SMITH, R., 'Justification in "The New Perspective on Paul"' *Reformed Theological Review* 58/1 (1999), 16–30.
–, 'A Critique of the "New Perspective" on Justification', *ibid.* 58/2 (1999), 98–113
SMITH, T.E., 'Hostility to Wealth in Philo of Alexandria', *JSNT* 19 (1983), 85–97.
SNAITH, N.H., *The Distinctive Ideas of the Old Testament* (London 1950).
SNODGRASS, K.R., 'Justification by Grace — to the Doers: An Analysis of the Place of Romans 2 in the Theology of Paul', *NTS* 32/1 (1986), 72–93.
SOARDS, M.L., 'Käsemann's "Righteousness" Re-examined', *CBQ* 49/2 (1987), 264–267.
SOLMSEN, F., 'Theophrastus and Political Aspects of the Belief in Providence', *GBRS* 19/1 (1978), 91–98.
SPICQ, C., *Théologie morale du Nouveau Testament* Tome 1 (Paris 1965).
–, *Theological Lexicon of the New Testament* (Peabody 1994: Fr. orig. 1978). 3 Vols.
SPILSBURY, P., 'God and Israel in Josephus: A Patron–Client Relationship', in S. Mason (ed.), *Understanding Josephus: Seven Perspectives* (Sheffield 1998), 172–191.
–, 'Josephus', in D.A. Carson (*et al.*, ed.), *Justification and Variegated Nomism. Volume 1 — The Complexities of Second Temple Judaism* (Tübingen 2001), 241–260.
STÄHLIN, G., 'Ἴσος, ἰσότης, ἰσότιμος', in G. Kittel (ed.), *TDNT* Vol.3 (Grand Rapids 1965), 343–355.
STAMBAUGH, J.E., 'Social Relations in the City of the Early Principate: State of Research', in P.J. Achtemeier (ed.), *Society of Biblical Literature 1980 Seminar Papers* (Missoula 1980), 75–99.
STANLEY, D., 'Become Imitators of Me: The Pauline Conception of Apostolic Tradition', *Bib* 40 (1959), 859–877.
–, 'Imitation in Paul's Letters: Its Significance for His Relationship to Jesus and to His Own Christian Foundations', in P. Richardson and J.C. Hurd (eds), *From Jesus to Paul: Studies in Honour of Francis Wright Beare* (Waterloo 1984), 127–141.
STANSELL, G., 'The Gift in Ancient Israel', *Semeia* 87 (1999), 65–90.
STAUFFER, E., *Christ and the Caesars: Historical Sketches* (London 1955).
STEEN, H.A., 'Les clichés épistolaires dans les lettres sur papyrus grecques', *C & M* 1 (1938), 119–176.
STEGNER, W.R., 'The Ancient Jewish Synagogue Homily', in D.E. Aune (ed.), *Greco–Roman Literature and the New Testament* (Atlanta 1988), 51–69.
STENDAHL, K., *Paul among Jews and Gentiles* (London 1977).
STEVENSON, T.R., 'The Ideal Benefactor and the Father Analogy in Greek and Roman Thought', *CQ* 42/2 (1992), 421–436.
STOEBE, H.J., '*haésaed*', in E. Jenni and C. Westermann (Hrsg.), *Theologisches Handwörterbuch zum Alten Testament* Bd.I (Zürich 1971), 600–621.
STONE, M.E., *Jewish Writings of the Second Temple Period: Apocrypha, Pseudepigrapha, Qumran Sectarian Writings, Philo, Josephus* (Assen 1984).
STONEHOUSE, N.B., *Paul before the Areopagus and Other New Testament Studies* (London 1957).
STOWERS, S.K., 'Social Status, Public Speaking and Private Teaching: The Circumstances of 'Paul's Preaching Activity', *NovT* 26/1 (1984), 59–82.
–, 'The Social Sciences and the Study of Early Christianity', in W.S. Green (ed.), *Approaches to Ancient Judaism: Studies in Judaism and Its Greco–Roman Context* Vol.5 (Atlanta 1985), 149–181.
–, *Letter Writing in Greco–Roman Antiquity* (Philadelphia 1986).

–, 'Social Typification and the Classification of Ancient Letters', in J. Neusner (ed.), *The Social World of Formative Christianity and Judaism* (Philadelphia 1988), 78–90.
–, *A Rereading of Romans: Justice, Jews, and Gentiles* (New Haven and London 1994).
STRACHAN, R.H., *The Second Epistle of Paul to the Corinthians* (London 1935).
STRELAN, J.G., 'Burden–Bearing and the Law of Christ: A Re-examination of Galatians 6:2', *JBL* 94/2 (1975), 266–276.
STROM, M., *Reframing Paul: Conversations in Grace and Community* (Downers Grove 2000).
STUHLMACHER, P., *Das paulinische Evangelium I: Vorgeschichte* (Göttingen 1968).
–, 'The Apostle Paul's View of Righteousness', in *id., Reconciliation, Law and Righteousness* (Philadelphia 1986).
–, *A Challenge to the New Perspective: Revisiting Paul's Doctrine of Justification with an Essay by Donald Hagnar* (Downers Grove 2001).
STYLER, G.M., 'The Basis of Obligation in Paul's Christology and Ethics', in B. Lindars and S.S. Smalley (eds), *Christ and Spirit in the New Testament: Studies in Honour of C.F.D. Moule* (Cambridge 1973), 175–187.
SURBURG, R.F., 'Pauline *Charis*: A Philological, Exegetical, and Dogmatical Study', *CTM* 29/10 (1958), 721–741.
SYME, R., *The Roman Revolution* (Oxford 1939).
TALBERT, C.H., 'Money Management in Early Mediterranean Christianity: 2 Corinthians 8–9', *RevExp* 86/3 (1989), 232–262.
TASKER, R.V.G., *The Second Epistle of Paul to the Corinthians* (London 1958).
TAYLOR, L.R., *Party Politics in the Age of Caesar* (Berkeley 1971).
THEISSEN, G., *The Social Setting of Pauline Christianity: Essays on Corinth* (Philadelphia 1982).
–, *Social Reality and the Early Christians: Theology, Ethics, and the World of the New Testament* (Edinburgh 1992).
THEOBALD, M., *Die überströmende Gnade: Studien zu einem paulinischen Motivfeld* (Würzburg 1982).
THIELMAN, F., *From Plight to Solution: A Jewish Framework for Understanding Paul's View of the Law in Galatians and Romans* (Leiden 1989).
THRAEDE, K., *Grundzüge griechisch–römischer Brieftopik* (München 1970).
THRALL, M.E., *The First and Second Letters of Paul to the Corinthians* (Cambridge 1965).
–, *A Critical and Exegetical Commentary on the Second Epistle to the Corinthians* Vol.2 (Edinburgh 2000).
THYEN, H., *Studien zur Sündenvergebung im Neuen Testament und seinen alttestamentlichen und jüdischen Voraussetzungen* (Göttingen 1970).
TIEDE, D.L., *Jesus and the Future* (Cambridge 1990).
TOD, M.N., 'Clubs and Societies in the Greek World', in *id., Ancient Inscriptions: Sidelights on Greek History* (Chicago 1932), 71–96.
TOMSON, P.J., *Paul and the Jewish Law: Halakha in the Letters of the Apostle to the Gentiles* (Assen 1990).
TORRANCE, T.F., *The Doctrine of Grace in the Apostolic Fathers* (Edinburgh 1948).
TRAVIS, S.H., 'Paul's Boasting in 2 Corinthians 10–12', *SE* 6 (1973), 527–532.
TREBILCO, P., 'Asia', in D.W.J. Gill and C. Gempf (eds), *The Book of Acts: Vol.2. Graeco–Roman Setting* (Carlisle 1994), 291–362.
TRENCH, R.C., *Synonyms of the New Testament* (Grand Rapids 1948).
TROMPF, G.W., *Payback: The Logic of Retribution in Melanesian Religions* (Cambridge 1994).

TUCKETT, C.M., 'A Cynic Q?', *Bib* 70/2 (1989), 349–376.
TURNER, M., *The Holy Spirit and Spiritual Gifts Then and Now* (Carlise 1996).
URBACH, E.E., *The Sages: Their Concepts and Beliefs* (Jerusalem 1987).
VAAGE, L.E., *Q: The Ethos and Ethics of an Itinerant Intelligence* (unpub. Ph.D. diss. Claremont Graduate School 1987).
–, *Galilean Upstarts: Jesus' First Followers According to Q* (Valley Forge 1994).
VALENTIN, L., 'De l'idée de Dieu dans Plutarche', *RevThom* 14 (1914), 313–327.
VAN BAAL, J., *Reciprocity and the Position of Women: Anthropological Papers* (Assen–Amsterdam 1975).
VAN DER HORST, P.W., *Ancient Jewish Epitaphs* (Kampen 1991).
VANDERLIP, V.F., *The Four Greek Hymns of Isidorus and the Cult of Isis* Vol.12 (Toronto: American Studies in Papyrology 1972).
VASSILIADIS, P., 'ΣΤΑΥΡΟΣ: Centre of the Pauline and Apostolic Ministry', in A. Vanhoye (ed.), *L' apôtre Paul: personnalité, style et conception du ministère* (Leuven 1986), 247–253.
–, 'The Collection Revisited', *Delt. Bib. Mel.* 21/2 (1992), 42–48.
–, 'Equality and Justice in Classical Antiquity and in Paul: The Social Implications of the Pauline Collection', *St. Vladimir's Theological Quarterly* 36/1–2 (1992), 51–59.
VELIGIANNI, C., 'Ehrendekret aus Gazoros (Ostmakedonien)', *ZPE* 51 (1983), 105–114.
–, 'Χάρις in den attischen Ehrendekreten der klassischen Zeit und die Ergänzung in IG I. 3(101), Z. 35–37, 51–52', *The Ancient History Bulletin* 3/2 (1989), 36–39.
VERBRUGGE, V.D., *Paul's Style of Church Leadership Illustrated by His Instructions to the Corinthians on the Collection: To Command or not to Command* (San Francisco 1992).
VERSNAL, H.S., 'Religious Mentality in Ancient Prayer', in *id.* (ed.), *Faith, Hope, and Worship* (Leiden 1981), 1–64.
VEYNE, P., *Bread and Circuses: Historical Sociology and Political Pluralism* (Oxford 1990: Fr. orig. 1976).
VIDMAN, L., *Sylloge Inscriptionum Religionis Isiacae et Sarapiacae* (Berlin 1969).
VON LIPS, H., 'Der Apostolat des Paulus — ein Charisma? Semantische Aspekte zu χάρις–χάρισμα und anderen Wortpaaren im Sprachgebrauch des Paulus', *Bib* 66/3 (1985), 305–343.
VOM BROCKE, B., *Thessaloniki – Stadt des Kassander und Gemeinde des Paulus. Eine frühe christliche Gemeinde des Paulus* (Tübingen 2001).
WAGNER, G., 'Le Scandale de la croix expliqué par le chant du Serviteur d'Isaïe 53. Réflexion sur Philippiens 2/6–11', *ETR* 61 (1986), 177–187.
WAITHE, M.E., *A History of Women Philosophers Volume 1: Ancient Women Philosophers 600 BC—500 AD* (Dordrecht 1987).
WALDMANN, H., *Die kommagenischen Kultreformen unter König Mithridates I. Kallinikos und seinem Sohne Antiochus I* (Leiden 1973).
WALLACE–HADRILL, A., 'The Golden Age and Sin in Augustan Ideology', *P&P* 95 (1982), 19–36.
–, (ed.), *Patronage in Ancient Society* (London and New York 1990).
WALTERS, J.C., *Ethnic Issues in Paul's Letter to the Romans: Changing Self–Definitions in Earliest Roman Christianity* (Valley Forge 1993).
WALTZING, J.–P., *Étude historique sur les corporations professionnelles chez les Romains* (New York 1970: Fr. orig. 1895). 4 Vols.
WANAMAKER, C.A., 'A Case against Justification by Faith', *Journal of Theology for Southern Africa* 42 (1983), 37–49.
WATSON, F., *Paul, Judaism and the Gentiles* (Cambridge 1986).

WEAVER, P.R.C., *Familia Caesaris: A Social Study of the Emperor's Freedmen and Slaves* (Cambridge 1972).
WEDDERBURN, A.J.M., *The Reasons for Romans* (Edinburgh 1988).
–, 'Paul's Collection: Chronology and History', *NTS* 48/1 (2002), 95–110.
WELBORN, L.L., 'The Runaway Paul', *HTR* 92/2 (1999), 115–163.
WELLES, C.B., *Royal Correspondence in the Hellenistic Period* (London 1934).
WENGST, K., *Humility: Solidarity of the Humiliated* (Philadelphia 1988: Gmn. orig. 1987).
WESTERHOLM, S., *Israel's Law and the Church's Faith: Paul and His Recent Interpreters* (Grand Rapids 1988).
WETTER, G.P., *Charis: Ein Beitrag zur Geschichte des ältesten Christentums* (Leipzig 1913).
WETTSTEIN, J., *Novum Testamentum Graecum* (Amsterdam 1752). 2 Vols.
WHELAN, C.F., 'Amica Pauli: The Role of Phoebe in the Early Church', *JSNT* 49 (1993), 67–85.
WHITE, J.L., 'Introductory Formulae in the Body of the Pauline Letter', *JBL* 90/1 (1971), 91–97.
–, *The Body of the Greek Letter* (Missoula 1972).
–, *The Form and Structure of the Official Petition: A Study in Greek Epistolography* (Missoula 1972).
–, *Id.*, and K.A. Kensinger, 'Categories of Greek Papyrus', in G. MacRae (ed.), *Society of Biblical Literature 1976 Seminar Papers* (Cambridge, Mass. 1976), 79–91.
–, 'The Greek Documentary Letter Tradition Third Century BCE to Third Century CE', *Semeia* 22 (1981), 89–106.
–, 'Saint Paul and the Apostolic Letter Tradition', *CBQ* 45/3 (1983), 433–444.
–, 'New Testament Epistolary Literature in the Framework of Ancient Epistolography', *ANRW* II 25/2 (1984), 1730–1756.
–, *Light from Ancient Letters* (Philadelphia 1986).
–, *The Apostle of God: Paul and the Promise of Abraham* (Peabody 1999).
WHITE, L.M., 'Social Authority in the House Church Setting and Ephesians 4:1–16', *ResQ* 29/4 (1987), 209–228.
–, *Building God's House in the Roman World: Architectural Adaptation among Pagans, Jews, and Christians* (Baltimore and London 1990).
–, 'Finding the Ties that Bind: Issues from Social Description', *Semeia* 56 (1992), 3–22.
WIEDEMANN, T.W., *Greek and Roman Slavery* (London and Canberra 1981).
WIEFEL, W., 'The Jewish Community in Rome and the Origins of Roman Christianity', in K.P. Donfried (ed.), *The Romans Debate: Revised and Expanded Edition* (Peabody, Mass. 1991), 85–101.
WILCKENS, U., *Der Brief an die Römer* (Zürich 1980).
WILES, G.P., *Paul's Intercessory Prayers: The Significance of the Intercessory Prayer Passages in the Letters of Paul* (Cambridge 1974).
WILKEN, R.L., 'Collegia, Philosophical Schools, and Theology', in S. Benko and J.J. O'Rourke (eds), *The Catacombs and the Colosseum: The Roman Empire as the Setting of Primitive Christianity* (Valley Forge 1971), 268–291.
–, *The Christians as the Romans Saw Them* (New Haven 1984).
WILLIAMS, D.J., *Paul's Metaphors: Their Context and Character* (Peabody 1999).
WILLIAMS, S.K., 'The "Righteousness of God" in Romans', *JBL* 99/2 (1980), 241–290.
WINGER, M., 'From Grace to Sin: Names and Abstractions in Paul's Letters', *NovT* 41/2 (1999), 145–175.
WINKLER, R., 'Die Gnade im Neuen Testament', *ZST* 10 (1933), 642–680.

WINTER, B.W., 'The Lord's Supper at Corinth: An Alternative Reconstruction', *Reformed Theological Review* 37/3 (1978), 73–82.
–, 'The Public Honouring of Christian Benefactors: Romans 13:3–4 and 1 Peter 2:14–15', *JSNT* 34 (1988), 87–103.
–, 'Secular and Christian Responses to Corinthian Famines', *TynBul* 40 (1989), 86–106.
–, '"If a man does not wish to work ...". A Cultural and Historical Setting for 2 Thessalonians', *TynBul* 40/2 (1989), 305–315.
–, 'Is Paul among the Sophists?', *The Reformed Theological Review* 53/1 (1994), 28–38.
–, *Seek the Welfare of the City: Christians as Benefactors and Citizens* (Grand Rapids 1994).
–, *Philo and Paul among the Sophists* (Cambridge 1997).
WINTER, J.G., *Life and Letters in the Papyri* (Ann Arbor 1933).
WINTER, S.C., 'Paul's Letter to Philemon', *NTS* 33/1 (1987), 1–15.
WISCHNITER, M., 'Notes to a History of the Jewish Guilds', *HUCA* 33/2 (1950), 245–263.
WITHERINGTON III, B., 'Christology', in G.F. Hawthorne (*et al.*, ed.), *Dictionary of Paul and His Letters* (Downers Grove–Leicester 1993), 100–115.
–, *Conflict and Community in Corinth: A Socio–Rhetorical Commentary on 1 and 2 Corinthians* (Carlisle 1995).
–, *Grace in Galatia: A Commentary on Paul's Letter to the Galatians* (Grand Rapids 1998).
WOBBE, J., *Der Charis–Gedanke bei Paulus: Ein Beitrag zur neutestamentlichen Theologie* (Münster 1932).
WOLFSON, H.A., *Philo: Foundations of Religious Philosophy in Judaism, Christianity, and Islam* (Cambridge, Mass. 1962).
WOODHEAD, A.G., 'Competitive Outlay and Community Profit: φιλοτιμία in Democratic Athens', *C&M* 34 (1983), 55–74.
WOODHEAD, A.G., *The Study of Greek Inscriptions* (Oxford 1959).
WORTHINGTON, I., *Greek Orators II: Dinarchus and Hyperides* (Warminster 1999).
WREDE, W. *Paul* (Boston 1908).
WRIGHT, C.J.H., *Living as the People of God: The Relevance of Old Testament Ethics* (London 1983).
–, *God's People in God's Land: Family, Land, and Property in the Old Testament* (Exeter 1990).
WRIGHT, N.T., 'The Paul of History and the Apostle of Faith', *TynBul* 29 (1978), 61–88.
–, *The Messiah and the People of God: A Study in Pauline Theology with Particular Reference to the Argument of the Epistle of Romans* (unpub. Ph.D. diss. Oxford University 1980).
–, *The Climax of the Covenant: Christ and the Law in Pauline Theology* (Edinburgh 1991).
YOUNG, N.H., 'An Aristophanic Contrast to Philippians 2:6–7', *NTS* 45/1 (1999), 153–155.
YOUTIE, H.C., 'The Kline of Sarapis', *HTR* 41 (1948), 9–29.
ZAHN, T., *Der Brief des Paulus an die Römer ausgelegt* (Leipzig 1910).
ZAPPELLA, M., 'A proposito di Febe PROSTATIS (Rm 16,2)', *RivB* 37/2 (1989), 167–171.
ZELLER, D., *Charis bei Philon und Paulus* (Stuttgart 1992).
ZIELINSKI, T., '*Charis* and *Charites*', *CQ* 18 (1924), 158–163.
ZIESLER, J.A., *The Meaning of Righteousness in Paul: A Linguistic and Theological Study* (Cambridge 1972).
–, *Paul's Letter to the Romans* (London 1989).
ZOBEL, H.–J., 'ḥesed', *TDOT* 5 (1986), 44–64.

Index of Modern Authors

Abegg, M. 103
Achtemeier, P.J. 221, 243
Alexander, P.S. 157, 158, 159
Allo, E.B. 308
Amaru, B.H. 134, 135, 136, 137
Andrews, S.B. 333
Armstrong, A.H. 172, 173, 197
Arnold, C.E. 91, 243, 244
Arzt, P. 65, 328
Ascough, R.S. 32, 257
Attridge, H.W. 134, 136, 172, 197
Aune, D.E. 90, 222, 252, 257
Aus, R.D. 304, 305
Austin, M.M. 41
Avemarie, R. 102

Badian, E. 15
Bagnall, R.S. 238
Baird, W. 67
Balch, D.L. 169
Bammel, E. 265
Banks, R. 278, 279, 280
Barclay, J.M.G. 105, 152, 305, 328, 329, 330
Barnett, P. 296, 297, 304
Barr, J. 100
Barrett, C.K. 152, 162, 168, 220, 247, 252, 296, 324, 332
Bartchy, S.S. 236, 328, 330
Barth, K. 213
Barth, M. 328, 329
Barton, S.C. 216
Bassler, J.M. 303, 304, 309, 313
Bauckham, R. 102
Baumert, N. 279
Becker, J. 212, 278, 308
Beckheuer, B. 292
Beker, J.C. 105, 212, 226, 283, 284, 286

Bell, H.I. 79, 93
Bellinger, W.H. 263
Benedum, J. 47, 302, 316
Benko, S. 90, 213
Berger, K. 10, 65, 226, 294, 305, 309
Best, E. 252, 300, 320, 342
Betz, H.D. 67, 90, 91, 93, 252, 272, 275, 284, 296, 302, 303, 307, 314, 327, 332
Bilde, P. 134
Black, D.A. 247
Black, M. 221
Blanke, H. 328, 328
Blau, P.M. 19
Bloch, M. 19
Boak, A.E.R. 29
Boccaccini, G. 169
Bockmuehl, M. 262
Boers, H. 10
Boobyer, G.H. 273
Bolt, P.G. 197, 198, 222
Botha, P.J.J. 29
Bolkestein, H. 5, 15, 41, 290, 291
Bonz, M.P. 147
Borgen, P. 151
Bormann, L. 16, 327
Bornkam, G. 278
Bowersock, G.W. 225
Brady, T.A. 85
Brandt, L.W. 294
Branick, V.P. 32
Brant, J.A. 320
Bray, G. 99
Bréhier, É. 116
Brenk, F.E. 186
Briggs, S. 236
Brockhaus, U. 238, 279, 280
Brooks, R. 164
Brooten, B. 31, 147, 148

Brown, C. 223, 263, 265
Brown, M.J. 236
Brown, J.P. 251
Bruce, F.F. 17, 168, 220, 242, 277, 296, 304
Bruck, E.F. 323
Buchanan, G.W. 157
Bultmann, R. 252
Burke, T.H. 342
Burkert, W. 53, 54
Burnish, R.F.G. 9, 107, 110, 117
Burstein, S.M. 238, 248, 316
Byrne, B. 102, 217, 221

Cadbury, H.J. 31
Callahan, A.D. 328, 329
Capes, D.B. 250
Carson, D.A. 100, 102, 103, 119, 158, 159, 160
Case, S.J. 216, 283, 289
Cassidy, R.J. 333
Castelli, E.A. 315
Cerfaux, L. 9, 281
Chacko, J. 300
Chambry, É. 173, 177, 180, 186, 198, 201, 205
Charlesworth, J.M. 100, 111, 112
Chaumartin, F.-R. 167
Chow, J.K. 7, 16, 291
Clark, G.R. 109
Clark, M.E. 230
Clark, W.P. 4, 38, 39, 339
Clarke, A.D. 7, 16, 31, 224, 225, 282
Clements, R.E. 217
Cohen, S.J.D. 146
Collins, J.N. 296
Combes, I.A. 235
Connolly, A.L. 216
Conzelmann, H. 9, 35, 115, 116
Cooper, K.T. 104
Cope, L. 212
Corrigan, G.M. 214, 219, 220
Corriveau, R. 255, 271, 294
Countryman, L. Wm. 30, 32, 243, 255, 290, 291, 295

Craddock, F.B. 251
Craffert, P.F. 15, 22, 23
Cranfield, C.E.B. 99, 212, 221, 251, 326
Crossan, J.D. 170, 322
Cullmann, O. 308

Dahl, N.A. 300
Daniélou, J. 115
Danker, F.W. 6, 15, 16, 17, 26, 29, 35, 41, 59, 85, 148, 216, 223, 225, 227, 230, 234, 245, 249, 251, 252, 254, 255, 269, 275, 282, 291, 296, 323, 333, 334, 335, 336, 341
Davies, G.N. 160, 221
Davies, W.D. 97, 160
Davis, S. 4
de Boer, W.P. 319
de Lacey, D.R. 250
de Roo, J.C. 99
deSilva, D.A. 7, 12, 13, 14
de St Croix, G.E.M. 15
DeWitt, N.W. 167, 172, 197, 306
de Witt Burton, E. 310
Deichgräber, K. 9, 34, 285
Deidun, T. 104, 159, 160, 242
Deines, R. 103
Deissmann, A. 31, 64, 67, 85, 237, 238, 275
Delling, G. 123
Den Boer, W. 264, 291
Denis, A.-M. 277
Deonna, W. 232
Derow, P. 238
Derrett, J.D.M. 328
Dibelius, M. 167
Di Bella, M.P. 20
Dickie, M.W. 46
Dihle, A. 15, 168
Dittmann, H. 107, 110, 119, 158
Dodd, C.H. 107, 221
Donfried, K.P. 213
Donlan, W. 15
Dörrie, H. 10
Doty, W.G. 65, 67, 68

Doughty, D.J. 9, 108, 226
Downing, F.G. 27, 118, 172, 198, 258, 261, 273
Drexler, H. 28
Dunn, J.D.G. 98, 99, 100, 103, 104, 159, 212, 221, 223, 224, 250, 251, 252, 268, 279, 280, 284, 285, 286, 287, 310, 319
du Toit, A.B. 11

Eastman, B. 10, 11, 99, 101, 227, 234, 247, 249
Eckhert, J. 306
Edgar, C.C. 211
Ehrenberg, V. 228, 229, 231, 239, 241
Elliott, J.H. 13, 14, 16, 46
Ellis, E.E. 32, 212, 305
Engberg-Pedersen, T. 172
Engelmann, H. 85
Enns, P. 242
Ernst, M. 31
Erskine, A. 15
Esler, P.F. 13, 104
Evans, C.A. 102
Exler, F.X. 67

Falk, D. 103
Farmer, W.R. 263
Fee, G.D. 294
Feldman, L.H. 135
Festugière, A.J. 197
Filson, F.V. 322
Finley, M.I. 42
Fiore, B. 320
Fitzgerald, J.T. 302, 332, 334
Fitzmyer, J.A. 79, 103, 221
Flack, E.E. 9, 107, 109
Foerster, W. 162
Forbes, C. 67, 275, 276, 278, 332, 334, 339
Forbes, C.A. 29
Fortenbaugh, W.W. 188
Fowl, S. 327
France, R.T. 250
Frank, R. 21

Franklin, W.M. 297
Franzmann, J.W. 8, 15, 53
Fridrichsen, A. 333
Friesen, S.J. 52
Frisch, E. 114, 148
Fung, R.Y.K. 212, 242, 279
Funk, R.W. 65
Funke, H. 258
Furnish, V.P. 105, 252, 296, 306

Gager, J.G. 13, 159
Gagnon, R.A. 213
Gardiner, A.W. 14
Garland, D.E. 252, 339
Garnet, P. 105
Garrett, S.R. 90
Gärtner, B. 168
Gaston, L. 103, 159
Gelzer, M. 15
Georgi, D. 10, 177, 227, 232, 233, 271, 272, 273, 282, 284, 285, 291, 296, 297, 304, 307, 308, 323, 327
Giannantoni, G. 258
Gill, C. 15
Gill, D.W.J. 31
Ginsburg, M. 29
Glad, C.E. 167, 213
Glombitza, O. 248
Glueck, N. 109
Goodspeed, E.J. 67
Goudge, H.I. 252
Goulet-Cazé, M.-O. 198
Gowan, D.E. 102
Graf, F. 243
Grant, M. 139
Green, W.S. 158
Greenberg, M.S. 14
Gregory, C.A. 19, 21
Guerra, A.J. 222
Guerra, A.T. 167
Guillet, J. 227, 277
Gundry, R.H. 100, 101, 104, 105, 159, 160, 242, 248
Gundry Volf, J.M. 241, 249
Gurval, R.A. 230

Index of Modern Authors

Grundmann, W. 9, 226
Hadzsits, D.P. 196
Hagnar, D.A. 97, 101, 162
Hainz, J. 298
Hamel, G. 255, 305
Hammond, M. 238
Hands, A.R. 5, 15, 36, 56, 250, 286, 289, 290, 314, 318, 319, 322
Hansen, G.W. 152
Hanson, R.P.C. 168, 252
Harnack, A. 307-308
Harris, M.J. 235, 250, 269, 328, 331
Harris, W.V. 29
Harrison, J.R. 32, 222, 227, 283, 325
Hatch, E. 32
Hauck, F. 265
Hawthorne, G.F. 36, 241
Hays, R.B. 220, 223
Headlam, A.C. 220, 226, 231
Hellegouarc'h, J. 15, 28
Hendrix, H.L. 6, 16, 17, 211. 239, 245
Hengel, M. 11, 103, 113, 151, 159, 169, 187, 212, 222, 225
Herford, R.T. 97, 103, 163
Héring, J. 252
Herman, G. 6, 7, 15, 310, 342
Herrmann, P. 239
Hershbell, J. 186, 192
Hewitt, J.W. 35, 40
Hickling, C.J.A. 212
Hock, R.F. 276, 332
Hodgson, R. 199
Höistad, R. 252, 257, 279
Holl, K. 309
Holmberg, B. 13, 305, 308, 309, 342
Hooker, J.T. 58
Hooker, M.D. 262
Horn, R.C. 66
Horsley, G.H.R. 17, 25, 26, 28, 32, 46, 56, 66, 216, 223, 236, 243, 245, 269, 285, 286, 294
Horsley, R.A. 236, 237, 319, 328
Horrell, D.G. 13, 32
Howell, D.N. 212
Hubert, H. 17

Hughes, P.E. 252, 295
Hummel, P. 8
Hunt, A.S. 211
Hunter, A.M. 220
Hurtado, L.W. 250, 262, 295

Jacob, E. 107
Jaubert, A. 123
Jauncey, E. 9, 107
Jervell, J. 247, 298
Jervis, L.A. 213
Jewett, R. 31, 326
Johnson, L.T. 305
Johnson, V.L. 171
Jones, A.H.M. 228, 229, 231, 239, 241
Jones, C.P. 170
Joubert, S. 7, 8, 11, 13, 14, 15, 16, 109, 251, 290, 296, 297, 306, 310, 311, 315, 342
Judge, E.A. 7, 14, 15, 16, 22, 23, 26, 27, 30, 31, 32, 45, 52, 67, 168, 213, 236, 238, 239, 241, 267, 275, 281, 282, 292, 293, 294, 301, 320, 322, 323, 326, 331, 332, 339, 340

Kamsler, H.M. 109
Kant, L.H. 149
Käsemann, E. 221, 223, 248
Kasher, A. 147
Kea, P.V. 328
Kearsley, R.A. 31, 224, 243, 244, 246, 290, 295
Keck, L.E. 300, 305
Kennedy, H.A.A. 116, 119
Keyes, C.W. 67
Kidd, R.M. 7, 32, 132, 170
Kim, C.-H. 65, 67
Kim, S. 11, 104, 159, 277
Kittel, G. 282
Klauck, H.-J. 185
Kloppenborg, J.S. 32
Koenig, J. 252, 272, 295, 304, 314, 327, 330
Koester, H. 232
Koskenniemi, H. 65, 68, 83, 84, 86, 298

Kötting, B. 4
Kraemer, D. 222
Kreitzer, L.J. 233
Krentz, E. 217
Kruse, C.G. 104, 252

Laato, T. 101
Lachs, S.T. 157
Lagrange, P.M.-J. 221
Lambrecht, J. 249
Lampe, P. 328
Lane, W.L. 114
Lane Fox, R. 215
LaPorte, J-M. 14, 119, 120, 123
Lassen, E.M. 342
Laum, B. 28, 56, 66, 218, 248
Leenhardt, F.-J. 220, 238
Lenski, R.C.H. 221, 252, 296
Levick, B. 89
Lévi-Strauss, C. 19
Lewis, L.A. 328
Lewis, N. 132
Liefeld, W.L. 277
Lieu, J.M. 230
Lifshitz, B. 122, 147, 148, 149
Lim, D.S. 279
Linss, W.C. 300
Llewelyn, S.R. 83, 223, 235, 237
Loader, B. 104
Lofthouse, W.F. 107, 109
Lohse, E. 331
Loew, O. 9, 34, 324
Loewe, H. 114, 164
Lombard, H.A., 279
Longenecker, B.W. 99, 152
Longenecker, R.N. 164, 310
Louis Martyn, J. 105, 310
Lutz, C.E. 258
Lyall, F. 235

MacLachlan, B. 8, 15
MacMullen, R. 29, 30
Malan, F.S. 235, 279

Malherbe, A.J. 32, 65, 68, 168, 169, 172, 178, 258, 259, 261, 295, 298, 300, 306
Malina, B.J. 13, 126
Malinowski, B. 20
Manson, W. 9, 34, 91, 107, 117
Marmorstein, A. 160, 164
Marshall, I.H. 25
Marshall, P. 7, 36, 42, 276, 306, 325, 332, 337
Martin, B.L. 160
Martin, D.B. 235, 240, 257, 258, 261
Martin, R.P. 248, 252, 261, 262, 296, 306
Mattingly, H. 233
Mason, S. 101, 104, 214
Masson, O. 44
Matera, F.J. 310
Mathews, J.B. 35
Matthews, V.H. 109
Mattingly, H. 15
Mauss, M. 17, 19, 91
McCant, J.W. 333
McCown, C.C. 243
McGrath, A. 9
McGuire, M.R.P 291
McKnight, S. 307
McLean, B.H. 32
Mealand, D.L. 118
Meeks, W.A. 4, 30, 31, 32, 66, 168, 234, 237, 290, 292, 298, 305, 314, 327
Meggitt, J.J. 31, 32
Meijer, P.A. 188
Melick, R.R. 251, 299, 302, 304, 307, 314
Menzies, A. 252
Michel, O. 226, 238
Mihaly, E. 159
Millar, F. 15, 49
Miller, J.C. 213
Milligan, G. 35
Mitchell, M.M. 306
Mitchell, S. 56, 249
Mitford, T.B. 239

Moffatt, J. 9, 10, 34, 35, 107, 116, 134, 226, 286
Montefiore, C.G. 97, 114, 162, 164
Montgomery, J.A. 107, 134
Moo, D. 105, 114, 221, 226, 227, 231
Moon, W.G. 124
Moore, G.F. 97, 160
Moore, R.K. 223
Morris, L. 221
Mott, S.C. 1, 5, 6, 15, 16, 18, 36, 118, 125, 133, 173, 245, 252, 284, 290, 314, 315
Moule, C.F.D. 105, 241, 242
Moulton, J.H. 35
Moussy, C. 28
Moxnes, H. 215, 216
Mullins, T.Y. 65
Munck, J. 277, 304
Murphy-O'Connor, J. 148
Murray, J. 221

Nachmanson, E. 301
Nanos, M.D. 213
Nardoni, E. 279, 281
Neusner, J. 65, 67, 100, 123, 158
Newell, K.N.E. 198
Newsome, J.D. 169
Neyrey, J.H. 13
Nicholson, G.C. 291
Nickelsburg, G.W.E. 169
Nickle, K.F. 170, 296, 297, 300, 304, 305, 308, 309, 313
Nock, A.D. 5, 29, 90, 93, 152, 289
Nolland, J. 244
Nordling, J.G. 328
North, H.F. 223
Nutton, V. 49
Nygren, A. 221

Obbink, D. 188
O'Brien, P.T. 261, 262, 269
Oikonomides, A.N. 45
Oliver, J.H. 34
Olyan, S.M. 114
Onwu, N. 320

Oostenendorp, W.D. 304, 305
Oster, R. 214, 233, 244

Panagopoulos, C. 37, 38
Panikulam, G. 251, 297, 299, 300
Pao, D.W. 11, 14, 217, 269
Pardee, D. 79
Patterson, O. 237
Peek, W. 33, 45
Penna, R. 214
Peristiany, J.G. 14, 18, 19, 20
Peterman, G.W. 7, 8, 14, 15, 69, 82, 84, 128, 140, 225, 255, 286, 298, 299, 309, 325, 326, 327, 329, 330, 331, 333, 342
Petersen, N.R. 13, 328, 329, 330
Peterson, B.K. 333, 342
Peterson, D. 216
Pfitzner, V.C. 273
Philipp, G.B. 41
Philippson, R. 196
Pickett, R.W. 215, 224, 240
Piepkorn, A.C. 279
Pitt-Rivers, J. 14, 18, 19, 20
Plummer, A. 252, 296
Pobee, J.S. 225
Pouilloux, J. 55
Price, S.R.F. 53, 211
Probst, H. 65

Quarles, C.L. 162
Quet, M.-H. 37

Rajak, T. 146
Rapske, B.M. 328
Reed, W.L. 107
Rendall, F. 307
Rengstorf, K.H. 273, 279
Reumann, J. 223
Reynolds, J.M. 53
Rich, A.N.M. 282
Ridderbos, H. 212
Riddle, D.W. 295
Rigaux, B. 65
Robert, L. 45, 46, 49, 342

Roberts, E.S. 27
Robinson, J.A.T. 221
Roehrs, W.R. 106, 107
Rogers, G.M. 42
Rohrbaugh, R.L. 32, 255
Roller, O. 65
Roniger, L. 15
Ross, A. 250
Roussillon, J. 107
Routledge, R. 109
Ryberg, I.S. 230
Ryder Smith, C. 9

Sakenfield, K.D. 109
Saldarini, A.J. 158
Saller, R.P. 15, 16, 22, 49, 265
Sampley, J.P. 67, 298, 332
Sanday, W. 220, 226, 231
Sanders, B. 320
Sanders, E.P. 24, 97, 98, 100, 101, 102, 103, 134, 158, 159, 160, 162, 212, 221, 242
Sandmel, S. 118, 124
Satake, A. 277
Savage, T.B. 263
Schechter, S. 97, 162
Schermann, T. 12, 119, 120, 269
Schlatter, A. 134
Schlier, H. 226, 231
Schmid, W. 197
Schneider, J. 68
Schoeps, H.J. 107, 164
Schreiner, T.R. 100, 101, 103, 105, 221, 225, 279
Schrenk, G. 222, 223
Schubert, P. 12, 24, 33, 64, 65, 119, 185, 213, 269
Schulz, T.N. 9, 35, 107, 117, 294
Schütz, J.H. 13, 247
Schwabe, M. 122, 147
Schwemer, A.M. 11, 151, 154
Schwer, W. 290
Scott, M. 8
Scroggs, R. 97, 105, 152, 226
Seaford, R. 15, 42

Seeley, D. 225, 257, 262
Seesemann, H.J. 296, 297, 300
Segal, A.F. 158, 160, 162
Seifrid, M.A. 101, 102, 103
Sevenster, J.N. 199
Shapiro, S.P. 14
Sharper, P.J. 333
Sherk, R.K. 28, 44, 88, 224, 228, 254
Shutt, R.J.H. 134
Siegert, F. 151, 153, 154, 155, 156, 157
Silva, M. 100, 102
Simon, M. 257
Simpson, A.D. 190
Skard, E. 4, 143, 252
Sloan, R.B. 105, 242
Smith, C.R. 107
Smith, D.E. 35, 37
Smith, J.Z. 292
Smith, M. 157
Smith, R. 99, 100
Smith, T.E. 118
Snaith, N.H. 107
Snodgrass, K.R. 286
Soards, M.L. 221
Solmsen, F. 188
Spicq, C. 12, 33, 55, 227, 229, 238, 243, 244, 267, 271
Spilsbury, P. 101
Stählin, G. 257
Stambaugh, M. 30
Stanley, D. 319, 320
Stansell, G. 17, 109
Stauffer, E. 228, 232, 233
Steen, H.A. 66
Stegner, W.R. 151
Stendahl, K. 98-99
Stevenson, T.R. 342
Stoebe, H.J. 107
Stone, M.E. 169
Stonehouse, N.B. 168
Stowers, S.K. 14, 64, 65, 66, 67, 68, 105, 213, 245, 275, 276
Strachan, R.H. 252
Strom, M. 286
Stuhlmacher, P. 97, 105, 223, 229

Styler, G.M. 241
Surburg, R.F. 9, 35, 91, 107, 117
Sykutris, J. 68
Syme, R. 15

Talbert, C.H. 304, 308, 314
Tasker, R.V.G. 252
Taylor, L.R. 15
Tcherikover, V. 79
Theissen, G. 13, 31, 32, 236, 282, 289, 291, 293
Theobald, M. 10, 11, 73, 226, 231, 272, 273, 296
Thielman, F. 105, 160
Thomas, G.S.R. 213
Thraede, K. 68, 298
Thrall, M.E. 252, 296, 306, 307, 308, 309
Thyen, H. 117
Tiede, D.L. 233
Tod, M.N. 29
Tomson, P.J. 284
Torrance, T.F. 9, 35, 107, 108, 117
Travis, S.H. 332
Trebilco, P. 244, 245, 246
Trench, R.C. 107, 109, 171
Trompf, G.W. 17, 20
Tuckett, C.M. 172
Turner, M. 279

Urbach, E.E. 160

Vaage, L.E. 172, 252
Valentin, L. 186
Van Baal, J. 14
van der Horst, P.W. 79, 149
Vanderlip, V.F. 54
Vassiliadis, P. 292, 309, 327, 340
Veligianni, C. 33, 319
Versnal, H.S. 44, 53
Verbrugge, V.D. 292, 311
Veyne, P. 6, 15, 27, 49, 230, 251, 290, 291, 314, 316
Vidman, L. 46, 47
vom Brocke, C. 17

von Lips, H. 277

Wagner, G. 262
Waithe, M.E. 178
Waldmann, H. 59
Wallace-Hadrill, A. 6, 15, 232
Walters, J.C. 214
Waltzing, J.-P. 29
Wanamaker, C.A. 23, 212
Watson, F. 13, 159
Weaver, P.R.C. 234
Wedderburn, A.J.M. 213, 305
Welborn, L.L. 333
Welles, C.B. 27, 29, 128, 334
Wengst, K. 262
Westerholm, S. 100, 105, 159, 160, 164
Wetter, G.P. 10, 12, 33, 34, 64, 91, 115, 116, 117, 120, 134, 138, 238, 244, 279, 285
Wettstein, J. 252, 256
Whelan, C.F. 31, 290, 325, 326
White, J.L. 10, 65, 67, 84, 100, 228, 235
White, L.M. 146-147, 148, 170, 214, 290, 293, 323, 325, 326
Whitehead, D. 41
Wiedemann, T.W. 235
Wiefel, W. 214
Wilckens, U. 238
Wiles, G.P. 64, 269, 272, 273
Williams, D.J. 235
Williams, S.K. 220, 223
Wilken, R.L. 30, 32
Wilson, S. 32
Winger, M. 10
Winkler, R. 9
Winter, B.W. 7, 16, 17, 31, 36, 39, 41, 42, 168, 228, 236, 276, 291, 320, 333
Winter, J.G. 66
Winter, S.C. 328
Wischniter, M. 147
Witherington III, B. 57, 227, 265, 282, 299, 310, 313, 315, 327

Wobbe, J. 9, 227, 238, 246, 269, 278, 279, 280, 285
Wolfson, H.A. 117
Woodhead, A.G. 37, 39
Woodhead, D. 39
Worthington, I. 336
Wrede, W. 98
Wright, C.J.H. 327
Wright, N.T. 99, 159

Young, N.H. 263

Youtie, H.C. 85

Zappella, M. 31, 295
Zeller, D. 12, 13, 120, 227, 269, 270, 271, 272, 279, 280, 281, 307
Zielinski, T. 9, 34
Zahn, T. 238
Ziesler, J. 221, 223
Zimmerli, W. 9, 107
Zobel, H.-J. 109

Old Testament

Genesis	
3:17-19	233
6:8	122, 136
6:9	108, 124, 136
9:8	136
9:11	124
9:11-13	136
9:15-17	136
15:6	156
17:2	123, 123
17:4	125
18:3	108
19:19	107
21:23	109
21:27	109
30:27	108
32:5	108
33:8	108
33:10	108
33:15	108
34	156
34:11	108
37:21-22	136
38	156
39	129
39:2-3	129
39:4	108
39:5	129
39:7-20	156
39:9b	129
39:21	107, 108, 129, 161
39:23	129
40:14	109
43:14	108
45:8	127
47:25	108
47:29	108
50:4	108
50:15ff	142
50:19-20	142

Exodus	
3:21	108
11:3	108
12:1-13	123
12:21-27	123
12:36	108
12:43-49	123
16:18	327
19:4-5	113
20:12	130
22:5	130
22:27	162
33:12	108
33:13	108
33:16	108
33:17	108
33:19	161
34:9	108

Leviticus
19:10	264
19:15	218
19:18	321
22:35-37	130
23:22	264
25:23	137
25:36	130
25:38	130

Numbers
11:11	108
11:15	107
14:7	137
15:37-41	162
18:18ff	327
32:5	108

Deuteronomy
1:7	218
4:37	113
6:4-9	162
7:7-9	113
8:7-9	137
8:18	130
9:5	123
9:6	113, 137
10:14-15	113
10:17	218
11:12	137
11:13-21	162
15:8	122
16:1-8	123
16:19	218
23:19	143
24:3	108
24:19	264
25:4	327
30:9-10	125
32:10-11	113
32:35	321

Joshua
2:12	109
2:14	109

Judges
1:24	109
6:17	107
8:35	109
13:1-25	154
16:15ff	155

Ruth
2:2	108
2:10	108
2:13	108

1 Samuel
2:30	114
8:7	228
20:8	109
20:14ff	109
28	145
28:16-19	145

2 Samuel
2:5-6	109
7:14-15	109
9:1	109
10:2	109

1 Kings
1:18	108
2:7	109
3:6	109
8:23	114, 145
8:23-25	109
16:22	108
20:3	108
20:29	108
25:8	108
27:5	108

2 Kings
14:22	108
15:25	108

1 Chronicles
16:26-27	114
17:13-14	109
19:2	109

Index of Passages

2 Chronicles
6:14	114, 145
19:7	218

Ezra
10:3	138

Nehemiah
1:5	114
9:32	114

Esther
	109
2:9	107, 108
2:15	108, 161
2:17	107
5:8	108
7:3	108
8:5	108

Job
29:12	264
34:19	218
34:28	264
35:7	321
41:11	321

Psalms
9:2(10:2)	263
9:30(10:9)	263
11(12):5	263
13(14):5	263
14:20	263
19:7	263
21(22):24	263
24:7ff	228
29:1-2	114
33(34):6	263
36(37):14	263
37:21-22	162
39(40):17	263
40(41):1	263
42:9	163
69(70):5	263
71(72):4	264
71(72):12	264
71(72):13	264
83(84):11	108
85(86):1	264
87(88):15	263
89:1-4	109
89:28	109
89:28-29	109
89:33	109
91:15	114
95:5-6	114
101(102) tit.	264
104:1	114
106:45	109, 114
108(109):16	264
111:5	114
111:9	114
111(112):9	265, 307
112(113):15	264
123:2-3	161
123:3	161
136	114
139(140):12	264

Proverbs
	107
1:9	108, 160
3:4	108, 160
3:9-10	114
3:22	108
3:34	108, 162
4:9	108, 160
5:19	108
7:5	108
10:14	338
10:32	108
11:1	338
11:16-18	338
11:21	338
11:27	108
12:2	108
12:6	338
13:15	108
14:3	338
14:31	114
15:2	338

15:7	108	*Jeremiah*	
15:14	338	1:5	277
17:5	263	1:16	277
17:7	338	9:24	338
17:8	108	51:57	228
18:6-7	338		
18:22	108	*Ezekiel*	
19:1	338	16:1-52	113
21:26	290	18:12	263
22:1	108	22:29	263
22:7	263		
25:10	108	*Daniel*	
28:23	108, 263	1:8	112
		1:9	161
Ecclesiastes		2:28-29	245
5:3	338	4:24	290
9:11	108	9:4	114
10:12	108		
10:14	338	*Hosea*	
		2:14-23	113
Song of Solomon		9:10	113
7:2	162	10:12	304, 307, 322
Isaiah		*Amos*	
3:15	263	2:7	263
6:5	228	3:2	113
10:2	263	4:1	263
30:18	161	5:11	263
32:2	161	8:4	263
42:6-7	277		
43:20	114	*Zephaniah*	
49:1	277	3:10	304
49:5-6	277		
53:5-6	262	*Haggai*	
53:10-12	262	1:6	114
55:5	307		
55:10	304, 307, 322	*Zechariah*	
60:1-7	304	6:14	108
61:6	304	12.10	108, 161
66:18-20	304		
66:19	304	*Malachi*	
66:20	304, 305	1:6	114

Apocrypha

Baruch	
1.12	110
2.14	110

1 Esdras	
6.5	110
8.4	110, 111
8.80	110

2 Esdras	
4.29ff	226

Judith	
8.23	111
10.8	110

1 Maccabees	
1.9	111
5.20	111
10.60	110
14.25	111

2 Maccabees	
2.21	97
3.33	111
6-7	262
8.1	97
9.20	111
14.38	97

4 Maccabees	
	169
4.26	98
5.8	110
11.2	110

Prayer of Manasseh	
12-14	162

Sirach	
	109, 169
1.13	110
3.3	102
3.18	110
3.30	102, 114
3.31	111
4.2	263
7.19	110
7.27-28	340
7.33	279
8.19	110
10.23	263
12.1	111
12.1-2	226
13.20	264
13.21	263
17.24	111
24.16	111
24.17	110
26.13	110
26.15	110
30.6	111
30.16	110
31.4	263
32.2	110
35.10	110
35.21	110
38.30	279
40.17	111
40.22	110
42.2	110
44.24	110

Tobit	
1.13	110
4.7	264
4.7ff	114
7.18	110
9.20	264
12.8	114
12.18	110
14.10	114

Wisdom		4.15	107, 110
	116, 169	8.21	110
2	262	13-15	153
3.9	107, 110	14.26	110, 111
3.10	110	18.2	111
3.14	110	29.21-28	111
3.19	110		

Pseudepigrapha

Joseph and Aseneth		Life of Adam and Eve	
4.7	112		102
13.15	112		
		Lives of the Prophets	
2 Baruch		4.3	112
	102		
		Odes of Solomon	
1 Enoch			113
5.7	111	5.3	113
32.3	234	7.5	113
60.8	234	7.10	113
60.23	234	7.22	113
70.3	234	7.26	113
77.3	234	9.5	113
		15.8	113
Epistle of Aristeas		20.7	113
	113, 116, 165, 169	20.9	113
226	113	21.1	113
230	113	21.2	113
238	113	25.4	113
249	111	29.3	113
278	113	29.5	113
		33.1	34-35, 113
4 Ezra		31.7	113
	102	33.10	113
4.50	227	34.6	113
13.13	304	41.3	113
Pseudo-Phocylides		Psalms of Solomon	
9	113		103
23	290		114

17.34	304

Sibylline Oracles
2.54	279
4	112
4.46	112
4.189	112
5	112
5.59	111
5.328-332	112

Testament of Dan
6.10	221

Testament of Job
11.1-3	296

Testament of Joseph
3.4	111
11.16	111
12.3	112

Testament of Judah
2.1	112
24.2	112

Testament of Levi
18.9	112

Testament of Reuben
4.8	111

Testament of Simeon
4.5	111
5.2	111

Rabbinic Literature

Mishnaic tractates and related literature

m. Abot
1.3 III A, B	164
3.15	162
6.7	160

m. Ber.
1.1 5.2	162

m. Sheqalim
3.2	160

t. Peah
4.5	147

t. Sanh.
13.2	102

b. 'Abod. Zar.
10b	102

b. B. Bat.
Vol.XXII. B.	162

Appendix 1(I:33)

b. Bavli. Ned.
Vol.XV.	162

Appendix 2 (1-19)

b. Ketub.
Vol.XIV.C. Ch.13(III.46)	163

b. Meg.
Ch.4(25a)	163

b. Menah.
Vol.XXIX. Ch.3(II.7)	162

b. Moed Qat.
Vol.XI. Ch.3(II.25)	162
Vol.XI Ch.2(I.9)	163

b. Ned.		*Pisqa*	
Vol.XV. B. Appendix 2 (1)	162	312	159
Vol.XV. B. Appendix 2 (2)	162	*Gen. Rab.* 33.1	161, 163
Vol.XV. B. Appendix 2 (6)	162	*Exod. Rab.* 31.1	164
Vol.XV. B. Appendix 2 (11)	162	*Lev. Rab.*	
Vol.XV. B. Appendix 2 (18)	162	1.11	102
		Num. Rab.	
b. Yev.		11.1	161
47a	255	11.6	161
y. Pe'a		*Deut. Rab.*	
1.1	102	2.1	161
Other rabbinic works		2.23	164
'Abot R. Nat B		4.10	164
10	102	*Sifre Deut.*	
Mek.		48	161
13.III.(8G)	161	304	164
16.III.(4B)	164	311	164
16.III.(4C)	164	329	164
22.I.(17A)	164	*Sifre Lev.*	
34.I.(5B)	164	5.17	226
40.II.(8D, F)	164		
Midr. Deut.		*Sifre Num.*	
33.2	102	41.2	161
Pesachim		*Anthology of rabbinic literature*	
101a	147	Montefiore and Loewe (eds), *A Rabbinic Anthology*	
Pesiq. R.		§587	114
1.8.II.(8)	164	§588	114
2.28.II.(4)	161	§590	164
		§597	164

New Testament

Matthew
5:43ff	208
5:45	218
6:25ff	208
10:10	327
11:29	262
20:25-28	262
23:11	262

Mark
9:35	262
10:35-45	262
10:42-45	297
12:41-44	253, 289, 297

Luke
3:11	294
6:27-38	352
7:3-5	148
10:7-8	327
14:12-14	352
22:24-27	262, 352

John
1:1ff	352
1:14	184
13:3-17	262
15:12	187
15:12-17	187
15:13	187
15:14	187
15:15	187
15:17	187

Acts
1:8	275
2:43-47	187
4:32-35	187
6:1-2	294
6:9	151
8:1a	151
8:9ff	346
8:14ff	90
9:2	151
9:11	175
9:20	151
13:4ff	91
13:5	151
13:14	151
13:16ff	152
13:38-41	152
13:42	151
13:43	152
14:1	151
14:8ff	346
14:11-14	168
14:17	168
14:18	168
15:21	151
15:31	26
16:1-2	31
16:14ff	31
16:15b	31
16:16ff	346
16:23	31
17:1	151
17:1-9	31
17:2	151
17:10	151
17:16-34	347
17:17	151
17:18	222
17:22ff	346
17:23	32, 346
17:32	222
18:1-3	275
18:2	213
18:2-3	31
18:3	31
18:3-4	148
18:4	151

18:7	151	1:16-2:10	218
18:8	148	1:16b	306
18:19	151	1:17	220, 221, 224
18:26	151	1:18	216, 218
19:8	151	1:18-19	216
19:9	275	1:19-20	218
19:13-17	243	1:19-23	153
19:17-20	346	1:20	218
19:19	90, 243	1:21	217
19:23ff	346	1:21-22	18
19:23-25	244	1:22a	216
19:27-28	246	1:23	216
19:31	243	1:23a	216
20:4	308	1:23b	216
20:14	304	1:24	217, 218
20:34	275	1:24-32	18
20:34-35	31, 246	1:24a	216
20:35	175	1:25	216, 240
21:27-30	308	1:25b	216
21:39	175	1:26	217, 218
22:3	175	1:28	218
22:15	274	1:29	218
22:19	151	1:30	276
22:21	275	1:32	216, 218
24:12	151	1:32a	218
24:17	324	2:2-3	218
24:17-19	293	2:4	217, 219, 222
26:11	151	2:5	218
26:16	274	2:6	218, 220, 321
		2:7	215, 218, 219
Romans		2:8	218
1-3	220, 346	2:9	220
1-4	152	2:10	219, 230
1:1	274, 276	2:11	218
1:2	233	2:11-12	220
1:3-4	233, 236	2:14-16	220
1:5	274, 278, 279, 285	2:17	217
1:5-6	213, 214	2:17ff	160
1:7	230	2:17-20	217, 306
1:8	269	2:20	223
1:11	272, 280	2:23	217
1:11-12	272, 326	2:23-24	220
1:13-15	214	2:23a	217
1:14	248, 313	2:29b	219
1:16	218	3-4	98

3:1-2	306	4:20	216
3:2	220	5-6	238
3:3	216, 217, 220	5:1	224
3:4	220	5:1-2	224
3:4-7	220	5:2	223, 224, 230, 234, 350, 351
3:5	220, 221		
3:5b	218	5:2b	219
3:5-6	220, 222	5:3-5	234
3:7	216, 220	5:4-5	230
3:8	220	5:5	351
3:8b	218	5:5a	268
3:9	105, 220	5:5b	268
3:10	224	5:6	225, 231
3:18	216	5:6-8	266, 311, 350
3:19-20	220	5:7	223, 225
3:20	103, 223	5:7b	225
3:21	220, 221, 223	5:8	225, 267
3:21a	220	5:10	225, 266
3:21b	221	5:12	105, 227
3:22	220	5:12ff	226
3:22-31	224	5:12-14	233
3:23	218, 220	5:12-21	226, 231, 350, 352
3:24	221, 224, 249, 333	5:14	105, 215, 227
3:24-25	221	5:14a	227
3:25	221	5:14b	233
3:25-26	221	5:15	224, 227
3:25b	220, 221	5:15a	226, 280
3:26	221	5:15b	226
3:26a	220	5:16a	226
3:26b	221	5:16b	226, 234, 280
3:27	219	5:17	105, 215, 224, 227, 278
3:27-28	217	5:17a	227
3:27a	217	5:17b	226, 227, 228, 234
3:28	103, 220	5:18	227
3:29-30	221	5:18-19	226
4:1-7	223	5:18b	230, 234
4:1-22	224	5:19b	230, 234
4:1-25	346	5:20	227, 242
4:4	74, 224	5:21	105, 215, 227, 228, 231, 242, 278
4:4-5	104, 267		
4:13ff	138	5:21a	227
4:15	106	5:21b	227, 234
4:16	73, 138, 181, 224	6	236, 237, 240
4:17	67	6:1	279
4:18	216	6:3-11	237

6:4	221	7:8-13	242
6:6	105, 237	7:11b	106
6:6b	235	7:12-14	105
6:9	105	7:13	105, 231
6:10	237	7:14	105
6:12	105, 237	7:16	105
6:12-23	234, 235, 350, 352	7:22	105
6:13	238	7:24	105
6:13a	235	7:24-25a	238, 270
6:13b	235, 238	7:25a	270
6:14	105, 242, 278	8:2	242
6:14-23	18	8:3	105
6:14a	237	8:3-4	106
6:14b	237	8:3-4a	242
6:15	237, 279	8:4	242
6:16	235	8:4-5	242
6:16-17	105	8:5b	242
6:16-18	237, 241	8:6	230
6:16-22	235	8:6b	242
6:16a	235	8:7	105
6:16b	235, 238	8:10	105
6:17	238, 240, 270	8:13b	242
6:17ff	270	8:14-17	241
6:17-19	235	8:18	223, 234
6:17a	235	8:18ff	352
6:18	238	8:18b	219
6:18a	240	8:19-23	106
6:18b	235	8:20	222, 230, 234
6:19	235	8:20b-21	233
6:19b	235, 238, 240	8:21	223
6:20	105, 227	8:22	233
6:20-23	237	8:23	234
6:20a	235	8:23b	233
6:20b	235	8:24-25	230, 234
6:21	240	8:28	268
6:22	240	8:29	233, 245
6:22-23	215, 236	8:30b	219
6:22a	240	8:32	222, 234, 266
6:22b-23	235	8:35	268
6:23	226, 238	8:35b-36	222
7:4	237	8:35-38	351
7:5	105	8:35-39	234
7:6	242, 346	8:37	268
7:7	105	8:38	105
7:7-11	105	8:38-39	231, 237

8:39	268	11:25	304, 305
9-11	152, 286, 305	11:25-26	305
9:1-4	306	11:26	304
9:1-5	103	11:28	160, 164, 165
9:1-18	151	11:29	220, 280, 306
9:4	280, 313	11:30-32	286
9:4-5	217, 220	11:33	217
9:5	160, 164, 250	11:35	217, 268, 285, 300, 321, 350
9:6a	220		
9:11-12	159	11:36	216
9:14	220	12:1	216
9:15-16	286	12:2	276
9:16	159	12:3	278, 285
9:18	286	12:4-8	281
9:21b	217	12:5	307
9:22b	217	12:6	280, 294
9:23	217, 286	12:7	294
9:30-32	224	12:8	294, 295
9:30-10:4	151	12:10	18, 21, 223, 267
9:32	159	12:10b	283
10:1	103	12:12	230
10:2-3	104, 159	12:12b	283
10:3	159, 221	12:13	295, 298, 301
10:4	159, 160, 231, 276	12:19	322
10:4-5	306	13:1-6	237
10:6ff	159	13:6-10	267
10:6-17	224	13:7	18, 223
10:15	230	13:8	299
10:16	160, 240	13:8-10	21, 242, 313, 324, 326, 331, 342, 348, 349
10:21	160		
11:1-6	151	13:11b-14	238
11:2-4	217	14:1-23	213
11:5	217, 304	14:1-15:13	214
11:5-6	138, 224, 267	14:5-6	270
11:6	104	14:15	268
11:6a	217	14:17	230
11:6b	218	14:19	230
11:7-9	306	15:4	230
11:9	322	15:5	285
11:11ff	304	15:8	261, 262
11:13	213, 274	15:8-9	138, 220
11:13-14	214	15:9	286
11:13-24	20	15:11	219
11:20	224	15:13	230
11:22	242	15:15	276, 278

15:15-18	214	1:10-17	298
15:15-19	276	1:11-16	270
15:15-21	248	1:17	274
15:15-33	304	1:18-25	340,
15:16	216, 304	1:18a	256
15:18	240, 279	1:18ff	283
15:24	21, 305, 325, 326, 348	1:18-23	276
15:25	294, 301	1:21b	256
15:25-27	311	1:23	256, 262, 274
15:25-31	303, 305	1:25a	256
15:26	265, 298, 301	1:25b	247, 256
15:26ff	306	2:1	274
15:26-27	308, 309, 342	2:6	236, 238
15:27	21, 298, 301, 305, 306, 313, 325, 327	2:6-8	222
		2:8	236, 238, 256
15:28	301, 304, 305	3:1-9	298
15:28-29	304	3:10	278
15:29	298	3:16-23	298
15:30	233	3:21	252
15:30ff	305	3:30	283
15:30-31a	308	4:1	274
15:30-32	293	4:7	266, 267, 300, 321, 350
15:31	298, 301, 334	4:9-13	247
15:31b	308	4:10	223
15:33	230	4:14-15	342
16	67, 325	4:16	320
16:1-2	21, 326, 342, 348	4:20	276
16:2	21, 294, 295, 348	4:20-21	276
16:4	269, 334	5:7	216
16:11	235	6:1-7	298
16:20	88, 230 242	6:1-11	291
16:23	295	6:9	31
16:25-26	233	6:9-11	242
16:26	215, 279	6:11	242
16:27	216	7:7	280, 282
		7:22	235, 330
1 Corinthians		8:4	283
1:1	274, 276	8:4ff	352
1:3	230	8:4-5	283
1:4	241, 269, 281, 302	8:5	235
1:4-5a	245	8:6	283
1:5	302, 303	9:1	277
1:6	274	9:3-11	342
1:7	280	9:3b-4	283
1:8-9	241	9:4-5	327

406 *Index of Passages*

9:7b	327	12:24-26	18
9:9	327	12:25	334
9:11	325, 327, 348	12:25b-26	281
9:12-23	342	12:26b	283
9:13	327	12:28	281
9:14	327	12:30-31	280
9:14-15	275	12:31	231
9:16	276	12:31-14:1	281
9:18	275	13:1-3	270
9:19-20	242	13:3	321, 324
9:19-22	261	13:13	303, 349
9:19a	261	14:3-5	281
9:19b	261	14:12	281
9:20a	261	14:16ff	270
9:20b	261	14:16-17	270
9:21	327	14:17	281
9:21b	261	14:18	270
9:22a	261	14:26	281
9:22b	261	15:3	266
9:25	215, 340	15:8	277
9:27	274	15:9	274
10:7-8	283	15:9-10	278
10:14-22	283	15:10a	248
10:30	270	15:10b	300
11:1	320	15:11-12	274
11:17-18	283	15:15	274
11:17-34	291, 298	15:20-28	231
11:24	270	15:21-22	233
12:1	216, 281	15:26	105
12:2	168, 283, 346	15:28	283
12:4	280	15:30	334
12:4-6	281	15:31	247, 262
12:7	281	15:43	223
12:8	281	15:45-48	233
12:9	280	15:45b	234
12:11	281	15:51-57	231
12:12-13	281	15:56b	105
12:12-27	281	16:1	300
12:13	307	16:1-4	308
12:14-21	281	16:2	300
12:14-26	291	16:3	294, 301
12:22ff	323	16:6	326
12:22-25a	281	16:10ff	67
12:23-26	223	16:11	326
12:24	21	16:22	267

New Testament

16:23	88, 242	4:5	227, 274
		4:6	217, 277, 346
2 Corinthians		4:7	231
	304	4:7-11	271
1:1	276	4:10-12	262
1:2	230	4:10a	247
1:6	326	4:10b	247
1:8-19	247	4:11a	247
1:11	271, 280	4:11b	247
1:12	276	4:12a	247
1:15	294, 301	4:12b	247
1:15-22	298	4:15	227, 271, 272
1:15-23	342	4:17	215
1:16	326	4:18-5:1	215
1:16a	294	5:14-15	351
1:16b	294	5:15	248
1:19	274	5:17	351
1:19-20	178	5:18	274
1:22-2:11	298	5:18-19	351
1:23	340	5:21	266
2:4	311	6:1	248
2:7	282	6:1-2	98
2:8	221	6:3	274
2:9	240	6:4-10	247
2:10	282	6:7	274
2:12	281	6:8	255
2:13	298	6:8a	223
2:14	270	6:8b-9a	306
2:17	248	6:9	255, 262
3	98, 104	6:10	251, 252, 265, 297, 334, 347, 349
3:1-3	67		
3:1-18	248	6:10b	266
3:4-18	159, 346	6:11-13	248
3:7	106, 274	6:11b	325
3:8	98, 274	6:13	21, 325, 342, 348
3:9	274	6:13a	342
3:10	231	6:13b	325
3:10-11	105	6:14-16	283
3:15	105	7:2	325
3:17	310	7:2-3	248, 306
3:18	217, 223	7:5	298
4:1	274, 346	7:8	311
4:2	274	8	306
4:2-6	248	8-9	10, 272, 299, 305, 310, 311, 349
4:4	217		

Index of Passages

8:1	73, 292, 294, 297, 298, 321	8:14c	327
		8:16	269, 292, 294, 305, 308
8:1-2	251, 266, 294	8:16ff	67
8:1-4	314, 320	8:16-23	306
8:1-5	297, 298, 347	8:16-24	308
8:1-6	315	8:19	292, 294, 298, 301, 313
8:1a	266, 296, 297	8:20	298, 301
8:2	266, 296, 301, 349	8:24	301, 308, 321, 327, 349
8:2a	296	9:1-4	298, 306
8:2b	297	9:1-5	266
8:3	297, 306, 308	9:2	294, 301, 312, 314, 321, 347
8:4	178, 292, 294, 295-299, 301, 308, 343, 349	9:3-5a	347
8:4b	295	9:3-5	19
8:5	294, 297	9:3b	321
8:6	257, 294, 298, 301, 313	9:4	294
8:6-7	347	9:5	301, 306, 308, 312, 347
8:6-8	19	9:5-11	299, 349
8:7	227, 292, 294, 297, 298, 301, 302, 313	9:5b	307
		9:6	301
8:7a	294, 297, 302, 303	9:6-11	322
8:7b	303	9:6-14	307, 349
8:8	301, 308, 321, 349	9:6-15	294
8:8-9	276, 294, 304, 309, 342	9:6b	307
8:8a	347	9:7	255, 306, 307, 308, 313, 313, 323, 347
8:8b	266		
8:8b-15	266	9:7-11	321
8:9	250-269, 285, 292, 294, 297, 308, 311, 313, 321, 328, 350, 351	9:7a	266
		9:7b	324
		9:7b-8	307
8:9a	255, 263, 265, 266, 297	9:7b-9	266
8:9b	255, 266, 297, 349	9:8	227, 282, 292, 294, 301
8:10	320	9:9	265, 307
8:10-12	19, 347	9:10	301, 304, 307, 321
8:11	257, 301, 320	9:10a	272, 307
8:11a	347	9:10b	272, 307
8:12	301, 306, 308	9:11	251, 301, 349
8:13	327	9:11-15	255, 271, 311, 351
8:13-14	291	9:11a	272, 307, 321
8:13-15	20, 21, 136, 180, 251, 306, 308, 309, 311, 325, 327, 348	9:11b	272, 308
		9:11b-12	271
		9:11c	272
8:14	313	9:12	294, 298, 301, 313
8:14a	304	9:12a	272
8:14a-b	327	9:12b	271, 272, 308

New Testament

9:12ff	324	11:16a	338
9:12-13	273	11:17b	338
9:12-14	308	11:19	334
9:12b-13	271, 272	11:19-29	335
9:13	257, 294, 298, 301	11:20	338
9:13a	272, 321	11:20-12:11	277
9:13b	298	11:21	267, 334, 335
9:14	231, 257, 272, 285, 292, 294, 298	11:21a-29	338
		11:21b	338
9:14-15	324	11:22	283
9:14a	272, 298	11:23	334, 335
9:14b	272, 298, 321	11:23-29	339
9:15	224, 272, 292, 294, 308	11:23-33	339
10-13	305, 332, 334-335, 336, 337, 344, 347	11:23a	338
		11:24	151
10:1	334	11:26	334, 347
10:1-13:14	248	11:27	334, 347
10:1b	342	11:28-29	334
10:3-6	247	11:29	334
10:9-10	246, 312	11:29-30	267
10:10	342	11:30	334
10:12a	334, 338	11:30-33	339
10:13-18	247	11:31	340
10:17	338	12:1	335
11:1	334, 335	12:1-10	247
11:3	247	12:1b	338
11:3-5	338	12:5	267
11:5	340	12:7	231, 244, 274
11:6	247, 312	12:7a	247
11:7-9	306	12:8-10	246, 262
11:7-11	246, 275, 332, 334, 342, 347	12:9	247, 276
		12:9a	246, 276
11:7b	333, 349	12:9b	246
11:8-9	275	12:9-10	267
11:9	333	12:10b	247
11:9-11	247	12:11	335
11:10	274	12:11-13	338
11:11	298	12:11-19	246
11:12-15	338	12:12	247
11:12-18	338	12:13	282, 342
11:13-15	247	12:13-15	347
11:16-18	334	12:13b	334
11:16-19	335	12:13-14	333
11:16-23	338	12:13-15	334
11:16-33	247	12:13-18	306

12:14-15	332, 341, 342	2:4	274
12:14-16a	349	2:4-5	104
12:14-16	275, 335	2:5	274
12:14b	341	2:6a	310
12:15	298, 334	2:6b	310
12:15a	341	2:9	278, 285, 298, 310, 311
12:16	333	2:9-10	19, 308, 310, 324
12:16-18	306, 332	2:10	265, 309
12:19-13:9	334, 347	2:11-14	104
12:20-21	298	2:14	104, 274
12:20-13:10	247	2:16	103
12:21	334	2:20	266, 268
13:3	247	2:20-21	311
13:4	266, 340	2:20b	351
13:4-5	262	2:21	104, 224, 248
13:4a	247, 256	3:1	242, 248
13:4b	247, 276	3:1-5	350
13:5-7	334	3:1-9	164
13:8	274	3:2	103, 248
13:8b	342	3:2-3	104, 105
13:13	88, 242	3:2-5	242
		3:3	104
Galatians		3:4-5	248
	104	3:5	103, 104, 248
1:1	276, 310	3:6-25	346
1:3	230	3:7	106
1:6	104, 248, 285	3:10	103, 106
1:6-9	104, 248	3:10ff	152
1:10	98, 310	3:13	106, 256, 266, 267
1:12	277	3:14	138, 346
1:13	231	3:18	138, 224
1:14	97, 283	3:19b-20	105-106
1:15	274, 277, 285	3:20	283
1:15-16a	277	3:21-22	105
1:15-16	248, 277, 278, 346	3:22	105
1:15-17	310	3:23-25	106
1:15a	277	3:28	307
1:15b	278	3:28-29	330
1:18-19	310	4:1-7	106, 242
1:16	278	4:3	105
1:16b	277	4:4	231
1:22	310	4:4b-5	267
2:2	274	4:6	248
2:2b	310	4:8	168, 284
2:3-5	104	4:8-9	105, 283, 346, 350

4:9	265	1:7b-8	227
4:9-10	242	1:9	243
4:12	320	1:9-10	245
4:21ff	152	1:10	246
4:21-31	105, 242, 346	1:12	243
5:1	248	1:14	243
5:1-5a	242	1:15-16	269
5:1-12	104	1:17	243
5:4	104, 248, 350	1:18	217, 243
5:4a	248	1:19	231, 243, 246
5:5	242	1:19-21	246
5:6	104, 303	1:20-21	245
5:6b	242	1:21	243
5:11	242, 248, 274	1:22-23	281
5:11b	256	2:2	243
5:13-15	249	2:4	243, 245, 268
5:13b-14	242, 351	2:4-8	311
5:16-18	242	2:5	245
5:16-24	248	2:5-6	245
5:22	242, 351	2:7	231, 243, 245
5:24	242	2:8	245
5:25	104, 242	2:8b-9	245
6:2	242, 295, 351	2:8-9	241
6:2-4	249	2:8-10	104
6:6	248, 327, 320	2:11-16	245
6:6-10	295	2:18	307
6:8	215, 242	2:19	245
6:12-14	104	3:2	246, 278
6:14	242	3:2a	245
6:14-15	249	3:2-3	243
6:15	104, 106, 248	3:2-4	245
6:18	88, 242	3:3	243
		3:4	243
Ephesians		3:6	246
1:1	276	3:7	224, 243, 246, 274, 278
1:2	230	3:7a	245
1:3	245	3:7b	245
1:3ff	352	3:8	243, 245, 246, 278
1:3-14	245	3:8a	245
1:4	245	3:8-9	245
1:5-6	73, 181	3:9	243, 246
1:6	243, 268	3:10	243
1:6a	243, 245	3:13	243
1:6b	243, 245	3:16	217, 243
1:7	243, 245	3:17b-19	268

412 *Index of Passages*

3:19	231	2:1	268
3:20	243	2:5-8	262
3:21	243	2:6	262, 328
4-6	239	2:6-7	263
4:1	348	2:6-8	254, 262
4:4-6	307	2:7	254, 261, 262, 263, 350
4:6	283	2:8	254, 256, 262
4:7	224, 280	2:8b	245
4:11	281	2:9-10	246
4:11-12	281	2:11	221
4:12-13	281	2:12	240
4:28	294	2:17	216
4:29	282	2:20	334
4:32	245, 282	2:22	274, 342
5:1	320	2:30	334
5:2	266, 268	3:2-6	338
5:4	270	3:2-10	104
5:20	270	3:5	159, 283
5:21	243	3:5ff	159, 261
5:22	268	3:5-6	104, 159
5:25	266, 268	3:5-7	261
5:27	245	3:5b	283
5:32	243, 245	3:6	159
6:2	223	3:6b	283
6:10-20	245	3:7	159, 261
6:12	243	3:7a	261
6:19	243, 245, 246	3:7b	338
6:24	242	3:8	159, 261
		3:8a	338
Philippians		3:8b	262, 338
1:1	320	3:8c	338
1:3	269	3:9a	159
1:5	269, 310	3:9b	159
1:6	241, 241, 278	3:10	261
1:7	247, 278	3:10b	247
1:12-14	262	3:12b	277
1:15-18	262	3:15	276
1:18	274	3:17	320
1:19	262	3:20-21	262
1:21b	262	3:21	223
1:24-26	262	4:1	340
1:27	348	4:6	270
1:29	247	4:8	164
1:29-30	262	4:10-19	275
1:32	262	4:10-20	21, 298, 325, 326

New Testament 413

4:11	282
4:15	7, 21, 298, 325, 348
4:19	217
4:22	235
4:23	88, 242

Colossians

1:1	276
1:2	73
1:3-4	269
1:5-6	274
1:6	240
1:6a	240
1:10	348
1:10b	240
1:12	270
1:13	268
1:15ff	352
1:18	233
1:18-19	281
1:23	274
1:24	262
1:27	217, 223
1:28	276
2:7	270
2:8	168
2:13	245
2:14	106
2:19	281
3:12a	268
3:12b-14	268
3:13	282
3:13b	245
3:15	270
3:17	270
3:24	322
4:2	270
4:6	178, 282
4:12	276
4:16	26
4:18	242

1 Thessalonians

	172
1:1	230, 320
1:2-3	269
1:3	172
1:4	268
1:6	261, 262
1:6a	320
1:9	168, 279
1:9-10	283, 346
2:9	31, 274, 333
2:11	274, 342
2:12	348
2:14	320
2:13-15	269
2:15-16	104
2:19	340
3:6-9	269
3:9	271, 321, 348
5:27	26
5:28	88, 242

2 Thessalonians

1:1	320
1:2	230
1:3	269, 271
1:6	321
1:8	240
1:9	215
1:11	348
1:12	245
1:13	20
2:13	268
2:16	215, 224, 268
3:6-13	349
3:7	320
3:7-9	31
3:7-10	320
3:8	275
3:9	320
3:11-12	320
3:13	320
3:14	240
3:18	89, 242

1 Timothy

1:1	276
1:2	230, 274

1:12	269	3:3-7	118
1:14	89, 227, 268	3:4	295
1:17	216	3:7	224
2:5	283	3:13	326
3:2	295	3:15	242, 267
4:3-4	216		
4:14	280	*Philemon*	
5:1	325		21, 67, 328-332
5:3	223	1	331
5:4	21, 325, 348	1-2	31, 328
5:10	295	2	330
5:17	21, 223, 348	3	230, 330
5:17-18	327	3-4	269
5:17-19	342	4	330
5:18	327	5	328, 330, 331
6:1	223	7	328, 330, 331
6:6	282	8-9	330
6:12	215	9	330, 331
6:16	215, 216	10	328, 342
6:21	242	11	331
		12	331
2 Timothy		13	331
	72	14	330
1:2	230	16	329, 331
1:3-5	269	16-17	331
1:6	280	17-19	329
1:8	274	17b	331
1:9	245	18	329
1:11	274	18-19	330
1:16	281	19b	328, 329
2:1	245	20	330
2:5	340	20a	330
2:10	215	21	330
2:14	148	21b	330
3:2	270	22	31, 282, 295, 328, 330
4:8	340	25	88, 242, 331
4:14-16	72		
4:22	242	*Hebrews*	
		1:1ff	352
Titus			
1:3	276	*Revelation*	
1:4	230	10:6	233
2:10-14	118	14:7	233
2:11	245	22:21	89
2:13	250		

Index of Ancient Non-Literary Sources

Austin, *The Hellenistic World from Alexander to the Roman Conquest*
§72   41

Bagnall and Derow (eds), *Greek Historical Documents: The Hellenistic Period*
§29B   238

Benedum, 'Griechische Arztinschriften aus Kos', *ZPE* 25 (1977), 265-276.
No. 2   47, 316
No. 4   47, 302

BGU
VIII 1787   82

Bosch.
108   231
131   231

BMI
455   27
894   229

Bologna Papyrus 5
II.1-4   71
IV.14-25   71

Burstein, *The Hellenistic Age from the Battle of Ipsos to the Death of Kleopatra VII*
§22   238
§33   316
§36   248

Caria. Aphro.
270   231
CIG

II 2059   38, 128, 325, 342
III 5361   148

CIL
I. 2   230

CIJ
I 25   301
I 173   301
I 652   301
II 732   301
II 772   149, 322
II 793   147
II 798   301
II 799a   301
II 803   301
II 1451   150
II 1510   150

CPJ
I 4   79
II 153   79
II 158a   80
II 159b   80
II 418   80
III 162   149
III 1530   150

Daniel and Maltimi (eds), *Supplementum Magicum* Vol. II
§63   93

Danker, *Benefactor*
§12   334
§20   41, 323
§21   323
§22   323
§27   86, 275
§28   269
§29   341

§30	334	Herrmann, *Der römische Kaisereid*	
§41	59, 216	§1	239
§42	59, 86, 216	§3	239
		§6	239

Ephesos BMI 455
455   148

Horsley and Mitchell (eds),
The Inscriptions of Central Pisidia
5A.I   56
5B.XXVII   56

Ehrenberg and Jones (eds), *Documents Illustrating the Reigns of Augustus and Tiberius*

§98a	228, 229, 231	Hunt and Edgar (eds), *Select Papyri* Vol.II	
§98b	228, 229	§211	211
§315	239, 241		

I. Assos

FD		7	42, 48
III(1) 546a	231	8	47, 48, 148, 302
III(4) 77	43, 270		
III(4) 287	47	*I. Délos*	
III(4) 313	47, 48	IV 1504	47, 302
III(4) 308	49	IV 1507	47, 125, 302
		IV 1517	128

Foucart, *Des associations religieuses chez les Grecs*

		IV 1518	47
		IV 1519	31, 141, 301, 318
§6	29, 31	IV 1520	29, 132, 254, 315, 317
§7	29, 31	IV 1521	41, 132, 152, 317
§8	29, 31	IV 1540	47
§10	29, 31		
§30	29, 31	*I. Ephesos*	
§43	29, 31	Ia. 6	27, 28, 43, 52, 215, 317

F.Gr.		Ia. 17	231
90 F 125.1	228	Ia. 18	231
		Ia.18b	244

Graf, 'An Oracle against Pestilence from a Western Anatolian Town', *ZPE* 92 (1992), 267-279.

		Ia. 20	32
		Ia. 21	300
	243	Ia. 27	42, 246, 320
		II. 233	52, 322
		VII(1). 3072	243
		VII(1). 3420	231

Hands, *Charities and Social Aid in Greece and Rome*

		IG	
§D.9	56, 284	II(2) 971	128
§D.13	250, 318, 320	IV 2	47, 149
§D.28	289	V(1) 1	47

V(1) 14	47	*I. Keramos*	
V(1) 931	42, 47, 315	6	128
V(1) 1175	29, 47		
V(1) 1361	47		
V(2) 472	46	*I. Kyme*	
VII(1) 18	47	19	211
VII(1) 21	47, 302		
VII(1) 121	143	*I. Kyzikos*	
VII(1) 412	47	II 2 col.1	45
VII(2) 2712	47, 48, 290, 317		
VII(2) 4130	302, 315	*I. Magnesia*	
VII(2) 4132	47	31	47
VII(2) 4133	43	61	47
VII(2) 4262	47	92a	42, 47, 48, 315
IX(2) 11	43, 315		
IX(2) 66a	47	*I. Mylasa*	
IX(2) 512	47	106	43, 149, 302
IX(2) 639	47	107	149
IX(2) 1230	47, 143, 224	110	43, 218, 272, 302
XI(4) 1061	29, 42, 47, 48, 121, 125, 141, 215, 316	*I. Perge*	
XI(4) 1299	85	381	233
XII(3) 1020	45		
XII(9) 239	29, 42, 48, 317	*I. Priene*	
XII(9) 899	42, 47, 48, 317	53	47, 48, 143, 148, 302
XIII(7) 395	231	108	47, 48
		112	39, 47, 58, 121, 182, 216, 224, 275, 302, 333
IGRR			
I 864	47, 302,		
III 148	48	113	39, 50, 59, 224, 302
III 493	47	114	27, 28, 59, 149
III 1031	147	117	50, 302
IV 351	47	118	47
IV 598	48		
IV 1156b	47	*I. Prusa Olymp.*	
		2	231
I. Hadrianoi			
24	233	*I. Stratonikeia*	
		15	47, 149
I. Iasos		29	60
152	128	1044	44
I. Kalchedon		*I. Tralles*	
1	47, 125, 302	81	231

Laum, *Stiftungen in der griechischen und römischen Antike* Vol.II
§50   28
§78a   66, 248
§104   28
§174   218

Lewis, *Leitourgia Papyri*
No. 4   132
No. 5   132

Lifshitz, *Donateurs et fondateurs dans les synagogues juives*
§1   149
§9   149
§10   149
§13   148, 149
§15   149
§20   149
§22   149
§33   149
§70   149
§72   149
§73a   149
§77   147
§79   147
§88   149

Mattingly, *Coins of the Roman Empire* Vol.I
59 (no. 323-328)   233

Meritt, *Corinth. Vol.VIII. Pt.I*
120   46
130   33

Michel
64   27, 50
163   47, 149, 341
235   27, 42, 47, 48, 302, 317
236   47, 128, 141, 341
297   39, 47
327   275

334   47, 55
372   27, 28, 43, 48, 126
475   43, 48, 126, 132, 149, 254
477   47, 48, 148, 302
515   47, 125, 302
541   39, 141, 143, 341
542   47, 148
550   302
803   301
982   39, 302
983   302, 316
984   29, 33, 323
985   27, 39, 43, 125, 302, 317
998   29, 47, 47, 128, 132, 147, 254, 302, 341
1007   43, 149, 341
1011   43, 125, 317
1101   29
1109   323
1553   323
1561   39, 43

Mitchell, *Regional Epigraphic Catalogues of Asia Minor. The Ankara District: The Inscriptions of North Galatia II*
392   249

New Docs
1 (1981), §1   286
1 (1981), §2   46
2 (1982), §16   285
3 (1983), §1   236
4 (1987), §22   243
4 (1987), §25   216
4 (1987), §28   245
4 (1987), §91   216
6 (1992), §29   243
7 (1994), §10   224, 290

Nouveau choix d'inscriptions grecques
§9   27
§11   27

Index of Ancient Non-Literary Sources

OGIS		III 260	95
229	334	III 580	93
248	41, 47, 316	III 591-596	93, 95
383	59	III 601-602	94
441	44	IV 197	91
666	28, 39, 49	IV 1061-1062	95
669	48, 333	IV 1615-1616	91
248	47	IV 1650	93
		IV 3165-3170	93
Pap. Agon		VII 215-216	93
6	67, 89, 322	VII 386	94
		VII 391-392	94
P. Ath. Univ. Inv.		VII 699	92
2782	45	VIII 5	92
		VIII 16-20	92, 244
P. Bon.		VIII 26	92
17	73	VIII 36	92
43	78	XIa 12-16	95
		XII 69	93
P. Brem.		XII 105	91
8	81	XII 225	92
49	69, 81	XII 226-227	92
52	75	XII 271	91
54	75	XIII 705-708	94
57	77	XV 8	93
63	76, 79	XVIIa 8-20	94
		XXII 5-6	94
Peek, 'Grabepigramm aus Aegypten',		XXIIa 20	93
ZPE 21 (1976), 133-134.		XXIIb 6	92
	33	XXIIb 20	92
	45	XXV 26	91
		XXXVI 35	91
P. Erasm.		XXXVI 225	91
I 6	78	XXXVI 275	92
		LII 17	93
P. Fam. Tebt.		LXI 9	93
43	76	LXII 37-39	95
		LXX 1	91
P. Fouad.			
8	79	*P. Gr.*	
21	88, 225	1236	73
25	77	*P. Herc.*	
		1417	167
PGM			
III 195	95	*P. Lond.*	

VI 1912	79	VIII 492	76
		VIII 498	78
P. Louvre		VIII 502	331
	79	VIII 510	75
P. Mert.		XII 1481	76
I 12	82-83, 84, 95, 171, 194, 203, 322, 327		
		Pouilloux, *Choix d'inscriptions grecques*	
II 62	78	§48	55
P. Mich.		P. Princ.	
II 123-124	224	162	78
II 123 Col 2.32	73		
II 123 Col 2.36	73	P. Oxy.	
II 123 Col 2.37	73	II 215	197
II 123 Col 4.15	73	II 273	73
II 123 Col 4.26	73	II(2) 292	77
II 123 Col 4.44	73	III 610	73
II 123 Col 5.33	73	IV 705	90
II 123 Col 6.4	73	VII 1021	87
II 123 Col 6.11	73	VII 1061	78
II 123 Col 6.21	73	VIII 1082	198
II 123 Col 7.3	73	XI 396	77
II 123 Col 8.7	73	XLII 3057	82, 305, 333
II 123 Col 8.26	73	XLII 3059	77
II 123 Col 8.34	73		
II 123 Col 12.4	73	P. Oxy. Hels.	
II 123 Col 12.18	73	47a	77
II 123 Col 13.17	73	47c	77
II 123 Col 14.8	73		
II 123 Col 14.27	73	P. Ross. Georg.	
II 123 Col 15.27	73	II 26	73
II 123 Col 16.16	73		
II 123 Col 16.19	73	PSI	
II 123 Col 20.25	73	IV 435	64, 275
II 123 Col 21.32	73		
II 124 Col 2.21	73	P. Sarap.	
II 128 Col 1.6	73	52	77
II 128 Col 1.7	73		
VIII 465	76	P. Soter	
VIII 466	77	24	73
VIII 473	73	P. Stras.	
VIII 476	73	II 117	78
VIII 477	73		
VIII 478	73, 76	P. Tebt.	
VIII 485	73, 178	III(1) 766	78

P. Turner
18   83, 322

P. Warren
13   86, 271, 284

P. Wash. Univ.
II 106   76

P. Wisc.
II 48   73

P. Würzb.
21   77

P. Yale Inv.
1536   79

RDGE
49   132

Reynolds, *Aphrodisias and Rome*
§1   53

Robert, *Bulletin epigraphique* 5 (1964-1967)
340   49

Roberts, *An Introduction to Greek Epigraphy. Pt.1.*
§180   27
§181   27

SB
VI 9017 No.23   76
VIII 9668   88
X 10288   76
X 15071   73
XII 10790   77
XII 11012   88, 333
XIV 11645   76
XVI 12589   76

Schwabe and Lifshitz (eds), *Beth She'arim. Volume II: The Greek Inscriptions*
§61   147
§79   147
§127   122
§168   147
§188   147

SEG
I 358   27
II 564   43, 47, 51
II 663   39, 149
IV 598   29, 47, 48, 271
IV 663   27
VII 11   27
VIII 496   27
VIII 527   28, 50, 218
VIII 549   54, 121
VIII 550   55, 244
IX 4   28, 39
X 131   27
XI 334   33
XI 344   37, 46
XI 435   27
XI 948   27, 43, 48, 51, 69, 126, 126, 131, 255, 316, 322
XII 94   43
XII 306   27, 47, 302, 317
XII 390   27
XII 472   27
XIII 255   28
XIII 258   27, 61, 66, 121, 290
XIII 526   48, 55
XIV 461   27
XV 111   27
XV 113   27
XV 670   44, 150
XV 877   27
XVI 73   27
XVI 94   43, 317
XVI 255   27, 43, 316
XVII 120   27
XVIII 20   27, 47, 302

XVIII 27	27, 47, 318	Sherk, *Roman Documents from the Greek East*	
XVIII 33	27		
XVIII 143	47, 48, 50, 148, 149	§12	44
XVIII 197	27	§20	44
XVIII 333	27	§21	44
XVIII 365	33, 46, 365	§49	28, 254
XIX 4	43		
XIX 728	33	Sherk, *The Roman Empire*	
XXI 419	43, 302, 317	§7II.E	225
XXI 452	43, 317	§31	228
XXI 469	55	§42B	228
XXI 469C	284	§67B	89
XXI 525	27		
XXII 128	27, 231	SIG^3	
XXIV 1094	27	22	27
XXIV 1100	42, 47, 148	64	39
XXIV 1108	48	117	278
XXV 564	29	204	27
XXVI 564	48	226	27
XXVI 1021	27, 47, 48, 215	227	27
XXVII 71	27	249	27
XXVII 261	37, 137	285	27
XXVIII 721	33, 46	330	27
XXVIII 964	27	336	27
XXIX 121	43	346	27
XXIX 977	44	374	27
XXX 30	27	391	27
XXX 65	27	475	27, 39
XXX 140	27	485	27
XXXII 1021	48	540	27
XXXII 1243	48, 224, 290	547	27
XXXIII 276	27	559	27
XXXV 80	27	587	39, 43, 48
XXXV 104	27	590	43, 48
XXXVI 139	27	593	47
XXXVI 155	27	613(A)	47, 316
XXXVII 70	27	615	47
XXXVII 1210	231	618	47
XXXVIII 127	27	674	44
XXXVIII 675	44	705	44
XXXVIII 1103	46	708	43, 56
XXXVIII 1270	44	709	47, 48
XXXVIII 1476	27	711(L)	47
XL 1672	46	721	27, 39, 42, 47, 48, 316
		736 Sect.1	280, 282

748	47, 48, 126, 341	I 59-60	85
764	44	I 64	76, 78
798	50, 62	I 71	128
799	47, 149	II 199	77
800	27, 28, 41, 47, 48, 302, 316		
814	27, 28, 48, 62, 286	Vidman, *Sylloge Inscriptionum Religionis Isiacae et Sarapiacae*	
826	37, 137	42	46
836	48	165	47
876	47		
912	27	Waldmann, *Die kommagenischen Kultreformen unter König Mithridates I. Kallinikos und seine Sohne Antiochus I*	
983	315		
985	280, 282		
997	216		
1007	39		62-67, 82-87
1109	280, 282, 283		
1240	34	Waltzing, *Étude historique sur les corporations professionnelles chez les romains* Vol.III	
TAM			
II(1-3) 579	231	§106	29
V 62	231	§114	29
		§141	29
UPZ			
I 34	87	Welles, *Royal Correspondence in the Hellenistic Period*	
I 35	87		
I 36	87	§35	27
I 41	86, 284	§52	334
I 59	76	§63	128, 334

Index of Ancient Literary Sources

Aeschines		170	338
In Ctes.		175-176	338
	333, 336	215-235	337
42	337	226	338
49-52	337	236	337
54-168	336	239-240	337
99	340	246	337
159	338	250	337
169-170	338	253	338
169-214	337		

Aesop
Chambry, Ésope: Fables
6	180
20	186
84	180
103	177
122	201
166	205
174	177
224	201
242	180

Alciphron
Ep.
3.17.4	279

Aristophanes
Women in Government
777-783	263

Aristotle
Eth. Nic.
4.1.8	176
5.5.4	179
5.5.6	180
5.5.6-7	180, 327
5.5.7	180
5.5.8	180, 188
9.1.7	180
9.2.1-5	180
9.8.1168b	187

Mag. Mor.
2.12.1	181, 340

Pol.
7.14.2	340
7.14.12	181

Rh.
2.7.4-6	174
3.2	275

Cicero
Amic.
9.31	202

Att.
9.11a	200

Cat.
4.3	206

Fam.
3.5.1	203
5.5.2-3	203
5.11.1	200
10.11.1	203
10.24.1	203
12.28.2	203
13.18.2	203
14.4.1-2	206

Fin.
2.35.117	208
3.22.73	206

Inv. Rhet.
2.22.65	202
2.22.65-67	199
2.34.115	200
2.53.161	199, 202

Leg.
1.15.43	200
1.18.48	208

Mur.
41	200
65	200

Nat. D.
1.17.45	208
1.43.121	208
1.44.122-123	208
1.44.123	208
1.44.124	208
1.121	132
3.17.44	206
3.36.87-88	206

Off.
1.15.47	202
1.15.48	202
1.15.49	202
1.16.51	187
2.20.69	202
3.63	167

Paradoxa Stoicorum
33-41	240

Phil.
3.6.14	202

Index of Ancient Literary Sources

Planc.	200
28.68	203
32.77	200
33.80	200
QFr.	
1.1.36	200
Red. Sen.	
9.23-24	202
Tusc.	
1.49.118	206

Cornutus
Summary of Greek Theology
8	188
15	188, 324

The Cynic Epistles
Pseudo-Anacharis
5	183

Pseudo-Crates
10.2	215
19	257
34.3	240

Pseudo-Diogenes
7.2	258
34.2	258
38.3	176

Socratics
30.3	176

Pseudo-Socrates
1.2	275, 276
1.7	276
1.9-10	276
1.23	176
6.9	183

Demosthenes
De Corona
	219, 333
1-2	340
8	340
112	335
141	340
173	337
197	337
256	335
256-258	336
258-264	336
265-266	336
268	335
269	336

De Viris Illustribus
54	205
56	177

Diels, *Vorsokr.* §89(82): *Anonymus Iamblichi*
3.4	264

Dinarchus
Against Demosthenes
	336
12-13	338
36	338
37	338
47	340
64	340
71	337
80-82	337
86	340

Dio Cassius
56.32.2	238
59.2.1ff	238

Dio Chrysostom
Or.
1-4	278
1.20	176
1.21	252
1.61-62	252
3.97	188
3.110	187
3.115	187
6.49	176
7.12	278
7.88	195
7.89	131, 195
8.5	277

Index of Ancient Literary Sources

9.2	277	75.6	174
12.42-43	181, 340		
13.9	275	*Diodorus Siculus*	
13.14ff	277	7.1	177
14.1ff	278		
14-15	241	*Diogenes Laertius*	
14.22	252, 258	1.15	257
20.21	184	2.93	175
27.7	277	4.37	175
31.7	174	4.49	175
31.37	188	5.48	167
31.50	174	5.81	167
31.53	182	6.13	257
31.54	244	6.72	187
31.60	182	7.167	167
31.68-69	182	7.175	167
31.125	176, 182	10.28	167
32.8	275	10.139	197
32.8-11	275		
32.10	277	*Eclogues of Nero*	
32.12-13	276		227
33.15	258		
34.4	275	*Epictetus*	
34.5	275	Arr., *Epict. Diss.*	
34.7	175	1.4.31-32	184
34.25	175	1.12.32-35	184
34.43	179	1.14.15-17	241
38.20	186	1.14.16	241
40.2	254	1.19.8-9	192
40.3	183	1.19.9	237
40.3-4	313	1.19.16	192
41.5	181, 224	1.19.19-23	192
41.6	181	1.19.19-29	193
43.3	179	1.19.23	192
44.4	175	1.19.25	193
45.5ff	278	1.19.26-29	192
45.7	175, 183	1.19.32	236
45.10	183	1.29.47	274
46.4	175	1.29.47-49	274
47.20	253	2.14:11-13	285
47.21	254	2.17.23-25	192
47.22	176	2.17.24	193
48.10	342	2.17.25	193
62	278	2.23.5-15	184
74.21	186	3.2.2	185

3.5.7-11	185	*Horace*	
3.13.9-11	230	*Carm.*	
3.22.23-25	273	1.2	232
3.22.49	278	1.12.46-48	230
3.22.69-70	274	1.12.49-60	230
3.22.81-82	325	3.14.14-16	230
3.22.82	274	3.25.4-5	230
3.22.90	178	4.2.41-52	230
3.24.64-66	267	4.5.16-24	232, 245
3.24.67-70	268	4.15	232
3.24.112	274	4.15.17-20	230
3.24.113-114	274	*Carm. Saec.*	
3.26.31-32	252	29-32	229, 232
4.1	240	37-48	232
4.1.4	286	49-56	232
4.1.12-14	239	57-60	232
4.1.33-38	236	*Ep.*	
4.1.103-105	185	7	167
4.4.7	270	*Epod.*	
4.4.18	186	9	230
4.5.35	184		
4.7.20	237	*Iamblichus*	
4.10.13	185	*Vit. Pyth.*	
4.10.14-15	186	30.167-168	187
4.10.16	186	38	181, 340
Frag. 11	258	50	185
		91-92	292
Epicurus			
Principal Doctrines		*Josephus*	
1	197	*Ap.*	
Sententiae Vaticanae		2.135-136	134
17	176	2.190	136
39	194	2.190-192	144
55	176	2.193-197	138
69	176	2.206	143
75	176	2.248-250	144
		AJ	
Hierocles		1.5	135
On Duties (Stobaeus)		1.10-12	134
3.52	181	1.100	136
		1.224	138
Homer		1.249	140
Od.		1.264	139
17.10ff	194	2.27-28	136
		2.56	143

2.140-158	139	11.149	138
2.141	139	11.165	138
2.142	139	12.48	142
2.143	139	12.48-57	134
2.144	139	12.53-54	142
2.145	139	13.5	319
2.147	139	13.48	142
2.151	107, 139	13.171-173	169
2.152	139	13.388	143
2.157	139	14.146	142
2.196	141	14.148	142
2.197	142	14.149-150	134
2.206	143	14.182-183	143
2.212	141	15.7	135
2.261-262	141	15.18	142
2.263-263	141	15.19	142
2.339	143	15.233	143
3.7	136	15.310	142
3.14	137	15.310-316	142
3.31	137	15.311	142
3.34-35	137	15.312	142
3.65	143	15.315	142
3.312	143	15.316	142
4.41	143	15.348	139
4.266	143	16.31-33	139
4.311	138	16.60	139
5.12-13	143	16.209	143
5.54	137	17.201-204	143
6.121	138	17.321	140
6.280	137	18.11-25	169
6.248	139	18.289	317
6.277	139	19.66	140
6.321	139	19.167	144
6.341-342	145	19.225	140
6.352	141	19.247	238
7.8	141	19.272	143
7.95	143	*BJ*	
7.111-113	141	1.237	143
7.299	143	1.401	143
7.305	143	1.457-458	143
7.387	141	2.119-166	169
8.11	144	5.530	143
8.327	137	*Vit.*	
10.41	138	10-12	169
10.139	143	419	140

Julian
Fragment of a Letter to a Priest
305B-C   289
Letter to Arsacius, High-Priest of Galatia
429C-431B   289

Lucian
Alexander the False Prophet
36   275
Apology
11   237
The Dance
41   177
The Dead Come to Life
5   177
The Dialogues of The Dead
              260
Disowned
13   177, 183
19   177
My Native Land
5   188
7   183
On Sacrifices
1   195
2   196
3   196
On Salaried Posts in Great Houses
7-9   236
9   236
20-21   236
23   236
42   240
The Parasite
10   258
49   260
The Passing of Peregrinus
12   277
Timon
5   253

Maximus Confessor
Commonplaces
46   175

Menander
Dyskolos
767-769   255

Musonius Rufus
Περὶ σκέπης
§19   193
Frag. 10   258

Pempelos
Περὶ γονέων (Stobaeus)
4.25.52   341

Petronius
Sat.   57

Philo
Abr.
17   122
52-54   123
54   243
143-146   121
177   129
Agr.
81   126
89-90   122
93   121
126   121
Cher.
84   121
122-123   322
123-124   130
Conf.
123   122
127   133
Decal.
111-112   129
112-115   130
Ebr.
32   122
107   121
112   133
145-146   133
224   121

Flacc.		*Mut.*	
57	147	39-40	125
Fug.		52	125
28-29	132	58	125
29	132	52-53	123
66	122	144	123
140-141	123	155	122, 133
141	126	218-219	126
Gig.		267	122
63ff	119	*Op.*	
Jos.		23	121, 122
46	129	169	126
46-47	129	*Plant.*	
99	126	130	129
229-230	107, 122	*Post.*	
241	127	32	121, 123
242	127	35-36	122
243	127	41	122
239	127	142	122
249	125	145	122
Leg.		*Quaest in Gn.*	
105	123	3.3-4	116
118	126	*Quis Her.*	
144-145	233	30-31	122
147	228	121	121
Leg. All.		226	126
1.34	227	302	126
1.82	270	*Quod Deus*	
2.32-33	133	5-6	123
3.10	129	5ff	270
3.14	125	7	126
3.77ff	119	48	126
3.78	279	70-71	122
3.106	122	71	108
3.163	227	74	107, 122, 126
3.164	125	104-108	116, 125
3.378	116	107	121
Mig.		*Quod Omn. Prob.*	
25	123		240
31	123	35	236
70	133	42	240
73	125	75-78	187
Mos.		*Sac.*	
1.58	126	52-58	117
2.7	123	57-58	123

58	126		14B	188
63	126		Leg.	
Som.			5.729C-D	174
1.162-163	121		11.931A	190, 191, 284
1.163	115		7.796C	190
2.176-178	125		Phd.	
2.177	125		231B-C	178
2.213	300		233D-E	174
Spec. Leg. I			234B-C	178
43-44	127		241A-C	178
152	126		Prt.	
187	133		343A-B	45
224	129		Resp.	
283	300		3.6.A	188
284	126		5.46.2c	
Spec. Leg. II			7.2.486D-487A	179
78	130		Ti.	
138	107		28c	153
219	121			
Virt.			Pliny	
83	130		Ep.	225
94	121		9.30.1	225
165-166	126			
168-169	126		Pliny the Elder	
184-186	119		NH	
			7.45.147-150	337
Philodemus				
De Dis			Plutarch	
III Frag. 84	187		Alex.	
Περὶ εὐσέβειας			43.4	191
Frag. 38	197		59.4	175
Περὶ παρρησίας			Cam.	
Xb 11	178		13.2	191
XIVb 2-3	178		Cat. Mai.	
			5	171
Philostratus			C. Gracch.	
Vit. Apol.			16.5	191
4:10-11	243		Comparison of Agesilaus and Pompey	
			3.3-5	337
Plato			Cor.	
Ap.			4.4.	181, 183, 340
23b	276		36.3	181, 340
29d	276		Crass.	
30e-31a	276		12.1	183
Euthphr.			Dem.	

Index of Ancient Literary Sources

5.4	183	497B	181
6.3	183	548-568	197
27.8	179	558B	182
Dion		558C	182
10.4	179	581C	252
43.5	191	582F	175
47.9	179	583C	183
52.1	253	584C	175
Flam.		610E	185
1.1-2	175	697D	178
Fragments		758A-B	185
85	185	759F	184
Letter on Friendliness		764E	184
Frag. 160	176	778C-D	188
Luc.		786F	176, 179
23.1-2	183	817D	317
Marc.		818C-D	189
10.3	183	842B-C	183
Mor.		844D	179
63C-D	174	966B	175
63F	186	987C	257
64A	175	1068D-E	179
67F	178	1098E	175
72F	178	1101B	197
92C-D	317	1101B-C	197
140D	190	1102A	189, 195
141F	188, 190	1102E	187, 197
172B	254	1102F	187
178C	175	1107C	197
235E	256	*Num.*	
329C	277	3	184
351C-D	184	4	296
355D	195	*Pel. and Mar.*	
356D	86	3.6	183
385D-E	45	*Phil.*	
401E-F	191	21.6	176
423D	132, 186	*Phoc.*	
470C-D	185	1.3	177
479B	340	7.2	183
479F	191	*Pomp.*	
480C	185	21.5	183
482E	178	*Pyrrh.*	
485A	179	3-4	198
485D	185	8.4	182
495B	194	*Sol.*	

2.1	254	55	70
Tim.		57	69
3.3	177	64	71, 306
8	256	76	68
		80	72, 306
Polybius		82	69
29:27	310		

Pseudo-Philo
De Jona

	151
	151-154
21	153
39	153
52	153

Posidonius
(Diod. Sic.)

34/35.2.8-9	183
34/35.2.40-41	183
34/35.38.2	183

De Sampsone

	151
	154-157
3	154
4	155
24-25	155
25	156
26	157

Proculus
Digest

	328
21.1.17.4	328
21.1.17.5	328
21.1.43.1	328

Pseudo-Aristotle
Ep.

4.1-5	180-181

Res Gestae

1	240
3	230
4	228
5	230, 232
8	232
12	230
13	230
15-24	49, 230
16	230
25	230, 239
26	230
27	228
31-33	228
34	229

Pseudo-Cebes
Tabula

9	240
22	240

Pseudo-Demetrius,
Τύποι 'Επιστολικοί

	69
3	70, 306
4	70
12	70
21	69, 225, 330

Pseudo-Heraclitus
Epistles

9.5-8	240

Sallust
Cat.

12	265

Seneca
Ben.

Pseudo-Libanius,
'Επιστολιμαῖοι Χαρακτῆρες

	68
53	70, 306

1.2.4	68	4.25.1-2	132
1.3.1	201	4.25.1-3	208
1.3.1-10	123	4.26.1-3	201, 208
1.3.2	123	4.27.5	201, 225, 307
1.4.3	201, 330	4.28.1-3	218
1.4.4	43	4.28.1-6	208
1.9.4	72	4.28.6	208
1.10.5	70	4.31.1-4.32.4	222
2.1.2	183, 200, 312	4.32.1-4	207
2.5.2	183, 200, 312	4.34.2	201, 225, 307
2.11.1-6	202	5.5.2	80
2.11.5	340	5.5.2-4	340, 340
2.15.1-3	200	5.22.2	201
2.17.6	205	5.25.6	201
2.18.5	84	6.4.1	201
2.18.5-6	205	6.5.1	201
2.21.5-6	306	6.6.2-3	201
2.22	81	6.23.1-3	218
2.23.1-2	201	6.23.3-7	207
2.23.3	71	6.23.6-7	207
2.24.4	201, 205	6.23.7	207
2.29-30	215	6.24.1-2	80, 340
2.29.3	206	6.25.1-6.27.7	207
2.30.2	206	6.27.1-2	206
2.31.2-3	208	6.29.1	207
2.35.1-5	205	6.30.1	218
2.35.3	69	6.34.5	84
3.1.1	71, 205	6.35.1-5	206
3.4.1-2	201	6.40.2	218
3.7.2-3	208	7.31.3-4	208
3.15.4	208	7.31.4	218
3.17.3	207, 218	9.9-10	70
3.18-28	81	*De Prov.*	
3.18-38	80	5.6	241
3.29.1	80	*Clem.*	
4.4.1-3	222	1.7.3	179
4.9.1	218	*Ep.*	
4.13.1-4.14.4	208	73.9	205
4.16.1-3	201	74.11	207
4.18.1	71	74.13	205
4.19.1-4	222	80.32	201
4.20.3	201	81	201
4.21.1-3	201, 205	81.7	201
4.24.2	201	81.8ff	201
4.25.14.26	218	81.9-10	206

81.10ff	201		*Divus Augustus*	
81.12	201		10	238
81.13ff	201		28.2	231
81.15ff	201		98	229
81.17ff	201		*Divus Claudius*	
81.18-19	206		10	238
81.19ff	201		25.4	213
81.23-26	206		*Nero*	
81.24ff	201		7	238
81.31-32	206		16:2	236
93.8	207			
98.11	206		*Tacitus*	
Hercules Furens			*Ann.*	
1337-1338	205		1.8	238
			2.48	265
Socraticorum Reliquiae Vol.2			12.41	238
53 (5-6)	260		14.11	238
53 (9)	258		15.44	236
53 (4, 7)	258		*Germ.*	
54 (1)	259		24	235
54 (2)	259			
54 (2-4)	260		*Teles*	
54 (3)	259		*On Exile*	
54 (5)	259		3.26H	176
54 (6-7)	259			
54 (8)	259		*Theano*	
54 (8-9)	259		*Ep.* (Hercher,	178
54 (9)	259, 263		604 No.5)	
54 (10)	259, 260			
			Theophrastus	
Statius			*Gnomologium Vaticanum*	
Silv.			328	176
4.1-3	228		Περὶ εὐσέβειας	
			9.1	188
Stobaeus			12.2	189
Eclogae			12.3-4	189
3.1.173	44		12.4	189
3.52	322		12.46	190
			12.51	190
Strabo			12.77	190
8.6.23	148		15.3	189
			24.1-5	189
Suetonius				
Divus Iulius				
88	230			

Valerius Maximus		2.675ff	230
Noteworthy Doings and Sayings		2.680-684	233
4.8. Ext.1	202 253	*Ecl.*	
4.8.4	205	4	230
4.7.5	204, 225	9.46-50	230
5.2.1	204	*G.*	
5.2. Ext. 1.2	205	1.24-42	232
5.2.5	204	1.498-514	230
5.2.7	254	2.170-172	230
5.3.2ff	207		
5.3.2b	204	*Vitruvius*	
		De Arch.	
Velleius Paterculus		9.1.2	153-154
2.89.1-6	230		
2.126.3-4	230	Xenephon	
		Cyr	
Virgil		7.5.45	224
Aen.			

Index of Subjects

Ancient benefactors
- and genuine expressions of affection 38, 48
- and inscriptional honorifics 120
- and peace 230
- and the reversal of obligation 183
- and σωτήρ terminology 228-229, 233
- Antiochus I of Kommagene 59-60
- Aristagoras of Istropolis 56
- Augustus 2-3, 213-214, 227-232, 345, 351, 352
- Caesars 48-49, 63, 79-80, 87-90, 95, 139-140, 192, 193, 211, 227-232, 234-242, 345-346, 351-352
- Caligula 12, 61-62, 351
- Claudius 79-80, 89-90
- Diogenes 267, 351
- Domitian 52-53
- Fabius Maximus 253
- Hadrian 55
- Heracles 252, 257

- impoverished benefactors 252-255, 263-265, 350
- Krateia of the Piraeus 40
- Metellus Pius 254
- Nero 12, 61-62, 33, 88-89, 95, 351-352
- Odysseus 257-261, 351
- Patron of Delos 30-31
- Phainios of Gytheion 60-61
- Phoebe 325-326
- Poseidippos of Cardamylae 43, 51-52, 69
- Theokles of Olbia 38, 325
- Timon 253-254, 256
- Vespasian 80
- Zosimos of Priene 38-39, 58-59, 224, 255, 334

Aristocratic literature
- its limitations compared to the inscriptional evidence 26-27, 29-30, 37, 38

437

Associations 29-33, 89-90, 147-148, 211, 215, 279-283, 291, 345, 351

Benefaction
- beneficence of the gods 6, 7, 39-40, 44, 53-57, 64, 78, 85-88, 183-191, 206-208, 208-209, 243-246, 349-351
- Christian benefaction and Julian the Apostate 289
- critiques of the benefaction system 84-85, 95, 111, 130-132, 192-199, 208-209, 322-324, 343, 349
- in Epicurean and Pythagorean groups 187, 209-210, 350
- misrepresentations of Graeco-Roman benefaction 290-291
- modern scholars on 3-8
- motivations for the gods' beneficence 186-188, 218, 285, 346, 350
- 'novelty' of Christian philanthropy 289-293

Charites 9, 34, 187-188, 210, 285, 313, 324, 327, 350

Delphic canon 44-45, 345

Divine wrath 215-216, 218, 248

Epistolary theorists
- letter of recommendation 68, 70, 78-79
- Paul's familiarity with 334, 347
- positive and negative tone of 70
- social world of 68-72
- usefulness in benefaction studies 65-66

Friendship 65, 68, 70, 80, 83-84, 89, 93, 95-96, 183, 187, 194, 202, 267-268, 292-293

Gift-giving
- and Christians 4
- in pre-Christian antiquity 5
- social-scientific perspectives on 21-22

Grace
- and Cynic debates about patronal leadership 212, 257-260
- and cult(s) 188-190, 195-196, 284, 349, 350
- and divine love 155, 225, 268, 290, 349, 351
- and justification 179, 199, 210, 346-347
- and language of abundance 11, 22, 226-227, 231, 348
- and language of excess 231, 348
- and language of peace and hope 230
- and language of power, glory, wealth and mystery 22, 243-246, 348, 350
- and regnal language 22, 60, 226-227, 228
- as central description of divine beneficence 212, 313-314
- as *gratis* 73-74
- as 'unalterable' 73
- as unilateral and covenantal 35, 56-57, 101, 112-113, 124, 133, 138, 284, 345, 346, 348-349, 350
- ἄχαρις χάρις 249
- δωρεάν 224, 333
- election and predestination 154
- *gratia* 7, 199-206
- hellenisation of χάρις 150, 345
- hypostatisation of χάρις 34-35
- inscriptional epithets attached to χάρις 33, 59-60, 62
- in the Apocrypha and Pseudepigrapha 110-114
- in Dead Sea Scrolls 5
- in Greek inscriptions 44-49
- in Greek papyri 72-78
- in Jewish funerary inscriptions 149-150
- in Jewish papyri 79-80
- in Jewish synagogal inscriptions 146-150
- in Jewish synagogal sermons 150-157
- in LXX 106-110
- in magical papyri 12, 90-95

- in popular philosophers 3, 6, 44, 153, 131-132, 133, 174-179, 199-202, 257-260, 273-279
- in rabbinic literature 157-164
- modern scholarship on 8-13
- modern scholarship on χάρις in the Greek inscriptions 33-37
- modern scholarship on χάρις in the Greek papyri 63-66
- modern scholarship on χάρις in Philo 114-120
- modern scholarship on χάρις in the philosophers 170-173
- negative connotations to χάρις 37
- semantic versatility of χάρις 2
- threats of withdrawal of grace 61, 62, 248

Graeco-Roman honour system
- ἀρετή 36, 58, 62, 72
- deflected honour 18
- δικαιοσύνη 36, 223-224, 287, 351
- hierarchy of honour 18
- honour-and-shame dynamic 214-219
- language of eternity in the inscriptions 215
- operation of 50-53
- reciprocity and the quest for φιλοτιμία 1, 30, 40
- return of honour 21
- role of inscriptions in 1, 4-5, 12, 27-33
- τιμή and δόξα 215, 217, 351
- χάρις as the central leit-motif of 2, 345

Ingratitude 53, 70-72, 77, 95, 111, 126, 143, 176-177, 182, 192-193, 201-202, 217, 334, 335, 347

Jerusalem collection 291-2, 293, 294-324, 332, 343
- and inscriptional motifs of rivalry and imitation 314-321
- and social-scientific studies 19-20
- and reciprocity 306, 323-324, 347, 349
- as χάρις 294-299

- as cycle of grace 54, 271-272
- ecumenical interpretation of 298, 307-308
- elements of reciprocity in 35, 298, 307, 310-311
- eschatological interpretation of 304-307
- Graeco-Roman 'parallels' to the collection 292
- obligation interpretation of 309-314
- pairings and triads of virtue 302-303
- Paul's profuse 'grace' language 10
- Paul's spread of terminology 301
- Paul's use of circumloculution 300, 301-302
- 'pilgrimage' theology 304, 305
- ritualised handshakes 310
- tensions regarding the collection 298, 305-306, 311-314, 314-315, 347

Josephus
- and Caesars 139-140
- and divine beneficence 135-138, 346
- and Old Testament benefactors 138-139
- and reciprocity 140-143
- apologetic aims of 134-135
- critique of the benefaction system 144-145
- use of benefaction parlance 133-135

Magic 12, 46, 64, 90-95, 243, 244, 350

Mercy and its relation to grace
- ἔλεος 2, 5, 106-110, 286-287, 348
- *hen* 106-110, 158, 160-163, 285-286
- *hesed* 2, 106-110, 348

Merit theology 100, 102-103, 113-114, 123, 124-125, 146, 159-160, 164, 196, 346, 351

Motivations for erecting inscriptions 28

'New Perspective' on Paul
- E.P. Sanders and 'covenantal nomism' 97-98, 346

- J.D.G. Dunn and the particularism of Jewish law 98-99
- critique of 100-106, 241-242

Occasion of Romans 213-214

Papyri
- their usefulness for benefaction studies 66-68, 345

Paul
- agrarian theology 307, 327
- alternative terminology used with χάρις 285
- and ἀγάπη 319, 320-321, 349, 351
- and Augustan eschatology 233-234
- and Caesarian loyalty oaths 238-242
- and Christ as πτωχός 263-267
- and cruciform grace 3, 220-226, 250-268, 351
- and cultic approaches to God 216
- and δικαιοσύνη 223-224
- and dishonoured benefactor 224-226, 346, 350-351
- and dishonouring of God 218, 220
- and divine δόξα 223
- and divine grace experienced as weakness 246-247
- and divine impartiality 218-219
- and divine justice 220-223, 346-347
- and 'enslaved leader' motif 257-268, 297, 350
- and epistolary theorists 334, 347
- and equality (ἰσότης) 130, 136, 228, 327-328
- and ethos of reciprocity 321-332
- and *familia Caesaris* 234-237, 352
- and gifts of grace (χαρίσματα) 156, 279-283, 294-295, 351
- and gods of the Gentiles 283-287
- and grace of apostleship 273-289
- and gratitude to God 269-273
- and human inability to recompense God 285, 300, 350
- and 'impoverished' benefactor motif 250-256, 350
- and inscriptional language of competition 320
- and interrelationship of χάρις, κοινωνία, and διακονία 60, 178, 295-299, 308, 343, 349
- and responding worthily to the divine benefactor 247-249
- and speech 178
- and wandering philosophers 168, 275-276, 350, 351
- apocalyptic framework of Paul's theology 105-106, 226-227
- as 'cowardly' benefactor 335-340
- as 'endangered' benefactor 334, 335-340
- as father/benefactor 328-332, 340-343
- avoidance of the plural χάριτες 285-286
- Damascus road experience 11, 151-152
- exposure to philosophical discussions of χάρις 167-169
- preference for χάρις over ἔλεος 285-287
- refusal to be a burden 333
- servant theology and Christology 261-263
- spending terminology 334, 341
- trade association contacts 32, 166
- use of benefaction terminology 28, 292, 333-344, 350

Philo
- and divine beneficence 120-128, 346
- and reciprocity 128-130, 352
- critique of benefaction system 130-132
- use of benefaction parlance 121, 126-128, 133
- view of covenantal grace 123-124

Rabbinic literature
- methodological issues 157-160

Reciprocity
- and magic 91
- bilateralness of reciprocity rituals 5
- '*do ut des*' mentality 17-18, 284, 350
- divine grace as reciprocal contract 217, 284-285
- Homer on 9, 42, 69, 194-195, 287
- in family 80, 83, 129-130, 143, 181-182, 194, 325-326
- in Greek inscriptions 50-53
- in Josephus 140-143
- in Greek papyri 81-85
- in Paul 225, 321-332, 340-343
- in popular philosophers 128-130, 179-183, 189-191, 202-206
- language of commensurability 11, 20-21, 271, 348
- inscriptional 'manifesto' clause: return of 'favour' or 'thanks'? 40-43, 47
- reciprocity terminology 41, 50, 51, 92-93, 190, 348

Roman patronal system
- in Greek East 1, 6, 15-17, 23, 210, 352
- Romanisation 8

Social-scientific approaches to the study of benefaction
- danger of anachronism 14
- deficiencies of 22-23
- patronage 13-17
- usefulness of 17-22

Structure of honorific decrees 39

Thanksgiving 11-12, 40-43, 55-56, 75-75, 94-95, 143, 175-178, 184-186, 217, 269-273, 351

'Works of the law' as boundary markers 103-104

www.ingramcontent.com/pod-product-compliance
Lightning Source LLC
Chambersburg PA
CBHW052048290426
44111CB00011B/1660